Carrying on the Anatomical Studies

Left to right: Thorstein Veblen, Joseph Schumpeter, John Maynard Keynes, and Alfred Marshall.

The Economic Problem

FOR Adolph Lowe

Robert L. Heilbroner wrote The Worldly Philosophers *while he was still a graduate student and was foolish enough not to use it as a dissertation. As a compensation, it has sold over a million copies in more languages than its author can identify. After* The Worldly Philosophers, *Robert Heilbroner went on to write several more widely acclaimed books* (The Future as History, The Great Ascent, *and* The Making of Economic Society), *before completing his doctoral dissertation and settling down into full-time academic life at the New School for Social Research, where he is now Norman Thomas Professor of Economics.* The Economic Problem *itself was many years in the writing before it appeared, in 1968; but since the first edition of that popular text, Professor Heilbroner has produced two more books:* The Limits of American Capitalism *and* Between Capitalism and Socialism. *As a speaker on many campuses and before a variety of audiences, including television audiences, Robert Heilbroner is known for the realism and directness that characterize his writing. Dr. Heilbroner and his wife, Joan, who is a librarian and an author of children's books, spend their summers on Martha's Vineyard, where (he tells us) he takes regular lessons in relevance from his two teen-aged sons.*

ABOUT THE AUTHOR

THE WORLDLY PHILOSOPHERS
THE FUTURE AS HISTORY
THE GREAT ASCENT
A PRIMER ON GOVERNMENT SPENDING (with Peter L. Bernstein)
THE MAKING OF ECONOMIC SOCIETY
UNDERSTANDING MACROECONOMICS
THE LIMITS OF AMERICAN CAPITALISM
UNDERSTANDING MICROECONOMICS
BETWEEN CAPITALISM AND SOCIALISM

OTHER BOOKS BY ROBERT HEILBRONER

Robert L. Heilbroner

Englewood Cliffs, New Jersey

The Economic Problem

third edition

PRENTICE-HALL, INC.

ACKNOWLEDGMENTS

I am happy to acknowledge permission from the
New York Review of Books to use material on ecology,
the arms economy, and the multinational corporation. The
material first appeared (in somewhat different form) in its
pages. I should like to thank, as well, *Trans-action* for
permission to use material on social neglect in America,
published first in that journal and also to appear in a volume
of essays, *Is Law Dead?* to be published by the New York Bar
Association. Some of the material in this new edition
has also been published, in altered form, in my book
Between Capitalism and Socialism (Random House, Inc., 1970).

ISBN   0-13-226910-4

Library of Congress Catalog Card No.: 70-37146

10 9 8 7 6 5 4 3 2 1

LONDON   PRENTICE-HALL INTERNATIONAL, INC.
SYDNEY   PRENTICE-HALL OF AUSTRALIA, PTY. LTD.
TORONTO   PRENTICE-HALL OF CANADA, LTD.
NEW DELHI PRENTICE-HALL OF INDIA PRIVATE LTD.
TOKYO   PRENTICE-HALL OF JAPAN, INC.

CONTENTS

part THREE   **Prosperity and Recession—The Economics of the Macro System**

part **FOUR**   **Microeconomics—Anatomy of a Market System**

The first two editions of this book began by saying that the cry in the land was "economic literacy"—a cry accompanied by dire predictions concerning the fate of a nation of economic illiterates. It will hardly come as news that the slogan has changed in the past few years: it is not *literacy* but *relevance* that is now on everyone's lips—or at least on every student's lips.

Although the word itself is rapidly becoming a cliché, I have considerable sympathy with the sentiments behind the call for relevance. I have always suspected a good deal of cant and some rather conservative ideologizing behind the emphasis on literacy; and although other kinds of cant and ideologizing are behind the banner of relevance, there is an honesty and an urgency to the call that is basically correct.

The question is: what to do about it? There are two things I do *not* intend to do. The first is to deny indignantly that economics ever smacks of irrelevance, or to write off the cry of the student as no more than the product of insufficient education, immaturity, or simply the generation gap. Although, like every other economist of my generation, I feel defensive before the charge of irrelevance, I am prepared to admit that a great deal of economic writing is concerned with unimportant matters and that parts of economic theory are more elegant than useful (I once irreverently wrote that much neoclassical theorizing was characterized by "rigor but, alas, also by mortis"). The student, however unprepared, young, or generationally remote, is right in insisting that economics teach him something—not merely by way of getting a job or rounding out his general education, but in understanding better what ails our society and how that society can be improved.

The other thing I do not intend to do is to accept the criticism without reservation, abjectly confessing that the apparently clear-sighted gaze of economics is actually only the stare of the extremely myopic, and that the foolishness of marginal analysis, equilibrium, and all the rest of standard micro- and macroanalysis should be relegated to the museum of antiquities. There may indeed be a need for deep-seated changes in economic thought, but economics must remain *thought,* and it must not become merely indignation. If economic analysis is irrelevant, it must be improved, not discarded.

What kind of improved analysis? I have, since the first edition of this book, urged the importance of adding historical dimension as an indispensable constituent of what we call economics. In support of my position, let me call on a most distinguished economist, Joseph Schumpeter:

What distinguishes the "scientific" economist from all the other people who think, talk, or write about economic topics is a command of techniques that we class under three heads: history, statistics, and "theory." The three together make up what we call Economic Analysis.

Of these fundamental fields, economic history—which issues into and includes present-day facts—is by far the most important. I wish to state right now that if, starting my work in economics afresh, I were told that I could study only one of the three but could have my choice, it would be economic history that I would choose. And this on three grounds. First, the subject matter of economics is essentially a unique process in historic time. Nobody can hope to understand the economic phenomena of any, including the present, epoch who has not an adequate command of historical *facts* and an adequate amount of historical *sense* or of what might be described as historical *experience.* Second, the historical report cannot be purely economic but must inevitably reflect also "institutional" facts that are not purely economic: therefore it affords the best method for understanding how economic and non-economic facts *are* related to one another and how the various social sciences *should* be related to one another. Third, it is, I believe, the fact that most of the fundamental errors currently committed in economic analysis are due to the lack of historical experience more often than to any other shortcoming of the economist's equipment.[1]

All this is, of course, grist for my mill; and it explains why I have maintained and even strengthened the historical and institutional material in this edition of *The Economic Problem,* as a first step toward bringing out the relevance that I believe economics does indeed have to offer. It explains as well why I believe that economic analysis, in a historical and an institutional setting, can indeed illumine problems of burning importance and of "radical" portent, provided that the tools of analysis are directed to historical and social issues and not used as mere exercises of the imagination.

What, then, are the main changes that I have introduced into this book? The first and most striking change is an effort to bring history home to the student at the very outset by a broadside exposure to some of the more sobering and disturbing aspects of the cutting edge of history—the present. In my new first chapter, "America Today," the "relevant" issues of our time are laid out for unsparing examination. Here is poverty, the military economy, pollution, racism, and other unpleasant realities of American life, not presented as a rounded picture of our life today, but as a direct confrontation with the facts to which economics must address itself. What does economics have to say about these problems? *What does it have to say about the historical process that produced them?* These are questions to which answers must be given, and to which the subsequent analysis is directed.

The stage set, we begin our analysis as before, by retracing the long and tortuous evolution of capitalism up to and into the troubled period in which we live. A few facts and figures from the previous historical section

[1] Joseph Schumpeter, *History of Economic Analysis* (New York: Oxford University Press, 1954), pp. 12–13. Elizabeth Boody Schumpeter points out that her husband added a fourth basic field, economic sociology, later in his analysis.

have been changed and added, but the essential outline remains unaltered, save for some policy-oriented suggestions in the later chapters.

Thereafter we are ready for what Schumpeter calls "theory"—standard macro- and microanalysis. I have not significantly altered the underlying *analytics* in either of these sections, but I have materially strengthened their connection with the historical panorama with which we began. Thus we return to poverty and pollution and the arms economy and the facts of racial discrimination and the paradox of unemployment and inflation, in greater depth and detail, seeking to show with examples from the recent past how our analytical framework can elucidate these problems and also how it can suggest ways of coping with them in part or whole. Thus by the time a student has finished his basic micro and macro work, I hope he will have learned not only the ways certain curves cross and equations work, but also how these curves and formulas apply to the externalities of pollution, to the imperfections of the labor market, to the economy-within-an-economy of the military sector or of the ghettos, and so forth.

It is for this same reason that I have added a new chapter to the section on international trade—the least "historical" portion of the previous edition. The rise of the multinational corporation is a historical fact of the greatest interest and importance; and it lends, I think, a concrete dimension to the always rather abstract considerations of the international division of labor or the balance of payments.

In the last section of the book we return, as before, to the sweep of history—first in Europe, then in the planned economies and in the underdeveloped world, and finally in America itself. But now I end with a new chapter that will, I believe, tie the book together by relating directly to the relevancies of the first chapter on America Today. For in this last chapter we examine the question posed at the outset but not yet squarely answered—the question of the degree to which it is American capitalism that is responsible for the disorders of American society. Because this is well outside the limits of standard analysis, I revert to the first person in telling the student what I believe to be the complex answer to that central question—an answer that stresses the historical realities behind the word *American,* considerably more than those behind the word *capitalism.* But that is a chapter with which I fully expect both student and instructor to argue if they wish. I am not trying to give textbook answers to so profound a query, but to suggest avenues of thought that may clarify it.

These changes, in themselves, give a new color to *The Economic Problem,* even though (or perhaps just because) its basic historical-institutional-analytical framework is left the same. But an additional change may interest the instructor. It relates to the third aspect of economic analysis that Schumpeter mentions: statistics. *The Economic Problem* has always combined history and theory, but statistics has been egregiously missing. Nor do I think it is possible within the confines of a single introductory text to *teach* the statistical techniques that properly belong in a course by themselves. Instead, following the first eight chapters of the macro portion, I have added short supplements to introduce the student to the *meaning* of quantitative methods.

My purpose, let me be clear, is not to try to cram even the beginnings of statistical expertise into students, who will not be able to calculate a standard deviation or a simple regression after finishing these short sections. But I hope they will be able to understand what statistics is about. In particular, I hope they will become wary of data, alive to problems of bias and selection, generally informed about what correlation seeks to do, and able to describe the kinds of problems to which econometrics addresses itself, although not the techniques it uses.

As before, I am very hesitant about suggesting to an instructor how he can best use this book. I know from much correspondence that some instructors spend a great deal of class time on the history section; others skip over it and assign it for background reading only. Some start with the micro section and take macro second; others go straight through as it is. I believe the book works best when it is followed from start to finish (and I do hope that every instructor will want to open with the dissonances of Chapter 1), but I know from talking with many teachers that there is no single right way to teach anything—only the way that suits that teacher best.

Hence let me conclude by wishing the instructor well. To instill in a single course what Schumpeter called a historical *sense,* and to combine this with a solid grasp of the prime movers of the macro and micro systems is a great deal; and to make that instillation permanent is a pedagogical triumph. No textbook, no matter how organized, explicit, lucid, or dramatic, can do this task alone. In the end, teaching remains a great art, one whose importance is too often overlooked. I only hope that those who have previously used *The Economic Problem* as a supplement to their teaching will find that the new edition eases their task and that those who will be using it for the first time will find its pace and methods to their taste—and perhaps, what is more important, to their students' taste.

Finally, I must add a note of thanks for those who have helped me at various stages of this enterprise. For this edition I have had the indispensable services of Eugene Epstein, a graduate student at the New School. I am much indebted to him, in particular for the initial drafting of all the statistical sections. John Owen, my colleague at the New School, and Maurice A. Girgis of Ball State University have kindly looked over these sections and have added many valuable suggestions of their own. To all the economists who have helped build the foundation on which this third edition stands, my gratitude is undiminished: Richard Attiyeh, Peter Bernstein, David Borfeld, Abraham Falick, John Hannaford, Peter John, Harry Johnson, Wylie Logan Jones, Don Kline, John M. Kuhlman, Hans Neisser, Goran Ohlin, Richard O'Rourke, Paul Phillips, and others including, above all, the dedicatee of this book, Adolph Lowe. To my editor at Prentice-Hall, Maurine Lewis, undying affection; to my straw boss there, Charles Briqueleur, dagger looks and much appreciation. To my students everywhere, deep thanks.

I can hardly imagine a student not reading the pages addressed to his professors, so I will begin by assuming that the main purpose of this book, as set forth in the preceding Introduction, is already clear to you. Yet, before the actual text begins and I drop the first person pronoun for the decent anonymity of textbook prose, there is a personal word I would like to address to students (and to their teachers who are no doubt trespassing in these pages).

The word, as I have said, is *relevance,* and *The Economic Problem* is as relevant as I can make it. Yet I do not want to raise false expectations with regard to what the bulk of this book is about. It begins with a "documentary"—America Today—but very quickly thereafter it settles into the serious and sober task of economic *analysis.* If Chapter 1 shocks you—as it shocked me to write it—the remaining thirty-five chapters are there to make you think, not to keep your blood pressure up. Hence you must be prepared for a long, eventful voyage through history, and then across the uncharted plains of something called macro- and microanalysis, and then further yet into international economics and still more history before you can claim to have thought *as an economist* about the problems of Chapter 1.

Is the trip a difficult one? I don't think the question should have an airily reassuring answer. Economics *is* difficult in a special way for certain people, and it is wise to face this fact honestly at the beginning. At the same time, it is important to understand the reasons for its difficulty. They do not lie in the inherent complexity of economic analysis. Economics, at least on the level of this book, presents no undue strains on anyone's powers of memory or computation or creative ability; and even in its most technically involved parts, where graphs and a few simple equations come into use, it is far from forbidding.

What is the nature of the difficulty then? I believe there are two causes, one relatively easily overcome and the second not so easily. The first is the need to acquire a new vocabulary when you speak or write economics. Like every technical discipline, from engineering to psychology, economics seeks to define its concerns as precisely as possible, and this necessitates creating words and phrases that have an unambiguous meaning, but that are unfamiliar in ordinary talk. To become an economist you have to learn at least a dozen words that have meanings different from those they have in daily use—I think of *capital, investment, consumption,* or *demand,* for instance— and another dozen phrases that come at first awkwardly to the tongue (and sometimes not at all to the mind): *marginal propensity to consume, average variable cost,* and some others.

In economics as in French, some people acquire new words and phrases easily, and some do not; and in economics as in French, until you can say things correctly, you are apt to say things very wrongly. So when the text says *gross domestic private investment,* those are the words that should be learned and not just any combination of three of them because they seem to mean almost the same thing. Fortunately, the necessary economic vocabulary is a good deal smaller than French, and the long and awkward phrases get shorter and easier as you say them a few times.

Economics is not really a hard language to learn. The second and more fundamental difficulty is that it is a hard language to think. This is because of an attribute of economics that comes as a surprise to many students. It is the *abstractness* of the subject. By *abstractness,* I most emphatically do not mean dullness, for economics is anything but dull. I mean that the matters with which economics is concerned—inflation, poverty, even racism—undergo a curious fading as they come under the economic lens. The color, the variety, the passion of life is bleached out, and what remains for investigation is schematized, as in a blueprint.

There is a very good reason for this blueprinting process. It is that economics is not primarily interested in the *description* of social happenings, but in the *analysis* of their causes and effects. If you want a rollicking account of the late 1920s, for example, you must go to the books of a social historian, such as Frederick Lewis Allen's *Only Yesterday,* and not to a book of economics that deals with the same period, such as Joseph Schumpeter's *Business Cycles.* Allen is trying to reconstitute in the reader's mind what it was like to live in those times; Schumpeter is interested in discovering the subterranean forces that were at work during the period and that eventually blew it up like a great volcano. Thus economics tries to go to the root of things. It tries to establish the long-lasting causes of, and connections among, events that emerge on the surface of life—the *reasons* for prosperity and depression rather than the characteristics of either; the consequences of inflation or racial prejudice, rather than the injustices of both.

The point is, then, that it takes a special effort of mind to learn to think of or to view things as an economist does, and this is not a turn of mind that everyone has. Further, the very injustices and failures about which economics *is* ultimately concerned often get in the way of putting a certain distance between ourselves and the problem at hand. The capacity to think in the generalizing fashion of economics, rather than in the individualizing fashion of daily life, is a gift that is distributed unevenly among people. Some take to this unaccustomed but powerful mode of thought as a duck to water; others have to swim for their lives. For the latter, I have no lifesaver ready at hand; but it may at least be helpful for a student who finds himself sinking to know what the trouble may be.

Finally, I must offer a word of advice to all students, easy swimmers or not. Accompanying the text you will find questions and problems, some at the end of chapters, others in a very skillfully prepared workbook by Dr. John Hannaford. *Do them.* Economics is not a subject that will just "sink in" by reading about it. It has to be learned by working in and with it. Even economic history, unlike the lists of kings or Presidents we all once learned, cannot simply be memorized, but must be thought about, for it is essentially explanatory and not merely narrative history. And certainly the operation of the economy as a whole, in Part Three, or of its constituent parts, in Part Four, cannot be learned by merely reading or listening to the instructor, no matter how attentively. The relationships that economics seeks to clarify must be figured out by yourself, by drawing your own diagrams (without looking at the text) or by calculating your own answers to the problems in the workbook. If you are like most students, you will find that when you sit down to reproduce a "simple" diagram, you will not get it quite right the first time, or your calculations will somehow go astray. It is only by making mistakes and then discovering what went wrong that what the psychologist calls the "Aha!" sensation will come.

But this is enough by way of a pre-game pep talk. The thing now is to take the plunge. In the first chapter you will find the "documentary" I mentioned at the beginning of this Introduction. Let us reserve further talk about economics until we have looked at that film.

Prologue

We Americans tend to think of ourselves as members of the richest society on earth. And so we are, for by the measure usually employed to count riches—gross national product—the American economy is beyond doubt the wealthiest in the world. In the winter of 1970, gross national product (GNP) crossed the trillion dollar mark for the first time in our history. Per capita, that amounted to approximately $5,000 for every man, woman, and child in the land. This is one third higher than the next richest country, Sweden; 40 percent higher than the next after Sweden: Canada; more than double that of West Germany; almost four times that of the Netherlands; and incomparably greater than the per capita GNP of India, which amounts to the equivalent of one week's American income per Indian—per year.[1]

Yet, these gargantuan figures mask a seamy side of American life. The wealth is there—but so is an extraordinary carelessness in its use; so that far from enjoying the highest standard of general well-being of any nation on earth, we find that our overall riches coexist with a degree of social neglect comparable to that of some of the poorest nations on earth.[2]

Take, for example, what is probably the most meaningful indicator of social welfare—the sheer statistical chances of remaining alive in a given society. Since the United States spends a higher proportion of its GNP on health services than any other nation, we might suppose that life expectancy in this country would be the highest in the world. It is not. In 1965 the United States ranked 22nd in male life expectancy and 10th in female life expectancy. Perhaps even more shocking, it ranked 24th in infant survival, putting it roughly at the level of Hong Kong.[3]

Or take the quality, rather than the "quantity," of life as an indicator of relative well-being. There exists no official index of the extent of slums or

[1] *Statistical Abstract of the United States* (Washington, D.C.: U.S. Bureau of the Census, 1970), p. 810. Let the reader be warned that intercountry comparisons of GNP are very shaky for reasons that will become clearer when we study GNP in Chapter 10. Nevertheless, GNP is the most commonly used measure of comparative international well-being.

[2] See R. Heilbroner, "The Roots of Social Neglect in the United States" in *Is Law Dead?* ed. Eugene Rostow (New York: Simon & Schuster, 1971).

[3] *Toward a Social Report* (Washington, D.C.: Department of Health, Education and Welfare, 1969), pp. 1-13; also N. Glazer "Paradoxes of Health Care," *The Public Interest,* No. 22 (Winter 1971), 72.

urban decay here or in other nations, but anyone who has traveled abroad knows that to match the lower depths of the New York, Detroit, Chicago, or any large American city one must visit not Europe but the underdeveloped world. To put it the other way around, any traveler knows that the general cleanliness and decency to be found in virtually *all* Scandanavian, West German, Swiss, or Dutch cities is simply not to be found in *any* large United States city at all.

Nor is it merely a matter of urban blight. The rural slums in America also vie with those of the underdeveloped world in sheer misery and neglect. Nearly a quarter of the (white) population of eastern Kentucky, for example, cannot read or write;[4] and malnutrition to the point of actual starvation has been discovered in some sections of the South and Southwest (including the presence of kwashiorkor, an illness formerly associated only with areas of extreme privation such as Central Africa).

Thus, if we are the richest nation in the world, we are also one of the more socially neglectful—ignorant of, or acquiescent in, conditions that other, less wealthy nations no longer tolerate.

POVERTY

This brings us to the broad problem of poverty in America. Poverty is, of course, a relative concept. A Calcutta family of street-dwellers would consider itself unimaginably well-off if it were given rupees equal to welfare payments made to a family in Mississippi (1969: $47 per month). A Mississippi family on welfare, transported to New York (average welfare per month $248) might also feel prosperous (a situation that helps explain the influx of rural poor to the big cities). So, too, some Americans who are officially "poor" may have incomes higher than those of some Norwegians who think of themselves as comfortable—perhaps because no Norwegian suffers the ill effects of slum conditions so common in America.

Yet, with all the problems of defining poverty, few would call the present U.S. definition extravagant. The U.S. Department of Labor establishes a poverty threshold that ranges from an income of $1,748 for a single

[4] Paul Good, *The American Serfs* (New York: Putnam, 1968), p. 166.

person living in a metropolitan area to $5,789 for a city-dwelling family of seven ($2.27 per person per day). By this definition, about 10 percent of urban Americans in 1968 were poor. The poverty threshold is appreciably lower for rural areas ($1,487 for a single person; $4,916 for a seven-member family), where 23 percent of all families fall below the threshold. For the nation as a whole, roughly one family in seven is officially considered "poor," and perhaps double that number "near-poor."[5]

But these overall figures dilute what poverty means to those who suffer from it, for the incidence of poverty is not random. It affects some groups much more severely than others. In 1968, for example, among families headed by a person 65 or older, 31 percent were poor. Among Negro families, 33 percent were poor; and among families (black or white) in which no adult male breadwinner was present, almost 39 percent were poor. For large groups of Americans, in other words—the aged, the blacks, the broken families—poverty is more likely to be a near-normal state of affairs than an unhappy accident. Put differently, whereas 41 percent of all white American families enjoy incomes of more than $10,000 a year, only 19 percent of Negro families have reached this degree of modest affluence; and whereas only 9 percent of white families fall below $3,000 a year, 24 percent of Negro families are clustered in this lowest range.[6]

Because of this clustering we cannot regard poverty with complacency, secure in the knowledge that the problem will gradually disappear. Although poverty has been slowly shrinking within American society as a whole, it rose 5 percent from 1969 to 1970, reversing a 10-year trend. Furthermore, poverty is not shrinking in certain critical areas. As the racial composition of the cities changes, for example, the concentration of poverty becomes worse, not better. It is estimated that we can expect an *additional* 1.4 million nonwhite poor children in our central cities by 1985.[7] What effect that will have on the crime rate, the drug problem, and the general civility of those cities can be imagined.

Poverty must be considered an aspect of social neglect by any nation affluent enough to eliminate it. And for Americans, this is perhaps the most disturbing aspect of all, for the elimination of poverty in America would not be a difficult task. To transfer enough money to bring all officially "poor" families up to the poverty threshold level would require approximately $10 to $15 billions per annum—between 1 and 1.5 percent of our GNP. Alternatively, if the 85 percent of households who are not poor would acquiesce in having the *growth* in their annual incomes reduced from an average of about 3 percent a year to about 2.5 percent, allowing the difference to be trans-

[5] *Statistical Abstract of the United States,* (1970), p. 327. See also *Economic Report of the President 1969* (Washington, D.C.), p. 151*f*; and Anthony Downs, *Who Are the Urban Poor?* (Washington, D.C.: Committee for Economic Development, 1970), *passim.*

[6] *Statistical Abstract,* 1970, p. 328.

[7] Downs, *Who Are the Urban Poor?* p. 55.

ferred to the poor, within less than five years all families below the poverty line would have been brought up to levels of minimum decency.[8]

But so far no such willingness has been visible, either within Congress or in any "grass roots" movement. As one observer has bitterly commented: "The middle class knows that the economists are right when they say that poverty could be eliminated if only we will it; they simply do not will it."[9]

Now let us turn to another aspect of our economic troubles. It is that perhaps 8 to 9 percent of the trillion dollars of total output of the American economy consists of military goods and services—missiles, bombs, planes, tanks, payrolls of the armed forces, military subsidies to foreign nations, and the like. The "perhaps" refers to the fact that we cannot give a very precise estimate of total military spending, because its full extent is only now being revealed. Recently, for example, the Senate Foreign Relations Committee discovered that direct and indirect military assistance to foreign nations for 1971 totalled $6.9 billion, whereas the item for Military Assistance in the President's Budget Message to Congress listed it at only $625 million. It was discovered as well that under the Food for Peace Program, $691 million had been transferred to foreign nations *for the purchase of arms;* that the United States had spent $1.5 billion in supporting South Vietnamese currency, of which $680 million was lost because of an overvaluation of that currency; and that the Pentagon had a surplus weapons stock worth $17 billion.[10]

After listening to three days of testimony with regard to the hitherto undisclosed flow of military assistance abroad, a senator said: "Most of us in Washington have seen a lot of mismanagement in government programs. But military assistance is the first program I have come across that appears to be characterized by unmanagement.... In some respects, the United States has been transformed from an 'arsenal of democracy' to a gigantic discount supermarket with no check-out counters, no store managers—only clerks who blithely deliver to foreign governments of practically any political persuasion whatever they happen to see and like."

If there is much that we do not yet know about the extent of our military economy, what we do know is sobering enough. The Department of Defense (DOD) is the largest planned economy outside the Soviet Union. Its property—plant and equipment, land, inventories of war and other commodities—amounts to some $202 billion, equal to about 8 percent of the assets of the entire American economy. It owns 39 million acres of land, roughly an area the size of Hawaii. It rules over a population of 4 million—direct employees or soldiers—and spends an "official" budget of over $75 billion, a

[8] *Economic Report of the President,* 1969, p. 160.

[9] Adam Walinsky in *The New Republic,* July 4, 1964, p. 15.

[10] Reported in *Sane World* (February 1971); figures from hearings before the Joint Subcommittee on Economy in Government (January 1971).

budget three-quarters as large as the entire gross national product of Great Britain.[11]

This makes the DOD richer than any small nation in the world and, of course, incomparably more powerful. That part of its assets represented by nuclear explosives alone gives it the equivalent of six tons of TNT for every living inhabitant of the globe, to which must be added the awesome military power of its "conventional" weapons. The conventional explosives dropped in Indochina *before* the extension of the war to Laos amounted to well over 3 million tons, or 50 percent *more* than the total bomb tonnage dropped on all nations in both European and Pacific theaters during World War II.

The DOD system embraces both men and industry. In 1969 the men (and women) included, first, some 3 million soldiers deployed in 2,257 bases or locations abroad and at home, plus another one million civilians located within the United States and abroad. No less important are at least 2.3 million civilian workers who are directly employed on war production, in addition to a much larger number employed in the secondary echelon of defense-related output. This does not include still further millions who owe their livelihood to the civilian services they render to the military. Symptomatic of the pervasive influence of military spending is the rise in unemployment in Connecticut to 8.1 percent of the labor force when a first small effort was made in 1971 to cut back on military output. What would be the effect of a major contraction in defense spending is a problem we will have to defer for later consideration, but no one denies that such a major contraction—*unless counteracted by vigorous expansion of peacetime spending*—could plunge this country into a severe depression.

The web of DOD expenditures extends to more areas of the economy than one might think. One expects Lockheed Aircraft, with 88 percent of its sales to the government, to be a ward of the DOD, which explains why the government agreed to rescue the company from bankruptcy in 1971 with an enormous advance of funds. One does not expect the DOD to show up as the source of some 44 percent of the revenues of Pan Am or to be, through its Post Exchange (PX) system the third largest marketing chain in the country, just after Sears Roebuck and the A&P; or to be a major factor in the construction business, spending more for military housing facilities between 1956 and 1967 than the total spent by federal government on all other public housing.[12]

All in all, some 22,000 firms are prime contractors with the DOD, although the widespread practice of subcontracting means that a much

---

[11] Adam Yarmolinsky, *The Military Establishment* (New York: Harper, 1971), p. 10. Note that this *excludes* the military component in our AID program, any military portion of NASA, and all CIA expenses. For further data on DOD employment and on the extent and distribution of military expenditure, see *Economic Report of the President,* 1971, pp. 42-49, and Seymour Melman, *Pentagon Capitalism* (New York: McGraw-Hill, 1970), pp. 72-73, 79.

[12] Melman, *Pentagon Capitalism,* pp. 72-73, 79.

larger number of enterprises—perhaps 100,000 in all—look to defense spending for a portion of their income. Within the main constituency, however, a very few firms are the bastion of the DOD economy. The hundred largest defense contractors supply about two-thirds of the $40-odd billion of manufactured deliveries; and within this group, an inner group of ten firms by themselves accounted for 30 percent of the total. Incidentally, many of these largest contractors owe not only their sales to the military economy, but a considerable portion of their capital as well. As of 1967, defense contractors used $2 billion worth of government-owned furniture and office machines, $4.7 billion worth of government-owned materials, and over $5 billion worth of government plant and equipment, on all of which they were allowed to make profits just as if they were using their own property.[13]

The military establishment, as the largest single customer in the economy, not only supports a central core of industry but also penetrates that core with 2,072 retired military officers who were employed in 1969 by the 95 biggest contractors (the 10 largest firms averaging 106 officers each). Meanwhile, the establishment has a powerful political arm as well. The DOD employs some 339 lobbyists on Capitol Hill and (a conservative estimate) some 2,700 public relations men in the U.S. and abroad. This close political relationship undoubtedly has some bearing on the Pentagon's requests for funds being given, until recently, only the most cursory congressional inspection, leading among other things to cost "overruns" of $24 billion on 38 weapons systems.

This is not to say, of course, that the United States does not need a strong defense capability today. But at what point does a "defense" capability become an instrument for aggressive use in its own right? To what extent has the sheer weight of military power been the cause of the *fifty* acts of military intervention officially listed since the end of World War II?[14]

To many of these questions we will return later, for it is clear that our military-industrial subeconomy poses a tremendous problem for (perhaps *of*) American capitalism. Meanwhile, it is worth pondering the words of Professor Seymour Melman, a well-known expert on military economics:

Rarely does a single social force have a controlling influence in changing, swiftly, the character of life in a large and complex society. The expansion of the Pentagon and its state-management is such a force. Failing decisive action to reverse the economic and other growth of these institutions, then the parent state, if it is saved from nuclear war, will surely become the guardian of a garrison-like society dominated by the Pentagon and its state-management."[15]

[13] Melman, *Pentagon Capitalism,* p. 80.
[14] Yarmolinsky, *The Military Establishment,* Chaps. 13, 14; also *The Pentagon Watchers,* Leonard Rodberg and Derek Sherer, eds. (Garden City, N.Y.: Doubleday, 1970), pp. 99–140, 143.
[15] Melman, *Pentagon Capitalism,* p. 227.

Neglect, poverty, militarism are aspects of American society to which critics have been sensitive for some time. But with startling swiftness, a new, almost wholly overlooked problem has come to the fore. This is the problem of pollution, the frightening rate at which we are narrowing the margin of safety in the air we breathe, the water we drink, the wastes we discharge into the environment.

ITEM: *Annual throwaway list:*

214 million tons of carbon monoxide, sulfur oxides, hydrocarbons, particulates, and nitrous oxides (over a ton per American)

55 billion tin cans (275 for each of us)

20 billion bottles (100 apiece)

65 billion metal and plastic bottle caps (325 each)

7 million cars (our annual output has to go *somewhere* after 100,000 miles or so)

10 million tons of steel and iron scrap (an average of 1,000 pounds each)

150 million tons of garbage and trash (4.1 pounds per person daily)

3 billion tons of tailings, mine debris, and waste (4 tons for each of us each day)

ITEM: In August, 1969, inhabitants of Los Angeles and St. Louis were warned against indulging in any kind of exercise, including jogging, golf, etc., because deep breathing was dangerous.

ITEM: Nitrates and phosphates in fertilizers and detergents cause water pollution problems that are beyond the control of present technology. The use of these chemicals is estimated to increase by tenfold before the year 2000. Professor Barry Commoner, ecologist, predicts a major agricultural crisis in the United States from this source alone within 50 years.

ITEM: It is estimated that by the year 2000, there will be, at any time, some 3,000 six ton trucks in transit carrying dangerous radioactive wastes to burial sites.

ITEM: With 6 percent of the world's population, the United States annually consumes about 40 percent of the world's output of raw materials and discharges into the environment about the same percentage of the world's waste products. Thus each American is roughly the equivalent of seven Asians or Africans or South Americans in his ecological disturbance. There are, in round numbers, some 2.2 billion inhabitants of Asia, Africa, and South America. What does this imply for the long-run chances of economic development in those areas? What does it imply about the long-run acceptable levels of economic "development" in the United States?[16] Clearly, here is a situation in which something must "give." Will it be the chance for economic development for the world's peoples, or will it be our profligate use of resources?

[16] See Paul and Anne Ehrlich, *Population, Resources, Environment* (San Francisco: Freeman, 1970), *passim.*

The troubles of the United States, it must be clear, are closely inter-twined. This is why it is difficult to deal with them individually. Social neglect is closely associated with poverty; and the failure to cope with social neglect and poverty are both connected with the vast military claim on our output; and all these in turn aggravate, and are aggravated by, the increasing pollution of the environment. Hence it is perhaps redundant to single out the special miseries of the ghetto as something apart from the issues we have already considered. Yet ghetto life, with its violence, its crime, its concentrated squalor, takes us more closely than any issue we have previously considered into what is surely one of the most troublesome problems that America faces today—racial discrimination. Let us therefore take a moment to sketch out its dimensions and peculiar difficulties.

How many people live in the black ghettos? No one is exactly sure. We have discovered that the census counts may be off by at least 10 percent in neighborhoods where addresses are often impermanent and where citizens avoid interviews by census takers, fearing them to be investigators from the welfare department, bill collectors, or process servers. But a reasonably reliable estimate puts the number of ghetto citizens at about 14 million, as of 1970. More important, because there continues to be an in-migration of blacks from the depressed rural South, we can expect the number to grow rapidly during the next decade. By 1985, the ghetto population is likely to have risen to over 20 million (and because of the high birthrate, will reach 17 million, even if in-migration comes to a halt).[17]

Life in the ghetto is mean, hard, and poor. Crime rates are higher than elsewhere in the country. Housing is scarcer and more expensive. Living is not cheap but expensive: a Federal Trade Commission study has revealed that prices in Washington, D.C., ghetto stores averaged $255 for each $100 of wholesale cost, compared with $159 for stores in nonghetto areas of the city.[18]

Typically, unemployment is rife in the ghetto. In 1970, the unemployment rate in poor urban neighborhoods was 60 percent higher than in the country at large. Among black teenagers, it reached a catastrophic level of 42 percent.[19] And even this may be an understatement of the problem, for a study of the slum labor market in New York City in 1966 revealed a "subemployment" rate that was three times higher than the official "unemployment" figure.[20] (This is a rate that takes into consideration the special problems of very low-wage employment and of the failure of official statistics to report on those who were so discouraged that they were no longer even looking for work.)

[17] W.K. Tabb, *The Political Economy of the Ghetto* (New York: Norton, 1970), p. 8: Carolyn Shaw Bell, *The Economics of the Ghetto* (New York: Pegasus, 1970), *passim.*

[18] Tabb, *ibid.,* pp. 38–40; Bell, *ibid.,* pp. 142–43.

[19] *The New York Times,* Jan. 25, 1971, p. 1.

[20] *Poverty and Economic Development in New York City,* First National City Bank (December 1968), p. 25.

Perhaps worst of all is the outlook for those who grow up in the ghetto and want to escape. The same New York City study revealed how tragically mismatched were the skills (or lack of skills) offered by the ghetto resident and those wanted by the outside world.

TABLE 1•1

THE SKILLS GAP

	Occupational distribution of ghetto unemployed, 1966	Estimated job openings, 1965–1975
White collar	13.6	65.7
Craftsmen	2.8	7.4
Operatives	14.7	7.7
Service	16.6	18.6
Laborers and others	52.3	0.6

Source: First National City Bank, *op cit.*, p. 12.

As the table shows, in only one category—service—was the prospective demand for labor roughly in line with the skills that were available. This meant a reasonable employment prospect for maids, restaurant workers, bellhops, and the like—among the lowest-paid occupations in the nation. As for the common laborer, who comprised over half the "skill pool" of the New York ghetto, the outlook for his services was bleak indeed—less than 1 percent of the estimated new jobs would fall in that category. Conversely, for the widest job market in the outside world, the white-collar trades that will offer over two-thirds of the new jobs over the decade ahead—the ghetto was able to offer only one-seventh of its residents as adequately trained. If these figures have any meaning at all, it is that ghetto poverty is here to stay, short of a herculean effort to retrain the trapped ghetto resident.

PROBLEMS VS. SOLUTIONS

This is not a balanced view of America, and it is not meant to be. On the one hand it omits everything that is reassuring or healthy on our economic scene; but it also omits areas in which economic problems remain to be explored. Unemployment *outside* the ghetto; the seemingly intractable problem of inflation; the power of giant corporations and strategically located labor unions; the relationship of rich America to the economies of the underdeveloped world—all these and still other problems remain for examination.

Hence what we have covered is no more than a partial inventory of America's debits and none of its credits. More important, we have only described in a journalistic way the things that are troubling America's conscience and we have as yet made no effort to probe into their origins or to assess their consequences. In short, we have done little more than make explicit some of the questions that we have in mind when we ask "Is economics relevant?" and some of the problems to which a textbook on economics should address itself.

Now it is time to conclude this initial plunge into some of the realities of the American scene, and to prepare ourselves for the lengthy and careful analysis that is to follow. That analysis will take us with disconcerting suddenness from the concerns of today to those of the ancient—and yet, as we will see, not entirely "remote"—past. We are going to take a detour through history before we come out again upon the present, to look around with new perspectives on today's problems. That, in turn, will prepare the way for a tour through the "principles" of economics itself—that is, through an analysis of the ways in which the society we live in can be understood as an economic mechanism.

Throughout this journey through economic history we shall be dealing with problems in some ways different from those we have raised in this first documentary view of America. Some problems will be remote in time; later, when we get to theory, they may seem remote in concern. Yet, by the time we have completed our historical and analytical tour, I hope that America's problems will be understandable in ways that they were not before we started. Moreover, we shall not lose sight of the contemporary issues themselves, for at many points in our historical and analytic exposition we will stop to consider the matters we have raised in this chapter.

There remains only one question before we embark on our historical search. It is the question of what is the root cause of the panorama of problems we have encountered in America Today. All through the 1960s we tended to think of these problems as faults and flaws within an essentially sound economic system, for which specific remedies could be found. But in the 1970s a more disturbing question is in the air. It asks: are the problems the consequence of the system itself? Can our kind of economic society produce a decent, peaceful, compassionate way of life? *Or can the troubles of our time be corrected only drastically, by dismantling American capitalism and creating a new economic system?*

That is the fundamental question to which this entire book is ultimately directed. But it is not a question to be taken on at once. To cope with it, we will need to draw on a considerable understanding of economic history and of the complex mechanics by which a system such as ours operates. Hence, only when we have gained some perspective on capitalism, both in history and in theory, will we attempt to risk an answer to a question so profound and momentous as whether American capitalism is salvageable, despite its problems.

So we shall have to complete a course of study before the final answer. But meanwhile, I trust that one thing has become indisputably clear: that economics is concerned with dramatic and decisive issues that are likely to affect you for the rest of your life. Many years ago, when I wrote *The Worldly Philosophers,** I said:

A man who thinks that economics is only a matter for professors forgets that this is the science that has sent men to the barricades. A man who has looked into an economics textbook and concluded that economics is boring is like a man who has read a primer on logistics and decided that the study of warfare must be dull.

I hope that this book will not be boring and that those who read it will not conclude that economics had best be left to the professordom, because the problems of America Tomorrow will depend to no small degree on the economic understanding of those who are studying America Today.

CONCEPTS, WORDS, AND QUESTIONS

All the following chapters end with summaries of key concepts—to help you focus on the important propositions in that chapter—key words to add to your vocabulary, and questions to make you think out for yourself the main points at issue. But in this first chapter, I think a summary is out of place, and questions are premature. This is not a chapter to be "studied," but one to be thought about. If it has made you angry or troubled, it has served its purpose. Now you are in the right mood to begin to study modern economics itself.

* On the front endpapers of the book, the reader will find a gallery of those sometimes very worldly and sometimes out-of-this worldly characters drawn by Bernarda Bryson. I am grateful to the *Scientific American* for permission to use one of Miss Bryson's drawings.

The emergence

of modern

economic

society

Having decided on our course of exploration, it would be convenient if we could immediately begin to examine our economic past. But not quite yet. Before we can retrace economic history, we need to know what economic history *is*. And that, in turn, requires us to take a moment to clarify what we mean by economics and by the economic problem itself.

The answer is not a complicated one. Economics is essentially the study of a process we find in all human societies—"the" economic problem is simply *the process of providing for the material well-being of society.* In its simplest terms, economics is the study of how man earns his daily bread.

This hardly seems like a particularly exciting subject for historical scrutiny. Indeed, when we look back over the pageant of what is usually called "history," the humble matter of bread hardly strikes the eye at all. Power and glory, faith and fanaticism, ideas and ideologies are the aspects of the human chronicle that crowd the pages of history books. If the simple quest for bread is a moving force in human destiny, it is well concealed behind what one philosopher historian has called "that history of international crime and mass murder which has been advertised as the history of mankind."[1]

Yet, if man does not live by bread alone, it is obvious that he cannot live without bread. Like every other living thing, the human being must eat—the imperious first rule of continued existence. And this first prerequisite is less to be taken for granted than at first appears, for the human organism is not, in itself, a highly efficient mechanism for survival. From each hundred calories of food it consumes, it can deliver only about twenty calories of mechanical energy. On a decent diet, man can produce just about one horsepower-hour of work daily, and with that he must replenish his exhausted body. With what is left over, he is free to build a civilization.

As a result, in many countries, the sheer continuity of human existence is far from assured. In the vast continents of Asia and Africa, in the Near

[1] Karl Popper, *The Open Society and Its Enemies,* 3rd ed. (London: Routledge, 1957), II, 270.

East, even in some countries of South America, brute survival is the problem that stares humanity in the face. Millions of human beings have died of starvation or malnutrition in our present era, as countless hundreds of millions have died over the long past. Whole nations are acutely aware of what it means to face hunger as a condition of ordinary life; it has been said, for example, that the Egyptian fellah, from the day he is born to the day he dies, never knows what it is to have a full stomach. In many of the so-called underdeveloped nations, the life span of the average person is less than half of ours. Not many years ago, an Indian demographer made the chilling calculation that of one hundred Asian and one hundred American infants, more Americans would be alive at age sixty-five than Indians at age *five!* The statistics, not of life but of premature death throughout most of the world, are overwhelming and crushing.

Thus we can see that economic history must focus on the central problem of survival and on how man has solved that problem. For most Americans, this may make economics seem very remote. Few of us are conscious of anything resembling a life-or-death struggle for existence. That it might be possible for us to experience severe want, that we might ever know in our own bodies the pangs of hunger experienced by an Indian villager or a Bolivian peon is a thought nearly impossible for most of us to entertain seriously.

Short of a catastrophic war, it is highly unlikely that many of us ever will know the full meaning of the struggle for existence. Nonetheless, even in our prosperous and secure society, there remains, however unnoticed, an aspect of life's precariousness, a reminder of the underlying problem of survival. *This is our helplessness as economic individuals.*

For it is a curious fact that as we leave the most impoverished peoples of the world, where the human being with his too few calories scratches out for himself a bare subsistence, we find the economic insecurity of the individual many times multiplied. The solitary Eskimo, Bushman, Indone-

THE INDIVIDUAL AND SOCIETY

sian, Nigerian, left to his own devices, will survive a considerable time. Living close to the soil or to his animal prey, such an individual can sustain his own life, at least for a while, singlehanded. With a community numbering only a few hundred, he can live indefinitely. Indeed, a very large percentage of the human race today lives in precisely such fashion—in small, virtually self-contained peasant communities that provide for their own survival with a minimum of contact with the outside world. This large portion of mankind suffers great poverty, but it also knows a certain economic independence. If it did not, it would have been wiped out centuries ago.

When we turn to the New Yorker or the Chicagoan, on the other hand, we are struck by exactly the opposite condition, by a prevailing ease of material life coupled with an extreme *dependence* on others. We can no longer envisage the solitary individual or the small community surviving unaided in the great metropolitan areas where most Americans live, unless they loot warehouses or stores for food and necessities. The overwhelming majority of Americans have never grown food, caught game, raised meat, ground grain into flour, or even fashioned flour into bread. Faced with the challenge of clothing themselves or building their own homes, they would be hopelessly untrained and unprepared. Even to make minor repairs in the machines which surround them, they must call on other members of the community whose business it is to fix cars or repair plumbing or whatever. Paradoxically, perhaps, the richer the nation, the more apparent is this inability of its average inhabitant to survive unaided and alone.

DIVISION OF LABOR

There is, of course, an answer to the paradox. We survive in rich nations because the tasks we cannot do ourselves are done for us by an army of others on whom we can call for help. If we cannot grow food, we can buy it; if we cannot provide for our needs ourselves, we can hire the services of someone who can. This enormous *division of labor* enhances our capacity a thousandfold, for it enables us to benefit from other men's skills as well as our own.

Along with this invaluable gain, however, comes a certain risk. It is a sobering thought, for example, that we depend on the services of less than 150,000 men—only one out of every five hundred people working in the nation—to provide us with that basic commodity, coal. An even smaller number of workers—only one third as many—are responsible for running the locomotives that haul all the nation's rail freight and passenger service. A still smaller number—roughly 20,000—comprises our total commercial aircraft pilot crew. A failure of any one of these very small groups to perform its functions would cripple us: in the case of airplane pilots, slightly; in the case of locomotive engineers, badly; in the case of coal miners, perhaps disastrously. As we know, when from time to time we face a bad strike, our entire economic machine may falter because a strategic group ceases to perform its accustomed tasks.

Thus along with the abundance of material existence as we know it goes a hidden vulnerability: our abundance is assured only insofar as the organized cooperation of huge armies of people is to be counted upon. Indeed, our continuing existence as a rich nation hinges on the tacit precondition that the mechanism of social organization will continue to function effectively. *We are rich, not as individuals, but as members of a rich society, and our easy assumption of material sufficiency is actually only as reliable as the bonds that forge us into a social whole.*

Strangely enough, then, we find that man, not nature, is the source of most of our economic problems, at least above the level of subsistance. To be sure, the economic problem itself—that is, the need to struggle for existence—derives ultimately from the *scarcity* of nature. If there were no scarcity, goods would be as free as air, and economics—at least in one sense of the word—would cease to exist as a social preoccupation.

And yet if the scarcity of nature sets the stage for the economic problem, it does not impose the only strictures against which men must struggle. For scarcity, as a felt condition, is not solely the fault of nature. If Americans today, for instance, were content to live at the level of Mexican peasants, all our material wants could be fully satisfied with but an hour or two of daily labor. We would experience little or no scarcity, and our economic problems would virtually disappear. Instead, we find in America—and indeed in all industrial societies—that as the ability to increase nature's yield has risen, so has the reach of human wants. In fact, in societies such as ours, where relative social status is importantly connected with the possession of material goods, we often find that "scarcity" as a psychological experience and goad becomes more pronounced as we grow wealthier: our desires to possess the fruits of nature race out ahead of our mounting ability to produce goods.

Thus the "wants" that nature must satisfy are by no means fixed. But, for that matter, nature's yield itself is not a constant. It varies over a wide range, depending on the social application of human energy and skill. Scarcity is therefore not attributable to nature alone but to "human nature" as well; and economics is ultimately concerned not merely with the stinginess of the physical environment, but equally with the appetite of the human being and the productive capability of the community.

ECONOMICS AND SCARCITY

Hence we must begin a systematic analysis of economics by singling out the functions that social organization must perform to bring human nature into social harness. And when we turn our attention to this funda-

ECONOMICS AND SOCIAL ORGANIZATION

mental problem, we can quickly see that it involves the solution of two related and yet separate elemental tasks:

1. *A society must organize a system to assure the production of enough goods and services for its own survival.*
2. *Society must also arrange the distribution of the fruits of its production so that more production can take place.*

These two tasks of economic continuity are, at first look, very simple.* But it is a deceptive simplicity. Much of economic history, as we shall see, is concerned with the manner in which various societies have sought to cope with these elementary problems; and what strikes us in surveying their attempts is that most of them were partial failures. (They could not have been total failures, or society would not have survived.) Hence it behooves us to look more carefully into the two main economic tasks, to see what hidden difficulties they may conceal.

Production and Distribution Problems

MOBILIZING EFFORT

What are the obstacles that a society encounters in organizing a system to produce the goods and services it needs?

Since nature is usually stingy, it seems that the production problem must be essentially one of applying engineering or technical skills to the resources at hand, of avoiding waste and utilizing social effort as efficaciously as possible.

This is indeed an important task for any society, and a great deal of formal economic thought, as the word itself suggests, is devoted to economizing. Yet this is not the core of the production problem. Long before a society can even concern itself about using its energies "economically," it must first marshal the energies to carry out the productive process itself. That is, *the basic problem of production is to devise social institutions that will mobilize human energy for productive purposes.*

This basic requirement is not always so easily accomplished. For example, in the United States in 1933, the energies of nearly thirteen million people—one-quarter of our work force—were not directed into the produc-

---

* In Chapter 21 we will return to the Economic Problem in a somewhat more technical perspective. There we will note that the production problem is itself a twofold task, involving both a choice of different *ends* to which effort may be put and also of different *methods* by which those ends may be sought. Here, where the challenge of social organization is emphasized, we combine these two tasks into a single overarching concern.

tion process at all. Although these unemployed men and women were eager to work, although empty factories were available for them to work in, despite the existence of pressing wants, somehow a terrible and mystifying breakdown short-circuited the production process, with the result that an entire third of our previous annual output of goods and services simply disappeared.

We are by no means the only nation that has, on occasion, failed to find work for willing workers. In the very poorest nations, where production is most desperately needed, we frequently find that unemployment is a chronic condition. The streets of the Asian cities are thronged with people who cannot find work. But this, too, is not a condition imposed by the scarcity of nature. There is, after all, an endless amount of work to be done, if only in cleaning the filthy streets or patching up the homes of the poor, building roads, or digging ditches. Yet, what seems to be lacking is a social mechanism to put the unemployed to work.

Both these examples point out to us that the production problem is not solely a physical and technical struggle with nature. On these "scarcity" aspects of the problem will depend the speed with which a nation may forge ahead and the level of well-being it can reach with a given effort. But the original mobilization of productive effort itself is a challenge to its *social organization*, and on the success or failure of that social organization will depend the volume of the human effort that can be directed to nature.

ALLOCATING EFFORT

But putting men to work is only the first step in the solution of the production problem. Men must not only be put to work; they must be put to work *in the right places*. They must produce the goods and services that society needs. Thus, *in addition to assuring a large enough quantity of social effort, the economic institutions of society must also assure a viable allocation of that social effort.*

In a nation such as India or Bolivia, where the great majority of the population is born in peasant villages and grows up to be peasant cultivators, the solution to this problem offers little to vex our understanding. The basic demands of society—food and fiber—are precisely the goods that its peasant population "naturally" produces. But in an industrial society, the proper allocation of effort becomes an enormously complicated task. People in the United States demand much more than bread and cotton. They need, for instance, such things as automobiles. Yet no one "naturally" produces an automobile. On the contrary, in order to produce one, an extraordinary spectrum of special tasks must be performed. Some people must make steel; others must make rubber. Still others must coordinate the assembly process itself. And this is but a tiny sampling of the far from "natural" tasks that must be performed if an automobile is to be produced.

As with the mobilization of its total production effort, society does not always succeed in the proper allocation of its effort. It may, for instance, turn out too many cars or too few. Of greater importance, it may devote its energies to the production of luxuries while large numbers of its people are starving. Or it may even court disaster by an inability to channel its productive effort into areas of critical importance. In the early 1950s, for instance, the British suffered a near economic collapse because they were unable to get enough of their workers to mine coal.

Such allocative failures may affect the production problem quite as seriously as a failure to mobilize an adequate quantity of effort, for a viable society must produce not only goods, but the right goods. And the allocative question alerts us to a still broader conclusion. It shows us that the act of production, in and of itself, does not fully answer the requirements for survival. Having produced enough of the *right* goods, society must now *distribute* those goods so that the production process can go on.

DISTRIBUTING OUTPUT

Once again, in the case of the peasant who feeds himself and his family from his own crop, this requirement of adequate distribution may seem simple enough. But when we go beyond the most primitive society, the problem is not always so readily solved. In many of the poorest nations of the East and South, urban workers have often been unable to deliver their daily horsepower-hour of work because they have not been given enough of society's output to run their human engines to capacity. Worse yet, they have often languished on the job while granaries bulged with grain and the well-to-do complained of the ineradicable laziness of the masses. At the other side of the picture, the distribution mechanism may fail because the rewards it hands out do not succeed in persuading people to perform their necessary tasks. Shortly after the Russian Revolution, some factories were organized into communes in which managers and janitors pooled their pay, and from which all drew equal allotments. The result was a rash of absenteeism on the part of the previously better-paid workers and a threatened breakdown in industrial production. Not until the old unequal wage payments were reinstituted did production resume its former course.

As was the case with failures in the production process, distributive failures need not entail a total economic collapse. Societies can exist—and indeed, in the majority of cases, do exist—with badly distorted productive and distributive efforts. It is only rarely, as in the instances above, that maldistribution actively interferes with the actual ability of a society to staff its production posts. More frequently, an inadequate solution to the distribution problem reveals itself in social and political unrest or even in revolution.

Yet this, too, is an aspect of the total economic problem. For if society is to insure its steady material replenishment, it must parcel out its production in a fashion that will maintain not only the capacity but the willingness to go on working. And thus again we find the focus of economic inquiry directed to the study of human institutions. For a viable economic society, we can now see, is not only one which can overcome the stringencies of nature, but one which can contain and control the intransigence of human nature.

The Three Solutions
to the Economic Problem

Thus to the economist, society presents itself in what is to us an unaccustomed aspect. Underneath the problems of poverty or pollution or the arms economy, he sees a process at work that he must understand before he can turn his attention to the issues of the day, no matter how pressing. That process is society's basic *mechanism for survival,* a mechanism for accomplishing the complicated tasks of its production and distribution necessary for its own continuity.

But the economist sees something else as well, something that at first seems quite astonishing. Looking not only over the diversity of contemporary societies, but back over the sweep of all history, he sees that man has succeeded in solving the production and distribution problems in but three ways. That is, within the enormous diversity of the actual social institutions that guide and shape the economic process, the economist divines but three overarching *types* of systems which separately or in combination enable humankind to solve its economic challenge. These great systemic types can be called economies run by *Tradition,* economies run by *Command,* and economies run by the *Market.* Let us briefly see what is characteristic of each.

TRADITION

Perhaps the oldest and, until a very few years ago, by far the most generally prevalent way of solving the economic challenge has been that of tradition. It has been a mode of social organization in which both production and distribution were based on procedures devised in the distant past, rigidified by a long process of historic trial and error, and maintained by heavy sanctions of law, custom, and belief.

Societies based on tradition solve the economic problems very manageably. First, they deal with the production problem—the problem of assuring that the needful tasks will be done—by assigning the jobs of fathers to their sons. Thus a hereditary chain assures that skills will be passed along and jobs will be staffed from generation to generation. In ancient Egypt, wrote Adam Smith, the first great economist, "every man was bound by a principle of religion to follow the occupation of his father and was supposed to commit the most horrible sacrilege if he changed it for another."[2] And it was not merely in antiquity that tradition preserved a productive orderliness within society. In our own Western culture, until the fifteenth or sixteenth centuries, the hereditary allocation of tasks was also the main stabilizing force within society. Although there was some movement from country to town and from occupation to occupation, birth usually determined one's role in life. One was born to the soil or to a trade; and on the soil or within the trade, one followed in the footsteps of one's forebears.

Thus tradition has been the stabilizing and impelling force behind a great repetitive cycle of society, assuring that society's work would be done each day very much as it had been done in the past. Even today, among the less industrialized nations of the world, tradition continues to play this immense organizing role. In India, for example, until very recently, one was born to a caste which had its own occupation. "Better thine own work is, though done with fault," preached the Bhagavad-Gita, the great philosophic moral poem of India, "than doing other's work, even excellently."

Tradition not only provides a solution to the production problem of society, but it also regulates the distribution problem. Take, for example, the Bushmen of the Kalahari Desert in South Africa who depend for their livelihood on their hunting prowess. Elizabeth Marshall Thomas, a sensitive observer of these peoples, reports on the manner in which tradition solves the problem of distributing their kill.

The gemsbok has vanished ... Gai owned two hind legs and a front leg, Tsetchwe had meat from the back, Ukwane had the other front leg, his wife had one of the feet and the stomach, the young boys had lengths of intestine. Twikwe had received the head and Dasina the udder.

It seems very unequal when you watch Bushmen divide the kill, yet it is their system, and in the end no person eats more than any other. That day Ukwane gave Gai still another piece because Gai was his relation, Gai gave meat to Dasina because she was his wife's mother ... No one, of course, contested Gai's large share, because he had been the hunter and by their law that much belonged to him. No one doubted that he would share his large amount with others, and they were not wrong, of course; he did.[3]

The manner in which tradition can divide a social product may be, as the illustration shows, very subtle and ingenious. It may also be very crude and, by our standards, harsh. Tradition has often allocated to women, in nonindustrial societies, the most meager portion of the social product. But

---

[2] *The Wealth of Nations* (New York: Modern Library, 1937), p. 62.
[3] *The Harmless People* (New York: Knopf, 1959), pp. 49–50.

however much the end-product of tradition may accord with, or depart from, our accustomed moral views, we must see that it is a workable *method* of dividing society's production.

Traditional solutions to the economic problems of production and distribution are most commonly encountered in primitive agrarian or nonindustrial societies where, in addition to serving an economic function, the unquestioning acceptance of the past provides the necessary perseverance and endurance to confront harsh destinies. Yet even in our own society, tradition continues to play a part in solving the economic problem. It plays its smallest role in determining the distribution of our own social output, although the persistence of such traditional payments as tips to waiters, allowances to minors, or bonuses based on length of service are all vestiges of old traditional ways of distributing goods, as is the differential between men's and women's pay for equal work.

More important is the continued reliance on tradition, even in America, as a means of solving the production problem—that is, in allocating the performance of tasks. Much of the actual process of selecting an employment in our society is heavily influenced by tradition. We are all familiar with families in which sons follow their fathers into a profession or a business. On a somewhat broader scale, tradition also dissuades us from certain employments. Sons of American middle-class families, for example, do not usually seek factory work, even though factory jobs may pay better than office jobs, because blue-collar employment is not in the middle-class tradition.

Thus, even in our society—clearly not a "traditional" one—custom provides an important mechanism for solving the economic problem. But now we must note one very important consequence of the mechanism of tradition. *Its solution to the problems of production and distribution is a static one.* A society that follows the path of tradition in its regulation of economic affairs does so at the expense of large-scale rapid social and economic change.

Thus the economy of a Bedouin tribe or a Burmese village is in few essential respects changed today from what it was a hundred or even a thousand years ago. The bulk of the peoples living in tradition-bound societies repeat, in the daily patterns of their economic life, much of the routine that characterized them in the distant past. Such societies may rise and fall, wax and wane, but external events—war, climate, political adventures and misadventures—are mainly responsible for their changing fortunes. Internal, self-generated economic change is but a small factor in the history of most tradition-bound states. *Tradition solves the economic problem, but it does so at the cost of economic progress.*

A second manner of solving the problem of economic continuity also displays an ancient lineage. This is the method of imposed authority, of

COMMAND

economic command. It is a solution based not so much on the perpetuation of a viable system by the changeless reproduction of its ways, as on the organization of a system according to the orders of an economic commander-in-chief.

Not infrequently we find this authoritarian method of economic control superimposed upon a traditional social base. Thus the Pharaohs of Egypt exerted their economic dictates above the timeless cycle of traditional agricultural practice on which the Egyptian economy was based. By their orders, the supreme rulers of Egypt brought into being the enormous economic effort that built the pyramids, the temples, the roads. Herodotus, the Greek historian, tells us how the Pharaoh Cheops organized the task.

[He] ordered all Egyptians to work for himself. Some, accordingly, were appointed to draw stones from the quarries in the Arabian mountains down to the Nile, others he ordered to receive the stones when transported in vessels across the river.... And they worked to the number of a hundred thousand men at a time, each party during three months. The time during which the people were thus harassed by toil lasted ten years on the road which they constructed, and along which they drew the stones; a work, in my opinion, not much less than the Pyramid.[4]

The mode of authoritarian economic organization was by no means confined to ancient Egypt. We encounter it in the despotisms of medieval and classical China which produced, among other things, the colossal Great Wall, or in the slave labor by which many of the great public works of ancient Rome were built. Of course, we find it today in the dictates of the communist economic authorities. In less drastic form we find it also in our own society; for example, in the form of taxes—that is, in the preemption of part of our income by the public authorities for public purposes.

Economic command, like tradition, offers solutions to the twin problems of production and distribution. In times of crises, such as war or famine, it may be the only way in which a society can organize its manpower or distribute its goods effectively. Even in America, we commonly declare martial law when an area has been devastated by a great natural disaster. On such occasions we may press people into service, requisition homes, impose curbs on the use of private property such as cars, or even limit the amount of goods a family may consume.

Quite aside from its obvious utility in meeting emergencies, command has a further usefulness in solving the economic problem. Unlike tradition, the exercise of command has no inherent effect of slowing down economic change. Indeed, the exercise of authority is the most powerful instrument society has for *enforcing economic change.* Authority in modern China or Russia, for example, has effected radical alterations in the systems of pro-

[4] *Histories,* trans. Cary (London: 1901), Book II, p. 124.

duction and distribution. But again, even in our own society, it is sometimes necessary for economic authority to intervene into the normal flow of economic life, to speed up or bring about change. The government may, for instance, utilize its tax receipts to lay down a network of roads that will bring a backwater community into the flux of active economic life. It may undertake an irrigation system that will dramatically change the economic life of a vast region. It may deliberately alter the distribution of income among social classes.

To be sure, economic command which is exercised within the framework of a democratic political process is very different from that which is exercised by a dictatorship: there is an immense social distance between a tax system controlled by Congress and outright expropriation or labor impressment by a supreme and unchallengeable ruler. Yet whilst the means may be much milder, the *mechanism* is the same. In both cases, command diverts economic effort toward goals chosen by a higher authority. In both cases it interferes with the existing order of production and distribution, to create a new order ordained from "above."

This does not in itself serve to commend or condemn the exercise of command. The new order imposed by the authorities may offend or please our sense of social justice, just as it may improve or lessen the economic efficiency of society. Clearly, command can be an instrument of a democratic as well as of a totalitarian will. There is no implicit moral judgment to be passed on this second of the great mechanisms of economic control. Rather, it is important to note that no society—certainly no modern society—is without its elements of command, just as none is devoid of the influence of tradition. *If tradition is the great brake on social and economic change, so economic command can be the great spur to change.* As mechanisms for assuring the successful solution to the economic problem, both serve their purposes, both have their uses and their drawbacks. Between them, tradition and command have accounted for most of the long history of man's economic efforts to cope with his environment and with himself. The fact that human society has survived is testimony to their effectiveness.

THE MARKET

But there is also a third solution to the economic problem, a third way of maintaining socially viable patterns of production and distribution. This is the *market organization of society*—an organization that, in truly remarkable fashion, allows society to insure its own provisioning with a minimum of recourse either to tradition or command.

Because we live in a market-run society, we are apt to take for granted the puzzling—indeed, almost paradoxical—nature of the market solution to the economic problem. But assume for a moment that we could act as economic advisers to a society that had not yet decided on its mode of economic organization. Suppose, for instance, that we were called on to act as consultants to one of the new nations emerging on the continent of Africa.

We could imagine the leaders of such a nation saying, "We have always experienced a highly tradition-bound way of life. Our men hunt and cultivate the fields and perform their tasks as they are brought up to do by the force of example and the instruction of their elders. We know, too, something of what can be done by economic command. We are prepared, if necessary, to sign an edict making it compulsory for many of our men to work on community projects for our national development. Tell us, is there any other way we can organize our society so that it will function successfully—or better yet, more successfully?"

Suppose we answered, "Yes, there is another way. Organize your society along the lines of a market economy."

"Very well," say the leaders. "What do we then tell people to do? How do we assign them to their various tasks?"

"That's the very point," we would answer. "In a market economy, no one is assigned to any task. In fact, the main idea of a market society is that each person is allowed to decide for himself what to do."

There is consternation among the leaders. "You mean there is no assignment of some men to mining and others to cattle raising? No manner of designating some for transportation and others for weaving? You leave this to people to decide for themselves? But what happens if they do not decide correctly? What happens if no one volunteers to go into the mines, or if no one offers himself as a railway engineer?"

"You may rest assured," we tell the leaders, "none of that will happen. In a market society, all the jobs will be filled because it will be to people's advantage to fill them."

Our respondents accept this with uncertain expressions. "Now look," one of them finally says, "let us suppose that we take your advice and allow our people to do as they please. Let's talk about something specific, like cloth production. Just how do we fix the right level of cloth output in this 'market society' of yours?"

"But you don't," we reply.

"We don't! Then how do we know there will be enough cloth produced?"

"There will be," we tell him. "The market will see to that."

"Then how do we know there won't be *too much* cloth produced?" he asks triumphantly.

"Ah, but the market will see to that too!"

"But what is this market that will do these wonderful things? Who runs it?"

"Oh, nobody runs the market," we answer. "It runs itself. In fact there really isn't any such *thing* as 'the market.' It's just a word we use to describe the way people behave."

"But I thought people behaved the way they wanted to!"

"And so they do," we say. "But never fear. They will want to behave the way you want them to behave."

"I am afraid," says the chief of the delegation, "that we are wasting our time. We thought you had in mind a serious proposal. What you suggest is inconceivable. Good day, sir."

Could we seriously suggest to such an emergent nation that it entrust itself to a market solution of the economic problem? That will be a problem to which we shall return at the very end of our book. But the perplexity which the market idea would rouse in the mind of someone unacquainted with it may serve to increase our own wonderment at this most sophisticated and interesting of all economic mechanisms. How does the market system assure us that our mines will find miners, our factories workers? How does it take care of cloth production? How does it happen that in a market-run nation each person can indeed do as he wishes and, withal, fulfill needs that society as a whole presents?

Economics, as we commonly conceive it and as we shall study it in much of this book, is primarily concerned with these very problems. Societies that rely primarily on tradition to solve their economic problems are of less interest to the professional economist than to the cultural anthropologist or the sociologist. Societies that solve their economic problems primarily by the exercise of command present interesting economic questions, but here the study of economics is necessarily subservient to the study of politics and the exercise of power.

It is a society that solves its economic problems by the market process that presents an aspect especially interesting to the economist. Clearly, many (although not all) of the problems we encounter in America today have to do with the workings or misworkings of the market system. And precisely *because* our contemporary problems often arise from the operations of the market, we study economics itself. Unlike the case with tradition and command, where we quickly grasp the nature of the economic mechanism of society, when we turn to a market society we are lost without a knowledge of economics. For in a market society it is not at all clear that even the simplest problems of production and distribution will be solved by the free interplay of individuals without guidance from tradition or command; nor is it clear how and to what extent the market mechanism is to be blamed for society's ills—after all, we can find poverty and neglect and pollution and armaments in nonmarket economies too!

In subsequent parts of this book we shall analyze these puzzling questions in more detail. But the task of our initial exploration must now be clear. As our imaginary interview with the leaders of an emergent nation has suggested, the market solution appears very strange to someone brought up in the ways of tradition or command. Hence the question arises: how did the market solution itself come into being? Was it imposed, full-blown, on

ECONOMICS AND THE MARKET SYSTEM

our society at some earlier date? Or did it arise spontaneously and without forethought? This is the focusing question of economic history to which we now turn, as we retrace the evolution of our own market system out of the tradition and authority dominated societies of the past.

KEY CONCEPTS AND KEY WORDS

Provisioning wants

1. Economics is the study of how man assures his material sufficiency, of how societies arrange for their *material provisioning*.

Scarcity

2. Economic problems arise because the wants of most societies exceed the gifts of nature, giving rise to the general condition of *scarcity*.

3. Scarcity, in turn (whether it arises from nature's stinginess or man's appetites) imposes two severe tasks on society:

Production

a) It must mobilize its energies for *production*—producing not only enough goods, but the right goods, and

Distribution

b) It must resolve the problem of *distribution*, arranging a satisfactory solution to the problem of Who Gets What?

Division of labor

4. These problems exist in all societies, but they are especially difficult to solve in advanced societies in which there exists a far-reaching *division of labor*. Men in wealthy societies are far more socially interdependent than men in simple societies.

5. Over the course of history, there have evolved three types of solutions to the two great economic problems. These are *Tradition, Command,* and the *Market System*.

Tradition

6. Tradition solves the problems of production and distribution by enforcing a continuity of tasks and rewards through social institutions such as the caste system. *Typically, the economic solution imposed by Tradition is a static one*, in which little change occurs over long periods of time.

Command

7. Command solves the economic problem by imposing allocations of effort or reward by *governing authority*. Command can be a means for achieving rapid and far-reaching economic *change*. It can take extreme totalitarian or mild democratic forms.

Market

8. The market system is a complex mode of organizing society in which order and efficiency emerge "spontaneously" from a seemingly uncontrolled society. We shall investigate the market system in great detail in the chapters to come.

QUESTIONS

1. If everyone could produce all the food he needed in his own backyard, and if technology were so advanced that we could all make anything we wanted in our basements, would an "economic problem" exist?

2. Suppose that everyone were completely versatile—able to do everyone else's work just as well as his own. Would a division of labor still be useful in society? Why?

3. Modern economic society is sometimes described as depending on "organization men" who allow their lives to be directed by the large corporations for which they work. Assuming that this description has some glimmer of truth, would you think that modern society should be described as one of Tradition, Command, or the Market?

4. In what way do your own plans for the future coincide with or depart from the occupations of your parents? Do you think that the so-called generational split is observable in all modern societies?

5. Economics is often called the science of scarcity. How can this label be applied to a society of considerable affluence such as our own?

6. What elements of Tradition and Command do you think are indispensable in a modern industrial society? Do you think that modern society could exist without any dependence on Tradition or without any exercise of Command?

7. Much of production and distribution involves the creation or the handling of *things*. Why are production and distribution *social* problems rather than engineering or physical problems?

8. Do you consider man's wants to be insatiable? Does this imply that scarcity must always exist?

9. Take the main problems that disturbed us in "America Today": neglect, poverty, armaments, pollution, racial discrimination. To what extent do you find such problems in societies run by Tradition? By Command? What is your feeling about the responsibility the market system bears for these problems in America?

"Nobody ever saw a dog make a fair and deliberate exchange of one bone for another with another dog," wrote Adam Smith in *The Wealth of Nations.* "Nobody ever saw one animal by its gestures and natural cries signify to another, this is mine, that yours; I am willing to give this for that."[1]

Smith was writing about "a certain propensity in human nature . . . ; the propensity to truck, barter, and exchange one thing for another." That such a propensity exists as a universal characteristic of humankind is perhaps less likely than Smith believed, but he was certainly not mistaken in putting the act of exchange at the very center of his scheme of economic life. For there can be no doubt that exchange, buying and selling, lies at the very heart of a market society such as he was describing. And so, as we now begin to study the rise of the market society, what could be more natural than to commence by tracing the pedigree of markets themselves?

It comes as something of a surprise, perhaps, to discover how very ancient is that pedigree. Men have traded with one another at least as far back as the last Ice Age. We have evidence that the mammoth-hunters of the Russian steppes obtained Mediterranean shells in trade, as did also the Cro-Magnon hunters of the central valleys of France. In fact, on the moors of Pomerania in northeastern Germany, archeologists have come across an oaken box, replete with the remains of its original leather shoulder strap, in which were a dagger, a sickle head, and a needle—all of Bronze Age manufacture. According to the conjectures of experts, this was very likely the sample kit of a prototype of the traveling salesman, an itinerant representative who collected orders for the specialized production of his community.[2]

And as we proceed from the dawn of civilization to its first organized societies, the evidences of trade and of markets increase rapidly. As Miriam Beard has written:

Millennia before Homer sang, or the wolf suckled Romulus and Remus, the bustling damkars (traders) of Uruk and Nippur . . . were buckling down to business. Atidum the merchant, in need of enlarged office facilities, was agreeing to rent a suitable

[1] Smith, *The Wealth of Nations,* p. 13.
[2] *Cambridge Economic History of Europe* (Cambridge: Cambridge University Press, 1952), II, 4.

location from Ribatum, Priestess of Shamash, for one and one-sixth shekels of silver per year—so much down and the rest in easy installments. Abu-wakar, the rich shipper, was delighted that his daughter had become Priestess of Shamash and could open a real estate office near the temple. Ilabras was writing to Ibi: "May Shamash and Marduk keep thee! As thou knowest, I had issued a note for a female slave. Now the time to pay is come."[3]

Thus at first glance it seems as if we can discover evidences of a market society deep in the past. But these disconcerting notes of modernity must be interpreted with caution. If markets, buying and selling, even highly organized trading bodies were well-nigh ubiquitous features of ancient society, they must not be confused with the equally ubiquitous presence of a *market society*. Trade existed as an important adjunct to society from earliest times, but the fundamental impetus to production, or the basic allocation of resources among different uses, or the distribution of goods among social classes was largely divorced from the marketing process. That is, *the markets of antiquity were not the means by which those societies solved their basic economic problems.* They were subsidiary to the great processes of production and distribution rather than integral to them; they were "above" the critical economic machinery rather than within it. As we shall see, between the deceptively contemporary air of many markets of the distant past and the reality of our contemporary market economy lies an immense distance over which society would take centuries to travel.

The Economic Organization of Antiquity

We must ourselves traverse that distance if we are to understand how contemporary market society came into being and, indeed, if we are to understand what it is. For only by immersing ourselves in the societies of the past, only by seeing how they did, in fact, solve their economic prob-

---

[3] *A History of the Business Man* (New York: Macmillan, 1938), p. 12.

lems, can we begin to understand clearly what is involved in the evolution of the market society which is our own environment.

Needless to say, it would make an enormous difference which of the many pre-market societies of the past we visited as general observers. To trace economic history from the monolithic temple-states of Sumer and Akkad to the "modernity" of classical Greece or Rome is to undertake a cultural journey of fantastic distance. Yet, traveling only as economic historians, we will find that it makes much less difference in which of the societies of antiquity we light. For as we examine these societies, we can see that underlying their profound dissimilarities of art or political rule or religious belief, there are equally profound similarities of economic structure, similarities we call to mind less frequently because they are in the "background" of history and rarely adorn its more exciting pages. But these identifying characteristics of economic organization are the ones that now interest us as we turn our gaze to the past. What is it that we see?

AGRICULTURAL FOUNDATION OF ANCIENT SOCIETIES

The first and perhaps the most striking impression is the overwhelmingly agricultural aspect of all these economies.

In a sense, of course, all human communities, no matter how industrialized, live off the soil: all that differentiates the "agricultural" society from the "industrial" is the number of the nonagricultural population that its food growers can support. Thus an American farmer, working a large acreage with abundant equipment, maintains more than thirty nonfarmers; while an Asian peasant, tilling his tiny plot with little more than a stick-plow, is often hard pressed to sustain his own family.

Over all of antiquity the capacity of the agricultural population to sustain a nonfarming population was very limited. Exact statistics are unavailable, but we can project backwards to the situation that prevailed in all these ancient nations by looking at the underdeveloped regions of the world today where the levels of technique and the productivity of agriculture bear a close—too close—resemblance to antiquity. Thus in India, in Egypt, in the Philippines, Indonesia, Brazil, Colombia, Mexico, we find that it takes two farm families to support one nonfarm family; while in tropical Africa, a survey tells us: "the productivity of African agriculture is still so low that it takes anywhere from two to ten people—men, women, and children—to raise enough food to supply their own needs and those of *one* additional—non-food-growing—adult."[4]

Antiquity was not *that* badly off; indeed at times it produced impressive agricultural outputs. But neither was it remotely comparable to American farm productivity with its enormous capacity to support a nonagricultural population. All ancient economic societies were basically rural econo-

[4] George H. T. Kimble, *Tropical Africa* (New York: Twentieth Century Fund, 1960), I, 572. (Italics added.)

mies. This did not preclude, as we shall see, a very brilliant and wealthy urban society nor a far-flung network of international trade. Yet the typical economic personage of antiquity was neither trader nor urban dweller. He was a tiller of the soil, and it was in his rural communities that the economies of antiquity were ultimately anchored.

But this must not lead us to assume that economic life was therefore comparable to that of a modern agricultural community like Denmark or New Zealand. Contemporary farmers, like businessmen, are very much bound up in the web of transactions characteristic of a market society. They sell their output on one market; they buy their supplies on another. The accumulation of money, and not of wheat or corn, is the object of their efforts. Books of profit and loss regularly tell them if they are doing well or not. The latest news of agricultural technology is studied and put into effect if it is profitable.

None of this properly describes the "farmer" of ancient Egypt, of antique Greece or Rome, or of the great Eastern civilizations. With few exceptions, the tiller of the soil was a peasant, and a peasant is a social creature very different from a farmer. He is not technologically alert but, on the contrary, clings with stubborn persistence—and often with great skill—to his well-known ways. He must, since a small error might mean starvation. He does not buy the majority of his supplies but, to a large extent, fashions them himself; similarly, he does not produce for a "market," but principally for himself. Finally, he is often not even free to consume his own crop, but typically must hand over a portion—a tenth, a third, half, or even more—to the owner of his land.

For in the general case, the peasant of antiquity did not own his land. We hear of the independent citizen—farmers of classical Greece and republican Rome, but these were exceptions to the general rule in which peasants were but tenants of a great lord. And even in Greece and Rome, the independent peasantry tended to become swallowed up as the tenantry of huge commercial estates. Pliny mentions one such enormous estate or latifundium (literally: broad farm) with a quarter of a million livestock and a population of 4,117 slaves.

Hence the peasant, who was the bone and muscle of the economies of antiquity, was in himself a prime example of the nonmarket aspect of these economies. Although some cultivators freely sold a portion of their own crop in the city marketplaces, the great majority of agricultural producers scarcely entered the market at all. For many of these producers—especially when they were slaves—this was, accordingly, an almost cashless world, where a few coppers a year, carefully hoarded and spent only for emergencies, constituted the only link with a world of market transactions.*

---

* This is not, let us note, only an ancient condition. Traveling in Morocco, John Gunther reported of the local peasant-serfs: "formerly they got no wages—what would they need money for—but this is changing now." *Changing now—in 1953!* (*Inside Africa.* New York: Harper, 1955, p. 104.)

Thus, whereas the peasant's legal and social status varied widely in different areas and eras of antiquity, in a broad view the tenor of his economic life was singularly constant. Of the web of transactions, the drive for profits of the modern farmer, he knew little or nothing. Generally poor, tax-ridden and oppressed, prey to nature's caprices and to the exploitation of war and peace, bound to the soil by law and custom, the peasant of antiquity—as the peasant today who continues to provide the agricultural underpinnings to the civilizations of the East and South—was dominated by the economic rule of tradition. His main stimulus for change was command—or, rather, obedience. Labor, patience, and the incredible endurance of the human being were his contributions to civilization.

ECONOMIC LIFE OF THE CITIES

The basic agricultural cast of ancient society and its typical exclusion of the peasant-cultivator from an active market existence makes all the more striking another common aspect of economic organization in antiquity. This is the diversity, vitality, and ebullience of the economic life of the cities.

Whether we turn to ancient Egypt, classical Greece, or Rome, we cannot help but be struck by this contrast between the relatively static countryside and the active city. In Greece, for example, a whole panoply of goods passed across the docks of the Piraeus: grain from Italy, metal from Crete and even Britain, books from Egypt, perfume from still more distant origins. Isocrates, in the *Panegyricus,* boasts: "The articles which it is difficult to get, one here, one there, from the rest of the world; all these it is easy to buy in Athens." So, too, Rome developed a thriving foreign and domestic commerce. By the time of Augustus, 6,000 loads of ox-towed barges were required to feed the city annually,[5] while in the city forum a crowd of speculators converged as on "an immense stock exchange."[6]

Thus something which at least superficially approximated our own society was visible in many of the larger urban centers of antiquity. And yet we must not be beguiled into the conclusion that this was a market society similar to our own. In at least two respects the differences were profound.

The first of these was the essentially restricted character and scope of the market function of the city. Unlike the modern city, which is not only a receiver of goods shipped in from the hinterlands but also an important exporter of goods and services back to the countryside, the cities of antiquity tended to assume an economically parasitic role vis-à-vis the rest of the economy. Much of the trade that entered the great urban centers of Egypt, Greece, and Rome (over and above the necessary provisioning of the city masses) was in the nature of luxury goods for its upper classes, rather than raw materials to be worked and then sent out to a goods-consuming

[5] *Cambridge Economic History of Europe,* II, 47.
[6] W. C. Cunningham, *An Essay on Western Civilization* (New York: 1913), p. 164.

economy. The cities were the vessels of civilization; but as centers of economic activity, a wide gulf separated them from the country, making the cities enclaves of economic life rather than nourishing components of integrated rural-urban economies.

SLAVERY

Even more important was a second difference between the ancient city economies and a contemporary market society. This was their reliance on *slave labor.*

For slavery on a massive scale was a fundamental pillar of nearly every ancient economic society. In Greece, for instance, the deceptively modern air of the Piraeus masks the fact that much of the purchasing power of the Greek merchant was provided by the labor of 20,000 slaves who labored under sickening conditions in the silver mines of Laurentium. At the height of "democratic" Athens, it is estimated that at least one-third of its population were slaves. In Italy of 30 B.C., some 1,500,000 slaves—on the latifundia, in the galleys, the mines, the "factories," the shops—provided a major impetus in keeping the economic machinery in motion.[7] Seneca even tells us that a proposal that they wear special dress was voted down lest recognizing their own number, they might know their strength.

Slaves were not, of course, the only source of labor. Groups of free artisans and workmen, often banded together in *collegia* or fraternal bodies, also serviced the Roman city, as did similar free workmen in Greece and elsewhere. In many cities, especially latter-day Rome, a mass of unemployed (but not enslaved) laborers provided a source of casual work. Yet, without the motive power of the slave, it is doubtful if the brilliant city economies of the past could have been sustained. And this brings us to the central point. It is that the flourishing market economy of the city rested atop an economic structure run by tradition and command. Nothing like the free exercise and interplay of self-interest guided the basic economic effort of antiquity. If an astonishingly modern urban market structure greets our eye, we must not forget that its merchants are standing on the shoulders of innumerable peasants and slaves.

WEALTH AND POWER

The presence of great agglomerations of urban wealth amid a far poorer rural setting alerts us to another characteristic of ancient economic society. This is the special relationship between its wealth and its underlying economic organization.

In any society, wealth implies that a *surplus* has been wrung from nature, that a social organization has not alone solved its economic produc-

[7] K. J. Beloch, *Die Bevölkerung der Griechisch-Römischen Welt* (Leipzig: 1886), p. 478.

tion problem but has achieved a margin of effort above that required for its own existence. Perhaps what first astonishes us when we regard the civilizations of the ancient world is the size of surplus which could be got from a basically poor peasant population. The temples of the ancient Assyrian kings, the extraordinary treasures of the Aztecs, the pyramids and pleasure craft of the Pharaohs of Egypt, the Acropolis of Athens, and the magnificent roads and architecture of Rome all testify to the ability of an essentially agricultural civilization to achieve a massive surplus, to pry considerable amounts of labor loose from the land, support it at whatever low level, and put it to work building for posterity.

But the stupendous achievements of the past testify as well to something else. The surplus productive potential that society manages to achieve (whether by technology or by adroit social organization) can be applied in many directions. It can be directed to agricultural improvements, such as irrigation ditches or dams, where it is apt to increase the bounty of the harvest still further. It can be applied to the tools and equipment of the city workman, where it is apt to raise his ability to produce. Or the surplus may be used to support a nonworking religious order or a class of courtiers and idle nobility. If it were not for its amazing capacity to produce a surplus, the United States could never support its armed forces—anymore than the U.S.S.R. could, if *its* economy did not also give rise to more output than it required for sheer self-perpetuation.

Thus the social form taken by the accumulation of wealth reveals a great deal about any society. "To whom does the surplus accrue?" is a question which invariably sheds important light on the structure of power within that society.

To whom did the wealth of antiquity accrue? At first glimpse it seems impossible to answer in a phrase. Emperors, nobles, religious orders, merchant traders—all enjoyed the wealth of antiquity at one time or another. But at second look, an interesting and significant generalization becomes possible: most wealth did not go to those who played a strictly *economic* role. Although there are records of clever slaves in Egypt and Rome who became wealthy, and although rich merchants and bankers are visible throughout the annals of antiquity, theirs was not the primary route to wealth. Rather, *in ancient civilization wealth was generally the reward for political, military, or religious power or status, and not for economic activity.*

There was a reason for this. Societies tend to reward most highly the activities they value most highly; and in the long and turbulent centuries of antiquity, political leadership, religious tutelage, and military prowess were unquestionably more necessary for social survival than trading *expertise*. In fact, in many of these societies, economic activity itself was disdained as essentially ignoble. As Aristotle wrote in his *Politics,* "in the best-governed polis . . . the citizens may not lead either the life of craftsmen or of traders, for such a life is devoid of nobility and hostile to perfection of character." It was a theme on which Cicero would later expand in his essay *De Officiis* (Book I).

The toil of a hired worker, who is paid only for his toil and not for artistic skill, is unworthy of a free man and is sordid in character. For in his case, money is the price of slavery. Sordid too is the calling of those who buy wholesale in order to sell retail, since they would gain no profits without a great deal of lying. . . . Trade on a small retail scale is sordid, but if it is on a large wholesale scale including the import of many wares from everywhere and their distribution to many people without any misrepresentation, it is not to be too greatly censured. . . .

Especially, added the great lawyer, "if those who carry on such trade finally retire to country estates, after being surfeited or at least satisfied with their gains."

Over and above the lesser social function of the merchant compared with the general, the consul, or the priest, this disdain of wealth obtained from "ignoble" economic activity reflected an economic fact of great importance: society had not yet integrated the production of wealth with the production of goods. Wealth was still a surplus to be seized by conquest or squeezed from the underlying agricultural population; it was not yet a natural adjunct of a system of continuously increasing production in which some part of an expanding total social output might accrue to many classes of society.

And so it would be for many centuries. Until the smallest as well as the largest activities of society would receive their price tag, until purchases and sales, bids and offers would penetrate down to the lowest orders of society, the accumulation of wealth would always remain more a matter of political, military, or religious power than of economics. To sum it up: *in premarket societies, wealth tended to follow power; not until the market society would power tend to follow wealth.*

Before we move on to view the economic system of antiquity in transition and evolution, we must ask one more question. What did contemporary economists think of it?

The answer we find is an interesting one: there were no contemporary "economists." Historians, philosophers, political theorists, writers on manners and morals abounded during the long span of history we here call "antiquity," but economists, as such, did not exist. The reason is not far to seek. The economics of society—that is, the mode by which society organized itself to meet the basic tasks of economic survival—were hardly such as to provoke the curiosity of a thoughtful man. There was little or no "veil" of money to pierce, little or no complexity of contractual relationship in the marketplace to unravel, little or no economic rhythm of society to interpret. As the harvest flourished, as the justice or injustice of the tax gathering system varied, as the fortunes of war and politics changed, so went the lot of the peasant proprietor, the slave, the petty craftsman, and trader. As relative military strength rose or fell, as individual merchants fared luckily or otherwise, as the arts prospered or declined, so went the pulse of trade. As his prowess in war or politics permitted, as his chance at ransoms, local monopolies, or marriage dictated, so fared the individual acquisitor of wealth. In all of this there was little to tax the analytic powers of social observers.

If there was a problem of economics—aside from the eternal problems of poor harvests, fortunes of war, etc.—it was inextricably mingled with the problem of social justice. As far back as the early Assyrian tablets, we have records of reformers who sought to alleviate taxes on the peasantry, and throughout the Bible—indeed, down through the Middle Ages—a strain of primitive communism, of egalitarian sharing, runs through the background of religious thought. In the Book of Leviticus, for example, there is mentioned the interesting custom of the *jubilee* year, one year in each fifty, in which the Israelites were to "return to each man unto his possession."* But despite the fact that religion was concerned with riches and poverty, and thus with the distributive problem of economics, the span of antiquity saw little or no systematic inquiry into the *social system* which produced riches or poverty. If riches were an affront, this was due to the personal failings of greedy men; and if social justice were to be obtained, it must be achieved by personal redistribution, by alms and charity. The idea of an "economic" study of society, as contrasted with a political or moral one, was conspicuous largely by its absence.

There was, however, one exception which we should note. Aristotle, the great pupil of Plato, turned his powerful scrutiny to economic affairs, and with him the systematic study of economics, as such, truly begins. Not that Aristotle, any more than the majority of the Church fathers, was a radical social reformer. Much is summed up in his famous sentence: "From the hour of their birth, some are marked out for subjection, others for rule."[8] But the student of the history of economic thought turns first to Aristotle for questions whose treatment he can subsequently trace down through the present time: questions such as "What is value?" "What is the basis of exchange?" "What is interest?"

We will not linger here over Aristotle's formulations of these ideas. But one point we might note, for it accords with what we have already seen of the attitude of antiquity to economic activity itself. When Aristotle examined the economic process, he differentiated it into two branches—not

---

* That is, lands which had been forfeited in debt, etc., were to be restored to their original owners. The wrath of the later prophets such as Amos indicates that the injunction must have been observed largely in the breach.

[8] *Politics,* Book I.

production and distribution, as we have done, but *use* and *gain*. More specifically, he differentiated between *oeconomia*—whence "economics," and *chrematistike*, from which we have no precise derivative term. By *oeconomia* the Greek philosopher meant the art of household management, the administration of one's patrimony, the careful husbanding of resources. *Chrematistike*, on the other hand, implied the use of nature's resources or of human skill for acquisitive purposes: *chrematistike* was trade for trade's sake, economic activity that had as its motive and end not use, but profit. Aristotle approved of *oeconomia* but not of *chrematistike*, and within the scope of the essentially limited market structure of antiquity, where the city trader all too frequently exploited the country peasant, it is not hard to see why. The much more difficult problem of whether a market society, in which *everyone* strives for gain, might warrant approval or disapproval never appears in Aristotle's writings, as it never appeared in ancient history. The market society with its genuinely perplexing questions of economic order and economic morality had yet to come into being. Until it did, the philosophy needed to rationalize that order was understandably lacking.

Economic Society in the Middle Ages

Our conspectus of economic organization has thus far scanned only the great civilizations of antiquity. Now we must turn in somewhat closer focus to a society far nearer in time and, what is more important, immediately precedent to ours in terms of social evolution. This is the vast expanse of history we call the Middle Ages, an expanse which stretches over and describes the Western world, from Sweden to the Mediterranean, "beginning" with the fall of Rome and "ending" with the Renaissance.

Modern scholarship emphasizes more and more the diversity which characterizes that enormous span of time and space, a diversity not alone of social appearance from century to century but of contrast from locality to locality within any given period. It is one thing to speak of "life" in the Middle Ages if one has in mind a tenth century peasant community in Normandy where, it is estimated, the average inhabitant probably never saw more than two hundred or three hundred persons in his lifetime or commanded a vocabulary of more than six hundred words,[9] and another if we mean the worldly city of Florence about which Boccaccio wrote so engagingly.

Even more relevant for our purposes is the need to think of the Middle Ages in terms of economic variety and change. The early years of feudal

---

[9] George G. Coulton. *Medieval Village, Manor and Monastery* (New York: Harper, Torchbooks, 1960), p. 15.

economic life are very different from the middle or later years, particularly insofar as general well-being is concerned. The commencement of feudalism coincided with a period of terrible retrenchment, deprivation, depopulation. During the fifth century the population of Rome actually fell from 1,500,000 to 300,000. But by the twelfth century, towns had again expanded (after 600 years!) to the limits of their old Roman walls and even spilled out beyond; and by the beginning of the fourteenth century, a very considerable prosperity reigned in many parts of Europe.* Then came a series of catastrophes: a ghastly two-year famine in 1315; thereafter, in 1348, the Black Death, which carried off between one-third and two-thirds of the urban population; a century-long devastating struggle between England and France and among the petty principalities of Germany and Italy. All of these misfortunes pulled down the level of economic existence to dreadful depths. Neither stasis nor smooth linear progress, but enormous and irregular secular tides mark the long history of feudalism, and they caution us against a simplistic conception of its development.

Our purpose, however, is not to trace these tides, but rather to form a generalized picture of the *economic structure* which, beneath the swings of fortune, marks the feudal era as a unique way-station of Western economic history. And here we can begin by noting the all-important development which underlay the genesis of that economic structure. *This was the breakdown of large-scale political organization.*

For as Rome "fell" and as successive raids and invasions from north, east, and south tore apart the European countryside, the great administrative framework of law and order was replaced by a patchwork quilt of small-scale political entities. Even in the ninth century, when Charlemagne's Holy Roman Empire assumed such impressive dimensions on the map, beneath the veneer of a unified "state" there was, in fact, political chaos: neither a single language nor a coordinated central government nor a unified system of law, coinage, or currency nor, most important, any consciousness of "national" allegiance bound the statelets of Charlemagne's day into more than temporary cohesion.

We note this striking difference between antiquity and the Middle Ages to stress the tremendous economic consequences that came with political dissolution. As safety and security gave way to local autarky and anarchy, long voyages of commodities became extremely hazardous, and the once vigorous life of the great cities impossible. As a common coin and a common law disappeared, merchants in Gaul could no longer do business with merchants in Italy, and the accustomed network of economic connec-

---

* There is some evidence that in England around the year 1500, real wages for common laborers achieved a level that they would not again surpass for at least three centuries. (*Economica*, November 1956, pp. 296-314.)

tions was severed or fell into disuse. As disease and invasion depopulated the countryside, men turned of necessity to the most defensive forms of economic organization, to forms aimed at sheer survival through self-sufficiency. A new need arose, a need to compress the viable organization of society into the smallest possible compass. For centuries this insularity of economic life, this extreme self-reliance would be the economic hallmark of the Middle Ages.

The need for self-sufficiency brought with it a new basic unit of economic organization: the *manorial estate.*

What was such an estate like? Typically, it was a large tract of land, often including many thousands of acres, which was "owned" by a feudal lord, spiritual or temporal.* The word "owned" is properly in quotation marks, for the manor was not first and foremost a piece of economic property as such. Rather, it was a social and political entity in which the lord of the manor was not only landlord, but protector, judge, police chief, administrator. Although himself bound into a great hierarchy in which each lord was some other lord's servant (and even the pope was *servus servorum Dei),* the feudal noble was, within the confines of his own manor, quite literally "lord of the land." He was also undisputed owner and master of many of the people who lived on the land, for the serfs (or villeins) of a manor, although not slaves, were in many respects as much the property of the lord as were his (or their) houses, flocks, or crops.

At the focal point of the estate was the lord's homestead, a great manor house, usually armed against attack from marauders, walled off from the surrounding countryside, and sometimes attaining the stature of a genuine castle. In the enclosed courtyard of the manor were workshops in which cloth might be spun or woven, grapes pressed, food stored, simple ironwork or blacksmithing work performed, coarse grain ground. Extending out around the manor was a patchwork of fields, typically subdivided into acre or half-acre "strips," each with its own cycle of crops and rest. Half or more of all of these belonged directly to the lord; the remainder "belonged," in various senses of that legal term, to the hierarchy of free, half-free, and unfree families who made up an estate.

The exact meaning of the word "belonged" hinged on the obligations and rights accruing to a serf, a freeman, or whatever other category one might be born into. Note however that even a freeman who "owned" his land could not sell it to another feudal lord. At best, his ownership meant

---

* That is, the lord might be the abbot or the bishop of the locality, or he might be a secular personage, a baron who came into his possessions by inheritance or by being made a knight and given lands for exceptional service in battle or for other reasons.

that he could not himself be displaced from his land short of extraordinary circumstances. A lesser personage than a freeman did not even have this security. A typical serf was literally tied to "his" plot of land. He could not, without specific permission and, usually, without specific payment, leave his homestead for another, either within the domain of the manor or within that of another. With his status came, as well, a series of obligations which lay at the very core of the manorial economic organization. These consisted of the necessity to perform labor for the lord—to till his fields, to work in his shops, to provide him with a portion of one's own crop. From manor to manor, and from age to age, the labor-dues varied: in some localities they amounted to as much as four or even five days of labor a week, which meant that only by the labor of a serf's wife or children could his own fields be maintained. And finally, the serfs owed small money-payments: head taxes, like the *chevage;* death-duties, like the *heriot;* or *merchet,* a marriage fee, or dues to use the lord's mill or his ovens.

There was, however, an extremely important *quid pro quo* for all of this. If the serf gave the lord his labor and much of the fruits of his toil, in exchange the lord provided some things which the serf alone could not have obtained.

The most important of these was a degree of physical security. It is difficult for us to reconstruct the violent tenor of much of feudal life, but one investigator has provided a statistic which may serve to make the point. Among the sons of English dukes, 46 percent of those born between 1330 and 1479 died violent deaths. Their life expectancy when violent death was excluded was 31 years; when violent death was included, it was but 24 years.[10] The peasant, although not a warrior and therefore not occupationally exposed to the dangers of continual combat, assassination, etc., was pre-eminently fair prey for the marauding lord, defenseless against capture, unable to protect his poor possessions against destruction. Hence we can begin to understand why even free men became serfs by "commending" themselves to a lord who, in exchange for their economic, social, and political subservience, offered them in return the invaluable cloak of his military protection.

In addition, the lord offered a certain element of *economic* security. In times of famine, it was the lord who fed his serfs from the reserves in his own manorial storehouses. And, although he had to pay for it, the serf was *entitled* to use the lord's own beasts and equipment in cultivating his own strips as well as those of the lord himself. In an age when the average serf possessed almost no tools himself, this was an essential boon.[11]

---

[10] T. H. Hollingsworth, "A Demographic Study of the British Ducal Families," *Population Studies,* XI (1957-58). I am indebted to Dr. Goran Ohlin for this reference.

[11] For a picture of life among the various classes in medieval Europe, one might turn to Eileen Power's *Medieval People* (Garden City, N.Y.: Doubleday, Anchor Books, 1954), a scholarly but

These facts should not incline us to an idyllic picture of feudal life. The relation between lord and serf was often and even usually exploitative in the extreme. Yet we must see that it was also mutually supportive. Each provided for the other services essential for existence in a world where overall political organization and stability had virtually disappeared.

Despite the extreme self-sufficiency of manorial life, there is much here that resembles the economic organization of antiquity.

ECONOMICS OF MANORIAL LIFE

To begin with, like those earlier societies, this was clearly a form of economic society organized by tradition. Indeed, the hand of custom—the famous "ancient customs" of the medieval manor court which served frequently as the counsel for the otherwise undefended serf— was never stronger. Lacking strong unified central government, even the exercise of command was relatively weak. As a result, the pace of economic change, of economic development, although by no means lacking, was extremely slow during the early years of the medieval period.

Second, even more than with antiquity, this was a form of society which was characterized by a striking absence of money transactions. Unlike the latifundium of Rome, which sold its output to the city, the manor supplied only itself, and perhaps a local town. No manorial estate was ever quite so self-sufficient that it could dispense with monetary links with the outside world; even serfs bought a few commodities and sold a few eggs; and the lord, on occasion, had to buy considerable supplies which he could not produce for himself. But on the whole, very little money changed hands. As Henri Pirenne, an authority on medieval economic history, has put it:

... the tenants paid their obligations to their lord in kind. Every serf ... owed a fixed number of days of labour and a fixed quantity of natural products or of goods manufactured by himself, corn, eggs, geese, chickens, lambs, pigs, and hempen, linen or woollen cloth. It is true that a few pence had also to be paid, but they formed such a small proportion of the whole that they cannot prevent the conclusion that the economy of the domain was a natural economy ... since it did not engage in commerce it had no need to make use of money....[12]

charming account of the reality of human existence which lies behind history. For a sense of the violent tenor of the times, see J. Huizinga, *The Waning of the Middle Ages* (Garden City, N.Y.: Doubleday, Anchor Books, 1954), Chap. I. Let me call attention also to two other books that convey a vivid sense of feudal economic life. One is by H. S. Bennett, *Life on the English Manor* (Cambridge: Cambridge University Press, 1965); the other, by Marc Bloch, *French Rural History* (Berkeley: University of California Press, 1966). *French Rural History,* especially, is one of the real masterworks of economic history.

[12] *Economic and Social History of Medieval Europe* (New York: Harcourt, Harvest Books, 1956), p. 105.

It would, however, be a misrepresentation of medieval life to conclude that cash and cash transactions and the bargaining of a market society were wholly foreign to it. Rather, as was the case with antiquity, we must think of medieval economic society as consisting of a huge, static, virtually moneyless foundation of agricultural production atop which flourished a considerable variety of more dynamic activities.

For one thing, in addition to manors, there also existed the shrunken descendants of Roman towns (and as we shall later see, the nuclei of new towns) and these small cities obviously required a network of markets to serve them. Every town had its stalls to which peasants brought some portion of their crop for sale. More important, towns were clearly a different social unit from manors, and the laws and customs of the manors did not apply to their problems. Even when towns fell under manorial protection, townspeople little by little won for themselves freedom from feudal obligations of labor and, more important, from feudal obligations of law.* In contrast to the "ancient customs" of the manor, a new, evolving "law of merchants" regulated much of the commercial activity within the town walls.

Another locus of active economic life was the fair. The fair was a kind of traveling market, established in fixed localities for fixed dates, in which merchants from all over Europe conducted a genuine international exchange. Held usually but once a year, the great fairs were tremendous occasions, a mixture of social holiday, religious festival, and a time of intense economic activity. At some fairs, like those at Champagne in France or Stourbridge in England, a wide variety of merchandise was brought for sale: silks from the Levant, books and parchments, horses, drugs, spices. Anyone who has ever been to the Flea Market, the famous open-air bazaar outside Paris, or to a country fair in New England or the Middle West has savored something of the atmosphere of such a market. One can imagine the excitement which fairs must have engendered in the still air of medieval life.

And finally, within the towns themselves, we find the tiny but highly important centers of medieval "industrial" production. For even at its grandest, the manor could not support every craft needed for its maintenance, much less its extension. The services or products of glaziers and masons, expert armorers and metalworkers, fine weavers and dyers had to be bought

---

* Hence the saying "City air makes men free"; for the serf who escaped to a city and remained there a year and a day was usually considered to have passed from the jurisdiction of his lord to that of the city burghers.

when they were needed, and typically they were to be found in the medieval institutions as characteristic of town life as the manors themselves were of life in the country.

These institutions were the *guilds*—trade, professional, and craft organizations of Roman origins. Such organizations were the "business units" of the Middle Ages; in fact, one could not usually set oneself up in "business" unless one belonged to a guild. Thus the guilds were a kind of exclusive union, but not a union of workers so much as of managers. The dominant figures in the guild were the guildmasters—independent manufacturers, working in their own houses and banding together to elect their own guild government which then laid down the rules concerning the internal conduct of affairs. Under the master guildsmen were their few journeymen (from the French *journée* or day), who were paid by the day, and their half-dozen or so apprentices, ten to twelve years old, who were bound to them for periods of three to twelve years as their legal wards. In time, an apprentice could become a journeyman and then, at least in medieval romance, graduate to the status of a full-fledged guildmaster on completion of his "masterpiece."

Any survey of medieval town life delights in the color of guild organization: the broiders and glovers, the hatters and scriveners, the shipwrights and upholsterers, each with its guild hall, its distinctive livery, and its elaborate set of rules. But if life in the guilds and at the fairs provides a sharp contrast with the stodgy life on the manor, we must not be misled by surface resemblances into thinking that it represented a foretaste of modern life in medieval dress. It is a long distance from the guild to the modern business firm, and it is well to fix in mind some of the differences.

In the first place, the guild was much more than just an institution for organizing production. While most of its regulations concerned wages and conditions of work and specifications of output, they also dwelt at length on "noneconomic" matters: on the charitable contributions expected from each member, on his civic role, on his appropriate dress, and even on his daily deportment. Guilds were the regulators not only of production but of social conduct: when one member of the mercer's guild in London "broke the hed" of another in an argument over some merchandise, both were fined £10 and bonded for £200 not to repeat the disgrace. In another guild, members who engaged in a brawl were fined a barrel of beer, to be drunk by the rest of the guild.

But between guild and modern business firm there is a much more profound gulf than this pervasive paternalism. *Unlike a modern firm, the purpose of a guild was not first and foremost to make money.* Rather, it was to preserve a certain orderly way of life—a way which envisaged a decent income for its master craftsmen but which was certainly not intended to allow any of them to become a "big" businessman or a monopolist. On the contrary, guilds were specifically designed to ward off any such outcome of an uninhibited struggle among their members. The terms of service, the wages, the route of advancement of apprentices and journeymen were all fixed by custom. So, too, were the terms of sale: a guild member who cornered the supply of an item was guilty of *forestalling*, for which rigorous penalties were invoked, and one who bought wholesale to sell at retail was similarly punished for the faults of *engrossing* or *regrating*. Thus competition was strictly limited and profits were held to prescribed levels. Advertising was forbidden, and even technical progress in advance of one's fellow guildmen was considered disloyal.

In the great cloth guilds of Florence in the fourteenth century, for instance, no merchant was permitted to tempt a buyer into his shop or to call out to a customer standing in another's doorway, nor even to process his cloth in a manner different from that of his brethren. Standards of cloth production and processing were subject to the minutest scrutiny. If a scarlet dye, for instance, were found to be adulterated, the perpetrator was condemned to a crushing fine and, failing payment, to loss of his right hand.[13]

Surely the guilds represent a more "modern" aspect of feudal life than the manor, but the whole temper of guild life was still far removed from the goals and ideals of modern business enterprise. There was no free play of price, no free competition, no restless probing for advantage. Existing on the margin of a relatively moneyless society, the guilds perforce sought to take the risks out of their slender enterprises. Their aim was not increase, but preservation, stability, orderliness. As such, they were as drenched in the medieval atmosphere as the manors.

MEDIEVAL ECONOMICS

Beyond even these differences, we must note a still deeper chasm between medieval economic society and that of a market economy. This is the gulf between a society in which economic activity is still inextricably mixed with social and religious activity, and one in which economic life has, so to speak, emerged into a special category of its own. In our next chapter we shall be talking about the ways in which a market society creates a special sphere of economic existence. But as we complete our introduction to medieval economic society, the main point to which we should pay heed is that no such special sphere then existed. *In medieval society, economics was a subordinate and not a dominant aspect of life.*

And what was dominant? The answer is, of course, that in economic matters as in so many other facets of medieval life, the guiding ideal was religious. It was the Church, the great pillar of stability in an age of disorder, that constituted the ultimate authority on economics, as on most other matters.

But the economics of medieval Catholicism was concerned not with the credits and debits of successful business operation so much as with the

---

13 G. Renard, *Histoire du Travail à Florence* (Paris: 1913), pp. 190 ff.

credits and debits of the souls of business operators. As R. H. Tawney, one of the great students of the problem, has written:

. . . the specific contributions of medieval writers to the technique of economic theory were less significant than their premises. Their fundamental assumptions, both of which were to leave a deep imprint on social thought of the sixteenth and seventeenth centuries, were two: that economic interests are subordinate to the real business of life, which is salvation; and that economic conduct is one aspect of personal conduct, upon which, as on other parts of it, the rules of morality are binding. Material riches are necessary . . . since without them men cannot support themselves and help one another . . . But economic motives are suspect. Because they are powerful appetites men fear them, but they are not mean enough to applaud them. Like other strong passions, what they need, it is thought, is not a clear field, but repression. . . .[14]

Thus what we find throughout medieval religious thought is a pervasive uneasiness with the practices of economic society. Essentially, the Church's attitude toward trade was wary and nicely summed up in the saying: "Homo mercator vix aut numquam Deo placere potest"—the merchant can scarcely or never be pleasing to God.

We find such a suspicion of business motives in the Church's concern with the idea of a "just price." What was a just price? It was selling a thing for what it was worth, and no more. "It is wholly sinful," wrote Thomas Aquinas, "to practise fraud for the express purpose of selling a thing for more than its just price, inasmuch as a man deceives his neighbor to his loss."[15]

But what *was* a thing "worth"? Presumably, what it cost to acquire it or make it. Suppose, however, that a seller had himself paid too much for an article—then what was a "just price" at which he might resell it? Or suppose a man paid too little—was he then in danger of spiritual loss, offsetting his material gain?

These were the questions over which the medieval "economist-theologians" mulled, and they testify to the mixture of economics and ethics, characteristic of the age. But they were not merely theoretical questions. We have records of the dismay that economic theology brought to actual participants in the economic process. One St. Gerald of Aurillac in the tenth century, having bought an ecclesiastical garment in Rome for an unusually low price, learned from some itinerant merchants that he had picked up a "bargain"; instead of rejoicing, he hastened to send to the seller an additional sum, lest he fall into the sin of avarice.[16]

---

[14] *Religion and the Rise of Capitalism* (New York: Harcourt, 1947), p. 31.

[15] A. E. Monroe, ed., "Summa Theologica," in *Early Economic Thought* (Cambridge, Mass.: Harvard University Press, 1924), p. 54.

[16] Henri Pirenne, *Economic and Social History of Medieval Europe* (New York: Harcourt, Harvest Books, 1956), p. 27.

St. Gerald's attitude was no doubt exceptional. Yet if the injunction to charge fair prices did not succeed in staying men's appetites for gain, it did stay their unbridled enthusiasm. Men in ordinary business frequently stopped to assess the condition of their moral balance sheets. Whole towns would, on occasion, repent of usury and pay a heavy amend, or merchants like Gandoufle le Grand would, on their deathbeds, order restitution made to those from whom interest had been extracted. Men of affairs in the twelfth and thirteenth centuries occasionally inserted codicils in their wills urging their sons not to follow their footsteps into the snares of trade, or they would seek to make restitution for their commercial sins by charitable contributions. One medieval merchant of London founded a divinity scholarship with £14 "forasmoche as I fynde myn conscience aggrugged that I have deceived in this life divers persons to that amount."[17]

Thus the theological cast of suspicion injected a wholly new note into the moneymaking process. For the first time it associated the making of money with *guilt*. Unlike the acquisitor of antiquity who unashamedly reveled in his treasures, the medieval profiteer counted his gains in the knowledge that he might be imperiling his soul.

Nowhere was this disapproval of moneymaking more evident than in the Church's horror of usury—lending money at interest. Moneylending had, since Aristotle's day, been regarded as an essentially parasitic activity, an attempt to make a "barren" commodity, money, yield a return. But what had always been a vaguely disreputable and unpopular activity became, under Church scrutiny, a deeply evil one. Usury was decreed to be a *mortal* sin. At the Councils of Lyons and Vienne in the thirteenth and fourteenth centuries, the usurer was declared a pariah of society, to whom no one, under pain of excommunication, might rent a house, whose confession might not be heard, whose body might not have Christian burial, whose very will was invalid. Anyone even defending usury was to be suspected of heresy.

These powerful churchly sentiments were not produced merely by theological scruples. On the contrary, many of the Church's injunctions against both usury and profiteering arose from the most secular of realities. Famine, the endemic scourge of the Middle Ages, brought with it the most heartless economic gouging; loans commanded 40 and 60 percent—for bread. Much of the dislike of profit seeking and interest taking rose from its identification with just such ruthless practices, with which medieval times abounded.

Finally, another, perhaps even more fundamental, reason underlay the disrepute of gain and profit. This was the essentially static organization of economic life itself. Let us not forget that that life was basically agricultural

[17] S. L. Thrupp, *The Merchant Class in Medieval London* (Chicago: University of Chicago Press, 1948), p. 177. Also Renard, *Histoire du Travail à Florence*, pp. 220 ff.

and that agriculture, with its infinite complexity of peasant strips, was far from efficient. To quote once more from Henri Pirenne:

. . . the whole idea of profit, and indeed the possibility of profit, was incompatible with the position occupied by the great medieval landowner. Unable to produce for sale owing to the want of a market, he had no need to tax his ingenuity in order to wring from his men and his land a surplus which would merely be an encumbrance, and as he was forced to consume his own produce, he was content to limit it to his needs. His means of existence was assured by the traditional functioning of an organization which he did not try to improve.[18]

What was true of the country was also true of the city. The idea of an *expanding* economy, a *growing* scale of production, an *increasing* productivity was as foreign to the guildmaster or fair-merchant as to the serf and lord. Medieval economic organization was conceived as a means of reproducing, but not enhancing, the material well-being of the past. Its motto was perpetuation, not progress. There is little wonder that in such a static organization, profits and profitseeking were viewed as essentially disturbing rather than welcome economic phenomena.

Prerequisites of Change

We have traced the broad outlines of the economic organization of the West roughly up to the tenth or twelfth century. Once again it is wise to emphasize the diversity of currents concealed within a landscape we have too often been forced to treat as undifferentiated. At best, our journey into antiquity and the Middle Ages can give us a few glimpses of the prevailing flavor of the times, a sense of the ruling economic climate, of the main institutions and ideas by which men organized their economic efforts.

But one thing is certain. We are very far from the temper and tempo of modern economic life. The few stirrings we have witnessed in the slow world of the manor and the town are but the harbingers of a tremendous change which, over the course of the next centuries, would dramatically alter the basic form of economic organization itself, replacing the old ties of tradition and command with new ties of market transactions.

We shall have to wait until our next chapter to witness the actual process of change itself. But perhaps it will help us put into focus both what we have already seen and what we are about to witness if we anticipate our line of advance. We now have an idea of a pre-market society, a society in

[18] *Economic and Social History of Medieval Europe,* p. 63.

which markets exist but which does not yet depend on a market mechanism to solve the economic problem. What changes will be required to transform such a society into a true market economy?

1. *A new attitude toward economic activity will be needed.*

For such a society to function, men must be free to seek gain. The suspiciousness and unease which surrounded the ideas of profit, of change, of social mobility must give way to new ideas which would encourage those very attitudes and activities. In turn this meant, in the famous words of Sir Henry Maine, that the *society of status* must give way to the *society of contract*, that the society in which men were born to their stations in life must give way to a society in which they were free to define those stations for themselves.

Such an idea would have seemed to the medieval mind without any possible rationale. The idea that a general free-for-all should determine men's compensations, with neither a floor to prevent them from being ground down nor a ceiling to prevent them from rising beyond all reason, would have appeared senseless—even blasphemous. If we may listen again to R. H. Tawney:

To found a science of society upon the assumption that the appetite for economic gain is . . . to be accepted, like other natural forces . . . would have appeared to the medieval thinker as hardly less irrational or less immoral than to make the premise of social philosophy the unrestrained operation of such necessary human attributes as pugnacity or the sexual instinct.[19]

Yet some such freeing of the quest for economic gain, some such aggressive competition in the new contractual relationship of man to man would be essential for the birth of a market society.

2. *The monetization of economic life will have to proceed to its ultimate conclusion.*

One prerequisite of a market economy should by now be clear: such an economy must involve the process of exchange, of buying and selling, at every level of society. But for this to take place men must have the wherewithal to enter a market; that is, they must have cash. And, in turn, if society is to be permeated with cash, men must earn money for their labors. In other words, *for a market society to exist, nearly every task must have a monetary reward.*

Even in our highly monetized society we do not pay for every service: most conspicuously not for the housekeeping services of a wife. But all through the pre-market era, the number of unpaid services—the amount of

[19] *Religion and the Rise of Capitalism,* pp. 31-32.

work performed by law without monetary compensation—was vastly larger than in our society. Slave labor was, of course, unpaid. So was most serf labor. Even the labor of apprentices was remunerated more in kind, in food and lodging, than in cash. Thus probably 70 to 80 percent of the actual working population of an ancient or medieval economy labored without anything resembling full payment in money.

Clearly, in such a society the possibilities for a highly involved exchange economy were limited. But a still more important consequence must be noted. The absence of a widespread monetization of tasks meant the absence of a widespread *market for producers*. Nothing like the flow of "purchasing power" which dominates and directs our own productive efforts could be forthcoming in a society in which money incomes were the exception rather than the rule.

3. *The pressures of a free play of market "demand" will have to take over the regulation of the economic tasks of society.*

All through antiquity and the Middle Ages, as we have seen, tradition or command solved the economic problem. These were the forces that regulated the distribution of social rewards. But in a market society, another means of control must rise to take their place. *An all-encompassing flow of money demand, itself stemming from the total monetization of all economic tasks, must become the great propulsive mechanism of society.* Men must go to their tasks not because they are ordered there, but because they will make money there; and producers must decide on the volume and the variety of their output not because the rules of the manor or the guild so determine, but because there is a market demand for particular things. From the top to the bottom of society, in other words, a new marketing orientation must take over the production and distribution tasks. The whole replenishment, the steady provisioning, the very progress of society must now be subject to the guiding hand of a universal demand for labor and goods.

What forces would ultimately drive the world of medieval economic organization into a world of money, of universal markets, of profit-seeking? The stage is now set for us to attempt to answer this profoundly important and difficult question. Let us turn to a consideration of the causes capable of effecting so vast a change.

KEY CONCEPTS AND KEY WORDS

1. We must differentiate between markets, which have a very ancient pedigree, and market societies, which do not. *In a market society, the economic problem itself—both production and distribution—is solved by means of a vast exchange between buyers and sellers.* Many ancient societies had markets, but these markets did not organize the fundamental activities of these societies.

Markets

Peasant farming

2. The economic societies of antiquity had several features in common, which contrast sharply with those of modern market economies:
   - They rested on an agricultural base of *peasant farming*.

Slavery

   - Their cities were—from an economic point of view—parasitic *centers of consumption, not active centers of production*.
   - *Slavery* was a common and very important form of labor.

Surplus

   - They produced very considerable *surplusses*.

3. As a result, in the economic societies of antiquity we find the economic side of life subservient to the political side. Priest, warrior, and statesman were superior to merchant or trader; *wealth followed power*, not—as in market societies to come—the other way around.

Wealth and power

Feudalism

4. Medieval economic life emerged from the catastrophic disorganization that followed the decline of Roman law and order. It was characterized by a unique form of organization called the *manorial* system in which:
   - *Local lords were the centers of political, military, economic, and social power.*

Lords

Serfs

   - *Most peasants were bound as serfs to a particular lord*, for whom they were required to work and to whom they owed both labor and taxes or dues.
   - *Physical security* against brigands or other lords was provided by the lord, as well as some economic security in times of distress.

Manorial system

5. *The manorial system*, particularly in its earlier days (sixth to tenth centuries), *was a static economic system*, in which monetary payments played only a minor role. Self-sufficiency was the main purpose and the most outstanding characteristic of the manor.

Fairs

6. Side by side with the manor existed the economic life of the *towns*. Here monetary exchange always played a more important role, as did the organization of a more active economic life in the institution of *fairs*.

Guilds

7. The *guild* was the main form of organizing production in the towns and cities. *Guilds were very different from modern-day businesses*, insofar as they discouraged competition or profit seeking and sought to impose general rules on the methods of production, rates of pay, practices of marketing, and so on.

Usury

8. All through medieval times the church—the main social organization of the age—was suspicious of buying and selling activity. In part this reflected a dislike of the exploitative practices of the times, in part it was a consequence of an ancient contempt for moneymaking (remember Aristotle's dislike of *chrematistike*) and especially for money-lending (usury). The religious leaders of the day worried about "just" prices, and did not admit that unregulated buying and selling gave rise to just prices.

Market society

9. Three profound and pervasive changes would be needed to convert medieval society into a market society:
   - *A new attitude toward moneymaking* as a legitimate activity would have to replace the medieval suspicion of profit seeking.

Monetization

   - *The web of monetization would have to expand* beyond its narrow confines—that is, buying and selling would have to control the output of all products and the performance of nearly all tasks.
   - The flux of *"demand" and "supply" would have to be allowed to take over the direction of economic activity* from the dictates of lords and the usages of custom.

1. What differences, if any, characterize the economic attitudes and behavior of the American farmer and the American businessman? Can this comparison also describe the behavior and attitude of the Egyptian peasant and the Egyptian merchant? What accounts for the difference between the two societies?

2. Julius Caesar and J. P. Morgan were both wealthy and powerful men. What is the difference in the origins of their wealth and their power? Does power still follow wealth in modern economic societies? Does wealth still follow power in nonmarket societies? If not, why not?

3. To what uses was the surplus of society put in ancient Rome? In feudal society? In modern America? In the U.S.S.R.? What significance attaches to these different uses? What do they tell us about the structure of these societies?

4. What do you think of the validity of Aristotle's distinction between economic activity for *use* and *gain?*

5. In what ways is a serf a different *economic* creature from a modern farm worker? How is a slave different from an industrial worker?

6. What changes would have to take place within a guild before it resembled a modern business?

7. The Bible has numerous hostile references to moneymaking—"It is easier for a camel to go through the eye of a needle than for a rich man to enter into the kingdom of God." How do you account for this ancient churchly antipathy toward wealth? Is religion today still suspicious of moneymaking? Why?

8. Is the idea of a "just" price (or a "just" wage) still encountered in our own society? What is usually meant by these terms? Do you think these ideas are compatible with a market system?

9. The manorial system persisted for nearly 1,000 years. Why do you think change was so slow in coming?

10. Ancient Greece and Rome are a great deal more "modern" in their temper than feudal Europe. Yet neither was remotely a modern economic system. Why not?

Tradition, changelessness, order—these were the key concepts of economic society in the Middle Ages, and our preceding chapter introduced us to this unfamiliar and static way of economic life. But our purpose in this chapter is different. It is no longer to describe those factors which preserved the economic stability of medieval society, but to identify those forces which eventually burst it asunder.

Once again we need to begin with a word of caution. Our chapter spans an immense variety of historical experience. We must beware of thinking that the forces of change which dominate this chapter were identical from region to region or from century to century, or that the transition which they effected was uniform throughout the broad expanse of Europe. On the contrary, the great evolution which we will witness in these pages was not sharp and clear, but muddy and irregular. At the same time that the first evidences of a truly modern market society were beginning to manifest themselves in the medieval cities of Italy or Holland, the most archaic forms of feudal relationship still persisted in the agricultural sectors of these nations, and indeed in the city life of other nations. We must bear in mind that the historic processes of this chapter extended from the tenth to the seventeenth (and even eighteenth and nineteenth) centuries and manifested themselves in no two countries in precisely the same way.

With these cautions in mind, now let us turn to the great evolution itself. What agents were powerful enough to effect the major historic changes needed to bring about a market society?

THE ITINERANT MERCHANT

We meet the first of these forces of change in an unexpected guise. It is a small irregular procession of armed men, jogging along one of the rudimentary roads of medieval Europe: standard-bearer with colors in the lead, then a military chief, then a group of riders carrying bows and swords, and finally a caravan of horses and mules laden with casks and bales, bags and packs.

Someone unacquainted with medieval life might easily take such a troop for part of the baggage train of a small army. But he would be mistaken. These were not soldiers but merchants, the traveling merchants whom the English of the twelfth century called "pie-powers," from *pieds poudreux,* dusty feet. No wonder they were dusty; many of them came immense distances along routes so bad that we know of one instance where only the intervention of a local ecclesiastical lord prevented the "road" from being plowed up as arable land. In their bags and packs were goods which had somehow made a perilous journey across Europe, or even all the way from Arabia or India, to be sold from town to town, or from halt to halt, as these merchant adventurers wound their way across the medieval countryside.

And adventurers they were indeed. For in the fixed hierarchies of the great manorial estates of Europe there was no natural place for these unlanded peddlers of goods, with their unfeudal attributes of calculation and (often very crude) bookkeeping and their natural insistence on trade in money. The traveling merchants ranked very low in society. Some of them, without doubt, were the sons of serfs, or even runaway serfs themselves. Yet since no one could prove their bondage, they had, if only by default, the gift of "freedom." It is no wonder that in the eyes of the nobility, the merchants were upstarts and a disturbing element in the normal pattern of things.

Yet no one would have dispensed with their services. To their brightly canopied stalls at the fairs flocked the lords and ladies of the manors as well as the Bodos and Ermentrudes of the fields. After all, where else could one buy pepper, or purple dye, or acquire a guaranteed splinter from the Cross? Where else could one buy the marvelous cloths woven in Tuscany or learn such esoteric words, derived from the Arabic, as "jar" or "syrup"? If the merchant was a disturbing leaven in the mix of medieval life, he was also the pinch of active ingredient without which the mixture would have been very dull indeed.

We first note the traveling merchant in Europe in the eighth and ninth century, and we can follow his progress until the fourteenth and fifteenth century. By this time, largely through the merchants' own efforts, commerce was sufficiently organized so that it no longer required these itinerant journeyers.* For what these travelers brought, together with their wares, was the first breath of commerce and commercial intercourse to a Europe which had sunk to an almost tradeless and self-sufficient manorial stagnation. Even to towns as minuscule and isolated as Forcalquier in France—a dot on the map without so much as a road to connect its few hundred souls to the outer world—these hardy traders beat their path: we know from a primitive book of accounts that in May, 1331, thirty-six itinerant merchants visited Forcalquier to transact business at the home and "shop" of one Ugo Teralh, a notary.[1] And so, in a thousand isolated communities, did they slowly weave a web of economic interdependence.

URBANIZATION

An important by-product of the rise of the itinerant merchant was the slow urbanization of medieval life, the creation of new towns and villages. When the traveling merchants stopped, they naturally chose the protected site of a local castle or burg, or of a church. And so we find growing up around the walls of advantageously situated castles—in the *foris burgis*, whence *faubourg*, the French word for "suburb"—more or less permanent trading places, which in turn became the inner core of small towns. Nestled close to the castle or cathedral wall for protection, the new burgs were still not "of" the manor. The inhabitants of the burg—the burgesses, burghers, bourgeois—had at best an anomalous and insecure relation to the manorial world within. As we have seen, there was no way of applying the time-hallowed rule of "ancient customs" in adjudicating their disputes, since there *were* no ancient customs in the commercial quarters. Neither were there clear-cut rules for their taxation or for the particular degrees of fealty they owned their local masters. Worse yet, some of the growing towns began to surround themselves with walls. By the twelfth century, the commercial burg of Bruges, for example, had already swallowed up the old fortress like a pearl around a grain of sand.

Curiously, it was this very struggle for existence in the interstices of feudal society which provided much of the impetus for the development of a new social and economic order within the city. In all previous civilizations, cities had been the outposts of central government. Now, for the first time,

* Records of an order for goods placed on the occasion of a funeral of a Swedish nobleman in 1328 include saffron from Spain or Italy, caraway seed from the Mediterranean, ginger from India, cinnamon from Ceylon, pepper from Malabar, anise from southern Europe, and Rhine and Bordeaux wines. The order was placed for immediate delivery from one local merchant, despite the fact that Sweden was then a laggard and even primitive land. Cf. Fritz Rorig, *Mittelalterliche Weltwirtschaft* (Jena: 1933), p. 17. (I am again indebted to Dr. Goran Ohlin for this reference.)
[1] *Cambridge Economic History of Europe*, II, 325-26.

they existed as independent entities outside the main framework of social power. As a result, they were able to define for themselves—as they *had* to define for themselves—a code of law and social behavior and a set of governing institutions which were eventually to displace those of the feudal countryside.

The process was long drawn out, for the rate of growth of towns was often very slow. In the nearly two centuries between 1086 and 1279, for example, the town of Cambridge, England, added an average of but one house *per year*.[2] One important reason for this almost imperceptible rate of expansion was the difficulty of moving men or materials over the terrible roads. Not the least consequence of the decline of Roman power had been the decay of its once magnificent system of highways, the very stones of which were pilfered for building materials during the years of worst social disorganization. Until the roads recovered, economic movement was perforce limited and limping. And it is worth remarking that in many parts of Europe, a system of transportation as efficient as that of ancient Rome was not enjoyed until the eighteenth or even nineteenth centuries.

Yet if growth was slow, it was steady; and in some locales it was much faster than in Cambridge. During the 1,000 years of the Middle Ages nearly 1,000 towns were fathered in Europe, a tremendous stimulus to the commercialization and monetization of life, for each town had its local marts, its local toll gates, often its local mint; its granaries and shops, its drinking places and inns, its air of "city life" which contrasted so sharply with that of the country. The slow, spontaneous growth of urban ways was a major factor in introducing a marketing flavor to European economic life.

THE CRUSADES

The rise of the itinerant merchant and the town were two great factors in the slow evolution of a market society out of medieval economic life; a third factor was the Crusades.

It is an ironic turn to history that the Crusades, the supreme religious adventure of the Middle Ages, should have contributed so much toward the establishment of a society to which the Church was so vigorously opposed. If we consider the Crusades, however, not from the point of view of their religious impulse, but simply as great expeditions of exploration and colonization, their economic impact becomes much more understandable.*

The Crusades served to bring into sudden and startling contact two very different worlds. One was the still slumbering society of European

---

[2] George Gordon Coulton, *Medieval Panorama* (New York: World Publishing, Meridian Books, 1955), p. 285.

* We might note here some of the complex interaction of the process we are watching. For the Crusades were not only a cause of European economic development, but also a *symptom* of the development which had previously taken place.

feudalism with all its rural inertia, its aversion to trade, and its naïve conceptions of business; the other was the brilliant society of Byzantium and Venice, with its urban vitality, its unabashed enjoyment of money-making, and its sophisticated business ways. The Crusaders, coming from their draughty castles and boring manorial routines, thought they would find in the East only untutored heathen savages. They were astonished to be met by a people far more civilized, infinitely more luxurious, and much more money-oriented than they.

One result was that the simple-minded Crusaders found themselves the pawns of commercial interests which they little understood. During the first three Crusades, the Venetians, who provided ships, gulled them as shamelessly as country bumpkins at a fair. The fact that they were fleeced, however, did not prevent the Crusaders from reaching the Holy Land, albeit with inconclusive results. But in the notorious Fourth Crusade (1202-1204) Dandolo, the wily 94-year-old Doge of Venice, managed to subvert the entire religious expedition into a gigantic plundering operation for Venetian profit.

First Dandolo held up the voyagers for an initial transportation price of 85,000 silver marks, an enormous sum for the unmoneyed nobility to scrape up. Then, when the funds had been found, he refused to carry out his bargain until the Crusaders agreed first to attack the town of Zara, a rich commercial rival of Venice. Since Zara was a *Christian*, not an "infidel" community, Pope Innocent III was horrified and suggested that the attack be directed instead against heathen Egypt. But Egypt was one of Venice's best customers, and this horrified Dandolo even more. The Crusaders, stranded and strapped, had no choice: Zara soon fell—after which, at Dandolo's urging, Christian Constantinople was also sacked. The "heathen" Orient was never reached at all, but Venice profited marvelously.

It was not only Venice which gained, however. The economic impact on the Crusaders themselves was much more formidable than the religious. On many this impact was disastrous, as knights who had melted down their silver plate to join the Crusades came back penniless to their ruined manor houses. To others, however, the Crusades brought a new economic impetus. When in 1101, for example, the Genoese raided Caesarea, a Palestinian seaport, 8,000 soldiers and sailors reaped a reward of some forty-eight *solidi* each, plus two pounds of pepper—and thus were 8,000 petty capitalists born.[3] And in 1204 when Constantinople fell, not only did each knight receive twenty marks in silver as his share of the booty, but even the squires and archers were rewarded with a few marks each.

Thus the Crusades provided an immense fertilizing experience for Europe. The old, landed basis of wealth came into contact with a new moneyed basis which proved much more powerful. Indeed, the old conception of life itself was forcibly revised before a glimpse of an existence not

[3] *Cambridge Economic History of Europe*, II, 306.

only wealthier, but gayer and more vital. As a means of shaking a sluggish society out of its rut, the Crusades played an immense role in speeding along the economic transformation of Europe.

GROWTH OF NATIONAL POWER

Yet another factor in the slow commercialization of economic life was the gradual amalgamation of Europe's fragmented economic and political entities into larger wholes. As the disintegration of economic life following the break-up of the old Roman Empire had shown, a strong economic society requires a strong and broad political base. Hence as political Europe began its slow process of reknitting, once again its economic tempo began to rise.

One of the most striking characteristics of the Middle Ages, and one of its most crippling obstacles to economic development, was the medieval crazy quilt of compartmented, isolated areas of government. Over a journey of a hundred miles, a traveling merchant might fall under a dozen different sovereignties, each with different rules, regulations, laws, weights, measures, money. Worse yet, at each border there was apt to be a toll station. At the turn of the thirteenth and fourteenth centuries there were said to be more than thirty toll stations along the Weser River and at least thirty-five along the Elbe; along the Rhine, a century later, there were more than sixty such toll stations, mostly belonging to local ecclesiastical princes: Thomas Wykes, an English chronicler, described the system as "the raving madness of the Teutons." But it was not only a German disease. There were so many toll stations along the Seine in France in the late fifteenth century that it cost half its final selling price to ship grain 200 miles down the river.[4] Indeed, among the European nations, England alone enjoyed an internally unified market during the middle and late Middle Ages. This was one powerful contributory factor to England's emergence as the first great European economic power.

The amalgamation of Europe's fragmented markets was essentially a political as well as an economic process; it followed the gradual centralization of power which changed the map of Europe from the infinite complexity of the tenth century to the more or less "modern" map of the sixteenth. Here, once again, the burgeoning towns played a central and crucial role. It was the city burghers who became the allies of the nascent monarchies, thereby disassociating themselves still further from their local feudal lords while, in turn, supplying the shaky monarchs with an absolutely essential prerequisite for kingship: cash.

Thus monarch and bourgeois combined to bring about the slow growth of centralized governments, and from centralized government, in turn, came not alone a unification of law and money but a direct stimulus to the

---

[4] *Ibid,* pp. 134–35.

development of commerce and industry as well. In France, for example, manufacturing was promoted by royal patronage of the famous Gobelin tapestry and Sèvres porcelain works, and business was created for innumerable craftsmen and artisans by the demands of the royal palaces and banquet halls. In other fields, growing national power also imparted a new encouragement: navies had to be built, armies had to be equipped, and these new "national" armed forces, many of whom were mercenaries, had to be paid. All this set into faster motion the pumps of monetary circulation.

EXPLORATION

Another economic impetus given by the gradual consolidation of political power was the official encouragement of exploration. All through the long years of the Middle Ages a few intrepid adventurers, like Marco Polo, had beat their way to remote regions in search of a short route to the fabled riches of India; and as a matter of fact, by the early fourteenth century the route to the Far East was well enough known so that silk from China cost but half the price of that from the Caspian area, only half the distance away.

Yet the network of all these hazardous and brave penetrations beyond Europe formed only the thinnest of spider webs. There still remained the systematic exploration of the unknown, and this awaited the kingly support of state adventurers. Columbus and Vasco da Gama, Cabral and Magellan did not venture on their epoch-making journeys as individual merchants (although they all hoped to make their fortunes thereby) but as adventurers in fleets bought with, and equipped by, royal money, bearing the royal mark of approval, and sent forth in hope of additions to the royal till.

The economic consequences of those amazing adventures were incalculably great. For one thing, they opened up an invigorating flow of precious metals into Europe. Gold and silver, coming from the great Spanish mines in Mexico and Peru, were slowly redistributed to other nations as Spain paid in gold specie for goods it bought abroad. As a result, prices rose throughout Europe—between 1520 and 1650 alone, it is estimated that they increased 200 to 400 percent, bringing about both stimulus and stress to industry, but setting in motion a great wave of speculation and commerce.

In addition, of course, the longer-run results of exploration brought an economic stimulus of still greater importance. The establishment of colonies in the sixteenth and seventeenth centuries and the subsequent enjoyment of trade with the New World provided a tremendous boost in propelling Europe into a bustling commercial society. The discovery of the New World was, from the beginning, a catalytic and revolutionizing influence on the Old.

CHANGE IN
RELIGIOUS
CLIMATE

The forces of change that we have thus far summarized were actually visible. At any time during the long transition from a nonmarket into a market society we could have witnessed with our own eyes the traveling merchants, the expanding towns, the Crusades, the evidences of a growing national power. Yet these were not the only forces that undermined the feudal system and brought into being its commercial successor. There were, as well, powerful but invisible currents of change, currents which affected the intellectual atmosphere, the beliefs, and attitudes of Europe. One of these, of special importance, was a change in the religious climate of the times.

In our last chapter we saw how deeply the Catholic church was imbued with theological aversions to the principle of gain—and especially to interest taking or usury. An amusing story of the times sums up the position of the Church very well. Humbertus de Romanis, a monk, tells of someone who found a devil in every nook and cranny of a Florentine cloister, although in the marketplace he found but one. The reason, Humbertus explains, was that it took only one to corrupt a marketplace, where every man harbored a devil in his own heart.[5] In such a disapproving climate, it was hard for the commercial side of life to thrive.

To be sure, for all its fulminations against gain and usury, the Church itself grew in time to a position of commanding economic importance. Through its tithes and benefices it was the largest collector and distributor of money in all of Europe; and in an age in which banks and safe deposit boxes did not exist, it was the repository of much feudal wealth. Some of its sub-orders, such as the Knights Templar, became immensely wealthy and served as banking institutions, lending to needy monarchs on stiff terms. Nonetheless, all of this faintly disreputable activity was undertaken despite, and not because of, the Church's deepest convictions. For behind the ecclesiastical disapproval of wealth seeking was a deep-seated theological conviction, a firm belief in the transient nature of this life on earth and the importance of preparing for the Eternal Morrow. The Church lifted its eyes and sought to lift the eyes of others above the daily struggle for existence. It strove to minimize the importance of life on earth and to denigrate the earthly activities to which an all too weak flesh succumbed.

What changed this dampening influence on the zest of wealth making? According to the theories of the German sociologist Max Weber and the English economic historian R. H. Tawney, the underlying cause lay in the rise of a new theological point of view contained in the teachings of the Protestant reformer John Calvin (1509–1564).

Calvinism was a harsh religious philosophy. Its core was a belief in *predestination*, in the idea that from the beginning God had chosen the saved and the damned, and that nothing man could do on earth could alter that inviolable writ. Furthermore, according to Calvin, the number of the damned exceeded by a vast amount the number of the saved, so that for the average person the chances were great that this earthly prelude was but the momentary grace given before eternal Hell and Damnation commenced.

[5] Beard, *A History of the Business Man,* p. 160.

Perhaps only a man of Calvin's iron will could have borne life under such a sentence. For we soon find that in the hands of his followers in the Lowlands and England, the inexorable and inscrutable quality of the original doctrine began to be softened. Although the idea of predestination was still preached, it was now allowed that in the tenor of one's worldly life there was a *hint* of what was to follow. Thus the English and Dutch divines taught that whereas even the saintliest-seeming man might end in Hell, the frivolous or wanton one was certainly headed there. Only in a blameless life lay the slightest chance of demonstrating that Salvation was still a possibility.

And so the Calvinists urged a life of rectitude, severity and, most important of all, diligence. In contrast to the Catholic theologians who tended to look upon worldly activity as vanity, the Calvinists sanctified and approved of endeavor as a kind of index of spiritual worth. Indeed in Calvinist hands there grew up the idea of a man *dedicated* to his work: "called" to it, as it were. Hence the fervid pursuit of one's calling, far from evidencing a distraction from religious ends, came to be taken as evidence of a dedication to a religious life. The energetic merchant was, in Calvinist eyes, a *Godly* man, not an ungodly one; and from this identification of work and worth, it was not long before the notion grew up that the more successful a man, the more worthy he was. Calvinism thus provided a religious atmosphere which, in contrast to Catholicism, encouraged wealth seeking and the temper of a businesslike world.

Perhaps even more important than its encouragement in seeking wealth was the influence of Calvinism on the *use* of wealth. By and large the prevailing attitude of the prosperous Catholic merchants had been that the aim of worldly success was the enjoyment of a life of ease and luxury, while Catholic nobility displayed on occasion a positively grotesque disdain for wealth. In an orgy of gambling that gripped Paris at the end of the seventeenth century, a prince who sent his mistress a diamond worth 5,000 *livres* had it pulverized and strewn over her reply when she rejected it as being too small. The same prince eventually gambled away an income of 600,000 *livres* a year. A *maréchal* whose grandson turned up his nose at a gift of a purse of gold threw it into the street: "Let the street cleaner have it then."[6]

The Calvinist manufacturer or trader had a very different attitude toward wealth. If his religion approved of diligence, it most emphatically did not approve of indulgence. Wealth was to be accumulated and put to good use, not frittered away.

Calvinism promoted an aspect of economic life of which we have hitherto heard very little: *thrift*. It made saving, the conscious abstinence

---

[6] Werner Sombart, *Luxury and Capitalism* (New York: Columbia University Press, 1938), pp. 120ff. Also Thirion, *La Vie Privée des Financiers au XVIIIe Siècle* (Paris: 1895), p. 292.

from the enjoyment of income, a virtue. It made investment, the use of saving for productive purposes, an instrument of piety as well as profit. It even condoned, with various *quids* and *quos,* the payment of interest. In fact, Calvinism fostered a new conception of economic life. In place of the old ideal of social and economic stability, of knowing and keeping one's "place," it brought respectability to an ideal of struggle, of material improvement, of economic growth.

Economic historians still debate the precise degree of influence which may properly be attributed to "the Protestant Ethic" in bringing about the rise of a new gain-centered worldly philosophy. After all, there was nothing much that a Dutch Calvinist would have been able to teach an Italian Catholic banker about the virtues of a businesslike approach to life. Yet, looking back on the subsequent course of economic progress, it is striking that without exception it was the Protestant countries with their "Puritan streak" of work and thrift which forged ahead in the economic race. As one of the powerful winds of change of the sixteenth and seventeenth centuries, the new religious outlook must be counted as a highly favorable stimulus for the evolution of the market society.

The enumeration of all these currents does not exhaust the catalog of forces bearing against the old fixed economic order in Europe. The list could be expanded and greatly refined.* Yet, with all due caution we can now begin to comprehend the immense coalition of events—some as specific as the Crusades, some as diffuse as a change in religious ideals—that jointly cooperated to destroy the medieval framework of economic life and to prepare the way for a new dynamic framework of market transactions.

BREAKDOWN OF THE MANORIAL SYSTEM

One important aspect of this profound alteration was the gradual *monetization of feudal obligations.* In locality after locality we can trace the conversion of the old feudal payments in *kind*—the days of labor or chickens or eggs which a lord received from his tenants—into payments of *money* dues and money rents with which they now discharged their obligations to him.

A number of causes lay behind this commutation of feudal payments. One was the growing urban demand for food, as town and city populations began to swell. In concentric circles around the town, money filtered out into the countryside, at one and the same time raising the capacity of the

---

* An extremely important influence (to which we will specifically turn in our next chapter) was the rise of a new interest in technology, founded on scientific inquiry into natural events. Another important causative factor was the development of modern business concepts and techniques. The German economic historian Werner Sombart has even said that if he were forced to give a single date for the "beginning" of modern capitalism he would choose 1202, the year in which appeared the *Liber Abaci,* a primer of commercial arithmetic. Similarly, the historian Oswald Spengler has called the invention of double-entry bookkeeping in 1494 an achievement worthy of being ranked with that of Columbus or Copernicus.

rural sector to buy urban goods and whetting its desire to do so. At the same time, in a search for larger cash incomes to buy a widening variety of goods, the nobility looked with increasing favor on receiving its rents and dues in money rather than in kind. In so doing, however, it unwittingly set into motion a cause for the further serious deterioration of the manorial system. Usually, the old feudal services were converted into *fixed* sums of money payments. This temporarily eased the cash position of the lord, but soon placed him in the squeeze which always hurts the creditor in times of inflation. And even when dues were not fixed, rents and money dues lagged sufficiently behind the growing monetary needs of the nobility, so that still further feudal obligations were monetized to keep the lord in cash. But as prices rose and the monetized style of life expanded still further, these too failed to keep him solvent.

The result was that the rural nobility, which now depended increasingly on rents and dues for its income, steadily lost its economic power.* Indeed, beginning in the sixteenth century we find a new class coming into being— the *impoverished* nobility. In the year 1530 in the Gevaudan district of France, we find that 121 lords had an aggregate income of 21,400 *livres,* but one of these seigneurs accounted for 5,000 *livres* of the sum, another for 2,000—and the rest averaged but a mean 121 *livres* apiece.[7] In fact, the shortage of cash afflicted not only the lesser nobility but even the monarchy itself. Maximilian I, Emperor of the Holy Roman Empire, on occasion lacked the cash to pay for even the overnight lodgings of his entourage on tour; and when two of his grandchildren married children of the King of Hungary, all the trappings of the weddings—2,000 caparisoned horses, jewels, and gold and silver plate—were borrowed from merchant bankers to whom Maximilian had written wheedling letters begging them not to forsake him in his moment of need.

Clearly, the manorial system was incompatible with a cash economy; for while the nobility was pinched between rising prices and costs and static incomes, the merchant classes, to whom cash naturally gravitated, steadily increased their power. In the Gevaudan district, for example, where the richest lord had his income of 5,000 *livres,* the richest town merchants had incomes up to 65,000 *livres.* In Germany, while Maximilian scratched for cash, the great banking families of Augsburg commanded incomes far larger than Maximilian's entire kingly revenue. In Italy, the Gianfigliazzi of Florence, who began as "nobodies" lending money to the Bishop of Fiesole, ended up stripping him of his possessions and leaving him a pauper; while in Tuscany, the lords who looked down their noses at usurers in the tenth

---

* This process of economic decline was considerably enhanced by the ineptitude of the nobility as managers of their estates. The descendants of the Crusaders were not much more businesslike than their ancestors.

[7] *Cambridge Economic History of Europe,* I, 557-58.

century lost their estates to them in the twelfth and thirteenth. All over Europe men of mean social standing turned the monetary economy to good account. One Jean Amici of Toulouse made a fortune in English booty during the Hundred Years War; Guillaume de St-Yon grew rich by selling meat at rapacious prices to Paris; and Jacques Coeur, the most extraordinary figure of all, rose from merchant to King's coiner, then to King's purchasing agent, then to financier not for, but *of*, the King, during the course of which he accumulated a huge fortune estimated at 27 million *écus.* *

Appearance of the Economic Aspect of Life

Behind all of these profoundly disturbing events we can discern an immense process of change that literally revolutionized the economic organization of Europe. Whereas in the tenth century, cash and money transactions were only peripheral to the solution of the economic problem, by the sixteenth and seventeenth centuries cash and transactions were already beginning to provide the very molecular force of economic cohesion.

But over and above this general monetization of life, another and perhaps even more profound change was taking place. This was the emergence of a separate *economic* sphere of activity visible within, and separable from, the surrounding matrix of social life. It was the creation of a whole aspect of society which had never previously existed, but which was thenceforth to constitute a commanding facet of human existence.[8]

In antiquity and feudal times, as we have seen, one could not easily separate the economic motivations or even the economic actions of the great mass of men from the normal round of existence itself. The peasant following his immemorial ways was hardly conscious of acting according to "economic" motives; indeed, he did not: he heeded the orders of his lord or the dictates of custom. Nor was the lord himself economically oriented. His interests were military or political or religious, and not basically oriented toward the idea of gain or increase. Even in the towns, as we have seen, the conduct of ordinary business was inextricably mixed with non-economic concerns. The undeniable fact that men were acquisitive, not to say avaricious, did not yet impart its flavor to life in general; the making of money,

---

* Note, however, that Coeur eventually fell from power, was imprisoned, and died in exile. The counting house was not yet fully master of the castle.

[8] The following section owes much to the insights of Karl Polanyi's famous *The Great Transformation* (Boston: Beacon Press, 1957, paperback ed.), Part II.

as we have been at some pains to indicate, was a tangential rather than a central concern of ancient or medieval existence.

LABOR, LAND,
AND CAPITAL
COME
INTO BEING

With the ever-widening scope of monetization, however, a genuinely new element of life came slowly to the fore. Labor, for example, emerged as an activity quite different from the past. No longer was "labor" part of an explicit social relationship in which one man (serf or apprentice) worked for another (lord or guildmaster) in return for at least an assurance of subsistence. Labor was now a mere quantum of effort, a "commodity" to be disposed of on the marketplace for the best price it could bring, quite devoid of any reciprocal responsibilities on the part of the buyer, beyond the payment of wages. If those wages were not enough to provide subsistence— well, that was not the buyer's responsibility. He had bought his "labor," and that was that.

This emergence of "pure" labor—labor as a quantity of effort detached from a man's life and bought on the market in fixed amounts—had a parallel in two other main elements of economic life. One of these was land. Formerly conceived as the territory of a great lord, as inviolable as the territory of a modern nation-state, land was now also seen in its economic aspect as something to be bought or leased for the economic return it yielded. An estate which was once the core of political and administrative power became a "property" with a market price, available for any number of uses, even as a site for a factory. The dues, the payments in kind, the intangibles of prestige and power which once flowed from the ownership of land gave way to the single return of *rent;* that is, to a money return derived from putting land to *profitable* use.

The same transformation became true of property. As it was conceived in antiquity and throughout most of the Middle Ages, property was a sum of tangible wealth, a hoard, a treasury of plate, bullion, or jewels. Very logically, it was realized in the form of luxurious homes, in castles and armaments, in costly robes and trappings. But with the monetization and commercialization of society, property, too, became expressible in a monetary equivalent: a man was now "worth" so many *livres,* or *écus,* or pounds, or whatever. Property became *capital,* manifesting itself no longer in specific goods, but as an abstract sum of infinitely flexible use whose "value" was its capacity to earn *interest* or *profits.*

None of these changes, it should be emphasized, was planned, clearly foreseen, or for that matter, welcomed. It was not with equanimity that the feudal hierarchies saw their prerogatives nibbled away by the mercantile classes. Neither did the tradition-preserving guildmaster desire his own enforced metamorphosis into a "capitalist," a man of affairs guided by market signals and beset by competition. But perhaps for no social class was the transition more painful than for the peasant, caught up in a process of history that dispossessed him from his livelihood and made him a landless laborer.

This process, which was particularly important in England, was the *enclosure movement*, a by-product of the monetization of feudal life. Starting as early as the thirteenth century, the landed aristocracy, increasingly squeezed for cash, began to view their estates not merely as the ancestral fiefs, but as potential sources of cash revenue. In order to raise larger cash crops, they therefore began to "enclose" the pasture which had previously been deemed "common land." Communal grazing fields, which had in fact always belonged to the lord despite their communal use, were now claimed for the exclusive benefit of the lord and turned into sheepwalks. Why sheepwalks? Because a rising demand for woolen cloth was making sheep-raising a highly profitable occupation. The medieval historian Eileen Power writes:

The visitor to the House of Lords, looking respectfully upon that august assembly, cannot fail to be struck by a stout and ungainly object facing the throne—an ungainly object upon which in full session of Parliament, he will observe seated the Lord Chancellor of England. The object is a woolsack, and it is stuffed as full of pure history as the office of the Lord Chancellor itself. . . . The Lord Chancellor of England is seated upon a woolsack because it was upon a woolsack that this fair land rose to prosperity.[9]

The enclosure process in England proceeded at an irregular pace over the long centuries; not until the late eighteenth and early nineteenth centuries did it reach its engulfing climax.* By its end, some ten million acres, nearly *half* the arable land of England, had been "enclosed"—in its early Tudor days by the more or less high-handed conversion of the "commons" to sheep-raising; in the final period, by the forcible consolidation of strips and plots into tracts suitable for commercial farming, for which tenants presumably received "fair compensation."

From a strictly economic point of view, the enclosure movement was unquestionably salutary in that it brought into productive employment land which had hitherto yielded only a pittance. Indeed, particularly in the

---

[9] *Medieval People* (Garden City, N.Y.: Doubleday, Anchor Books, 1954), p. 125.

* In other European nations an enclosure process also took place, but at a much slower pace. In France, Italy, and southern Germany the small-holder peasant persisted long after he had virtually ceased to exist in England; in northeastern Germany, on the other hand, the small peasant was deprived of his holdings and turned into a landless proletarian.

eighteenth and nineteenth centuries, enclosure was the means by which England "rationalized" its agriculture and finally escaped from the inefficiency of the traditional manorial strip system. But there was another, crueler side to enclosure. As the common fields were enclosed, it became ever more difficult for the tenant to support himself. In the fifteenth and sixteenth centuries, when the initial enclosure of the commons reached its peak, as many as three-fourths to nine-tenths of the tenants of some estates were simply turned off the farm. Whole hamlets were thus wiped out. Sir Thomas More described it savagely in Book I of his *Utopia*.

Your sheep that were wont to be so meek and tame, and so small eaters, now, as I hear say, be become so great devourers and so wild, that they eat up and swallow down the very men themselves. They consume, destroy and devour whole fields, houses and cities. For look in what parts of the realm doth grow the finest, and therefore dearest wool, there noblemen and gentlemen, yea and certain abbots, holy men Got wot, not contenting themselves with the yearly revenues and profits that were wont to grow to their forefathers and predecessors of their land ... leave no ground for tillage, they enclose all into pastures, they throw down houses, they pluck down towns and leave nothing standing, but only the church to make of it a sheep house ...

The enclosure process provided a powerful force for the dissolution of feudal ties and the formation of the new relationships of a market society. By dispossessing the peasant, it "created" a new kind of labor force—landless, without traditional sources of income, however meager, impelled to find work for wages wherever it might be available.

Together with this agricultural proletariat, we begin to see the emergence of an urban proletariat, partly brought about by a gradual transformation of guilds into more "business-like" firms, partly by the immigration into the cities of some of the new landless peasantry. And then to exacerbate the whole situation, from the middle of the eighteenth century a rising population (itself traceable in large measure to the increase in food output resulting from the enclosures) began to pour growing numbers onto the labor market. As a result of this complicated interplay of causes and effects, we find England plagued with the problem of the "wandering poor." One not untypical proposal of the eighteenth century was that they be confined in what a reformer candidly termed "Houses of Terror."

Thus did the emergence of a market-oriented system grind into being a "labor force," and though the process of adjustment for other classes of society was not so brutal, it, too, exacted its social price. Tenaciously the guildmasters fought against the invasion of their protected trades by manufacturers who trespassed on traditional preserves or who upset established modes of production with new machinery. Doggedly the landed nobility sought to protect their ancient privileges against the encroachment of the moneyed *nouveaux riches*.

Yet the process of economic enlargement, breaking down the established routines of the past, rearranging the power and prestige of all social classes, could not be stopped. Ruthlessly it pursued its historic course and impartially it distributed its historic rewards and sacrifices. Although stretched out over a long period, it was not an evolution but a slow revolution which overtook European economic society. Only when that society had run its long gauntlet, suffering one of the most wrenching dislocations of history, would the world of transactions appear "natural" and "normal" and the categories of "land," "labor," and "capital" become so matter-of-fact that it would be difficult to believe they had not always existed.

Yet, as we have seen, it was not at all "natural" and "normal" to have free, wage-earning, contractual labor or rentable, profit-producing land or fluid, investment-seeking capital. They were *creations* of the great transformation of a pre-market into a market society. Economics calls these creations the *factors of production,* and much of economics is concerned with analyzing the manner in which these three basic constituents of the productive process are combined by the market mechanism.

What we must realize at this stage of our inquiry, however, is that "land," "labor," and "capital" do not exist as eternal categories of *social* organization. Admittedly, they are categories of *nature,* but these eternal aspects of the productive process—the soil, human effort, and the artifacts which can be applied to production—do not take on, in every society, the specific separation that distinguishes them in a market society. In pre-market economies, land, labor, and capital are inextricably mixed and mingled in the figure of slave and serf, lord and guildmaster—none of whom enters the production process as the incarnation of a specific economic function offered for a price. The slave is not a "worker," the guildmaster is not a "capitalist," nor is the lord a "landlord." Only when a social system has evolved in which labor is sold, land is rented, and capital is freely invested do we find the categories of economics emerging from the flux of life.

Modern economics thus describes the manner in which a certain kind of society, with a specific history of acculturation and institutional evolution, solves its economic problems. It may well be that in another era there will no longer be "land," "labor," and "capital." If, for example, a pure communist society ever evolves, the method by which the social product will be assured or distributed need not bear any more relation to our present system of wage payments or rental incomes or profit-shares than our own system bears to its feudal predecessor. In that case, "economics" as we know it will have to be revised to correspond to the new social relationships by which the production and distribution problems will be solved.

But the emergence of a market society, with its new factors of production, was not yet the only creation of the forces of change we have examined in this chapter. Along with the new relationships of man to man in the marketplace, there arose a new form of *social control* to take over the guidance of the economy from the former aegis of tradition and command.

RISE OF THE "PROFIT MOTIVE"

What was this new form of control? Essentially, it was a pattern of social behavior, of normal, everyday action that the new market environment imposed on society. And what was this pattern of behavior? In the language of the economist, it was the drive to *maximize one's income* (or to minimize one's expenditures) by concluding the best possible bargains on the marketplace. In ordinary language, it was the drive to buy cheap and sell dear, or in business terminology, the *profit motive*.

The market society had not, of course, invented this motive. Perhaps it did not even intensify it. But it did make it a *ubiquitous* and *necessitous* aspect of social behavior. Although men may have *felt* acquisitive during the Middle Ages or antiquity, they did not enter en masse into market transactions for the basic economic activities of their livelihoods. And even when, for instance, a peasant sold his few eggs at the town market, rarely was the transaction a matter of overriding importance for his continued existence. Market transactions in a fundamentally nonmarket society were thus a subsidiary activity, a means of supplementing a livelihood which, however sparse, was largely independent of buying or selling.

With the monetization of labor, land, and capital, however, transactions became *universal* and *critical* activities. Now everything was for sale, and the terms of transactions were anything but subsidiary to existence itself. To a man who sold his labor on a market, in a society that assumed no responsibility for his upkeep, the price at which he concluded his bargain was all-important. So it was with the landlord and the budding capitalist. For each of these a good bargain could spell riches—and a bad one, ruin. Thus the pattern of economic maximization was generalized throughout society and given an inherent urgency which made it a powerful force for shaping human behavior.

The new market society did more than merely bring about an environment in which men were forced to follow their economic self-interest. It brought into being at the same time a social environment in which men could be *controlled* in their economic activities. With the emergence of a generalized drive to maximize income, it now became possible to steer the application of men's energies in various directions by raising or lowering the rewards offered for different tasks. If more effort was needed in the making of shoes, the market mechanism could attract that effort by raising the rewards for land, labor, and capital employed in shoe manufacture. Or if society wished to diminish the amount of social energy employed in making hats, it had but to lower the market rewards—wages, rents, profits—of hat manufacture, and there would ensue an exodus of the factors of the production from hat-making toward other, more profitable fields. Thus, in the universalized presence of a drive toward income maximization, society possessed a powerful tool for *allocating its resources.*

Note, however, that this regulatory device required more than just the profit motive. Equally necessary was a *mobility of the factors of production.* To the extent that labor was tied to its manorial estates or to its guild establishments, or that guildmasters were forbidden to expand their scales of operation or to venture into new endeavors, the control mechanism would not work. In that case, raising rewards for shoes or lowering rewards for hats could only increase or decrease the incomes of those already engaged in the field, but could not bring about any substantial increase or decrease in the quantity of social effort put into each pursuit.

An essential part of the evolution of the market society was thus not only the monetization of life but the mobilization of life—that is, the dissolution of those ties of place and station which were the very cement of feudal existence. And this essential requirement of mobility leads to a further point. Mobility meant that any job or activity was now open to all comers. *Competition appeared.* The traditional compartmented division of feudal labor had to give way to a universal rivalry among employments. No longer was each employment a protected haven for apprentice and guildmaster alike. Now any worker and any employer could be displaced from his task by a competitor who would do the job more cheaply.

THE WORKINGS
OF
COMPETITION

For those who *were* displaced, the institution of competition must have seemed a harsh and unjust one; but for society as a whole, it provided an essential safeguard. Having freed the drive of economic self-interest from the limitations of feudalism, society seemed in danger of being endlessly gouged by profiteering merchants or demanding workmen—the very fear of the medieval social philosopher. What competition did, however, was to *contain* the economic drive. By pitting seller against seller, it made it difficult for any single participant to gain a strategic position for his own advantage. Even though every seller in a competitive market would *like* to charge monopolistic prices, the presence of a crowd of eager competitors at his elbow, each ready to steal away the lucrative business of the next by shading his price, assured society that ultimate selling prices would be no more than the minimum required to make continued production possible.

Competition not only prevented the seller from using his economic power to general social disadvantage, but it also assured a similar restraint on the buyer. No single purchaser could force prices below the cost of production, for other eager buyers would quickly outbid him. And this competitive mechanism worked not only in the market for commodities but in the market for factors, as well. Clearly, no laborer could ask for more than the "going" wage if he wanted to secure employment. But neither would he have to take less from any single wage-cutting employer, for he could always find better wages elsewhere.

Even if all employers in, say, the shoe trade paid lower wages than employers in the hat trade, again competition would provide the remedy. For labor would then leave the shoe trade for the hat trade, thereby bringing about a shortage of workers in the shoe plants and a surplus in hats. Wages would therefore rise in the shoe trade as manufacturers sought to bid labor back into their plants, and they would decline in hats.

Now we begin to see the complex nature of the price control mechanism provided by the competitive struggle. Across the market, buyer and seller faced one another in a contest wherein every buyer sought to pay as little as possible and every seller sought to gain as much as possible. By itself this would be merely a tug of war about the outcome of which one could say very little. But because sellers on one side of the tug of war were themselves engaged in a contest with one another, and because buyers at the other end of the rope were engaged in a similar contest, the outcome of the contest was quite predictable. While prices of goods might sway back and forth in the short run, the interaction of supply and demand operated to bring them always back toward *costs of production* in the long run. And while incomes of factors in different employments might fluctuate temporarily upward or downward, again the competitive mechanism operated always to bring the rewards for similar tasks into a common alignment.

We shall investigate this process more carefully in Part Four. Now, only one final point should be noted. We have seen how a competitive market economy operated to fulfill the wants of society. But who was to say what its wants were?

In pre-market economies, such a question did not pose subtle problems. The "wants" of such societies were either codified by ageless tradition or specifically formulated by its rulers. But in a market society, the specification of wants suddenly takes on a new dimension. It now consists of demands of everyone who has the wherewithal to enter the market. *The "wants" of society are thus expressed by millions of daily orders placed on the market by an entire community.* As these orders enter the marketplace they affect the prices at which goods sell. Thus shifts in prices become, in effect, signals to producers: rising prices betokening an increase in demand and an actual or prospective increase in rewards; falling prices signaling the opposite.

In this way the market society catapults the consumer into a position of extraordinary importance. On his ability and willingness to buy hinges the panoply of demands which confront society's producers. If consumers do not want a good or service, or if they do not wish to buy it at its offered price, that good or service will go unsold. In that case, the production effort needed to supply it will not pay for itself and will soon terminate. *In a market society, the consumer is the ultimate formulator of the pattern of economic activity.* He is now the sovereign of the economic process—sovereign not as an individual, but as a member of an entire society which collectively guides and controls its on-going productive effort through a market mechanism.

Does the market really work as this first introduction to it suggests? Much of the rest of this book will be devoted to that very question—that is, to what extent the outcome of the market process in actuality corresponds with its outcome in a "pure" market system. But we are not yet ready to consider that problem. We have so far traced the market only to its first half-formed appearance when the "theory" of a market was still far from formulated in men's minds. Let us therefore return to our historical narrative as the market system begins to evolve into capitalism itself. For the slow evolution of the market system cannot be considered merely as the rise of a new mechanism of social control. It must also be seen as the evolution of a new socio-economic organization of society, a new structure of law, of political organization, of social institutions, of ideas.

For example, a market society could not coexist with a form of legal organization that did not recognize the freedom of the individual to contract for employment as he wished. Nor could it exist under a code of law that barely recognized "private property" as we know it. Neither could it flourish under a political system in which privilege accrued to birth rather than to achievement, or in which the landed nobility by law and usage possessed the main power to regulate society's affairs. Feudalism as a legal, political, and social organization had to give way to another form of society with a very different set of laws, customs, and political institutions.

We call that other form of society *capitalism,* and the long process of change which we have studied in its economic aspects can be given a wider interpretation as the evolution (and revolution) of feudalism into capitalism. The student of government notes the growth of political representation on the part of the middle classes, a growth most dramatically symbolized in the overthrow of feudal power in the French Revolution, but most fully realized in the long rise of parliamentary power in England. So, too, a student of law notes the rise of the law of contract, or the decline of the legal restrictions of serfdom or in the legal prerogatives of the aristocracy. Without a study of these changes, we cannot fully comprehend the manner in which capitalism arose from feudalism. Yet without an understanding of the deeper-seated economic changes which took place, so to speak, spontaneously and without conscious human intervention, the accompanying legal and political changes cannot themselves be understood.

Many of those necessary changes did not take place until the sixteenth and seventeenth centuries, or even later. After all, serfdom was not formally abolished in France until 1789; and in Germany, not until a half century later. Certainly by 1700, the market society had not yet reached a stage in which capitalism had achieved full legal and political status. Although "land," "labor," and "capital" had come into being, although a highly monetized society characterized France and England and Holland, although the merchant classes were strong and rich, there was still lacking a final achievement of economic "freedom," a final throwing off of traditional bonds and restrictions on labor and capital, a final loosening of controls and commands from above. In England in the late 1700s, for example, no master hatter could employ more than two apprentices, or no master cutler more than one, and these and similar guild regulations did not vanish until the medieval Statute of Artificers was repealed in 1813. Likewise in France, an immense web of regulations bound the would-be capitalist. Rules and edicts, many of them seeking to standardize production, laid down the exact number of threads to be woven into the cloths of the French textile manufacturers, and to disregard these laws was to risk pillorying—first for the cloth, then for the manufacturer.

Thus in the decades before the opening of the eighteenth century—indeed, well into that century—we find the great revolution of the market still incomplete; or rather, we find the nearly complete process of monetization and commercialization contained uncomfortably within a frame of legal and social organization not yet fully adapted to it.

We call this stage of pre-capitalism *mercantilism*, but we must not think of mercantilism solely as a time in which a nascent capitalism was held back by an outmoded social and economic order. On the contrary, it was also a time when the final achievement of capitalism was powerfully stimulated and accelerated. For the policies of mercantilism were devoted to building up national economic strength—in part by highly protectionist foreign trade policies, in part by subsidy; in part by urging the rising manufacturer to expand. Colbert, France's finance minister to Louis XIV, told the butterfly court of Versailles that the greatness of the country depended on its wealth; its wealth, on its work; and its work, on the encouragement of those industrial, commercial, and agricultural producers who were, in the main, regarded with supercilious disdain. Colbert, therefore, struggled to encourage the rising *bourgeoisie* and to promote the interests of manufacture and commerce in general.

He did so in a curiously self-defeating way, with a web of regulations, tariffs, and ordinances which suffocated the entrepreneurial impulse at the same time that it sought to foster it; and the social benefits of his economic policy were largely vitiated by the necessity to abide by a feudal system of taxation which was harsh, iniquitous, and corrupt. Yet, as in no previous period, the seeds for subsequent growth were deliberately sown all through the mercantile era by the royal patronage of shipyards and porcelain factories, tapestry works and arsenals. It is curious that the zest for expansion was often more notable on the part of the monarch than the manufacturer: Frederick the Great complained in the margin of one of his edicts that his commoners had to be dragged to their profits "by their noses and ears."[10]

And one significant anomaly is also to be remarked. Despite the multiplicity of regulations which mercantilism imposed, it was also during these years—perhaps because of the very difficulties of regulation—that the idea of a totally free and unhampered market began to gain acceptance. "Que faut-il faire pour vous aider?" (How may we help you?) wrote Colbert to the merchant Gournay. "Nous laissez faire" (Leave us alone) was the answer. Colbert scarcely heeded the advice, but soon it would become the slogan of the new capitalist world.

A full-scale review of economic history must study European mercantilism at length, for it is a critical era of economic history, an era in which industrial growth was first launched as a deliberate act of national economic policy. Yet it was, so to speak, a position of unstable rest, not fully emancipated from the past, not fully entrant upon the future. The basic elements of capitalism had been created and waited for a full trial. The trial was soon to come, first in England, later throughout Europe and in the United States. We shall soon watch this major chapter of economic history unfold.

KEY CONCEPTS AND KEY WORDS

1. *Powerful forces of change* were operative within European feudalism, and served gradually to introduce the structure of a market society. Primary among these forces were:

   Feudalism

   - The role of *the itinerant merchant* in introducing trade, money, and the acquisitive spirit into feudal life.
   - The *process of urbanization* as a source of economic activity, and as the locus of a new, trade-centered seat of power.
   - *The Crusades* as a force for the disruption of feudal life and the introduction of new ideas.
   - The rise of unifying, commerce-supporting *national states.*
   - The stimulus of the *Age of Exploration* and of the *gold* it brought into Europe.
   - The emergence of *new religious ideas* more sympathetic to business activity than Catholicism had been.
   - The *monetization of dues* within the manorial system.

[10] Lowe, *Economics and Sociology* (London: Allen, 1935), p. 23.

2. As a consequence of these forces, we begin to see *the separation of economic from social life.* The processes of production and distribution were no longer indistinguishably melded into the prevailing religious, social, and political customs and practices, but now began to form a sharply distinct area of life in themselves.

Enclosures

3. With the rise of the economic aspect of life, we see *deep-seated transformations* taking place. The peasant-serf is no longer bound to the land, but becomes a free, mobile laborer; the guildmaster is no longer hobbled by guild rules but becomes an independent entrepreneur; the lord of the land becomes (in the modern sense of the word) a landlord. The transformation was a long and often violent one, especially in the complex case of the *enclosures.*

Factors of production

4. The advent of free laborers, capitalists, and landlords, each selling his services on the market for land and capital and labor, made it possible to speak of the *"factors of production."* By this was implied two things: the *physical categories* of land, labor, and capital as distinguishable agents in the production process, and the *social categories* of laborers, landowners, and capitalists as distinct groups or classes entering the marketplace.

Profit motive

5. The emergence of the factors of production signaled the entrance of the full-fledged *market system.* Its earmarks were:
   - The appearance of the *"profit motive"* as a guide for economic behavior.

Mobility
   - The greatly increased legal and social *mobility* of the factors of production.
   - A widespread *competition* among all individuals in their economic activities.

Demand
   - The *appearance of "demand"*—the amounts that consumers were willing and able to spend—as the new regulator of production.
   - The *elevation of the consumer,* en masse, to a new position of economic control.

6. The market system required not alone the economic innovations of the market process, but a whole panoply of *legal and political changes* as well. The freedom and independence of the economic person, an idea quite incompatible with feudalism, was an essential precondition for a fluid market system.

Mercantilism

7. The transformation was not achieved in one bound. The evolution of feudalism into a free market system led to a transitional stage called *mercantilism.* Mercantilism was characterized by an effort to regulate commerce and production in great detail, while at the same time supporting and encouraging it.

Capitalism

Laissez faire

8. The complexities and difficulties of mercantilist regulation gave rise to the slogan that was to be the rallying cry of the new philosophy of *capitalism: laissez faire* (leave us alone).

1. What was so disruptive to feudal life about the activities of the merchant? Are business activities today also the causes of social stress?

2. The underdeveloped nations today often resemble the economies of antiquity or of the Middle Ages, at least insofar as their poverty and stagnation is concerned. Discuss what relevance, if any, the forces of change mentioned in this chapter have on the modernization of these areas. Are there new forces of change?

3. The leading nations in the world, so far as per capita income is concerned, are the U.S., New Zealand and Australia, and the Scandinavian states. Among the less affluent Western nations are Ireland, Spain, Portugal, and Italy. Do you think this proves the validity of the Weber-Tawney thesis as to the importance of the Protestant ethic in economic growth? Does the addition of Latin America change the argument? Japan?

4. The process of monetization and commercialization was often a violent one in Europe. Do you think the Civil War, which ended slavery and displaced the southern semifeudal plantation system, could be considered as part of the same transformation in America?

5. Is economic life distinctly separate from social and political life in America?

6. Do you think most people in the United States obey the profit motive? Are most people mobile in the United States? Do you know anyone who has changed his residence because of economic considerations? His profession?

7. Profit-making is certainly as old as man. Do you think we can speak of the origins of capitalism as being equally old?

8. How would you define *feudalism? Mercantilism? Capitalism?*

9. What legal and political changes were necessary to change feudalism into a market system?

Heretofore, in our survey of economic history, we have concentrated almost entirely on two main currents of economic activity: agriculture and commerce. Yet there was, from earliest days, a third essential source of economic wealth—industry—which we have purposely let slip by unnoticed. For in contrast to agriculture and commerce, industrial manufacture did not leave a major imprint on economic society itself. As a peasant, a serf, a merchant, or a guildsman, the actors in the economic drama directly typified the basic activities of their times, but this would not have been true of someone in industry. Such a person as a "factory worker"—indeed, the very idea of an *industrial* "proletarian"—was singularly absent from the long years before the late seventeenth century.

Let us note as well that the "industrial capitalist" was also lacking. Most of the moneymakers of the past gained their fortunes by trading, or transporting, or lending—not by making. It is amusing—more than amusing: instructive—to mark the best ways of getting rich enumerated by Leon Battista Alberti, a fifteenth-century architect, musician, and courtier. They are: (1) wholesale trade; (2) seeking for treasure trove; (3) ingratiating oneself with a rich man to become his heir; (4) usury; (5) the rental of pastures, horses, and the like. A seventeenth-century commentator adds to this: royal service, soldiering, and alchemy. Manufacturing is conspicuously absent from both lists.[1]

Granted, in ancient Greece, Demosthenes had an armor and a cabinet "factory"; and from long before his time, in ancient Egypt we even have the attendance record of workers in "factories" for the production of cloth. Yet it is clear that this form of production was far less important than either agriculture or commerce in shaping the economic texture of the times. For one thing, the typical scale of manufacture was small. Note that the very word "manufacture" (from the Latin *manus*, hand, and *facere*, to make) implies a system of hand, rather than machine, technology. Demosthenes' enterprises, for example, employed no more than fifty men. It is true that

[1] Werner Sombart, *The Quintessence of Capitalism* (New York: Dutton, 1915), pp. 34-35.

from time to time we do come across quite large manufacturing operations; already in the second century A.D. a Roman brickworks employed forty-six foremen; and by the time we reach the seventeenth century, enterprises with several hundred workers are not unheard of. Yet such operations were the exception rather than the rule. In 1660, for instance, a steelmaker in France needed no more than three tons of pig iron a year for his output of swords or sickle blades or artistic cutlery. Similarly, most guild operations, as we have seen, were small. As late as 1843, a Prussian census showed only sixty-seven working people for every hundred masters.[2] In the past—as today in the East and Near East—most "industry" was carried on in the backs of small shops or the dim cellars of houses, in sheds behind bazaars, or in the scattered homes of workers to whom materials would be supplied by an organizing "capitalist."

In addition to the smallness of the scale of industry, another aspect of the times delayed industrial manufacture from making known its social presence. This was the absence of any sustained interest in the development of an *industrial technology.* Throughout antiquity and the Middle Ages, little of society's creative energy was directed toward a systematic improvement of manufacturing techniques. It is indicative of the disinterest attached to productive technology that so simple and important an invention as the horse collar had to await the Middle Ages for discovery: the Egyptians, Greeks, and Romans, who were capable of a magnificent technology of architecture, were simply not fundamentally concerned with the techniques of everyday production itself.[3] Even well into the Renaissance and Reforma-

PACE OF TECHNICAL CHANGE

[2] *Cambridge Economic History of Europe,* II, 34; John U. Nef, *Cultural Foundations of Industrial Civilization* (New York: Harper, Torchbooks, 1960), p. 131; R. H. Tawney, *Equality,* 4th ed. (London: Macmillan, 1952), p. 59.

[3] E. M. Jope, in *History of Technology,* eds. Charles J. Singer *et al.* (New York: Oxford University Press, 1956), II, 553. There was, however, considerable improvement in mining techniques, especially for silver and copper.

tion, the idea of industrial technology hardly attracted serious thought. With the exception of Leonardo da Vinci, whose fecund mind played with inventions of the most varied kind, the serious thinkers of Europe, until well into the seventeenth century, were both ignorant of, and uninterested in, the technology of basic production.

There was good reason for this prevailing indifference: in the societies of the pre-market world, the necessary economic base for any large-scale industrial manufacture was totally lacking. In economies sustained by the labor of peasants, slaves, and serfs, economies in which the stream of money was small and the current of economic life, accidents of war and nature aside, relatively changeless from year to year, who could dream of a process in which avalanches of goods would be turned out? The very idea of industrial production on the large scale was inconceivable in such an unmonetized, static setting.*

For all these reasons, the pace of industrialization was slow. It is a question whether Europe in the year 1200 was significantly more technologically advanced than it had been in the year 200 B.C. The widespread use of waterpower in industry, for instance, did not appear until the fifteenth century, and it would be still another century before windmills provided a common means of tapping the energy of nature. The mechanical clock dates from the thirteenth century, but not for 200 years would significant improvements be made in instruments for navigation, surveying, or measuring. Movable type, that indispensable forerunner of mass communication, did not appear until 1450.

In short, despite important pockets of highly organized production, notably in the thirteenth-century Flanders cloth industry and in Northern Italian towns, not until the late sixteenth century can we discern the first signs of a general ground swell of industrial technology, and even in that day it would have been impossible to foresee that one day industry would be the dominant form of productive organization. As a matter of fact, as late as the eighteenth century, when manufacturing had already begun to reach respectable proportions as a form of social endeavor, it was not generally thought of as inherently possessing any but secondary importance. Agriculture, of course, was the visible foundation of the nation itself. Trading was regarded as useful insofar as it brought a nation gold. But at best, industry was seen as a hand-maiden of the others, providing the trader with the goods to export, or serving the farmer as a secondary market for the products of the earth.†

---

* Even today, one sees the difficulties of the unmonetized, static, underdeveloped societies in finding an industrial-minded, rather than commercial-minded, entrepreneurial group.

† It was in the mid-eighteenth century that the French doctor François Quesnay propounded one of the first systematic explanations of economic production and distribution. It is noteworthy that in his system (called *Physiocracy*) only the farmer was regarded as a producer of net worth; and the manufacturer, while his utility was not ignored, was nonetheless relegated to the "sterile" (i.e., non-wealth-producing) classes.

What finally conspired to bring manufacturing into a position of overwhelming prominence?

It was a complex concatenation of events that finally brought about the eruption we call the industrial revolution. As with the Commercial Revolution and the Mercantile era which preceded it and formed its indispensable preparation, it is impossible in a few pages to do justice to the many currents which contributed to that final outburst of industrial technology. But if we cannot trace the process in detail, we can at least gain an idea of its impetus and of the main forces behind it if we turn now to England around 1750. Here, for the first time, industrial manufacture as a major form of economic activity began to work its immense social transformations. Let us observe the process as it took place.

Why did the industrial revolution originally take place in England and not on the Continent? To answer the question we must look at the background factors which distinguished England from most other European nations in the eighteenth century.

The first of these factors was simply that England was relatively wealthy. In fact, a century of successful exploration, slave trading, piracy, war, and commerce had made her the richest nation in the world. Even more important, her riches had accrued not merely to a few nobles, but to a large upper-middle stratum of commercial *bourgeoisie*. England was thus one of the first nations to develop, albeit on a tiny scale, a prime requisite of an industrial economy: a "mass" consumer market. As a result, a rising pressure of demand inspired a search for new techniques. Very typically, the Society for the Encouragement of Arts and Manufactures (itself a significant child of the age) offered a prize for a machine that would spin six threads of cotton at one time, thus enabling the spinner to keep up with the technologically more advanced weaver. It was this which led, at least in part, to Arkwright's spinning jenny, of which we shall hear more shortly.

Second, England was the scene of the most successful and thoroughgoing transformation of feudal society into commercial society. The process of enclosures was a significant clue to a historic change that sharply marked off England from the Continent. It was that in England alone the aristocracy had made its peace with (and more than that, found its profits in) commerce. Although sharp conflicts of interest remained between the "old" landed power and the "new" monied power, by 1700 the ruling orders in England had decisively opted for adaptation rather than resistance to the demands of the market economy.[4]

Third, England was the locus of a unique enthusiasm for science and engineering. The famous Royal Academy, of which Newton was an early

ENGLAND
IN 1750

---

[4] See Barrington Moore, *Social Origins of Dictatorship and Democracy* (Boston: Beacon Press, 1966), Chap. I.

president, was founded in 1660 and was the immediate source of much intellectual excitement. Indeed, a popular interest in gadgets, machines, and devices of all sorts soon became a mild national obsession: *Gentlemen's Magazine,* a kind of *New Yorker* of the period, announced in 1729 that it would henceforth keep its readers "abreast of every invention"—a task which the mounting flow of inventions soon rendered quite impossible. No less important was an enthusiasm of the British landed aristocracy for scientific farming: English landlords displayed an interest in matters of crop rotation and fertilizer which their French counterparts would have found quite beneath their dignity.

Then there were a host of other background causes, some as fortuitous as the immense resources of coal and iron ore on which the British sat; others as purposeful as the development of a national patent system which deliberately sought to stimulate and protect the act of invention itself.* And then, as the Revolution came into being, it fed upon itself. The new techniques (especially in textiles) simply destroyed their handicraft competition around the world and thus enormously increased their own markets. But what finally brought all these factors into operation was the energy of a group of New Men who made of the latent opportunities of history a vehicle for their own rise to fame and fortune.

RISE OF THE NEW MEN

One such, for instance, was John Wilkinson. The son of an old-fashioned small-scale iron producer, Wilkinson was a man possessed by the technological possibilities of his business. He invented a dozen things: a rolling mill and a steam lathe, a process for the manufacture of iron pipes, and a design for machining accurate cylinders. Typically, he decided that the old-fashioned leather bellows used in the making of iron itself were not efficient, and so he determined to make iron ones. "Everybody laughed at me," he later wrote. "I did it and applied the steam engine to blow them and they all cried: 'Who could have thought of it?'"

He followed his success in production with a passion for application: everything must be made of iron: pipes, bridges, even ships. After a ship made of iron plates had been successfully launched, he wrote a friend: "It

* Phyllis Deane, in *The First Industrial Revolution* (paperback ed., Cambridge: Cambridge University Press, 1965) ascribes the onset of industrialism in England to a somewhat different set of causes: a rise in population, better food-producing techniques, a boom in foreign trade, and a vast improvement in transportation. There is no doubt that these were also indispensable elements in the process. I mention Miss Deane's book so that a student will not think that there is only one "right" way of accounting for very complex historical transformations. For yet another exceedingly good general account of the process, one might turn to the fascinating chapter by David Landes, "Technological Change and Development in Western Europe" in the *Cambridge Economic History* (Cambridge: Cambridge University Press, 1965), VI, esp. pp. 274–350, where the emphasis is focused on the process of technological advance, and in particular on the strategic inventions of steam power, and textile machinery. Landes' essay has been extended and published as a separate book, *The Unbound Prometheus* (Cambridge: Cambridge University Press, 1969).

answers all my expectations, and has convinced the unbelievers, who were nine hundred and ninety-nine in a thousand. It will be a nine-days wonder, and afterwards, a Columbus' egg."[5]

But Wilkinson was only one of many. The most famous was, of course, James Watt, who, together with Matthew Boulton, formed the first company for the manufacture of steam engines. Watt was the son of an architect, shipbuilder, and maker of nautical instruments. At thirteen he was already making models of machines, and by young manhood he was an accomplished artisan. He planned to settle in Glasgow, but the guild of hammermen objected to his making mathematical instruments—the last remnants of feudalism thus coming into an ironic personal conflict with the man who, more than any other, would create *the* invention that would destroy guild organization. At any rate, Watt found a haven at the university and there, in 1764, had his attention turned to an early and very unsatisfactory steam engine invented by Newcomen. In his careful and systematic way, Watt experimented with steam pressures, cylinder designs, and valves, until by 1796 he had developed a truly radical and (by the standards of those days) extraordinarily powerful and efficient engine. Interestingly, Watt could never have done so well with his engines had not Wilkinson perfected a manner of making good piston-cylinder fits. Previously, cylinders and pistons were made of wood and rapidly wore out. Typically, too, it was Wilkinson who bought the first steam engine to be used for purposes other than pumping: it worked the famous iron bellows.

There was needed, however, more than Watt's skill. The new engines had to be produced and sold, and the factory that made them had to be financed and organized. Watt at first formed a partnership with John Roebuck, another iron magnate, but it shortly failed. Thereafter luck came his way. Matthew Boulton, already a wealthy and highly successful manufacturer of buttons and buckles, took up Roebuck's contract with Watt, and the greatest combination of technical skill and business acumen of the day was born.

Even then the firm did not prosper immediately. Expenses of development were high, and the new firm was not out of debt for twelve years. Yet from the beginning, interest was high. By 1781 Boulton was able to claim that the people of London, Birmingham, and Manchester were all "steam mill mad"; and by 1786, when two steam engines were harnessed to fifty pairs of millstones in the largest flour mill in the world, all of London came to see and marvel.

The steam engine was the greatest single invention, but by no means the sole mainstay, of the industrial revolution. Hardly less important were a group of textile inventions, of which the most famous was Arkwright's

[5] Paul Mantoux, *The Industrial Revolution in the Eighteenth Century,* 2nd ed. (New York: Harcourt, 1928), pp. 313 n., 315.

jenny, or water frame, as it was called to distinguish it from other hand-operated spinning jennies.*

Arkwright's career is, in itself, interesting. A barber, he plied his trade near the weaving districts of Manchester and so heard the crying need for a machine that would enable the cottage spinners to keep up with the technically more advanced weavers. Good fortune threw him into contact with a clockmaker named John Kay, whom he hired to perfect a machine that Kay had already begun with another employer-inventor. What happened thereafter is obscure: Kay left the business accused of theft and embezzlement, and Arkwright appeared as the "sole inventor" of a spinning jenny in 1769.

He now found two rich hosiers, Samuel Need and Jedediah Strutt, who agreed to set up business with him to produce water frames, and in 1771 the firm built its own spinning mill. It was an overnight success; by 1779 it had several thousand spindles, more than 300 workmen, and ran night and day. Within not many years Arkwright had built an immense fortune for himself and founded an even more immense textile industry for England. "O reader," wrote Carlyle, looking back on his career, "what a historical phenomenon is that bag-cheeked, pot-bellied, much enduring, much inventing barber! ... It was this man that had to give England the power of cotton."[6]

THE INDUSTRIAL ENTREPRENEUR

It is interesting, as we watch the careers of these New Men to draw a few generalizations concerning them. For these were an entirely new class of economically important persons. Peter Onions, who was one of the inventors of the puddling process, was an obscure foreman; Arkwright was a barber; Benjamin Huntsman, the steel pioneer, was originally a maker of clocks; Maudslay, who invented the automatic screw machine, was a bright young mechanic at the Woolwich Arsenal. None of the great industrial pioneers came of noble lineage; and with few exceptions, such as Matthew Boulton, none even possessed money capital. In agriculture, the new revolutionary methods of scientific farming enjoyed aristocratic patronage and leadership, especially from the famous Sir Jethro Tull and Lord Townshend; but in industry, the lead went to men of humble origin and descent.

Let us note, therefore, that this required a social system flexible enough to permit the rise of such obscure "adventurers." It is not until we see the catalytic effect of unleashing and harnessing the energies of talented men in the lower and middle ranks of the social order that we begin to appreciate the immense liberating effect of the preceding economic and political revolutions. In the medieval hierarchy the meteoric careers of such New Men would have been unthinkable. In addition, the New Men were the product

---

* Essentially what the water frame did was to enable cotton thread of much greater strength to be produced. As a result, for the first time it was possible to use cotton thread instead of linen thread for the warp (the vertical threads that take most of the strain in weaving) as well as for the weft. Not until Arkwright's invention was "cotton cloth" made wholly of cotton. The new cloth was incomparably superior to the old and instantly enjoyed a huge demand.

[6] Mantoux, *The Industrial Revolution in The Eighteenth Century*, p. 225.

of the unique economic preparation of England itself. They were, of course, the beneficiaries of the rising demand and the technical inquisitiveness of the times. Beyond that, many of the small manufacturers were, themselves, former small proprietors who had been bought out during the late period of the enclosure movement and who determined to use their tiny capital in the promising area of manufacture.

Many of these New Men made great sums of money. A few, like Boulton and Watt, were modest in their wants. Despite an iron-clad patent, they charged for their engines only the basic cost of the machine and installation plus one-third the saving in fuel which the customer got. Some, like Josiah Wedgwood, founder of the great china works, actually refused, on principle, to take out patents. But most of them did not display such fine sensibilities. Arkwright retired a multi-millionaire living in ostentatious splendor; Huntsman, Wilkinson, Samuel Walker (who began life as a nail-smith and stole the secret of cast steel)—all went on to roll up huge fortunes.* Indeed, Wilkinson's iron business became a minor industrial state with a credit stronger than many German and Italian principalities. It even coined its own money, and its copper and silver tokens (with a profile and legend of John Wilkinson, Ironmaster) were much in use between 1787 and 1808.

Beyond mere avarice, the manufacturers have been described by the economic historian, Paul Mantoux, as

tyrannical, hard, sometimes cruel: their passions and greeds were those of upstarts. They had the reputation of being heavy drinkers and of having little regard for the honour of their female employees. They were proud of their newly acquired wealth and lived in great style with footmen, carriages and gorgeous town and country houses.[7]

Pleasant or unpleasant, the personal characteristics fade beside one overriding quality. These were all men interested in expansion, in growth, in investment for investment's sake. All of them were identified with technological progress, and none of them disdained the productive process. An employee of Maudslay once remarked, "It was a pleasure to see him handle a tool of any kind, but he was *quite splendid* with an 18-inch file."[8] Watt was tireless in experimenting with his machines; Wedgwood stomped about his factory on his wooden leg scrawling, "This won't do for Jos. Wedgwood," wherever he saw evidence of careless work. Richard Arkwright was a bundle of ceaseless energy in promoting his interests, jouncing about England over execrable roads in a post chaise driven by four horses, pursuing his correspondence as he traveled.

---

* In contrast to the manufacturers, the inventors did not usually fare successfully. Many of them, who did not have Watt's good fortune in finding a Boulton, died poor and neglected, fruitlessly suing for stolen inventions, unpaid royalties, ignored claims.

[7] Mantoux, *The Industrial Revolution in The Eighteenth Century*, p. 397.

[8] Lewis Mumford, *Technics and Civilization* (New York: Harcourt, 1934), p. 210.

"With us," wrote a French visitor to a calico works in 1788, "a man rich enough to set up and run a factory like this would not care to remain in a position which he would deem unworthy of his wealth."[9] This was an attitude entirely foreign to the rising English industrial capitalist. His work was its own dignity and reward; the wealth it brought was quite aside. Boswell, on being shown Watt and Boulton's great engine works at Soho, declared that he never forgot Boulton's expression as the latter declared, "I sell here, sir, what all the world desires to have—Power."[10]

The New Men were first and last *entrepreneurs*—enterprisers. They brought with them a new energy, as restless as it proved to be inexhaustible. In an economic, if not a political, sense, they deserve the epithet "revolutionaries," for the change they ushered in was nothing short of total, sweeping, and irreversible.

INDUSTRIAL AND SOCIAL REPERCUSSIONS

The first and most striking element of that change was a sharp rise in the output of the newly industrialized industries. The import of raw cotton for spinning weighed 1 million pounds in 1701; 3 million pounds in 1750; 5 million in 1781. That was a respectable rate of increase. But then came the sudden burst in textile technology. By 1784 the figure was over 11 million pounds; by 1789 it was three times greater yet, and still it grew: to 43 million pounds in 1799; 56 million in 1800; 60 million in 1802.[11] So was it with much else where the new technology penetrated. The output of coal increased tenfold in forty years; that of pig iron leaped from 68,000 tons in 1788 to 1,347,000 tons in 1839.[12]

Thus, the first impact of the industrial revolution was an immense quickening of the pace of production in the new industrial sector of the economy, an effect which we find repeated in every nation which goes through an "industrial revolution." In France, for example, the impact of industrial techniques did not make its influence felt until about 1815: between that date and 1845, the French output of pig iron grew fivefold; her coal production, sevenfold; her rate of importation, tenfold.[13]

The industrial revolution, itself, did not immediately exert a comparable leverage on the *over-all* increase of output. The industrial sector, to begin with, was small; and the phenomenal rates of increase in those industries where its leverage was first and most fruitfully applied were by no means mirrored in every industry. What is of crucial importance, however,

[9] Mantoux, *The Industrial Revolution in The Eighteenth Century*, p. 404.
[10] H. R. Fox Bourne, *English Merchants* (London: 1866), p. 119.
[11] Mantoux, *The Industrial Revolution in The Eighteenth Century*, p. 258.
[12] J. L. and B. Hammond, *The Rise of Modern Industry* (New York: Harcourt, 1937), p. 160.
[13] A. Dunham, *The Industrial Revolution in France, 1815-48* (New York: Exposition Press, 1955), p. 432.

is that the industrial revolution ushered in the technology by which large-scale, sustained growth was eventually to take place. This is a process into which we must look more carefully at the end of this chapter.

But first we must pay heed to another immediate and visible result of the industrial revolution in England. We can describe it as the transformation of an essentially commercial and agricultural society into one in which industrial manufacture became the dominant mode of organizing economic life. To put it more concretely, the industrial revolution was characterized by *the rise of the factory to the center of social as well as economic life.* After 1850, the factory was not only the key economic institution of England, but it was the economic institution that shaped its politics, its social problems, the character of its daily life, just as decisively as the manor or the guild had done a few centuries earlier.

It is difficult for us today to realize the pace or the quality of change which this rise of factory work brought about. Until the mid-eighteenth century, Glasgow, Newcastle, and the Rhondda Valley were mostly waste or farm land, and Manchester in 1727 was described by Daniel Defoe as "a mere village." Forty years later there were a hundred integrated mills and a whole cluster of machine plants, forges, leather and chemical works in the area. A modern industrial city had been created.

By the 1780s the shape of the new environment was visible. A French mineralogist visiting England in 1784 wrote:

[The] creaking, the piercing noise of the pulleys, the continuous sound of hammering, the ceaseless energy of the men keeping all this machinery in motion, presented a sight as interesting as it was new ... The night is so filled with fire and light that when from a distance we see, here a glowing mass of coal, there darting flames leaping from the blast furnaces, when we hear the heavy hammers striking the echoing anvils and the shrill whistling of the air pumps, we do not know whether we are looking at a volcano in eruption or have been miraculously transported to Vulcan's cave ...[14]

The factory provided not merely a new landscape but a new and uncongenial social habitat. In our day, we have become so used to urban-industrial life that we forget what a wrench is the transition from farm to city. For the peasant, this transfer requires a drastic adjustment. No longer does he work at his own pace, but at the pace of a machine. No longer are slack seasons determined by the weather, but by the state of the market. No longer is the land, however miserable its crop, an eternal source of sustenance close at hand, but only the packed and sterile earth of the industrial site.

It is little wonder that the English laborer, still more used to rural than urban ways, feared and hated the advent of the machine. Throughout the

[14] Mantoux, *The Industrial Revolution in The Eighteenth Century,* p. 313.

early years of the industrial revolution workmen literally attacked the invading army of machinery, burning and wrecking factories. During the late eighteenth century, for instance, when the first textile mills were built, whole hamlets rose in revolt rather than work in the mills. Headed by a mythical General Ludd, the Luddites constituted a fierce but fruitless opposition to industrialism. In 1813, in a mass trial which ended in many hangings and transportations, the movement came to an end.*

Distasteful as was the advent of the factory itself, even more distasteful were the conditions within it. Child labor, for instance, was commonplace and sometimes began at age four; hours of work were generally dawn to dusk; abuses of every kind were all too frequent. A Committee of Parliament appointed in 1832 to look into conditions gives this testimony from a factory overseer.

Q. At what time in the morning, in the brisk time, did these girls go to the mills?

A. In the brisk time, for about six weeks, they have gone at three o'clock in the morning and ended at ten or nearly half past at night.

Q. What intervals were allowed for rest and refreshment during those nineteen hours of labour?

A. Breakfast a quarter of an hour, and dinner half an hour, and drinking a quarter of an hour.

Q. Was any of that time taken up in cleaning the machinery?

A. They generally had to do what they call dry down; sometimes this took the whole time at breakfast or drinking.

Q. Had you not great difficulty in awakening your children to the excessive labour?

A. Yes, in the early time we had to take them up asleep and shake them.

Q. Had any of them any accident in consequence of this labour?

A. Yes, my eldest daughter ... the cog caught her forefinger nail and screwed it off below the knuckle.

Q. Has she lost that finger?

A. It is cut off at the second joint.

Q. Were her wages paid during that time?

A. As soon as the accident happened the wages were totally stopped.[15]

---

* Even in our day, however, we use the word "Luddite" to describe an attempt to "fight back" at the threat of machinery.

[15] Tawney, Bland, and Brown, *English Economic History, Selected Documents* (London: Bell, 1914), p. 510.

It was a grim age. The long hours of work, the general dirt and clangor of the factories, the lack of even the most elementary safety precautions, all combined to give early industrial capitalism a reputation from which, in the minds of many people of the world, it has never recovered. Worse yet were the slums to which the majority of workers returned after their travail. A government commissioner reports in 1839 on one such workers' quarter in Glasgow called "the wynds."

The wynds ... house a fluctuating population of between 15,000 and 30,000 persons. This district is composed of many narrow streets and square courts and in the middle of each court there is a dunghill. Although the outward appearance of these places was revolting, I was nevertheless quite unprepared for the filth and misery that were to be found inside. In some bedrooms we visited at night we found a whole mass of humanity stretched on the floor. There were often 15 to 20 men and women huddled together, some being clothed and others naked. There was hardly any furniture there and the only thing which gave these holes the appearance of a dwelling was fire burning on the hearth. Thieving and prostitution are the main sources of income of these people.[16]

Without question, the times were marked by tremendous social suffering. But it is well, in looking back on the birth years of industrial capitalism, to bear several facts in mind:

1. *It is doubtful if the poverty represented a deterioration in life for the masses in general.*

In at least some sections of England, industrialism brought immediate benefits. Wedgwood (an exceptionally good employer, it is true) used to tell his employees to ask their parents for a description of the country as *they* first knew it and to compare their present state. So, too, the twelve-hour day in Arkwright's mills was a two-hour *improvement* over previous Manchester standards. Furthermore, the existing poverty was not by any means new. As we know from Hogarth's etchings, long before the industrial revolution, "Gin Lane" already sported its pitiful types. As one reformer of the mid-nineteenth century wrote, those whose sensibilities were revolted by the sight of suffering factory children thought "how much more delightful would have been the gambol of free limbs on the hillside; the sight of the green mead with its spangles of buttercups and daisies; the song of the bird and the humming of the bee ... [but] we have seen children perishing from sheer hunger in the mud hovel or in the ditch by the wayside."[17]

[16] Quoted in F. Engels, *The Condition of the Working Class in England* (New York: Macmillan, 1958), p. 46

[17] Friedrich Hayek, ed., *Capitalism and the Historians* (Chicago: University of Chicago Press, 1954), p. 180.

2. *Much of the harsh criticism to which early industrial capitalism was subjected derived not so much from its economic but from its political accompaniments.*

For coincident with the rise of capitalism, and indeed contributory to it, was a deep-seated change in the vantage point of political criticism. New ideas of democracy, of social justice, of the "rights" of the individual charged the times with a critical temper of mind before which *any* economic system would have suffered censure.

To be sure, the political movements by which capitalism was carried to its heights were not working-class movements, but middle-class, bourgeois movements: the rising manufacturers in England and France had little "social conscience" beyond a concern for their own rights and privileges. But the movement of political liberalism which they set into motion had a momentum beyond the narrow limits for which it was intended. By the first quarter of the nineteenth century, the condition of the working classes, now so exposed to public view in the new factory-slum environment, had begun to curry public sympathy.

Thus, one of the unexpected consequences of the industrial revolution was a sharp reorientation of political ideas. In the creation of an industrial working class and an industrial environment, the revolution bequeathed a new economic framework to politics. Karl Marx and Friedrich Engels were to write in 1848 that "all history" was the history of class struggle, but never did that struggle emerge so nakedly into the open as after the industrial environment had been brought into being.

Equally important was that the rise of political liberalism not only roused feelings of hostility toward the prevailing order, but initiated the slow process of amelioration. *From the outset, a reform movement coincided with capitalism.* In 1802, pauper apprentices were legally limited to a twelve-hour day and barred from night work. In 1819, the employment of children under nine was prohibited in cotton mills; in 1833, a 48- to 69-hour week was decreed for workers under eighteen (who comprised about 75 per cent of all cotton mill workers), and a system of government inspection of factories was inaugurated; in 1842, children under ten were barred from the coal mines; in 1847 a 10-hour daily limit (later raised to $10\frac{1}{2}$) was set for children and women.

The nature of the reforms is itself eloquent testimony to the conditions of the times, and the fact that the reforms were bitterly opposed and often observed in the breach is testimony to the prevailing spirit. Yet capitalism, unlike feudalism, was from the beginning subject to the corrective force of democracy. Karl Marx, drawing on the material of the 1830s, drew a mordant picture of the capitalist process in all its economic squalor, but he overlooked (or shrugged off) this countervailing force whose power was steadily to grow.

3. *The most important effect of the industrial revolution we have left for last: its long-term leverage on economic well-being.*

The ultimate impact of the industrial revolution was to usher in a rise of living standards on a mass scale unlike anything that the world had ever known before.

This did not happen overnight. In 1840, according to the calculations of Arnold Toynbee, Sr., the wage of an ordinary laborer came to eight shillings a week, which were six shillings less than he needed to buy the bare necessities of life.[18] He made up the deficit by sending his children or his wife, or both, to work in the mills. If, as we have noted, some sections of the working class gained from the early impact of industrialization, others suffered a *decline* from the standard of living enjoyed in 1795 or thereabouts. A Committee of Parliament in the 1830s, for example, discovered that a hand weaver at that earlier date could have bought more than three times as many provisions with his wages as at the later date. Although not every trade suffered equally, the first flush of the industrial revolution brought its hardships to bear full force, while its benefits were not as immediately noticeable.

By 1870, however, the long-run effects of the industrial revolution were beginning to make themselves felt. The price of necessaries had by then risen to fifteen shillings, but weekly earnings had crept up to meet and even exceed that sum. Hours were shorter, too. At the Jarrow Shipyards and the New Castle Chemical Works, the workweek had fallen from 61 to 54 hours; and even in the notoriously long-worked textile mills, the stint was down to "only" 57 hours. It was still a far cry from an abundant society, much less an "affluent" one, but the corner had been turned.

The Industrial Revolution in the Perspective of Theory

We have reviewed very briefly the salient historic features of the rise of industrial capitalism. Now we must reflect back on the great economic and social changes we have witnessed and ask a pertinent economic question: *How did the process of industrialization raise material well-being?* To answer the question, we must turn to economic theory to elucidate systematically what we have thus far only described.

Let us begin by asking what is necessary for a rise in the economic well-being of a society. The answer is not difficult. If we are to enjoy a greater material well-being, generally speaking, we must produce more. This

[18] *The Industrial Revolution* (Boston: Beacon Press, 1956), p. 113.

is particularly true when we begin at the stage of scarcely-better-than-subsistence which characterized so much of Europe before the industrial revolution. For such a society to raise the standard of living of its masses, the first necessity is unquestionably higher production. Despite all the inequities of distribution which attended the society of serf and lord, capitalist and child-employee, underlying the meanness of the times was one overriding reality: the sheer inadequacy of output. There was simply not enough to go around, and if somewhat less lopsided distributive arrangements might have lessened the moral indignity of the times, they would not have contributed much to a massive improvement in basic economic well-being. Even assuming that the wage of the city laborer and the income of the peasant could have been doubled had the rich been deprived of their share—and this is a wildly extravagant assumption—still, the characteristic of rural and urban life would have been its poverty.

We must add only one important qualification to this emphasis on increased output as the prerequisite of economic improvement. Over-all living standards will not improve if a country's population is growing even faster than its increased output. The production of goods and services must rise *faster* than population if individual well-being is to improve.

How does a society raise its *per capita* output?

We will not fully analyze this problem until we study growth in Chapter 20. But the industrial revolution enables us to understand a great deal about the problem. For clearly, *the key to higher output lies in enhancing the human energies of the community with the leverage of industrial capital.* Our analytic understanding of the growth must begin by looking further into this extraordinary power which capital possesses.

CAPITAL AND PRODUCTIVITY

We have already frequently used the word "capital," but we have not yet defined it. We can see that in a fundamental sense, capital consists of anything which can enhance man's power to perform economically useful work. An unshaped stone is capital to the cave man who can use it as a hunting implement. A hoe is capital to a peasant; a road system is capital to the inhabitants of a modern industrial society. Knowledge is capital, too—indeed, perhaps the most precious part of society's stock of capital.

When economists talk of capital, however, they usually confine their meaning to *capital goods*—the stock of tools, equipment, machines, and buildings which society produces in order to expedite the production process.* All these capital goods have one effect in common on the productive

---

* Is money capital? It certainly is to the individual who possesses it. But it is not capital for society as a whole. For money only represents *claims* to society's real wealth, which is its goods and services. If an individual's money disappears, he loses his claim on those goods and services, and we can indeed say that he has lost his "capital." But if *all* money disappeared, we could not say that society had lost its claim on its own wealth. It would only have to devise another system of tickets. More about this, too, in Part Three.

process: they all operate to make human labor more productive. They make it possible for a worker to produce more goods in an hour (or a week, or a year) than he could produce without the aid of that capital. Capital is therefore a method of raising per capita *productivity,* which is an individual's output in a given span of time. For example, in a forty-hour week a typical modern worker using power-driven mechanical equipment can physically outproduce three men working seventy hours a week with the simpler tools of a half-century ago. To put it differently, in one day a modern worker will turn out as much output as his counterpart of 1900 in a full week—not because the modern worker works harder, but because he has at his command thousands of dollars worth of capital equipment rather than the few hundred dollars worth available to a worker in 1900.

Why does capital make labor so much more productive?

The most important reason is that capital goods enable man to use principles and devices such as the lever and the wheel, heat and cold, combustion and expansion in ways that the unaided body cannot. *Capital gives men mechanical and physicochemical powers of literally transhuman dimensions.* They magnify enormously his muscular strength; they refine his powers of control; they endow him with endurance and resilience far beyond those of the flesh and bone. In using capital, man utilizes the natural world as a supplement to his own feeble capacities.

Another reason for the augmentation of production lies in the fact that capital facilitates the *specialization of man's labor.* A team of men working together, each man tending to one job alone in which he is expert, can usually far outproduce the same number of men, each of whom does a variety of jobs. The prime example is, of course, the auto production line in which a thousand men cooperate to produce an immensely larger output of cars than could be achieved if each man built a car by himself. Auto assembly lines, of course, use prodigious quantities of capital in the overhead conveyor belts, the inventories of parts on hand, the huge factory with its power system, and so on. And while not all specialization of labor depends on capital, capital is usually necessary for the large-scale industrial operations in which specialization becomes most effective.

In our next chapter we will return to these important matters in the context of the development of modern industry. But while we are still discussing the basic question of the rise of industry itself, there is a fundamental problem to be disposed of. This is the question of how capital is made in the first place, of how a society generates the capital equipment it needs in order to grow.

This brings us for the first time to a relationship that we will encounter many more times in our study of economics, both in a perspective of history and from a later vantage point of theory. The relationship is between the creation of those physical artifacts we call capital, and the inescapable prior act that we call *saving*.

When we think of saving, we ordinarily picture it in financial terms; that is, as a decision not to spend part of our income. Behind this financial act, however, lies a "real" act that we must now clearly understand. *When we save money we also abstain from using a certain quantity of goods and services we might have bought.* To be sure, our money savings represent a claim on goods and services, a claim that we may later exercise. Until we do, however, we have freed resources which would otherwise have been used to satisfy our immediate wants. From these freed resources, society builds its capital or, in more technical language, carries out the act of *investment*.

In the simplest example, we can see this real meaning of saving in the case of a primitive hunter who abstains from a full meal today, so that he will not have to hunt tomorrow. By saving half of today's kill, he frees the resource of (his own) labor: instead of hunting, tomorrow, he will make a better spear. In a much more indirect and complex fashion, when we save money we are also giving up a potential meal (or some other consumption good), so that society can then make capital out of the goods and services we would otherwise have consumed.

Thus the acts of saving and investment are inextricably linked: saving is the releasing of resources from consumption; investment is the employment of these resources in making capital. Indeed, from society's point of view, saving and investment are only two sides of the same coin. Why do we then separate them in economic discourse? The reason is that different people may perform the saving and investing functions, especially in modern societies. We are no longer hunters and spear makers. Those who release the resources of society are usually not the same individuals as those who gather up those resources for investment purposes. Nonetheless, we can see that every act of investment, no matter who performs it, requires the presence of released resources.*

This does not mean that investment necessarily entails a *diminution* of consumption. A rich society does not feel its normal, recurrent saving as a "pinch" on its spending. A society with unemployed factors can put its idle resources to work building capital without diminishing its expenditure on consumption. (It is still saving, of course, insofar as it is not using those newly employed resources to make consumption goods.) But—and this is a crucial point—when a *fully employed* society builds more capital, it *must* curtail its consumption. In this case, there is nowhere whence the needed

---

* Note, however, that an act of saving—i.e., an abstention from consumption—does not *automatically* bring about an act of purposive investment. This leads to serious problems to which we shall turn in Chapter 8, and in still greater detail in Part Three.

capital-building resources can come but from their erstwhile consumption employments.

Let us go on still further. We can now see that the *rate* at which an economy can invest—that is, the size of the yearly addition it can make to its stock of capital goods—depends on its capacity to save. If its living standards are already close to the margin of existence, it will not be able to transfer much labor from consumption effort to capital-building effort. However badly it may wish for more tools, however productive those tools would prove to be, it cannot invest beyond the point at which its remaining consumption activity would no longer be adequate to maintain subsistence. At the other extreme, if a society is well-to-do, it may be able to abstain from a great deal of current consumption effort to provide for the future. Accordingly, its growth will be fast. *It is a hard economic reality that the amount of construction for the future can never exceed the amount of resources and effort which are unused, or which can be released from consumption in the present.*

This seems to imply that the process of economic growth must perforce be very slow in a poor economy. And so it is. In England, as we have already seen, nearly three-quarters of a century elapsed before the new process of industrialization brought about an increase in productivity sufficiently large to be felt as a general improvement in the lot of the working-man. In the underdeveloped nations, as we shall see in Part Six, the prospect is equally or even more sluggish. At its best, growth is a gradual and cumulative, rather than an "instant" phenomenon; and where the initial level of savings is low because of poverty, the rate of advance is correspondingly slower.

Perhaps we can better appreciate this over-all determinant of the pace of growth if we now examine the actual social circumstances under which saving arose in early nineteenth-century England.

For who did the saving? Who abstained from consumption? Well-to-do agriculturalists and manufacturers (for all their ostentatious ways) were certainly important savers who plowed substantial sums into more new capital investments. Yet the savers were not just the manufacturers or the gentry but also another class—the industrial workers. Here, in the low level of industrial wages, a great sacrifice was made—not voluntarily, by any matter of means, but made just the same. From the resources the workers could have consumed was built the industrial foundation for the future.

We can also see something which is perhaps even more significant. This is the fact that England *had* to hold down the level of its working class consumption in order to free productive effort for the accumulation of capital goods. In point of historic actuality, the "holding-down" was accomplished largely by the forces of the market place—with a liberal assist, to be sure, from the capitalists and from a government quick to oppose the demands of labor in the interests of its upper classes. But social inequities aside, the hard fact remains that had industrial wages risen very much, a vast demand for consumers' goods would have turned the direction of the English economy away from capital-building, toward the satisfaction of current wants. This would certainly have redounded to the immediate welfare of the English worker (although the increase in per capita consumption would have been small). At the same time, however, it would have *postponed* the day when society's overall productive powers were capable of generating an aggregate output of very large size.

This bitter choice must be confronted by every industrializing society, capitalist or socialist, democratic or totalitarian. To assuage the needs of today or to build for tomorrow is *the* decision which a developing society must make. As we shall see in Part Six, it is a decision which lies behind much of the political and economic agony of a large part of the world today.

INCENTIVES FOR GROWTH

There remains but one last question. We have gained some insight into the mechanics of growth, but we have not yet answered the question: how are these mechanics brought about? How does society arrange the reallocation of its factors of production to bring about the creation of the capital it needs?

This query brings us again to a consideration of our original division of economic societies into three types: traditional, command, and market. It also leads to some very important conclusions.

The first of these is obvious: it is that tradition-bound societies are not apt to grow. In such societies there is *no* direct social means of inducing the needed reallocation of factors. Worse yet, there are often strong social and religious barriers which create obstacles to the needed shifts in employment.

The situation is very different, however, when we turn to command societies. We have seen a striking use of command as the industrializing-agency in modern times. In at least one country, the Soviet Union, command has been the principal mechanism for a dramatic transition from peasanthood into industrialization, and in many other collectivist economies, command is now trying to bring into effect such a transition.

In Part Six we shall return to the Russian experience. Meanwhile, let us not forget that command was also one of the principal ways by which Europe began its industrialization. In the state-directed establishment of shipyards and armories, the construction of royal palaces and estates, tapestry works and chinaware factories, a very important organizing impetus was given to the creation of an industrial sector in the mercantilist era. True, of course, that in those days, command was never so ruthlessly applied nor so widely directed as with the Communist states. But however much milder the dosage, the medicine was in essence the same: the *initial* transfer of labor from the traditional pursuits of the land to the new tasks of the factory depended on a commanding authority which ordered the new pattern into being.*

But command was by no means the main agency for the final industrialization of the West. Rather, the organizing force which put men to work in making capital equipment was the market.

How did the market bring about this remarkable transformation? It achieved its purposes by the lure of monetary rewards. It was the hope of *profits* that lured manufacturers into turning out more capital goods. It was the attraction of better *wages* (or sometimes of *any* wages) that directed workers into the new plants. It was the signal of rising prices that encouraged, and falling prices that discouraged, the production of this or that particular capital good.

And what, we may next ask, opened the prospect of profits large enough to induce entrepreneurs to risk their savings in new capital goods? The answer brings us full circle to the focal point of this chapter. For the answer is to be found primarily in the body of technological advance constituting the core of the industrial revolution.

Not that every new invention brought with it a fortune for its pioneering promoters, or that every new product found a market waiting for it. The path of technical advance is littered with inventions born "too soon" and with enterprises founded with great hopes and closed down six months later. But looking back over the vast process of capital accumulation which, beginning in the late eighteenth century, lifted first England and then America into the long flight of industrial development, there is little doubt that the impelling force was the succession of inventions and innovations that successively opened new aspects of nature to human control. Steam power, the cheap and efficient spinning and weaving of cloth, the first mass production of iron, and later steel—these were the great breakthroughs of industrial science that opened the way for the massive accumulation of capital. And once the great inventions had marked out the channel of advance, secondary improvements and subsidiary inventions took on an important supporting role. To the enterpriser with a cost-cutting innovation went the prize of a market advantage in costs and a correspondingly higher profit. More than that, once one pioneer in a field had gained a technical

---

* As Barbara Ward has written in *India and the West:* "A developing society must at some point begin to save, even though it is still poor. This is the tough early stage of growth which Marx encountered in Victorian England and unfortunately took to be permanent. It is a difficult phase in any economy—so difficult that most societies got through it by *force majeure* ... No one asked the British laborers moving into the Manchester slums whether they wanted to save.... The Soviet workers who came to Sverdlovsk and Magnitogorsk from the primitive steppes had no say in the scale or the condition of their work. Nor have the Chinese in their communes today."

advantage, competition quickly forced everyone else in the field to catch up as quickly as they could. Most of the cost-cutting innovations involved adding machinery to the production process—and this in turn boosted the formation of capital.

Capitalism as a whole proved an unparalleled machine for the accumulation of capital. In its development we find the first economic system in history in which economic growth became an *integral* part of daily life. As Marx and Engels were to write in the *Communist Manifesto:* "The bourgeoisie, during its scarce one hundred years, has created more massive and more colossal productive forces than have all preceding generations together." And the compliment, all the more meaningful coming from the two archenemies of its social order, was true.

KEY CONCEPTS AND KEY WORDS

Industrial revolution

1. The industrial revolution *is a* great *turning period* in history, during which manufacturing and industrial activity become primary forms of social production.

2. The industrial revolution began in England in the mid- to late eighteenth century (although its roots are far deeper). There are numerous reasons why it occurred there and then:
   - England was *a wealthy trading nation* with a well-developed middle class.
   - England's *aristocracy was much more commerce-minded* than the aristocracies of the Continent.
   - England was the home of a widespread vogue of *scientific investigation* and of "gentlemen farmers" interested in *agricultural innovation.*
   - England's relatively *open social structure* permitted the rise of New Men, such as Watt or Wilkinson, who brought to manufacturing a burst of new social energies.
   - Many other causes could be cited as well. The industrial revolution was a *many-sided, complex chain* of events.

Output

3. The revolution brought with it changes of the greatest importance in society.
   - It ushered in a slow, but cumulative *rise in output* that was eventually to lift the industrial world out of an age-old poverty.
   - It brought the *factory* (and the *industrial slum*) as a new environment for work and life.
   - It gave rise to new kinds of *social abuses* and greatly sharpened the general *awareness of economic conditions.*

Capital-building

4. The industrial revolution was essentially a *capital-building process* (machines, buildings, canals, railways), as a result of which the productivity of labor was greatly increased.

Productivity

5. *Capital generally enhances productivity* because it gives man for greater physical and chemical capabilities than he enjoys with unaided labor alone. It also enables men to combine and *specialize* their labor, as in modern factory production lines.

Saving

6. *Capital-building requires saving.* Capital can be built only if society has the use of resources normally used for filling its consumption needs. Saving releases these resources; investing puts them to use.

7. Society cannot devote more resources or energies to capital-building than those it releases from other uses (or those it has available as unemployed resources). Hence, by and large, *saving regulates the pace at which investment can proceed.* Poor societies, in which it is difficult to give up consumption, accordingly have great problems in amassing enough resources for investment.

Investment

Consumption

8. The saving necessary for investment can come from agriculture, manufacturing enterprises, and many other sources. In poor nations, it must also often be wrung from workers or peasants by denying them the use of all the nation's economic potential to fill their consumption needs.

9. Hence *saving in poor nations is usually an involuntary process.* Capital-building in many developing nations today, particularly those under collectivist regimes, is accomplished by the agency of command. In the industrial revolution, it was accomplished in part by command, but mainly by the market system. The remarkable inventions of the industrial revolution served as sources of profits that resulted in great accumulations of capital.

Q U E S T I O N S

1. It is interesting to note that technical improvements in agriculture or manufacturing have generally been slow to arise in countries that have relied on slave labor. Can you think of a reason why this might be so?

2. What forces do you think would be necessary to bring a new "industrial revolution" to the underdeveloped world today? Is an industrial revolution there apt to resemble that in England in the eighteenth century?

3. Industrialization in England was marked by a sharp growth of bitter political feeling on the part of the new factory proletariat. Do you think this must be an accompaniment of industrialization everywhere, or was it a particular product of early capitalism?

4. How does capital help human productivity? Discuss this in relation to the following kinds of labor: farm labor, office help, teaching, government administration.

5. When General Motors devotes a billion dollars to new investment (building new factories, warehouses, offices, etc.), who does the saving that is required? Stockholders? Workers? The public? Buyers of cars?

6. It is estimated that the value of the capital structures and equipment in the U.S. is some $2 trillion (Chap. 10). Assume that half of it were wiped out in some catastrophe. What would happen to U.S. productivity? To average U.S. well-being? How could the damage be repaired?

7. Does all investment require saving? Why?

8. Is capital-building in the U.S. today directed by the market alone? Does the government accumulate capital? Does public capital improve productivity as well as private capital?

9. Is building a school "investment"? Is building a hospital? A sports stadium? A housing project? A research lab? What do you think distinguishes investment, in general, from consumption?

With this chapter, we enter a new major period of economic history. Formerly we have dealt largely with the past, giving only an occasional glance to later echoes of the problems we have encountered. Commencing with this chapter, our focus turns toward and into the actual present. We have reached the stage of economic history whose nearest boundary is our own time. Simultaneously, our point of geographic focus shifts. As economic history enters the mid-nineteenth century, the dynamic center of events comes increasingly to be located in the United States. Not only do we now begin to enter the modern world, but the economic trends in which we will be interested take us directly into our own society.

What will be the theme of this chapter? Essentially it will be a continuation of a motif we began with the industrial revolution—the impact of technology on economic society. Looking back, we can see that the burst of inventions which marked "the" revolution was not in any sense the completion of an historic event. Rather, it was merely the inception of a process of technological change which would continually accelerate down to the present time.

We can distinguish three or even four stages of this continuous process. The "first" industrial revolution was largely concentrated in new textile machinery, improved methods of coal production and iron manufacture, revolutionary agricultural techniques, and steam power. It was succeeded in the middle years of the nineteenth century by a "second" industrial revolution: a clustering of industrial inventions centering on steel, railroad and steamship transportation, agricultural machinery, and chemicals. By the early years of the twentieth century there was a third wave of inventions: electrical power, automobiles, the gasoline engine. In our own time there is a fourth: the revolution of electronics, air travel, automation, and, of course, nuclear energy.

It is difficult, perhaps impossible, to exaggerate the impact of this continuing industrial revolution. Now advancing rapidly, now slowly; now on a broad front, now on a narrow salient; now in the most practical of inventions, again in the purest of theoretical discoveries, the cumulative application of science and technology to the productive process was *the* great change of the nineteenth and twentieth centuries. The initial industrial revolution was thus in retrospect a kind of discontinuous leap in human history; a leap as important as that which had lifted the first pastoral settlements above the earlier hunting communities. We have already noted that in the factory the new technology brought a new working place for man, but its impact was vastly greater than that alone. The enormously heightened powers of transportation and communication, the far more effective means of wresting a crop from the soil, the hugely enhanced ability to apply power for lifting, hauling, shaping, binding, cutting—all this conspired to bring about a literal remaking of the human environment, and by no means an entirely benign one.

In this book we cannot do more than inquire into some of the economic consequences of the incursion of industrial technology into modern society, but it may help us gain some insight into the dimensions of that penetrative process if we follow for a short distance the repercussions of a single invention.

IMPACT
OF ONE
INVENTION

Let us therefore look in on the Paris Exposition of 1867, where curious visitors are gathered around an interesting exhibit: a small engine in which illuminating gas and air are introduced into a combustion chamber and ignited by a spark. The resulting explosion pushes a piston; the piston turns a wheel. There is but one working stroke in every four, and the machine requires a large flywheel to regularize its movement, but as the historian Allan Nevins writes, the effect of the machine "was comparable to the sudden snapping on of an electric globe in a room men had been trying to light with smoky candles."[1] It was the world's first internal combustion engine.

It was not long before the engine, invented by Dr. N. A. Otto of Germany, was a regular feature of the American landscape. Adapted to run on gasoline, a hitherto uninteresting by-product of kerosene manufacture, it was an ideal stationary power plant. Writes Nevins, "Soon every progressive farm, shop, and feed-mill had its one-cylinder engine chugging away, pumping water, sawing wood, grinding meal, and doing other small jobs."[2] By 1900 there were more than 18,500 internal combustion engines in the United

[1] *Ford, the Times, the Man, the Company* (New York: Scribner's, 1954), I, 96.
[2] *Study in Power, John D. Rockefeller* (New York: Scribner's, 1953), II, 109.

States; and whereas the most powerful model in the Chicago World's Fair in 1893 was 35 horsepower, at the Paris Exposition seven years later it was 1,000 horsepower.

The internal combustion engine was an extraordinary means of increasing, diffusing, and giving mobility to a basic requirement of material progress: power. And soon the new engine opened the way for a yet more startling advance. In 1886, Charles E. Duryea of Chicopee, Massachusetts had already decided that the gasoline engine was a far more promising power source than steam for a self-propelling road vehicle. By 1892 he and his brother had produced the first gas-powered "automobile," a weak and fragile toy. The next model in 1893 was a better one, and by 1896 the Duryea brothers actually sold thirteen cars. In that same year, a thirty-two-year-old mechanic called Henry Ford sold his first "quadricycle." The history of the automobile industry had begun.

Its growth was phenomenal. By 1905 there were 121 establishments making automobiles, and 10,000 wage earners were employed in the industry. By 1923 the number of plants had risen to 2,471, making the industry the largest in the country. In 1960 its annual payroll was as large as the national income of the United States in 1890. Not only that, but the automobile industry had become the single greatest customer for sheet steel, zinc, lead, rubber, leather. It was the buyer of one out of every three radios produced in the nation. It absorbed twenty-five billion pounds of chemicals a year. It was the second largest user of engineering talent in the country, bowing only to national defense. It was the source of one-sixth of all the patents issued in the nation and the object of one-tenth of all consumer spending in the country. In fact, it has been estimated that no less than one job out of every seven and one business out of every six owned their existences directly or indirectly to the car.

Even this impressive array of figures by no means exhausts the impact of the internal combustion engine and its vehicular mounting. Roughly eight out of every ten families today own a car; nearly six out of ten own two or more cars. As a result, some fifty thousand towns managed to flourish without rail or water connections, an erstwhile impossibility; and seven out of ten workers no longer live within walking distance of their places of employment but drive to work. To an extraordinary extent, in other words, our entire economy has become "mobilized"—which is to say, dependent for its very functioning on the existence of wheeled, self-propelled transportation. If by some strange occurrence our automotive fleet were put out of commission—say by a spontaneous change in the nature of the gasoline molecule, rendering it incombustible—the effect would be as grave and as socially disastrous as a catastrophic famine in the Middle Ages.*

---

* I believe it was the economist Kenneth Boulding who suggested that if the United States were to be visited by intelligent beings from another part of the universe, their initial impression would likely be that the dominant form of life here consists of hard-shelled creatures with soft pulpy insides, who are propelled by wheels, although the creatures are capable of sluggish motion on their own when not encased in their natural exoskeletons.

We dwell on the impact of the car, not because it is the most significant of technological changes. Before the car, there was the startling economic transformation caused by the train, and after it came the no less totally transforming effects of electrical communication. Rather, we touch on the profound economic implications of the automobile to illustrate the diffuse effects of all industrial technology—effects which economics often cannot measure and which exceed its normal area of study but which must, nonetheless, be borne in mind as the ever-present and primary reality of the technological revolution itself. Let us mention a few of these general effects on the society in which we live.

The first has been a *vast increase in the degree of urbanization of society.* To an extraordinary extent (as we shall see in our next chapters) technology has enhanced the ability of the farmer to support the nonfarmer. As a result, society has more and more taken on the aspects and problems of the city rather than the country. In 1790 only 24 towns and cities in all of the United States had a population of more than 2,500, and together they accounted for only 6 percent of the total population. By 1860 the 392 biggest cities held 20 percent of the population; by the late 1960s, from Boston through Washington, D.C., 168 great metropolitan areas along the eastern seaboard had become virtually one huge, loosely connected city with over 60 percent of the nation's people. Industrial technology has literally refashioned the human environment, bringing with it all the gains—and all the terrible problems—of city life on a mass scale.

Second, *the steady growth of industrial technology has radically lessened the degree of economic independence of the average citizen.* In our opening chapter we noted the extreme vulnerability of the "unsupported" inhabitant of a modern society, dependent on the work of a thousand others to sustain his own existence. This, too, we can now trace to the effect of the continuing industrial revolution. Technology has not only moved men off the soil and into the city, but has vastly increased the specialized nature of work. Unlike the "man of all trades" of the early nineteenth century—the farmer who could perform so many of his necessary tasks himself—the typical factory worker or office worker is trained and employed to do only one small part of a social operation which now achieves staggering complexity. Technology has vastly increased the degree of economic interdependence of the modern community and has made the solution of the economic problem hinge on the smooth coordination of an ever-widening network of delicately connected activities.

Third, *the expansion of industrial technology has radically altered the character of work.* For the greater part of man's history, work has been a strenuous physical activity, largely carried on alone or in small groups in the open air, requiring considerable dexterity to match human strength to the infinite variations of the natural environment, and culminating in an end product as unambiguously identifiable as the grain in the field or the cloth on a loom.

The industrial revolution profoundly altered these attributes of work.

Work now consisted more and more of repetitive movements which, however exhausting after a full day, rarely involved more than a fraction of a man's full muscular ability. In place of the judgments and aptitudes required to meet the variations of nature, it demanded only the ability to repeat a single task adapted to a changeless work surface. No longer alone in nature, the worker performed his job in vast sheds with regiments like himself. And most wrenching of all, in place of "his" product, what he saw emerging from the factory was an object in which he could no longer locate, much less appreciate, his own contribution.

A worker in an automobile plant reports:

I work on a small conveyor which goes around in a circle. We call it a "merry-go-round." I make up zigzag springs for front seats. Every couple of feet on the conveyor there is a form for the pieces that make up the seat springs. As the form goes by me, I clip several pieces together, using a clip gun. I then put the pieces on the form, and it goes around to where other men clip more pieces together.... The only operation I do is work the clip gun. It takes just a couple of seconds to shoot six or eight clips into the spring and I do it as I walk a few steps. Then I start right over again....[3]

What has been the effect on workers of this basic alteration in the pace and pattern of labor? Looking around us at factories (and offices), we find that industrial technology often subjects men to a stultifying and enervating discipline—that it makes work a singularly joyless and meaningless process to which they must subordinate their individual personalities. This is an aspect of technology that has disturbed observers since Adam Smith commented, two hundred years ago, that a man who endlessly performed the same task "generally becomes as stupid and ignorant as it is possible for a human creature to become."[4] Later, Karl Marx wrote with passion and perception about the terrible effects of industrial capitalism in divorcing the worker from the fruits of his own toil; and since Marx, writers in socialist as well as in capitalist nations have articulated the feelings of impotence and estrangement experienced in a vast, mechanized environment.

Is industrial technology in fact the cause of a pervasive "alienation" of man? We do not really know. Man today is certainly as much the servant as the master of his industrial apparatus. Yet we must guard against too easy an indictment of technology as the great dehumanizer. Let us not forget the terrible toll on the human personality of preindustrial labor, with its exhausted peasants and its brutalized common laborers. Further, let us bear in mind that if the repressive and disciplinary aspects of technology predominate in our time, it may be because we are still only in the inception of the industrial history of humankind. In a longer perspective, this same technology holds forth at least the promise of an eventual emancipation of man, as machinery gradually takes over his onerous, monotonous tasks.

[3] Charles R. Walker and Robert H. Guest, *The Man on the Assembly Line* (Cambridge: Harvard University Press, 1952), p. 46.

[4] *The Wealth of Nations* (New York: Modern Library, 1937), p. 734.

We will return again to some of these problems of technology. But meanwhile we must pay heed to another important aspect of the technological invasion. This is the striking alteration it has brought about in the tasks of social provisioning. It is obvious that the inventory of work-skills that we possessed in 1800 would never suffice to operate the social machine of the 1960s. But even in the much shorter span since 1900, the required distribution of skills has significantly changed, as Table 6-1 shows.

Note how different is our profile of occupations today from the not too distant past. We have already commented on the sharp drop in the number of people needed to feed the nation, but we can also see a shift within the "blue collar" group from unskilled to skilled and semiskilled jobs, as more people labor with capital equipment than with their hands. In addition, as the sharp increase in the number of managers and clerical workers indicates, a swifter and more complex production process requires ever more people to coordinate and oversee the actual making of goods. In 1899 there was one nonproduction worker for every thirteen production workers in manufacturing; in 1964, one for three.

Before we leave this discussion of the general impact of technology on economic society, we must briefly look into one last attribute of industrialism—the rise of labor unions within the market system during the late nineteenth and early twentieth centuries.

| | Percent of labor force | |
	1900	1968
Managerial and professional		
Professional and technical workers	4.1	14.4
Managers, officials, and proprietors (nonfarm)	5.9	10.5
White-collar		
Clerical workers	3.1	17.9
Sales workers	4.8	6.0
Blue-collar		
Skilled workers and foremen	10.3	12.7
Semiskilled workers	12.8	17.6
Unskilled workers	12.4	4.6
Household and other service workers	8.9	12.4
Farm		
Farmers and farm managers	20.0	2.2
Farm laborers	17.6	1.9

TABLE 6•1

OCCUPATIONAL DISTRIBUTION OF THE LABOR FORCE 1900–1968

Source: 1900 figures calculated from *Historical Statistics of the United States*, Series D 72–122, p. 74; 1968 figures from *Statistical Abstract*, 1970, p. 225. Totals do not add to 100 percent, owing to rounding. Farmers and farm laborers partly estimated (*Statistical Abstract*, p. 228).

Actually we can trace the origins of trade unionism back to early Roman times, when some workmen joined into semifraternal orders. But unionism as an important social institution obviously had to await the creation of a free labor force, and that, as we know, did not occur until relatively recent times. Even after labor had been pried loose from its feudal status and thrown upon the market for survival, unionism still awaited as a final stimulus the advent of an industrial technology that brought masses of men together in the insecure and impersonal environment of the factory.

Thus, all through the nineteenth century, as industrial technology entered nation after nation, we also find a strong impetus toward union organization. In nearly every nation, it should also be noted, these movements were met at first with determined and often ferocious resistance: under the so-called Conspiracy Doctrine and the Combination Laws (1800) of Great Britain, for example, thousands of workmen were punished for combining to raise wages—although in no case were employers punished for combining to lower them. Indeed, for a quarter of a century, British unionists were treated as rebels or common criminals, as they also were, for that matter, in France or Germany.

In America, trade union progress was also slow. The strong American belief in "rugged individualism"—a belief shared by many workers as well as by their bosses—a reliance on docile immigrant labor in the heavy industries, and the use of every legal and many illegal weapons on the part of employers kept American unionism largely limited to the skilled crafts long after the union movement had finally gained acceptance and some measure of power in Europe.

During the 1920s, for example, union membership *dropped* some 30 percent, partly as a result of an all-out attack by the National Association of Manufacturers; partly as a consequence of labor's own indifference to unionism. By 1929 less than one nonagricultural worker in five belonged to a union, and not a single industrial union of consequence had yet organized a mass production industry.*

The coming of industrial unionism in America was compressed into a few dramatic years in the mid-1930s. Then, under the combined impetus of the New Deal and the newly-formed Congress for Industrial Organization (CIO), the long pent-up pressures of labor frustration finally broke the barriers of corporate resistance. In a series of dramatic strikes, the CIO won contracts from Ford and General Motors, United States Steel and Bethlehem Steel, all bastions of antilabor resistance. It was not the terms of the contracts that mattered so much as the fact that in signing any contract at all, the companies *for the first time* recognized the unions as bargaining agents for their workers regarding wages, hours, and working conditions.

As a result unionism boomed. By 1940 the number of the unionized

---

* Craft unions seek to organize the workers of a particular skill (regardless of where they work) into one union; examples are the Newspaper Guild and the carpenters' or the plumbers' unions. Industrial unions, on the other hand, join all the members of a given industry (regardless of their craft or level of skill); examples are the Steelworkers and the United Auto Workers.

had jumped from less than 4 million to over 8 million, and big business resistance to union was effectively finished.

It is difficult today to reconstruct that era, not so very long past, when Walter Reuther, the great organizer of the United Auto Workers, was thrown down a flight of concrete stairs and kicked by the hired strongmen of the Ford Motor Company, when coal miners carried rifles to fight the local police, or when strikers actually seized and occupied General Motors and Chrysler plants. The tumultuous history of this turning point in labor history has today given way to a much calmer era, in which tensions and conflicts continue to mark the relations of business and labor (as they always will in a market society), but the attitudes and actions of the antilabor past already seem to be ancient history.

We cannot trace here the full story of American unionism (including the very important and checkered history of its efforts at self-government), but one point seems worth making before we return to our main narrative. It is that a high point in union membership seems to have been reached in the late 1950s when just over 18 million workers, or about 32 percent of all nonagricultural employment, belonged to affiliates of the AFL-CIO or to independent unions. Since then there has been a stagnation in union growth, all the more noticeable against a rising total labor force. Today only about 23 percent of the total labor force is unionized, and less than 28 percent of all workers in nonagricultural establishments belong to unions.

Why has the union movement ceased to grow? The single, most cogent reason seems to lie in the very shift in the job spectrum we have already examined. Blue-collar jobs, where trade unionism has traditionally been strongest, are now a static or perhaps slowly declining fraction of the work force. Conversely, the fastest growing area of employment is in the service and white-collar sectors, where the antipathy to unionism has traditionally been greatest.

Out of this shift in occupations may come a new era in labor relations—and in labor problems. It is unlikely, as we have seen, that industrial unionism will experience much further dynamic growth. But this does not mean that the power of organized labor is therefore on the wane. For the stability or shrinkage in industrial unionism has been compensated in recent years by a sudden rise of union activity in the service and white-collar areas, particularly in the public sector. Strikes of sanitation workers and teachers can be very disruptive and, more important, may be difficult to settle without large wage increases. Unlike the case of a union dealing with a corporation, a union dealing with a municipality or a state does not have to temper its demands to the ability of its adversary to pay wages out of its *sales*. Instead, wage increases are ultimately limited only by the amount of additional *tax revenues* that the union can force the public authority to allocate to its members. Thus, restraints on public wages are very hard to impose.

There is a second and even more cogent reason for labor's gain in the balance of power between employer and worker. Traditionally, the employer has held the whip hand over the union, because in all labor disputes, sooner or later, the pressure of sheer need would compel the union to agree to the employer's offer. But this inherent inequality is changing as technology increases the general affluence of the economy. When workers' bank balances and union treasuries are full, and when it is easy for strikers to find temporary employment, the traditional pressures on the union to "settle" lose much of their effect.

All this implies that considerable labor problems may lie ahead, for which there are no simple solutions. What is necessary is to recognize that these problems, which we tend to blame on this union leader or on that company or public official, have their roots in a much deeper change of situation—indeed, that they ultimately spring, as we have said, from the power of technology to increase productivity and to alter the occupational mix. Another way of putting it is that technology has rearranged the priorities of society, lessening the pressing nature of the production problem and exacerbating that of the distribution problem; and while such reflections do not solve our problems, they help us to understand them better.

ECONOMIES OF LARGE-SCALE PRODUCTION

Thus far we have examined some of the diffuse effects of industrial technology on the life-ways of society. Now we must turn back to a more technical aspect of the industrial process—but one that in many ways underlies the larger and more general effects we have been studying. This is the development of a new method of industrial production first visible after the 1860s, although not fully realized until the turn of the twentieth century. This is the method of *mass production*.

Allan Nevins has described what mass production techniques looked like in the early Ford assembly lines.

Just how were the main assembly lines and lines of component production and supply kept in harmony? For the chassis alone, from 1,000 to 4,000 pieces of each component had to be furnished each day at just the right point and right minute; a single failure, and the whole mechanism would come to a jarring standstill .... Superintendents had to know every hour just how many components were being produced and how many were in stock. Whenever danger of shortage appeared, the shortage chaser—a familiar figure in all automobile factories—flung himself into the breach. Counters and checkers reported to him. Verifying in person any ominous news, he mobilized the foreman concerned to repair deficiencies. Three times a day he made typed reports in manifold to the factory clearing-house, at the same time chalking on blackboards in the clearing-house office a statement of results in each factory-production department and each assembling department.[5]

Such systematizing in itself resulted in astonishing increases in productivity. With each operation analyzed and subdivided into its simplest components, with a steady stream of work passing before stationary men, with a relentless but manageable pace of work, the total time required to assemble

[5] *Ford, the Times, the Man, the Company*, I, 507.

a car dropped astonishingly. Within a single year, the time required to assemble a motor fell from 600 minutes to 226 minutes; to build a chassis, from 12 hours and 28 minutes to 1 hour and 33 minutes. A stopwatch man was told to observe a 3-minute assembly in which men assembled rods and piston, a simple operation. The job was divided into three jobs, and half the men turned out the same output as before.[6]

But what interests us in the context of our study are not the technical achievements of mass production as much as its economic results. For increases in productivity bring reductions in cost. Even though the machinery needed for mass production is extremely expensive, output increases so fast that costs *per unit* of output drop dramatically.

Imagine, for instance, a small plant turning out 1,000 items a day with the labor of ten men and a small amount of equipment. Suppose each man is paid $10, each item before manufacture costs 10¢, and the daily amount of "overhead"—that is, the daily share of costs such as rent, plant maintenance, office salaries, and wear-and-tear on equipment—comes to $100. Then our total daily cost of production is $300 per day ($100 of payroll, $100 of raw material costs, and $100 of overhead). Divided among 1,000 items of output, our cost per item is 30¢.

Now imagine that our product lends itself to mass production techniques. Our payroll may then jump to $1,000 and with our much larger plant and equipment, our daily overhead to $5,000. Nevertheless, mass production may have boosted output as much as 100 times. Then our total daily cost of production will be $16,000 ($1,000 of payroll, $5,000 of overhead, and $10,000 of raw material costs). Divided among our 100,000 items of output, our cost per item has fallen to 16¢. Despite a quintupling of over-all expense, our cost per unit has almost halved.

This is not a far-fetched example of what economists call *the economies of large-scale production*. A glance at Table 6-2 shows how mass production

TABLE 6•2

Year	Unit sales, Ford cars	Price of typical model (touring)	
1907–1908	6,398	$2,800 (Model K)	
1908–1909	10,607	850	
1909–1910	18,664	950	
1910–1911	34,528	780	
1911–1912	78,440	690	
1912–1913	168,304	600	Model T
1913–1914	248,307	550	
1914–1915	221,805 (10 mos.)	490	
1915–1916	472,350	440	
1916–1917	730,041	360	

Compiled from Nevins, *Ford, the Times, the Man, the Company,* pp. 644, 646–47.

[6] *Ibid,* pp. 504, 506.

techniques did, in fact, boost output of Ford cars by more than one hundred times while reducing their cost by seven-eighths.

Nor do the dynamics of the industrial process come to a halt with these formidable economies of large-scale production. For this technological achievement brings into the market system itself a new element of primary importance. That element is *size*.

It is not difficult to see why. Once a firm—by virtue of adroit management, improved product, advantages of location, or whatever other reason—steps out decisively in front of its competitors in size, *economies of large-scale production operate to push it out still further in front.* Bigger size usually means lower cost, at least for a young expanding industry. Lower cost means bigger profits. Bigger profits mean the ability to grow to still larger size. Thus the techniques of large-scale manufacture bring about a situation threatening to alter the whole meaning of competition. From a mechanism that prevents any single firm from dominating the market, competition now becomes a force that may drive an ever-larger share of the market into the hands of the largest and most efficient producer.

THE GREAT ENTREPRENEURS

We shall have much more to say about the economics of the drive to bigness when we study the market system in Part Four. Yet, it may be helpful if we look once again at the actual historic scene in which this internal growth took place. For the processes of economic change described in this chapter did not occur in a vacuum. They were brought about by a social "type" and a business milieu which powerfully accelerated and abetted the process of industrial enlargement, much as the New Men had speeded along the initial industrializing process in England in the late eighteenth century.

The agents of change during the late nineteenth century in America were very much the descendants of their industrial forebears a century earlier. Like Arkwright and Watt, many of the greatest American entrepreneurs were men of humble origin endowed with an indomitable drive for business success. There was Carnegie in steel, Harriman in railroads, Rockefeller in oil, Frick in coke, Armour and Swift in meat packing, McCormick in agricultural machinery—to mention but a few. To be sure, the *typical* businessman was very different from these Horatio Alger stereotypes of the business hero. Economic historians, such as F. W. Taussig, looking back over the careers of the business leaders of the late nineteenth century, have discovered that the average entrepreneur was not a poor, industrious immigrant lad, but the son of well-circumstanced people often in business affairs themselves. Nor was the average businessman nearly so successful as a Carnegie or a Rockefeller.

Yet in nearly every line of business, at least *one* "captain of industry" appeared who dominated the field by his personality and ability. Though few achieved their supreme degree of pecuniary success, the number who climbed into the "millionaire class" was impressive. In 1880 it had been estimated that there were 100 millionaires in the country. By 1916 the number had grown to 40,000.

Interesting and significant differences distinguish these nineteenth century business leaders from those of a century earlier. The American captains of industry were not typically men whose leadership rested on inventive or engineering skills. With the growth of large-scale production, the engineering functions became the province of salaried production experts, of second-echelon plant managers. What was required now was the master touch in guiding industrial strategy, in making or breaking alliances, choosing salients for advance, or overseeing the logistics of the whole operation. More and more the great entrepreneurs were concerned with the strategy of finance, of competition, of sales, rather than with the cold technics of production itself.

Then, too, we must make note of the entrepreneurial tactics and tone of the period. In a phrase that has stuck, Matthew Josephson once called the great men of business in this era "the robber barons." In many ways, they did indeed resemble the predatory lords of the medieval era. For example, in the 1860s a small group of California entrepreneurs under the guiding hand of Collis Huntington performed the astonishing feat of building a railroad across the hitherto impassable Rockies and Sierras. Aware that Huntington and his associates would thereby have a monopolistic control of all rail traffic to California, the Congress authorized the construction of three competing lines. But the legislators had not taken the measure of the wily pioneers. Before their own line was completed, they secretly bought the charter of one competitive line; and when the second proved somewhat harder to buy out, they simply built it out, recklessly flinging their lines into its territory until it, too, was forced to surrender. Thereafter it was no great trick to buy out the third, having first blocked it at a critical mountain pass. Only one competitive source of transportation remained: the Pacific Mail Steamship Company. Fortunately, this was owned by the obliging Jay Gould, a famous robber baron in his own right; and for the payment of a proper tribute, he agreed to eliminate San Francisco as a cargo port. There was now *no* way of bringing goods across the nation into southern California except those which the Huntington group controlled. Counting the smaller lines and subsidiaries which passed into their grasp, *nineteen* rail systems, in all, came under their domain. It was not surprising that to the residents of California the resulting unified system was known as "the Octopus" and that its average freight rate was the highest in the nation.

And it was not just the railroad industry that used economic power to create a monopoly position. In whisky and in sugar, in tobacco and cattle-feed, in wire nails, steel hoops, electrical appliances, tin plate, in matches and meat there was an octopus similar to that which fastened itself on

California. One commentator of the late 1890s pictured the American citizen born to the profit of the Milk Trust and dying to that of the Coffin Trust.

If the robber barons milked the public as consumers (and to an even greater extent bilked them as stockholders), they also had no compunctions about cutting each other down to size. In the struggle for financial control of the Albany and Susquehanna Railroad, for instance, James Fisk and J. P. Morgan found themselves in the uncomfortable position of each owning a terminal at the end of a single line. Like their feudal prototypes, they resolved the controversy by combat, mounting locomotives at each end and running them full tilt into each other—after which the losers still did not give up, but retired, ripping up the line and tearing down trestles as they went. In similar spirit, the Huntington group that built the Central Pacific hired General David Colton to run a subsidiary enterprise for them, and the General wrote to his employers:

I have learned one thing. We have got *no true* friends outside of us five. We cannot depend upon a human soul outside of ourselves, and hence we must all be good-natured, stick together, and keep to our own counsels.

whereupon he proceeded to swindle his friends out of several millions.

With this buccaneering went as well another identifying mark of the times: what the economist Thorstein Veblen was to call Conspicuous Consumption. One repentant member of the gilded age recalled in his memoirs parties at which cigarettes were wrapped in money for the sheer pleasure of inhaling wealth; a dog that was presented with a $15,000 diamond collar; an infant, resting in a $10,000 cradle, attended by four doctors who posted regular bulletins on the baby's (excellent) health; the parade of fabulous chateaux stuffed with fabulous and not-so-fabulous works of art on New York's Fifth Avenue; and the collection of impecunious European royalty as sons-in-law of the rich.

The age was a rollicking, sometimes cruel, but always dynamic one. Yet what interests us here is not to recount its colorful social history as much as to understand its deeper economic consequences. It is impossible to consider the period with which we have been concerned without taking into account the social type of the robber baron and the milieu in which he operated. Bold, aggressive, acquisitive, competitive, the great entrepreneur was the natural agent to speed along the process for which the technology of the day prepared the way. But as yet we have only begun to sketch out the changes wrought by the joint impact of strong men and ever-more complex machinery. Now we must look more carefully into the effect that this combination produced.

1. The industrial revolution brought not one but *successive waves of technical progress* and economic advance.

            Technical progress

2. In studying the impact of these industrial discoveries, we must broaden our lens to look beyond the effect on productivity alone (although that was no doubt the single most important result). Industrialization brought:
   - A vast increase in *urbanization*.

            Urbanization

   - A cumulative rise in the degree of *economic interdependence* of individuals within society.
   - A new climate for and character of work, including *the disturbing problems of monotonous industrial work* (alienation).

            Alienation

   - A *sweeping redistribution of occupations* away from unskilled toward semiskilled, technical, and managerial labor.
   - The rise of *unionism*.

            Unions

3. The new technology brought as well a change in the character of both production and competition. Production became more and more a process of highly intergrated subassemblies, making possible the *mass production* of goods. The large amounts of capital required for mass production led to very great *economies of scale*.

            Mass production

            Economies of scale

4. With the advent of mass production, *the nature of competition also changed into a destructive force.* Economies of scale led to situations in which a leading firm could undersell all competitors and thus dominate a market.

            Destructive competition

5. The dynamic potential of the new technology was given further impetus by the *aggressive "Robber baron" era* of business leadership.

            "Robber baron"

Q U E S T I O N S

1. Describe the social, as well as economic, repercussions of the following inventions: the typewriter, the jet airplane, television, penicillin. Which do you think is greater in each case—the social or economic impact?

2. The philosopher Karl Jaspers has claimed that modern technology brings an "immense joylessness." Do you agree? Is factory work unpleasant, to your mind? Office work, in a very large organization such as an insurance company? Do you think the nature of industrial work can be basically changed?

3. White-collar jobs have always proved harder to unionize than so-called blue-collar (factory floor) jobs. Why do you think this is so? Do you think it might change?

4. Suppose that you have a business in which you hire five men, to whom you pay $2 an hour; suppose further that you have overhead costs of $100 a day and that you pay $1 in materials cost for each item that your business manufactures. Assuming that you keep all five men, what is your average cost per unit of output if your plant turns out 10 items per 8-hour day? 100 items? 1,000?

5. Which is more economical, a plant with a payroll of $400 a week, with $100 of overhead a week, and with an output of 100 units per week, or a plant with a payroll of $80,000 a week, an overhead of $100,000 a week, and with an output of 50,000 units per week?

6. How do you explain economies of large-scale production? Why do certain businesses, such as cigarette manufacture, seem to enjoy them, whereas other businesses, such as barbering, do not?

So far we have investigated the impact of the new technology of mass production mainly insofar as it exerted its pervasive influence on "social" life, and we have only glanced at its effects on the workings of the economic system proper. Now we must look more carefully into this latter problem. For under the joint impetus of the drive of bold entrepreneurs and the self-feeding tendencies of economies of large-scale production dramatic changes began to appear in many sectors of the economy by the end of the nineteenth century. A system originally characterized by large numbers of small enterprises was starting to give way to one in which production was increasingly concentrated in the hands of a relatively few, very big and very powerful business units.

By 1900, for example, the number of textile mills, although still large, had dropped by a third from the 1880s; over the same period, the number of manufacturers of agricultural implements had fallen by 60 percent, and the number of leather manufacturers by three-quarters. In the locomotive industry, two companies ruled the roost in 1900, contrasted with nineteen in 1860. The biscuit and cracker industry changed from a scatter of small companies to a market in which one producer had 90 percent of the industry's capacity by the turn of the century. Meanwhile in steel there was the colossal U.S. Steel Corporation, which alone turned out over half the steel production of the nation. In oil, the Standard Oil Company tied up between 80 to 90 percent of the nation's output. In tobacco, the American Tobacco Company controlled 75 percent of the output of cigarettes and 25 percent of cigars. Similar control rested with the American Sugar Company, the American Smelting and Refining Company, the United Shoe Machinery Company, and dozens more.

From an overall view, the change was even more impressive. In the early 1800s, according to the calculations of Myron W. Watkins, no single plant controlled as much as 10 percent of the output of a manufacturing industry. By 1904, 78 enterprises controlled over half the output of their industries, 57 controlled 60 percent or more, and 28 controlled 80 percent or more. From industry to industry, this degree of "concentration" varied—from no significant concentration at all in printing and publishing, for instance, to the highly concentrated market structure of industries like copper or rubber. But there was no mistaking the overall change. In 1896, railroads excepted, there were not a dozen $10 million companies in the nation. By 1904, there were over 300 of them with a combined capitalization of over $7 billion. Together, these giants controlled more than two-fifths of the industrial capital of the nation and affected four-fifths of its important industries.[1]

Clearly something akin to a major revolution in market structure had taken place. Let us examine more closely the course of events which led up to it.

The initial impact of the trend to big business was an unexpected one. Rather than diminishing the degree of competitiveness of the market structure, it extended and intensified it. In the largely agricultural, handicraft, and small factory economy of the early nineteenth century, "the" market consisted mainly of small, localized markets, each insulated from the next by the high cost of transportation and each supplied by local producers who had neither the means nor the motivation to invade the market on anything resembling a national scale.

CHANGE IN COMPETITION

The rise of mass production radically changed this fragmented market structure and, with it, the type of competition within the market. As canals and railroads opened the country and as new manufacturing techniques vastly increased output, the parochial quality of the market system changed. More and more, one unified and interconnected market bound together the entire nation, and the petty semimonopolies of local suppliers were invaded by products from large factories in distant cities.

Quickly, a second development followed. As the new production techniques gained momentum, aggressive businessmen typically not only built, but overbuilt. "As confident entrepreneurs raced to take advantage of every ephemeral rise in prices, of every advance in tariff schedules, of every new market opened by the railroads and puffed up immigration," write Thomas Cochran and William Miller in a history of these industrializing times, "they

---

[1] John Moody, *The Truth about Trusts* (Chicago: Moody, 1904). See also Ralph Nelson, *Merger Movements in American Industry, 1895-1956* (Princeton, N.J.: National Bureau of Economic Research, 1959).

recklessly expanded and mechanized their plants, each seeking the greatest share of the new melon."[2]

The result was a phenomenal burst in output but, simultaneously, a serious change in the nature of competition. Competition now became not only more extensive, but more *expensive*. As the size of the plant and the complexity of equipment grew, so did the "fixed charges" of a business enterprise—the interest on borrowed capital, the depreciation of capital assets, the cost of administrative staff, the rent of land, and "overhead," generally. These costs tended to remain fairly constant, regardless of whether sales were good or bad. Unlike the payment of wages to a working force, which dropped when men were fired, there was no easy way to cut down the steady drain of payments for these fixed expenditures. The result was that the bigger the business, the more vulnerable was its economic health when competition cut into its sales.

The ebullience of the age, plus the steady growth of a technology that required massive investments, made competition increasingly drastic. As growing giant businesses locked horns, railroad against railroad, steel mill against steel mill, each sought to assure the coverage of its fixed expenses by gaining for itself as much of the market as it could. The outcome was the emergence of "cutthroat competition" among massive producers, replacing the more restricted, local competition of the small business, small market world. In 1869, for example, the New York-Chicago railway freight rate on a hundredweight of grain crashed from $1.80, on February 4, to 40¢ twenty days later, climbed back to $1.88 in July, and then plummeted to 25¢ in August when another "war" broke out. In the oil fields, the coal fields, among the steel and copper producers, similar price wars repeatedly occurred as producers sought to capture the markets they needed to achieve a profitable level of production. All this was unquestionably favorable to the consumer, as indeed competitive situations always are, but it threatened literal bankruptcy for the competing enterprises themselves—and furthermore, bankruptcy on a multimillion dollar scale.

LIMITATION OF COMPETITION

In these circumstances, it is not difficult to understand the next phase of economic development. The giants decided not to compete.

But how were they to avoid competition? Since common law invalidated any contract binding a competitor to fixed prices or production schedules, there seemed no alternative but voluntary cooperation: trade associations, "gentleman's agreements," or "pools," informal treaties to divide the market. By the 1800s there were a cordage pool and a whiskey pool, a coal pool, a salt pool, and endless rail pools, all calculated to relieve the individual producers from the mutually suicidal game of all-out competition. But to little avail. The division of the market worked well during

[2] *The Age of Enterprise*, rev. ed. (New York: Harper, Torchbooks, 1961), p. 139.

good times; but when bad times approached, the pools broke down. As sales fell, the temptation to cut prices was irresistible, and thus began again the old, ruinous game of competition.

The robber baron ethics of the day contributed to the difficulties. "A starving man will usually get bread if it is to be had," said James J. Hill, a great railway magnate, "and a starving railway will not maintain rates."[3] Typically, at a meeting of rail heads called to agree upon a common freight schedule, the president of one road slipped out, during a brief recess, to wire the new rates to his road, so that it might be the first to undercut them. (By chance, his wire was intercepted, so that when the group next met it was forced to recognize that even among thieves there is not always honor.)

During the 1880s, a more effective device for control became available. In 1879, Samuel Dodd, lawyer for the new Standard Oil Company, had a brilliant idea for regulating the murderous competition that regularly wracked the oil industry. He devised the idea of a trust. Stockholders of companies that wished to join in the Standard Oil Trust were asked to surrender their actual shares to the board of directors of the new trust. Thereby they would give up working control over their companies, but in return they would get "trust certificates" which entitled them to the same share in the profits as their shares earned. In this way, the Standard Oil directors wielded control over all the associated companies, while the former stockholders shared fully in the profits.

Eventually, as we shall see, the trusts were declared to be illegal. But by that time, still more effective devices were created. In 1888 the New Jersey legislature passed a law allowing a corporation chartered in the state to buy stock in another corporation. This was a privilege that had not previously been available to corporations chartered anywhere in the United States. The result was the rapid appearance of the corporate merger, the coming together of two corporations to form a new, bigger one. In manufacturing and mining, alone, there were 43 mergers in 1895 (affecting $41 million dollars worth of corporate assets); 26 mergers in 1896, 69 mergers in 1897. Then in 1898 there were 303—and finally in 1899 a climactic *1,208 mergers combined some $2.26 billion in corporate assets.*[4] Another great wave of mergers occurred in the 1920s. In all, from 1895 to 1929, some $20 billion of industrial corporate wealth were merged into larger units.*

[3] Cochran and Miller, *The Age of Enterprise,* p. 141.

[4] *Historical Statistics of the United States,* Series V, pp. 30-31.

* We must take a footnote to call attention to a development that deserves a chapter in itself. This is the importance of the *corporation,* as a marvelously adaptive legal form of organizing production, in spurring on the growth of the economy. Unlike the personal proprietorship or partnership, the corporation existed quite independently of its owners, survived their deaths, and could enter into binding contracts in "its" own name. Further, by limiting the liability of its owners to the value of the stock they had bought, it protected a capitalist against limitless loss. Much has been written, quite rightly, about the abuses of corporations, but it is important to recognize how valuable was this ingenious legal innovation in encouraging the accumulation of capital and in creating the organizational means to supervise and direct that capital into production.

Another effective means of limiting competition was the *holding company*. Having passed a law permitting its corporations to buy stock in one another, New Jersey now allowed its corporations to do business in any state. Thus the legal foundation was laid for a central corporation which could control subsidiary enterprises by the simple means of buying a controlling share of their stock. By 1911, when the Standard Oil combine was finally dissolved, Standard Oil of New Jersey had used this device to acquire direct control over seventy companies and indirect control over thirty more.

Yet we must not think that it was only the movement toward trustification and merger that brought about the emergence of the giant firm with its ability to limit—or eliminate—competition. Equally, perhaps more, important was simply the process of internal growth. Ford and General Motors, General Electric and A.T.&T., DuPont and Carnegie Steel (later to be the core of U.S. Steel) grew essentially because their market was expanding and they were quick, able, efficient, and aggressive enough to grow faster than any of their competitors. All of them gobbled up some small businesses along the way, and most of them benefited from agreements not to compete. But their gradual emergence to a position of dominance within their industries was not, in the last analysis, attributable to these facts. It was the dynamism of their own business leadership, coupled with a production technique which made enormous size both possible and profitable.

THREAT OF ECONOMIC FEUDALISM

Certainly, size became enormous. By the end of the nineteenth century, some business units were already considerably larger than the states in which they were located. Charles William Eliot pointed out in 1888 that a single railway with headquarters in Boston not only employed three times as many people as the entire government of the Commonwealth of Massachusetts, but enjoyed gross receipts nearly six times that of the state government which had created it. But by comparison with the findings of the Pujo Committee of the U.S. Senate, not quite twenty-five years later, the railway was still small. The committee pointed out that the Morgan banking interests held 341 directorships in 112 corporations whose aggregate wealth exceeded by three times the value of *all* the real and personal property of New England. And not only was the process of trustification eating away at the competitive structure of the market, but the emergence of enormous financially controlled empires posed as well a political problem of ominous portent. As Woodrow Wilson declared: "If monopoly persists, monopoly will always sit at the helm of government. I do not expect to see monopoly restrain itself. If there are men in this country big enough to own the government of the United States, they are going to own it."[5]

[5] Richard Hofstadter, *The Age of Reform* (New York: Knopf, 1955), p. 231.

Not surprisingly, from many quarters the trend to bigness was vehemently opposed. From the 1880s on, a series of state laws strove to undo the trusts which squeezed their citizens. Louisiana sued the Cottonseed Oil Trust; New York, the Sugar Trust; Ohio, the Oil Trust—but to little avail. When one state, like New York, clamped down on its trusts, other states, seeing the revenue available from a change in corporate headquarters, virtually invited the trust to set up business there. When the Supreme Court ruled that corporations, as "persons," could not be deprived of property without "due process of law," state regulation became almost totally useless.

It was soon clear that if something further were to be done, the federal government would have to do it. "Congress alone can deal with the trusts," said Senator Sherman in 1890, "and if we are unwilling or unable, there will soon be a trust for every production and a master to fix the price for every necessity of life."[6]

The result was the Sherman Antitrust Act, an act which, on its surface, was an effective remedy for the problem. "Every contract, combination . . . or conspiracy, in restraint of trade" was declared to be illegal. Violators were subject to heavy fines and jail sentences, and triple damages could be obtained by persons who proved economic injury because of unfair price rigging.

Indeed, under the Sherman Act a number of trusts were prosecuted; and in a famous action in 1911, the great Standard Oil Trust was ordered dissolved. Yet, despite the break-up of a few trusts, the act was singularly weak. Fines for violations were too small to be effective, and in any case, few were levied: not until Franklin Roosevelt's time would the Antitrust Division of the Department of Justice have as much as a million dollars with which to investigate and control the affairs of a multi-billion dollar economy. In fact, during the first fifty years of its existence, only 252 criminal actions were instituted under the Sherman law. And then too, the prevailing judicial opinion of the 1890s and early 1900s was not much in sympathy with the act. The Supreme Court early dealt it a severe blow by finding, in the American Sugar Refining case, that manufacturing was not "commerce," and therefore the American Sugar Refining Company, which had bought controlling stock interests in its four largest competitors, was not to be considered as acting "in restraint of trade." It is not surprising that the concentration of business was hardly slowed in such a climate of opinion. As a humorist of the times put it: "What looks like a stone wall to a layman is a triumphal arch to a corporation lawyer."

These weaknesses led to further acts in 1914: primarily, the Clayton Antitrust Act, prohibiting specific kinds of price discrimination and mergers by the acquisition of stock in competing corporations; and the Federal Trade Commission, which sought to define and prevent "unfair" business

---

[6] Cochran and Miller, *The Age of Enterprise,* p. 171.

practices. As we shall see later, these acts were not without their effect. Yet, undermining the entire antitrust movement there remained one critical and vitiating fact. The purpose of antitrust was essentially to restore competitive conditions to markets which were in danger of becoming "monopolized" by giant firms. Against this tendency, antitrust legislation could pose a deterrent only insofar as the monopolization process resulted from the outright *combination* of erstwhile competitors. Against a much more fundamental condition—the ability of large businesses to enjoy decisive advantages in finance, merchandising, and research over small businesses—it could offer no remedy. While antitrust effort concentrated its fire against collusion or amalgamation, it was powerless against the fact of spontaneous internal growth.

And therefore growth continued. Through most of the first quarter of the twentieth century, the biggest corporations not only grew, but grew much *faster* than their smaller competitors. As Adolf Berle and Gardiner Means pointed out in a famous study in 1932, between 1909 and 1928 the 200 largest nonfinancial corporations increased their gross assets over 40 percent more rapidly than all nonfinancial corporations.[7] Looking into the future, Berle and Means concluded:

Just what does this rapid growth of the big companies promise for the future? Let us project the trend of the growth of recent years. If the wealth of the large corporations and that of all corporations should each continue to increase for the next twenty years at its average annual rate for the twenty years from 1909 to 1929, 70 percent of all corporate activity would be carried on by two hundred corporations in 1950. If the more rapid rates of growth from 1924 to 1929 were maintained for the next twenty years 85 percent of corporate wealth would be held by two hundred huge units. . . . If the indicated growth of the large corporations and of the national wealth were to be effective from now until 1950, half of the national wealth would be under the control of big companies at the end of that period.[8]

Indeed, warned the authors, if the trend of the past continued unchecked, it was predictable that in 360 years all the corporate wealth in the nation would have become fused into one gigantic enterprise, which would then have an expected life span equal to that of the Roman Empire.

STRUCTURE OF THE NATIONAL MARKET: PERIPHERY AND CENTER

Has the Berle and Means projection come true? The question brings to a climax our long survey of the changing market structure. We have been concerned with gathering up the various forces that created and shaped the market as a great system of economic control. Now we must see what the outcome of that process has been.

[7] *The Modern Corporation and Private Property* (New York: Macmillan, 1948), p. 36.
[8] *Ibid.,* pp. 40-41.

Let us begin by looking at the market system in the United States today. Immediately, we notice one thing: there is not one market system in America, but two. One of them, with which we are all familiar at firsthand, consists of the millions of small enterprises that make up the large stratum of the population known as "small-business men." Here are the stores we pass every day on the avenues, the columns of names in the yellow pages of the phone books.

There are roughly 12 million "small" businesses in America, counting every one from the newsstand through the farm (2.9 million farms) up to enterprises that employ several hundred people and count their dollar volume in tens of millions.* Among these 12 million business units, corporations number only about 1.5 million, but these 1.5 million corporations do nearly *five times* as much business as all the small proprietorships and partnerships. In turn, however, most of the 1.5 million corporations are small, even when measured by a small-business yardstick. Over half do less than $100,000 a year in sales, with the result that the whole group of little corporations accounts for only 2 percent of all corporate sales.

Thus, in terms of sales (or assets), little business is little indeed. Yet, by virtue of its numbers, the small businesses of America are by no means unimportant in the national economic picture. Small business collectively employs roughly 40 percent of the American labor force. (This compares with 35 percent of the labor force that works for the "not-for-profit" sector—state, local, and federal government, hospitals, social services agencies, clubs, etc.—and with 25 percent that works for big business.) Millions of small entrepreneurs constitute the very core of the American "middle class," and thus give a characteristic small-business view to much of American political and social life.

Yet it must be emphasized that even as a collectivity, the 12 million minibusinesses do not begin to match the economic power of a tiny number of giant enterprises at the other end of the scale. In the apt phrase of Robert Averitt, small business constitutes the Periphery, but the giants constitute the Center.[9] For here, in a few hundred large industrial corporations, is an economy within an economy, a "system" unto itself. All by itself, this very small core of corporations—500 at the most—accounts for a third of all industrial sales, and within that core there is an inner core that by itself produces the main flow of industrial production on which the economy rests.

* Just to get an idea of scale: the 500th largest American industrial firm in 1969 (in terms of sales) was Montfort of Colorado, a meatpacking firm with sales of $161 million. The 500th biggest in terms of *assets* was another meatpacker, Missouri Beef Packers, worth $19.8 million. At the other end of the list, the largest industrial corporation in terms of sales was General Motors, with a sales volume of $24 *billion*. Biggest in terms of assets was Standard Oil (N.J.) with assets of almost $15 billion. This does not count A.T.&T., which is not classified as an "industrial" company, but which is the largest enterprise in the nation, by far, in terms of assets—$49.6 billion in 1970.

[9] Robert T. Averitt, *The Dual Economy* (New York: Norton, 1968).

Table 7-1 gives us a first overview of the strategic position of the giant corporation within various divisions of the economy.

TABLE 7 • 1

GIANT
CORPORATIONS

RELATIVE SHARES OF LARGE CORPORATIONS IN VARIOUS SECTORS, 1967

Sector	All corporations		Corporations with assets of $250 million or more	
	Number	Total assets ($ billion)	Number	Percent of assets in that sector
Mining	14,441	$ 18.1	12	31%
Manufacturing	197,023	448.0	243	58
Transportation, communication, utilities	66,045	221.1	95	79
Finance, insurance, real estate	388,115	1,097.3	517	55
Wholesale and retail trade	465,841	144.1	29	20
All industrial divisions [a]	**1,534,360**	**2,010.7**	**958**	**53**

Source: *Statistical Abstract*, 1970, p. 475. (Data calculated from tax returns.)
[a] Including divisions not shown in table.

The table speaks for itself. Note that the giant corporation is much more dominant in some sectors, such as transportation and communication, than in others, such as retail and wholesale trade. The Center and the Periphery stand out particularly in the latter sector where we find nearly a half-million corporate enterprises (note that we are not even counting the millions of proprietorships and partnerships), but where 29 giant companies, such as Sears Roebuck, A&P, Safeway, and others, nonetheless control almost 30 percent of the total assets.

These figures, however, do not give us a sense of the movement toward corporate concentration that is still going on. For in recent years there has been a burst of merger activity comparable to the great merger movement of the late nineteenth century. Between 1951 and 1960, one-fifth of the top 1,000 corporations disappeared—absorbed within the remaining four fifths. As a result of this and other growth, by 1968 the *100* largest manufacturing corporations owned 49.3 percent of the assets of all manufacturing corporations—*a larger percentage than the top 200 corporations had held in 1948!*

Moreover, the pace of this centralizing activity has been steadily growing. Between 1963 and 1966 the value of assets acquired by the big mining and manufacturing companies averaged $4 billion to $5 billion a year. This rate rose to $10 billion in 1967, then to $15 billion in 1968, and reached an all-time peak *rate* of $20 billion in the first quarter of 1969. The subsequent break in the stock market thereupon brought mergers to an abrupt halt, but the total for 1969 was nonetheless almost at the 1968 level.[10]

Here is a trend that seems to confirm the worst fears of Berle and Means. Does the conclusion they feared also follow? For in *The Modern Corporation and Private Property* (p. 46), they wrote: "a society in which production is governed by blind market forces is being replaced by one in which production is carried on under the ultimate control of a handful of individuals." In the light of our historical study, we can rephrase that conclusion very simply. It meant that the market as the basic control mechanism within capitalism was about to be replaced by another system, akin to a new economic feudalism. Is that the conclusion to which the statistics on corporate size now force us?

CONGLOMERATES AND THE MARKETPLACE

The answer is not a simple one. There is no question that a massive concentration of corporate power exists in America and that the degree of concentration within business as a whole is increasing. At the same time, rather surprisingly, the degree of concentration in the *marketplace*—an area of critical importance for the control mechanism of the capitalist society— does not seem to be getting significantly worse.

How can that seemingly contradictory state of affairs exist? How can corporations be getting bigger and not be increasingly monopolistic? The answer is that the merger wave that has so dramatically boosted the figures for the national concentration of business wealth has taken place largely by the rise of so-called *conglomerates*—corporations that have grown by merging with other corporations not *within* a given market but in a *different* market. Consider the case of International Telephone and Telegraph. Originally a much smaller company wholly engaged in running foreign communications systems, ITT determined in 1961 to embark on a major acquisition and diversification program. During the next 7 years it acquired 52 domestic and 55 foreign companies with combined assets of 1.5 billion. In 1969 alone, the directors approved an additional 22 domestic and 11 foreign acquisitions. As a result it has jumped from 34th to 9th in industrial size, with sales and assets of $5 billion each and 353,000 employees—the 5th largest private

---

[10] *Statistical Abstract,* 1970, pp. 476, 483. See also Federal Trade Commission, *Staff Report on Corporate Mergers,* October 1969, esp. pp. 184-98.

employer in the world. More important, whereas it had once been a "one-product" company, selling and operating telecommunications systems, by 1970 ITT rented cars (Avis), operated motels and hotels (Sheraton), built homes (Levitt), baked bread (Continental), sold insurance, produced glass, made consumer loans, managed a mutual fund and processed data—among other things.

We do not yet know what may be the long-term consequences of the rise of such giant, diversified companies. Many of them have been put together more with an eye to realizing the profits that could be had from exchanges of shares than with any careful consideration of operating efficiencies, and some have already come unglued in the 1969-1970 stock market decline. Others may indeed prove to be efficient combinations of diverse activities that will enjoy the advantages of access to a central pool of capital and a topflight supermanagement. Still others may run afoul of antitrust laws and may be forced to dissolve.

STABILITY OF MARKET SHARES

But as matters now stand, it seems unlikely that the conglomerates will be adding to their size by buying up *competitors*. Hence it is likely that the structure of the individual markets in which they operate will show no more change than they have in the past. And here, in the critical area of the marketplace, we discover a truly surprising long-run stability. For more than half a century, now, there has been no substantial increase in "monopoly" in the nation's markets, considered as a whole. Going back to 1901, we find some industries—tobacco, chemicals, stone, clay and glass, transportation equipment—where industrial concentration has risen; but in others, no less important—food, textiles, pulp and paper, petroleum and coal products, rubber, machinery—concentration has fallen since 1901.

The same conclusion holds for more recent years. If we take the four largest companies in any industry between 1947 and 1966 (the latest year for which figures are available) and compare the value of their total shipments to the value of all shipments in the industry, we find a similar mixed trend. In a few instances, such as the automobile industry, where some early postwar competitors were shaken out, the concentration ratio has increased appreciably: in the case of autos, from 56 percent in 1947 to 79 percent in 1966. In the majority of industries, however, the movement toward concentration was insubstantial; and in a considerable number, concentration actually declined.

Perhaps most convincing of all is a recent government study that shows the degree of concentration within 213 industrial markets to be virtually unchanged between 1947 and 1966. In 1947, the average share of all markets going to the top four firms was 41.2 percent; in 1966 it was 41.9 percent. Moreover, the number of highly concentrated industries—where the top four firms did three-quarters or more of all sales—showed a sharp drop during the period.[11]

[11] *The New York Times,* January 26, 1969.

What has produced this stabilization of concentration within industry? Two reasons suggest themselves.

The first is the *restraining effect of antitrust legislation.* At the point at which we left our historical narrative, we had seen only the ineffectiveness of early antitrust legislation. But beginning in the 1930s under Franklin Roosevelt, a much stronger enforcement of the various antitrust laws began to gain favor. A vigorous campaign to block the drift toward concentration resulted in a number of suits brought against major corporations for restraint of trade. No less important was a change in the prevailing judicial view, which now construed much less narrowly the powers of the Constitution to impose social controls over business enterprise. In more recent years, new amendments to the antitrust acts and a growing stringency of Justice Department rulings have made the marriage of competitive firms increasingly difficult.

One result of these obstacles in the way of direct "concentration-affecting" mergers is that corporations have been forced to seek acquisitions in fields considerably removed from their original base of operations. This is one source of that trend toward conglomerates we noted above. What interests us here is that this process of diversification has put many large corporations into fields in which they are not the dominant companies by any means. One study shows that in a thousand different product markets, the 100 biggest firms are not even among the four biggest sellers in almost half these markets.[12] By way of illustration, in 1965 the Radio Corporation of America acquired Random House, a book publisher. In its manufacturing activities, RCA is a large producer in a moderately concentrated field (the top four companies make just under half of all radios); in its broadcasting activities, as the owner of NBC, it is one of three great broadcasting networks; but as a book publisher it sails in a highly competitive race.

A second reason for the stabilization within markets is more diffuse, but no less significant. It lies in a decisive *change in the character of business management.*

We have already noticed a certain change in the evolution of the great entrepreneur, from the production-oriented industrialist of the early nineteenth century to the sales and strategy-oriented "captain of industry" of the late nineteenth. Yet throughout the first century of rapid corporate expansion, one characteristic marked both types of business leaders. Both were the direct owners of their enterprises. The men who ran the corporations were themselves the men who had put up the capital or who owned large blocks of stock in the enterprises. The Carnegie Steel Company, the Standard Oil Company, the Ford Motor Company were all extensions of the personalities of Carnegie, Rockefeller, and Ford. This personal direction of affairs was

---

[12] A. D. H. Kaplan, *Big Enterprise in a Competitive System* (Washington, D.C.: Brookings, 1964), p. 286.

the case in the overwhelming majority of the other large and small enterprises of the day.

But with time, a significant change set in. As the original founders of the great businesses died, their stock was inherited by heirs who often did not have business ability and who receded into the background. In addition, the widening dispersion of stock ownership among more and more small investors made it unnecessary for any group to own an actual majority of the stock to exercise control over a company. In 1928, for example, the board of directors of U.S. Steel (which included two of the largest stockholders in the company) held only 1.4 percent of the company's stock. In that year, the biggest stockholder in A.T.&T. held but seven-tenths of 1 percent of the company's total stock and the biggest shareowners of the Pennsylvania Railroad held less than 3 percent of the firm's stock.

The result was that the active direction of the big firms passed from owner-capitalists to a new group of "managers" who ruled the corporation by virtue of their *expertise* rather than because they owned it. The new management was different in many ways from its predecessors. In 1900, for example, half the top executives of the biggest corporations had followed paths to the top that could be described as "entrepreneurial" or "capitalist"—that is, half had built their own businesses or had risked their own capital as the means to business preeminence. By 1925 only a third of the top corporate executives had followed this path, and in 1960 *less than 3 percent* had done so. More and more, the route to success lay through professional skills, whether in law or engineering or science, or in the patient ascent of the corporate hierarchical ladder. Significantly there was a visible change as well as a marked change in the educational background of the top corporate officials. As recently as the 1920s, a majority of the topmost corporate leaders had not gone to college; today over 90 percent have college degrees and a third hold graduate degrees.[13]

The new management brought important changes in its wake. The affairs of big companies increasingly became matters to be handled in systematized, "professional" ways, rather than in the often highly personal, Haroun-al-Raschid mode of the founders. A certain bureaucratization thus crept into the conduct of business life, at the very time that the business community was waxing most vocal about the dangers of bureaucracy in government. More important, the new management now adopted a new strategy for corporate growth—or rather, abandoned an older one. Advances in technology, changes in product design, vigorous advertising, the wooing of businesses to be acquired in other fields—all these provided ample outlets for the managerial impulse toward expansion. But one mode of growth—the mode that the founders of the great enterprises had never hesitated to use—was now ruled out: growth was no longer to be sought by the direct head-on competition of one firm against another in terms of *price*.

---

[13] Mabel Newcomer, *The Big Business Executive* (New York: Columbia University Press, 1955), pp. 61-63; and Jay Gould, *The Technical Elite* (New York: Augustus Kelley, 1966), pp. 160-71.

Thus, the evolution of a more "statesmanlike" attitude in business affairs brought a significant change in business tactics. But the change cannot be ascribed solely to a new outlook on the part of big-business men. Behind that new outlook was *a change in the market environment.*

We call this new kind of market situation *oligopoly,* meaning a market shared by a few sellers. Note that it is not *monopoly,* which is a market entirely served by one seller. Neither is it "pure competition," such as we envisaged when we first looked into the theory of a market economy.

What is the essential difference? We cannot investigate it thoroughly until Part Four, but the main points of the contrast are not difficult to grasp. Classical competition implies a situation in which there are so many firms (of roughly the same order of size) that no one of them by itself can directly influence market prices. This is the case—more or less—within much of the Periphery. In oligopoly, by way of contrast, the numbers of firms are few enough (or the disparity in size among the few large ones and the host of smaller ones is so great) that the large firms cannot help affecting the market situation. Here is the typical situation at the Center. As a result, whereas in classical competition firms must accept whatever prices the market thrusts upon them, in oligopolistic markets, prices can be "set," at least within limits, by the direct action of the leading firms.

In many of the most important industrial markets, as we have seen, it is oligopoly rather than pure competition that is the order of things today. In industry after industry, economies of large-scale production have brought about a situation in which a few large producers divide the market among themselves. Often these markets are dominated by one very large firm that serves as "price leader," raising or lowering its prices as general economic conditions warrant, and being followed up or down by everyone else in the field. U.S. Steel in the steel industry, General Motors in the auto field, Corn Products Refining in the cornstarch industry have more or less consistently "led" their industries in this fashion. By and large, as we would expect, these prices are considerably higher than the prices that a pure competitive market would enforce. General Motors, for instance, "targets" its prices to attain a 15 to 20 percent return after taxes, *calculating its costs on the assumption that it will use only 60 to 70 percent of its total plant capacity.* U.S. Steel sets its prices high enough so that it can earn a small profit *even if it operates only two days out of five.* In fact "target pricing" has come to be the established procedure for many leading manufacturing firms.[14]

Prices set by leading firms, rather than by the interplay of competition among many firms, are called *administered prices.* This does not mean that in each of these industries firms do not vie with one another. On the contrary, if you ask a General Motors or a U.S. Steel executive, he will tell you of vigorous competition. He may show you that Ford had edged out General Motors in such-and-such a line, or that Bethlehem Steel has cap-

[14] *Study of Administered Prices in the Steel Industry* and *Study of Administered Prices in the Automobile Industry,* Senate Report 1387, 85th Cong., 2nd sess.; see also R. F. Lanzillotti, "Pricing Objectives of Large Companies," *American Economic Review,* December 1958, pp. 921–40.

tured some of U.S. Steel's business. The point, however, is *that the competition among oligopolists typically utilizes every means except one: price cutting.* The tactics of lowering price to secure a rival's business is not regarded as "fair play," although once in a while it breaks out, just as it did in the days of cutthroat competition of the 1880s.* But what was common practice then is rare now. Competition among oligopolists today means winning business away from another by advertising, customer service, or product design—but not by "chiseling" on price. Everyone recognizes that it is to his advantage not to disturb the market. There have been few instances in steel, or oil, or automobiles, or chemicals, or cigarettes when out-and-out price "warfare" has taken the place of nonprice "competition."

CHALLENGE TO CONSUMER SOVEREIGNTY

Our inquiry has led us from the emergence of the giant corporation—a process that we have seen to be still going on—to a consideration of the change in corporate tactics within industrial markets. Now we must stand back a pace and once again look at the operation of the market system as a whole, seeking an answer to the questions we posed at the outset. What is the consequence of the giant corporation for American society? What are its effects on the operation of a market economy?

The second question is easier to cope with than the first. We will remember that a distinguishing feature of the market system was that the *power of control was vested in the consumer.* There were two aspects of this power. First, a market society enabled consumers to have the ultimate decision as to the allocation of the factors of production. *Their* desires arranged the productive pattern of society, not the desires of society's rulers, its keepers of traditions, or its producers. Second, the market society assured the consumer that he would be able to buy the output of society at the lowest price compatible with a continued flow of production. While producers might wish to make exorbitant profits from consumers, they would be prevented from doing so by the pressure of competition from other producers.

Does the consumer still exercise this economic sovereignty? In a general sense he does. If the consumer does not choose to buy the goods produced by giant concerns, those concerns have no choice but to curtail the production of those goods. For example, in the mid-1950s the Ford Motor Company poured nearly a quarter of a billion dollars into the production of a new car, the Edsel. The car was rejected by consumers, and after a few years its production was quietly discontinued. Familiar, too, is the effect of a swing in consumer tastes. From the mid-1950s on, imports of foreign

---

* On occasion, the administered prices in an oligopoly are maintained by out-and-out collusive agreement, which is strictly illegal. This was the case when General Electric, Westinghouse, and a number of smaller manufacturers were discovered in 1959 to be rigging prices and sharing the market for heavy electrical equipment. A number of top executives in the main concerns were sent to jail, heavy fines were imposed, and the purchasers of the equipment sued for triple damages. More frequently, however, oligopolistic prices are maintained simply by tacit consent.

sports and small cars rose steadily—from 57,000 vehicles in 1955 to 668,000 in 1959. With the exception of American Motors, the major car manufacturers insisted that the trend to compacts was only a fad and that Americans "wanted" bigger cars. But there was no brooking the contrary opinion of consumers themselves. Eventually, all the major manufacturers were *forced* into the production of small cars.

What then is the difference between this state of affairs and that of the "ideal" market system? One major difference lies in the fact that the great corporations today do not merely "fill" the wants of consumers. They themselves help to *create* these wants by massive efforts to interest the public in buying the products they manufacture. In 1969, for example, business spent some $20 billion on advertising its products—an expenditure two-thirds as large as our total expenditures for public elementary and secondary education. By way of contrast, in 1867 we spent only $50 million on advertising; and in 1900, only $542 million. So it is that while consumers still move the factors of production to satisfy their "wants," these wants are themselves increasingly influenced by the producers. In contrast to the ideal market where producers hasten at the beck of an imperious consumer demand, in the new market, consumers are to some extent themselves at the beck of an imperious producer demand.

We might note, for instance, that no sooner was the first small Ford placed on the market than the company announced a "luxury" small car, and this example was quickly followed by other producers. It may very well be that consumers prefer a large spectrum of sizes and shapes of automobiles. But it is difficult to square the original image of serving the consumers' uninfluenced wants with the process by which new models are designed and touted. We shall have a further word to say about this at the conclusion of our chapter.

PRESSURE ON PRICES

The second main attribute of the ideal market was that consumers' interests were satisfied as cheaply as possible because prices were forced down to the average cost of producing goods. Is this still true?

We have already seen that prices in oligopolistic industries are considerably higher than they would be under competitive conditions. Yet they are not wholly without controls. If a direct price struggle is conspicuously lacking within oligopolistic industries, there are other pressures that nonetheless enforce a certain degree of price discipline.

One of these pressures has been called by John Kenneth Galbraith "countervailing power."[15] By this, Galbraith means that in an oligopolistic world the opposition of interests across the market provides some compensation for the absence of a contest of interests on each side of the market. Today, powerful corporate sellers often face equally powerful corporate

---

[15] See John K. Galbraith, *American Capitalism, the Concept of Countervailing Power* (Boston: Houghton Mifflin, 1952), pp. 115ff.

buyers. The giant raw materials producer who faces little or no competition within his industry must sell to the giant chemical or other processing plant; the giant steel mill to the giant auto firm; the giant canner to the giant supermarket chain. Not least important, the large firm no longer bargains with the individual employee, but with large and powerful unions. This kind of neutralization of economic power does not hold true in every market nor in every situation, but, Galbraith contends, it is true in enough markets and in enough situations to constitute a powerful restraining force on the unhindered exercise of oligopolistic power.

A second restraining force is the competition among different *products.* Even if all steel prices are kept at "administered" levels, steel as a whole must compete with aluminum. Nor does the competition end here. What we find, indeed, is an immense chain of interproduct competition—steel against aluminum, aluminum against glass, glass against plastics, plastics against wood, wood against concrete, concrete against steel. And this competition is without doubt effective. Note that automobile engines are now made of cast aluminum as well as of steel; that buildings are now sheathed in glass as well as brick or concrete; that cooking utensils are made of glass as well as of aluminum; that drinking "glasses" are often made of plastic.

Thus prices are not *wholly* free from control. That does not mean that they are therefore adequately controlled. Oligopoly does not mean *arbitrarily* high prices, but it does mean a price structure considerably higher than those which a more competitive system might enjoy. "What few will question," writes Gardiner Means in a study of steel pricing, "is that the after-tax target rates of 16 and 20 percent and the actual earnings in excess of these targets are well above a competitive rate of return. Prices set to achieve these targets must involve substantial premiums over costs, taxes and a legitimate rate of return. To this extent, the public interest is not served. . . ."[16]

UNRESOLVED
PROBLEM OF
ECONOMIC
POWER

How shall we summarize this complicated situation with its pluses and minuses?

Without doubt, many of the aspects of a system of giant oligopoly are disquieting departures from the rationale of a market economy as the *servant* of the consumer. Yet is would be erroneous to conclude that the emergence of these new attributes is nothing but a threat to the market system. On the contrary, in part at least, they can also be seen as new functional mechanisms for the *support* of that system.

Take first the phenomenon of advertising and the manipulation of consumers' wants. This seems at first glance a direct assault upon a prime principle of the market system—the sovereignty of consumers' wants. Yet, before we jump to that conclusion, we must note that the wants themselves have changed. In the nineteenth century, consumer wants were essentially

[16] *Pricing Power and the Public Interest* (New York: Harper, 1962), p. 268.

focused on the basic requirements of simple existence: food, clothing, shelter. In the rich nation of the mid-twentieth century, however, these basic wants have been largely satisfied. Consumer demand is no longer driven to essentials, but hesitates before a whole range of possible luxuries and semiluxuries.

Thus the fact that producers can create and manipulate these wants testifies to the much more important fact that *the wants themselves are now amorphous and vague and susceptible to influence.* Curiously, then, we can view the rise of advertising as an attempt to introduce an orderliness and regularity of demand into a society where purely "spontaneous" demand would no longer firmly indicate which patterns of economic activity producers should follow.

In similar vein, we cannot conclude that the price-setting power of oligopolistic firms has no economic function. For the achievement of a certain market stability, which is the purpose of administered pricing, is not without its benefits to the economy. Indeed, a return to the uninhibited price competition of the nineteenth century might very well lead to a resumption of cutthroat tactics from which would emerge not a nicely balanced competitive market, but an array of triumphant monopolies.

And then, too, it has often been pointed out that the most "ideally" competitive industries, such as agriculture, are typically those which offer the worst wages and which display the least progressive economic characteristics. On the other hand, in those industries where oligopoly has permitted larger than competitive profits to accrue, we tend to find not only higher wages and more "social conscience," but the most forward-looking (and expensive) commitment to research and expansion. As Galbraith has written in a wry commentary on this situation: "The showpieces (of the economy) are, with rare exceptions, the industries which are dominated by a handful of large firms. The foreign visitor, brought to the United States . . . visits the same firms as do attorneys of the Department of Justice in their search for monopoly."[17]

Thus the changing market structure has its uses as well as its abuses. We must see in it not only a departure from the ideal market system, but also an attempt to find an accommodation within the real market system for a powerful new technology which impels all organizations—labor and government, as well as private industry—toward large-scale operations.* We must understand that if oligopoly undermines the market system in some regards, it strengthens it in others.

Beyond this mixed economic judgment, there are, however, other considerations that return us to the basic question of the relation between giant

---

[17] *American Capitalism, The Concept of Countervailing Power,* p. 96.

* We should note that the situation is not peculiar to America. In every industrial market society, a similar concentration of production has occurred. Studies of concentration in England, France, Italy, Japan, Canada, Holland, and Scandinavia reveal that in most cases it has proceeded further than in the United States. See Andrew Schonfield, *Modern Capitalism* (New York: Oxford University Press, 1965), p. 241 n.

business and society at large. For in the end, the strictly economic consequences of oligopoly may be less important than the social and political consequences of business giantism. The deliberate endless titillation of the consumer is not a pretty spectacle for those who see in man something more than a voracious consumer of goods. Neither is the emergence within a democratic society of a fortress of well-nigh impregnable economic power a wholly reassuring political sight. When we contemplate the enormous corporations of the Center in whose unsupervised hands rests so much of the economic future of this nation, we cannot but feel that here is a structure of power that is simply immune to our normal processes of community control. As Professor Berle has said, "Some of these corporations can be thought of only in somewhat the way we have heretofore thought of nations." Unlike nations, however, their power has not been rationalized in law, fully tested in practice, or well defined in philosophy. Unquestionably, the political and social influence of the great corporations poses problems with which capitalism will have to contend for many years to come. In Chapter 29, when we review our analytical exploration of the market mechanism, and again in Chapter 32, when we look into the multinational corporation, we will pursue this question a good deal further than we can now.

KEY CONCEPTS AND KEY WORDS

Concentration

1. A combination of aggressive entrepreneurship and the economies of scale typical of industrial technology brought about a *concentration of economic power* in many markets in the late nineteenth and early twentieth centuries.

Merger

2. The emergence of large firms with massive capital structures led to "cutthroat" competition that was exceedingly dangerous for the firms concerned. Hence there were *many attempts to stabilize the competitive struggle* by means of pools, trusts, holding companies, and mergers.

Antitrust

3. As the great trusts and combines rose to power, there was a "countervailing" thrust of political *antitrust legislation,* culminating in the Sherman Antitrust Act (1890), later in the Clayton Antitrust Act (1914), and in subsequent amendments designed to make mergers more difficult.

Internal growth

4. None of these laws prohibited or interfered with *internal growth.* As a result, large businesses continued to expand. A famous survey by Berle and Means in 1933 predicted that if the rate of growth of the top 200 nonfinancial corporations continued, they would soon own virtually the entire economy.

Conglomerates

5. This prediction has been partly borne out, especially in the recent rise of the *conglomerates*—enormous diversified corporations—that have dramatically increased the concentration of all manufacturing wealth held by the top 100 corporations. At the same time, the very diversification of these enterprises has precluded any marked change in concentration within industrial markets.

6. This stability within markets can be traced to several causes:
   - More effective *antitrust* legislation.
   - The *diffusion of corporate growth* into new, competitive markets.
   - The *bureaucratization* of business management.
   - The rise of *more stable market structures.*

7. We call the new market structures *oligopoly,* meaning few sellers. *The outstanding difference between oligopoly and traditional competition is that oligopolistic firms can set the levels of their prices more or less at their own discretion, whereas competitive firms have no alternative but to meet the "going" price of the market.*

8. The effect of oligopoly is twofold. First, it greatly *reduces the role of price competition.* Second, it opens the consumer to the *influence of advertising.*

9. The shift of power from consumer to producer is not total. Consumer tastes, however influenced, cannot be shaped at will or ignored. And *competition among products* still exercises an important restraint on firms.

10. The great corporation is at best only partially disciplined by the market. The presence of oligopoly poses *an unresolved problem* for capitalism.

Monopoly

Bureaucratization

Oligopoly

Stability of market structures

Q U E S T I O N S

1. Can you name the chief corporate executives of the top ten industrial firms in the U.S. (General Motors, Standard Oil of New Jersey, Ford, General Electric, Socony, U.S. Steel, Chrysler, Texaco, Gulf, Western Electric)? How many names of leading businessmen do you know? What does this suggest as to the character of business leadership today contrasted with the 1890s?

2. Why does heavy overhead cost lead to "cutthroat competition"? Why is this kind of competition dangerous?

3. Suppose Congress decided to foster a return to classical competition in the United States. What changes would have to be wrought in the American business scene? Do you think this is a practical possibility?

4. Compare the situation of a farmer selling fruit on a roadside stand and an executive of a large auto company selling a new model. How much latitude does each have in pricing his product?

5. Do you believe that tastes are ever created by advertising? Have your own been?

6. What do you consider to be the most desirable characteristic of bigness in business? The most undesirable?

7. Suppose you wanted to measure concentration in an industry. What attributes of the firms in that industry would interest you: their respective sales? their assets? their number of employees? Might different measures give different concentration ratios?

8. What are the important differences between "pure" competition and oligopoly as regards the position of the consumer? The producer? On net balance which do you think is preferable? Why?

In the preceding chapter we concentrated on important aspects of the developing industrial economy—the swift rise in productivity, the impact of mass production, the thickening texture of the market. But we purposely ignored one effect of technology which, in retrospect, towers over the others. This was the tremendous impetus it gave to the process of economic growth.

In Chapter 5, "The Industrial Revolution," we commented on the importance of technology for growth. Prior to that time, a chart of the well-being of the average person in Europe would have shown a distressingly horizontal profile, rising in some years or even centuries, falling in others, perhaps tilted slightly upward as a whole, but certainly displaying nothing like a steady year-by-year increase in the output of goods and services available per capita. Even with the initial introduction of the new technology we noted that the standard of living did not immediately improve. But starting in the third quarter of the nineteenth century, the accumulations of capital and the accretion of *expertise* began to display their hidden powers. In nearly every industrializing country, and most dramatically in the United States, the profile of economic well-being now began to show that steady and regular improvement that has become the very hallmark of modern economic times.

Figure 8-1 shows us the general path of this growth in the United States from the 1870s, when the process was in full swing, to 1929 when it reached a dramatic peak, to which we will shortly return. If we draw a line through the irregularly upward-moving graph to express the average rate of growth taking good years and bad together, we find it to be about 3.5 percent (with all price changes eliminated), which means that the total volume of output was doubling about every 22 years. Since the number of mouths was also doubling, although more slowly, *per capita* shares in this mounting volume of goods obviously grew more slowly. Roughly, we can estimate that individuals improved their lot at a rate of about $1\frac{1}{2}$ to 2 percent a year, doubling their real incomes every 40 years on the average. In Chapter 10 we will learn to interpret these growth figures with a certain caution. But there is no doubt that the period as a whole was one of unprecedented progress and improvement. How strange then that it should have ended in the greatest disaster in the history of the market system—one that very nearly spelled the end of capitalism and that permanently altered the system in ways that we must now learn about.

We in America today are nearer to the final triumph over poverty than ever before in the history of any land. The poorhouse is vanishing from among us. We have not yet reached the goal, but, given a chance ... we shall soon with the help of God be in sight of the day when poverty will be banished from this nation.

Thus spoke Herbert Hoover in November 1928, and indeed by 1929 the American economy had shown extraordinary progress. Population had grown from 76 million in 1900 to over 121 million, while ten years had been added to the expectation of life at birth for whites and thirteen for non-whites. To hold and feed and sustain its growing numbers, the nation had built up two new cities to a million each, five to over half a million, nearly 1,500 from rural to urban classification; $75 billion worth of homes, $9 billion worth of new farm structures; over $30 billion worth of new industrial equipment. Meanwhile, there were jobs for 48 million people—all save 3.2 percent of the labor force in 1929. Furthermore, these job holders had

FIG. 8•1 REAL GNP (1929 PRICES) AGGREGATE AND PER HEAD

seen average weekly hours of work in manufacturing drop from nearly 60 in 1900 to 44. Average hourly earnings rose from 20 cents in 1909 to 56 cents, while consumer prices lagged sufficiently behind to allow a rise in real wages of some 10 to 20 percent. It was not surprising, then, that an atmosphere of optimism gripped America in 1929 and that President Hoover's official words only reflected an informal sentiment throughout the nation.

Certainly few Americans suspected that a major economic calamity might be just around the corner. On the contrary, most people were concerned with quite another prospect of the American economy, and a highly attractive one. This was the great stock market boom—a boom which by 1929 had pulled perhaps 10,000,000 people into "the market," where they had the pleasure of watching their money painlessly and effortlessly grow. As Frederick Lewis Allen, the social historian of the Twenties, described it:

The rich man's chauffeur drove with his ears laid back to catch the news of an impending move in Bethlehem Steel; he held fifty shares himself on a twenty point margin. The window cleaner at the broker's office paused to watch the ticker, for he was thinking of converting his laboriously accumulated savings into a few shares of Simmons. Edwin Lefevre (an articulate reporter on the market at this time who could claim considerable personal experience) told of a broker's valet who made nearly a quarter of a million in the market, of a trained nurse who cleaned up thirty thousand following the tips given her by her grateful patients; and of a Wyoming cattleman, thirty miles from the nearest railroad, who bought or sold a thousand shares a day.[1]

It was, of course, admittedly speculative, and yet the risks seemed eminently justified. Someone who had put $1,000 each year, from 1921 on, into a group of representative stocks would have found himself worth over $6,000 in 1925, almost $9,000 in 1926, well over $11,000 in 1927, and an incredible $20,000 in 1928. And that was just the beginning: during June and July of 1929 industrial stock averages went up nearly as much as they had during the entire year of 1928, which had been, in its time, a year of unprecedented rise. By August 1929, the three-months' summer spurt had already outdistanced the entire 1928 rise. In those three months alone, an investor who had bought 100 shares of Westinghouse would have almost doubled his money; even a buyer of staid A.T.&T. would have been richer by a third. It seemed that everyone had but to beg or borrow money to buy shares in order to get rich.

THE GREAT CRASH

What pricked the bubble? No one knows exactly what final event was to blame. But when the boom did break, it was as if an enormous dam had suddenly crumbled. All the frenzy that had stretched out over two years in

[1] *Only Yesterday* (New York: Bantam, 1946), p. 349.

sending stocks up was concentrated in a few incredible weeks beating them down. On Tuesday, October 29, 1929 an avalanche of selling crushed the exchanges. On occasion there were *no* offers to buy stock at all—just to sell it. Goldman Sachs, a much sought-after investment trust, lost almost half its quoted value on this single day. By the end of the trading session (the ticker, lagging behind, stretched out the agony two-and-a-half hours longer than the actual market transactions) 16,410,000 shares of stock had been dumped. In a single day, the rise in values of the entire preceding year had been wiped out. A few weeks later, $30 billion of "wealth" had vanished in thin air. Millions who had counted their paper gains and thought themselves well off discovered they were poor.

The great crash is in itself a fascinating chapter in the "madness of crowds." At first it seemed unconnected with anything bigger. In fact, the early weeks after the crash were regularly marked with expressions of confidence: the general cliché of the day was that things were "fundamentally sound." Yet things were *not* fundamentally sound. The terrifying Crash ushered in the much more terrifying Depression.

Frederick Lewis Allen wrote:

It was an oddly invisible phenomenon, this Great Depression. If one observed closely, one might note that there were fewer people on the streets than in former years, that there were many untenanted shops, that beggars and panhandlers were much in evidence; one might see breadlines here and there, and "Hoovervilles" in vacant lots at the edge of town (groups of tar-paper shacks inhabited by homeless people); railroad trains were shorter, with fewer Pullmans; and there were many factory chimneys out of which no smoke was coming. But otherwise there was little to see. Great numbers of people were sitting home, trying to keep warm.[2]

However invisible to the casual observer, the Depression was far from being a mere figment of the imagination. To begin with, gross national product—the measure of the nation's total output—fell precipitously from $104 billion in 1929 to $56 billion in 1933. Almost one dollar's worth of final output out of every two simply disappeared. As a result, unemployment soared. In 1929, the unemployed had numbered 1.5 million. By 1933 the number had risen eightfold until *one person out of every four in the entire labor force was without a job.* In the nation as a whole, residential construction fell by 90 percent: there were virtually no houses built. Nine million savings accounts were lost as banks closed their doors. Eighty-five thousand businesses failed. In Pennsylvania in 1932, it was reported by the State Department of Labor that wages had fallen to 5 cents an hour in sawmills, 6 cents in brick and tile manufacturing, 7.5 cents in general contracting. In Tennessee, women in mills were paid as little as $2.39 for a 50-hour week. In Kentucky, miners ate the weeds that cows ate; in West Virginia, people

[2] *The Big Change* (New York: Harper, 1952), p. 248.

began to rob stores for food. In California, a child starved to death and was discovered to have been living on refuse.[3]

CAUSES OF THE DEPRESSION: SPECULATION

How did this tragedy come about?

An immediate, precipitating cause was, of course, the speculative fever that had engulfed the economy by 1929. The mania was not just confined to Wall Street. Throughout the nation, a get-rich-quick philosophy had destroyed normal business and banking caution. Foreign bonds of the most dubious validity were eagerly (and sometimes ruthlessly) pushed by the banks into investors' hands or, worse folly, put into their own portfolios.* In addition, huge pyramided structures of investment trusts and holding companies erected a house of cards atop the operating base of enterprise. For instance, Georgia Power & Light Company was controlled by the Seaboard Public Service Corporation, which was controlled by the Middle West Utilities Company, which was controlled by Insull Utility Investments, Inc., which was controlled by the Corporation Securities Company of Chicago (which was controlled, in turn, by Insull Utility Investments, which presumably *it* controlled). Of these companies, only one—Georgia Power—actually produced electricity. The rest produced only profits and speculative opportunities. And the Insull empire was only one of *twelve* holding companies that owned 75 percent of all the utility operating plants in the country.

All these manipulative activities helped to pave the way for the Depression. When the stock market finally crashed, it brought down with it an immense flimsy structure of credit. Individual investors who had borrowed to the hilt to buy securities had their stock sold out from under them to meet their indebtedness to brokers. Banks and financial institutions, loaded with dubious foreign bonds, were suddenly insolvent. Meanwhile, to compound the terrible panic, the monetary authorities pursued policies that unwittingly weakened the banking system still further.[4]

WEAKNESS ON THE FARM

In the vulnerability of an economy bound up with a rickety and speculative financial superstructure we have located one reason for the Great Depression—or, more specifically, one reason why the Wall Street Crash pulled down with it so much business activity. But we have far from exhausted the explanations for the Depression itself. For the Crash, after all,

[3] Arthur Schlesinger, Jr., *The Crisis of the Old Order* (Boston: Houghton Mifflin, 1957), pp. 249-50.

* Many of these deals were unsavory to the point of malfeasance. The son of the President of Peru, for instance, was paid $450,000 by the securities affiliate of the National City Bank for his services in connection with a $50 million bond issue which the bank's affiliate then floated for Peru. The President's son's "services" consisted almost entirely of an agreement not to block the deal. Eventually, of course, the bonds went into default. (John K. Galbraith, *The Great Crash, 1929.* Boston: Houghton Mifflin, 1955, p. 186.)

[4] See Milton Friedman and Anna Schwartz, *The Great Contraction* (Princeton, N.J.: Princeton University Press, 1965).

might have been no worse than many previous speculative disasters. Why was it protracted into a chronic and deep-rooted ailment?

The question turns our attention away from the spectacular misfortunes of 1929 to a consideration of the state of the economy as a whole in the years preceding the collapse. We have already characterized the first quarter of the twentieth century as a time of unprecedented expansion. Could it be, however, that behind the overall figures of rising output and incomes there were concealed pockets of trouble?

There was no question that one such worrisome sector existed. This was the farm sector, especially the all-important grains. All through the 1920s, the farmer was the "sick man" of the American economy. Each year saw more farmers going into tenantry, until by 1929 four out of ten farmers in the nation were no longer independent operators. Each year the farmer seemed to fall further behind the city dweller in terms of relative well-being. In 1910 the income per worker on the farm had been not quite 40 percent of the nonfarm worker; by 1930, it was just under 30 percent.

Part of this trouble on the farm, without question, stemmed from the difficult heritage of the past. Beset now by drought, now by the exploitation of powerful railroad and storage combines, now by his own penchant for land speculation, the farmer was proverbially an ailing member of the economy. In addition, the American farmers had been traditionally careless of the earth, indifferent to the technology of agriculture. Looking at the average individual farmer, one would have said that he was poor because he was unproductive. Between 1910 and 1920, for instance, while nonfarm output per worker rose by nearly 20 percent, output per farm worker actually fell. Between 1920 and 1930, farm productivity improved somewhat, but not nearly so fast as productivity off the farm. For the great majority of the nation's agricultural producers the trouble appeared to be that they could not grow or raise enough to make a decent living.

If we had looked at farming as a whole, however, a very different answer would have suggested itself. Suppose that farm productivity *had* kept pace with that of the nation. Would farm income as a whole have risen? The answer is disconcerting. The *demand* for farm products was quite unlike that for manufactured products generally. In the manufacturing sector, when productivity rose and costs accordingly fell, the cheaper prices of manufactured goods attracted vast new markets, as with the Ford car. Not so with farm products, however. When food prices fell, people did not tend to increase their actual consumption very greatly. Increases in over-all farm output resulted in much lower prices but not in larger cash receipts for the farmer. Faced with what is called an *inelastic demand*—a demand that does not respond in proportion to price changes—a flood of output only leaves sellers *worse* off than before, as we shall see in Chapter 23.

That is very much what happened during the 1920s. From 1915 to 1920, the farmer prospered because World War I greatly increased the demand for his product. Prices for farm output rose, and his cash receipts rose as well; in fact, they more than doubled. But when European farms resumed their output following the war, the American farmers' crops simply glutted the market. Although prices fell precipitously (40 percent in the single year 1920-1921), the purchases of farm products did not respond in anything like equal measure. As a result, the cash receipts of the farmer toppled almost as fast as prices. Meanwhile, his taxes were up by some 70 percent, and his mortgage payments and his cost of living in general had approximately doubled. Matters improved somewhat during the later 1920s but not enough to bring the crop farmers back to substantial prosperity.

There is a lesson here in economics as well as history. Had farmers constituted an oligopolistic market, the decline in farm income might have been limited. A few producers, facing an inelastic demand for their products, can see the sense in mutually curtailing output. Rather than flooding a market which does not want their product, they can agree, tacitly or otherwise, to hold back production to some amount which the market will absorb at a reasonable price. But the individual farmer is about as far from an oligopolist as one can imagine. When the price for his crop falls, it gains the individual farmer nothing to decrease his output. On the contrary, in his highly competitive situation, the best that he can do is to rush to sell as much as he can before things get worse—thereby unwittingly *making* things worse.

As its core, the trouble with the farm sector was that the market mechanism in this particular case did not yield a satisfactory result.* That might not have been so serious, had it not been for another development: while agriculture remained static and stagnant, the manufacturing sector was growing by leaps and bounds. Yet its growth was undermined because a fifth of the nation—the agricultural sector—was unable to match the growing volume of production with a growing volume of purchasing power. As the farmers' buying power lagged, it pulled down the demand for tractors, cars, gasoline and electric motors, and manufactured consumers' goods, generally. Weakness on the farm was thus symptomatic of a weakness throughout the economy, a failure of purchasing power across the whole lower stratum of the nation to keep up with the tempo of national industrial production.

WEAKNESS IN THE FACTORY   Most economists of the 1920s, as we have said, would have agreed that there was a source of potential trouble on the farm. Had we suggested that there might be another potential breeding ground for trouble in the factory

---

* In theory, we will remember (pp. 71-73) there was a cure for situations in which the producers of one commodity were undercompensated relative to other pursuits: producers would leave the undercompensated field for more lucrative occupations. Indeed, the American farmer tried this cure. It has been estimated that 20 farmers left the soil to seek city work for every urban worker who came to the land. Unfortunately, the cure did not work fast enough. While the agricultural sector steadily diminished in relative size, it could not shrink its absolute numbers significantly. From 1910 to 1930 approximately 10 million farmers remained "locked" on the farm, perhaps half of them barely contributing to national output beyond their own meager livelihoods.

or the mine, however, few would have given their assent. Most people's eyes, during the 1920s, were fixed on only one aspect of the industrial sector—production—and here there was surely little reason for complaint.

Yet had scrutiny penetrated a bit deeper, very serious signs might well have been spotted in this presumably most buoyant section of the economy. For while production was steadily rising, *employment* was not. In manufacturing, for example, physical output in 1929 was up 49 percent over 1920, while employment was precisely unchanged. In mining, output was up 43 percent, while employment had shrunk some 12 percent. In transportation and in the utility industry again output was higher—slightly in transportation, spectacularly in utility's electrical output—and again employment had actually declined.

Overall employment had not, of course, declined. It was significantly up in construction, in trade and finance, in the service industries, and in government. But note that all these employment-absorbing industries were characterized by one common denominator: they were all relatively devoid of technological advance. Or to put it the other way around, all the employment-static or declining industries were singularly characterized by rapid technological advance. In other words, pressing against the overall upward tendency of the economy was an undertow of *technological displacement.*

Heretofore in our frequent consideration of technology, we have never stopped to inquire what its effects might be on employment. Rather, we have implicitly assumed those effects to be positive, as we dwelt on the capacity of industrial technology to increase output. Yet it is not difficult to see that technology need not always be favorable for employment. When a new invention creates a new industry, such as the automobile, it is clear that its employment-creating effect can be enormous. Yet, even in such an instance there is an undertow, albeit a small one, as the growing automobile industry crowds out the old carriage industry. When we turn to inventions that do not create new *demands* but merely make an established industry more productive, it is clear that the initial impact of technical change can generate serious unemployment.

How are such technologically displaced workers re-employed? We will return to this question later in our chapter and again in more detail in Chapter 19. At this juncture, however, we want to examine still further the effect of rapid technological change in the "displacing industries" themselves, during the 1920s. And here we see an interesting fact. As production soared and employment sagged, the output per man-hour rose rapidly; in fact, between 1920 and 1929 it increased over 30 percent in transportation, over 40 percent in mining, and over 60 percent in manufacturing.* This much larger flow of production per hour meant that wages *could have* been raised substantially or prices cut sharply. But this is not what we find to have been the case. Only on the unionized railroads did wage rates rise (by about 5 percent). In mining, hourly earnings fell by nearly 20 percent, and

---

* These productivity indexes cannot be computed from our previous output and employment figures, since weekly hours changed. For the original figures, see *Historical Statistics,* Series W.

in manufacturing they remained steady. Since the hours of work per week were also declining, the average annual earnings of employees in these industries were far from keeping pace with the rise in their productivity. In mining, average yearly earnings fell from $1,700 to $1,481. In transportation and manufacturing, yearly earnings fell from 1920 through 1922 and did not regain 1920 levels until 1928 and 1929.

Thus the gains from higher productivity were not passed along to the industrial worker in terms of higher wages. Were they passed along via lower prices? Yes, to some extent. The overall cost of living between 1920 and 1929 fell by about 15 percent. Part of this reduction, as we have seen, was due to falling food prices. Nonfood goods fell sharply in price from 1920 postwar peaks to 1921; thereafter they, too, declined about about 15 percent up to 1929, but the fall was not enough to distribute all the gains from industrial technology. How do we know this? Because the *profits* of large manufacturing corporations soared between 1920 and 1929. From 1916 through 1925, profits for these companies had averaged around $730-odd million a year; from 1926 through 1929, they averaged $1,400 million. Indeed, in the year 1929, profits were triple those of 1920.[5]

MALDISTRIBUTION OF INCOME

Now we can generalize from what we have just discovered about the trend of wages and profits, to state one further reason for the sudden weakness which overcame the economy, beginning in 1929. Income was distributed in such a way as to make the system vulnerable to economic shocks.

This does *not* mean that somehow the American economy was failing to generate "enough" purchasing power to buy its own output. An economy always creates enough *potential* buying power to purchase what it has produced (for reasons we shall investigate very carefully in Chapters 11-12).

There can, however, be a very serious *maldistribution* of the income payments arising from production. For not all the proceeds arising from production may be placed in the hands of people who will *exercise* their purchasing power. Incomes paid out to the lower-paid strata of the labor force do, indeed, return to the stream of purchasing power, for the working-man tends to spend his wages quickly. But incomes which take the form of profits, or business accruals, or as very high individual compensations may not quickly turn over as purchasing power. Profits or high incomes may be saved. They may eventually return to the great stream of purchasing demand, but income which is saved does not "automatically" return via the route of consumption expenditure. Instead, it must find a different route—the route of investment, of capital-building.

Returning to the economy in 1929, we can now see as well what was perhaps the deepest-seated reason for its vulnerability: the fact that its income payments were not going in sufficient volume to those who would

[5] *Historical Statistics*, V, 236.

surely spend them. We have already understood why farmers and working men, who were indeed possessed of a "limitless" desire to consume, were pinched in their *ability* to buy. Now we must complete the picture by seeing how the failure to distribute the gains of productivity to the lower-income groups swelled the incomes of those who were potential *non*spenders.

TABLE 8 • 1

TOP INCOMES

PERCENTAGE SHARES OF TOTAL INCOME RECEIVED BY THE TOP
1 PERCENT AND TOP 5 PERCENT OF TOTAL POPULATION *

Year	Top 1 percent	Top 5 percent
1919	12.2	24.3
1923	13.1	27.1
1929	18.9	33.5

* The table shows the "disposable income variant": i.e., income after payment of taxes and receipt of capital gains.
Source: *Historical Statistics,* G135–6.

What we see here is an extraordinary, and steadily worsening, concentration of incomes. By 1929, the 15,000 families or individuals at the apex of the national pyramid, with incomes of $100,000 or more each, probably received as much income as 5 to 6 million families at the bottom of the pyramid. And more was involved here than just a matter of moral equity. It meant that the prosperity of the Twenties—and for the majority of the nation it *was* a prosperity of hitherto unequalled extent—in fact covered over an economic situation of grave potential weakness. For *if* the nation's on-going momentum should be checked, in this lopsided distribution of purchasing power lay a serious problem. So long as the high profits and salaries and dividends continued to be returned to the income stream, all was well. But what if they should not be?

CRITICAL
ROLE OF
CAPITAL
FORMATION

The question brings us to a critical relationship that has gradually been emerging throughout these pages as the central dynamic process in determining the level of activity in a market society. The relationship is that between the savings that a society desires to make on the one hand, and its opportunities for profitable investment, on the other. Much of the next section of this book—Part Three on macroeconomics—will be devoted to investigating that relationship in some detail. But we cannot explain the main events of the Great Depression unless we have a general grasp of the problem now.

Actually we have already understood half the saving-investment relationship. In our chapter on the industrial revolution we saw that saving was an indispensable prerequisite for capital formation. Now we must complete our understanding by adding the next step in the growth process. *Unless we make large enough capital expenditures to absorb our saving, we will not be able to keep the economy moving forward.* If saving is essential for investment, investment is essential for prosperity.

Indeed, because investment expenditure is the way we return savings to the income flow, we can see that the rate at which we add to our stock of capital equipment will have a deep effect on our over-all economic well-being. When spending for investment is sluggish, bad times are upon us. When spending for capital formation quickens, good times are again at hand. In other words, *the rate of capital formation is really the key to prosperity or recession.*

That does not yet tell us why the rate of capital expenditure should fluctuate. But a moment's reflection makes the answer clear enough. Spending for consumption purposes tends to be a reliable and steady process. Most consumer goods are quickly used up and must be replaced. The desire to maintain a given standard of living is not subject to sudden shifts or changes. As consumers, we are all to a considerable extent creatures of habit.

Not so with capital expenditures. Unlike consumer goods, most capital goods are durable and their replacement can therefore easily be postponed. Again in contrast to consumer goods, capital goods are not bought out of habit or for personal enjoyment. They are bought only because they are expected to yield a *profit* when put to use. We commonly hear it said that a new store, a new machine, or an additional stock of inventory must "pay for itself." And so it must. New investment increases output and that additional output must have a profitable sale. If for any reason a profit is not anticipated, the investment will not be made.

This enables us to see that the *expectation* of profit (which may be greater or less than profits actually being realized at the moment) plays a crucial role in the rate of capital formation. But why—and this is the last and obviously the key question—should a profit not be expected from a new investment good?

The answers all bring us back to our point of departure in the early 1930s. One answer may be that a speculative collapse, such as the Great Crash, destroys "confidence" or impairs financial integrity and leads to a period of retrenchment while financial affairs are put in order. Another reason may be that costs shoot up and monetary troubles impede the boom: the banks may become loaned up and money for new capital projects may suddenly become "tight" and dear. Still another reason may be that consumption expenditures are sluggish, owing perhaps to a maldistribution of income, such as that of the late 1920s, thereby discouraging plant expansion. Or the rate of population growth or of family formation may decline, bringing a slowdown in the demand for housing. Or the boom may simply die a "natural death"—that is, the wave of technological advance on which it rode may peter out, the great investments needed to build up a tremendous industry may be completed, and no second wave of equal capital-attracting magnitude may immediately rise to take its place.

Many of these reasons, as we have seen, served to bring capital formation to a halt in the Great Depression. The Crash itself, with its terrible blow to confidence and to the solvency of banks and holding companies, the weakness of the agricultural sector, the drag of technological displacement, and the maldistribution of income, all combined to bring about a virtual cessation of economic growth. The figures in Table 8-2 for gross private domestic investment—the proper nomenclature for private capital formation—tell their own grim story.

TABLE 8 • 2

GROSS PRIVATE
DOMESTIC
INVESTMENT

	BILLIONS OF CURRENT DOLLARS			
Year	Residential nonfarm construction	Other construction	Producers' durable equipment	Change in inventories
1929	$3.6	$5.1	$5.9	$+1.7
1932	.6	1.2	1.6	−2.6

Thus the Great Depression can be characterized essentially as a tremendous and long-lasting collapse in the rate of capital formation. In housing, in manufacturing plant and equipment, in commercial building, in the accumulation of inventories, a paralysis afflicted the economy. Between 1929 and 1933 investment goods output shrank by 88 percent in real terms—that is, after allowances for price changes. Although the capital goods industries employed only one-tenth of the total labor force in 1929, by 1933 one-third of total unemployment had been caused by the shrinkage of these critical industries.

Here is a major key to the Depression. But the trouble did not end there. When savings are not returned to active purchasing power because of inadequate investment, the fall in buying begins to spread. Let us say that a steelworker is laid off because of the slump in building. He will certainly pare his family's budget to the bone. But this in turn will create a further loss in income for the businesses where the steelworker's family ordinarily spent its income. Others will lose their jobs or have their wages reduced. In this way a kind of snowball effect, or to use the proper term, a *multiplier effect,* is brought about.

This helps us understand the mechanism of the Great Depression. As capital expenditures fell during the early 1930s, they pulled down consumption expenditures with them; and because of the multiplier effect, by an even larger amount than the fall in investment. From 1929 to 1933, consumption declined from $79 to $49 billion, nearly twice as large a drop as the absolute fall in investment. And the fall of consumption, in turn, pulled down still further the flow of capital expenditures.

To be sure, the process works the other way around, as well. When capital expenditures again begin to mount, consumption expenditures typically climb by an even larger amount. For example, President Truman pointed out in a radio address in 1949 that $1 billion of new public expenditures, which gave initial income to some 315,000 people, also added to the incomes of some 700,000 more. In expansion as well as in contraction, there is a typical *cumulative* pattern to economic activity, as success breeds further success, and failure breeds further failure.

Our brief excursion into the theory of economic fluctuations comes to an end at this point, to be pursued at much greater length in the macroeconomic portion of the text to follow. But the understanding we have gained enables us to see the Great Depression not only as an historical phenomenon, but as an instance of a more endemic problem of a market society. We have seen how that society paved the way for the Great Depression by its malfunctions in the 1920s. Now let us follow the struggles of the economy in the 1930s as it sought to escape from the deepest and most destructive depression it had ever known.

KEY CONCEPTS AND KEY WORDS

Growth

1. The outstanding economic fact of the hundred years prior to 1929 was the long trend of *economic growth*—a trend that doubled per capita incomes in the United States roughly every forty years and that brought U.S. prosperity in 1929 to unprecedented heights.

Depression

2. The long trend of growth came to a disastrous stop—for nearly a decade—with the advent of the *Great Depression.* The causes of the Depression were many:

Credit structure

Technological unemployment

   • A *speculative and shaky credit structure* that was demolished by the *stock market crash* of 1929, and by *inept monetary policy.*

   • A *steady deterioration of farm purchasing power* aggravated by the inelastic demand for farm products.

Distribution of income

   • A considerable undertow of *technological unemployment.*

   • A bad and *worsening distribution of income.*

Capital formation

3. The joint effect of these causes was a tremendous *collapse in capital formation.* Between 1929 and 1933 investment (in real terms) declined by 88 percent.

National income

4. A *fall in investment is a prime cause of a fall in national income,* because investment is the route over which savings return to the flow of national spending. When investment fails to return savings, recession begins.

5. Investment is thus a critical element in determining the level of prosperity. It is, however, a highly volatile element, since *investment spending depends on expected profits.* When expectations are not optimistic, new capital will not be built.

Investment spending

6. A relatively small decline in investment spending can spread through the economy. This is called the *multiplier effect.*

Multiplier

Q U E S T I O N S

1. Discuss the causes of the Great Depression in terms of what you know about the economy today. Do you think another Great Depression is possible? Another stock market crash?

2. Among the families you know, how many work for companies that provide goods or services for capital formation—that is, for investment purposes rather than for consumption?

3. Suppose that you were a businessman who intended to build a plant to turn out a promising new item—say, a pencil that would last twice as long as present kinds. What sorts of developments might discourage you from making this investment? How much would your final decision hinge on what you anticipated for the future, compared with what you knew to be the situation today?

4. How can the money you put into a savings bank get back into someone's hands as his income? The money you put into a newly-formed business? The money you put into insurance?

5. If your income (or your parents') was suddenly reduced to half, by how much would your expenditures fall? What sorts of businesses would be hit by your reduced spending? Would they in turn curtail their expenditures?

6. Why is investment so critical in determining the level of prosperity?

"This nation asks for action, and action now.... We must act and act quickly."

The words are from the inaugural address of the incoming President Franklin Delano Roosevelt. It is hard today to reconstruct the urgency, the sense of desperation, against which the words were addressed on March 4, 1933. A few hours before the actual inauguration ceremony, every bank in America had locked its doors. The monetary system was at the point of collapse. Nearly thirteen million Americans were without work. A veterans' march on Washington, 15,000 strong, in the previous year had been dispersed with tear gas, tanks, and bayonets. On the farms, mortgage-lifting parties, at which a noose was tactfully displayed, served as powerful deterrents to any representatives of insurance companies or banks who might be thinking of bidding in foreclosed land. Meanwhile, a parade of business leaders before the Senate Finance Committee had produced a depressing sense of impotence. Said the president of a great railroad: "The only way to beat the depression is to hit the bottom and then slowly build up." "I have no solution," said the president of one of New York's biggest banks. "I have no remedy in mind," testified the president of U.S. Steel. "Above all we must balance the budget," urged a long string of experts.[1] The crisis was a deep and genuine one; it is doubtful if the United States has ever stood closer to economic collapse and social violence.

THE NEW DEAL

The new President's response was immediate and vigorous: in the three months after Roosevelt's inauguration, writes Arthur Schlesinger, "Congress and the country were subjected to a presidential barrage of ideas and programs unlike anything known to American history." This was the famous Hundred Days of the New Deal—the days in which, half by design, half by accident, the foundation was laid for a new pattern of government

[1] Arthur Schlesinger, Jr., *The Crisis of the Old Order* (Boston: Houghton Mifflin, 1957), pp. 457-58.

relationship to the private economy, a pattern that was to spell a major change in the organization of American capitalism.

We begin to trace its general outline in the main measures of the Hundred Days. In all, some fifteen major bills were passed: the Emergency Banking Act, which reopened the banks under what amounted to government supervision; the establishment of the Civilian Conservation Corps to absorb at least some of the young unemployed; the Federal Emergency Relief Act to supplement the exhausted relief facilities of states and cities; the Emergency Farm Mortgage Act, which loaned four times as much to farmers in seven months as all federal loans in the previous four years; the Tennessee Valley Authority Act, setting up TVA, a wholly new venture into government enterprise; the Gass-Steagall Banking Act, divorcing commercial banks from their stock-and-bond floating activities and guaranteeing bank deposits; the first of the Securities Acts aimed at curbing stock speculation and reckless corporate pyramiding.

The Hundred Days only inaugurated the New Deal; it did not by any means complete it. Social Security, housing legislation, the National Recovery Act, the dissolution of public utility holding companies, the establishment of a Federal Housing Authority were yet to be passed. So was the Wagner Act. Indeed, it would not be until 1938 that the New Deal would be "completed" with the passage of the Fair Labor Standard Acts, establishing minimum wages and maximum hours and banning child employment for interstate commerce.

It would take us beyond the boundaries of our survey of general economic history to investigate the content of each of these important pieces of legislation, but we can gain an over-all view of the New Deal by summarizing its achievements against the backdrop of the problems and issues of economic history that we have already encountered. Then we can see that the New Deal is important as marking a genuine change in the development of the market economy itself. With its advent we begin to trace the evolution of a new kind of capitalism, different in significant ways from that which we have heretofore studied. We must understand the nature of this evolution if we are to bring our survey of general economic history to its contemporary terminus in our own society.

One general problem that confronted the New Deal, we have noted earlier in this chapter. It was the severe misfunction of the market mechanism in agriculture.

The problem, we will remember, arose in large part from two causes: the nature of the inelastic demand for farm products, and the highly competitive, "atomistic" structure of the agricultural market itself. The New Deal could not alter the first cause, the inelasticity of demand, for this arose from the nature of the consumers' desire for food. But it could change the condition of supply which hurled itself, self-destructively, against an unyielding demand. Hence, one of the earliest pieces of New Deal legislation—the Agricultural Adjustment Act—sought to establish machinery by which farmers, as a group, could accomplish what they could not as competitive individuals: curtailment of output.

The curtailment was sought by offering payments to farmers who agreed to cut back their acreage or in other ways hold down their output. In the first year of the act, there was no time to cut back acreage, so that every fourth row of growing cotton had to be plowed under, and six million pigs were slaughtered. In a nation still hungry and ill-clad, such a spectacle of waste aroused sardonic and bitter comment. And yet, if the program reflected an appalling inability of a society to handle its distribution problem, its attack on over-production was not without results. In both 1934 and 1935 more than thirty million acres were taken out of production in return for government payments of $1.1 billion. Farm prices rose as a result. Wheat, which had slumped to 38¢ a bushel in 1932, rose to $1.02 in 1936. Cotton doubled in price, hog prices tripled, and the net income of the American farmer climbed from the fearful low of $2.5 billion in 1932 to $5 billion in 1936.

We need not here retrace the many later developments in the agricultural programs of the New Deal and its successors. Suffice it rather to make the point that the *central idea* of the AAA has remained. Farmers' incomes no longer reflect the extreme fluctuations characteristic of an inelastic demand, but are cushioned by government payments earned by adhering to some form of crop limitation. The uncontrolled competitive struggle to market crops has given way to a continuing effort to achieve a balance between supply and demand by limiting supply itself.

Has the idea worked well? It might have, but for one thing. Belatedly, technology caught up with American agriculture. Starting in the years before World War II and continuing thereafter with accelerating effect, productivity on the farm began to soar—in fact, it rose faster than productivity in industry. Hence, despite the limitation of *acreage*, the actual output of *crops* increased steadily: between 1940 and the late 1960s, for instance, the amount of harvested acreage declined by 15 percent, but the yield per acre increased by *more than 70 percent.* The result was a flood of output, huge quantities of which had to be purchased and stored by the government under its support programs. Only the gradual distribution of these surpluses to the underdeveloped lands during the 1960s prevented the surplus problem from becoming a permanent national embarrassment.*

At best, the attempt to solve the farm problem has been but a partial success. It has not, for instance, succeeded in much improving the economic status of the million-and-a-half least productive small farmers, for these farmers are not able to raise enough crops to benefit substantially from crop supports. Nor has it succeeded in bringing about a sufficient reduction in farm output, so that the normal interplay of supply and demand would lift crop prices above their support levels and relieve the government of its purchase obligations.

Yet the attempt to improve the farm picture must not be brushed aside as ineffective. Without doubt, agriculture, as an income-producing activity, has benefited substantially—especially for the million-odd successful farmers who produce 90 percent of our marketed farm products. Between 1940 and 1964 the farm operator families enjoying the use of electricity increased from 33 percent to more than 95 percent; telephones increased from 25 percent to 76 percent; refrigerators from 15 percent to more than 90 percent. In the West, Midwest, and Northeast, the independent farm operator is today, as he was never before, at a close parity to the urban middle class in terms of living standards.

Our primary interest, however, is not to assess the relative success or failure of the farm programs from early New Deal days to the present. It is, rather, to note that all of the programs spelled a fundamental change in the role of the government in a market society. *The essence of that change was that the government sought to alter the structure of certain markets to allow the competitive process to produce socially acceptable results.*

For it was not only in the agricultural sector that the government tried to ameliorate the functioning of the competitive process. In the industrial sector, as well, a new policy of active intervention tried to bring about a better working of the economic mechanism.

In industry as in agriculture, during the first years of acute economic distress, intervention mainly took the form of an attempt to limit supply. Under the provisions of the National Industrial Recovery Act (NIRA) passed in 1933, business was permitted to make sweeping price-and-production agreements (in return for wage agreements designed to better the

---

* Actually, technology had been catching up with—and creating problems for—the farmer for a long time. One of the reasons for the overproduction of the 1920s was that we were steadily cutting back on the acreage needed to sustain horses and mules, as tractors came into general use. Before World War I, we used to devote over a quarter of our cropland to sustaining draft animals. After 1940, this fell to just over 10 percent. Much of the land not needed for animals went into production for the market, thereby adding its load of straw to the camel's back. I am indebted to Professor Eldon Weeks for this point.

incomes of the poorest paid). In other words, recovery was aimed at by legalizing the partial oligopolization of business.

The NIRA was greeted with great enthusiasm, and nearly 800 industrial "codes" were elaborated under it. But as the demoralized markets of the early 1930s regained some degree of orderliness, a new source of complaint arose. Smaller producers within many industries claimed that the codes favored the large producer. By the time the experiment was declared unconstitutional by the Supreme Court in 1935, it had already become apparent that the problem was not too much competition, but too little.

There arose a radical shift in policy signaled by the vigorous prosecution of the antitrust laws, a development we traced in Chapter 7. Yet, although the angle of attack had changed completely, the objective was much the same: *to make the market work.*

To what extent can the government make markets work? The answer, as we have seen, is far from clear-cut. Against the powerful forces of oligopoly on the one hand, and the self-defeating competition of "atomistic" industries on the other, the market-shaping powers of government may well prove to be inadequate. But in the formulation of the aim itself is evidence of a profoundly important change in the philosophy of the market society. No longer does laissez faire constitute the ideal relationship between government and economy. *Slowly there has arisen the conception of active public intervention to insure the orderly operation of the system.*

COUNTERING THE DEPRESSION

But the market system had broken down in a much more important way than was revealed in the farm glut or even in the troubles of the manufacturing sector. Its real collapse in the 1930s was its inability to solve the basic production problem itself—its inability to put together human beings, capital, and land, in order to produce a satisfactory level of output for the nation.

It is curious that the Roosevelt administration had little clear idea of how to remedy this situation when it first took office. Neither, as we have seen, did the business community. Indeed, for nearly everyone, economists included, the only "remedy" for the Depression was thought to be a balanced budget for the government.

Yet there were emergencies to be faced that could not be deferred, even if they unbalanced the budget. Many of the unemployed were literally at the brink of starvation, and the resources of private, state, and local charities were in most instances exhausted. President Roosevelt, unlike his predecessor, did not believe that the receipt of federal relief would "demoralize" the unemployed any more than the receipt of federal loans from the Reconstruction Finance Corporation had "demoralized" business. By May of the inaugural year, a relief organization had been established; and a year later, nearly one out of every seven Americans was receiving relief. In nine states, one out of five families—in one state one out of three families—was dependent on public support. Not that relief did much more than keep these unfortunate families from starvation—the average grant per family was less than $25 per month—but it did provide an economic floor, no matter how rickety.

The immediate aims of relief were humanitarian. Shortly, however, they were followed by thoughts of the *useful* possibilities of relief expenditures. Soon the great bulk of relief spending was being paid for public works of various sorts: schools, roads, parks, hospitals, slum clearance—and even federal art, theater, and writing projects.

As the public-works program grew, however, the finances of the federal government took a turn for the worse, until, by the mid-1930s, it was clear that something like a chronic deficit of $2 to $3 billion a year had been achieved. Each year the government spent more than it took in through taxes—not only for relief, but for conservation, farm subsidies, veterans' bonuses, public housing, aid to the states. To meet its bills it borrowed the necessary money from the public through the sale of government bonds to private individuals, to corporations, and to the commercial banks. Obviously, as the total amount of bonds outstanding grew each year, so did the total debt of the nation. In 1929, the national debt totaled $16.9 billion. By 1935 it had risen to $28.7 billion, and each year it steadily rose: to $36 billion in 1937, to $40 billion in 1939, to $42 billion in 1940.

At first the heavy spending of the federal government was greeted with wary acceptance by the business and banking communities as a necessary temporary expedient. Before long, however, even within the administration itself, the mounting deficit was regarded with considerable misgivings. The recurrent excess of government expenditure over tax receipts was thereupon apologized for as "pump priming"—as an injection of government fuel which would, so to speak, start up the stalled motor of private expenditures, making further injections unnecessary. Thus, a few billions of government spending, it was hoped, would set into motion an upward spiral of spending and job expansion by the business sector.

But the upward spiral did not materialize. After 1933, helped by government spending, *consumption* expenditures began to rise, but private capital expenditures lagged behind. Although they, too, improved after 1933, by 1938 they were still 40 percent below 1929.

Why did private investment fail to rise? The answer lies partly in the fact that the very government deficits that were supposed to cure the Depression only frightened business into a condition of economic paralysis that prolonged it. Coupled with the reform legislation of the New Deal, the new presence of government's large-scale economic activity caused business to lose its former "confidence." The businessman felt uncomfortable and ill-at-ease in a changing economic and political climate and was in no mood to plan ahead boldly for the future. The general outlook stressed caution rather than promise; cycles rather than growth; safety rather than gain. And then behind the psychological factors, real forces were also at work. A much slower rate of population growth in the 1930s depressed the important housing market. Even more serious, no major industry-creating technological breakthrough, comparable to the railway or the automobile, held sufficient promise of profitable growth to tempt private capital into a major capital-building boom of its own.

Thus, for many reasons, the new federal expenditures did not prime the pump. Private investment did not spontaneously rise to take over its traditional propulsive function, now "temporarily" carried out by the government. This did not mean, however, that the economic influence of government was therefore relegated to a minor role. On the contrary, the failure of pump priming—conceived as an emergency measure—caused a widening in the conception of the government's role. Government now began to be envisioned as a *permanent stabilizing and growth-promoting agency for the market economy as a whole.*

COMPENSATORY GOVERNMENT SPENDING

The idea was slow in taking form and did not, in fact, receive its full-dress exposition until the middle 1930s.* As is often the case with new ideas, it seemed at first complicated and difficult, and even among professional economists its basic concepts were the subject of murky discussion for a number of years. Yet in retrospect, it appears as a very simple argument.

The key to prosperity or depression, it had become increasingly evident, lay in the *total volume of expenditure* that a market society laid out for its goods and services. When that volume was high, employment and incomes were high; when it declined, output and employment declined as well. And what determined the volume of expenditure? As we have seen, the stream of consumption spending tended to be a passive factor, rising when individuals' incomes rose and diminishing when they fell. The volatile item, as both history and theory made clear, was the stream of capital expenditure.

From this starting point it is not difficult to take the next step. If lagging private capital expenditures were responsible for lagging employment and output, why could not the government step in to make up whatever deficiencies arose from private expenditure? There had always been, after all, a fairly regular flow of public expenditure, much of it for capital-creating purposes, such as roads or schools. Why could not this flow of public spending be deliberately enlarged when the occasion demanded, to maintain the needed total volume of expenditure? True, this required the government to borrow and spend and thereby increase its debt. But did not much private capital spending also result in corporate debts? And why could not the debt, itself, be handled as corporate debts which were never

---

* The most influential book setting forth the concept—albeit, in highly technical terms—was John Maynard Keynes' *General Theory of Employment, Interest and Money* published in 1936. Few books have roused such controversy or left so permanent a mark. We shall learn more about it, beginning with the next chapter.

"paid off" in the aggregate but refunded, with new bond issues being sold to take the place of those coming due?*

To the economists of the Roosevelt administration, the answers to these questions seemed plain enough. The government not only could, but should, use its spending powers as an economic instrumentality for securing full employment. By this, they did not have in mind a "radical" revision of capitalism. Rather, they envisaged the evolution of a new form of *guided* capitalism—a market society in which the all-important levels of employment and output would no longer be left to the vagaries of the market but would be protected against decline and stimulated toward growth by public action.

This was not how matters appeared to many members of the nation, however, and especially to the business community. They saw government spending as inherently "wasteful," and the mounting debt as evidence that we would spend ourselves into "bankruptcy." Beneath these arguments there lurked a deeper suspicion, a suspicion that government spending, whatever the protestations to the contrary, was the entering wedge for socialism or worse.

The controversy raged through 1940. But in a sense, it was an empty debate. At its peak, the annual deficit never touched $4 billion, and federal government purchases never contributed more than 6 percent to gross national product. Judged by the importance of government in the economy, probably no industrial nation in the world was *less* socialist than the United States. Yet, if the fears of the conservatives were hardly realistic, neither were the hopes of the liberals. For in the prevailing atmosphere of distrust, the remedy of government spending could never be more than half-heartedly applied. Deficit spending in the 1930s was a holding operation and not an operation of growth. By 1939, although conditions had improved considerably over the levels of 1932, there were still 9.5 million people—17 percent of the labor force—without work.

In the end, it was not theory that settled the history of compensatory government spending, but history that settled the theory. With the outbreak of World War II came a tremendous forced expansion in government outlays. Year by year, spending for war purposes rose, until in 1944 federal expenditures totaled just over $100 billion, and with this unprecedented rise in expenditure came an equally swift rise in GNP. By 1945, our gross national product had risen by 70 percent in real terms over 1939, and unemployment had dwindled to the vanishing point. The demonstration that public spending could indeed impel the economy forward—indeed, could lift it beyond all previously imagined bounds—was unmistakable. So was the

IMPACT OF THE WAR

* In Chap. 16, we will look very carefully into the arguments for and against deficit spending.

fact that a government could easily carry an enormously much larger debt, a debt that now towered over $250 billion, provided that its gross national product was also much larger.

And then, with the war had come a marked change in attitude both toward the government and to the economy in general. After four years of unprecedented effort, the American people looked to massive government action with a more accustomed eye; so, too, after four years of record output, they looked back upon the days of mass unemployment with a new feeling of shame. Perhaps most important of all, they looked ahead to the postwar period with considerable trepidation. Virtually every economist, contemplating the huge cutback in spending consequent upon a termination of hostilities, feared the rise of a vast new army of the unemployed. Even the most conservative opinion was uneasy at the political possibilities of such a return to the 1930s.

The upshot of the change in attitude was the passage of the Employment Act of 1946, one of the truly historic pieces of American economic legislation. The act recognized (although in carefully circumspect terms) that it was "the continuing policy and responsibility of the Federal Government ... to promote maximum employment, production, and purchasing power." It was, as we shall see, one thing to write such an act and another thing to implement it; but without question, the Employment Act marked the end of an era. The idea that the best thing the government could do to promote recovery was to do nothing, the belief that a balanced budget was in all cases the goal for government fiscal policy, and beyond that the trust in the blind forces of the market as inherently conducive to prosperity—all these once firmly held ideas of the past had been abandoned. The debate within capitalism was no longer whether or not government should undertake the responsibility for the overall functioning of the market system; only the specific means were questioned: how best to achieve that end.

AFTERMATH OF THE WAR: INFLATION

The war ended in 1945; within a year, federal spending dropped by $40 billion, and the nation waited tensely for the expected fall in employment, incomes, and prices.

Instead, it found itself confronting the least anticipated of all eventualities: a rousing inflationary boom. It is true that unemployment doubled, rising to two million, but this was still less than 4 percent of the labor force. Meanwhile, the number of people at work showed a steady rise: 54 million jobs in 1945; 57 million in 1946; 60 million in 1947; 63 million in 1950. Industrial production, after a brief postwar dip, was buoyant: by 1953 it would surpass its wartime peak with no sign of more than momentary turndown. Most striking of all was what happened to prices. Year by year, the cost of living rose: up a third between 1945 and 1948, up another 10 percent between 1948 and 1952, up still another 7 percent from then to 1957. In all, the purchasing power of the dollar declined by more than a third in the first twelve postwar years.

What was the cause of this totally unforeseen turn of events?

There was no one single cause, but several. To begin with, the end of the war found America in a situation of "classic" inflationary potential: too much money and too little goods. The too little goods was, of course, the result of four years of wartime shortage; the too much money was the result of having added $150 billion to liquid savings during those same years of high incomes and consumer scarcity. With the end of the war, Americans lost no time in entering upon a mammoth spending spree. In fact, it was this unexpected surge of consumption that was the main reason why the gloomy postwar economic forecasts were not fulfilled. Meanwhile, the nation's supply of money itself, in the form of bank deposits, was also high, owing to wartime financing. Banks and other credit institutions were all too happy to supply loans to consumers or corporations. Thus an enormous pressure of pent-up demand, financed out of past savings and current incomes, exerted its pressure on the price level.

A second reason for the inflationary boom was that spending was high in the nonconsumer areas. Government expenditures ceased falling in 1947 and sparked by rising state and local needs, began to increase again, augmented in 1950, when the Korean War added its fillip to federal expenditures. High exports and Marshall aid to Europe provided another stimulus. Perhaps more significant was that private capital expenditures proved themselves unexpectedly strong. Encouraged by the avalanche of consumer buying, by a host of new inventions and industries stemming from the war, by a new impetus toward research and development, the longest and steadiest period of capital accumulation in American history added its expenditures to the flow of purchasing power.

And then there was a third cause of the inflationary trend. In "pattern-setting" areas of industry, such as automobiles or steel, powerful unions succeeded in winning sharp wage increases. That, in itself, was not so unusual; but in these years of "easy money," there was nothing to prevent corporations from passing along the increases in terms of higher prices. What made matters still worse was that the wage increases (particularly in the mid-1950s) were often in excess of productivity increases, while the corporation price boosts (especially in the critical case of steel) were in excess of the wage boosts. Easy money, strong labor unions, and oligopolistic industry all combined to create inflationary pressure points at strategic locations of the economy.

This is by no means a full explanation of the inflationary problem from which America suffers, but we shall have to wait until we can examine the subject more analytically in Chapter 18, before we can go deeper into the matter. It is clear, however, that the nation faced a postwar situation very different from the one anticipated during the late 1930s by the fervent advocates of government spending. All through the 1950s it was the prob-

INSTRUMENTS OF POLICY

lem of inflation that occupied the authorities—and without much more success than had attended their efforts to curb mass unemployment twenty years earlier. Yet the confrontation with the problem of inflation was not without results; for out of the debate which it created, there emerged for the first time a general consensus on the nature of the mechanisms the government was entitled to use in seeking to affect the over-all operation of the system.

In our next section, on macroeconomics, we will look into these mechanisms in a technical way. Here, however, we need only to grasp the general nature of the three main devices of control.

The first were *monetary controls*, mainly centered in the Federal Reserve banking system. By easing or tightening the reserve requirements which all banks had to maintain behind their deposits, the Federal Reserve was able to encourage or discourage lending, the source of much economic activity. In addition, by buying or selling government bonds, the Federal Reserve was able to make the whole banking system relatively flushed with funds, when these were needed, or relatively short of funds when money seemed in excess supply.

The second were *tax adjustments*. The pressure of consumer buying during the postwar boom served as a reminder of the fact that the largest fraction of the volume of total expenditure was always consumption spending. By raising or lowering taxes, particularly income taxes, the government could quickly increase or diminish this broad flow of purchasing power.

The third was *the federal budget*. By the 1950s, the great debate over the virtues of a balanced government budget had virtually come to an end. Among academic groups and in a widening circle of business leaders, the budget was recognized as a tool for regulating total national expenditure. In inflationary times, a budget surplus would serve to "mop up" part of the inflationary purchasing flow. In depressed times, a budget deficit (covered by borrowing) was a mechanism for generating a desired increase in that flow.

The idea of monetary controls was not new, but the general consensus on the use of taxes and budgets as deliberate instruments of economic policy to counter boom and recession *was* new. Once again, as in the case with government spending, it was not the force of theoretical argument which had won this historic agreement. Rather, it was the fact of historic change which had placed theory in a new light. For essentially what commended the new means of influence over the market system were profound changes in the structure of that system. Let us see what those changes were.

REDISTRIBUTION
OF INCOME

In our concentration on the functional problems of the economy in its years of depression, war, and inflation, we have omitted one very significant development. This was a marked movement away from the extreme inequalities of reward which so vividly marked the capitalism of the past.

In part, this was brought about by a decline in unemployment, in part by aiding lower income groups through the support of trade unions, through the enactment of minimum wage floors, and through the passage of welfare legislation. The change was not entirely due to public policy, however. The occupational shifts which we noted at the commencement of our previous chapter also played a powerful role, as workers shifted out of low-paid agricultural and unskilled labor into the semiskilled and skilled categories of the factory.

However varied the causes, the results were striking.

TABLE 9•1

INCREASED
INCOME

PERCENT INCREASE IN PRE-TAX AVERAGE INCOME (1950 DOLLARS)

	1935–36 to 1962
Lowest fifth	120%
Second fifth	136
Third fifth	131
Fourth fifth	115
Highest fifth	74
Top 5 percent	47
All groups	98

Source: *Statistical Abstract*, 1965, p. 340.

Note in Table 9-1 that the lowest and second fifths benefited almost twice as much as the highest fifth and almost three times as much as the top 5 percent. While the bottom was moving up, owing to a variety of causes, the top was coming down—in large part owing to the pressure of higher tax rates. For beginning with the New Deal, then receiving an even stronger impetus from the war, stiffer tax schedules and stricter enforcement had borne down upon the relative affluence of upper income groups. Table 9-2 gives us some idea of the change.

TABLE 9•2

RELATIVE
AFFLUENCE

PERCENT SHARES OF TOTAL INCOME RECEIVED BY TOP 1 PERCENT AND TOP 5 PERCENT OF TOTAL POPULATION

	1929	1941	1946	1968
Top 1% (after tax)	19.1%	9.9%	7.7%	n.a.
Top 5% (before tax)	30.0	24.0	21.3	17.0

Source: *Historical Statistics*, G135, 105 (1929–1946). Figures for 1968 estimated from data, *Statistical Abstract*, 1970, p. 323.

What had happened was quite extraordinary. The share of income going to the top 1 percent had been cut by over 60 percent. That going to the top 5 percent had been cut by more than one third.

To be sure, we must exercise a good deal of caution in interpreting these figures. Without question they give evidence of a substantial improvement in the relative distribution of income in the United States since the lopsided days of the late 1920s. However we must not therefore leap to the conclusion that the existing distribution is "fair." Table 9-3 shows us the share of money income received by family units in 1960 and 1968. Note that the scales have begun to tilt slightly the other way and that the share of the top income group is beginning once again to rise faster than the bottom groups. Note as well that there has been virtually no change in the past eight to ten years; and that the top 10 percent of families get *thirty times* as much income as the bottom 10 percent.

TABLE 9•3

**SHARE OF
TOTAL INCOME BY
FAMILY UNITS**

Income rank	Percent of total income	
	1960	1968
Lowest tenth	1%	1%
Second tenth	3	3
Third tenth	5	4
Fourth tenth	7	6
Fifth tenth	8	8
Sixth tenth	9	9
Seventh tenth	11	11
Eighth tenth	13	13
Ninth tenth	16	15
Highest tenth	27	30

Source: *Statistical Abstract,* 1970, p. 323.

**INCOME
AND WEALTH**

Finally, two last and very important cautions. The official statistics of income distribution do not take into account very large flows of personal receipts that are legally exempted from classification as "income," such as stock options and expense accounts. We do not know the extent to which such legal (not to mention many illegal) ways of "smuggling" income reduce the reliability of the figures, but it may be by a very substantial amount.

Second, the data on incomes do not tell us about the distribution of *wealth*—bank accounts, home ownership, and above all, stocks and bonds. There is little evidence that wealth ownership has become less concentrated in the United States in recent years. For instance, it is estimated that the top 1 percent of all "spending units" own at least 65 percent of all corporate stock and that the wealthiest one-tenth of 1 percent own 35 percent of it—and here too concentration may be increasing.[2]

We shall have another opportunity, in Chapter 24, to examine these statistics of wealth and to comment on their influence on the distribution of income. At this juncture of our historic survey, however, that would be getting ahead of ourselves. For despite the remaining unfairness of income distribution, there is no doubt that a basic change has overtaken the economic profile of American society since the Great Depression. With all the misery that remains at the bottom of the nation and all the luxury at the top, what has emerged more and more clearly is a society in which "middle incomes" describes the facts and the psychology of the American people. In 1969 about 40 percent of all households received incomes of $10,000 or more before taxes, and 18 percent received over $15,000. If GNP grows at the rate of 4.3 percent for the next decade—a rate slightly higher than the historic trend, but by no means impossible of attainment—*40 percent of all families will be over the $15,000 mark (in terms of 1970 dollars) by 1980.*[3]

These present and projected realities go a long way in explaining the predominantly "middle-class" viewpoint of American society (and may help explain as well our indifference to the social neglect that penalizes those who are least fortunate in the competitive struggle for incomes). But in this chapter, where our main theme is the evolution of a new "guided" capitalism, it is important to stress that the *upward escalation of incomes has also provided the government with a new and powerful means of economic influence.* As Table 9-4 shows, the upward shift in the economic center of gravity of the nation has brought about a situation in which, for the first time, a change in income taxes can directly affect *mass* purchasing power.

TABLE 9 • 4

IMPACT OF INDIVIDUAL INCOME TAXES

Year	Number of individual returns (millions)	Total income tax paid ($ billions)	Total income tax as % of total consumption	Income tax liability of median family ($)
1929	2.5	$ 1.0	1%	$ 17
1940	7.4	1.4	2	101(1941)
1968	73.4	76.6	14	1,044

Source: *Statistical Abstract,* 1970, p. 387, *Historical Statistics,* Series Y 292, 299, 303, 307.

[2] See F. Lundberg, *The Rich and the Super Rich* (New York: Lyle Stuart, 1968), pp. 15ff., and supporting citations.

[3] *Fortune* Magazine (February 1971), p. 80.

The redistribution of income thus provides us with an understanding of why tax policy has become such a potent new instrument of economic manipulation. An insight into the second of our new instruments—fiscal policy, or the use of the government's budget—is provided if we examine another structural alteration in the economy: the change in the relative size of the government contribution to gross national product. Table 9-5 gives us the magnitude of the change.

TABLE 9•5

**GROWTH
OF THE
PUBLIC SECTOR
(current dollars)**

Year	GNP (billions)	Gov't. purchases of goods and services (billions)		All gov't. purchases as percent of GNP
		Federal	State & local	
1929	$104.4	$ 1.3	$ 7.2	8.1%
1940	100.6	6.2	7.9	14.0
1970	976.5	99.7	120.9	22.5

Source: *Historical Statistics,* Series F, 67, 81, 86; *Economic Indicators.*

It is clear from the table that a major shift has taken place. Whereas in 1929 less than one dollar in ten of national production owed its origin to government purchasing, today about one dollar in five of all goods and services produced is sold to some branch of the government.

What has accounted for this striking shift? Three-quarters of the rise in *federal* expenditures is due solely to the growth of the military subeconomy, whose economic significance we will examine in Chapter 16. But a second look at the table reveals that the growth of the public sector is by no means entirely a matter of federal spending. State and local expenditures have also grown enormously. In fact, federal nonwar expenditures plus state and local expenditures amount to about double the fraction of GNP represented by these public expenditures in 1929.

What lies behind this rise in the public sector? The cause of the growth of the armaments economy is the Cold War—a problem we will examine in our final chapter. As for the growth of the nonwar public sector, this is a phenomenon we find in all industrialized countries. It stems in part from the increase in population that has steadily spurred the growth of huge urban complexes; in part from a widening government concern with education and welfare; in part from the omnipresent automobile with its necessary road systems and supervisory personnel. Perhaps ultimately the cause is the growing dependence of man on man, of which we spoke in Chapter 6—a dependence in turn traceable to the relentless entrance of a technology that both heightens the collective productivity of man and intensifies his helplessness as an individual.

But at this juncture we are not as interested in tracing the reasons for the rise of the public sector, as we are in bringing home its consequences. For in the evolution of a guided, rather than laissez-faire capitalism, the growth of public economic activity, whether for war or peace, brought a signal change to the economy. It has meant that today the government is in a position of such commanding economic strength that it cannot *avoid* influencing the trend of total expenditure, even by relatively modest changes in its budgetary balance. For example, a 10 percent fall in government receipts and a 10 percent rise in expenditures will add to total GNP expenditures an amount equal to one-and-a-half times all manufacturing investment; in 1929, a similar change in the budget position would have contributed new purchasing power equal to much less than one-half of all manufacturing investment.

Does the existence of these government "stabilizers" and the general consensus on the mechanisms of influence mean that economic fluctuations such as the Great Depression cannot recur?

It is certainly unlikely in the extreme that the terrible experience of the early 1930s will be repeated. Many of its causes, as we noted, were rooted in particular excesses of the times, and these, to a very large extent, have been corrected. The flimsiness of the credit structure, the vulnerability of the banks—and perhaps most important of all, the barrier of inadequate economic understanding—have all been removed or much improved. Although history teaches us the virtues of caution in announcements of this kind, it seems fair to state that we now understand, as we never did before, the economic policies required to avoid or cure severe economic depressions.

In this regard the Kennedy tax cut proposed in 1962 is an interesting example of the New Economics in action. There had been a mild recession in 1960 from which the nation had not fully recovered by mid-1962, and President Kennedy's advisers were much concerned about the mounting level of unemployment in the country at large. To cure this unemployment, all agreed, the economy's rate of growth would have to increase, and this in turn required a major economic stimulus. But where was the stimulus to come from? Relying on the New Economics, the President's advisers recommended that taxes be cut across the board, despite mounting federal expenditures, so that a "deficit" in the nation's budget would be *deliberately* incurred.

As was to be expected, voices of disaster were raised. "At the heart of our national finances," declared Representative Cannon, then Chairman of the House Appropriations Committee, "is a simple inescapable fact, easily grasped by anyone. It is that our government—any government—like individuals and families—cannot spend and continue to spend more than they take in without inviting disaster."

What Representative Cannon did not seem to grasp, however, was that the government was not proposing to spend more than it took in. It was proposing to spend more than it took in *in taxes, borrowing the rest from the nation's savings.* This was an operation that was, economically speaking, in no way different from the nation's business sector which in a normal year of growth took in, in sales, less than it spent for its running expenses plus its capital investments, and which regularly borrowed the difference.

Thus at its core the so-called New Economics proposed that the government be considered not as an individual "household," but as a full economic *sector,* no different from the business sector in its operation, except that it was subject to deliberate public control and could thus be used to help move the economy in a desired direction. This is a central aspect of modern economic policy to which we will turn in detail in Part Three.

After much debate, the controversial tax cut was finally passed in early 1964. Was it a success? As is often the case in economics, we cannot produce laboratory proof. Certainly the economy responded vigorously and unemployment fell after the tax cut. But by then other factors were also at work, including higher spending for the Vietnam war. Indeed, by the end of 1965, spending on Vietnam had already strained the economy to the point that the President's advisers recommended a tax *increase* to dampen inflationary pressures.

Hence we can only say that economists *think* the New Economics works. Perhaps more important, it is increasingly clear that business thinks so too and bases its plans on the assumption that government will no longer "let" depressions go unchecked. It is perhaps too early to be absolutely certain that the suspicions and misunderstandings of the 1930s have been overcome. Yet it seems likely that the graduates of the colleges and business schools who now play an important part in the direction of corporate affairs are not so likely to be panicked by government action to cure a slump as were their fathers thirty years ago. There is a hypothesis that should cheer the despairing instructor of economics!

REMAINING PROBLEMS

This general reassurance should not lead us to the easy assumption that economic fluctuations of considerable severity and unemployment of uncomfortable magnitude are not still possibilities. The basic cause of instability in the market system remains; and so long as anticipated profit is the critical link between savings and investment, it will continue to remain. Irregular bursts of capital formation and recurrent downward revisions of profit anticipations are virtually inseparable from an economic system in which the process of technical change and its conversion into real capital are left to the unguided impulses of individual business firms.

Yet, we now possess powerful instruments of economic compensation against the *cumulative effects* of these shocks—protections we have never enjoyed (or understood) before. To be sure, the mere existence of these instruments does not guarantee that they will, in fact, be used. Lingering fears of an unbalanced budget may delay or even prevent the use of compensatory government expenditure. Then, too, nearly half our present total government expenditure (and 85 percent of our *federal* expenditure) goes for defense purposes. The effective use of a compensatory mechanism in a truly *peacetime* economy might be much more difficult than in an economy where a large defense sector offers a politically acceptable area for public spending. Finally, we must remember that the New Economics is designed to be an instrument of restraint as well as one of stimulus—that it is meant to be used against inflation as well as recession. Recently we have been discovering that to translate restraint into effective political action may be much more difficult than we had thought. The New Economics is no panacea against the old politics, if it calls for unpopular measures like raising taxes.

Nevertheless, there can be no doubting the change since the early days of the New Deal with which we began this chapter. However difficult to control or disconcerting to predict, something like a "guided" system has emerged. The great central problem of capitalism, which threatened the very existence of the system in the dark days of the 1930s, can be considered essentially solved.

Does that mean that capitalism is therefore secure—that its place in history will remain unchanged and unchallenged for many years? The panorama with which we began in Chapter 1 should be enough to make it clear that no such conclusion can be drawn. If the problem of deep depression has been more or less effectively diagnosed and strong remedies concocted, new problems of no less severity have risen to take its place. Social neglect, the stubborn continuance of poverty amid a growing general affluence, the growth of an arms subeconomy, the problem of pollution, the ghetto—to mention only some of the issues that agitate our times—are far from solved and pose dangers perhaps as grave as depression itself.

But are these new problems at least understood? That question serves well as an introduction to the next stage of our journey. Our long review of economic history has given us a sense of the main outlines of the development of our system. Now we need to leave history for a more careful analytical examination of exactly how the system works—and of why and where it does not work. Hence we turn now, at the point where history becomes big with the present to a much more detailed examination of the economic mechanism itself. Our study of economic history has prepared us for an understanding that only economic theory can now provide.

New Deal

1. *The New Deal* was a major effort to reverse the downward spiral of the Great Depression. A many-pronged attack, it sought both to correct the failures of the economy, and to strengthen its workings.

2. The New Deal *interfered with the structure of markets* to a greater extent than had been tried by an American government before. Not only agricultural, but many industrial markets were regulated in an effort to bring about an orderly economic recovery. Although many of these efforts failed or were declared unconstitutional, the heritage of the New Deal has been a new concept of *government intervention* and an effective end to the philosophy of laissez faire.

Pump-priming

3. The most important of the New Deal policies was the deliberate initiation of *government spending,* first for relief, then for public works, as a means of stimulating private investment—so-called priming the pump. Owing to the small scale of the public spending and the prevailing business attitude of fear and suspicion to government intervention, the pump priming did not work.

Compensatory government spending

4. Out of the New Deal experience evolved a new conception of how the economy operated, and of how government might counteract depression. The key was now recognized to be the *total volume of expenditure.* And the new conception urged that whenever private expenditure was insufficient to maintain full employment, the government should add *compensatory spending* of its own.

Employment Act of 1946

5. The war provided convincing evidence that public expenditure could indeed bring about a high level of employment and output. After the war, the *Employment Act of 1946* recognized the role of the government in promoting "maximum employment."

Fiscal policy

6. Postwar experience brought inflation, rather than the generally expected recession. But the period also saw the formulation of a general consensus on the tools of the *New Economics:*

Monetary controls

   • *Monetary controls* to encourage or discourage private spending.
   • *Tax adjustments* to induce or to dampen consumer and business spending.

Federal budget

   • The use of the *federal budget* as a balance wheel in the economy.

Public sector

7. These new tools were made more workable by a considerable *redistribution of income* that had taken place and by *the enlargement of the public sector.*

8. The New Economics is by no means a cure for all economic ills, but it does hold the promise of *greater economic stability* than in the past.

QUESTIONS

1. What do you think is the prevailing attitude of big businessmen to government today? Of little businessmen? Farmers? Students?

2. "Even if the Hoover administration had wanted to take a more active role in combatting the Depression, it would have been difficult in those times for it to do so." Why?

3. Do you consider inflation to be as dangerous a condition as depression?

4. The farm problem will always be difficult to solve as long as agriculture is a highly competitive industry, faced with an inelastic demand and with a technology that continuously increases productivity. Explain why.

5. Do you think that all government spending is wasteful? Some? All private spending? Some? How does one measure "waste"?

6. In what ways has history provided the testing ground for the theory of government spending? Was the war such a test? Was it conclusive? What would invalidate the theory that government spending can properly supplement private investment to cure a depression?

Prosperity

and recession—

the economics

of the

macro system

What does it mean to move from an emphasis on history to one of theory? Perhaps we can explain the change in our perspective by saying that we are now using an X-ray rather than a camera. Our purpose is no longer to construct a narrative that explains the present in terms of the past, but to penetrate beneath the "story" of events to processes and relationships that only a knowledge of macroeconomic theory will reveal.

Through our study of the Great Depression and its consequences, we are, in a sense, familiar with the broad outlines of macroeconomics. Prosperity and recession, inflation and deflation, unemployment and growth are the great problems of macroeconomic inquiry, and we learned a good deal about them in Chapters 8 and 9, when we followed the development of modern capitalism. Yet, as we shall see, there is much more to learn before we understand the causes of the phenomena that interest us. That is what we shall set out to do in the pages that follow.

THE MACROECONOMIC PERSPECTIVE

But what is "macroeconomics"? The word derives from the Greek *macro* meaning "big," and the implication is therefore that it is concerned with bigger problems than in microeconomics (*micro* = small). Yet as we shall see in Part Four, microeconomics wrestles with problems that are quite as large as those of macroeconomics. The difference is really not one of scale. It is one of approach, of original angle of incidence. *Macroeconomics begins from a viewpoint that initially draws our attention to aggregate economic phenomena and processes,* such as gross national product or saving and investment. Microeconomics begins from a vantage point that first directs our analysis to the individual constituents of economic behavior, mainly the actions of individuals and firms. Both views, as we shall see by the end of Part Four, are needed to comprehend the economy as a whole, just as it takes two different lenses to make a stereophoto jump into the round. But we can learn only one view at a time, and it is well to begin with the exciting spectacle of the entire national economy as it unfolds to the macroscopic gaze.

What does the economy look like from this perspective? The view is not unlike that from a plane. What we see first is the fundamental tableau of nature—the fields and forests, lakes and seas, with their inherent riches; then the diverse artifacts of man—the cities and towns, the road and rail networks, the factories and machines, the stocks of half-completed or unsold goods; and finally the human actors themselves with all their skills and talents, their energies, their social organization.

Thus our perspective shows us a vast panorama from which we single out for our special attention those elements and activities having to do with our worldly well-being, with our capacity to provide ourselves with the necessaries and luxuries of material life. It need hardly be said that this is at best only a partial view of society. An economist does not examine the flux of social goings-on, the quality of intellectual life, the spirituality or crassness of a community. Initially, at any rate, he concerns himself with only those aspects of society that bear on its *material provisioning,* and even here he often limits himself to things that he can measure in some fairly objective way.

National Wealth

Let us, then, begin to set our first economic impressions in order by directing our attention to an attribute of the landscape below us that is clearly important in the provisioning process, and that should be subject to roughly accurate measurement—our national wealth. By our wealth, we mean the very objects—or at least many of them—that have already caught our eye. Table 10-1 is the most recent estimate made of the national wealth of the United States for the year 1967.

Let us note immediately that this is not a full valuation of the riches of our society. No monetary worth is put on our human skills or even on the

TABLE 10·1

U.S. NATIONAL WEALTH 1967 VALUE

Billions of dollars, rounded

Structures	
Residential	$ 721
Business	373
Government	347
Equipment	
Producers (machines, factories, etc.)	331
Consumers durables (autos, appliances)	325
Inventories, business	206
Monetary gold and silver	17
Land	
Farm	147
Residential	136
Business	105
Public	62
Net foreign assets	**54**
Total	**2828**

Rather than encumber each table with sources that are, for the most part, identical, I have added the source only if the figures might be difficult to find or if they are the result of considerable arithmetical manipulation. All unidentified figures will be found in one or more of the following basic sourcebooks: *Historical Statistics of the United States* and *Statistical Abstract of the United States,* 1970, both published by the Bureau of the Census, Washington, D.C., and the National Income and Product Tables reported in *Survey of Current Business,* Department of Commerce, and in *Economic Indicators,* Joint Economic Committee.

presence of so many head of population. Nor does this table pretend to embrace, much less measure, all our material possessions. Such immense economic treasures as the contents of the Library of Congress or the Patent Office cannot be accurately valued. Nor can works of art, nor military equipment—neither of which is included in the total. Much of our public land is valued at only nominal amounts. Hence at best this is the roughest of estimates. Nonetheless, it gives us an idea of the magnitude of the economic endowment that we have at our disposal.

It would perhaps be a much more meaningful idea if we could now compare our own national wealth with that of a poor nation, such as India, or more precisely, compare the *per capita* value of our wealth—that is, the share of our wealth that is available to each of us—to the *per capita* wealth of India. Alas, as is so often the case with the less developed countries, these measurements do not exist for India. But a few statistics that are available (Fig. 10-1) give us a glimmering of what such a comparison might show.

It is clear enough that if we could total up all the items in both nations, the scales would tilt overwhelmingly in favor of the United States. That this has an immense significance for the relative well-being of the two countries

Per 1,000 people

Rooms, residential — U.S. 1430 / India 340

Motor vehicles in use — U.S. 422 / India 1

■ U.S.
■ India

Telephones — U.S. 430 / India 1

Radios — U.S. 944 / India 5

Years vary; see source: Statistical Abstract, 1967.

FIG. 10•1 COMPARATIVE WEALTH OF INDIA AND THE UNITED STATES, RECENT YEARS

is apparent. However, let us defer a consideration of exactly what that significance is, until we look a little more closely into the nature of national wealth itself.

One portion of the endowment of a nation's wealth has a special significance. This is its national *capital*—the portion of its productive wealth that is *man-made* and therefore *reproducible.* If we look back at the table, we can see that our own national capital in 1967 consisted of the sum total of all our structures, our producers' equipment and our consumer durables, our inventories, our monetary gold and silver, and our foreign assets—$2378 billions in all.

We can think of this national capital as consisting of whatever has been preserved out of the sum total of everything that has ever been produced from the very beginning of the economic history of the United States up to a certain date—here December 31, 1967. Some of that capital—inventories for example—might be used up the very next day. On the other hand, inventories might also be increased. In fact, our national capital changes from date to date, as we do add to our inventories or to our stocks of equipment or structures, etc., or, more rarely, as we consume them and do not replace them. But at any date, our capital still represents *all that the nation has produced*—yesterday or a century ago—*and that it has not used up or destroyed.*

The reason that we identify our national capital within the larger frame of our wealth is that it is constantly changing and usually growing. Not that a nation's inheritance of natural resources is unimportant; indeed, the ability of a people to build capital depends to no small degree on the bounties or obstacles offered by its geography and geology—think of the economic

CAPITAL

limitations imposed by desert and ice on the Bedouin and the Eskimo. But the point in singling out our capital is that it represents the portion of our total national endowment over which we have the most immediate control. As we shall later see, much of a nation's current economic fortunes is intimately related to the rate at which it is adding to its capital wealth.

WEALTH AND CLAIMS

There remains to be noted one more thing before we leave the subject of wealth. In our table of national wealth, two items are missing that would be the very first to be counted in an inventory of our personal wealth: our bank accounts and our financial assets, such as stocks or bonds or deeds or mortgages. Why are these all-important items of personal wealth excluded from our summary of national wealth?

The answer to this seeming paradox is not hard to find. We have already counted the *things*—the houses, factories, machines, etc.,—that constitute the real assets behind stocks, bonds, deeds, and the like. Indeed these certificates tell us only who *owns* the various items of our national capital. Stocks and bonds and mortgages and deeds are *claims* on assets, but they are not those assets in themselves. The reality of General Motors is its physical plant and its going organization, not the shares of stock that organization has issued. If by some curious mischance all its shares disintegrated, General Motors would still be there; but if the plants and the organization disintegrated instead, the shares would not magically constitute for us another enterprise.

So, too, with our bank accounts. The dollars we spend or hold in our accounts are part of our personal wealth only insofar as they command goods or services. The value of coin or currency as "objects" is much less than their official and legal value as money. But most of the goods over which our money exerts its claims (although not, it must be admitted, the services it also buys) are already on our balance sheet. To count our money as part of national wealth would thus be to count a claim as if it were an asset, much as in the case of stocks and bonds.

Why, then, do we have an item for monetary gold and silver (mainly gold) in our table of national wealth? The answer is that under existing international arrangements, foreigners will accept gold in exchange for their own real assets (whereas they are not bound to accept our dollar bills) and that, therefore, monetary gold gives us a claim against *foreign* wealth.* In much the same way, the item of *net foreign assets* represents the value of all real assets located abroad that are owned by U.S. citizens, less the value of any real wealth located in the United States and owned by foreigners.

Thus we reach a very important final conclusion. *National wealth is not quite the same thing as the sum of personal wealth.* When we add up our

---

* Gold has, of course, a value in itself—we can use it for jewelry and for dentistry. However, in the balance sheet of our national wealth, we value the gold at its international exchange price, rather than merely as a commodity.

individual wealth, we include first of all our holdings of money or stocks or bonds—all items that are excluded from our national register of wealth. The difference is that as individuals we properly consider our own wealth to be the *claims* we have against one another, whereas as a society we consider our wealth to be the stock of material *assets* we possess, and the only claims we consider are those that we may have against other societies. National wealth is thus a *real* phenomenon, the tangible consequence of past production. Financial wealth, on the other hand—the form in which individuals hold their wealth—is only the way the claims of ownership are established vis-à-vis the underlying real assets of the community. The contrast between the underlying, slow-changing reality of national wealth and the overlying, sometimes fast-changing financial representation of that wealth is one of the differences between economic life viewed from the vantage point of the economist and that same life seen through the eyes of a participant in the process. We shall encounter many more such contrasts as our study proceeds.

The Flow of Production

But why is national wealth so important? Exactly what is the connection between the wealth of nations and the well-being of their citizens?

The question is not an idle one, for the connection between wealth and well-being is not a matter of direct physical cause and effect. After all, India has the largest inventory of livestock in the world, but its contribution to Indian living standards is far less than that of our livestock wealth. Or again, our national capital in 1933 was not significantly different from that in 1929, but one year was marked by widespread misery and the other by booming prosperity. Clearly then, the existence of great physical wealth by itself does not guarantee—it only holds out the possibility of—a high standard of living. It is only insofar as wealth interacts with the working population that it exerts its enormous economic leverage, and this interaction is not a mechanical phenomenon that we can take for granted, but a complex *social* process, whose motivations we must explore.

As the example of Indian livestock indicates, local customs and beliefs can effectively sterilize the potential physical benefits of wealth. Perhaps we should generalize that conclusion by observing that the political and social system will have a primary role in causing an effective or ineffective use of existing wealth. Compare the traditional hoarding of gold or gems in many backward societies with the possibility of their disposal to produce foreign exchange for the purchase of machinery.

In a modern industrial society, we take for granted some kind of effective social and political structure. Then why do we at times make vigorous use of our existing material assets and at other times seem to put them to little or no use? Why do we have "good times" and "bad times"? The question directs our attention back to the panorama of society to discover something further about its economic operation.

INPUTS AND
OUTPUTS
This time, our attention fastens on a different aspect of the tableau. Rather than noticing our stock of wealth, we observe the result of our use of that wealth, a result we can see emerging in the form of a *flow of production*.

How does this flow of production arise? We can see that it comes into being as man combines his energies with his natural and man-made environment. We have already traced the long and painful history of his social and technical attempts to combine those energies and the environment successfully, and we take for granted, in our scrutiny of the production process, the very things that interested us in the first part of this book—the development of a "climate" of enterprise, the rise of an industrial technology, the underpinning of a vast capital equipment. Now we focus only on the growing edge of history, the present, where men gifted with the fruits of their past labors continue to cope with the material world.

Hence we take for granted the fact that men organize their struggle with nature according to the rules of a market process whose evolution was the main subject matter of Part Two. Later, in Part Four, we shall go back to examine in greater detail the interactions of the actors on the marketplace. But right now we want to know what happens to the flow of output emerging under our eyes from thousands of enterprises as their entrepreneurs hire the factors of production and combine their services as inputs to yield a saleable output.*

It may help us picture the flow as a whole if we imagine that each and every good and service that is produced—each loaf of bread, each nut and bolt, each doctor's call, each theatrical performance, each car, ship, lathe, or bolt of cloth—can be identified in the way that a radioactive isotope allows us to follow the circulation of certain kinds of cells through the body. Then if we look down on the economic panorama, we can see the continuous combination of land, labor, and capital giving off a continuous flow of "lights" as goods and services emerge in their saleable form.

Where do these lights go? Many, as we can see, are soon extinguished. The goods or services they represent have been incorporated into other products to form more fully finished items of output. Thus from our aerial perspective we can follow a product such as cotton from the fields to the spinning mill, where its light is extinguished, for there the cotton disappears into a new product: yarn. In turn, the light of the yarn traces a path as it

---

* It is well to remember two things about the factors of production from Part Two (see pp. 66 f.). The factors are both a representation of different *physical* elements of the production process (land and natural resources, man-made capital, and labor of all sorts); and also the incarnation of *social functions* (renting land, lending or risking capital, selling labor services) that must be combined if production is to be carried on.

leaves the spinning mill by way of sale to the textile mill, there to be doused as the yarn disappears into a new good: cloth. And again, the cloth leaving the textile mill lights a way to the factory where it will become part of an article of clothing.

And what of the clothing? Here at last we have what the economist calls a *final* good. Why "final"? Because once in the possession of its ultimate owner, the clothing passes out of the active economic flow. As a good in the hands of a consumer, it is no longer an object on the marketplace. Its light is now extinguished permanently—or if we wish to complete our image, we can imagine it fading gradually as the clothing "disappears" into the use and pleasure, the so-called *utility,* of the consumer. In the case of consumer goods like food or of consumer services like recreation, the light goes out faster, for these items are "consumed" when they reach their final destination.*

We shall have a good deal to learn in later chapters about the behavior of consumers. What we should notice in this first macroeconomic view is the supreme importance of this flow of production into consumers' hands. This is the vital process by which the population replenishes or increases its energies and ministers to its wants and needs; it is a process that, if halted for very long, would cause a society to perish. That is why we speak of consumption as the ultimate end and aim of all economic activity.

Nevertheless, for all the importance of consumption, if we look down on the illuminated flow of output we see a surprising thing. Whereas the greater portion of the final goods and services of the economy is bought by the human agents of production for their consumption, we also find that a lesser but still considerable flow of final products is not. What happens to it?

If we follow an appropriate good, we may find out. Let us watch the destination of the steel that leaves a Pittsburgh mill. Some of it, like our cotton cloth, will become incorporated into consumers' goods, ending up as cans, automobiles, or household articles of various kinds. But some steel will not find its way to a consumer at all; instead, it will end up as part of a machine or an office building or a railroad track.

Now in a way, these goods are not "final," for they are used to produce still further goods or services—the machine producing output of some kind, the building producing office space, the rail track producing transportation. Yet there is a difference between such goods, used for production, and

---

* In fact, of course, they are not *really* consumed but remain behind as garbage, junk, wastes, and so on. Economics used to ignore these residuals, but it does so no longer. However, we will not discuss the problems they pose until we reach Chapter 28.

consumer goods, like clothing. The difference is that the machine, the office building, and the track are goods that are used by business enterprises as part of their productive equipment. As a result, they are usually carefully maintained and replaced as they wear out. In terms of our image, these goods slowly lose their light-giving powers as their services pass into flows of production, but usually they are replaced with new goods before their light is totally extinguished. That is why we call them *capital goods* in distinction to consumers' goods. As part of our capital, they will be preserved, maintained, and renewed, perhaps indefinitely. Hence *the stock of capital, like consumers, constitutes a final destination for output.**

GROSS AND NET INVESTMENT

We call the great stream of output that goes to capital *gross investment.* The very word *gross* suggests that it conceals a finer breakdown; and looking more closely, we can see that the flow of output going to capital does indeed serve two distinct purposes. Part of it is used to replace the capital—the machines, the buildings, the track, or whatever—that has been used up in the process of production. Just as the human agents of production have to be replenished by a flow of consumption goods, so the material agents of production need to be maintained and renewed if their contribution to output is to remain undiminished. We call the part of gross investment, whose purpose is to keep society's stock of capital intact, *replacement investment,* or simply *replacement.*

Sometimes the total flow of output going to capital is not large enough to maintain the existing stock—for instance, if we allow inventories (a form of capital) to become depleted, or if we simply fail to replace worn-out equipment or plant. This running-down of capital, we call *disinvestment,* meaning the very opposite of investment: instead of building up capital, we are literally consuming it.

Not all gross investment is used for replacement purposes, however. Some of the flow may *increase* the stock of capital, by adding buildings, machines, track, inventory, and so on.† If the total output consigned to capital is sufficiently great not only to make up for wear and tear, but to increase the capital stock, we say there has been *new* or *net investment,* or *net capital formation.*

Sometimes it helps to have a homely picture in mind to keep things straight. The difference between replacement and net investment is made clear by using as an example the paving of streets. Each year some streets wear out, and we have to repave them to keep them passable. This is clearly

---

* We might note that some products, like automobiles, possess characteristics of both consumption goods and capital goods. We call such goods *consumer durables;* and unlike ordinary goods (such as clothing) held by consumers, we include them in our inventory of national wealth (see Table 10-1, p. 170).

† Note carefully that *increased* inventory is a form of investment. In Chapter 11, this will take on a special importance.

investment, but it does not add to our ability to enjoy surface transportation. Hence it is solely *replacement* investment. Only when we build *additional* streets do we undertake new or net investment. Also, sometimes we build a new street but allow an old one to deteriorate beyond usability. Here we have to offset the new investment with the *disinvestment* in our now unpassable road. Whether or not we have any net investment in street building as a whole depends on whether we have added or subtracted from street capacity when we consider the net investment and the disinvestment together.

One last important point. Who normally buys these additions to our capital wealth? As our example above shows, the government is one such buyer. But in the main, the purchasers of new capital goods are business firms who seek to increase their holdings of machines and buildings and equipment of various kinds. Since additions to business capital are additions to our nation's wealth, and since with more wealth we would expect to be able to produce still more goods and services, the act of business investment immediately stands out as a key element in the study of macroeconomics. In fact, as we shall see, in many ways the process and the problems of business investment will be a central point of focus in macroeconomic analysis.

CONSUMPTION AND INVESTMENT

A simple diagram may help us picture the flows of output we have been discussing.

Figure 10-2 calls to our attention three important attributes of the economic system.

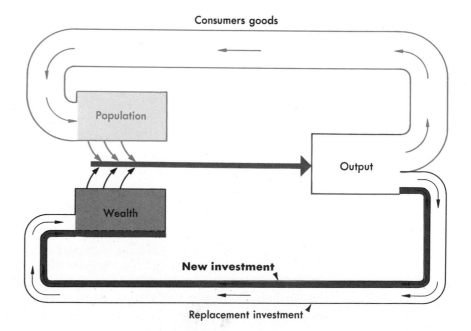

Consumers goods

Population

Output

Wealth

New investment

**FIG. 10 • 2
THE CIRCULAR
FLOW, VIEW I**

Replacement investment

1. It emphasizes the essential *circularity,* the self-renewing, self-feeding nature of the production flow. This circularity is a feature of the macroeconomic process to which we will return again and again.

2. It illumines a basic choice that all economic societies must make: *a choice between consumption and investment.* For the split flow of production reveals that any good entering the capital stream cannot also be in the consumption stream. At any given level of output, consumption and investment are, so to speak, rivals for the current output of society.

3. Finally, it makes clear that *society can invest* (that is, add to its capital) *only the output that it refrains from consuming.* We call this relinquishing of consumption *saving,* and saving thus becomes an economic act located at the very core of the wealth-creation process. For the economic meaning of saving, as our diagram shows, is to release resources from consumption so that they can be used for the building of capital. Whether they *will* be so used is a matter that will occupy us through many subsequent chapters.

GROSS NATIONAL PRODUCT

There remains but one preliminary matter before we proceed to a closer examination of the actual determinants of the flow of production. We have seen that the annual output of the nation is a revealing measure of its well-being, for it reflects the degree of interaction between the population and its wealth. Later we shall also find output to be a major determinant of employment. Hence it behooves us to examine the nature and general character of this flow and to become familiar with its nomenclature and composition.

We call the dollar value of the total annual output of final goods and services in the nation its gross national product. The gross national product (or GNP as it is usually abbreviated) is thus nothing but the dollar value of the total output of all consumption goods and of all investment goods produced in a year. As such we are already familiar with its general meaning. At this juncture, however, we must define GNP a little more precisely.

1. *GNP includes only final goods.*

We are interested, through the concept of GNP, in measuring the value of the *ultimate* production of the economic system—that is, the total value of all goods and services *enjoyed by its consumers or accumulated as new or replacement capital.* Hence we do not count the intermediate goods we have already noted in our economic panorama. To go back to an earlier example, we do not add up the value of the cotton *and* the yarn *and* the cloth *and* the final clothing when we compute the value of GNP. That kind of multiple counting might be very useful if we wanted certain information about our total economic activity, but it would not tell us accurately about the final value of output. For when we buy a shirt, the price we pay already included the cost of the cloth to the shirtmaker; and in turn, the amount the shirtmaker paid for his cloth already included the cost of the yarn; and in turn, again, the seller of yarn included in his price the amount he paid for raw cotton. Embodied in the price of the shirt, therefore, is the value of all the intermediate products that went into it. Thus in figuring the value for GNP, we add only the values of all final goods, both for consumption and for investment purposes. Note as well that GNP only includes a given year's production of goods and services. Therefore sales of used car dealers, antique dealers, etc., are not included, because the value of these goods was picked up in GNP of the year they were produced.

2. *There are four categories of final goods.*

In our first view of macroeconomic activity we divided the flow of output into two great streams: consumption and gross investment. Now, for purposes of a closer analysis, we impose a few refinements on this basic scheme.

First we must pay heed to a small flow of production that has previously escaped our notice. This is the net flow of goods or services that leaves this country; that is, the total flow going abroad minus the flow that enters. This international branch of our economy will play a relatively minor role in our analysis for quite a while; we will largely ignore it until Chapter 15, then again until Part Five. But we must give it its proper name: *net exports.* Because these net exports are a kind of investment (they are goods we produce but do not consume), we must now rename the great bulk of investment that remains in this country. We will henceforth call it *gross private domestic investment.*

The word *private* brings us to a second refinement. It concerns a subflow of goods and services within both the great consumption stream and the investment branch of activity. These are the goods and services bought or produced by the government (as contrasted with consumers or businesses). Some of these may be consumers' goods—policemen's services, say—and some may be investment goods, such as roads or schools or dams. Conventionally, however, we include all public purchases, whether for consumption or investment purposes, in a category called *government purchases of goods and services.*

This gives us four streams of "final" output, each going to a final purchaser of economic output. Therefore we can speak of gross national product as being the sum of consumption goods and services, gross private domestic investment, government purchases, and net exports, or (to abbreviate a long sentence) we can write that

$$\text{GNP} \equiv C + I + G + E.$$

This is a descriptive equation that should be remembered.

It helps, at this juncture, to look at GNP over the past decades. In Figure 10-3 we show the long irregular upward flow of GNP from 1929 to

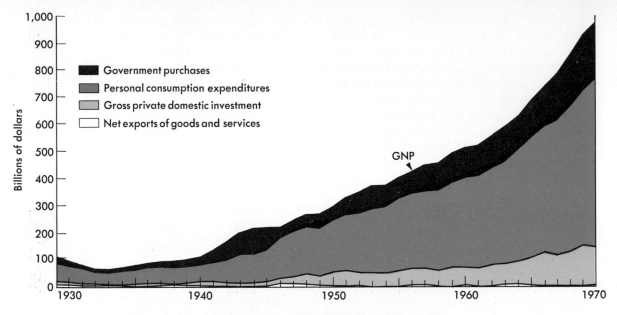

FIG. 10•3   GNP AND COMPONENTS, 1929–1970

the present, with the four component streams of expenditures visible. Later we will be talking at length about the behavior of each stream, but first we need to be introduced to the overall flow itself.

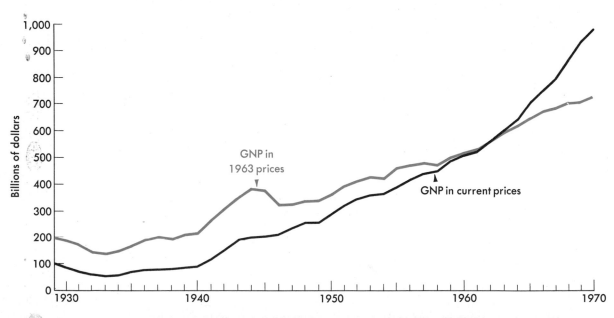

FIG. 10•4   GNP IN CONSTANT AND CURRENT PRICES, 1929–1970

One final point should be made about our basic equation. All through our discussion of GNP we have talked about *flows* of output. We do so to distinguish GNP, a "flow concept," from wealth or capital (or any asset) that is a *stock,* or a sum of wealth that exists at any given time.

A moment's reflection may make the distinction clear. When we speak of a stock of business capital or of land or structures, we mean a sum of wealth that we could actually inspect on a given date. GNP, however, does not "exist" in quite the same way. If our gross national product for a year is, say, $900 billion, this does not mean that on any day of that year we could actually discover this much value of goods and services. Rather, GNP tells us the average annual rate, for that year, at which production was carried out; so that if the year's flow of output had been collected in a huge reservoir without being consumed, at the end of the year the volume in the reservoir would indeed have totaled $900 billion. GNP is, however, constantly being consumed as well as produced. Hence the $900 billion figure refers to the value of the *flow of production over the year,* and should not be pictured as constituting a given sum of wealth at any moment in time.

GNP is an indispensable concept in dealing with the performance of our economy, but it is well to understand the weaknesses as well as the strengths of this most important single economic indicator. There are four of them.

1. *GNP deals in dollar values, not in physical units.*

That is, it does not tell us how many goods and services were produced, but only what their sales value was. Trouble then arises when we compare the GNP of one year with that of another, to determine whether or not the nation is better off. For if prices in the second year are higher, GNP will appear higher, even though the actual volume of output is unchanged.

We can correct for this price change very easily when all prices have moved in the same degree or proportion. Then it is easy to speak of "real" GNP—that is, the current money value of GNP adjusted for price changes—as reflecting the actual rise or fall of output. The price problem becomes more difficult, however, when prices change in different degrees or even in different directions, as they often do. Then a comparison of "real" GNP from one year to the next, and especially over a long span of years, is unavoidably arbitrary to some extent.*

Figure 10-4 shows us the previous totals for GNP corrected as best we can for price changes. In this chart, 1963 is used as the "base," and the GNP's of other years are raised or lowered so that price changes are

---

* A student who is unsure about how price indexes work should study the statistical supplement at the end of Chapter 11.

eliminated to the greatest possible extent. One can, of course, choose any year for a base. Although the basic dollar measuring rod will then change, the profile of "real" changes year to year will be the same.

2. GNP does not reflect changes in the quality of output.

The second weakness of GNP also involves its inaccuracy as an indicator of "real" trends over time. This time the difficulty revolves around the changes in the utility (or use and pleasure-producing capabilities) of goods and services. In a technologically advancing society, goods are usually improved from one decade to the next, or even more rapidly; and in an urbanizing, increasingly high-density society, the utility of other goods may be lessened over time. An airplane trip today, for example, is certainly highly preferable to one taken twenty or thirty years ago; a subway ride is not. Thus, to the extent that the quality of most goods and services improve, and as some deteriorate, GNP misrepresents the true value of output, especially over long stretches of time.

3. GNP does not reflect the purpose of production.

A third difficulty with GNP lies in its blindness to the ultimate use of production. If in one year GNP rises by a billion dollars owing to an increase in expenditure on education, and in another year it rises by the same amount because of a rise in cigarette purchases, the figures in each case show the same amount of "growth" of GNP. Even output that turns out to be wide of the mark or totally wasteful—such as the famous Edsel car that no one wanted or military weapons that are obsolete from the moment they appear—all are counted as part of GNP.

An extremely important aspect of this "blindness" of GNP is that it makes no allowance for expenditures made only to clean up the environmental harm that other parts of the GNP have caused. The cleaning bills that we pay to undo damage caused by smoke of the neighborhood factory become part of GNP, although cleaning our clothes does not increase our well-being; it only brings it back to what it was in the first place. We shall have much more to say about this problem in Chapter 28.

Thus, changes in GNP give us only a very rough indication of changes in the *quality* of life. That is why comparisons of GNP today and fifty or one hundred years ago—comparisons that show Americans today enjoying a vastly greater output than did their forebears—should not be interpreted to mean that life is therefore that much "better."

4. GNP does not include most goods and services that are not for sale.

Presumably GNP tells us how large our final output is. Yet it does not include one of the most important kinds of work and sources of consumer pleasure—the labor of wives in maintaining their households. Yet, curiously, if this labor were paid for—that is, if we engaged cooks and maids and babysitters instead of depending on our wives for these services, GNP *would* include their services as final output, since they would be purchased on the market. But the labor of wives being unpaid, it is excluded from GNP.*

The difficulty here is that we are constantly moving toward purchasing "outside" services in place of home services—laundries, bakeries, restaurants, etc., all perform work that used to be performed at home. Thus the process of *monetizing* activity gives an upward trend to GNP statistics which is not fully mirrored in actual output.

A related problem is that some parts of GNP are paid for by some members of the population and not by others. Rent, for example, measures the services of landlords for homeowners and is therefore included in GNP, but what of the man who owns his own home and pays no rent? Similarly, what of the family that grows some part of its food at home, and therefore does not pay for it? In order to include such items of "free" consumption into GNP, the statisticians of the Commerce Department add an "imputed" value figure to include goods and services like these not tallied on a cash register.

These problems lead economists to treat GNP in a skeptical and gingerly manner, particularly insofar as its "welfare" implications are concerned. Indeed, Kenneth Boulding has suggested that we relabel the monster *Gross National Cost* to disabuse ourselves once and for all of the notion that a bigger GNP is necessarily a better one.

It is doubtful that Boulding's idea will gain general currency—for better or worse, GNP has become part of the vocabulary of the modern world—but his cautions are worth taking very seriously indeed. We should remember that comparisons between GNPs are much more trustworthy for two close years than for two distant ones (prices and qualities are not apt to have changed so much in the shorter span of time); that GNP overlooks everything that does not pass through the cash register; that it counts dangerous, polluted, or pointless output just as proudly as beneficent, clean, and necessary output. Hence, as we saw in Chapter 1, the fact that the U.S. has a per capita GNP that is a third higher than that of Sweden carries no easy conclusion that life here is therefore a third "better." By the indices of health, longevity, quality of environment, or ease of retirement, it is worse.

Sobering comparisons such as these have led many economists in recent years to look beyond GNP toward development of more sensitive indices of real well-being. The Department of Health, Education and Welfare drew up the first such analysis of social indicators in 1968; the document, *Toward a Social Report* (1969) is well worth reading. Yet, with all its shortcomings GNP is still our best simple way of summarizing the overall *level of activity* (good or bad) of the economy. Gross national product today is a yardstick used by every nation in the world. It has become a term familiar to every

---

* This gives rise to an amusing anomaly. Every time a man marries his cook, GNP declines by the amount of the wages he formerly paid her, even though her cooking may continue. Even if he pays her an allowance as large as her wages, GNP still declines, since allowances are not presumed to cover "productive services" and therefore are not picked up in GNP.

congressman and editorial writer, although not many of them could describe very clearly exactly what it means. Hence, let us turn to a closer study of this critical economic concept by examining how GNP is actually generated and maintained.

KEY CONCEPTS AND KEY WORDS

Macroeconomics	1. *Macroeconomics* is not a separate part of economics, but an *approach to economic problems* through the study of certain aggregate processes.
Wealth **Capital**	2. We begin the study of macroeconomic processes by observing how a *flow of output comes from human resources interacting with our national wealth* (the most important part of which is our *capital*).
Claims	3. We note that capital consists of *real things,* and *not of the financial claims* against those things.
Production	4. The flow of output shows us *the circular nature of the process of production.* From the interaction of population and wealth emerges a stream of goods going back to replenish consumers (consumption goods) and a stream to replenish and add to our capital wealth (gross investment).
Replacement Investment	5. A study of the flow of output and its division into consumption and investment emphasizes the essential choice that must be made between these *two basic uses of output.*
Net Investment **Gross Investment**	6. The investment flow can be subdivided into two: one flow *replaces or renews capital* that has been worn out or used up. This is *replacement investment.* The other flow *adds to the stock of capital wealth,* and is called *new* or *net capital* or *investment.* The two flows together are called *gross investment.*
Consumption **Gross private domestic investment** **Government purchases**	7. The name for the total flow of output is *gross national product.* It is divided into four major categories: • *Consumption (C),* or the goods and services going to consumers. • *Gross private domestic investment (I),* or that portion of output going to private businesses as replacements for, and additions to, their real domestic capital. • *Government purchases (G),* or those goods and services (both consumers' and capital) bought by all public agencies. • *Net exports (E),* the net outflow of goods and services to other countries. • The formula GNP ≡ *C* + *I* + *G* + *E* conveniently summarizes these four subdivisions.
GNP **Final goods**	8. Note that GNP counts only the dollar value of *final goods and services* in each of these categories. Intermediate goods or services are not counted, since their value is included in the value of final goods.
	9. GNP is an indispensable concept in macroeconomics. Nonetheless, it must be used with caution, especially if it is to be used as an indication of relative "well-being." Remember that: • GNP deals in *dollar values, not physical units.* This can lead to problems in adjusting price changes from year to year so that GNP accurately reflects changes in output. • GNP does not show changes in the *quality* of output. • GNP does not reveal the *composition* of output. • GNP figures do not include *output* that is *not for sale.* Thus, comparisons from year to year should be made warily, particularly when comparing one nation with another or with itself at a point distant in time.

1. Why is capital so important a part of national wealth? Why is money not considered capital?

2. What is meant by the "circularity" of the economic process? Does it have something to do with the output of the system being returned to it as fresh inputs?

3. What is meant by net investment? by gross investment? What is the difference?

4. Write the basic formula for GNP and state *carefully* the exact names of each of the four constituents of GNP.

5. Suppose we had an island economy with an output of 100 tons of grain, each ton selling for $90. If grain is the only product sold, what is the value of GNP? Now suppose that production stays the same but that prices rise to $110. What is the value of GNP now? How could we "correct" for the price rise? If we didn't, would GNP be an accurate measure of output from one year to the next?

6. Now suppose that production rose to 110 tons but that prices fell to $81. The value of GNP, in terms of current prices, has fallen from $9,000 to $8,910. Yet, actual output, measured in tons of grain, has increased. Can you devise a price index that will show the change in real GNP?*

7. Presumably, the quality of most products improves over time. If their price is unchanged, does that mean that GNP understates or overstates the real value of output?

8. When more and more consumers buy "do-it-yourself" kits, does the value of GNP (which includes the sale price of these kits) understate or overstate the true final output of the nation?

9. Do you think that we should develop measures other than GNP to indicate changes in our basic well-being? What sorts of measures?

10. What is an intermediate good, and why are such goods not included in the value of GNP? Is coal sold to a utility company an intermediate good? Coal sold to a consumer? Coal sold to the army? What determines whether a good will or will not be counted in the total of GNP?

*If you have trouble with this, look into the statistical supplement that follows.

L E A R N I N G   A B O U T   S T A T I S T I C S

With our introduction to macroeconomic theory, we begin an introduction to statistics, in a series of short supplements that will continue through much of the macroeconomic section of our text. Why statistics? The reason is that economics, more than any other social science, involves things that can be counted, concepts that can be quantified, activities that can be measured. Prices, wages, GNP itself, as we have just learned, all express our ability to put magnitudes on certain aspects of social activity. *Statistics involves the manner in which we establish these numerical magnitudes and in which we use them.*

AN INTRODUCTION TO STATISTICS

Thus every economist must have a general working knowledge of statistics, and every student of economics should have at least a basic idea of what statistics is about. That basic idea is what these supplements are intended to provide. They will not teach you more than a smattering of rather easy statistics, but they should take away some of the mystery surrounding the compilation and use of the numbers on which economics depends; and they may interest you enough in the problems of the subject to lead you to take a course in statistics.

In the succeeding supplements, we will investigate numerous problems involving quantities—problems such as what we mean by an *average* or an *index* or a *correlation*. But in this first view of the quantitative side of economics it may be helpful to look at the subject of statistics as a whole, without going into particulars. Here are five general hints and cautions that will be useful to remember:

1. *Quality vs. quantity.*

There are two misconceptions about statistics that we should clear up immediately. The first might be called statistics worship. It finds expression in the view that if you can't count something, it doesn't count. The second is just the opposite. It scoffs at statistics because all the important things in life are qualitative and therefore can't be measured.

Both of these *are* misconceptions, and it is important to understand why. The statistics worshipper must realize that before anyone can count anything, he must *define* it, and that definition is ultimately an act of judgment, not measurement. And the statistics scoffer must realize that before he can bring his reason to bear on social problems involving good and evil, he must have at least some notion of how *large* a good or evil he is concerned with.

Take as an illustration the problem of poverty. When Professor Galbraith wrote *The Affluent Society* in 1958, he said that one family in thirteen in America was poor. In the first chapter of *The Economic Problem,* we have said that about one in seven is poor. Does that mean that a larger fraction of Americans are poor today? Of course not. The answer is that today the United States statistical authorities' *definition* of poverty is different from the definition used by Galbraith, so that the "growing" percentage of the poor reflects nothing more than a changing conception of what poverty means.*

Thus, the extent of poverty in America is a quantitative measure founded on a qualitative definition, and the person who places a blind faith in the "facts" must remember that many of these facts change as our definition of social problems change. But isn't that just the point, asks the statistical skeptic. Since definition is everything, the problem of poverty boils down in the end to what we *think* poverty is. What is important is not what the numbers tell us, but our moral judgments from which the numbers emerge.

Of course it is true that definitions *do* come first, but they establish the unit or yardstick by which we measure the problem. Poverty may rise or fall in America if we use an unchanged yardstick. It can also rise or fall because we change its definition. But once we have made that choice of the yardstick, we use the definition to learn the magnitude of the problem *as we have defined it.* For until we know its magnitude as measured by the *same* yardstick, we cannot know how serious a problem it is, much less determine what action will be needed to remedy it.

2. *The problem of definitions.*

The second lesson follows from the first. Words are slippery, even when no arbitrary judgments are involved. Any maker or user of statistics must be exceedingly careful that he knows exact meaning of the terms he is using. For example, in *The Statistical Abstract of the United States* (1970 edition), the annual official gold mine of national statistics, there are many tables dealing with poverty. Some

---

*In his most recent edition of *The Affluent Society,* Galbraith has adopted the newer definition.

show "households" and some show "families." Is a household a family? The answer is no, since a household can be a single individual, but a family always includes more than one person. Therefore we must expect to find more poor "households" than poor "families," since there are obviously more of the first category than of the second. And in fact if we look into the *Statistical Abstract* (p. 329) we find that 9.7 million households fell below the poverty line in 1968, compared with 5 million families. (A reason for the very large discrepancy is that a disproportionate number (34 percent) of "single individuals" are poor.

The moral is clear: *read all table headings and notes very carefully.* The numbers may not refer to the thing you think they do.

3. *Be skeptical of your data.*

Numbers, perhaps even more than words, have a magical authority inherent in them, but that does not mean that either are necessarily correct, even from the most impeccable sources. People make honest mistakes in gathering statistics, or mistakes creep in because of the difficulties in compiling statistics, some of which we will learn about later.

To take one example: if you examine the figure for GNP in 1968 in the *Statistical Abstract* (p. 312) you will find it to be $865.7 billion. But if you examine the most recent tables of GNP in publications such as the monthly *Economic Indicators,* you will discover that the figure for 1968 has been reduced to $865.0. What happened to the $700,000,000 in the first figure?

The answer is that many statistical series are refined and corrected as more complete data are collected, so that virtually all figures change until the "final" returns are in. Most economic statistics are necessarily based on fragmentary data and are gradually improved as fuller information is obtained. The latest statistics are *always* subject to revision and are often marked *prelim.,* or *est.,* to warn the reader that they will be subject to change. The changes are usually not large, but occasionally large enough to alter precise calculations based on earlier data.

At regular intervals the various government offices concerned with the collection of statistical information bring out revised—sometimes drastically revised— series of data. These revisions not only establish new "bases" and "weights" for many indices (see our next statistical supplement for the meaning of these terms), but involve recalculation of many past series based on new concepts, on more sophisticated data-handling techniques, and so on. (One recent controversy, for example, concerns the problem of whether or not we have accurately measured the value of the private capital stock in the United States. Economist Robert Gordon has claimed that we have "mislaid" $45 billion of this stock by failing to make allowance for various government transactions, such as the very low prices at which some companies acquired plants built during World War II by the government and subsequently sold at nominal figures to private enterprise.*)

Of course no ordinary user of official statistics can be aware of all these pitfalls or can anticipate the revisions that may alter the numbers on which he is relying. An excess of wariness would only paralyze the research that we must carry on with the only data we have at hand. But a healthy pinch of caution, allowing for moderate changes in the magnitudes at hand, has saved many a researcher from trying to prove a point by relying on very *small differences in magnitudes that may later disappear.*

* See *American Economic Review,* June 1969, and rejoinder, *ibid.,* September 1970.

4. *Be wary of the problems of aggregation.*

The previous example involved the problems of dealing with an *aggregate*—a number that includes many different kinds of things—called the private capital stock. In the chapter we have just finished, we discussed another tricky aggregate, called GNP; and in our next statistical supplement we will look into the pitfalls of aggregating such diverse entities. The point, no doubt, is already clear: aggregates can be deceptive. A more important point, however, may not be so clear: more things are actually aggregates than appear to be so on the surface.

Take, for example, something nice and unaggregated-sounding like steel. We all think we know what steel is, and therefore nothing could appear to be less ambiguous than a figure on steel prices. But what is "steel"? Oddly, you cannot go into the marketplace and buy a commodity called steel, because it doesn't exist. You can, of course, buy steel rods of various diameters and lengths, steel plates of various thicknesses and dimensions, steel ingots of various chemical purities, but "steel" as such is not for sale anywhere.

Thus the price of steel actually refers to the price of one *representative* kind of steel, or of a *given assortment* of kinds of steel. (You will find such a representative price index of "steel mill products" on p. 341 of the *Statistical Abstract.*) But the kind of steel that is representative of all the kinds of steel in the market is almost sure to change markedly over 20 years, as will the assortment that "represents" the steels a nation uses.

Result: the price of "steel" has to be an aggregate and is, therefore, a good deal less solid than it looks at first. And the same is true for the prices (or the quantities) of such seemingly standard items as coal or wheat or bread or oil, which in fact are also aggregates of many *kinds* of coal, and so on. The point is not that aggregates are to be avoided. *We have no alternative to aggregating things if we are to avoid a vast and unmanageable collection of data.* But an awareness that many figures *are* aggregates teaches us to be cautious about drawing inferences about "trends," especially when time periods are lengthy.

5. *Lying with numbers.*

Darrell Huff once wrote a very amusing book called *How to Lie with Statistics.* His point was that you can easily use numbers to "make a point," something that every perceptive reader of ads or viewer of TV commercials already knows.

But even when statistics are not used deliberately to deceive, they can often be innocently deceptive unless one thinks hard about the problem. Take, as an instance, the endless figures cited to prove the existence of crime waves. Usually these figures show how many more thefts, felonies, assaults, and other crimes took place this year compared with some year in the past.

Now it may be that the numbers are accurate. But before we can be sure that there really is a crime wave, our information about the period must include facts such as: (a) population increase, (b) change in crime reporting methods; (c) change in prices. If population rose, for example, we should expect a higher *number* of crimes, even though the *proportion* of crime to population remained constant. If police-reporting methods improved, we should also expect a higher number of *reported* crimes, even though the number actually committed may not have changed at all. And if prices rose, we would expect that more thefts would involve sums that made them, by law, major offenses rather than minor ones. Once again, the moral is simple: caution first, last, and always in dealing with reported numbers of anything.

These are very general warnings, but not to be taken lightly. More than one researcher has been in serious trouble because he didn't read the caption at the top of a table of figures or because he failed to check on the most recent compilations of data or because he swallowed an aggregate without examining it or because he was fooled by numbers that did not adequately reflect the changing nature of the problem he was trying to measure.

Now, at the end, a word to redress the balance. We have stressed skepticism toward statistics because the general attitude of the beginning student is generally one of blind acceptance. But too much skepticism is perhaps worse than none at all. *Carefully defined and collected data, clearly labeled and competently used, are the only way we have of measuring very important facets of our social activity.* This book would be impossible to write without statistics, and economics would be severely crippled if we could not rely on numerical magnitudes. Statistics really are an integral part of economics. The thing is to be wary of their weaknesses while appreciating their great virtues and absolute necessity.

So far, we have talked about output as it emerges from the interaction of wealth and labor, but we have not inquired very deeply into the manner in which that interaction takes place. Yet the output of our economy does not spring forth "automatically" by the pursuit of changeless tradition, as is the case in simple preindustrial societies. Nor is it brought into being because the labor force is more or less forcibly combined with material resources, as is the case in collectivized economics. Rather, in our kind of society, output results from innumerable activities and decisions on the marketplace where men buy and sell, largely as they wish. What we must now understand is precisely how this daily activity of the marketplace gives rise to the flow of gross national product.

Output and Demand

How does the market actually bring output into existence? How does it effect the combination of land, labor, and capital under the guidance of an entrepreneur? Any businessman will give you the answer. He will tell you that the crucial factor enabling him to perform his economic task (or in his language, "to run a business") is *demand* or *purchasing power;* that is, the presence of buyers who are willing and able to buy some good or service at the price for which he is willing to sell it.

But how does demand or purchasing power come into existence? If we ask any buyer, he will tell us that his dollars come to him because they are part of his *income* or his cash receipts.

But where, in turn, do the dollar receipts or incomes of buyers come from? If we inquire again, most buyers will tell us that they have money in their pockets because in one fashion or another they have contributed to the process of production; that is, because they have helped to make the output that is now being sold.

Thus our quest for the motive force behind the flow of production leads us in a great circle through the market system. We can see this in Fig. 11-1.

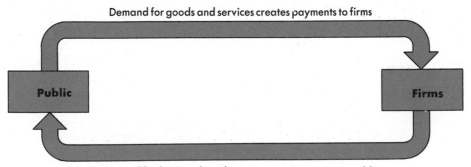

Demand for goods and services creates payments to firms

Public

Firms

Demand for factors of production creates payments to public

FIG. 11 • 1   THE CIRCULAR FLOW, VIEW II

At the top of the circle we see payments flowing from the public to firms, thereby creating the demand that brings forth production. At the bottom of the circle, we see more payments, this time flowing from firms back to the public, as businesses hire the services of the various factors in order to carry out production. Thus we can see that there is a constant regeneration of demand as money is first spent by the public on the output of firms, and then in turn spent by firms for the services of the public.

We must examine this chain of payments and receipts in great detail, for it contains the key to the operation of our economic system. First, however, we need a reminder about our method of inquiry. It must be obvious that it is impossible to depict the flux of buying and selling as it actually occurs on the marketplace of the nation. It would require us to fix in our minds more details than can be reported on all the financial pages of all the newspapers in the nation every day. Hence, to comprehend the basic processes of the economy, we must use a special method of reducing its confusion to understandable dimensions. This we do by extracting from the actual happenings of economic life those aspects that experience and analy-

**AN
ECONOMIC
MODEL**

sis have taught us to regard as central and critical. From these crucial links and processes we then create a imaginary *model* of an economy that exhibits, in its operation, all the essential movements of its real-life counterpart. We shall find our model to be an indispensable guide to the complicated reality of economic life around us.

Our model, to begin with, will be a very simple one. We must, of course, exclude from it all the variety of life itself: the differences in personality of one man and another, the peculiar ways that one market differs from another, the distinctions that separate one firm from its competitor. We reduce our economy, in other words, to a colorless and abstract reproduction of life in which we can speak of general *kinds* of relationships without having to qualify each and every statement to accommodate each and every existing situation. Thus our model will call upon our capacity to think in that abstract manner which is so much a part of economic reasoning.

But our model will be simple not only in its disregard of "life." We must also simplify it, at first, by ruling out some of the very events to which we will later turn as the climax of our study. For instance, we shall ignore changes in *people's tastes,* so that we can assume that everyone will regularly buy the same kinds of goods. We shall ignore differences in the *structure of firms* or *markets,* so that we can forget about differences in competitive pressures. We shall rule out *population growth* and, even more important, *inventive progress,* so that we can deal with a very stable imaginary world. For the time being, we will exclude even *saving* and *net investment* (although of course we must permit replacement investment), so that we can ignore growth. Later, of course, we are to be deeply concerned with just such problems of dynamic change. But we shall not be able to come to grips with them until we have first understood an economic world as "pure" and changeless as possible.

COST AND
OUTPUT

The very abstract model we have created may seem too far removed from the real world to tell us much about its operation. But if we now go back to the circle of economic activity, in which payments to firms and factors become their incomes, and in turn reappear on the marketplace as demand, our model will enable us to explain a very important problem. *It is how an economy that has produced a given GNP is able to buy it back.*

This is by no means a self-evident matter. Indeed, one of the most common misconceptions about the flow of economic activity is that there will not be enough purchasing power to buy everything we have produced—that somehow we will fail to generate enough demand to keep up with the output of our factories. So it is well to understand once and for all how an economy can sustain a given level of production through its purchases on the market.

We start, then, with an imaginary economy in full operation. We can, if we wish, imagine it as having just produced its year's output, which is now sitting on the economic front doorstep looking for a buyer. What we must now see is whether it will be possible to *sell* this gross national product to the people who have been engaged in producing it. In other words, *we must ask whether there is enough income or receipts generated in the process of production to buy back all the products themselves.*

How does production create income? Businessmen do not think about "incomes" when they assemble the factors of production to meet the demand for their product. They worry about *cost*. All the money they pay out during the production process is paid under the heading of *cost,* whether it be wage or salary cost, cost of materials, depreciation cost, tax cost, or whatever. Thus it would seem that the concept of cost may offer us a useful point of entry into the economic chain. For *if we can show how all costs become incomes,* we will have taken a major step toward understanding whether our gross national product can in fact be sold to those who produced it.

Costs and Incomes

It may help us if we begin by looking at the kinds of costs incurred by business firms in real life. Here is a hypothetical expense summary of General Manufacturing, which will serve as an example typical of all business firms, large or small. (If you will examine the year-end statements of any business, you will find that their costs all fall into one or more of the cost categories below.)

Wages, salaries, and employee benefits	$100,000,000
Rental, interest, and profits payments	5,000,000
Materials, supplies, etc.	50,000,000
Taxes other than income	15,000,000
Depreciation	20,000,000

TABLE 11•1

GENERAL MANUFACTURING COST SUMMARY

FACTOR COSTS AND NATIONAL INCOME

Some of these costs we recognize immediately as payments to factors of production. The item for "wages and salaries" is obviously a payment to the factor *labor*. The item "interest" (perhaps not so obviously) is a payment to the factor *capital*—that is, to those who have lent the company money in order to help it carry on its productive operation. The item for rent is, of course, a payment for the rental of *land* or natural resources from their owners.

Note that we have included profits with rent and interest. In actual accounting practice, profits are not shown as an expense; for our purposes, however, it will be quite legitimate and very helpful to regard profits as a special kind of factor cost going to entrepreneurs for their risk-taking function. In our next chapter, we shall go more thoroughly into the matter of profits.

Two things strike us about these factor costs. First, it is clear that they represent payments that have been made to secure production. In more technical language, they are payments for factor inputs that result in commodity outputs. All the production actually carried on within the company, all the value it has added to the economy, has been compensated by the payments the company has made to land, labor, and capital. To be sure, the company has incurred other costs, for materials and taxes and depreciation, and we shall soon turn to these. But whatever production, or assembly, or distribution the company itself has carried out during the course of the year has required the use of land, labor, or capital. Thus *the total of its factor costs represents the value of the total new output that General Manufacturing by itself has given to the economy.*

From here it is but a simple step to add up *all* the factor costs paid out by *all* the companies in the economy, in order to measure the total new *value added* by all productive efforts in the year. This measure is called *national income* (or sometimes national income at factor costs).* As we can see, it is less than gross national product, for it does not include other costs of output; namely, certain taxes and depreciation.

FACTOR COSTS AND HOUSEHOLD INCOMES

A second fact that strikes us is that *all factor costs are income payments.* The wages, salaries, interest, rents, etc., that were costs to the company were income to its recipients. So are the profits, which will accrue as income to the owners of the business.

Thus, just as it sounds, national income means the total amount of earnings of the factors of production within the nation. If we think of these factors as constituting the households of the economy, we can see that *factor costs result directly in incomes to the household sector.* Thus, if factor costs were the only costs involved in production, the problem of buying back the gross national product would be a very simple one. We should simply be paying out to households, as the cost of production, the very sum needed to buy GNP when we turned around to sell it. But this is not the case, as a glance at the General Manufacturing expense summary shows. There are other costs, besides factor costs. How shall we deal with them?

COSTS OF MATERIALS

The next item of the expense summary is puzzling. Called payments for "materials, supplies, etc.," it represents all the money General Manufactur-

---

* It might be well to add that not all production (and therefore not all national income) originates with companies. Governments also produce value, such as the output of firemen's services or of roads, and private individuals, like farmers or doctors, produce output as "proprietorships." For the purposes of exposition, however, we can think of government units or individual proprietorships as "companies" since they incur exactly the same kinds of costs.

ing has paid, not to its own factors, but to other companies for other products it has needed. We may even recognize these costs as payments for those intermediate products that lose their identity in a later stage of production. How do such payments become part of the income available to buy GNP on the marketplace?

Perhaps the answer is already intuitively clear. When the General Manufacturing sends its checks to, let us say, U.S. Steel, or General Electric, or to a local supplier of stationery, each of these recipient firms now uses the proceeds of General Manufacturing's checks to pay its own costs. (Actually, of course, they have probably long since paid their own costs and now use General Manufacturing's payment only to reimburse themselves. But if we want to picture our model economy in the simplest way, we can imagine U.S. Steel and other firms sending their products to General Manufacturing and waiting until checks arrive to pay their own costs.)

And what are those costs? What must U.S. Steel or all the other suppliers now do with their checks? The answer is obvious. They must now reimburse their own factors and then pay any other costs that remain.

FIG. 11•2 HOW MATERIALS COSTS BECOME OTHER COSTS

Figure 11-2 may make the matter plain. It shows us, looking back down the chain of intermediate payments, that what constitutes material costs to one firm is made up of factor and other costs to another. Indeed, as we unravel the chain from company to company, it is clear that all the contribution to new output must have come from the contribution of factors somewhere down the line, and that all the costs of new output—all the value added—must ultimately be resolvable into payments to land, labor, and capital.

Another way of picturing the same thing is to imagine that all firms in the country were bought up by a single gigantic corporation. The various production units of the new supercorporation would then ship components and semifinished items back and forth to one another, but there would not have to be any payment from one division to another. The only payments that would be necessary would be those required to buy the services of factors—that is, various kinds of labor, or the use of property or capital—so that at the end of the year, the supercorporation would show on its expense summary only items for wages and salaries, rent, and interest (and as we shall see, taxes and depreciation) but it would have no item for materials cost.

We have come a bit further toward seeing how our gross national product can be sold. To the extent that GNP represents new output made during the course of the year, the income to buy back this output has already been handed out as factor costs, either paid at the last stage of production or "carried along" in the guise of materials costs. But a glance at the General Manufacturing expense summary shows that entrepreneurs incur two kinds of costs that we have still not taken into account: taxes and depreciation. Here are costs employers have incurred that have not been accounted for on the income side. What can we say about them?

TAX COSTS

Let us begin by tracing the taxes that General Manufacturing pays, just as we have traced its materials payments. In the first instance, its taxes will go to government units—federal, state, and local. But we need not stop there. Just as we saw that General Manufacturing's checks to supplier firms paid for the suppliers' factor costs and for still further interfirm transactions, so we can see that its checks to government agencies pay for goods and services that these agencies have produced—goods such as roads, buildings, or defense equipment; or services such as teaching, police protection, and the administration of justice. General Manufacturing's tax checks are thus used to help pay for factors of production—land, labor, and capital—that are used in the *public sector*.

In many ways, General Manufacturing's payments to government units resemble its payments to other firms for raw materials. Indeed, if the government *sold* its output to General Manufacturing, charging for the use of the roads, police services, or defense protection it affords the company, there would be *no* difference whatsoever. The reason we differentiate between a company's payment to the public sector and its payments for intermediate products is important, however, and worth looking into.

The first reason is clearly that, with few exceptions, the government does *not* sell its output. This is partly because the community has decided that certain things the government produces (education, justice, or the use of public parks, for instance) should not be for sale but should be supplied to all citizens without charge. In part, it is also because some things the government produces, such as defense or law and order, cannot be equitably charged to individual buyers, since it is impossible to say to what degree anyone benefits from—or even uses—these communal facilities. Hence General Manufacturing, like every other producer, is billed, justly or otherwise, for a share of the cost of government.

There is also a second reason why we consider the cost of taxes as a new kind of cost, distinct from factor payments. It is that when we have finished paying the factors we have not yet paid all the sums that employers must lay out. Some taxes, in other words, are an addition to the cost of production.

These taxes—so-called *indirect taxes*—are levied on the productive enterprise itself or on its actual physical output. Taxes on real estate, for instance, or taxes that are levied on each unit of output, regardless of whether or not it is sold (such as excise taxes on cigarettes), or taxes levied on goods sold at retail (sales taxes) are all payments that entrepreneurs must make as part of their costs of doing business.

Note that not all taxes collected by the government are costs of production. Many taxes will be paid, not by the entrepreneurs as an expense of doing business, but by the *factors* themselves. These so-called *direct* taxes (such as income taxes) are *not* part of the cost of production. When General Manufacturing adds up its total cost of production, it naturally includes the wages and salaries it has paid, but it does not include the taxes its workers or executives have paid out of their incomes. Such direct taxes transfer income from earners to government, but they are not a cost to the company itself.

In the same way, the income taxes on the profits of a company do *not* constitute a cost of production. General Manufacturing does not pay income taxes as a regular charge on its operations, but waits until a year's production has taken place, and then pays income taxes on the profits it makes *after* paying its costs. If it finds that it has lost money over the year, it will not pay any income taxes—although it will have paid other costs, including indirect taxes. Thus direct taxes are not a cost that is paid out in the course of production and must be recouped, but a payment made by factors (including owners of the business) from the incomes they have earned through the process of production.

Thus we can see two reasons why taxes are handled as a separate item in GNP and are not telescoped into factor costs, the way materials costs are. One reason is that taxes are a payment to a *different sector* from that of business and thus indicate a separate stream of economic activity. But the second reason, and the one that interests us more at this moment, is that *certain taxes—indirect taxes—are an entirely new kind of cost of production, not previously picked up.* As an expense paid out by entrepreneurs, over and above factor costs (or materials costs), these tax costs must be part of the total selling price of GNP.

Will there be enough incomes handed out in the process of production to cover this item of cost?

We have seen that there will be. The indirect tax costs paid out by entrepreneurs will be received by government agencies who will use these tax receipts to pay incomes to factors working for the government. Thus the new item of tax costs will eventually become income to factors working in the public sector, and will be available, together with all other factor incomes, to create demand on the marketplace.

But there is still one last item of cost. At the end of the year, when the company is totting up its expenses to see if it has made a profit for the period, its accountants do not stop with factor costs, material costs, and indirect taxes. If they did, the company would soon be in serious straits. In producing its goods, General Manufacturing has also used up a certain amount of its assets—its buildings and equipment—and a cost must now be charged for this wear and tear if the company is to be able to preserve the value of its physical plant intact. If it did not make this cost allowance, it would have failed to include all the resources that were used up in the process of production, and it would therefore be overstating its profits.

Yet, this cost has something about it clearly different from other costs that General Manufacturing has paid. Unlike factor costs or taxes or materials costs, depreciation is not paid for by check. When the company's accountants make an allowance for depreciation, all they do is make an entry on the company's book, stating that plant and equipment are now worth a certain amount less than in the beginning of the year.

At the same time, however, General Manufacturing *includes* the amount of depreciation in the price it intends to charge for its goods. As we have seen, part of the resources used up in production was its own capital equipment, and it is certainly entitled to consider the depreciation as a cost. Yet, it has not paid anyone a sum of money equal to this cost! How, then, will there be enough income in the marketplace to buy back its product?

The answer lies in the fact that we are not dealing with a single company but with a vast assemblage of companies, all of which are depreciating their assets—that is, adding to their costs sums equal to the wear and tear on their equipment—and *some of which are also busy replacing their equipment as it becomes completely worn out.*

Suppose we had 10 companies, each with machines worth $1,000 that deteriorated at a rate of $100 a year. If these companies originally bought their machines in different years, then we can see that each year the sum of depreciation costs would be $1,000 (10 companies each adding $100 to their costs), but that this would be nicely offset by the actual expenditure of $1,000 as, each year, one company bought itself a new machine to take the place of the unit that had finally worn out. Ten companies might not space their replacement expenditures so evenly. But when we deal with the thousands of companies in the economy and with the widely varying lifetimes of their equipment, we can make the quite realistic assumption that there will be a steady flow of replacement spending.*

This enables us to see that insofar as there is a steady stream of replacement expenditures going to firms that make capital goods, there will be payments just large enough to balance the addition to costs due to depreciation. As with all other payments to firms, these replacement expenditures will, of course, become incomes to factors, etc., and thus can reappear on the marketplace.

ANOTHER VIEW OF COSTS AND INCOMES

Because it is very important to understand the relationship between the "selling price" of GNP and the amount of income available to buy it back, it may help to look at the matter from a different point of view.

This time let us approach it by seeing how the economy arranges things so that consumers and government and business, the three great sectors of final demand, are each provided with enough purchasing power to claim the share of GNP they need. Suppose, to begin with, that the economy paid out income only to its factors and priced its goods and services accordingly. In that case, consumers could purchase the entire value of the year's output, but business and government would be unable to purchase any portion of that output for themselves.

This would obviously lead to serious trouble. Hence we must arrange for business and government to have a claim on the total output by taking a portion of the factors' purchasing power and transferring it to these two sectors. One means of doing this is by taxation. Direct (income) taxes simply transfer money directly from factors' pockets to the government, thereby lowering consumers' purchasing power. Indirect taxes accomplish the same thing by pricing goods above their factor costs, thus making it impossible for factors to claim the entire output.

In exactly the same way, business also reserves a claim on output by pricing its products to include a charge for depreciation. By so doing, it again reduces the ability of consumers to buy back the entire output of the economy, while it gives business the purchasing power to claim the output it needs (just as taxes give purchasing power to government). Now, after paying direct and indirect taxes and depreciation, the consumer is finally free to spend all the remainder of his income without danger of encroaching on the output that must be reserved for public activity and for the replacement of capital.

* But wait, some bright student will object. Suppose one of the 10 companies decides not to replace its machine, but to junk it, or suppose it decides to go out of business or to go into some other line. Then there won't be a flow of replacement spending equal to depreciation costs! Our student is quite right. But that brings us ahead of ourselves to consider a highly dynamic economy. In our calm model, we just ignore such complexities of the actual economic world. Furthermore, we are not too unrealistic in doing so. Save for the most severely depressed years, the economy as a whole *does* replace its depreciated assets.

Chapter 11 **199**

In other words, we can look at taxes and depreciation not merely as "costs" that the consumer has to pay, or as "incomes" that accrue to government and business, but also as the means by which the output of the economy is made available to two important claimants besides the public.

THE THREE
STREAMS OF
EXPENDITURE

Our analysis is now essentially complete. Item by item, we have traced each element of cost into an income payment, so that we now know there is enough income paid out to buy back our GNP at a price that represents its full cost.

Perhaps this was a conclusion we anticipated all along. After all, ours would be an impossibly difficult economy to manage if somewhere along the line purchasing power dropped out of existence, so that we were always faced with a shortage of income to buy back the product we made. But our analysis has also shown us a more unexpected thing. We are accustomed to thinking that all the purchasing power in the economy is received and spent through the hands of "people"—by which we usually mean households. Now we can see that this is not true. There is not only one, but there are *three* streams of incomes and costs, all quite distinct from one another.

1. Factor costs→Households→Consumers goods

2. Indirect Taxes→Government agencies→Government goods

3. Depreciation→Business firms→Replacement investment

To help visualize these three flows, imagine for an instant that our money comes in colors (all of equal value): black, orange, and gray. Now suppose that firms always pay their factors in black money, their taxes in orange money, and their replacement expenditures in gray money. In point of fact, of course, the colors would soon be mixed. A factor that is paid in black bills will be paying some of his black income for taxes; or a government agency will be paying out orange money as factor incomes; or firms will be using gray dollars to pay taxes or factors, and orange or black dollars to pay for replacement capital.

But at least in our mind we could picture the streams being kept quite separate. An orange tax dollar paid by General Manufacturing to the Internal Revenue Service for taxes could go from the government to another firm, let us say in payment for office supplies, and we can think of the office supply firm keeping these orange dollars apart from its other receipts, to pay its taxes with. Such an orange dollar could circulate indefinitely, from government agencies to firms and back again, helping to bring about production but never entering a consumer's pocket! In the same way, a gray replacement expenditure dollar going from General Manufacturing to, let us say U.S. Steel, could be set aside by U.S. Steel to pay for *its* replacement needs; and the firm that received this gray dollar might, in turn, set it aside for its own use as replacement expenditure. We could, that is, imagine a circuit of expenditures in which gray dollars went from firm to firm, to pay for replacement investment, and never ended up in a pay envelope or as a tax payment.

There is a simple way of explaining this seemingly complex triple flow. Each stream indicates the existence of a *final taker* of gross national product: consumers, government, and business itself.* Since output has final claimants other than consumers, we can obviously have a flow of purchasing power that does not enter consumers' or factors' hands.

The Crucial Role of Expenditures

The realization that factors do not get paid incomes equal to the total gross value of output brings us back to the central question of this chapter: can we be certain that we will be able to sell our GNP at its full cost? Has there surely been generated enough purchasing power to buy back our total output?

We have thus far carefully analyzed and answered half the question. *We know that all costs will become incomes to factors or receipts of government agencies or of firms making replacement items.* To sum up again, factor costs become the incomes of workers, managements, owners of natural resources and of capital; and all these incomes together can be thought of as comprising the receipts of the household sector. Tax costs are paid to government agencies and become receipts of the government sector. Depreciation costs are initially accrued within business firms, and these accruals belong to the business sector. As long as worn-out capital is regularly replaced, these accruals will be matched by equivalent new receipts of firms that make capital goods.

What we have not yet established, however, is that these sector receipts will become sector *expenditures.* That is, we have not demonstrated that all households will now *spend* all their incomes on goods and services, or that government units will necessarily *spend* all their tax receipts on public goods and services, or that all firms will assuredly *spend* their depreciation accruals for new replacement equipment.

What happens if some receipts are not spent? The answer is of key importance in understanding the operation of the economy. A failure of the sectors to spend as much money as they have received means that some of the costs that have been laid out will *not* come back to the original entrepreneurs. As a result, they will suffer losses. If, for instance, our gross national product costs $900 billion to produce but the various sectors spend only

---

* We continue to forget about net exports until Chapter 15. We can think of them perfectly satisfactorily as a component of gross private investment.

$890 billion in all, then some entrepreneurs will find themselves failing to sell all their output. Inventories of unsold goods will begin piling up, and businessmen will soon be worried about "over-producing." The natural thing to do when you can't sell all your output is to stop making so much of it, so that businesses will begin cutting back on production. As they do so, they will also cut back on the number of people they employ. As a result, businessmen's costs will go down; but so will factor incomes, for we have seen that costs and incomes are but opposite sides of one coin. As incomes fall, the expenditures of the sectors might very well fall further, bringing about another twist in the spiral of recession.

This is not yet the place to go into the mechanics of such a downward spiral of business. But the point is clear. *A failure of the sectors to bring all their receipts back to the marketplace as demand can initiate profound economic problems.* In the contrast between an unshakable equality of costs and incomes on the one hand and the uncertain connection between receipts and expenditures on the other, we have come to grips with one of the most important problems in macroeconomics.

THE COMPLETE CIRCUIT

We shall have ample opportunity later to observe exactly what happens when receipts are not spent. Now let us be sure that we understand how the great circle of the economic flow is closed when the sectors *do* spend their receipts. Figure 11-3 shows how we can trace our "black, orange, and gray" dollars through the economy and how these flows suffice to buy back GNP for its total cost.

We can trace the flow from left to right. We begin on the left with the bar representing the total cost of our freshly produced GNP. As we know, this cost consists of all the factor costs of all the firms and government units in the nation, all the indirect tax costs incurred during production, and all the depreciation charges made during production. The bar also shows us the amount of money demand our economy must generate in order to buy back its own output.

The next bars show us the transmutation of costs into sector receipts for householders, government units, and business firms (who retain their own depreciation accruals). This relationship between costs and sector receipts is one of *identity*—all costs *must* be receipts. Hence we use the sign $\equiv$ to indicate that this is a relation of identities—of definitional differences only.

Thereafter we notice the crucial link. Each sector dutifully spends all its receipts, as it it supposed to. Our household sector buys the kinds of goods and services householders do in fact buy—consumption goods and services. Our government sector buys government goods and services, and our business sector buys replacement investment. This time we use an arrow ($\rightarrow$) because this is emphatically *not* a relationship of identity.

Now note the next bar. Here we see what happens to these expenditures when they are received by the firms who make consumer goods, or by

FIG. 11·3 THE CIRCULAR FLOW, VIEW III

the firms or individuals who make goods and services bought by governments, or by the manufacturers of capital equipment. Each of these recipients will use the money he has received to cover factor payments, taxes, and depreciation for his own business. (What we show in our diagram are not these costs for each and every firm, but the aggregate costs for all firms selling to each sector.)

We are almost done. It remains only to aggregate the sector costs; that is, to add up all the factor costs, all the taxes, and all the depreciation accruals of *all* firms and government agencies—to reproduce a bar just like the one we started with. A circle of production has been completed. Firms and government units have received back on the marketplace a sum just large enough to cover their initial costs, including their profits for risk. The stage is set for another round of production, similar to the last.

GNP as a Sum of Costs and a Sum of Expenditures

Our bar graph also enables us to examine again the concept of gross national product, for now we can see that GNP can be looked at in one of two ways. We can think of measuring a year's gross national product as a sum of all the costs that have been paid out during that year: factor costs, indirect taxes, and depreciation.* Or we can think of measuring the same GNP as the sum of the expenditures that bought this output; that is, consumption expenditure, government expenditure, and gross private investment expenditure. Since the final output is one and the same, we can see that the two methods of computing its value must also be the same.

An illustration may make it easier to grasp this identity of the two ways of measuring GNP. Suppose once again that we picture the economy as a gigantic factory from which the flow of production emerges onto a shipping platform, each item tagged with its selling price. There the items are examined by two clerks. One of them notes down in his book the selling price of each item and then proceeds to analyze that price into its cost components: factor cost (including profit), indirect taxes, and depreciation. The second clerk keeps a similar book in which each item's selling price is also entered, but his job is to note which sector—consumer, government, business investment, or export—is its buyer. Clearly, at the end of the year, the two clerks must show the same value of total output. But whereas the books of the first will show that total value broken down into various costs, the books of the second will show it broken down by its "customers"; that is, by the expenditures of the various sectors.

But wait! Suppose that an item comes onto the shipping platform without an order waiting for it! Would that not make the sum of costs larger than the sum of expenditures?

The answer will give us our final insight into the necessary equality of the two measures of GNP. For what happens to an item that is not bought by one of the sectors? It will be sent by the shipping clerk into inventory *where it will count as part of the business investment of the economy!* Do not forget that increases in inventory are treated as investment because they are a part of output that has not been consumed. To be sure, it is a very unwelcome kind of investment; and if it continues, it will shortly lead to changes in the production of the firm. Such dynamic changes will soon lie at the very center of our attention. In the meantime, however, the fact that unbought goods are counted as investment—as if they were "bought" by the firm that produced but cannot sell them—establishes the absolute identity of GNP measured as a sum of costs or as a sum of expenditures.

To express the equality with the conciseness and clarity of mathematics, we can write:

$$C + I + G + E \equiv F + T + D$$

Where C, I, G, and E are the familiar categories of expenditure, and F, T, and D stand for factor costs, indirect taxes, and depreciation.

---

* This is, of course, Boulding's Gross National Cost.

It is now also very easy to understand the meaning of two other less frequently used measures of output. One of these is called *net national product* (NNP). As the name indicates, it is exactly equal to gross national product *minus depreciation*. The other measure, national income, we have already met. It is GNP *minus depreciation and indirect taxes*. This makes it equal to the sum of factor costs only. Figure 11-4 should make this relationship clear.

FIG. 11•4

The "self-reproducing" model economy we have now sketched out is obviously still very far from reality. Nevertheless, the particular kind of unreality that we have deliberately constructed serves a highly useful purpose. An economy that regularly and dependably buys back everything it produces gives us a kind of bench mark from which to begin our subsequent investigations. We call such an economy, whose internal relationships we have outlined, an economy in *stationary equilibrium,* and we denote the changeless flow of costs into business receipts and receipts back into costs a *circular flow.*

We shall return many times to the model of a circular flow economy for insights into a more complex and dynamic system. Hence it is well that we summarize briefly two of the salient characteristics of such a system.

1. *A circular flow economy will never experience a "recession."*

Year in and year out, its total output will remain unchanged. Indeed, the very concept of a circular flow is useful in showing us that an economic system can maintain a given level of activity *indefinitely,* so long as all the sectors convert all their receipts into expenditure.

2. *A circular flow economy also will never know a "boom."*

That is, it will not grow, and its standard of living will remain unchanged. That standard of living may be high or low, for we could have a circular flow economy of poverty or of abundance. But in either state, changelessness will be of its essence.

In the chapters that follow, we must successively reintroduce the very elements that we have so carefully excluded. First, net saving and net investment, then technological change and population growth must one by one find their way back into our model. Thus, gradually it will approximate itself to the realities around us, allowing us to return from the abstract world of ideas to the concrete world of reality.

KEY CONCEPTS AND KEY WORDS

1. **A great *circle of payments and receipts constantly renews the demand* that keeps the economy going. Income is pumped out to the participants in the production process, who then spend their incomes to buy the output they have helped to make, thereby returning money to the firms that again pump it out.**

Model

2. **We seek to elucidate this circle by constructing a *model*—an economy stripped of everything that is not essential to the process we seek to understand. Our model simplifies and therefore highlights the relationships that underlie the macroeconomic process.**

Costs

3. **We use our model to show *how an economy can in fact buy back all of its own output*—how enough demand can be created to keep the economy going. To do so, we must show that *every item of cost to business firms can become demand* for them on the marketplace.**

Factor payments

4. **The first item of costs is *factor payments* (wages, rent, profits, interest). These payments for factor services are *the source of household income.* In turn, households can spend their incomes for *consumption goods.***

Indirect taxes

5. ***Indirect taxes* are costs paid by firms to government agencies. In turn, these agencies spend their tax receipts for *government purchases.***

Direct taxes

(Note that direct taxes—income taxes—are not a cost of production, but a levy imposed on factors after they have been paid.)

Depreciation

6. ***Depreciation costs* are costs incurred by *businesses* for the wear and tear of capital. They are accrued by business firms, who, in turn, are able to use them to purchase *replacement investment.***

Intermediate goods and final goods

7. ***Materials costs* are payments to other firms. Ultimately, they can all be broken down into factor costs, indirect tax costs, and depreciation costs.**

8. ***The total value of output (GNP) can be seen not only as a sum of expenditures (C + I + G + E), but as a sum of costs (F + T + D).***

Sector

9. ***All costs thus become sector receipts:* factor costs become household incomes; indirect tax costs become government receipts; depreciation costs become business re-**

ceipts. In turn, *these sector receipts can be returned to the market as new expenditures (demand).*

10. This gives us *three streams of cost—income—expenditure (demand):*
    factor costs→household incomes→consumption expenditure
    indirect taxes→government receipts→government expenditure
    depreciation→business receipts→replacement expenditure

Receipts

11. *The key linkage is that between receipts and expenditure. All costs must become receipts. But not all receipts need necessarily be spent.*

Expenditure

12. When all receipts are spent, then we have a perfect *circular flow.* In such a situation, the economy generates an unchanging flow of demand, and therefore experiences neither boom, recession, nor growth.

Circular flow

Q U E S T I O N S

1. How can a model elucidate reality when it is deliberately stripped of the very things that make reality interesting?

2. Why do we need a model to show that an economy can buy back its own production?

3. What are factor costs? What kinds of factor costs are there? To what sector do factor costs go?

4. What are direct taxes? What are indirect taxes? Which are considered part of production costs? Why?

5. To whom are materials costs paid? Why are they not part of the sum total of costs in GNP?

6. What is depreciation? Why is it a part of costs? Who receives the payments or accruals made for depreciation purposes?

7. Show in a carefully drawn diagram how costs become income or receipts of the different sectors.

8. Show in a second diagram how the incomes of the various sectors can become expenditures.

9. Why is the link between expenditure and receipt different from that between receipt and expenditure?

10. What is meant by a circular flow economy? Why does such an economy have neither growth nor fluctuation?

11. Explain the two different ways of looking at GNP and write the simple formula for each.

12. Can we have demand without expenditure?

L E A R N I N G   A B O U T   S T A T I S T I C S

Our first "Learning about Statistics" taught us to be cautious in handling data and, in particular, to be careful about problems involving aggregates. Now, in this introduction to statistical methods themselves, we shall learn something more about the problems of aggregates, by investigating an exceedingly important question raised earlier in the text. This is the question of how we "correct" the data of GNP (or any other set of data that are expressed in money-magnitudes) for the *price changes that affect the value of our dollars but not the real quantities of goods and services our dollars buy.*

THE PROBLEM
OF PRICE
INDEXES

Say that in 1967 you were earning $200 a week and that four years later, in 1971, your salary is $240 a week. Are you richer now than you were then? Anyone who is sure that the answer is *yes* suffers from a "money illusion," the impression that riches are measured by dollars rather than by the amount of goods and services that those dollars can buy. Of course, since inflation has been so much in the news, the money illusion is no longer as widespread as it used to be, although in one way or another it continues to persist. How many of us, while feeling good about the money we have "made" from our savings accounts, have to be reminded that if the bank's interest rate is 5 percent and the rate of inflation is 5 percent, we have in fact made nothing at all?*

A price index, in effect, allows us to retain the money illusion without falling into error. By reducing the buying power of one year's dollar to the buying power of another year's, it enables us to compare different amounts of goods and services in terms of dollar figures.

HOW IT WORKS   Can you, as the aforementioned wage earner, purchase more in 1971 than you could in 1967? The answer is no. According to the consumer price index put out by the U.S. Department of Labor, even though you receive $40 a week more, your *real* income has not changed.

Here is how we arrive at this conclusion. The Department of Labor tells us that a typical "basket" of goods and services cost about 20 percent more in 1971 than it did in 1967. It is customary to express such a relationship in terms of a *price index,* with 100 equal to the price level in whatever year we call *the base.* The Department of Labor now takes 1967 as its base year. Thus, the price index for 1967 is set at 100, and the price index for 1971 (20 percent higher) must be 120. If prices go down in 1980 to half the 1967 level, the index then will be 50.

We are now ready to express our two income figures in 1967 prices. We do it *by dividing each figure by the price index for that year* (and then by multiplying each result by 100). In the first case we get, of course, what we originally started with:

$$\frac{\$200 \text{ (our income in 1967)}}{100 \text{ (price index for 1967)}} = \$2; \qquad\qquad \$2 \times 100 = \$200$$

And in the second case the result is the same:

$$\frac{\$240 \text{ (our income in 1971)}}{120 \text{ (price index in 1971)}} = \$2; \qquad\qquad \$2 \times 100 = \$200$$

Thus, *our real income has not changed.*

In a similar fashion, with another, but basically similar, price index, called the *GNP deflator,* we can reduce figures for GNP to magnitudes that can be compared with one another. As with the income figure, we divide the GNP figure by its price index and then multiply the result by 100. Suppose GNP is $900 billion in the base year and $960 billion in the following year. Suppose the GNP deflator (the price index) has gone from 100 to 120. What has happened to real GNP? Answer:

$$\frac{\$900}{100} = \$9 \times 100 = \$900 \text{ billion in the base year}$$

$$\frac{\$960}{120} = \$8 \times 100 = \$800 \text{ billion in the following year}$$

* Anyone who has ever made such an error should think about the following: suppose we put $100 in the bank at 5 percent, so that by the end of the year we have $105. If in that same period prices have gone up by 5 percent, then it now must *cost* $105 to buy the same item that cost $100 a year ago. So we are back where we started from. Of course, if we had put the money in a mattress instead of in the bank, we would actually be poorer than when we began.

Thus, while "current-price" GNP has risen, "constant-price" GNP has fallen. In other words, money illusions to the contrary, output has actually gone down.

If we carry out these operations on a series of GNP figures, then we can draw the graph shown in Fig. 10-4. Notice that for the year 1963 the constant price GNP is the same as the current price GNP. The lines coincide at that point because in this graph 1963 is used as the base year. One can, in fact, use *any* year as a "base year" and build a price index that shows the relation of price levels in years before or after that year to the base. Caution: in using price indexes do not compare two series that have *different* base years. It is not difficult to "splice" one index to another, but that is a procedure that has to be learned in a course on statistical methods.

BUILDING A PRICE INDEX

So far, we have learned how to use a price index. Now we are going to work backward and find out how a price index is built.

Take an imaginary economy with only one consumer product, which we will call bread. Say that in the first year, which we will use as our base, bread sells for $2 per baker's dozen, and that in the second year its price is $4. What would the price index be for the second year? Elementary algebra gives us the answer:

$2 is to $4 as 100 is to X

$$\frac{2}{4} = \frac{100}{x}$$

Solving by cross-multiplying, we get:

$$2x = 400$$
$$x = 200$$

With 200 as our price index, we are now ready to compute real income in the second year in terms of base-year prices, just as we did earlier. Suppose a worker in our one-product economy was paid $5,000 the first year and $11,000 the second. What has happened to his real income? Answer:

$$\frac{\$5,000}{100} = \$50 \times 100 = \$5,000 \text{ (real income in Year 1)}$$

$$\frac{\$11,000}{200} = \$55 \times 100 = \$5,500 \text{ (real income in Year 2)}$$

Thus, his real income has risen, but not by nearly so much as the sheer dollar increase would indicate.

WEIGHTS

Now let's drop the assumption of a one-product economy and see what happens when there is more than one product. Assume an economy that consists of two products, bread and shoes. How would we compute a price index in this case?

Here we face a new problem. Before we can calculate *one* index for *two* products, we have to impute a proportional importance to each. For example, if more than half of consumer expenditures went for bread, then a doubling in its price would count more heavily than if the price of shoes doubled. The way we customarily deal with such a problem is *to take the amount of each product that the "typical" consumer purchased in the base year, and then to compute his rise in living costs under the assumption that he will buy each product in the same proportion in succeeding years.*

Let us say that we find he spent $100 in the base year and that he allotted the money in this way, between bread at $2 per unit and shoes at $10 per pair.

Product	No. units bought	×	Price	=	Total
Bread	35 dozen	×	$2	=	$70
Shoes	3 pairs	×	$10	=	$30
					$100

In the second year, the price of bread doubles to $4 and the price of shoes is cut in half to $5. If the consumer plans to buy the same number of units of each, then his new budget must look like this:

Product	No. units bought	×	Price	=	Total
Bread	35 dozen	×	$4	=	$140
Shoes	3 pairs	×	$5	=	$15
					$155

This gives us an aggregate expenditure for each year, from which we can compute the price index. Since it cost $100 to buy a typical basket of goods in the base year and $155 to buy *the same basket of goods* in the succeeding year, then the relevant index numbers are, of course, 100 and 155.

A more common way to go about this computation is *to derive "weights" from the proportional number of dollars spent on each product in the base year*. Since 70 percent of the typical consumer's money was spent on bread and 30 percent on shoes in 1967, the weights are .7 and .3, respectively.

In order to use the weights, however, we must first compute a separate price index for each product. For bread, which doubled in price, the index is 200 for the second year, and for shoes, which halved in price, the index is 50. Now we multiply the index for each product by its corresponding weight and add up the results. For the base year:

Product	Index	×	Weight	=	Total
Bread	100	×	.7	=	70
Shoes	100	×	.3	=	30
					100

For the succeeding year:

Product	Index	×	Weight	=	Total
Bread	200	×	.7	=	140
Shoes	50	×	.3	=	15
					155

Again, our index numbers are 100 and 155.

Generally speaking, we assign weights by the value of purchases of the base year. But what is more important is that the *same* weights must be used in the computation of each index number (or weights that are at least approximately the same). The consequences of doing otherwise are that an index number for one year would have little or no relation to an index number for another. If we are going to talk about fluctuations in a price level, then it must be a price level for the *same* basket of goods, as in the two products of our example, or for a basket of goods that is *relatively unchanging* in composition.

This procedure works very well in the short run because the output of each A SHORTCOMING commodity remains proportionately about the same from year to year. But in the long run, the composition of output can change drastically. A rise in the price of bread made more difference to a consumer in 1900 than it does in the Seventies, because in 1900 consumers spent a higher percentage of their income on bread than they do now. Similarly, a rise in the price of automobiles would inflate current price GNP a lot more today than in 1910; hence, a GNP deflator for 1971 would have to weight automobiles far more heavily than a GNP deflator for 1910.

Thus, not only does the quality of output change over the long run—a point we have discussed in the text—but the composition of that output also changes. For both reasons, when two income or GNP figures are separated by decades, any attempt to compare them with each other is bound to be misleading to some degree. If you want to make a precise comparison of economic life in, say, 1900 with that of 1971, it would be better to describe the different kinds of goods and services peculiar to each era (horse-and-buggy vs. automobile, e.g.) and to try to quantify these differences in terms of physical units. Dollar values would have limited usefulness at best.

But the great convenience of using dollar values should not be easily given up. Without it, we would not be able to draw the graph in Fig. 10-4, which at a glance gives us a general picture of the trend of economic output. And so long as dollar values *are* being used, price indexes will remain indispensable. But be sure that they are correctly applied and understood to be no more than rough approximations of the "real" changes that take place in a changing economy over time.

Let us return for a moment to our original perspective, an aerial view of the economic flow. We will remember that we could see the workings of the economy as an interaction between the factors of production and their environment, culminating in a stream of production—some private, some public—that was used in part for consumption and in part for the replacement or the further building up of capital. In our model of a circular flow economy we saw how such an economy can be self-sustaining and self-renewing, as each round of disbursements by employers found its way into a stream of purchasing power just large enough to justify the continuation of the given scale of output.

The Meaning of Saving

Yet we all know that such a circular flow is a highly unreal depiction of the world. Indeed, it omits the most important dynamic factor of real economic life—the steady accumulation of new capital (and the qualitative change in the nature of the capital due to technology) that characterizes a *growing* economy. What we must now investigate is the process by which society adds each year to its stock of real wealth—and the effect of this process on the circuit of production and purchasing.

We begin by making sure that we understand a key word in this dynamic analysis—*saving*. We have come across saving many times by now in this book and so we should be ready for a final mastery of this centrally important economic term. In Chapter 10 (and previously in our discussion of the Great Depression in Chapters 8 and 9) we spoke of saving in *real* terms as the act by which society relinquished resources that might have been used for consumption, thereby making them available for the capital-building stream of output. Now we must translate that underlying real meaning of saving into terms corresponding with the buying and selling, paying and receiving discussed in the preceding chapter.

What is saving in these terms? It is very simply *not spending all or part of income for consumption goods or services.** It should be very clear then why saving is such a key term. In our discussion of the circular flow, it became apparent that expenditure was the critical link in the steady operation of the economy. If saving is not-spending, then it would seem that saving could be the cause for just that kind of downward spiral of which we caught a glimpse in our preceding chapter.

And yet this clearly is not the whole story. We also know that the act of investing—of spending money to direct factors into the production of capital goods—requires an act of saving; that is, of not using that same money to direct those factors instead into the production of consumers goods. *Hence, saving is clearly necessary for the process of investment.* Now, how can one and the same act be necessary for economic expansion and a threat to its stability? This is a problem that will occupy us during much of this book.

THE
DEMAND GAP

It will help us understand the problem if we again have recourse to the now familiar diagram of the circular flow. But this time we must introduce into it the crucial new fact of net saving. Note *net* saving. Quite unnoticed, we have already encountered saving in our circular flow. In our model economy, when business made expenditures for the replacement of capital, it used money that *could* have been paid in dividends to stockholders or in additional compensation to employees. Before a replacement expenditure was made, someone had to decide not to allocate that money for dividends or bonuses. Thus, there is a flow of saving—that is, of nonconsumption—even in the circular flow.

---

* Note "for consumption goods and services." Purchasing stocks or bonds or life insurance is also an act of saving, even though you must spend money to acquire these items. What you acquire, however, are assets, not consumption goods and services. Some acts of spending are difficult to classify. Is a college education, for instance, a consumption good or an investment? It is probably better thought of as an investment even though in the statistics of GNP it is treated as consumption.

But the saving is not *net* saving. Like the regular flow of replacement investment itself, the flow of saving that finances this replacement serves only to maintain the existing level of capital wealth, not to increase it. Hence, just as with investment, we reserve the term *net saving* for that saving which makes possible a rise in the total of our capital assets.

Gross and net saving are thus easy to define. *By gross saving we mean all saving, both for replacement and for expansion of our capital assets, exactly like gross investment. By net saving, we mean any saving that makes possible an increase in the stock of capital, again exactly as in the definition of net investment.*

We have already seen that an economy can maintain a circular flow when it saves only as much as is needed to maintain its capital. But now suppose that it saves more than that, as is shown in Fig. 12-1. Here householders save a portion of their incomes, over and above the amount saved by business to insure the maintenance of its assets.

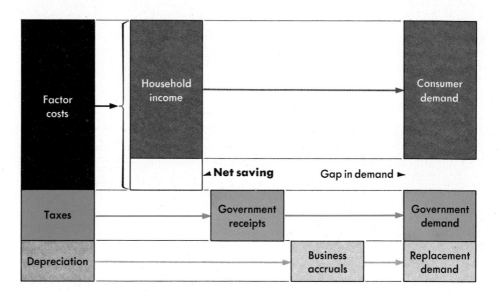

FIG. 12 • 1   THE DEMAND GAP

What we see is precisely what we would expect. There is a gap in demand introduced by the deficiency of consumer spending. This means that the total receipts of employers who make consumer goods will be less than the total amounts they laid out. It begins to look as if we were approaching the cause of economic recession and unemployment.

Yet, whereas we have introduced net saving, we have forgotten about its counterpart, net investment. Cannot the investment activity of a growing economy in some way close the demand gap?

This is indeed, as we shall soon see, the way out of the dilemma. But before we trace the way in which investment compensates for saving, let us draw some important conclusions from the analysis we have made up to this point.

1. *Any act of saving, in and by itself, creates a gap in demand, a shortage of spending. Unless this gap is closed, there will be trouble in the economic system, for employers will not be getting back as receipts all the sums they laid out.*

2. *If the gap is caused by saving that is implicit in depreciation, it can be closed by replacement expenditures. But if it is caused by net saving, over and above the flow needed to maintain the stock of capital, it will require net investment to be closed.*

3. *The presence of a demand gap forces us to make a choice. If we want a dynamic, investing economy, we will have to be prepared to cope with the problems that net saving raises. If we want to avoid these problems, we can close the gap by urging consumers not to save. Then we would have a dependable circular flow, but we would no longer enjoy economic growth.*

The Offset to Savings

How, then, shall we manage to make our way out of the dilemma of saving? The previous diagram makes clear what must be done. If a gap in demand is due to the savings of households, then *that gap must be closed by the expanded spending of some other sector.* There are only two other such sectors: government or business. Thus in some fashion or other, the savings of one sector must be "offset" by the increased activity of another.

But how is this offset to take place? How are the resources that are relinquished by consumers to be made available to entrepreneurs in the business sector or to government officials? In a market economy there is only one way that resources or factors not being used in one place can be used in another. Someone must be willing and able to hire them.

Whether or not government and business *are* willing to employ the factors that are not needed in the consumer goods sector is a very critical matter, soon to command much of our attention. But suppose that they are willing. How will they be able to do so? How can they get the necessary funds to expand their activity?

There are four principal methods of accomplishing this essential increase in expenditure.

1. The business sector can increase its expenditures by *borrowing* the savings of the public through the sale of new corporate bonds.

2. The government sector can increase its expenditures by *borrowing* savings from the other sectors through the sale of new government bonds.

3. The business sector can increase its expenditures by attracting household savings into partnerships, new stock, or other *ownership or equity.*

4. Both business and government sectors can increase expenditures by *borrowing* additional funds from commercial banks.

CLAIMS

There are other possibilities. Government has a very important means of increasing its command over resources, through taxing the household or business sectors. Business can also increase its expenditures by using its own accumulated past savings to finance new spending.

But the most important methods itemized above all have one attribute that calls them especially to our attention. Without exception they give rise to *claims* that reveal from whom the funds have been obtained and to whom they have been made available, as well as on what terms. Bonds, corporate or government, show that savings have been borrowed from individuals or banks by business and government units. Shares of stock reveal that savings have been obtained on an equity (ownership) basis, as do new partnership agreements. Borrowing from banks gives rise to loans that also represent the claims of one part of the community against another.

We can note a few additional points about claims, now that we see how many of them arise in the economy. First, many household savings are first put into banks and insurance companies—so-called financial intermediaries— so that the transfer of funds from households to business or government may go through several stages; e.g., from household to insurance company and then from insurance company to corporation.

Second, not *all* claims involve the offsetting of savings of one sector by expenditures of another. Many claims, once they have arisen, are traded back and forth and bought and sold, as is the case with most stocks and bonds. These purchases and sales involve the *transfer of existing claims,* not the creation of new claims.

Finally, not every new claim necessarily involves the creation of an asset. If A borrows $5 from B, bets it on the races, and gives B his note, there has been an increase in claims, but no new asset has been brought into being to match it.

PUBLIC AND
PRIVATE
CLAIMS

Now let us look at Fig. 12-2. This time we show what happens when savings are made available to the business sector by direct borrowing from households. Note the claim (or equity) that arises.

If the government were doing the borrowing, rather than the business sector, the diagram would look like Fig. 12-3. Notice that the claim is now a government bond.

We have not looked at a diagram showing business or government borrowing its funds from the banking system. (This process will be better

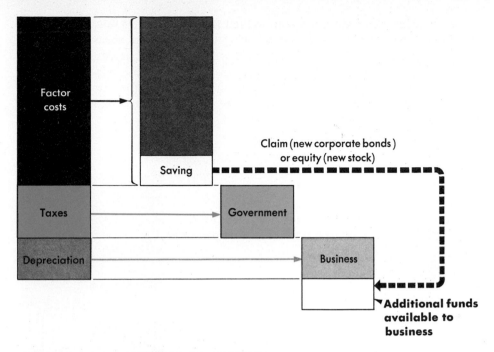

FIG. 12 • 2 "TRANSFER" OF SAVINGS

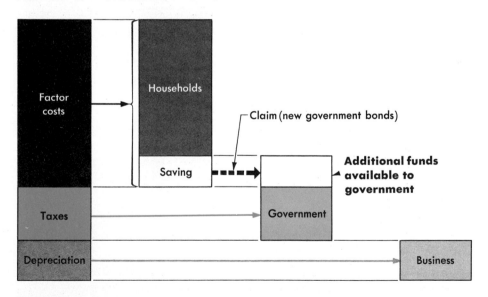

FIG. 12 • 3

understood when we take up the problem of money and banking, in Chapter 17.) The basic concept, however, although more complex, is much the same as above.

There remains only a last step, which must by now be fully anticipated. We have seen how it is possible to offset the savings in one sector, where they were going to cause an expenditure gap, by increasing the funds available to another sector. It remains only to *spend* those additional funds in the form of additional investment or, in the case of the government, for additional public goods and services. The two completed expenditure circuits now appear in Fig. 12-4.

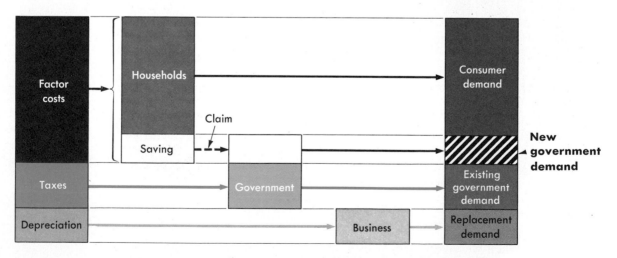

FIG. 12 • 4 TWO WAYS OF CLOSING THE DEMAND GAP

We shall not investigate further at this point the differences between increased public spending and increased business investment. What we must heed is the crucial point at issue: *if saving in any one sector is to be offset, some other sector (or sectors) must spend more than its income. A gap in demand due to insufficient expenditure in one sector can be compensated only by an increase in demand—that is, in expenditure—of another.*

Once this simple but fundamental point is clearly understood, much of the mystery of macroeconomics disappears, for we can then begin to see that an economy in movement, as contrasted with one in a stationary circular flow, is one in which sectors must *cooperate* to maintain the closed circuit of income and output. In a dynamic economy, we no longer enjoy the steady translation of incomes into expenditure which, as we have seen, is the key to an uninterrupted flow of output. Rather, we are faced with the presence of net saving and the possibility of a gap in final demand. Difficult though the ensuing problems are, let us not forget that saving is the necessary condition for the accumulation of capital. The price of economic growth, in other words, is the risk of economic decline.

This central importance of saving in a growing economy will become a familiar problem. At this juncture, where we have first encountered the difficulties it can pose, we must be certain that we understand two different aspects that saving assumes.

One aspect, noticed in our initial overview of the economy, is the decision to relinquish *resources* that can then be re-deployed into capital-building. This is the real significance of saving. But this "real" aspect of saving is not the way we encounter the act of saving in our ordinary lives. We think of saving as a monetary phenomenon, not a "real" one. When we save, we are conscious of not using all our incomes for consumption, but we scarcely, if ever, think of releasing resources for alternative employments.

There is a reason for this dichotomy of real and money saving. In our society, with its extraordinary degree of specialization, the individuals or institutions that do the actual saving are not ordinarily those that do the actual capital-building. In a simple society, this dichotomy between saving and investing need not, and usually does not, occur. A farmer who decides to build new capital—for example, to build a barn—is very much aware of giving up a consumption activity—the raising of food—in order to carry out his investment. So is an artisan who stops weaving clothing to repair his loom. Where the saver and the investor are one and the same person, there need be no "financial" saving, and the underlying real phenomenon of saving as the diversion of activity from consumption to investment is immediately apparent.

In the modern world, savers and investors are sometimes the same individual or group—as in the case of a business management that spends profits on new productive capacity rather than on higher executive salaries. More often, however, savers are not investors. Certainly householders, though very important savers, do not personally decide and direct the process of capital formation in the nation. Furthermore, the men and materials that households voluntarily relinquish by not using all their incomes to buy consumers goods have to be physically transferred to different industries, often to different occupations and locations, in order to carry out their investment tasks. This requires funds in the hands of the investors, so that they can tempt resources from one use to another.

Hence we need an elaborate system by which money saving can be "transferred" directly or indirectly into the hands of those who will be in a position to employ factors for capital construction purposes. Nevertheless, underlying this complex mechanism for transferring purchasing power remains the same simple purpose that we initially witnessed. Resources that have been relinquished from the production of consumption goods or services are now employed in the production of capital goods. Thus, *saving and investing are essentially real phenomena,* even though it may take a great deal of financial manipulation to bring them about.

A final important point. *The fact that the decisions to save and the decisions to invest are lodged in different individuals or groups alerts us to a basic reason why the savings-investment process may not always work smoothly.* Savers may choose to consume less than their total incomes at times when investors have no interest in expanding their capital assets. Alternatively, business firms may wish to form new capital when savers are interested in spending money only on themselves. This separation of decision-making can give rise to situations in which savings are not offset by investment, or in which investment plans race out ahead of savings capabilities. In our next chapters we will be investigating what happens in these cases.

Transfer Payments and Profits

We have talked about the transfer of purchasing power from savers to investors, but we have not yet mentioned another kind of transfer, also of great importance in the overall operation of the economy. This is the transfer of incomes from sector to sector (and sometimes within sectors).

Income transfers (called *transfer payments*) are a very useful and important means of reallocating purchasing power in society. Through transfer payments, members of the community who do not participate in production are given an opportunity to enjoy incomes that would otherwise not be available to them. Thus Social Security transfer payments make it possible for the old or the handicapped to be given an "income" of their own (not, to be sure, a currently *earned* income), or unemployment benefits give purchasing power to those who cannot get it through employment.

FIG. 12•5 TRANSFER PAYMENTS

Not all transfers are in the nature of welfare payments, however. The distribution of money *within* a household is a transfer payment. So is the payment of interest on the national debt.* So is the grant of a subsidy to a private enterprise, such as an airline, or of a scholarship to a college student. Any income payment that is not earned by selling one's productive services on the market falls in the transfer category.

It may help to understand this process if we visualize it in our flow diagram. Figure 12-5 shows two kinds of transfers. The upper one, from the government to the household sector, shows a typical transfer of incomes, such as veterans' pensions or Social Security; the transfer below it reflects the flow of income that might be illustrated by a payment to agriculture for crop support. Transfers *within* sectors, such as household allowances, are not shown in the diagram.

One thing we may well note about transfers is that they can only *rearrange* the incomes created in the production process; they cannot increase those incomes. Income, as we learned in the last chapter, is inextricably tied to output—indeed, income is only the financial counterpart of output.

Transfer payments, on the other hand, are a way of arranging individual claims to production in some fashion that strikes the community as fairer or more efficient or more decorous than the way the market process

---

* Curiously, the payment of interest on corporate debt is not considered a transfer payment, but a payment to a factor of production. Actually, much government interest should also be thought of as a factor payment (for the loan of capital for purposes of public output); but by convention, all government interest is classified as a transfer payment.

allocates them through the production process. As such, transfer payments are an indispensable and often invaluable agency of social policy. But it is important to understand that no amount of transfers can, in itself, increase the total that is to be shared. That can happen only by raising output itself.

TRANSFER
PAYMENTS
AND TAXES

We have mentioned, but only in passing, another means of transferring purchasing power from one sector to another: taxation. Heretofore, however, we have often spoken as though all government tax receipts were derived from indirect taxes that were added onto the cost of production.

In fact, this is not the only source of government revenue. Indirect taxes are an important part of state and local revenues, but they are only a minor part of federal tax receipts. Most federal taxes are levied on the incomes of the factors of production or on the profits of businesses after the other factors have been paid.

Once again it is worth remembering that the government taxes consumers (and businesses) because it is in the nature of much government output that it cannot be *sold*. Taxes are the way we are billed for our share—rightly or wrongly figured—of government production that has been collectively decided upon. As we can now see, taxes—both on business and on the household sector—also finance many transfer payments. That is, the government intervenes in the distribution process to make it conform to our politically expressed social purposes, taking away some incomes from certain individuals and groups, and providing incomes to others. Figure 12-6

FIG. 12 • 6   TRANSFERS AND INCOME TAXES

shows what this looks like in the flow of GNP. (Note that the business sector is drawn with profits, as our next section will explain.)

As we can see, the exchanges of income between the household and the government sectors can be very complex. Income can flow from households to government units via taxation, and return to the household sector via transfer payments; and the same two-way flows can take place between government and business.

The last diagram has already introduced a new element of reality in our discussion. Taxes on business *income* presuppose that businesses make *profits*. Let us see how these profits fit into the savings-investment process.

During our discussion of the circular flow, we spoke of profits as a special kind of factor cost—a payment to the factor *capital,* in return for its contribution of risk-taking. But since we are no longer in a changeless circular flow economy, we can introduce a much more dynamic conception of profits. Now we can think of profits not merely as a factor cost (although there is always a certain element of risk-remuneration in profits), but as a return to especially efficient or forward-thinking firms who have used the investment process to introduce new products or processes ahead of the run of their industries. We can think of profits, too, as being in part the return accruing to powerful firms who exact a semimonopolistic return from their customers. In Part Four we will look much more carefully into the question of the origin of profits.

What matters in our analysis at this stage is not the precise explanation we give to the origin of profits, but a precise explanation of their role in maintaining a "closed-circuit" economy in which all costs are returned to the marketplace as demand. A commonly heard diagnosis for economic maladies is that profits are at the root of the matter, in that they cause a "withdrawal" of spending power or income from the community. If profits were "hoarded," or kept unspent, this might be true. In fact, however, profits can be spent in three ways. They may be

1. distributed as income to the household sector in the form of dividends or profit shares, to become part of household spending
2. spent by business firms for new plant and equipment
3. taxed by the government and spent in the public sector

All three methods of offsetting profits appear in Fig. 12-7.

We can see that profits need not constitute a withdrawal from the income stream. Indeed, unless profits are adequate, businesses will very likely not invest enough to offset the savings of the household sector. They may, in fact, even fail to make normal replacement expenditures, aggravating the demand gap still further in this way.

Thus the existence of profits, far from being deflationary—that is, far from causing a fall in income—is, in fact, essential for the maintenance of a

FIG. 12 • 7 PROFITS IN THE CIRCULAR FLOW

given level of income or for an advance to a higher level. Nonetheless, there is a germ of truth in the contentions of those who have maintained that profits can cause an insufficiency of purchasing power. *For unless profits are returned to the flow of purchasing power as dividends that are spent by their recipients, or as new capital expenditures made by business, or as taxes that lead to additional public spending, there will be a gap in the community's demand.* Thus we can think of profits just as we think of saving—an indispensable source of economic growth or a potential source of economic decline.

SAVING, INVESTMENT, AND GROWTH

We are almost ready to leave our analysis of the circle of production and income, and to proceed to a much closer study of the individual dynamic elements that create and close gaps. Before we do, however, it is well that we take note of one last fact of the greatest importance. In offsetting the savings of any sector by investment, we have closed the production and income circuit, much as in the stationary circular flow, but there is one crucial difference from the circular flow. Now we have closed the flow by diverting savings into the creation of *additional* capital. Unlike the stationary circular flow where the handing around of incomes did no more than to maintain unchanged the original configuration of the system, in our new dynamic saving-and-investing model *each closing of the circuit results in a quantitative change—the addition of a new "layer" of capital.* Hence, more and more wealth is being added to our system; and thinking back to our first impressions of the interaction of wealth and population, we would expect more and more productiveness from our human factors. Bringing with it complications with which we shall have to deal in due course, *growth* has entered our economic model.

KEY CONCEPTS AND KEY WORDS

1. The critical element missing from the concept of the circular flow is *saving.* The key question is how an economy can buy back all its output when some of its receipts are saved rather than returned to the market through expenditure.

2. Saving poses a dilemma. On one hand, it breaks the circular flow and creates a *demand gap.* On the other hand, if there is *no saving,* there can be *no investment.*

   Demand gap

3. The answer to the dilemma is that *saving,* which is essential for growth, *must be offset by additional expenditure.* This means that another sector must spend more than its income.

4. There are four main ways in which a sector can spend more than its income:
   • The *business sector can borrow* from the household sector.
   • The *government sector can borrow* from the household sector.
   • The *business sector* can attract household savings into *equities.*
   • Business and government can borrow from the *commercial banks.*

   Inter-sectoral cooperation

5. Although saving involves money, it is essentially a "real" process (as is investment). That is, its real meaning is that resources are released from consumption. The acts of releasing resources (saving) and the acts of employing them (investment) are usually performed by different groups in modern society.

   Real saving

6. *Transfer payments,* from one sector to another or within one sector, play an important part in *redistributing* income, but do not increase the total GNP.

   Transfer payments

7. Profits can be returned to the expenditure flow by being: (1) paid out as dividends, etc., to the household sector, where they can be used for consumption; (2) spent by business firms for new investment; or (3) taxed by the government and spent by it.

   Profits and expenditure

8. Saving thus requires investment to assure that all payments will be returned to the market as demand. Note, however, that the process of *investment adds to capital* and thereby increases productivity. Saving and investment are therefore an integral part of the *process of growth.*

   Growth

QUESTIONS

1. What do we mean by a demand gap? Show diagrammatically.
2. How is a demand gap filled by business investment? Show diagrammatically.
3. Why is saving indispensable for growth?
4. Can we have planned business investment without saving? Saving without planned business investment?
5. Draw carefully a diagram that shows how savings can be offset by government spending.
6. How is it possible for a sector to spend more than its income? How does it get the additional money?

7. What is a transfer payment? Draw diagrams of transfers from government to consumers, from government to business. Is charity a transfer? Is a lottery?

8. Diagram the three ways in which profits can be returned to the expenditure flow. What happens if they are not?

9. Why is a problem presented by the fact that those who save and those who make the decision to invest are not the same people?

10. In what way is a circular flow economy different from an economy that saves and invests?

LEARNING ABOUT STATISTICS

**WHAT IS
AN AVERAGE?**

Which of these figures represents the average income received by families and individuals in the United States: $8,100 or $7,100? The answer is *both of them!* The first average, called the *arithmetic mean,* is what we usually have in mind when we use the term *average.* We get it by taking the total amount of income received and dividing it by the total number of families and individuals receiving it.

**Means
and medians**

But our second figure also qualifies as an average, and in this case, as we shall see, it is the more useful of the two. Called *the median,* it can be regarded as representing the level of the "middle" income; half the economic units receive more than this amount, and half receive less.

Why is the arithmetic mean larger than the median? A moment's thought tells us that if the median income is $7,100, then the range of income in the poorer half of the population must be smaller than the range in the half that is richer; 50 percent of the population must receive between $1 and $7,100, and 50 percent between $7,100 and the income of the richest person in the country. *This asymmetry in the distribution of income is at the root of the difference between the two averages.*

**A SIMPLE
ILLUSTRATION**

Perhaps the principle involved is clear to you by now. If not, an arithmetical example may help you to understand it.

Assume that there are two towns, A and B, and that each consists of five families. The following table represents the distribution of income.

| A | $4,000 | $6,000 | $7,000 | $8,000 | $10,000 |
| B | $4,000 | $6,000 | $7,000 | $8,000 | $15,000 |

In each town, the median is $7,000, the income of the family in the middle. But notice that in town A, the distribution of income is symmetrical; that is, the median family is $1,000 away from the second and fourth families, and $3,000 away from the first and fifth families. Note, however, that this is not true of town B; the income of the top (fifth) family is much further away from the median than the income of the first family.

In town A, the median should be equal to the arithmetic mean. And, of course, it is: total income of $35,000 of town A divided by 5 equals $7,000. But in town B, because of the imbalance of income toward the wealthier side, the arithmetic mean is higher than the median: total income of $40,000 of town B divided by 5 equals $8,000. So the mean is $1,000 greater than the median in B.

In its way, town B is a highly simplified version of the country as a whole. If we lined up all the approximately 50 million families in the U.S., from poorest to richest, and picked the middle family—that is, the family with 25 million families on either side—our designated *median* household would have an income of $7,100. If instead, we added up the *incomes* of all families, in any order, and divided by 50 million, the resulting *mean* income would be $8,100.

This asymmetry in distribution is called *skewness,* a term we shall make use of subsequently. A quick way of grasping skewness is to plot data on a graph. For example, in Fig. 12-8, *A* and *B* show two hypothetical distributions, one skewed and one not. In both graphs we measure income along the horizontal axis and the number of families along the vertical axis.

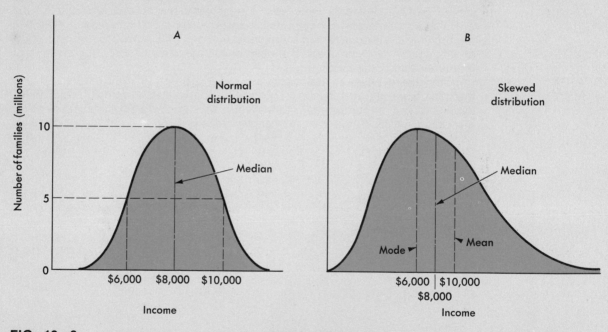

FIG. 12 • 8

The nonskewed distribution is shown in *A,* where we can see that the distribution of income is just the same on one side of the median as on the other. For example, if the median income is $8,000, we note that 5 million families have an income of $6,000 and that 5 million families have an income of $10,000, each income being the same $2,000 distance from the median figure.

This kind of unskewed frequency distribution is called a *bell-shaped curve* or a *normal* curve. Graph *B*, on the other hand, is skewed to the right. Suppose that $8,000 is the median income for this population, as it was for our first example. We can see from the shape of the curve that there is no longer an even pairing of families on either side of this median. The incomes of the families on the right "tail" of the curve are further from the median than the incomes of those on the left "tail," and so the mean (the "old-fashioned" average) must be above the median (middle) income.

Here the mean, as we know from our definition above, is higher than the median (we suppose it to be $10,000 on the graph).

Furthermore, we can now speak of *another* kind of average, called a *mode,* which shows the particular income level on which there are a *larger number* of families than are on any other income level. In our graph, this is represented by the figure of $6,000. Notice that in a bell-shaped distribution, the mode is the same as the median and the arithmetic mean, but this is true for only a normal, bell-shaped distribution.

WHICH AVERAGE TO USE? If we want to express the average income in the United States, which average should we use? Ordinarily, we choose the median because what we have in mind with the word *average* is indeed that income which is "middle-most." If we use the arithmetic mean we distort the picture of the middle family, for we now show an amount of "average" income swollen by the presence of very large incomes at the upper end of the income register.

Sometimes, however, the mean is a better average than the median. This is the case when the distribution of income is approximately normal. Under these circumstances, the arithmetic mean has the advantage that it takes into account the *actual value* of the money incomes received by rich and poor families,

FIG. 12 • 9

whereas the median counts only the number of families on either side of the middle figure.

But bear in mind that in some kinds of distributions, the use of either average can be misleading. Say we had a country where 95 percent of the population received about $500, and the other 5 percent received more than $500, ranging up to $1 million. This is not unlike the situation in India. With such a violent skewness, we probably should use the *mode*, $500. It tells us more than either the mean or the median about the distribution of income.

But suppose the upper 5 percent were all clustered around $10,000. Then we could separate the population into two frequency curves, one for the rich and one for the poor. Such a curve is likely to be *bimodal*, showing that a great many families cluster around one income level and another group clusters around a wholly different level. We show such a bimodal distribution in Fig. 12-9.

Statisticians are well aware of the difficulties of accurately representing such bimodal frequencies with "averages." Thus when you see well-conceived data that present averages—whether for IQs, academic grades, incomes, or other phenomena—you can be pretty confident that the data have only one mode and represent the kind of frequency distribution shown in Fig. 12-8.

With a basic understanding of the crucial role of expenditure and of the complex relationship of saving and investment behind us, we are in a position to look more deeply into the question of the determination of gross national product. For what we have discovered heretofore is only the *mechanism* by which a market economy can sustain or fail to sustain a given level of output through a circuit of expenditure and receipt. Now we must try to discover the *forces* that dynamize the system, creating or closing gaps between income and outgo. Hence, beginning with this chapter, we devote our attention to the actual behavior of the household, government, and business sectors and to their respective motivations for consumption, government purchases, and investment.

The Household Sector

Largest, most familiar, and in many respects more important of all the sectors in the economy is that of the nation's households—that is, its families and single-dwelling individuals (the two categories together called consumer units) considered as receivers of income and transfer payments, or as savers and spenders of money for consumption.

How big is this sector? In 1970 it comprised some fifty-one million families and some fourteen million independent individuals who collectively gathered in $801 billion in income and spent $617 billion.* As Fig. 13-1

---

* The Department of Commerce has recently redefined some categories of the national income accounts, and the word *consumption* today applies, strictly speaking, only to personal expenditures for goods and services. Included in total consumer spending, however, are sizeable amounts for interest (mainly on installment loans) and for remittances abroad, neither of which sums are included in the amount for goods and services. The proper nomenclature for the total of consumer spending (goods and services plus interest and remittances) is now *personal outlays.* We shall, however, continue to use the simpler term consumption, although our figures will be those for personal outlays.

Note, also, that the compilation of these figures is a time-consuming process in which earlier estimates are frequently subject to revision. Hence, figures for the components of consumption, or, for that matter, for almost all magnitudes in the economic process, are apt to vary slightly in successive printed statistics until, eventually, the "final" figures are arrived at. Recall our caution about preliminary data in our first "Learning about Statistics" section, p. 187.

All figures in billions*

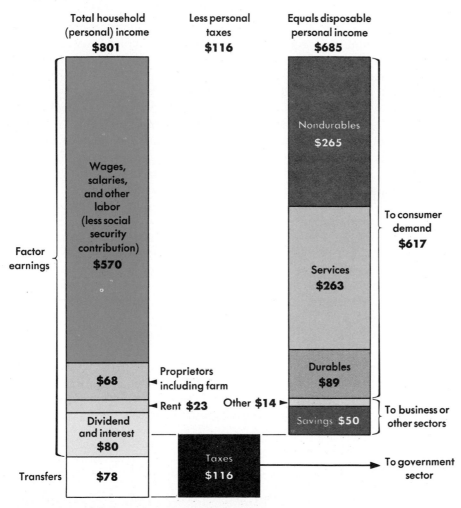

*Totals do not always add, owing to rounding

FIG. 13•1 CONSUMPTION SECTOR, 1970

shows, the great bulk of receipts was from factor earnings, and transfer payments played only a relatively small role. As we can also see, we must subtract personal tax payments from household income (or *personal income* as it is officially designated) before we get *disposable personal income*—income actually available for spending. It is from disposable personal income that the crucial choice is made to spend or save. Much of this chapter will focus on that choice.

SUBCOMPONENTS OF CONSUMPTION   Finally we note that consumer spending itself divides into three main streams. The largest of these is for *nondurable* goods, such as food and clothing or other items whose economic life is (or is assumed to be) short. Second largest is an assortment of expenditures we call consumer *services,* comprising such things as rent, doctors' or lawyers' or barbers' ministrations, theater or movie admissions, bus or taxi or plane transportation, etc., where we buy not a physical good but the work performed by someone or by some equipment. Last is a substream of expenditure for consumer *durable* goods which, as the name suggests, includes items such as cars or household appliances whose economic life is considerably greater than that of most nondurables. We can think of these goods as comprising consumers' capital.

There are complicated patterns and interrelations among these three major streams of consumer spending. As we would expect, consumer spending for durables is extremely volatile. In bad times, such as 1933, it has sunk to less than 8 percent of all consumer outlays; in the peak of good times in the 1960s, it has risen to nearly double that. Meanwhile, outlays for services have been a steadily swelling area for consumer spending in the postwar economy. As a consequence of the growth of consumer buying of durables and of services, the relative share of the consumer dollar going to "soft goods" has been slowly declining. It is interesting to note, for example, that between 1950 and the end of the 1960s, consumer spending for food fell from 23 percent of all consumption to 19 percent and that expenditures for apparel fell from 11 percent to less than 9 percent. Conversely, consumer spending on recreation and foreign travel and remittances climbed from 6.4 percent to more than 8 percent.

CONSUMPTION AND GNP   These internal dynamics of consumption are of the greatest interest to someone who seeks to project consumer spending patterns into the future—perhaps as an aid to merchandising. But here we are interested in the larger phenomenon of the relationship of consumption as a whole to the flow of gross national product.

Figure 13-2 shows us this historic relationship since 1929. Certain things stand out.

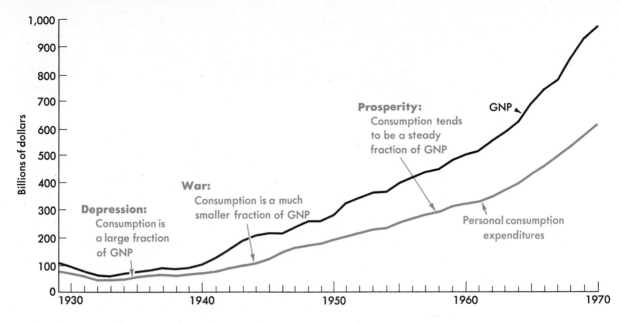

FIG. 13·2 CONSUMPTION AND GNP, CURRENT PRICES

1. *Consumption spending is by far the largest category of spending in GNP.*

Total consumer expenditures—for durable goods, such as automobiles or washing machines; nondurables, like food or clothing; and services, such as recreation or medical care—account for approximately two-thirds of all the final buying in the economy.

2. *Consumption is not only the biggest, it is also the most stable, of all the streams of expenditure.*

For consumption, as we have mentioned, is the essential economic activity. Unless there is a total breakdown in the social system, households will consume some bare minimum. Further, it is a fact of common experience that even in adverse circumstances, households seek to maintain their accustomed living standards. Thus consumption activities constitute a kind of floor for the level of overall economic activity. Investment and government spending, as we shall see, are capable of sudden reversals; but the streams of consumer spending tend to display a measure of stability over time.

3. *Consumption is nonetheless capable of considerable fluctuation as a proportion of GNP.*

Remembering our previous diagrams, we can see that this proportionate fluctuation must reflect changes in the relative importance of investment and government spending. And indeed this is the case. As investment spending fell in the Depression, consumption bulked relatively larger in GNP; as government spending increased during the war, consumption bulked relatively smaller. The changing *relative* size of consumption, in other words, reflects broad changes in *other* sectors rather than sharp changes in consuming habits.

4. *Despite its importance, consumption alone will not "buy back" GNP.*

It is well to recall that consumption, although the largest component of GNP, is still *only* two-thirds of GNP. Government buying and business buying of investment goods are essential if the income-expenditure circuit is to be closed. During our subsequent analysis it will help to remember that consumption expenditure by itself does not provide the only impetus of demand.

Saving in Historic Perspective

This first view of consumption activity sets the stage for our inquiry into the dynamic causes of fluctuations in GNP. We already know that the saving-investment relationship lies at the center of this problem, and that much saving arises from the household sector. Hence, let us see what we can learn about the saving process in historic perspective.

We begin with Fig. 13-3, which shows us the relationship of household saving to disposable income—that is, to household sector incomes after the payment of taxes.

What we see here are two interesting facts. First, during the bottom of the Great Depression there were *no* savings in the household sector. In fact, under the duress of unemployment, millions of households were forced to *dissave*—to borrow or to draw on their old savings (hence the negative figure for the sector as a whole). By way of contrast, we notice the immense savings of the peak war years when consumers' goods were rationed and households were urged to save. Clearly, then, the *amount* of saving is capable of great fluctuation, falling to zero or to negative figures in periods of great economic distress and rising to as much as a quarter of income during periods of goods shortages.

In Fig. 13-4, however, we are struck by another fact. However variable the amounts, the savings *ratio* shows a considerable stability in "normal" years. This steadiness is particularly noteworthy in the postwar period. From 1950 to the present, consumption has ranged between roughly 92 to 95 percent of disposable personal income—which is, of course, the same as saying that savings have ranged between 8 percent and 5 percent. If we take the postwar period as a whole, *we can see that in an average year we have consumed a little more than 94 cents of each dollar of income and that this ratio has remained fairly constant even though our incomes have increased markedly.*

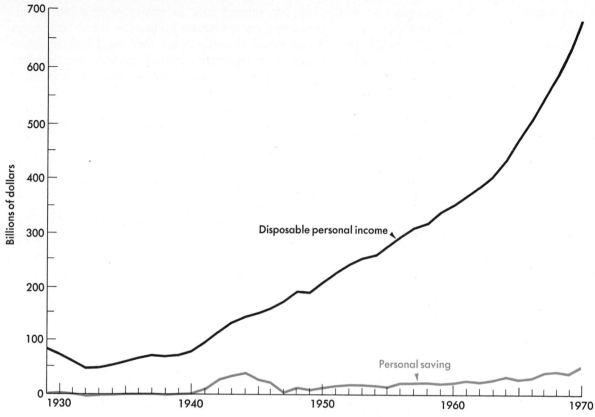

FIG. 13·3 SAVING AND DISPOSABLE INCOME

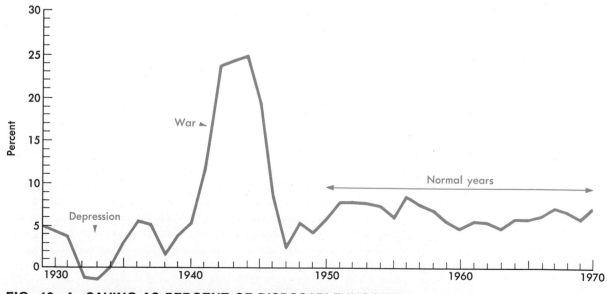

FIG. 13·4 SAVING AS PERCENT OF DISPOSABLE INCOME

This stability of the long-run savings ratio is an interesting and important phenomenon, and something of a puzzling one, for we might easily imagine that the savings ratio would rise over time. Statistical investigations of cross sections of the nation show that rich families tend to save not only larger amounts, but larger *percentages* of their income, than poor families do. Thus as the entire nation has grown richer, and as families have moved from lower income brackets to higher ones, it would seem natural to suppose that they would also take on the higher savings characteristics that accompany upper incomes.

Were this so, the economy would face a very serious problem. In order to sustain its higher levels of aggregate income, it would then have to invest an ever larger *proportion* of its income to offset its growing ratio of savings to income. As we shall see in our next chapter, investment is always a source of potential trouble because it is so much riskier than any other business function. If we had to keep on making proportionally larger investments each year to keep pace with our proportionally growing savings, we should live in an exceedingly vulnerable economic environment.

Fortunately, we are rescued from this dangerous situation, because our long-run savings ratio, as we have seen, displays a reassuring steadiness. In fact, there has been no significant upward trend in the savings ratio for the nation's households since the mid-1800s, and there may have been a slight downward trend.*

How do we reconcile this long-run stability with the fact that statistical studies always reveal that rich families *do* save a larger percentage of their incomes than poor families? As the nation has moved, en masse, into higher income brackets, why has it not also saved proportionately more of its income?

The answer hinges on important differences between the savings behavior of typical families over a short period of time and over a longer period. In the short run, families in every income bracket do indeed increase their savings sharply as their incomes rise. Much of a salary raise or a windfall is likely to be used *at first* for savings purposes. Debts may be quickly paid off. Money may be allowed to pile up in the bank while plans are made to readjust living standards. Even when the increase in income is used for a splurge such as the purchase of a new car, income may be allowed to lie idle for a short period. Thus, in the short run, savings ratios for additions to income are typically higher than they were before the increase was received.

What is true for the short run, however, is not true for the long run. From decade to decade, and even from year to year, powerful pressures and pervasive changes in our environment seem to operate on families at all

---

* Economists maintain a certain tentativeness about their assertions as to long-run trends, since the statistical foundation on which they are based is inevitably subject to some error and uncertainty.

levels, giving rise to a slow, secular decline in the desire to save. The growth of Social Security and pension plans, the impingement of higher income taxes, the steady expansion of advertising and consumer credit, the temptations of affluence, and the spirit of keeping up with the Joneses—all these influences appear to have worked a gradual decline in the long-run desires of *all* income groups. In addition, despite the statistics that show a steady rise in savings-ratios from income class to income class, it is likely that families in different income groups save much more nearly equal proportions of their incomes than our "cross section" data show.*

As a result of these and still other motivations, savings behavior in the long run differs considerably from that in the short run. Over the years, American households have shown a remarkable stability in their rate of over-all savings. Its importance has already been mentioned. In a shorter period of time, however—over a few months or perhaps a year—households tend to save higher fractions of increases in their incomes than they do in the long run. The very great importance of this fact we shall subsequently note.

The Consumption-Income Relationship

What we have heretofore seen are some of the historical and empirical relationships of consumption and personal saving to income. We have taken the trouble to investigate these relationships in some detail, since they are among the most important causes of the gaps that have to be closed by investment. But the statistical facts in themselves are only a halfway stage in our macroeconomic investigation. Now we want to go beyond the facts to a generalized understanding of what they mean. Thus our next task is to extract from the facts certain *relationships* that are sufficiently regular and dependable for us to build into a new dynamic model of the economy.

If we reflect back over the data we have examined, one primary conclusion comes to mind. This is the indisputable fact that the *amount* of saving generated by the household sector depends in the first instance upon the income enjoyed by the household sector. Despite the stability of the savings ratio, we have seen that the dollar volume of saving in the economy is susceptible to great variation, from negative amounts in the Great Depres-

---

* For instance, Professor Milton Friedman has suggested that middle-class families who have suffered temporary reverses (and who are therefore counted in lower than their "regular" income brackets) will typically maintain their living standards and reduce their savings, thereby causing a lower savings ratio for these lower brackets than would be found if we included only "permanent" members of it. Conversely, families that have had a lucky year and are temporary residents of a higher bracket may save more than is customary for regular residents of that bracket, thereby exaggerating the saving propensities of the upper groups. The motivation to save, in order to provide future well-being, may well result in surprisingly similar savings ratios, at least in the broad spectrum of income brackets between the very low and the very high.

sion to very large amounts in boom times. Now we must see if we can find a systematic connection between the changing size of income and the changing size of saving.

There is indeed such a relationship which lies at the heart of macroeconomic analysis. We call it the *consumption function* or, more formally, the *propensity to consume*, the name invented by John Maynard Keynes, who first formulated it.* What is this "propensity" to consume? It means that the relationship between consumption and income is sufficiently dependable so that we can actually *predict* how much consumption (or how much saving) will be associated with a given level of income.

We base such predictions on a *schedule* that enables us to see the income-consumption relationship over a considerable range of variation.

⟳ TABLE 13 • 1

A PROPENSITY TO CONSUME SCHEDULE

BILLIONS OF DOLLARS		
Income	Consumption	Savings
$100	$80	$20
110	87	23
120	92	28
130	95	35
140	97	43

Table 13-1 is such a schedule, a purely hypothetical one, for us to examine.

One could imagine, of course, innumerable different consumption schedules; in one society a given income might be accompanied by a much higher propensity to consume (or propensity to save) than in another. But the basic hypothesis of Keynes—a hypothesis amply confirmed by research—was that the consumption schedule in all modern industrial societies had a particular basic configuration, despite these variations. The propensity to consume, said Keynes, reflected the fact that on the average, men tended to increase their consumption as their incomes rose, but not by as much as their income. In other words, as the incomes of individuals rose, so did both their consumption *and their savings.*

Note that Keynes did not say that the proportion of saving rose. We have seen how involved is the dynamic determination of savings ratios. Keynes merely suggested that the *amount* of saving would rise as income rose—or to put it conversely again, that families would not use *all* their increases in income for consumption purposes alone. It is well to remember that these conclusions hold in going down the schedule as well as up.

* The name, incidentally, is pronounced "Kanes," not "Keenes."

Keynes' basic "law" implies that when there is a decrease in income, there will be some decrease in the *amount of saving,* or that a family will not absorb a fall in its income entirely by contracting its consumption.

What does the consumption schedule look like in the United States? We will come to that shortly. First, however, let us fill in our understanding of the terms we will need for our generalized study.

THE AVERAGE
PROPENSITY
TO CONSUME

The consumption schedule gives us two ways of measuring the fundamental economic relationship of income and saving. One way is simply to take any given level of income and to compute the percentage relation of consumption to that income. This gives us the *average propensity to consume.* In Table 13-2, using the same hypothetical schedule as before, we make this computation.

TABLE 13 • 2

CALCULATION
OF THE
AVERAGE
PROPENSITY
TO CONSUME

BILLIONS OF DOLLARS		Consumption divided by income (Average propensity to consume)
Income	Consumption	
$100	$80	.80
110	87	.79
120	92	.77
130	95	.73
140	97	.69

The average propensity to consume, in other words, tells us how a society at any given moment divides its total income between consumption and saving. It is thus a kind of measure of long-run savings behavior, for the ratios in which households divide their income between saving and consuming reflect established habits and, as we have seen, do not ordinarily change rapidly.

MARGINAL
PROPENSITY
TO CONSUME

But we can also use our schedule to measure another very important aspect of saving behavior: the way households divide *increases* (or decreases) in income between consumption and saving. This *marginal propensity to consume* is quite different from the average propensity to consume, as the figures in Table 13-3 (still from our original hypothetical schedule) demonstrate.

Note carefully that the last column in Table 13-3 is designed to show us something quite different from the last column of the previous table. Take a given income level—say $110 billion. In Table 13-2 the average propensity to consume for that income level is .79, meaning that we will actually spend

TABLE 13•3

CALCULATION
OF THE
MARGINAL
PROPENSITY
TO CONSUME

	BILLIONS OF DOLLARS			Marginal propensity to consume = Change in consumption ÷ change in income
Income	Consumption	Change in income	Change in consumption	
$100	$80	—	—	—
110	87	$10	$7	.70
120	92	10	5	.50
130	95	10	3	.30
140	97	10	2	.20

on consumption 79 percent of our income of $110 billion. But the corresponding figure opposite $110 billion in the marginal propensity to consume table (13-3) is .70. This does *not* mean that out of our $110 billion income we somehow spend only 70 percent, instead of 79 percent, on consumption. It *does* mean that we spend on consumption only 70 percent *of the $10 billion increase* that lifted us from a previous income of $100 billion to the $110 billion level. The rest of that $10 billion increase we saved.

Much of economics, in micro- as well as macroanalysis, is concerned with studying the effects of *changes* in economic life. It is precisely here that marginal concepts take on their importance. When we speak of the average propensity to consume, we relate all consumption and all income from the bottom up, so to speak, and thus we call attention to behavior covering a great variety of situations and conditions. But when we speak of the marginal propensity to consume, we are focusing only on our behavior toward *changes* in our incomes. Thus the marginal approach is invaluable, as we shall see, in dealing with the effects of short-run fluctuations in GNP.

A DIAGRAM OF THE PROPENSITY TO CONSUME

The essentially simple idea of a systematic relationship between income and consumption will play an extremely important part in the model of the economy we shall soon construct. But the relationships we have thus far defined are too vague to be of much usefulness. We want to know if we can extract from the facts of experience not only a general dependence of consumption on income, but a *fairly precise method of determining exactly how much saving will be associated with a given amount of income.*

Here we reach a place where it will help us to use diagrams and simple equations rather than words alone. So let us begin by transferring our conception of a propensity to consume schedule to a new kind of diagram directly showing the interrelation of income and consumption.

The *scatter diagram* (Fig. 13-5) on p. 241 shows precisely that. Along the vertical axis on the left we have marked off intervals to measure total consumer expenditure in billions of dollars; along the horizontal axis on the bottom we measure disposable personal income, also in billions of dollars.

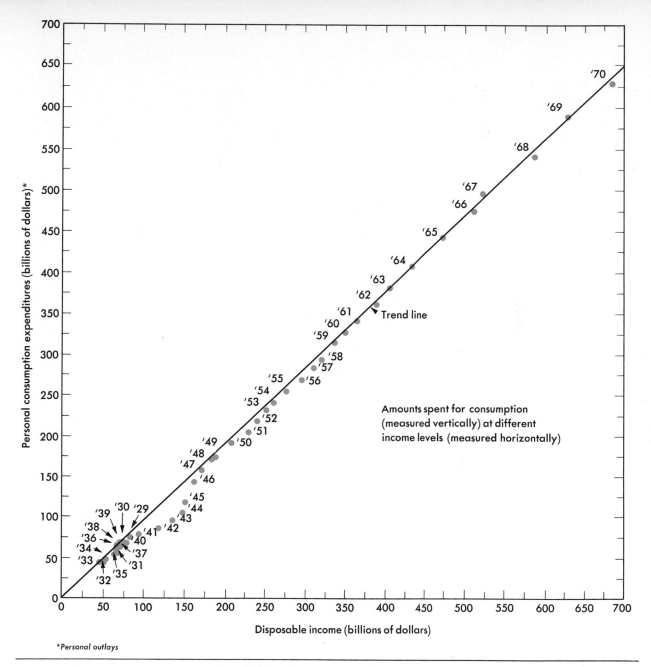

FIG. 13 • 5 UNITED STATES' PROPENSITY TO CONSUME, 1929–1970

The dots tell us, for the year that the numerals indicate, how large consumption and income were. For instance, if we take the dot for 1966 and look directly below it to the horizontal axis, we can see that disposable personal income for that year was roughly $510 billion. The same dot measured against the vertical consumption axis tells us that consumption for 1966 was a little more than $475 billion. If we now divide the figure for consumption by that for income, we get a value of 93.1 percent for our propensity to consume. If we subtract that from 100, our propensity to save must have been 6.9 percent.*

Returning to the diagram itself, we notice that the black line which "fits" the trend of the dots does not go evenly from corner to corner. If it did, it would mean that each amount of income was matched by an *equal* amount of consumption—in other words, that there was no saving. Instead, the line leans slightly downward, indicating that as income goes higher, consumption also increases, but not by quite as much.

Does the chart also show us our marginal propensity to consume? Not really. As we know, our short-run savings propensities are higher than our long-run propensities. This chart shows our "settled" position, from year to year, after the long-run, upward drift of spending has washed out our marginal (short-run) savings behavior.

Nevertheless, if we look at the movement from one dot to the next, we get some notion of the short-run forces at work. During the war years, for instance, as the result of a shortage of many consumer goods and a general exhortation to save, the average propensity to consume was unusually low. That is why the dots during those years form a bulge below the main trend line. After the war, we can also see that the marginal propensity to consume must have been very high. As a matter of fact, for a few years, consumption actually rose faster than income, as people used their wartime savings to buy things that were unavailable during the war. Between 1946 and 1947, for example, disposable income rose by some $9.8 billion, but personal outlays rose by almost $18 billion! By 1950, however, the consumption-income relationship was back to virtually the same ratio as during the 1930s.

PROPENSITY TO CONSUME, IN SIMPLE MATHEMATICS

There is another way of reducing to shorthand clarity the propensity to consume idea, particularly for those who find simple mathematics an expressive language. (For students who are uneasy in the face of formulas, there is a lesson in elementary math at the end of this chapter.)

We begin by giving letters to the words we use again and again.

$$C = \text{consumption}$$
$$I = \text{investment}$$
$$S = \text{saving}$$
$$Y = \text{income}$$

---

* It is difficult to read figures accurately from a graph. The actual values are: disposable income, $512 billion; consumption, $478 billion; average propensity to consume, 93.4 percent.

For more information on "fitting" a line to such a graph, see the statistical section following this chapter.

Finally, we use the symbol *f( )* to express the idea of *relationship*. Read it "function of (whatever is included in the parentheses)."

Now when we talk of $C = f(Y)$, we read it aloud as "consumption is a function of income." What this means is that consumption is related to income in some manner that can be described by a mathematical relationship.

What kind of relationship? Highly sophisticated and complex formulas have been tried to "fit" the values of *C* and *Y*. Their economics and their mathematics both are beyond the scope of this book. But we can at least get a clearer idea of what it means to devise a *consumption function* by trying to make a very simple one ourselves. If we look at Fig. 13-5 on p. 241, we can see that during the Depression years, at very low levels of income, around $50 billion, consumption was just as large as income itself. (In some years it was actually bigger; as we have seen, there was net dissaving in 1933.) Hence, we might hypothesize that a consumption function for the United States might have a fixed value representing this "bottom," plus some regular fraction designating the amount of income that would be saved for all income over that amount. Furthermore, recalling the stability of the savings ratio of about 6 percent in the postwar years, we might hypothesize that we will consume 94 percent of all income over the "bottom."

Such a formula would yield roughly accurate results. For 1979, for instance, it would predict that total consumption would equal $50 billion plus 94 percent of all disposable income over $50 billion. This gives us a figure of $674 billion for consumption in 1966—less than 2 percent off from the actual figure of $635 billion.*

Let the reader be warned, however, that devising a reliable consumption function is much more difficult than this simple and uncritical test would indicate. In a model of the economy that is currently being studied at the University of Michigan, for example, it takes 13 equations to represent the various components of consumption. One equation, concerned solely with predicting the demand for automobiles, depends on only *part* of disposable personal income—the portion received as cash earnings and not as transfer payments, etc.—and on factors such as the number of cars on the

---

* For those who are at home in simple algebra, we can generalize our results. We begin with a simple hypothetical formulation of the consumption function as follows:

$C = Y_0 + c(Y - Y_0)$, where
C = consumption
Y_0 = the value of disposable income at the "bottom" (where $Y = C$)
c = long-run ratio of *C* to *Y*, and
Y = current value of disposable income

Substituting values for the United States in 1970, we get
Y_0 = $50 billion
c = .94
Y = $685 billion. Thus,
C = $50 + .94 (685 − 50) = 646.9

More about this in "Learning about Statistics" at the end of the chapter.

road, the average age of the national fleet of cars, the size of consumers' assets, and still other variables.

Thus the process of translating economics into *econometrics*—that is, of finding ways to represent abstract theoretical relationships in terms of specific empirical relations—is a very difficult one.* Nonetheless, even our simple example gives one an idea of what the economist and the econometrist hope to find: a precise way of expressing functional interrelations (like those between consumption and income), so that the relations will be useful in making predictions.

PASSIVITY OF CONSUMPTION   Throughout this chapter we have talked of the dynamics of consuming and saving. Now it is important that we recall the main conclusion of our analysis, *the essential passivity of consumption as an economic process.* Consumption spending, we will recall, is a function of income. This means it is a *dependent* variable in the economic process, a factor that is acted *on,* but that does not itself generate spontaneous action.

To be sure, it is well to qualify this assertion. We have earlier paid special attention to the long-term stability of the savings ratio and pointed out that one cause of this stability was a general movement of all households toward consumption as their incomes grew. This dynamic, although slow-acting, behavioral trend has exerted a strong background force on the trend of the economy. Then, too, there have been occasions, the most famous being the years just following World War II, when consumption seemed to generate its own momentum and—as we have seen—raced out ahead of income. But this was a period when wants were intense, following wartime shortages, and when huge amounts of wartime savings were available to translate those wants into action. During the normal course of things, no matter how intense "wants" may be, consumers ordinarily lack the spendable cash to translate their desires into effective demand.

This highlights an extremely important point. Wants and appetites *alone* do not drive the economy upward; if they did, we should experience a more impelling demand in depressions, when people are hungry, than in booms, when they are well off. Hence the futility of those who urge the cure of depressions by suggesting that consumers should buy more! There is nothing consumers would rather do than buy more, if only they could. Let us not forget, furthermore, that consumers are at all times being cajoled and exhorted to increase their expenditures by the multibillion dollar pressures exerted by the advertising industry.

The trouble is, however, that consumers cannot buy more unless they have more incomes to buy with. It is true, of course, that for short periods they can borrow or they may temporarily sharply reduce their rate of savings; but each household's borrowing capacity or accumulated savings are limited, so

* In the statistical section following our next chapter the interested student will have a taste of the subject.

that once these bursts are over, the steady habitual ways of saving and spending are apt to reassert themselves.

Thus it is clear that in considering the consumer sector we study a part of the economy that, however ultimately important, is not in itself the source of major changes in activity. Consumption mirrors and, as we shall see, can magnify disturbances elsewhere in the economy, but it does not initiate the greater part of our economic fortunes or misfortunes. For that, we must turn to the two remaining great sectors, where we shall find the driving elements of our economic mechanism.

KEY CONCEPTS AND KEY WORDS

1. Consumption is the largest sector of economic activity, and accordingly the largest absolute source of demand with the economy. Nonetheless, *consumption alone will not create enough demand to buy all of the nation's output.*

    Consumption

2. Consumption in absolute amounts is capable of wide fluctuations, but *the relation of consumption to disposable income is relatively stable.*

    Disposable income

3. Over the long run (since the mid-1800s), *the fraction of disposable income that has been saved seems to have been more or less unchanged.* This has prevented the economy from facing the problem of a growing proportion of saving. In the short run, the ratio of saving to increases in income is apt to be higher than over the long run.

4. We call the relation between saving and disposable income the *consumption function.* We can represent this function (relationship) in a *schedule* showing the division of disposable income, at different levels of income, between consumption and saving.

    Consumption function

5. The consumption schedule shows that the *amount of consumption rises as income rises, but not by as much as income.* Therefore the amount of saving also rises as income rises.

    Schedule

6. From the consumption schedule we can derive two ratios. One shows us the relation between the *total income* and the *total consumption* of any period. We call this the *average propensity to consume.* The other shows us the relationship between the *change in income and the change in consumption* between two periods. This is called the *marginal propensity to consume.*

    Average propensity to consume

    Marginal propensity to consume

7. The average propensity to consume shows us how people behave with regard to consumption and saving over the *long run.* The marginal propensity to consume shows us how they behave over the *short run.*

8. The common abbreviations used in economics are: *C* for consumption, *I* for investment, *S* for saving and *Y* for income (note that *I* is used only for investment). We also use the symbol *f* followed by parentheses ( ) to express relationships. It is read "function of."

    Function

9. Consumption is generally regarded as a *passive economic force,* rather than an initiating active one. It is acted on by changes in income. Thus we generalize the force of consumption by saying that it is a *function of income: C = f(Y).*

    $C = f(Y)$

1. What are the main components of consumption? Why are some of these components more dynamic than others?

2. "The reason we have depressions is that consumption isn't big enough to buy the output of all our factories." What is wrong with this statement?

3. What do you think accounts for the relative stability of the savings ratio over the long run? Would you expect the savings ratio in the short run to be relatively stable? Why or why not?

4. What is meant by the consumption function? Could we also speak of a savings function? What would be the relation between the two?

5. Suppose that a given family had an income of $8,000 and saved $400. What would be its average propensity to consume? Could you tell from this information what its marginal propensity to consume was?

6. Suppose the same family now increased its income to $9,000 and its saving to $500. What is its new average propensity to consume? Can you figure out the family's marginal propensity to consume?

7. Draw a scatter diagram to show the following:

Family income	Savings
$4,000	$ 0
5,000	50
6,000	150
7,000	300
8,000	500

From the figures above, calculate the average propensity to consume at each level of income. Can you calculate the marginal propensity to consume for each jump in income?

8. How do you read $S = f(Y)$? From what you know of the propensity to consume, how would you describe the relation of S to Y?

9. Why can't we cure depressions by urging people to go out and spend?

LEARNING ABOUT STATISTICS

SIMPLE FUNCTIONAL RELATIONSHIPS

In this section we turn our attention away from statistics proper in order to learn a little more about a very important concept in mathematics, which is also widely used in statistical work. This is the concept of *functional relationships* to which Chapter 13 has introduced us.

Without a background in mathematics, many persons who begin to master economics feel at ease when looking at a diagram, but uncomfortable when forced to deal with equations. The purpose of this short, but very important, section is to make plain that *diagrams are nothing but geometrical representations of formulas and equations.* In other words, diagrams and equations are two different ways of expressing the same thing. Once this idea is grasped, much of the feeling of uneasiness about equations disappears.

Because we are familiar with the idea of the propensity to consume, let us use this as a central example for exploring the relationship between diagrams and formulas. We are acquainted now with the equation $c = f(y)$. Let us begin by acquiring a bit of mathematical vocabulary.

Variables

The letters C and Y in our formula are *variables,* because each of these entities can take on different—i.e., variable—values. As we know, Y varies according to the level of output and income, and C follows along behind, depending on our behavioral patterns or propensities.

Although both Y and C are variables, we distinguish between two *kinds* of variables, one *independent,* or causative; the other *dependent,* or passive (i.e., the effect of the other). In our formula, Y is the *independent variable.* Of course, Y may itself be the dependent variable of a different equation, but for the purposes of estimating the propensity to consume, we take Y as the independent variable.

By way of contrast, C is the *dependent variable* in this equation. That is, C is the variable whose value at any point in time is dependent upon the corresponding value of Y. In another equation, C might be the independent variable (for instance, an equation that portrayed the relationship between various amounts of consumption and, say, the amount we spent on food).

Thus in any equational system, whether it describes economics or physics, we commonly distinguish between the "moving force," which we describe as the independent variable, and the effect that this force produces, which is called the dependent variable. Note, however, as our examples show, that the independent variable in one equation can be the dependent variable in another. (Another example: we can write $I = f(P)$ where I is investment and P profits. Here, profits are treated as an independent variable and investment as a dependent variable—the formula, in other words, tells us how large investment will be, *given* such and such a level of profits. But we might also write $P = f(Y)$, or profits are a function of income. Now profits become a dependent variable—the effect of "given" income.

What is the point of the distinction between dependent and independent variables? The answer is that functional relationships help us express cause-and-effect linkages in the economy. As we shall later see when we look briefly into economic forecasting (p. 354), models of the economy can be tremendously complicated. In order to come to grips with the basic patterns of economic relationships, we need to pare away the inessentials and to lay bare the connections between a few central variables. Statistics, or econometrics, as our subsequent sections will explain, have very clever techniques for clarifying what those linkages are. But the idea of independent (causative) and dependent (passive) variables is indispensable to the more sophisticated search for linkages themselves.

Functions

So much for the variables. Now for the $f(\ )$; that is, for the *function* itself.

What is a function? It is a mathematical description of the relationship between variables. If we hypothesize that there is a relationship between sales volume of TV sets and antennas, then we may write: (antenna sales) $= f$(TV sales). This is read: antenna sales are a function of TV sales, or equivalently, antenna sales depend upon TV sales. Empirically, we may find that for every two TV sets sold, one antenna is sold. This finding can be written in a *formula* or *equation* form as: (antenna sales) $= \frac{1}{2}$ (TV sales). This means that for every value of TV sales, there is one corresponding value of antenna sales.

The relational idea expressed by a function brings us to the point from which we began. Relationships that are *depicted* on graphs can be *expressed* in equations. Take, for example, the propensity to consume. We have seen this relationship drawn in the graph on p. 241, and we have derived a very simple approximate "consumption function" in the footnote on p. 243. In our next statistical lesson we shall investigate the way in which we actually find the line that "fits" the dots shown on p. 241 (or what is the same thing, discover the actual formula for the function). At this juncture, however, let us postpone the problem of how we derive actual relationships, and make certain that we fully understand the connection between the diagram and the formula.

For this purpose let us take an imaginary consumption function, simpler than the one on the bottom of p. 243. Assume that the consumption function is this:

$$C = 2 + .8Y$$

This formula enables us to set up a table or schedule, relating C and Y, as follows:

If Y is equal to	then C is equal to	shown on graph as point
0	2 + .8(0) = 2 + 0 = 2	A
10	2 + .8(10) = 2 + 8 = 10	B
20	2 + .8(20) = 2 + 16 = 18	C
40	2 + .8(40) = 2 + 32 = 34	D
75	2 + .8(75) = 2 + 60 = 62	E
100	2 + .8(100) = 2 + 80 = 82	F

Let's now graph this relationship. Remember that each point in the two-dimensional graph represents *two* numbers; namely, C and Y.

FIG. 13 • 6

For instance, the point *D* shows us that if the income level (*Y*) is $40.00, consumption would be $34.00. Similarly, point *F* represents *Y* = 100 and *C* = 82; and point *A* = *Y* = O, *C* = 2. *If we now connect all the points A through F, we get a graphical representation of the function C* = 2 + .8Y. But how do we know that it is a *straight* line?

The answer is that the word *straight* means that the line has an *unchanging slope*. If it were not a straight line, the slope would be increasing or decreasing from place to place, as Fig. 13–7 shows.

Slope is decreasing

Slope is increasing

FIG. 13 • 7

By way of contrast, all lines of unchanging slope are always straight, although they need not all slope at the same angle. Figure 13–8 shows a variety of lines of *unchanging* slope, with very *different angles* of slope.

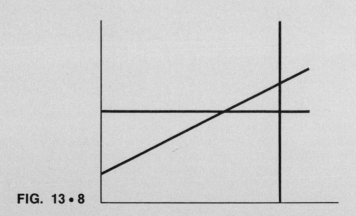

FIG. 13 • 8

What is it about our formula that tells us that the (hypothetical) consumption function of *C* = 2 +.8Y is a straight line? It is not the number 2, which simply tells us the value of *C* when *Y* = 0. This so-called intercept tells us where our line "begins" on the vertical axis, but it says nothing about its slope. That is determined by the second term, .8Y. In this term, the number .8 is called the *coefficient* of Y, and shows its steepness. The "linearity" (straight line) aspect of the equation depends on the fact that Y is of the "first order"—that is, is not squared or of a higher power. $C = 2 + .8Y^2$ would *not* be a linear function, but a curvilinear one. Generally speaking, a linear function is of the form $X = a + by$.

Coefficients

The coefficient of the independent variable tells us how much the dependent variable will change for each unit of change of the independent variable. That is, .8 tells us that for each variation of $1 in income, consumption will change by 80¢. Given our unchanging coefficient, this relationship will remain the same, whether we are dealing with $1 or with $1,000,000. In each case, the change in C will be 80 percent the change in Y. If, in fact, the coefficient did change—if, e.g., we consumed a larger fraction of a small income than of a large one—the line would not be straight, and the equation that represented that line would not be an equation of the very simple form we have used.*

FIG. 13•9

Coefficients, even of the simplest kinds, can represent all kinds of slopes. In Fig. 13-9 we show three coefficients that give rise to three slopes. The lowest line has a coefficient of zero, giving rise to a straight horizontal line parallel to the income axis. (Such a line depicts a situation in which we would not consume any more than a fixed amount, no matter how high our incomes—a highly implausible state of affairs.) The middle line shows a consumption function of approximately .4—a state of affairs in which we regularly consume 40¢ out of each additional $1 of income over the $2 intercept. The topmost line shows us our familiar coefficient of .8.

* The two numbers 2 and .8 in our formula are called *parameters*. A change in either or both parameters indicates a *shift* in the consumption line.

Note two things: (1) *the income coefficient determines the slope;* (2) *all these lines have unchanging slopes (are straight) because the coefficients are unchanging throughout.*

You will find this correspondence between diagrams and equations useful as we go further into economics and into statistical techniques called econometrics. In this lesson on functional relationships we do no more than recognize the equivalence between diagrams and equations in a somewhat intuitive way, and do not require more than a general grasp of the relationship between the two. But it should be clear that the relationship is not a difficult one.

Then why not use only diagrams or only equations? The answer is not difficult to give. Some relationships are much more simply grasped "pictorially" than in equations (and the equations themselves may be very complex, particularly if a line is *not* straight). At the same time, some equations allow us to perform calculations, or to make certain kinds of mathematic tests that graphs do not permit (or that would be very difficult to perform on graphs). Hence, sometimes graphs are easier to work with than equations, and sometimes equations are more convenient than graphs. We shall use both in this text. The thing to bear in mind is that the choice is a matter of convenience, not of a different mode of calculation.

Consumption is activity everyone knows as an experienced economic actor in his own right; investing, on the other hand, is an economy activity foreign to most of us. For investing, in the context of macroeconomic analysis, has very little to do with the kind of "investing" familiar to us in the selection of stocks or bonds as personal assets. Investing, as the economist sees it, is an activity that uses the resources of the community to maintain or add to its stock of capital wealth.

Now this may or may not coincide with the purchase of a security. When we buy an ordinary stock or bond, we usually buy it from someone who has previously owned it, and therefore our personal act of "investment" becomes, in the economic view of things, merely a *transfer* of claims without any direct bearing on the creation of new wealth. A pays B cash and takes his General Manufacturing stock; B takes A's cash and doubtless uses it to buy stock from C; but the transactions between A and B and C in no way alter the actual amount of real capital in the economy. Only when we buy *newly issued* shares or bonds, and then only when their proceeds are directly allocated to new equipment or plant, does our act of personal financial investment result in the addition of wealth to the community. In that case, A buys his stock directly (or through an investment banker) from General Manufacturing itself, and not from B. A's cash can now be spent for new capital goods, as presumably it will be.

Thus investment, as economists see it, is a little-known form of activity for the great majority of us. This is true not only because real investment is not the same as personal financial investment, but because the real investors of the nation usually act on behalf of an institution other than the familiar one of the household. The unit of behavior in the world of investment is typically the business *firm*, just as in the world of consumption it is the household. Boards of directors, chief executives, or small-business proprietors are the persons who decide whether or not to devote business cash to the construction of new facilities or to the addition of inventory; and this decision, as we shall see, is very different in character and motivation from the decisions familiar to us as members of the household sector.

The Investment Sector in Profile

Before we begin an investigation into the dynamics of investment decisions, however, let us gain a quick acquaintance with the sector as a whole, much as we did with the consumption sector.

Figure 14-1 gives a first general impression of the investment sector in a recent year. Note that the main source of gross private domestic investment expenditure is the retained earnings of business; that is, the expenditures come from depreciation accruals or from profits that have been kept in the business. However, as the next bar shows, gross investment *expenditures* are considerably larger than retained earnings. The difference represents funds that business obtains in several ways.

1. *It may draw on cash (or securities) accumulated out of retained earnings or depreciation accruals of* previous *years.*

2. *It may obtain savings from the household sector by direct borrowing or by sale of new issues of shares of stock or indirectly via insurance companies or savings banks or pension funds, and so on.*

3. *It may borrow from commercial banks.*

The last of these sources of funds we will not fully understand until we reach Chapter 17, when we study the money mechanism. But our chart enables us to see that most gross investment is financed by business itself from its *internal* sources—retained earnings plus depreciation accruals—and that external sources play only a secondary role. In particular, this is true of new stock issues which, during most of the 1960s, raised only some 3 to 8 percent of the funds spent by the business sector for new plant and equipment.*

---

* In 1969 and 1970 stock issues were unusually large because the interest rates on bonds were forbiddingly high. (See Special Assignment in Chap. 6 of the *Student Guide,* which deals with different kinds of corporate securities.)

All figures in billions*

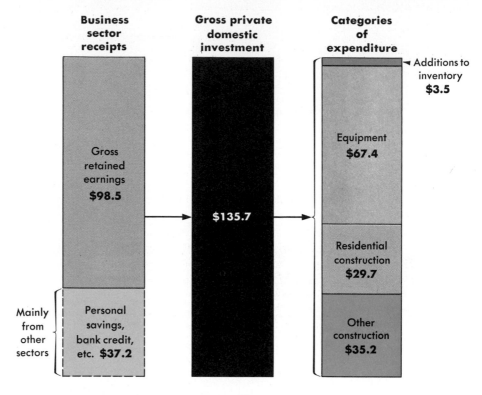

| Business sector receipts | Gross private domestic investment | Categories of expenditure |

Gross retained earnings $98.5

$135.7

◄ Additions to inventory $3.5

Equipment $67.4

Residential construction $29.7

Other construction $35.2

Mainly from other sectors

Personal savings, bank credit, etc. $37.2

Totals do not always add, owing to rounding

FIG. 14 • 1 BUSINESS SECTOR, 1970

CATEGORIES OF INVESTMENT

From the total funds at its disposal, the business sector now renews its worn-out capital and adds new capital. Let us say a word concerning some of the main categories of investment expenditure.

1. *Inventories.*

At the top of our bar we note an item of $7.6 billion for *additions to inventory.* Note that this figure does not represent total inventories, but only *changes* in inventories, upwards or downwards. If there had been no change in inventory over the year, the item would have been zero, even if existing inventories were huge. Why? Because those huge inventories would have been included in the investment expenditure flow of *previous* years when they were built up.

Additions to inventories are capital, but they need not be additions to capital *goods.* Indeed, they are likely to include farm stocks, consumers goods, and other items of all kinds. Of course, these are goods held by business, and not by consumers. But that is the very point. We count inventory additions as net investment because they are output that has been produced but that has not been consumed. In another year, if these goods pass from the hands of business into consumers' hands, and inventories decline, we will have a negative figure for net inventory investment. This will mean, just as it appears, that we are consuming goods faster than we are producing them—that we are disinvesting.

Investments in inventory are particularly significant for one reason. Alone among the investment categories, inventories can be *rapidly* used up as well as increased. A positive figure for one year or even one calendar quarter can quickly turn into a negative figure the next. *This means that expenditures for inventory are usually the most volatile element of any in gross national product.* A glance at Fig. 14-2 shows a dramatic instance of how rapidly inventory spending can change. In the second quarter of 1960, we were *disinvesting* in inventories at an annual rate of almost $5 billion. Two quarters later, we were building up inventories—*investing* in inventories—by roughly the same amount. Thus, within a span of six months, there was a swing of almost $10 billion in spending. And as the chart shows, this was by no means a unique occurrence.

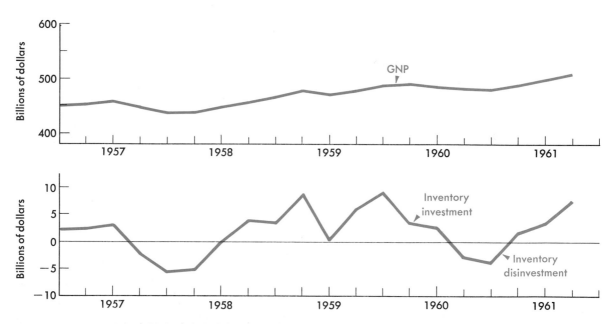

FIG. 14•2 INVENTORY SWINGS AND GNP

As we shall see more clearly later, this volatility of investment has a great deal of significance for business conditions. Note that while inventories are being built up, they serve as an offset to saving—that is, some of the resources released from consumption are used by business firms to build up stocks of inventory capital. But when inventories are being "worked off," this avenue for closing the demand gap is no longer available. As we would expect, this can give rise to serious economic troubles.

2. *Equipment.*

The next item in our bar is more familiar: $67.4 billion for *equipment.* Here we find expenditures for goods of a varied sort—lathes, trucks, generators, computers, office typewriters.* The total includes both new equipment and replacement equipment, and we need a word of caution here. Exactly what does it mean to "replace" a given item of equipment? Suppose we have a textile loom that cost $100,000 and that is now on it last legs. Is the loom "replaced" by spending another $100,000, regardless of what kind of machine the money will buy? Suppose loom prices have gone up and $100,000 no longer buys a loom of the same capacity? Or suppose that prices have remained steady; but that owing to technological advance, $100,000 now buys a loom of double the old capacity. Such questions make the definition of "replacement" an accountant's headache and an economist's nightmare. We need not involve ourselves deeper in the question, but we should note the complexities introduced into a seemingly simple matter once we leave the changeless world of stationary flow and enter the world of invention and innovation.

3. *Construction.*

Our next section on the diagrammatic bar is total *residential construction.* Why do we include this item of $29.7 billion in the investment sector when most of it is represented by new houses that householders buy for their own use?

The answer is that most houses are built by business firms (such as contractors and developers) who put up the houses *before* they are sold. Thus the original expenditures involved in building houses typically come from businessmen, not from households. Later, when the householder buys a house, he takes possession of an *existing* asset, and his expenditure does not pump new incomes out into the economy, but only repays the contractor who *did* pump new incomes out.

Actually this is a somewhat arbitrary definition, since, after all, businessmen own all output before consumers buy it. However, in macroeconomics, our goal is to understand growth and fluctuation in growth, and we define our terms to serve that purpose. Residential housing "behaves" very much like other items of construction, and it simplifies our understanding of the forces at work in the economy if we classify it as an investment expenditure rather than a consumer expenditure.

The last item on the bar, $35.2 billion of *other construction,* is largely made up of the "plant" in "plant and equipment"—factories and stores and

---

* But *not* typewriters bought by consumers. Thus the same good can be classified as a consumption item or an investment item depending on the use to which it is put.

private office buildings and warehouses. (It does not, however, include public construction such as roads, dams, harbors, or public buildings, all of which are picked up under government purchases.) It is interesting to note that the building of structures, as represented by the total of residential construction plus other private construction, accounts for over half of all investment expenditure, and this total would be further swelled if public construction were included herein. This accords with the dominant role of structures in the panorama of national wealth we first encountered in Chapter 10. It tells us, too, that swings in construction expenditure can be a major lever for economic change.

Investment in Historic Perspective

With this introduction behind us, let us take a look at the flow of investment, not over a single year, but over many years.

In Fig. 14-3, several things spring to our notice. Clearly, investment is not nearly so smooth an unperturbed flow of spending as consumption. Note that gross investment in the depths of the Depression virtually disappeared—that we almost failed to *maintain*, much less add to, our stock of

FIG. 14 • 3   GROSS PRIVATE DOMESTIC INVESTMENT, 1929–1970

wealth. (Net investment was, in fact, a negative figure for several years.) Note also investment was reduced during the war years as private capital formation was deliberately limited through government allocations.

Two important conclusions emerge from this examination of investment spending:

First, as we have already seen, investment spending contains a component—net additions to inventory—that is capable of drastic, sudden shifts. This accounts for much of the wavelike movement of the total flow of investment expenditure.

Second, investment spending as a whole is capable of more or less total collapses, of a severity and degree that are never to be found in consumption.

The prime example of such a collapse was, of course, the Great Depression. From 1929 to 1933, while consumption fell by 41 percent, investment fell by *91 percent,* as we can see in Fig. 14-3. Similarly, whereas consumption rose by a little more than half from 1933 to 1940, investment in the same period rose by *nine times.*

IMPORTANCE OF INVESTMENT

This potential for collapse or spectacular boom always makes investment a source of special concern in the economic picture. But even the tendency toward inventory fluctuations, or toward milder declines in other capital expenditures, is sufficient to identify investment as a prime source of economic instability. As we have said before, there is often a tendency among noneconomists to equate all buying in the economy with consumer buying. Let us never lose sight of the fact that the maintenance of, and addition to, capital is also a part of GNP spending and that a considerable part of the labor force depends for its livelihood on the making of investment goods. Remember, from Chapter 8, that at the bottom of the Great Depression in 1933, it was estimated that one-third of total unemployment was directly associated with the shrinkage in the capital goods industry.

We shall want to look more closely into the reasons for the sensitivity of investment spending. But first a question must surely have occurred to the reader. For all its susceptibility to change, the investment sector is, after all, a fairly small sector. In 1970, total expenditures for gross private domestic investment came to less than one-seventh of GNP, and the normal year-to-year variation in investment spending in the 1950s and 1960s was only about $5 billion to $10 billion, or 1 to 2 percent of GNP. To devote so much time to such small fluctuations seems a disproportionate emphasis. How could so small a tail as investment wag so large a dog as GNP?

The Multiplier

The answer—as we may also recall from our historical survey of the Depression era—lies in a relationship of economic activities known as the *multiplier.* The multiplier describes the fact that *additions to spending (or diminutions in spending) have an impact on income that is greater than the original increase or decrease in spending itself.* In other words, even small increments in spending can *multiply* their effects (whence the name).

It is not difficult to understand the general idea of the multiplier. Suppose that we have an island community whose economy is in a perfect circular flow, unchanging from year to year. Next, let us introduce the stimulus of a new investment expenditure in the form of a stranger who arrives from another island (with a supply of acceptable money) and who proceeds to build a house. This immediately increases the islanders' incomes. In our case, we will assume that our stranger spends $1,000 on wages for construction workers, and we will ignore all other expenditures he may make. (We also make the assumption that these workers were previously unemployed, so that our stranger is not merely taking them from some other task.)

Now the construction workers, who have had their incomes increased by $1,000, are very unlikely to sit on this money. As we know from our study of the marginal propensity to consume, they are apt to save some of the increase (and they may have to pay some to the government as income taxes), but the rest they will spend on additional consumption goods. Let us suppose that they save 10 percent and pay taxes of 20 percent on the $1,000 they get. They will then have $700 left over to spend for additional consumer goods and services.

But this is not an end to it. The sellers of these goods and services will now have received $700 over and above their former incomes, and they, too, will be certain to spend a considerable amount of their new income. If we assume that their family spending patterns (and their tax brackets) are the same as the construction workers, they will also spend 70 percent of their new incomes, or $490. And now the wheel takes another turn, as still *another* group receives new income and spends a fraction of it—in turn.

If our stranger now departed as mysteriously as he came, we would have to describe the economic impact of his investment as constituting a single "bulge" of income that gradually disappeared. The bulge would consist of the original $1,000, the secondary $700, the tertiary $490, and so on. If everyone continued to spend 70 percent of his new income, after ten rounds all that would remain by way of new spending traceable to the original $1,000 would be about $38. Soon, the impact of the new investment on incomes would have virtually disappeared.

But now let us suppose that after our visitor builds his house and leaves, another visitor arrives to build another house. This time, in other words, we assume that the level of investment spending *continues* at the higher level to which it was raised by the first expenditure for a new house. We can see that the second house will set into motion precisely the same repercussive effects as did the first, and that the new series of respendings will be added to the dwindling echoes of the original injection of incomes.

In Fig. 14-4, we can trace this effect. The succession of orange bars at the bottom of the graph stands for the continuing injections of $1,000 as new houses are steadily built. (Note that this means the level of new investment is only being maintained, not that it is rising.) Each of these orange bars now generates a series of secondary, tertiary, etc., bars that represent the respending of income after taxes and savings. In our example we have assumed that the respending fraction is 50 percent.

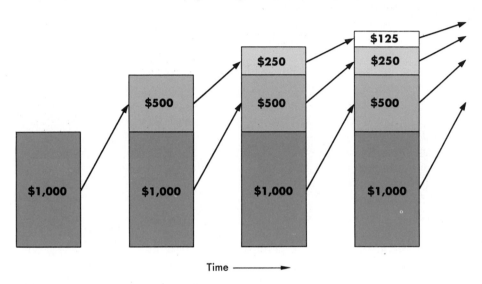

Time ⟶

FIG. 14 • 4   THE MULTIPLIER

Our diagram shows us two very important things.

1. *A steady flow of new investment generates an equally steady but larger flow of total incomes.*

It is very important to note that the incomes generated by respending are just as permanent as those due to the flow of investment itself.

2. *The rise in income due to a continuing flow of new investment gradually levels out.*

As the successive respending fractions become smaller, the rise in income approaches a plateau.

MARGINAL
PROPENSITY
TO SAVE

We can understand now that *the multiplier is the numerical relation between the initial new investment and the total increase in income.* If the initial investment is $1,000 and the total addition to income due to the respending of that $1,000 is $3,000, we have a multiplier of 3; if the total addition is $2,000, the multiplier is 2.

What determines how large the multiplier will be? The answer depends entirely on our marginal consumption (or, if you will, our marginal saving) habits—that is, on how much we consume (or save) out of each dollar of additional income that comes to us. Let us follow two cases below. In the first, we will assume that each recipient spends only one half of any new income that comes to him, saving the rest. In the second case, he spends three-quarters of it and saves one-quarter.

It is very clear that the amount of income that will be passed along from one receiver to the next will be much larger where the marginal propensity to consume is higher. In fact, we can see that the total amount of new incomes (the total amount of the boxes above) must be mathematically related to the proportion that is spent each time.

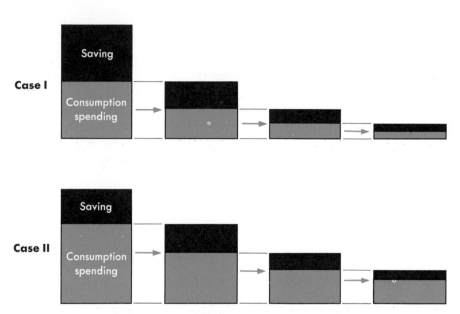

FIG. 14 • 5 COMPARISON OF TWO MULTIPLIERS

What is this relationship? The arithmetic is easier to figure if we use not the consumption fraction, but the *saving fraction* (the two are, of course, as intimately related as the first slice of cake and the remaining cake). If we use the saving fraction, the *sum of new incomes is obtained by taking the reciprocal of* (i.e., inverting, or turning upside down) *the fraction we save.* Thus, if we save $\frac{1}{2}$ our income, the total amount of new incomes generated by responding will be $\frac{1}{2}$ inverted, or 2—twice the original increase in income. If we save $\frac{1}{4}$, it will be the reciprocal of $\frac{1}{4}$ or 4 times the original change.

We call the fraction of new income that is saved the *marginal propensity to save* (often abbreviated as mps). As we have just said, this fraction is the complement of an already familiar one, the marginal propensity to consume. If our marginal propensity to consume is 80 percent, our marginal propensity to save must be 20 percent; if our mpc is three-quarters, our mps must be one-quarter.

Understanding the relationship between the marginal propensity to save and the size of the resulting respending fractions allows us to state a very simple (but very important) formula for the multiplier:

$$\text{change in income} = \text{multiplier} \times \text{change in investment}$$

Since we have just learned that the multiplier is determined by the reciprocal of the marginal propensity to save, we can write:

$$\text{multiplier} = \frac{1}{\text{mps}}$$

If we now use the symbols we are familiar with, plus a Greek letter Δ, delta, that means "change in," we can write the important economic relationship above as follows:

$$\Delta Y = \frac{1}{\text{mps}} \times \Delta I$$

Thus, if our mps is $\frac{1}{4}$ (meaning, let us not forget, that we save a quarter of increases in income and respend the rest), then an increase in investment of $1 billion will lead to a total increase in incomes of $4 billion ($1 billion $\times \frac{1}{1/4} = $4 billion). Note that the multiplier is a complex or *double* fraction—it is $\frac{1}{1/4}$ and *not* $\frac{1}{4}$. If the mps is $\frac{1}{10}$, $1 billion gives rise to incomes of $10 billion; if the mps is 50 percent, the billion will multiply to $2 billion. And if mps is 1? This means that the entire increase in income is unspent, that our island construction workers tuck away (or find taxed away) their entire newly earned pay. In that case, the multiplier will be 1 also, and the impact of the new investment on the island economy will be no more than the $1,000 earned by the construction workers in the first place.

The importance of the size of the marginal savings ratio in determining the effect that additional investment will have on income is thus apparent. Now, however, we must pass from the simple example of our island economy to the more complex behavioral patterns and institutional arrangements of real life. The average propensity to save (the ratio of saving to disposable income) runs around 6 to 7 percent. In recent years, the *marginal propensity to save* (the ratio of additional saving to increases in income) figured over the period of a year has not departed very much from this figure. If this is the case, then, following our analysis, the multiplier would be very high. If mps were even as much as 10 percent of income, a change in investment of $1 billion would bring a $10 billion change in income. If mps were nearer 6 percent—the approximate level of the average propensity to save—a change of $1 billion would bring a swing of over $16 billion. Were this the case, the economy would be subject to the most violent disturbances whenever the level of spending shifted.

In fact, however, the impact of the multiplier is greatly reduced because the successive rounds of spending are damped by factors other than personal saving. One of them we have already introduced in our imaginary island economy. This is the tendency of *government taxation* to "mop up" a fraction of income as it passes from hand to hand. This mopping-up effect of taxation is in actuality much larger than that of saving. For every dollar of change in income, federal taxes will take up to 30 cents, and state and local taxes another 6 cents.

Another dampener is the tendency of respending to swell *business savings* as well as personal incomes. Of each dollar of new spending, perhaps 10 cents goes into business profits, and this sum is typically saved, at least for a time, rather than immediately respent.

Still another source of dampening is the tendency of consumers and businesses to increase purchases from abroad as their incomes rise. These rising *imports* divert 3 to 4 percent of new spending to foreign nations and accordingly reduce the successive impact of each round of expenditure.

All these withdrawals from the respending cycle are called *leakages,* and the total effect of all leakages together (personal savings, business savings, taxes, and imports) is to reduce the overall impact of the multiplier from an impossibly large figure to a very manageable one. The combined effect of all leakages brings the actual multiplier in the United States in the 1970s to around 2 for a period of about a year.*

To be sure—and this is very important—all these leakages *can* return to the income stream. Household saving can be turned into capital formation; business profits can be invested; tax receipts can be disbursed in government spending programs; and purchases from foreign sellers can be returned as purchases *by* foreigners. What is at stake here is the regularity and reliability with which these circuits will be closed. In the case of ordinary income going to a household, we can count with considerable assurance on

---

* In dealing with the multiplier equation ($\Delta Y = \dfrac{1}{\text{mps}} \times \Delta I$), we can interpret mps to mean the total withdrawal from spending due to all leakages. This brings mps to around $\frac{1}{2}$, and gives us a multiplier of 2.

It is interesting to note that the leakages all tend to increase somewhat in boom times and to decline in recessions, which results in a slightly larger multiplier in bad times than in good.

a "return expenditure" of consumption. In the case of the other recipients of funds, the assurance is much less; hence we count their receipts as money that has leaked out of the expenditure flow, for the time being.

THE DOWNWARD MULTIPLIER

The multiplier, with its important magnifying action, rests at the very center of our understanding of economic fluctuations. Not only does it explain how relatively small stimuli can exert considerable upward pushes, but it also makes much clearer than before how the failure to offset a small savings gap can snowball into a serious fall in income and employment.

For just as additional income is respent to create still further new income, a loss in income will not stop with the affected households. On the contrary, as families lose income, they cut down on their spending, although the behavior pattern of the propensity to consume schedule suggests that they will not cut their consumption by as much as their loss in income. Yet each reduction in consumption, large or small, lessens to that extent the income or receipts of some other household or firm.

We have already noted that personal savings alone do not determine the full impact of the multiplier. This is even more fortunate on the way down than on the way up. If the size of the multiplier were solely dependent on the marginal propensity to save, an original fall in spending would result in a catastrophic contraction of consumption through the economy. But the leakages that cushion the upward pressure of the multiplier also cushion its downward effect. As spending falls, business savings (profits) fall, tax receipts dwindle, and the flow of imports declines.

All of these leakages now work in the direction of mitigating the repercussions of the original fall in spending. The fall in business profits means that less will be saved by business and thus less withdrawn from respending; the decline in taxes means that more money will be left to consumers; and the drop in imports similarly releases additional spending power for the domestic market. Thus, just as the various leakages pulled money away from consumption on the way up, on the way down they lessen their siphoning effect and in this way restore purchasing power to consumers' hands. As a result, in the downward direction as in the upward, the actual impact of the multiplier is about 2, so that a fall in investment of, say, $5 billion will lower GNP by $10 billion.

THE MULTIPLIER AND INVESTMENT

Even with a reduced figure, we can now understand how a relatively small change in investment can magnify its impact on GNP. If the typical year-to-year change in investment is around $5 to $10 billion, a multiplier of 2 will produce a change in GNP of $10 to $20 billion, by no means a negligible figure. In addition, as we shall shortly see, the multiplier may set up repercussions that feed back onto investment. But more of that momentarily. First let us make two final points in regard to the multiplier.

1. *Other multipliers.*

We have talked of the multiplier in connection with changes in investment spending. *But we must also realize that any change in any spending has a multiplier effect.* We have used investment as the "trigger" for the multiplier because it is, in fact, the component of spending that is most likely to evidence *large* and *sudden* changes. But an increase in foreigners' purchases of our exports has a multiplier effect, as does an increase in government spending or a decrease in taxes, or a spontaneous increase in consumption itself due to, say, a drop in the propensity to save. Any stimulus to the economy is thus not confined to its original impact, but gives a series of successive pushes to the system until it has finally been absorbed in leakages. We shall come back to this important fact in our next chapter.

2. *Idle resources.*

Finally, there is a very important proviso to recognize, although we will not study its full significance until Chapter 18. This is the important difference between an economy with idle resources—unemployed labor or unused machines or land—and one without them.

For *it is only when we have idle resources that the respending impetus of the multiplier is useful.* Then each round of new expenditure can bring idle resources into use, creating not only new money incomes but *new production and employment.* The situation is considerably different when there are no, or few, idle men or machines. Then the expenditure rounds of the multiplier bring higher money incomes, but these are not matched by increased real output.

In both cases, the multiplier exerts its leverage, bringing about an increase in total expenditure larger than the original injection of new spending. In the case without idle resources, however, the results are solely *inflationary,* as the increased spending results in higher incomes and higher prices, but not in higher output. In the case where idle resources exist, we can avoid this mere "money" multiplication and enjoy a rise in output as a result of our increased spending. Indeed, we can even speak of the *employment multiplier* in situations where there is considerable unemployment, meaning by this the total increase in employment brought about by a given increase in spending. We shall return in subsequent chapters to a fuller scrutiny of the difference between the case of idle and of fully employed resources, but we must bear the distinction in mind henceforth.

KEY CONCEPTS AND KEY WORDS

1. The investment sector is made up, not of households and their activities, but of *business firms adding to their capital assets.* By and large, these additions to business capital are financed out of *internal funds* (retained earnings and depreciation accruals) rather than from external sources (borrowing or new equities). The main categories of

Investment

investment expenditure are additions to inventory, new equipment, residential housing, and other construction.

Instability

2. The main characteristic of all investment expenditure is its *potential instability.* In times of serious recession, net investment can virtually cease. Even in ordinary times, inventory investment is capable of drastic changes.

Multiplier

3. Changes in investment (or in any other kind of spending) are given larger economic impact because of the *multiplier effect.* This arises because incomes received from a new investment (or any other source) are *partly respent,* giving rise to additional new incomes which, in turn, are respent.

4. A single "burst" of investment creates a bulge in incomes which disappears over time; but a *continuing level of new investment creates a continuing higher level of new incomes.*

5. The size of the multiplier depends on the fraction of additional income spent for consumption by each new recipient. *The more the spending* (or the less the saving) *the greater will be the multiplier.*

Marginal propensity to save

$$\Delta Y = \frac{1}{mps} \times \Delta I$$

6. *We calculate the multiplier by taking the reciprocal of the marginal propensity to save.* This gives us the important formula:

$$\Delta Y = \frac{1}{mps} \times \Delta I \text{ (change in income = multiplier} \times \text{ change in investment)}$$

Leakages

7. The *size of mps is determined by leakages.* There are four main leakages:
   • Saving
   • Taxation
   • Business profits
   • Imports
   Total leakages in the U.S. amount to about one-half of increases in income. Therefore the U.S. multiplier is about 2.

8. *Each of these leakages takes money out of the "automatic" respending circuit of consumption.* Money going into leakages *can* return to the economy via additional investment, but it does not do so as reliably as money that stays in the consumption flow.

9. Magnifying the effects on income of a fall in investment, the *multiplier works downward,* as well as upward.

10. The multiplier will have very different economic effects, depending on whether or not the economy is *fully employed.*

Q U E S T I O N S

1. If you buy a share of stock on the New York Stock Exchange, does that always create new capital? Why, or why not?

2. Why are additions to inventory so much more liable to rapid fluctuation than other kinds of investment?

3. Why is investment capable of much more complete collapse than consumption?

4. Draw a diagram showing the multiplier effect of $1,000 expenditure when the marginal propensity to save is one-tenth. Draw a second diagram, showing the effect when the marginal propensity to consume is nine-tenths. Are the diagrams the same?

5. Compare two multiplier diagrams: one where the marginal propensity to save is one-quarter; the other where it is one-third. The *larger* the saving ratio, the larger or smaller the multiplier?

6. Calculate the impact on income if investment rises by $10 billion and the multiplier is 2. If the multiplier is 3. If it is 1.

7. Income is $500 billion; investment is $50 billion. The multiplier is 2. If inventories decline by $10 billion, what happens to income?

8. Draw a diagram showing what happens to $1 billion of new investment given the following leakages: mps 10 percent; marginal taxation 20 percent; marginal propensity to import 5 percent; marginal addition to business saving 15 percent. What will be the size of the second round of spending? the third? the final total?

9. If the marginal propensity to consume is three-quarters, what is the size of the marginal propensity to save? If it is five-sixths? If it is 70 percent?

10. What is the formula for the multiplier?

LEARNING ABOUT STATISTICS

CORRELATION AND REGRESSION

In this section we begin to look into econometrics, a relatively new use for statistics. As the roots of the word indicate, *econo-metrics* refers to the measurement of economic concepts. As such, econometrics covers a wide range of applications and is much used in making economic predictions and in testing economic hypotheses. What is the difference between a study of economic statistics and a study of econometrics? Strictly speaking, the econometrician uses all the standard statistical concepts; then to those concepts he applies the tools of other branches of mathematics such as algebra or calculus to test how economic phenomena conform to economic theory.

Here, we are going to learn something about the fundamental problems of econometrics, and in particular, about two words much used in it, *correlation* and *regression.*

The analysis of relationships

We have already come into contact with an econometric problem in our study of the propensity to consume. There we were interested in examining the association between two variables, income and consumption. Much of econometrics is concerned with the kinds of *problems* exemplified by the income-consumption relationship, although the kinds of *activities* which econometrics investigates runs a vast gamut that includes price-quantity relations, interest rate-investment relationships, and wage-employment relationships.

What is it that we want to discover when we look into the relationship of two variables, such as income and consumption, wages and employment, or whatever? Generally, we seek to establish three things: (1) whether a change in one of these variables—say, income—or wages—is usually associated with a change in the second variable; (2) if there *is* such an association, whether a given change in one variable usually results in large or small change in the associated variable; and (3) once two variables have been shown to be linked in some way, just how precisely the relationship between the two can be specified.

Correlation and scatter diagrams

All of these problems use statistical techniques that we will not attempt to teach fully in this text. But for each of them there is also an intuitive representation that will make you familiar with the nature of these econometric questions.

The first such task, we have said, is to discover whether or not a relationship exists at all between two variables. The simplest way to test for the probable existence of such a relationship is to perform the operation we did on p. 241, where we made a *scatter diagram* of income and consumption. In Fig. 14–6, we show two such scatter diagrams, each a visual representation of the association between two variables. On the left, we show a diagram that depicts the relationship of the heights and weights of a group of male adults; on the right we show one that portrays the heights and IQs of a group of male adults (both diagrams are fictitious).

The difference between the two diagrams is obvious. There is a clear-cut relationship between height and weight—the taller the man, the heavier he tends to be (with exceptions, of course). But there is no clear-cut relation between height and IQ: tall men are neither brighter nor more stupid than short men. In the first case, there is prima facie evidence that a correlation exists; in the second case there is none.

FIG. 14 • 6

Regression
Once we have some evidence that a correlation exists, we would like to find a way of describing it. That is, we would like to discover the value of one variable, if we know the value of the other, or the rate of change in one variable, given a change in the other. For example, we would like to know the *average change* in weight associated with an additional inch of height, or the *average change* in consumption associated with an additional dollar of income. (The last is, of course, our familiar marginal propensity to consume.)

When econometricians seek to reduce this relationship to a numerical magnitude, they speak of "running a regression" of one variable (such as height or consumption) on the other (weight or income). How do you run such a regression? The details of computation are better reserved for a statistics course. We will just ask you to take on faith that there is a fairly simple arithmetical technique

FIG. 14 • 7

for deriving a regression line that will tell us what variable A will tend to be, given variable B.

In Fig. 14–7, we show a very simple height-weight scatter diagram (it could be, of course, an income-consumption scatter diagram) with *two* regression lines. Each line was drawn visually in an attempt to show the form of the relationship which the dots exhibit. Forget the colored lines for a moment. How do we know which is the better of the two, line *A* or *B?*

The answer is that we try to find the line that describes the relationship best, that is the line that lies closest to the dots. But how do we define "closest"? Here is where the colored lines enter. (1) From each dot we draw a vertical line to a given regression line (line *A* in our example). (2) We measure each "colored-line" distance and *square* it.* (3) We add together the squared distances.

Least squares

In our diagram we have shown the distances of the dots from line *A*. Now we would have to do the same thing for line *B*, or for any other line we could draw. In the end, *we choose the line that has the smallest sum of squared distances as being the best fit.* We call the technique of finding such a line "fitting a regression by least squares." The actual process of doing so must also be left for a statistics course, but the basic idea of a "least squares" fit should now be plain.

What does the resulting line show? We know the answer from the propensity to consume (note the least squares line fitted on the diagram on page 241). The regression coefficient, or the *slope* of the regression line, shows us the change in the dependent variable (C) associated with a change in the independent variable (Y). We know that this relationship can also be expressed (very roughly) in the formula to be found in the footnote on page 243 where the coefficient is

---

* Why do we square the distances? One answer is that this gives additional importance (weight) to any dots that lie considerably away from the regression line, thereby making our measure more sensitive to "exceptions" to what seems to be the rule.

.94*Y*. Thus once again we have shown that a diagram and an equation are only two ways of depicting the same thing—in this case, the relationship between consumption and income.*

Correlation coefficient

There remains one last problem. We know now what we mean by correlation and by a regression analysis. We even understand, in general, the criterion by which we fit a line to a group of "dots." But we do not know how we distinguish between two correlations to determine which is better.

Once again, an example will help make the answer clear. In Fig. 14-8 we show two regression lines, *each one of which is the best fit we can get by the least squares criterion.* Yet, clearly, the line on the right shows a better correlation of *Y* on *X* than the line on the left, simply because the dots lie directly on, or just off, the regression line, whereas in the second case they lie at some distance from it.

FIG. 14 • 8

There is a mathematical way of describing the difference in "closeness of fit" of the two lines; it is called a *correlation coefficient*. A correlation coefficient is a number that tells us how closely our regression line fits the actual data. This coefficient always has a value between +1 and −1. If the correspondence is perfect—that is, if the dots lie exactly *on* the line, the correlation coefficient is either +1 or −1 (depending on whether the two variables move in the same direction or in directions opposite to one another). If the correlation coefficient is 0, then no correlation exists, as in the case of our example of height and IQ.

---

* Note that we have been talking exclusively about *positive* coefficients; that is, about cases where an added inch of height is associated with an *added* amount of weight, or where an extra dollar of income is associated with *extra* consumption spending. We can also have negative regression coefficients, where the groups of "dots" would be downward sloping, and where the coefficient would have a minus sign in front of it. For example, if you graph weight on the vertical axis and life expectancy on the horizontal, you would find a downward sloping cluster of dots. Can you think of other such cases?

Once again, we leave the calculation of the coefficient itself to a statistics course. But you can now see that the closer a correlation coefficient (for which we use the symbol r) is to $+1$ or -1, the stronger is the relationship between the two variables, and the better is the correlation.

One further piece of information. Statisticians usually use the *square* of the correlation coefficient (r^2) to describe what percentage of a change in one variable we can attribute to the other. Suppose that the coefficient of correlation for the weight-height relationship were $+.8$. Then statisticians would say that changes in height account for 64 percent of changes in weight. Why 64? Because $.8 \times .8 = .64 = 64$ percent. In other words, a high r^2 is evidence of a "significant" relationship between two variables, and a low r^2 is evidence of the *lack* of such a relationship. This raises two questions: (1) by a "significant" correlation do we imply that changes in one variable *cause* changes in the other? and (2) how high an r^2 is "significant? These are questions that our next two statistical supplements will take up.

Multiple correlation

A last problem remains, to which we can only allude in passing in this introduction to correlation analysis. It is the question of how we deal with the problem of correlation when more than one variable is associated with changes in another. For instance, how do we figure out the relationship not merely between consumption and income, but between consumption and income *and* wealth *and* changes in prices *and* consumer expectations *and* still other variables that may influence consumption expenditures?

The answer is that we run what is called a *multiple regression analysis.* We do this by quantifying the relationship between the variable in which we are interested (the *dependent variable*) and the other variables (the *independent variables*), by techniques that enable us to discover the separate effect of each independent variable on the dependent variable. Once again, the techniques for doing this must be kept for a statistics course, but we should now be able to understand the meaning of the complicated formulas that emerge from multiple regression analysis.

Such a formula (purely imaginary in this case) might look like this:

$$C = .8Y + .3W - .2T \ldots$$

The purpose of such a multiple regression formula is to show us the different effects on our dependent variable, consumption (C), of various independent variables such as income (Y), wealth (W), taxes (T), and so on. What our particular formula tells us is that the net effect on consumption of $1 of added income is .80 cents, assuming that there is no change in wealth, taxes, etc.; that the net effect of an increase in wealth is 30 cents (again assuming that we have held the other variables constant); that the net effect of a rise in taxes is a *decline* in consumption (note the minus sign before the coefficient of .2), again with other variables held constant.

Multiple regression not only is a very widely used econometric technique, but it opens a new problem for our examination. This is the problem to which we have already referred—the relation of the "correlation" between two things and the idea of causation. That is the question to which we will turn next in our "Learning about Statistics."

We have spent some time investigating how variations in investment spending can induce powerful repercussions in the national economy. But we have not yet asked the all-important question of why the flow of capital expenditure should be variable in the first place. Nor have we understood how GNP will settle down after it has been raised or lowered by more or less investment. In this chapter, we must look into these matters—into the motives behind the investment expenditure of the firm, and into the way that changes in investment can shift GNP from one level to another.

The Motivation of Investment

Consumption spending, let us remember, is essentially directed at the satisfaction of the person. In an increasingly affluent society, we may not be able to say that consumer expenditure is any longer solely geared to necessity, but at least it obeys the fairly constant promptings of the cultural and social environment, with the result that consumer spending, in the aggregate, fluctuates relatively little, except as income fluctuates.

A quite different set of motivations drives the investment impulse. Whether the investment is for replacement of old capital or for the installation of new capital, the ruling consideration is virtually never the personal use or satisfaction that the investment yields to the owners of the firm. Instead, the touchstone of investment decisions is *profit*.

Figure 15-1 shows corporate profits since 1929, as well as their division into retained earnings, dividends, and taxes. What is strikingly apparent, of course, is the extreme fluctuation of profits between prosperity and recession. Note that corporations as a whole lost money in the depths of the Depression years, but that even in the lush postwar period, the swings from year to year have been considerable (compare 1958 and 1959).

Have corporate profits changed as a percent of GNP? Surprisingly little. In 1929, corporate profits before tax amounted to about 10 percent of GNP; from 1965 through 1968 they averaged about 11 percent; from 1969 through 1970, they slumped to 9 percent. Profits *after* taxes fell from some 8 percent of GNP in 1929 to under 7 percent in the 1965-1968 period, to only 5 percent from 1969 to 1970. Profits after tax plus depreciation accruals remain unchanged at under 12 percent. Corporate profits have, of course, increased sharply as a percent of GNP from their level in the early 1900s, but this is because corporations themselves were not a dominant form of business organization until after World War I.

EXPECTATIONS

The chart shows us how corporate profits looked to businessmen when the books were tallied at the end of each year. But the results of his last year's operation, although very important, is not the main thing that motivates a businessman to invest. Primarily, he is interested in the profits he expects from *next year's* operations. His view is never backward, but always forward.

Note the important stress on *expectations.* One firm may be enjoying large profits on its existing plant and equipment at the moment; but if it anticipates no profits from the sale of goods that an *additional* investment would make possible, the firm will make no additions to capital. Another firm may be suffering current losses; but if it anticipates a large profit from the production of a new good, it may launch a considerable capital expenditure.

There is a sound reason for this anticipatory quality of investment decisions. Typically, the capital goods bought by investment expenditures are expected to last for years and to pay for themselves only slowly. In addition, they are often highly specialized. If capital expenditures could be recouped in a few weeks or months, or even in a matter of a year or two, or if capital goods were easily transferred from one use to another, they would not be so risky and their dependence on expectations not so great. But it is characteristic of most capital goods that they *are* durable, with life expectancies of ten or more years, and that they tend to be limited in their alternative uses, or to have no alternative uses at all. You cannot spin cloth in a steel mill or make steel in a cotton mill.

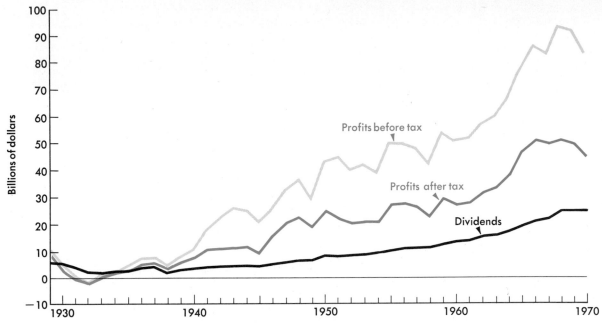

FIG. 15 • 1 PROFITS, TAXES, AND DIVIDENDS

The decision to invest is thus always forward-looking. Even when the stimulus to build is felt in the present, the calculations that determine whether or not an investment will be made necessarily concern the flow of income to the firm in the future. These expectations are inherently much more volatile than the current drives and desires that guide the consumer. Expectations, whether based on guesses or forecasts, are capable of sudden and sharp reversals of a sort rare in consumption spending. Thus in its orientation to the future we find a main cause for the volatility of investment expenditures.

Induced and Autonomous Investment

One kind of profit expectation, and the investment that stems from it, ties in closely with the analysis we have just made of the multiplier. This is an expectation of future profit derived from *an observed rise in current consumption spending.*

Many business firms decide to invest because they must expand their capacity to maintain a given share of a growing market. Real estate developers who build to accommodate an already visible suburban exodus, or supermarkets that build to serve a booming metropolis, or gas stations that must be built to serve a new highway, or additions to manufacturing capacity that must be made because existing facilities cannot keep up with demand—these are all examples of what we call *induced investment.*

When rising consumption induces investment, we call the relationship the *acceleration principle* or the *accelerator.* In many ways it resembles the multiplier effect. The multiplier describes the effect that investment has on income via consumption spending; the acceleration principle describes the effect that consumption can have on income via investment spending. When consumption is rising and plant capacity is already tight, investment is likely to be induced, and this induced investment in turn will generate still *additional* incomes through the multiplier effect. Thus the multiplier effect and the acceleration principle can interact to yield even larger "secondary" impacts than either can alone. It is interesting to note that when the Council of Economic Advisers was arguing for the Kennedy tax cut before the Joint Economic Committee of the 88th Congress, it estimated that the pure multiplier effect on GNP was only a little over 2, but that the combined multiplier-accelerator effect was 3 to 4.

The acceleration principle thus helps us understand further how small increases in one sector can be magnified and spread throughout the economy. But beyond that, it enlightens us about a surprising thing. Let us discover it by imagining an industry with rising sales and fully utilized equipment and, therefore, induced investment. We will assume that our industry needs a capital equipment twice as large in dollar value as its annual volume of sales, in order to produce effectively. We also assume that 10 percent of its capital equipment wears out and is replaced each year—that is, the average machine lasts ten years. Table 15-1 gives us a model of such an industry.

TABLE 15 • 1

Year	Sales	Existing capital	Needed capital (2 × sales)	Replacement	Induced new investment (2 × addition to sales)	Total investment
1	$100	$200	$200	$20	—	$20
2	120	200	240	20	$40	60
3	130	240	260	20	20	40
4	135	260	270	20	10	30
5	138	270	276	20	6	26
6	140	276	280	20	4	24
7	140	280	280	20	—	20
8	130	280	260	—	—	0
9	130	260	260	20	—	20

In our first view of the industry, we find it in equilibrium with sales of, let us say, 100 units, capital equipment valued at 200 units, and regular replacement demand of twenty units. Now we assume that its sales rise to 120 units. To produce 120 units of goods, the firm will need (according to our assumptions) 240 units of capital. This is forty units more than it has, so it must order them. Note that its demand for capital goods now shoots from twenty units to sixty units: twenty units for replacement as before, and forty new ones. Thus investment expenditures *triple,* even though sales have risen but 20 percent!

Now assume that in the next year sales rise further, to 130 units. How large will our firm's investment demand be? Its replacement demand will not be larger, since its new capital will not wear out for ten years. And the amount of new capital needed to handle its new sales will be only twenty units, not forty as before. Its total investment demand has *fallen* from sixty units to forty.

What is the surprising fact here? It is that *we can have an actual fall in induced investment, though consumption is still rising!* In fact, as soon as the *rate of increase* of consumption begins to fall, *the absolute amount* of induced investment declines. Thus a slowdown in the rate of improvement in sales can cause an absolute decline in the orders sent to capital goods makers. This helps us to explain how weakness can appear in some branches of the economy while prosperity seems still to be reigning in the market at large.

Now look at what happens to our model in the eighth year, when we assume that sales slip back to 130. Our existing capital (280 units) will be greater by twenty units than our needed capital. That year the industry will have no new orders for capital goods and may not even make any replacements, since it can use its new machines in place of the discarded old ones. Its orders to capital goods makers will fall to zero, even though its level of sales is 30 percent higher than at the beginning. The next year, however, if sales remain steady, it will again have to replace one of its old machines. Its replacement demand again jumps to 20. No wonder capital goods industries traditionally experience feast or famine years!*

There is, in addition, an extremely important point to bear in mind about the accelerator. *Its upward leverage usually takes effect only when an industry is operating at or near capacity.* When an industry is not near capacity, it is relatively simple for it to satisfy a larger demand for its goods by raising output on its underutilized equipment. Thus, unlike the multiplier, which yields its effects on output only when we have unemployed resources, the accelerator yields its effects only when we do *not* have unemployed capital. That is when induced investment is most likely to follow from increased consumption and when we are also most likely to suffer a decline in total investment, after an initial peak, once the rate of increase in consumption begins to taper off.

---

* Perhaps you have noticed a kind of wavelike movement in the orders for capital goods. We will return to this in Chap. 20 when we study business cycles.

Not all investment is induced by prior rises in consumption. In fact, perhaps the more significant category of investment is that undertaken in the expectation of a profit to be derived from a *new* good or a *new* way of making a good. This type of investment is usually called *autonomous* investment.

In autonomous investment decisions, prior trends in consumption have little or nothing to do with the decision to invest. This is particularly the case when new technologies provide the stimulus for investment. Then the question in the minds of the managers of the firm is whether the new product will create *new* demand for itself.

Technological advance is not, however, the only cause for autonomous investment, and therefore we cannot statistically separate autonomous from induced investment. With some economic stimuli, such as the opening of a new territory or shifts in population or population growth, the motivations of both autonomous and induced investment are undoubtedly present. Yet there is a meaningful distinction between the two, insofar as induced investment is sensitive and responsive to consumption, whereas autonomous investment is not. This means that induced investment, by its nature, is more foreseeable than autonomous investment.

At the same time, both spontaneous and induced investments are powerfully affected by the over-all investment "climate"—not alone the economic climate of confidence, the level and direction of the stock market, etc., but the political scene, international developments, and so on. Hence it is not surprising that investment becomes by far the most unpredictable of the components of GNP, and thus the key "independent" variable in any model of GNP.

The Determinants of Investment

The profit expectations that guide investment decisions are largely unpredictable. But there exists one guideline for investment decisions that works in a more determinable manner. This is the influence of the *rate of interest* on the investment decisions of business firms.

Typically, the rate of interest offers two guides to the investing firm. If the businessman must borrow capital, a higher rate of interest makes it more expensive to undertake an investment. For huge firms that target a return of 15 to 20 percent on their investment projects, a change in the interest rate from 5 to 6 percent may be negligible. But for certain kinds of investment—notably utilities and home construction—interest rates constitute an important component of the cost of investment funds. To these firms, the lower the cost of borrowed capital, the more the stimulus for investment. The difference in *interest costs* for $1 million borrowed for twenty years at 3 percent (instead of 4 percent) is $200,000, by no means a negligible sum. Since construction is the largest single component of investment, the interest rate therefore becomes an important influence on the value of total capital formation.

A second guide is offered to those businessmen who are not directly seeking to borrow money for investment, but who are debating whether to invest the savings (retained earnings) of their firms. This problem introduces us to an important idea: the discounting of future income.

DISCOUNTING THE FUTURE

Suppose that someone gave you an ironclad promise to pay you $100 a year hence. Would you pay him $100 *now* to get back the same sum 365 days in the future? Certainly not, for in parting with the money you are suffering an *opportunity cost* (a term we will encounter again and again in economics), or a cost than can be measured in terms of the opportunities that your action has foreclosed for you. Had the going rate of interest been 5 percent, for example, you could have loaned your $100 at 5 percent and had $105 at the end of the year. Hence, friendship aside, you are unlikely to lend your money unless you are paid something to compensate you for the opportunities you must give up while you are waiting for your money to return. Another way of saying exactly the same thing is that we arrive at the *present value* of a specified sum in the future by discounting it by some percentage. If the discount rate is 5 percent, the present value of $100 one year in the future is $100 ÷ 1.05, or approximately $95.24.

This brings us back to our businessman who is considering whether or not to make an investment. Suppose that he is considering investing $100,000 in a machine that he expects to earn $25,000 a year for 5 years, over and above all expenses, after which it will be worthless. Does this mean that the expected profit on the machine is therefore $25,000—the $125,000 of expected earnings less the $100,000 of original cost? No, it does not, for the expected earnings will have to be discounted by some appropriate percentage to find their present value. Thus the first $25,000 to be earned by the machine must be reduced by some discount rate; and the second $25,000 must be discounted *twice* (just as $100 to be repaid in *two* year's time will have to yield the equivalent of *two* years' worth of interest); the third $25,000, three times, etc.*

Clearly, this process of discounting will cause the present value of the expected future returns of the machine to be less than the sum of the

---

* The formula for calculating the present value of a flow of future income that does not change from year to year is:

$$\text{Present value} = \frac{R}{(1+i)} + \frac{R}{(1+i)^2} + \cdots + \frac{R}{(1+i)^n}$$

where R is the annual flow of income, i is the interest rate, and n is the number of years over which the flow will last.

returns. If, for example, its returns are discounted at a rate of 10 percent, the businessman will find that the present value of a five-year flow of $25,000 per annum comes not to $125,000 but to only $94,700. This is *less* than the actual expenditure for the machine ($100,000). Hence, at a discount rate of 10 percent, the businessman would not undertake the venture.

On the other hand, if he used a discount rate of 5 percent, the present value of the same future flow would be worth (in round numbers) $109,000. In that case, the machine *would* be a worthwhile investment.

What rate should our businessman use to discount his future earnings? Here is where the rate of interest enters the picture. Looking out at the economy, the businessman sees that there is a whole spectrum of interest rates, ranging from very low rates on bonds (usually government bonds) where the element of risk is very small, to high rates on securities of the same maturity (that is, coming due in the same number of years) where the risk is much greater, such as "low-grade" corporate bonds or mortgages. Among this spectrum of rates, he can then choose one that he thinks represents *the same degree of risk as his own venture,* and by applying that rate he can discover whether the estimated future earning from his venture, properly discounted, is actually profitable or not.

There is still another way in which the interest rate helps determine the volume of investment, although it is really only another version of the same idea. The businessman can calculate the rate of discount that would just suffice to make a particular investment pay. *This rate is called the marginal efficiency of capital (or investment).* In our illustration above, we saw that a rate of 10 percent proved the machine to be unprofitable and that one of 5 percent made it show an expected profit. There must be some rate, between these two, that would just make the discounted value of the expected returns equal the cost of the $100,000 machine; if we figure it out, the rate turns out to be approximately 8 percent.*

What has this to do with the rate of interest? The answer is that the businessman very likely has a choice among different investment projects from which he anticipates different returns. Suppose he ranks those projects,

---

* How did we arrive at the figure of 8 percent? By using the formula in the preceding footnote and solving for the value of *i* (the discount rate) that would make the sum of the terms on the right—the discounted future earnings—just equal to the *cost* of the machine, which we put on the left. The mathematics is a bit complicated, but the idea is not. Clearly, if we expect an investment to yield very high returns (*R* in the formula), it will have a very high marginal efficiency—that is, it will take a very high discount rate (*i* in the formula) to bring the sum of future earnings down to the level of cost. On the other hand, if the investment is expected to give only small returns, it will have a low marginal efficiency, for only a low discount rate will keep the discounted value of future earnings from falling below costs.

FIG. 15 • 2

as we have in Fig. 15-2, starting with the most profitable *(A)* and proceeding to the least profitable *(G)*. How far down the list should he go? The rate of interest gives the answer. Suppose the rate (for projects of comparable risk) is shown by *OX*. Then all his investment projects whose marginal efficiency is higher than *OX* (investments *A* through *D*) will be profitable, and all those whose marginal efficiency falls below *OX* (*E* through *G*) will be discarded or at least postponed.

Note that if the interest rate falls, more investments will be worthwhile; and that if it rises, fewer will be. By generalizing the relationship of expected investment-profitability with the interest rate, we arrive at a schedule of the marginal efficiency of capital (or investment) shown on the right. As we would expect, as interest falls (from *OX* to *OY*) the quantity of investment rises (from *OC* to *OG*).

Thus, whether we figure interest as a cost or as a guideline against which we measure the expected returns of a capital investment, we reach the important conclusion that *low interest rates tend to encourage investment spending*—or in more formal language, that *investment is inversely related to the rate of interest.* To be sure, the fact that a given investment, such as project *B* above, has a marginal efficiency higher than the interest rate is no guarantee that a business actually will undertake it. Other considerations—perhaps political, perhaps psychological—may deter management, despite its encouraging calculations. But assuredly a business will not carry out a project that yields less than the interest rate, because it can make more profit by lending the money, at the same degree of risk, than by investing it.

We have been talking about the determining factors that ultimately affect the rate of investment, the background forces to which we must turn to account for any given level of investment spending (much as we turn to the habits of householders as the background force determining the level of consumption). We have found that these background forces for investment are not a single variable, like a propensity to consume income, but a mixture of variables: *increases in consumption that may induce investment; expected levels of profitability of new inventions, techniques, discoveries, etc.; and the rate of interest with which we discount the future stream of investment income.*

Now we can go a step further. With a general understanding of the constellation of forces that determines investment, we can begin to understand how a particular level of output is set for the economy as a whole.

Saving and Investment

Let us begin as before, with a simple model; this time, a simple island economy having only two sectors: consumption and investment. We dispense with government and with the export sector for reasons of clarity in exposition. It will be easy enough to reintegrate them into the model, subsequently.

Next we establish schedules for consumption and saving at different levels of income. We have already worked with a hypothetical propensity to consume schedule, so let us merely repeat it here with a new column of figures that will represent the amount of investment spending at various levels of income.

TABLE 15•2

SCHEDULES OF SAVING AND INVESTMENT

FOR A HYPOTHETICAL ECONOMY (IN BILLIONS OF DOLLARS)			
Income	Consumption	Saving	Investment
$100	$80	$20	$28
110	87	23	28
120	92	28	28
130	95	35	28
140	97	43	28

From our previous discussion, we have seen that there is no simple functional relation between income and investment, but rather that many forces bear on the investment total. We could, for instance, imagine an investment schedule that rose with income (perhaps due to the accelerator) or one that fell because expectations turned sour. In our model, for the sake of simplicity, we have assumed a schedule of investment expenditures that remains constant at $28 billion. The subsequent analysis would be more difficult but not fundamentally different if we used a variable schedule.

INTERPLAY OF SAVING AND INVESTMENT

If we now look at the last two columns, those for saving and investment, we can see a powerful cross play that will characterize our model economy at different levels of income, for the forces of investment and saving will not be in balance at all levels. At some levels, the propensity to save will outrun the act of purposeful investment; at others, the motivations to save will be less than the investment expenditures made by business firms. In fact, our island model shows that at only one level of income—120—will the savings and investment schedules coincide.

What does it mean when intended savings are greater than the flow of intended investment? It means that people are *trying* to save out of their given incomes a larger amount than businessmen are willing to invest. Now if we think back to the exposition of the economy in equilibrium, it will be clear what the result must be. The economy cannot maintain a closed circuit of income and expenditure if savings are larger than investment (or if investment is smaller than savings). This will simply give rise to a demand gap, the dangerous repercussions of which we have already explored.

But a similar lack of equilibrium results if intended savings are less than intended investment expenditure (or if investment spending is greater than the propensity to save). Now businessmen will be pumping out more than enough to offset the savings gap. The additional expenditures, over and above those that compensate for saving, will flow into the economy to create new incomes—and out of those new incomes, new savings.

Income will be stable, in other words, only when the flow of intended investment just compensates for the flow of intended saving. Investment and saving thus conduct a tug of war around this pivot point, driving the economy upward when intended investment exceeds the flow of intended saving; downward when it fails to offset saving.

The careful reader may have noticed that we speak of *intended* savings or of *intended* investments. This is because there is a formal balance between *all* saving and *all* investment in the economy at every instant. After all, saving and investment are only different names for the portion of economic output that is not consumed: from one point of view, this portion is "saved"; from another it is "invested." But this strict balance between saving and investment is of no more analytic interest than the fact that both sides of a balance sheet always balance, whether a firm is making money or losing it. What matters in the determination of GNP are the *actions* people are taking—actions leading them to try to save, or actions leading them to seek to invest. These are the activities that must be brought into balance and that will drive the economy upward or downward when they are out of balance. Meanwhile, a formal balance of saving and investment will be maintained because there will be temporary *unintended* saving (for instance, unexpected profits) or *unintended* investment (such as inventories that pile up or become depleted, not on purpose, but because business took an unexpected turn). These unintended items can provide our "balance sheet equality" of S and I, but they are important in dynamic analysis only insofar as they affect the powerful currents of our propensity to save and of our willingness to invest.

CONSUMPTION
DIAGRAM
RE-EXAMINED

We can clarify the idea of equilibrium by reverting to a familiar figure, the propensity-to-consume diagram. Let us explore it more carefully than we have had a chance to, so far.

Suppose, for example, that a society consumed *all* its income at every level of income. In such a society, expenditures (consumption) would be exactly equal to income, and a line showing the relation of consumption to income would therefore lie exactly on the 45° "income line." The two diagrams in Fig. 15-3 should make this clear.

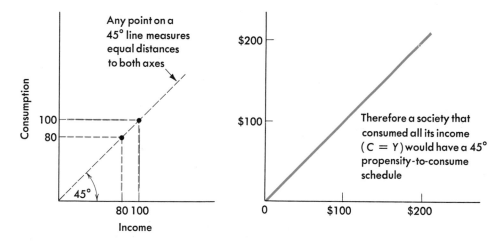

FIG. 15 • 3   THE 45° INCOME LINE

As we know, however, most societies do not consume an amount equal to their incomes, at least above the level of deep depression. For example, at a level of income represented on our chart by $100 billion, we could realistically imagine a society that consumed only $80 billion and saved the rest. How would we represent this on our graph?

The answer is shown in Fig. 15-4. Note that the dot measures $100 billion along the horizontal (income) axis, but only $80 billion on the vertical (expenditure) axis. Thus the dot represents the ratio of C to Y, at an income of $100 billion, or the propensity to consume at that level.

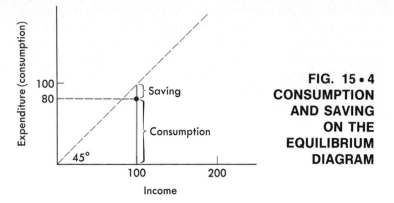

FIG. 15 • 4
CONSUMPTION
AND SAVING
ON THE
EQUILIBRIUM
DIAGRAM

But notice further that the vertical distance between the dot and the 45° income line measures the *difference* between our income and our expenditure. (If we spent all our income, the dot would be *on* the line; hence the distance between the line and dot shows us by how much our expenditure fell short of equaling our income.) This difference between income and expenditure on consumption is our saving. Thus Fig. 15-4 shows us our propensity to save at this given income, as well as our propensity to consume.

**THE COMPLETE
SCHEDULE
DIAGRAMMED**

Now there remains only one additional complication. Most societies have positive saving at high income levels; but at very low levels of incomes, rich societies like the United States will *dissave;* that is, they will draw on accumulated savings and spend more than they currently earn. To represent such a state of affairs on our graph, we would have to show expenditure larger than saving. In Fig. 15-5, there is such a situation, in which income is only $50 billion and expenditure comes to $60 billion. Here dissaving is represented by the length of the line above the 45° income slope.

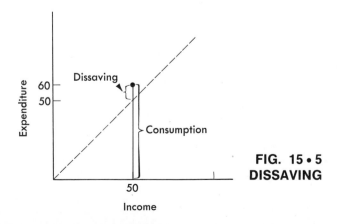

FIG. 15 • 5
DISSAVING

Perhaps the next step is already obvious. Our dots are in fact nothing but a depiction of the relation of C to Y at various levels of income. By drawing a line through them, we show the schedule of the propensity to consume at these levels of income. The slope of the line, which tells us by how much our consumption changes from one income level to the next, will be a geometric presentation of the marginal propensity to consume. The consumption schedule of our hypothetical economy would look like Fig. 15-6, where the varying amounts of saving and dissaving are clearly seen.

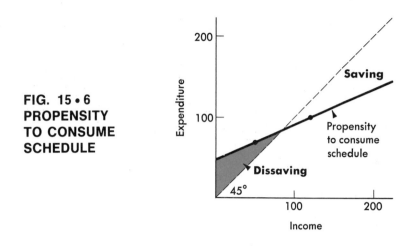

**FIG. 15 • 6
PROPENSITY
TO CONSUME
SCHEDULE**

The Determination of Equilibrium

We are now ready to show how the equilibrium level of income can be determined from our diagram. That level, we remember, is where intended investment is equal to intended saving. But so far, our graph shows us only a schedule of consumption and saving at different income levels. Which is the actual amount of saving? And how shall we put investment into the picture?

Let us answer the second question first. In Table 15-2, we note that investment expenditures are scheduled to be $28 billion at *every* level of income. If we now add a second line 28 units higher than the consumption line, we will show the total amount of expenditure that consumers and businessmen intend to make at all levels of income. Such a schedule is shown in Fig. 15-7.

We now have a schedule, represented by the $C + I$ line, that shows us how much total expenditure will be associated with *different* levels of income. Now we are ready for the first question. Given this schedule of investment desires and the slope of our propensity to consume, what will be the equilibrium level of expenditure and income? *We know the answer must be that the level of income at which investment equals saving.*

Our diagram now indicates exactly where this equilibrium level must

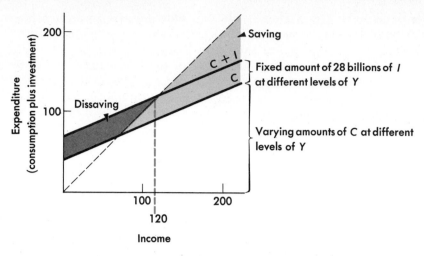

FIG. 15·7 ADDING INVESTMENT TO THE DIAGRAM

be. It must lie at that level where the total amount of expenditure (as represented by the $C + I$ line) is just equal to the level of total income (as represented by the 45° income line). On the graph, equilibrium lies—just as in our table—at an income of $120 billion.

How do we know that some other point would not also represent an equilibrium? Suppose, for example, that we look at point X to the left of the equilibrium position in Fig. 15-8. Here investment is larger than savings (which are negative to the left of the 45° line). Income would therefore be moving upwards, toward equilibrium. But similarly, a point such as Y, to the right of the equilibrium level, is also out of balance. Here investment can be seen to be less than savings, and income would therefore be falling toward the equilibrium point.

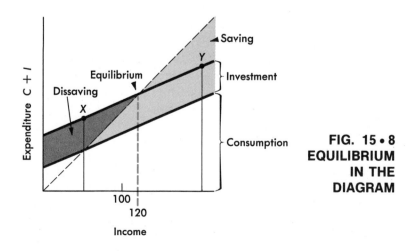

**FIG. 15·8
EQUILIBRIUM
IN THE
DIAGRAM**

Thus what our diagram shows us is that *the point of equilibrium can be only where income equals expenditure.* And that point, we can now see, is precisely where investment and saving are also alike.

Thus, given our investment schedule and our saving schedule, we see that there is one and only one equilibrium level at which income must settle. But this equilibrium need not be maintained. Suppose investment intentions now increase and that business firms spend *another* $28 billion for investment. Our line $C + I$ changes to $C + I'$, as shown in Fig. 15-9. Now what happens?

**FIG. 15 • 9
SHIFTS IN
EQUILIBRIUM**

By looking for the new intersection of the expenditure schedule $(C + I')$ and the 45° income line, we can see that the new equilibrium point lies at X'. If we now measure the amount of income represented by this new equilibrium point, we find it to be 175.

Here is a puzzle. We have increased our investment expenditure by 28. But our income has risen by 55. How can this be?

The answer lies in our now familiar multiplier. The increase of 28 in investment spending has brought about a *larger* increase in income because of the respending of the original additional income.

Another Approach to the Equilibrium Problem

The idea of equilibrium is never easy to grasp at first, but a second approach to the selfsame problem may clarify things. Suppose that we are back on our model island community and are asked by a group of businessmen to predict the island's income for the coming year. We know that income will be the sum of two expenditure streams—consumption and investment (we are still ignoring government)—so we send our two teams of researchers to discover people's intentions concerning their expenditures.

The first team goes to a sample of consumers' houses and asks, "How much will you be consuming next year?" The answer is a bit disconcerting: "It all depends on how large our incomes are," they tell us. What our poll-takers would find, in other words, is that consumption expenditures (or savings plans) could be predicted only in the form of a *schedule,* relating C to Y, or S to Y. In Fig. 15-10, we show this new (but quite obvious) saving/income relationship. Note that the vertical axis in this new diagram measures saving, not consumption.

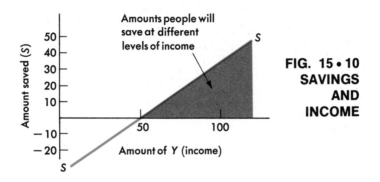

FIG. 15 • 10
SAVINGS
AND
INCOME

Now we turn to the poll of business intentions. Here, too, there is an element of "it depends," for some investment, as we know, will be induced by various consumption levels. Yet to a very large extent, businessmen *must* formulate their investment plans on a forward-looking basis, and we will assume that their capital budgets for the coming year are already set at a figure they divulge to us.

In Fig. 15-11 we show these budgets superimposed. It is obvious that the equilibrium level of income, measured along the horizontal axis, is determined by the point where the S and I curves intersect.

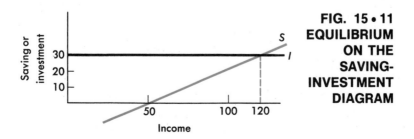

FIG. 15 • 11
EQUILIBRIUM
ON THE
SAVING-
INVESTMENT
DIAGRAM

FIG. 15 • 12
TWO METHODS OF SHOWING EQUILIBRIUM

It is helpful to see the integral relation between our two different looking diagrams for equilibrium; in fact, the second diagram is taken right out of the first. In Fig. 15-12 we show the two ways of depicting equilibrium, one above the other. Notice that the shaded triangle showing the propensity to save is transposed to the second diagram. There it looks "flatter" only because we now ignore consumption and therefore put the savings triangle on a horizontal base instead of a sloping one. Our fixed investment schedule is also exactly the same in both diagrams, although once again, in the lower figure it is shown as a horizontal line, rather than as a line that is parallel to the sloping line *C*. Now it should be obvious why the equilibrium intersection point must be at the same figure on the income axis of both diagrams.

And what if investment expenditures change? We see the effect in Fig. 15-13, where the *I* curve jumps to *I'*. This too is only a different depiction of the process that we have already drawn in Fig. 15-9. A good exercise is to pencil in a higher *I'* on both graphs in Fig. 15-12 and to prove to yourself that the new equilibrium point must be the same in both cases.

One last point before we move on. We know by now that the size of the multiplier depends on the marginal propensity to save. And we know

FIG. 15•13   THE MULTIPLIER AND EQUILIBRIUM—ANOTHER VIEW

further that the marginal propensity to save (like the marginal propensity to consume) determines the slope of the lines we draw on our diagrams. Fig. 15-14 has two propensity-to-save curves with different slopes. Indicate in pencil the original and new equilibrium points for each, and show that the lower the marginal propensity to save, the greater will be the multiplier effect, both for an increase or a decrease in investment spending.

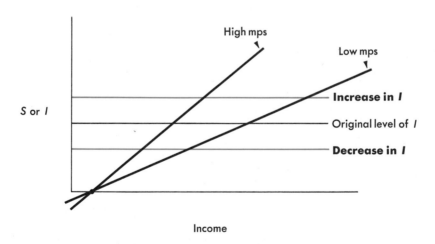

FIG. 15•14   MPS AND EQUILIBRIUM

THE IDEA OF EQUILIBRIUM

Thus we have begun to understand how GNP reaches an equilibrium position after a change in investment. Here it is well to remember, however, that the word "equilibrium" does not imply a static, motionless state. We use the word only to denote the fact that *given* certain behavior patterns of consumption and investment, there will be a determinate point to which their interaction will push the level of income; and *so long as the underlying patterns of consumption and investment remain unchanged, the forces they exert will keep income at this level.*

In fact, of course, the flows of consumption and investment are continually changing, so that the equilibrium level of the economy is constantly shifting, like a Ping-Pong ball suspended in a rising jet of water. Equilibrium can thus be regarded as a target toward which the economy is constantly propelled by the push-pull between saving and investment. The target may be attained but momentarily before the economy is again impelled to seek a new point of rest. What our diagrams and the underlying analysis explain for us, then, is not a single determinate point at which our economy will in fact settle down, but the *direction* in which it will go in quest of a resting place, as the dynamic forces of the system exert their pressures.

The fact that income must always move toward the level where the flows of intended saving and investment are equal leads to one of the most startling—and important—paradoxes of economics. This is the so-called paradox of thrift, a paradox that tells us that the *attempt to increase saving* may, under certain circumstances, lead to a *fall in actual saving.*

THE PARADOX OF THRIFT

The paradox is not difficult for us to understand at this stage. An attempt to save, *when it is not matched with an equal willingness to invest,* will cause a gap in demand. This means that businessmen will not be getting back enough money to cover their costs. Hence, production will be curtailed or costs will be slashed, with the result that incomes will fall. As incomes fall, savings will also fall, because the ability to save will be reduced. Thus, by a chain of activities working their influence on income and output, the effort to *increase* savings may end up with an actual *reduction* of savings.

This frustration of individual desires is perhaps the most striking instance of a common situation in economic life, the incompatibility between some kinds of individual behavior and some collective results. An individual farmer, for instance, may produce a larger crop in order to enjoy a bigger income; but if all farmers produce bigger crops, farm prices are apt to fall so heavily that farmers end up with less income. So too, a single family may wish to save a very large fraction of its income for reasons of financial prudence; but if all families seek to save a great deal of their incomes, the result—unless investment also rises—will be a fall in expenditure and a common failure to realize savings objectives. The paradox of thrift, in other words, teaches us that the freedom of behavior available to a few individuals cannot always be generalized to all individuals.*

---

* The paradox of thrift is actually only a subtle instance of a type of faulty reasoning called the fallacy of composition. The fallacy consists of assuming that what is true of the individual case must also be true of all cases combined. The flaw in reasoning lies in our tendency to overlook "side effects" of individual actions (such as the decrease in spending associated with an individual's attempt to save more, or the increase in supply when a farmer markets his larger crop) which may be negligible in isolation but which are very important in the aggregate.

A Note on Exports,
Injections, and Leakages

With an initial understanding of the mechanism of equilibrium and disequilibrium behind us, we have reached a very important stage in our inquiry. The interactions of the macroeconomic variables now begin to come together and the causes and mechanics of prosperity and depression begin to reveal themselves to us.

Before we go on to complete our understanding, however, we must mention, if only in passing, a sector we have largely overlooked in this book. This is the foreign sector, or more properly the sector of net exports.

If we lived in a European, South American, or Asian country, we could not be so casual in our treatment of foreign trade, for this sector constitutes the very lifeline of many, perhaps even most, countries. Our own highly self-sustained economy in which foreign trade plays only a small quantitative (although a much more important qualitative) role, is very much the exception rather than the rule.*

In part, it is the relatively marginal role played by foreign trade in the American economy that allows us to treat it so cavalierly. But there is also another problem. The forces that enter into the flows of international trade are much more complex than any we have heretofore discussed. Not alone the reactions of American consumers and firms, but those of foreign consumers and firms must be taken into account. Thus comparisons between international price levels, the availability of foreign or domestic goods, credit and monetary controls, exchange rates—a whole host of "extraneous" considerations—lie at the very heart of foreign trade. To begin to unravel these interrelationships, one must study international trade as a subject in itself, and that we will defer until Part Five. Nevertheless, we should try to understand the main impact of foreign trade on the level of GNP, even if we cannot yet investigate the forces and institutions of foreign trade as thoroughly as we might like.

IMPACT OF FOREIGN TRADE

We must begin by repeating that our initial overview of the economic system, with its twin streams of consumption and investment, was actually incomplete. It portrayed what we call a "closed" system, an economy with no flows of goods or services from within its borders to other nations, or from other nations to itself.

Yet such flows must, of course, be taken into account in computing our national output. Let us therefore look at a chart that shows us the main streams of goods and services that cross our borders, as well as a table of the magnitudes in our benchmark years.

---

* In Chapter 30 we shall see, however, that international currency problems can play a very important role in our economic affairs.

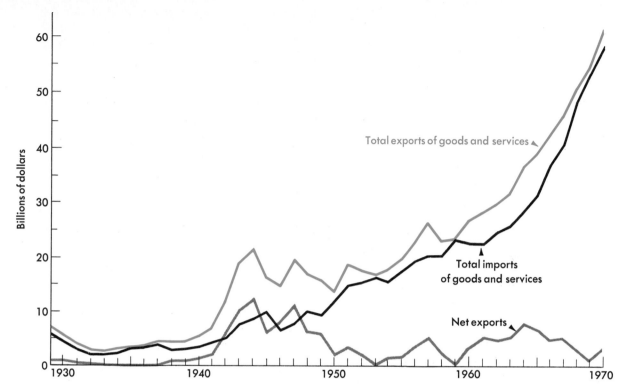

FIG. 15 • 15 EXPORTS, IMPORTS, AND NET EXPORTS

First a word of explanation. Exports show the total value of all goods and services we sold to foreigners. Imports show the total value of all goods and services we bought from foreigners. Our bottom line shows the net difference between exports and imports, or the difference between the value of the goods we sold abroad and the value we bought from abroad. This difference is called *net exports,* and it constitutes the net contribution of foreign trade to GNP.

If we think of it in terms of expenditures, it is not difficult to see what the net contribution is. When exports are sold to foreigners, their expenditures add to American incomes. Imports, on the contrary, are expenditures that we make to other countries (and hence that we do not make at home). If we add the foreign expenditures made here and subtract the domestic expenditures made abroad, we will have left a net figure that will show the contribution (if any) made by foreigners to GNP.

What is the impact of this net expenditure on GNP? It is much the same as net private domestic investment. If we have a rising net foreign trade balance, we will have a net increase in spending in the economy. And this increase in spending, just like that arising from the addition of plant or equipment, will exert a magnified impact on GNP via the multiplier. Conversely, if our imports rise more rapidly than our exports, so that our net foreign trade balance declines or becomes negative, our GNP would decline—not only by the drop in net exports, but by the net fall in spending again magnified by the influence of the marginal propensity to consume.

LEAKAGES AND INJECTIONS

Thus we can consider the effects of the foreign trade sector as if it were a part of the investment sector, even though the underlying forces are extremely different. But as we broaden the model of our economy, from its original simple conception as a society that only consumes and invests, to one that now imports and exports, and in our next chapter to one that has, as well, an active government sector, it becomes convenient to widen our terminology somewhat when we speak of the determinants of GNP.

Now, instead of referring only to "saving" as the cause of a downward pressure on the level of expenditure, or to "investment" as the only cause of upward pressures, we can speak of *leakages in, or withdrawals from, the expenditure flow* or of *injections or additions to that flow.* The word *leakage* is, of course, already familiar to us from our analysis of the multiplier. Here we use it as a general term to describe any activity that diminishes the flow of spending—be it saving or increasing imports, or rising government taxes or growing business profits. Similarly, we speak of *injections* as any activity—investment, exports, government spending, or a spontaneous rise in consumption—that will increase the flow of spending.

The determination of output can then be generally described as the outcome of the balance between leakages or withdrawals of all kinds and injections or additions of all kinds. So long as injections are outpacing leakages, GNP will rise; when leakages overbalance injections, GNP will fall; and when the two are in a state of balance, GNP will be in stable equilibrium.

KEY CONCEPTS AND KEY WORDS

Expectations

1. The motivation for investment expenditure is not personal use or satisfaction, but *expected profit.* Note that investment is always geared to forward profit *expectations* rather than to past or present results.

Induced Investment

Antonomous Investment

2. We distinguish between two kinds of investment motivation. When investments are made to meet an expected demand arising from present or clearly indicated changes in consumption, we speak of *induced investment.* When investment is stimulated by developments (such as inventions) that have little relation to existing trends, we speak of *autonomous investment.*

Acceleration principle

3. Induced investment is subject to the *acceleration principle* which describes how a given increase in *C* can give rise to a proportionally larger increase in *I*. The acceleration principle also shows us that the absolute level of induced investment can fall, even though the level of *C* is still rising. Thus it helps explain the onset of recessions. Note that the acceleration principle "takes hold" only when an industry is at or near full utilization.

4. In two ways, the rate of interest is an important determinant of investment: (1) it directly affects *the cost of investment* and (2) it gives us a rate (for investments with risks similar to the one we are contemplating) which allows us to calculate whether the *discounted future returns of our investment are greater than its cost.*

Rate of interest

Discounting future income

5. We can also discover the rate of discount that just makes the expected returns on an investment equal to its cost. This rate is called the *marginal efficiency of investment or the marginal efficiency of capital.* Unless the marginal efficiency of investment is greater than the rate of interest, an investment will not be profitable.

Marginal efficiency of investment

6. Note that whether we consider interest as a cost or as a guideline against which to compare the marginal efficiency of capital, *the lower the interest rate, the larger the volume of investment is likely to be.*

7. The level of income in the economy as a whole is moved upward or downward by the interplay of the schedules of intended saving and investment. *Only where intended S and intended I are equal will income be in equilibrium.*

Equilibrium

8. We can show the idea of equilibrium in two kinds of diagrams. In one we ascertain what point on the *C + I* expenditure schedule lies on the 45° income line. In the other diagram, we find the point of intersection between the saving and the investment schedules on a graph that relates saving and investment (on the vertical axis) to income (on the horizontal axis). *Both graphs are only visual ways of showing the point of mutual compatibility between schedules of intended saving and investment behavior at different income levels.*

45° income line

9. The graphs also show that changes in *I* lead to larger changes in *Y.* The reason for this is the slope of the *C + I* schedule (or in the saving-investment graph, of the *S* schedule). Since these slopes represent the marginal propensity to consume (or save), *the graphs merely present in visual form the familiar multiplier relationship.*

10. The new level of equilibrium of income, given a change in *I,* depends on two things: (1) *the size of the actual change in I:* and (2) *the multiplier.*

11. The fact that income must finally settle where the schedules of intended *S* and *I* converge leads to the famous *paradox of thrift.* This paradox tells us that the effort to save, unless matched by an equal effort to invest, will lead to an excess of *S* over *I,* and thereby drive income lower. At lower levels of income, there will be less *S,* rather than more. Thus the effort to save more has resulted in the economy's actually *saving less!* (Note that this occurs only if the effort to save is not matched by more investment.)

Paradox of thrift

Intended vs. actual saving

12. Exports and imports serve as stimuli for, or drags on, the expenditure flow. They act much as investment does in driving the level of income higher or lower. Therefore, we broaden our terminology to include exports and imports and similar stimuli by speaking of *injections* into, or *withdrawals* or *leakages* from, the expenditure flow.

Injections and leakages

Q U E S T I O N S

1. Discuss the difference in the motivation of a consumer buying a car for pleasure and the same person buying a car for his business.

2. Which of the following are induced, and which autonomous, investment decisions: a developer builds homes in a growing community; a city enlarges its water supply after a period of water shortage; a firm builds a laboratory for basic research; an entrepreneur invests in a new gadget.

3. What is the basic idea of the acceleration principle? Describe carefully how the acceleration principle helps explain the instability of investment.

4. What is meant by "discounting" the value of an expected return? If the rate of interest were 10 percent, what would be the *present value* of $100 due a year hence? What would be its present value two years hence? (Hint: the first year's discounted value has to be discounted *a second time*.)

5. Assume that it costs 7 percent to borrow from a bank. What is the minimum profit that must be expected from an investment before it becomes worthwhile? Could we write that $I = f(r)$ where r stands for the rate of interest? What would be the relation between a change in r and I? Would $I = f(r)$ be a complete description of the motivation for investment?

6. Suppose that an economy turns out to have the following consumption and saving schedule:

Income (billions)	Saving (billions)	Consumption (billions)
$400	$50	$350
450	55	395
500	60	440
550	70	480
600	85	515

Now suppose that firms intend to make investments of $60 billion during the year. What will be the level of income for the economy? If investment rises to $85 billion, then what will be its income? What would be the multiplier in this case?

7. Show the equilibrium income before and after the jump in investment on a $C = I$ graph and on an S and I graph.

8. Exactly what is meant by "equilibrium"? Is a balloon floating in mid-air in equilibrium? Why? If gravity is saving, and the lift of hydrogen is investment, what economic magnitude is represented by the height of the balloon?

9. Is there an opposite to the paradox of thrift? Suppose everyone tried not to save but to spend all his income, and that businessmen did not alter their investment plans. What would happen? (Since there would be no more goods and a good deal more spending, wouldn't someone have to end up holding money and not being able to use it for consumption? Wouldn't the "paradox of spendthrift" lead to more saving, despite the effort not to save?) What does this tell us about the need to coordinate S and I plans to achieve a desired macroeconomic goal?

10. Explain how exports stimulate income and how imports depress it. Does this mean than imports are bad? Are savings bad?

LEARNING ABOUT STATISTICS

CORRELATION AND CAUSALITY

In our preceding supplement, we described the aims of correlation analysis and familiarized ourselves with some of its vocabulary. Now we want to discuss a profoundly important problem that involves the uses of correlation. This is the relationship between *correlation* and *causation*—that is, between the observed association of two variables and the causal linkages that bind them.

As any student knows if he has ever dipped into a book on philosophy, the meaning of the word *cause* is elusive and perplexing. Econometrics does not really probe into the meaning of the word, but it sheds a good deal of light on some of the pitfalls associated with it. In particular it makes us very cautious about declaring that such-and-such an event is the cause of another, simply because there is a high degree of correlation between them.

Here are a few examples to think about.

1. *Wrong-way causation.*

It is a statistical fact that there is a positive correlation between the number of babies born in various cities of northwestern Europe and the number of storks' nests in those cities. Is this evidence that storks really do bring babies? The answer is that we are using a correlation to establish a causal connection in the wrong way. The true line of causation lies in the opposite direction: cities that have more children tend to have more houses, which offer storks more chimneys to build their nests in!

2. *Spurious causation.*

It is a statistical fact that there has been a positive correlation all during the 1960s between the cost of living in Paris and the numbers of American tourists visiting there. Does that imply that American visitors are the cause of price increases in that city?

Here at least there is little danger of getting the causal links back to front; few people would argue that more Americans visit Paris *because* its prices are going up. But it would be equally difficult to argue that American tourists are the cause of rising Parisian prices, simply because the total amount of American spending is small in relation to the total amount of expenditure in Paris (with the exception of a few tourist traps).

The answer, then, is that the correlation is "spurious" in terms of causality, although it is "real" in terms of sheer statistics. The true explanation for the correlation is that the rising numbers of American visitors and the rising costs of living in Paris are both aspects of a worldwide expansion in incomes and prices. Neither is the "cause" of the other; both are the results of more fundamental, broader-ranging phenomena.

3. *The problem of ceteris paribus.*

Finally, consider this problem. Suppose that we are quite sure that additional income really does "cause" us to spend more money for consumption. But suppose that we tested our belief by correlating figures for income and consumption during a particular period, and we find to our dismay that rising income was not associated with rising consumption. Does that lack of correlation disprove our causal hypothesis?

Not necessarily. Here our brief look at multiple correlation provides an answer. It may be that during the particular period we observed, other events were counteracting the effects of a rise in income on consumption. Perhaps the stock market had collapsed, or menacing headlines made people uneasy about spending money. In that case, their "normal" propensity to consume may have been swamped by a sudden propensity to save brought about by a loss in their wealth or a general apprehension about the economic future. To test out our hypothesis, in other words, we would have to make allowance for causal factors other than those explicit in the direct income-consumption relationship. In the famous economic phrase, we cannot test a hypothesis except under conditions of *ceteris paribus,* the Latin phrase for "other things being equal."

The same condition is true for all scientific tests, not just for economics. Scientists cannot test the law of gravitation unless "other things" are equal, such as an absence of air that would cause a feather to fall a great deal more slowly than Galileo predicted. But the trouble with the social sciences is that the "other things" are often more difficult to spot—or just to think of—than they are in the laboratory. For example, what are we to make of the fact that there is a positive correlation between shoe sizes and mathematical ability among school children? The answer, once we think about it, is that we have not held "other things" equal in one very important respect—the age of the school children. Of course older children, with bigger feet, will be able to do more arithmetic than little children. Hence the first thing to do is to see if there is a correlation between shoe sizes of children of *equal ages* and mathematical ability. Children of equal ages will also have different shoe sizes, but the correlation with problem solving ability is no longer there.

What can correlation tell us?

These (and still other) pitfalls makes econometricians extremely cautious about using correlations to "prove" causal hypotheses. *Even the closest correlation may not show in which direction the causal influences are working;* for instance, the high correlation between the number of corporate mergers and the level of stock prices in the 1960s does not show whether mergers caused stock prices to move up, or whether booming prices encouraged companies to merge and float their new securities on a favorable market.

So, too, *the interconnectedness of the economic process often causes many series of data to move together.* In inflationary periods, for example, most prices tend to rise, or in depression many indexes tend to fall, without establishing that any one of these series was directly responsible for a movement in another particular series.

And finally, econometricians are constantly on the lookout for factors that have not been held constant during a correlation, so that *ceteris paribus conditions were not in fact maintained.*

Is there an answer to these (and still other) very puzzling problems of correlation and causation? There is a partial answer. We cannot claim that a correlation is proof that a causal relationship exists. But a causal relationship is likely to exist when we can demonstrate a strong correlation, backed up by theoretical reasoning. That is, every valid economic hypothesis (or for that matter every valid hypothesis of any kind) *must* show a high and "significant" correlation coefficient between the "cause" and the "effect," provided that we are absolutely certain that our statistical test has rigorously excluded spurious correlations of various kinds and unsuspected "other things." Needless to say this is often very difficult and sometimes impossible to do with real world data. A physicist can hold "other things equal" in his laboratory, but the world will not stand still just so an economist can test his theories.

All this has a very important moral. Because economists deal with quantifiable data, correlation analysis is one of the most important tools in the economist's kit. All the "laws" of economics, from supply and demand to the various relationships of macroeconomics, are constantly being subjected to highly sophisticated econometric tests, *because these are the only objective methods we have for establishing whether variable X is associated with variable Y.* Thus we constantly use correlations to buttress—but not to prove—our belief in economic relationships such as those between consumer spending and income or between rising investment and a multiplier effect on income. Conversely, when careful correlation analysis fails to show high coefficients, there is good reason to look very skeptically at our economic hypotheses.

Hence, correlation is an indispensable part of economic science. But that is not the same thing as saying that it *is* economic science. Behind the tools of econometrics lies the process of *economic reasoning*—that is, the attempt to explain why people behave in certain ways on the marketplace, or how the hard realities of nature or technology shape and constrain the ongoing economic process. If the economic reasoning is faulty, econometrics will not set it straight. Econometrics is the most penetrative means of empirical analysis that economics has yet developed, and our understanding of the workings of the economy would be terribly handicapped if we did not command its powerful techniques. But ultimately it is to economic theory that we look for that basic understanding itself.

We turn now to the last of the main sources of GNP—the government, and as before we shall begin by familiarizing ourselves with the sector in its long historical profile.

Figure 16-1 shows us the emergence of the government sector as a significant contributor to GNP, a process we have already discussed in Part Two, and to which we will return later in this chapter.

Government in the Expenditure Flow

Now let us take a closer look at a recent year, to help us fit the government sector into the flow of national expenditure. Figure 16-2 shows us the familiar bars of our flow diagram. Note that indirect taxes, totaling some $92 billion in 1970, amounted to almost 10 percent of the value of GNP. As can be seen, however, income taxes on households and businesses are much more important than indirect taxes in providing total government revenues. (What the diagram does not show is that about two-thirds of the indirect taxes are state and local in origin: property taxes, excise taxes, motor vehicle and gasoline taxes, and others. Income taxes and social security contributions constitute about nine-tenths of the income of the federal government.)

On the expenditure side, we see that state and local purchases of goods and services are as important as federal purchases in providing public demand. Since two-thirds of all transfer payments are federal in origin, however, total federal *expenditures* (as contrasted with purchases of goods and services) run about one-fifth higher than all state and local expenditures.

Finally, it is worth reminding ourselves of the different significance and impact of public purchases and transfers. Public purchases of goods and services, whether they originate with local or federal government, require the use of land, labor, and capital. They are thus *public production,* and constitute a net addition to GNP. Transfer payments, on the other hand, do not increase output. They are simply a reallocation of income, from factors to various groups of the community in the business sector or the household sector. Transfers, therefore, do not require new production and are not a part of GNP.

How large does the public sector bulk in the total flow of GNP? Let us again try to put a perspective into our answer by observing the trend of government purchases over the years.

The striking change from prewar to postwar years is, of course, immediately visible. The government sector, taken as a whole, has changed from a very small sector to a very large one (see Chap. 9, p. 162). In 1929, total government purchases of goods and services were only half of total private investment spending; in 1970, total government purchases were over 50 percent *larger* than private investment. *In terms of its contributions to GNP, government is now second only to consumption.*

The public sector, whose operation we will have to examine closely, has become a major factor in the economy as a whole. Let us begin by learning to distinguish carefully among various aspects of what we call "government spending." As we shall see, it is very easy to get confused between "expenditures" and "purchases of goods and services"; between federal spending and total government spending (which includes the states and localities); and between war and nonwar spending.

1. *Government expenditures vs. purchases of goods and services.*

When we speak of government spending, we must take care to specify whether we mean total *expenditures of the government,* which include transfer payments, or *purchases of goods and services by the government,* which represent only actual economic activity performed for and bought by the government. In the latter category we include all "production" that owes its existence to public demand, whether from federal, state, or local agencies; in

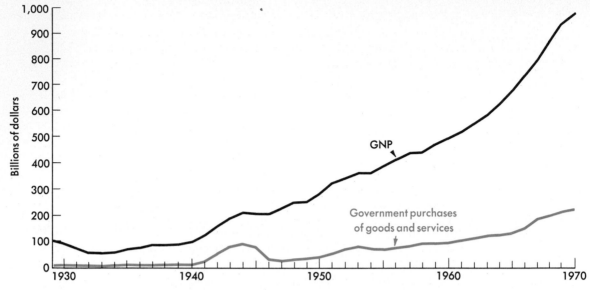

FIG. 16 • 1 GNP AND THE GOVERNMENT SECTOR

the former we include activities performed for the government *plus* transfer payments made by government, at all levels, as part of the redistribution of income. Thus, under "purchases" we include items such as arms and education and police and roads; under "expenditures" we count all these plus Social Security; interest on the debts of localities, states, and the federal government; welfare; and other such transfers.

The distinction is important in terms of the relative bulk of what we call government spending. The purchases of goods and services by all government agencies amounted in 1970 to about $221 billion (of which, as Fig. 16-2 shows, the federal government accounted for just under $100 billion). The larger "expenditure" category came to $313 billion. Thus government purchases were the direct cause of the production of about 22 percent of GNP itself, whereas government expenditures amounted in all to not quite one-third of GNP. Remember that GNP does not include transfers, so that the ratio is a comparison between differently defined flows.*

2. *Federal vs. state and local spending.*

In dealing with the public sector we must also be careful to distinguish between expenditures or purchases that originate with the federal govern-

---

* It is only fair to add that most economists carelessly use the term *government expenditure* to mean "purchases" or "purchases plus transfers." The point is to be careful about which figures you use before jumping to conclusions. Here is another example of the need to examine data carefully (see pp. 187–188).

ment and those that stem from state and local agencies. As we noted in Chapter 9, state and local spending for goods and services is *larger* than federal purchasing. This is the consequence of the rise of an urbanized, motorized, education-minded society that has imposed vast new burdens on state and local authorities: the supervision of vehicular traffic alone requires the employment of roughly one out of every ten state and local employees, and the support of education now runs to $35 billion a year. These have been increasing during the last decade, and now, annual state and local spending for such goods and services runs about 25 percent ahead of federal purchases.

On the other hand, federal expenditures, *including transfers,* make *total* federal spending larger than total state-and-local spending. In 1970, for example, federal expenditures, including transfers such as Social Security, interest on the debt, various subsidies, grants to the states, etc., brought total federal outlays of all kinds to above $200 billion, roughly double the amount it spent for goods and services alone.

Billions of dollars

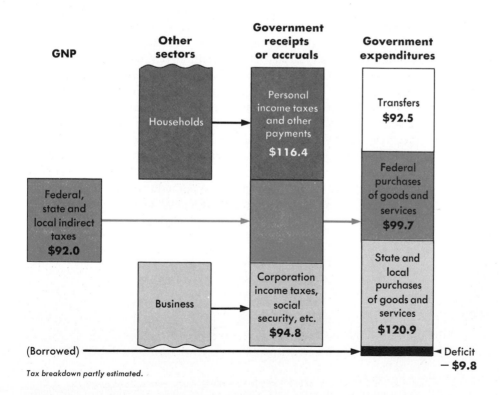

Tax breakdown partly estimated.

FIG. 16 • 2 GOVERNMENT SECTOR, 1970

3. *Welfare vs. warfare.*

Most of the rise in federal purchases of goods and services is the result of our swollen armaments economy, a problem to which we shall return at the end of this chapter. Defense spending in 1970 amounted to approximately 40 percent of our federal expenditures of all kinds including transfers, and to a much larger fraction—about 75 percent—of federal purchases of goods and services.

Federal spending for welfare has been much smaller than spending for warfare. It is interesting to note that federal purchases of nonwar goods and services as a percent of GNP is actually smaller than in the prewar days and has shown only a slight rise during the last decade.

TABLE 16 • 1

FEDERAL NONDEFENSE PURCHASES

Selected years	1929	1933	1940	1960-65	1966	1967	1968	1969	1970
Percent of GNP	1.0*	3.0*	4.0	2.1	2.2	2.3	2.5	2.5	2.4

* Estimated.

Meanwhile, social welfare expenditures of all kinds and of all government agencies (federal, state, and local), including such payments as Social Security, health and medical programs, public education, public housing, welfare assistance, etc., have risen from about 10 percent of GNP in the mid-1930s to about 14 percent today. This is not a large percentage by international standards. In 1967 (the last year for which we have comparative figures) at least 8 other nations spent a higher proportion of their GNP on education than we did. Other social welfare spending (excluding education) amounted to about 9 percent of our GNP, compared with an average of more than 15 percent among the industrialized nations of Europe. It is noteworthy that in 1969 the average Social Security check per married couple came to just over $100; in Scandanavian countries the payments, compared to average earnings, were roughly twice as generous as ours.

The Economic Character
of the Public Sector

Thus we see that the classification of public expenditure is far more complicated than that of the consumption or investment sectors. Yet, so far we have been concerned mainly with problems of a definitional kind.* Now we

---

* We could also attempt to divide public expenditures into categories comparable to consumption and investment. The division is not a simple one to make, however. We could have no trouble putting the tag "Investment" on construction for roads or airfields or dams. But what are we to

want to examine the public sector from a different angle; namely, its unique *economic* character. And here the appropriate place to begin seems to be in the difference in *motivations* that guide public, as contrasted with private, spending.

We recall that the motivations for the household sector and the business sector are lodged in the free decisions of their respective units. Householders decide to spend or save their incomes as they wish, and we are able to construct a propensity to consume schedule only because there seem to be spending and saving patterns that emerge spontaneously from the householders themselves. Similarly, business firms exercise their own judgments on their capital expenditures, and as a result we have seen the indeterminacy and variability of investment decisions.

But when we turn to the expenditures of the public sector, we enter an entirely new area of motivation. It is no longer fixed habit or profit that determines the rate of spending, but *political decision*—that is, the collective will of the people as it is formulated and expressed through their local, state, and federal legislatures and executives.

As we shall soon see, this does not mean that government is therefore an entirely unpredictable economic force. There are regularities and patterns in the government's economic behavior, as there are in other sectors. Yet the presence of an explicit political will that can direct the income or outgo of the sector *as a whole* (especially its federal component) gives to the public sector a special significance. *This is the only sector whose expenditures and receipts are open to deliberate control.* We can exert (through public action) very important influences on the behavior of households and firms. But we cannot directly alter their economic activity in the manner that is open to us with the public sector.

Fiscal Policy

The deliberate use of the government sector as an active economic force is a relatively new conception in economics. As we know from our historical survey, like so much of the apparatus of macroeconomic analysis, it stems essentially from the work of John Maynard Keynes during the Great Depression. At that time his proposals were regarded as extremely daring, but

---

make of education expenditures? Economists believe that education is fully as important as capital goods for long-term growth. Shall we then count it as investment? Or what shall we make of spending on recreational facilities or on defense? The line between consumption and investment in the public sector is evidently much harder to draw than in the private sector. For reasons that we shall shortly discuss, it might be useful to list separately those items that are unquestionably additions to public capital. But since the distinction between capital and consumption in the public sphere is often unclear, economists take the line of least resistance and lump all kinds of public purchases, however varied, in one undifferentiated public sector.

they have become increasingly accepted by economists.* Although the bold use of the economic powers of the public sector is far from commanding unanimous assent in the United States today, there is a steadily growing consensus in the use of fiscal policy—that is, the deliberate utilization of the government's taxing and spending powers—to help the stability and growth of the national economy.

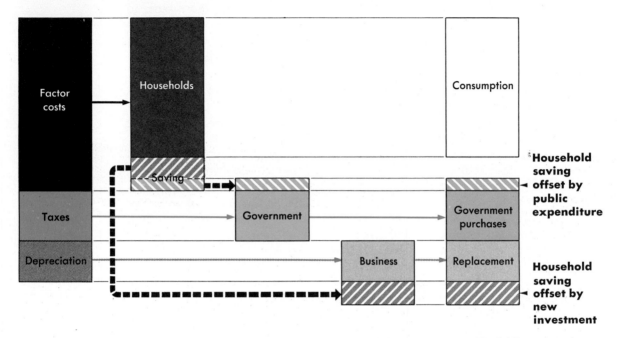

FIG. 16 • 3   PUBLIC EXPENDITURE AND THE DEMAND GAP

The basic idea behind modern fiscal policy is simple enough. We have seen that economic recessions have their roots in a failure of the business sector to offset the savings of the economy through sufficient investment. If savings or leakages are larger than intended investment or injections, there will be a gap in the circuit of incomes and expenditures that can cumulate downward, at first by the effect of the multiplier, thereafter, and even more

---

* Reviewing a book in 1964 with the word "macroeconomics" in its title, Harold Somers wrote: "The name of Keynes is anathema in some circles. . . . As a result, courses bearing the name of Keynes are very scarce and one publisher . . . even boasts that his elementary economics book contains no mention of Keynes.

"All is not lost. There is available a very competent economist called Macro. This economist, Macro, is most versatile. He . . . encompasses everything that Keynes taught, might have taught, and would have denied teaching. . . ." (*American Economic Review,* March 1964, p. 138.)

seriously, by further decreases in investment brought about by falling sales and gloomy expectations.

But if a falling GNP is caused by an inadequacy of expenditures in one sector, our analysis suggests an answer. Could not the insufficiency of spending in the business sector be offset by higher spending in another sector, the public sector? Could not the public sector serve as a supplementary avenue for the "transfer" of savings into investment?

As Fig. 16-3 shows, an expenditure gap can indeed by closed by "transferring" savings to the public sector and spending them.

The diagram shows savings in the household sector partly offset by business investment and partly by government spending. It makes clear that at least so far as the mechanics of the economic flow are concerned, the public sector can serve to offset savings or other leakages equally as well as the private sector.

How is the "transfer" accomplished? It is done much as business does it, by offering bonds that individuals or institutions can buy with their savings. Unlike business, the government cannot offer stock, for it is not run as a profit-making enterprise. However, we must note that the government can also tax incomes to finance its expenditures. This may have complicated results, for the taxes may not cause consumers to cut back their spending, but to curtail their saving—or more likely, to cut back some on both consumption and saving.

We will look more carefully into the question of how the government can serve as a kind of counterbalance for the private economy. But first we must discover something about the normal behavior of the public sector; for despite the importance of political decisions in determining the action of the public sector, and despite the multiplicity of government units and activities, we can nonetheless discern "propensities" in government spending and receiving—propensities that play their compensating role in the economy quite independently of any direct political intervention.

The reason for these propensities is that both government income and government outgo are closely tied to private activity. Government receipts are derived in the main from taxes, and taxes—direct or indirect—tend to reflect the trend of business and personal income. In fact, we can generalize about tax payments in much the same fashion as we can about consumption, describing them as a predictable function of GNP. To be sure, this assumes that tax *rates* do not change. But since rates change only infrequently, we can draw up a general schedule that relates tax receipts and the level of GNP. The schedule will show not only that taxes rise as GNP rises, but that they rise *faster* than GNP.

TAXES,
EXPENDITURES,
AND GNP

Why faster? Largely because of the progressive structure of the federal income tax.* As household and business incomes rise to higher levels, the percentage "bite" of taxes increases, from around 20 percent on the first dollar of taxable income to much higher percentages for high income brackets. Thus as incomes rise, tax liabilities rise even more. Conversely, the tax bite works downward in the opposite way. As incomes fall, taxes fall even faster, since households or businesses with lowered incomes find themselves in less steep tax brackets.

Government expenditures also show certain "propensities," which is to say, *some government spending is also functionally related to the level of GNP.* A number of government programs are directly correlated to the level of economic activity in such a way that spending *decreases* as GNP *increases,* and vice versa. For instance, unemployment benefits are naturally higher when GNP is low or falling. So are many welfare payments at the state and local level. So, too, are disbursements to farmers under various agricultural programs.

AUTOMATIC STABILIZERS

All these automatic effects taken together are called the *automatic stabilizers* or the *built-in stabilizers* of the economy. What they add up to is an automatic government counterbalance to the private sector. As GNP falls because private spending is insufficient, taxes decline even faster and public expenditures grow, thereby automatically causing the government sector to offset the private sector to some extent. In similar fashion, as GNP rises, taxes tend to rise even faster and public expenditures decline, thereby causing the government sector to act as a brake.

The public sector therefore acts as an automatic compensator, even without direct action to alter tax or expenditure levels, pumping out more public demand when private demand is slow and curbing public demand when private demand is brisk.

How effective are the built-in stabilizers? It is estimated that the increase in transfer payments plus the reduction in taxes offset about 35¢ of

---

* The overall tax structure, however, is much less progressive than is the federal tax structure, since state and local taxation is largely founded on sales and property taxes, which affect all income groups more or less equally (and which often affect lower income groups more than upper ones). A study by the Tax Foundation in 1965 showed that combined federal and state taxes took roughly the same proportion of income from all income groups, starting at the bottom, until the $15,000 bracket was reached, at which point overall progressivity began. It should be noted, however, that there is considerable evidence of tax evasion in the upper brackets, so that the degree of progressivity in the upper brackets is probably less than appears on the surface. For details about tax evasion, see Philip M. Stern, *The Great Treasury Raid* (New York: New American Library, 1964).

We must also recognize that some federal and state and local expenditures—especially welfare expenditures—benefit lower income groups more than upper ones. This redresses some of the balance. On the other hand, much public expenditure for things such as road systems, the aviation network, police, justice, and higher education benefits the middle and upper groups more than the lower ones. It is difficult to arrive at a wholly objective calculation of the net benefits that each income class derives from public expenditure.

each dollar of original decline in spending. Here is how this works. Suppose that private investment were to fall by $10 billion. Because of the multiplier, household spending might well fall by another $10 billion, causing a total decline of $20 billion in incomes.

The action of the stabilizers, however, will prevent the full force of this fall. First, the reduction in incomes of both households and firms will lower their tax liabilities. Since taxes take about 35¢ from each dollar, the drop of $10 billion in incomes will reduce tax liabilities by about $3.5 billion. Most of this—let us say $3 billion—is likely to be spent. Meanwhile some public expenditures for unemployment insurance and farm payments will rise, pumping out perhaps $1 billion into the consumption sector, all of which we assume to be spent by its recipients.

Thus, the incomes of firms and households, having originally fallen by $10 billion, will be roughly offset by $4 billion in additional transfer incomes and in income made available by lessened tax obligations. As a result, the net decline in expenditure will be reduced from $10 billion to $6 billion (actually $6.5 billion, according to the calculations of the Council of Economic Advisers). The multiplier will then indeed affect this net reduction in spending, so that total incomes in the economy will fall by twice as much, or $13 billion in all. But this is considerably less than the fall of $20 billion that would otherwise have taken place.

This is certainly an improvement over a situation with no stabilizers. Yet if the drop in investment is not to bring about some fall in GNP, it will have to be *fully* compensated by an equivalent increase in government spending or by a fall in taxes large enough to induce an equivalent amount of private spending. This will require public action more vigorous than that brought about automatically. Indeed, it requires that the government take on a task very different from any we have heretofore studied, the task of acting as the *deliberate* balancing mechanism of the economy.

There is nothing in our formal analysis to make us doubt that government can take on such a task. Government spending is just like private spending so far as its multiplier effects are concerned.* In the same fashion, government taxes serve to constrict private spending, much as additional saving would.

Hence we can draw a new diagram showing an equilibrium for an economy with various levels of public expenditure. In Fig. 16-4, we enlarge the familiar chart from the last chapter to include a new item on the

---

* Although we should note that different kinds of private and public spending programs may have different multipliers if they go to different spending groups. A government public works program that uses unskilled labor is not apt to have the same initial repercussions on GNP as a private investment project in computers. Additional transfer expenditures may also have initial multiplier effects different from direct purchases of goods and services. And finally, different tax structures will cause changes in GNP to affect private spending differently.

**FIG. 16 • 4
NEW
EQUILIBRIUM
WITH INCREASED
GOVERNMENT
EXPENDITURE**

expenditure axis—government purchases, or G—and a new item on the receipts or income axis—taxes, or T. Once again we draw our 45° slanting line and our schedule of income possibilities, this time as consumption plus investment plus government purchases ($C + I + G$).* Our new schedule shows an equilibrium point at X, where all expenditures, public or private, intersect the income line.

Now let us imagine that C and I remain unchanged but that the regular flow of government purchasing increases, raising total outlays from $C + I + G$ to $C + I + G'$, shown by the broken line. Our equilibrium point now shifts to X'. Once again we note that *the change in equilibrium income is greater than the change in initial expenditure.* The reason is, of course, the same as in the case with private investment. All additional injections of expenditure into the economy will exert a multiple income effect as they pass through successive (albeit diminishing) rounds of receipt and re-expenditure.

**ANOTHER
VIEW OF
EQUILIBRIUM**

For clarity, let us go back again to our island community to predict the equilibrium level of GNP for the coming year. Again we send out our teams of pollsters, and as before, we take note of household consuming and saving intentions and of businessmen's investment plans. This time, however, we also study the community's tax schedules and inquire into the island's projected public expenditures.

---

* Although we do not show it on the diagram, as we add government expenditures and taxation to our model, we must expect the slope of the previous propensity to consume schedule to change. We should picture the impact of taxes as reducing the slope of the curve, since rising income means even faster rising taxes. On the other hand, government expenditure may redistribute income away from savers toward spenders. Hence, one cannot generalize about the way in which the addition of G affects the slope of the propensity to consume schedule. The effect will vary according to the tax and expenditure programs. But it is well to bear this qualification in mind.

As a result, our diagram of equilibrium includes more factors than it did formerly. In Fig. 16-5, we show the schedule of savings plans *plus* additional taxes at various levels of income. In the same diagram, the stream of investment is now increased to include projected public expenditures. As a result, the levels and the slopes of the two lines—one now

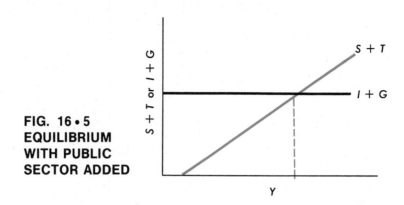

**FIG. 16•5
EQUILIBRIUM
WITH PUBLIC
SECTOR ADDED**

representing leakages and one injections—are different from our former simple model. Yet the intersection of the two lines again tells us what we want to know; that is, given the commitments and propensities of private spending and saving, and public spending and taxing, where the income of our community will settle.

Deficit Spending

Thus from an analytic standpoint we can treat the contribution of government very much as if it were investment. Our diagrams of the sectoral flows and equilibrium relationships make it perfectly plain that the government sector can offset saving just as efficiently as the business sector can, from the point of view of maintaining a given level of spending.

Yet the suggestion that the government deliberately exercise compensatory powers opens a new question for us to consider. The use of the government budget as a stabilizing device means that the government must be prepared to spend more than its normal tax receipts. It must purposefully plan a budget in which outgo exceeds income, leaving a negative figure called a *deficit*.

Like a business, however, a government cannot spend money it does not have in a bank account. Therefore it must *borrow* from individuals, firms, or banks in order to cover its planned deficit. Deficit spending, in other words, means the spending of borrowed money, money derived from the sale of government bonds.

**DEFICITS
AND LOSSES**

Can the government safely run up a deficit? Let us begin to unravel this important but perplexing question by asking another: can a private business afford to run up a deficit?

There is one kind of deficit that a private business *cannot* afford: a deficit that comes from spending more money on current production than it will realize from its sale. This kind of deficit is called a *business loss;* and if losses are severe enough, a business firm will be forced to discontinue its operations.

But there is another kind of deficit, although it is not called by that name, in the operations of a private firm. This is an excess of expenditures over receipts brought about by spending money on *capital assets.* When the American Telephone and Telegraph Company or the Consolidated Edison Company use their own savings or those of the public to build a new power plant, they do not show a "loss" on their annual statement to their stockholders, even though their total expenditures on current costs and on capital may have been greater than their sales. Instead, expenditures are divided into two kinds, one relating current costs to current income, and the other relegating expenditures on capital goods to an entirely separate "capital account." Instead of calling the excess of expenditures a "deficit," they call it "investment."*

**DEBTS
AND ASSETS**

Can A.T.&T. or Consolidated Edison afford to run deficits of the latter kind indefinitely? We can answer the question by imagining ourselves in an economic landscape with no disturbing changes in technology or in consumers' tastes, so that entrepreneurs can plan ahead with great safety. Now let us assume that in this comfortable economy, Consolidated Edison decides to build a new plant, perhaps to take care of the growing population. To finance the plant, it issues new bonds, so that its new asset is matched by a new debt.

Now what about this debt? How long can Consolidated Edison afford to have its bonds outstanding?

The answer is—forever!

Remember that we have assumed an economy remaining changeless in tastes and techniques, so that each year the new factory can turn out a quota of output, perfectly confident that it will be sold; and each year it can set aside a reserve for wear and tear, perfectly confident that the factory is being properly depreciated. As a result, each year the debt must be as good as the year before—no better and no worse. The bondholder is sure of getting his interest, steadily earned, and he knows that the underlying asset is being fully maintained.

---

* Investment does not *require* a "deficit," since it can be financed out of current profits. But many expanding companies do spend more money on current and capital account than they take in through sales and thereby incur a "deficit" for at least a part of their investment.

Admittedly, after a certain number of years the new factory will be worn out. But if our imaginary economy remains unchanged and if depreciation accruals have been properly set aside, when the old plant gives out, an identical new one will be built from these depreciation reserves. Meanwhile, the old debt, like the old plant, will also come to an end, for debts usually run for a fixed term of years. Consolidated Edison must now pay back its debtholders in full. But how? The firm has accumulated a reserve to buy a new plant, but it has not accumulated a second reserve to repay its bondholders.

Nevertheless, the answer is simple enough. When the bonds come due in our imaginary situation, Consolidated Edison issues *new* bonds equal in value to the old ones. It then sells the new bonds and uses the new money it raises to pay off the old bondholders. When the transaction is done, a whole cycle is complete: both a new factory and a new issue of bonds exist in place of the old. Everything is exactly as it was in the first place. Furthermore, as long as this cycle can be repeated, such a debt could safely exist in perpetuity! And why not? Its underlying asset also exists, eternally renewed, in perpetuity.

REAL CORPORATE DEBTS

To be sure, not many businesses are run this way, for the obvious reason that tastes and techniques in the real world are anything but changeless. Indeed, there is every reason to believe that when a factory wears out it will *not* be replaced by another costing exactly as much and producing just the same commodity. Yet, highly stable businesses such as Consolidated Edison or A.T.&T. do, in fact, continuously "refund" their bond issues, paying off old bonds with new ones, and never "paying back" their indebtedness as a whole. A.T.&T., for instance, actually did increase its total indebtedness from $1.1 billion in 1929 to $19.6 billion in 1970. Consolidated Edison Company actually did run up its debt from $240 million in 1929 to $2.3 billion in 1970. And the credit rating of both companies today is as good as, or better than, it was in 1929.

Thus some individual enterprises that face conditions of stability similar to our imaginary situations do actually issue bonds "in perpetuity," paying back each issue when it is due, only to replace it with another (and, as we have seen, *bigger*) issue.

TOTAL BUSINESS DEBTS

Only a few very strong individual businesses can carry their debts indefinitely, but the business sector *as a whole* can easily do so. For although most individual businesses must prudently seek to retire their debts, as we look over the whole economy we can see that as one business extinguishes its debt, another is borrowing an even larger sum. Why larger? Because the *assets* of the total business sector are also steadily rising.

Table 16-2 shows this trend in the growth of corporate debt.*

Note that from 1929 through 1940, corporate debt *declined*. The shrinkage coincided with the years of depression and slow recovery, when additions to capital plant were small. But beginning with the onset of the postwar period, we see a very rapid increase in business indebtedness, an increase that continues down to our present day.

TABLE 16 • 2

CORPORATE NET LONG-TERM DEBT*

Year	1929	1933	1940	1950	1966	1967	1968	1969
Billions of dollars	47	48	44	60	231	258	286	315

* Maturity over one year.

If we think of this creation of debt (and equity) as part of the savings-investment process, the relationship between debts and assets should be clear. Debts are claims, and we remember how claims can arise as the financial counterpart of the process of real capital formation. Thus, rising debts on capital account are a sign that assets are also increasing. It is important to emphasize the *capital account*. Debts incurred to buy capital assets are very different from those incurred to pay current expenses. The latter have very little close connection with rising wealth, whereas when we see that debts on corporate capital account are rising, we can take for granted that assets are probably rising as well. The same is true, incidentally, for the ever-rising total of consumer debts that mirror a corresponding increase in consumers' assets. As our stock of houses grows, so does our total mortgage debt; as our personal inventories of cars, washing machines, and other appliances grow, so does our outstanding consumer indebtedness.

GOVERNMENT DEFICITS

Can government, like business, borrow "indefinitely"? The question is important enough to warrant a careful answer. Hence, let us begin by comparing government borrowing and business borrowing.

One difference that springs quickly to mind is that businesses borrow in order to acquire productive assets. That is, matching the new claims on the business sector is additional real wealth that will provide for larger output. From this additional wealth, business will also receive the income to pay interest on its debt or dividends on its stock. But what of the government? Where are its productive assets?

We have already noted that the government budget includes dams, roads, housing projects, and many other items that might be classified as

---

* We do not show the parallel rise in new equities (shares of stock), since changes in stock market prices play so large a role here. We might, however, add a mental note to the effect that business issues new stock each year, as well as new bonds. During the 1960s, net new stock issues have ranged from about $2 to $8 billion per annum.

assets. During the 1960s, federal expenditures for such civil construction projects averaged about $5 billion a year. Thus the total addition to the gross public debt during the 1960s (it rose from roughly $239 billion in 1960 to $300 billion in 1970) could be construed as merely the financial counterpart of the creation of public assets.

Why is it not so considered? Mainly because, as we have seen, the peculiar character of public expenditures leads us to lump together all public spending, regardless of kind. In many European countries, however, public capital expenditures are sharply differentiated from public current expenditures. If we had such a system, the government's deficit on capital account could then be viewed as the public equivalent of business's deficit on capital account. Such a change might considerably improve the rationality of much discussion concerning the government's deficit.

SALES VS. TAXES

But there is still a difference. Private capital enhances the earning capacity of a private business, whereas most public capital, save for such assets as toll roads, does not "make money" for the public sector. Does this constitute a meaningful distinction?

We can understand, of course, why an individual business insists that its investment must be profitable. The actual money that the business will pay out in the course of making an investment will almost surely not return to the business that spent it. A shirt manufacturer, for instance, who invests in a new factory cannot hope that the men who build that factory will spend all their wages on his shirts. He knows that the money he spends through investment will soon be dissipated throughout the economy, and that it can be recaptured only through strenuous selling efforts.

Not quite so with a national government, however. Its income does not come from sales but from taxes, and those taxes reflect the general level of income of the country. Thus *any* investment money that government lays out, just because it enters the general stream of incomes, redounds to the taxing capacity or, we might say, the "earning capacity" of government.

How much will come back to the government in taxes? That depends on two main factors: the impact of government spending on income via the multiplier, and the incidence and progressivity of the tax structure. Under today's normal conditions, the government will recover about half or a little more of its expenditure.* But in any event, note that the government does not "lose" its money in the way that a business does. Whatever goes into the income stream is always *available* to the government as a source of taxes; but whatever goes into the income stream is not necessarily available to any single business as a source of sales.

---

* We can make a rough estimate of the multiplier effect of additional public expenditure as 2 and of the share of an additional dollar of GNP going to federal taxes as about ⅓ (see page 309). Thus $1 of public spending will create $2 of GNP, of which 65¢ will go back to the federal government.

This reasoning helps us understand why federal finance is different from state and local government finance. An expenditure made by New York City or New York State is apt to be respent in many other areas of the country. Thus taxable incomes in New York will not, in all probability, rise to match local spending. As a result, *state and local governments must look on their finances much as an individual business does.* The power of full fiscal recapture belongs solely to the federal government.

The National Debt

This difference between the limited powers of recoupment of a single firm and the relatively limitless powers of a national government lies at the heart of the basic difference between business and government deficit spending. It helps us understand why the government has a capacity for financial operation that is inherently of a far higher order of magnitude than that of business. We can sum up this fundamental difference in the contrast between the *externality of business debts* and the *internality of national government debts.*

What do we mean by the externality of business debts? We simply mean that business firms owe their debts to someone distinct from themselves, whether this be bondholders or the bank from which they borrowed. Thus, to service or to pay back its debts, business must transfer funds from its own possession into the possession of outsiders. If this transfer cannot be made, if a business does not have the funds to pay its bondholders or its bank, it will go bankrupt.

The government is in a radically different position. Its bondholders, banks, and other people or institutions to whom it owes its debts belong to the same community as that whence it extracts its receipts. In other words, the government does not have to transfer its funds to an "outside" group to pay its bonds. It transfers them, instead, from some members of the national community (taxpayers) to other members of the *same* community (bondholders). The contrast is much the same as that between a family that owes a debt to another family, and a family in which the husband has borrowed money from his wife; or again between a firm that owes money to another, and a firm in which one branch has borrowed money from another. *Internal debts do not drain the resources of one community into another, but merely redistribute the claims among members of the same community.*

A government cannot always borrow without trouble, however. Important and difficult problems of money management are inseparable from a large debt. More important, the people or institutions from whom taxes are collected are not always exactly the same people and institutions to whom interest is paid, so that servicing a government debt often poses problems of *redistribution of income.* For instance, if all government bonds were owned by rich people and if all government taxation were regressive (i.e., proportionately heavier on low incomes), then servicing a government debt would mean transferring income from the poor to the rich. Considerations of equity aside, this would also probably involve distributing income from spenders to savers, and would thereby intensify the problem of closing the savings gap.

In addition, a debt that a government owes to foreign citizens is *not* an internal debt. It is exactly like a debt that a corporation owes to an "outside" public, and it can involve payments that can cripple a firm.* Do not forget that the internality of debts applies only to *national* debts held as bonds by members of the same community of people whose incomes contribute to government revenues.

Finally, we must not overlook the practical difficulties of government spending. The problem is that there is usually a long lag between the time of recognition, when the need for more public spending is first admitted, and the actual expenditure of the money itself. The time lag may, in fact, be so long—eighteen to twenty-four months—that by the time the public expenditures take effect, the condition they were supposed to remedy may have disappeared or worsened. In either case, the original government program is no longer the proper one. To counteract this difficulty, many economists have urged that the government keep a "stockpile" of approved public works, to be rapidly put into effect when needed. Numerous political and technical difficulties surround this proposal, however.

EXPENDITURES
VS. TAX CUTS

Because of the time-lag problem, interest has recently focused on another method of achieving a government deficit: a deliberate tax cut (while holding expenditures steady). The purpose of such a tax cut is also to create a deficit in the government sector—but a deficit which is brought about not by increased government spending, but by encouraging increased *consumer* spending.

This is the method of stimulating the economy used in the now famous Kennedy tax cut of early 1964, and it is a method likely to be employed again when the need for government stimulus arises. It need hardly be said that cutting taxes is always politically popular and that tax cuts therefore have a somewhat easier time than increased spending programs have in getting through Congress. Yet even tax cuts take time to get through, and some economists have therefore suggested that we should have *flexible tax rates* that could be adjusted upward or downward, within limits, by presidential action to create quickly a budgetary deficit or surplus.

Despite their speedy impact, tax cuts still present some problems. One

---

* About 5 percent of the U.S. debt is held by foreigners.

problem is that some of the tax cut will undoubtedly result in higher consumer saving, so that the net effect on demand of a tax cut of $1 billion will be less than the net effect of increased expenditures of $1 billion. The other difficulty is that tax cuts are not likely to stimulate demand among those portions of the population who are most in need of help during a recession, because their incomes are so low that they pay no income taxes. On the contrary, the increased flow of private purchasing activity may well bypass the most afflicted portion of the community.

There is no reason, however, why both tax cuts and increased expenditures cannot be used jointly, the one for speedy effect and the other for purposeful social action. We should recognize, nevertheless, that increasing demand by public action is not a simple matter, but one that poses very substantial problems of its own.

PERPETUAL PUBLIC DEBTS

These important caveats nothwithstanding, can a national government have a perpetual debt even in a dynamic and changeful economy? We have seen that it can. To be sure, the debt must be constantly refunded, much as business refunds its debts, with new issues of bonds replacing the old. But like the business sector, we can expect the government debt in this way to be maintained indefinitely.

Will our public debt grow forever? That depends largely on what happens to our business debts and equities. If business debts and equities grow fast enough—that is, if we are creating enough assets through investment—there is no reason why government debts should grow. Government deficits, after all, are designed as *supplements* to private deficits. The rationale behind public borrowing is that it will be used only when the private sector is not providing enough expenditure to give us the GNP we need.

Nonetheless, the prospect of a rising national debt bothers many people. Some day, they say, it will have to be repaid. Is this true? It may aid us to think about the problem if we try to answer the following questions:

1. *Will public assets continue to increase?*

If so, we can understand why debts grow with them, just as is the case with private debts and private assets. Conversely, if we imagine that at some future date we will have enough public assets, then public debts should cease rising, just as one day when we have enough private capital, private debts and equities will cease growing. The reason will be simple enough: we will no longer need any more net saving or net investment. All our output will go for consumption and replacement.

2. *Can we afford to pay interest on a rising debt?*

The capacity to expand debts, both public and private, depends largely on the willingness of people to lend money, and this willingness in turn reflects their confidence that they will be paid interest regularly and will have their money returned to them when their bond is due.

We have seen how refunding can take care of the repayment problem. But what about interest? With a private firm, this requires that interest costs be kept to a modest fraction of sales, so that they can easily be covered. With government, similar financial prudence requires that interest costs stay well within the taxable capacity of government. The figures in Table 16-3 give us some perspective on this problem today.

	Net interest $ billions	Interest as proportionate cost
All corporations (1967)	$35.4	2.6 percent of receipts
Federal government (1970)	14.0	{ 7.2 percent of receipts { 1.4 percent of GNP

TABLE 16•3

DEBT AND INTEREST COSTS

It can be seen that interest is a much higher percentage of federal revenues than of corporate revenues. But there is a reason for this. Corporations are supposed to maximize their sales; the government is not supposed to maximize its tax income. Hence we must also judge the size of the federal interest cost in comparison with the size of GNP, the total tax base from which the government can draw. Finally, we should know that interest as a percentage of all federal expenditures has remained very steady in recent years, and it is actually much lower than in the 1920s, when interest costs amounted to about 20 to 30 percent of all federal outlays.

3. *Can we afford the burden of a rising debt?*

What is the "burden" of a debt? For a firm, the question is easy to answer. It is the *interest cost* that must be borne by those who owe the debt. Here, of course, we are back to the externality of debts. *The burden of a debt is the obligation it imposes to pay funds from one firm or community to another.*

But we have seen that there is no such cost for an internal debt, such as that of a nation. The *cost* of the debt—that is, the taxes that must be levied to pay interest—becomes *income* to the very same community, as checks sent to bondholders for their interest income. Every penny that the debt costs our economy in taxes returns to our economy as income.

The same is also true of the principal of the debt. The debts we owe inside the nation we also *own* inside the nation—just as the I.O.U. a husband owes his wife is also an I.O.U. owned by the family; or, again, just as an amount borrowed by Branch A of a multibranch firm is owed to Branch B of the same firm.

There is a further point here. Internal debts are debts that are considered as financial *assets* within the "family." Nobody within A.T.&T. considers its debts to be part of the assets of the firm, but many thousands of people in the U.S. consider the country's debts to be their assets. Indeed, everyone who owns a government bond considers it an asset. Thus in contrast to external debts, paying back an internal debt does not "lift a burden" from a community, because no burden existed in the first place! When a corporation pays off a debt to a bank, it is rid of an obligation to an outside claimant on its property. But when a husband pays back a wife, the *family* is no richer, any more than the *firm* is better off if one branch reimburses another. So, too, with a nation. If a national debt is repaid, the national economy is not rid of an obligation to an outside claimant. We would be rid only of obligations owed to one another.

REAL BURDENS

This is not to say—and the point is important—that government spending is costless. Consider for a moment the main cause of government spending over the past fifty years: the prosecution of three wars. There was surely a terrific cost to these wars in lives, health, and (in economic terms) in the use of factors of production to produce guns instead of butter. But note also that all of this cost is irrevocably and unbudgeably situated in the past. The cost of all wars is borne during the years when the wars are fought and must be measured in the destruction that was then caused and the opportunities for making civilian goods that were then missed. The debt inherited from these wars is no longer a "cost." Today it is only an instrument for the transfer of incomes within the American community.

So, too, with debts incurred to fight unemployment. The cost of unemployment is also borne once and for all at the time it occurs, and the benefits of the government spending to combat unemployment will be enjoyed (or if the spending is ill-advised, the wastes of spending will be suffered) when that spending takes place. Afterward, the debt persists as a continuing means of transferring incomes, but the debt no longer has any connection to the "cost" for which it was made.

Costs, in other words, are *missed opportunities,* potential well-being not achieved. Debts, on the other hand (when they are held within a country) only transfer purchasing power and do not involve the nation in giving up its output to anyone else.

INDIRECT EFFECTS

Does this mean that there are no disadvantages whatsoever in a large national debt?

We have talked of one possible disadvantage, that of transferring incomes from spenders to savers, or possibly of transferring purchasing power from productive groups to unproductive groups. But we must pay heed to one other problem. This is the problem a rising debt may cause indirectly, but nonetheless painfully, *if it discourages private investment.*

If government spending serves to turn business expectations downward, then for each dollar of government spending, we may find that we must allow for a dollar *less* of private investment spending. Were such to be the case, the real burden of government deficits would be the new productive resources that might have been laid down in the country but were not.

This could be a very serious, real cost of government debts, were such a reaction to be widespread and long-lasting. It may well be (we are not sure) that the long drawn-out and never entirely successful recovery from the Great Depression was caused, to a considerable extent, by the adverse psychological impact of government deficit spending on business investment intentions. Business did not understand deficit spending and interpreted it either as the entering wedge of socialism (instead of a crash program to save capitalism), or as a wastrel and a hare-brained economic scheme. To make matters worse, the amount of the government deficit (at its peak $4 billion), while large enough to frighten the business community, was not big enough to begin to exert an effective leverage on total demand, particularly under conditions of widespread unemployment and financial catastrophe.

Today, however, it is much less likely that deficit spending would be attended by a drop in private spending. A great deal that was new and frightening in thought and practice in the 1930s is today well-understood and tested. The war itself was, after all, an immense laboratory demonstration of what public spending could do for GNP. The experience of 1954, 1958, and above all, of 1964 gives good reason to believe that deficit spending in the future will not cause a significant slowdown in private investment expenditure.

In view of the fact that our national debt today figures out to approximately $1500 for every man, woman, and child, it is not surprising that we frequently hear appeals to "common sense," telling us how much better we would be without this debt, and how our grandchildren will groan under its weight.

Is this true? We have already discussed the fact that internal debts are different from external debts, but let us press the point home from a different vantage point. Suppose we decided that we would "pay off" the debt. This would mean that our government bonds would be redeemed for cash. To get the cash, we would have to tax ourselves (unless we wanted to roll the printing presses), so that what we would really be doing would be transferring money from taxpayers to bondholders.

Would that be a net gain for the nation? Consider the typical holder of a government bond—a family, a bank, or a corporation. It now holds the world's safest and most readily sold paper asset from which a regular income is obtained. After our debt is redeemed, our families, banks, and corporations will have two choices: (1) they can hold cash and get *no* income, or (2) they can invest in other securities that are slightly *less* safe. Are these investors better off? As for our grandchildren, it is true that if we pay off the debt they will not have to "carry" its weight. But to offset that, neither will they be carried by the comfortable government bonds they would otherwise have inherited. They will also be relieved from paying taxes to meet the interest on the debt. Alas, they will be relieved as well of the pleasure of depositing the green Treasury checks for interest payments that used to arrive twice a year.

THE PUBLIC SECTOR AGAIN IN PERSPECTIVE

We have spent enough time on the question of the debt. Now we must ask what is it that close examination of the problems of government finance reveals, making them look so different from what we expect. The answer is largely that we think of the government as if it were a firm or a household, when it is actually something else. *The government is a sector;* and if we want to think clearly about it, we must compare it, not to the maxims and activities of a household or a firm, but to those of the entire consumer sector or the entire business sector.

Then we can see that the government sector plays a role not too dissimilar from that of the business sector. We have seen how businesses, through their individual decisions to add to plant and equipment, act in concert to offset the savings of consumers. The government, we now see, acts in precisely the same way, except that its decisions, rather than reflecting the behavior of innumerable entrepreneurs in a search for profit, reflect the deliberate political will of the community itself.

Persons who do not understand the intersectoral relationships of the economy like to say that business must "live within its income" and that government acts irresponsibly in failing to do so. These critics fail to see that business does *not* live within its income, but borrows the savings of other sectors, and thus typically and normally spends more than it takes in from its sales alone. By doing so, of course, it serves the invaluable function of providing an offset for saving that would otherwise create a demand gap and thereby precipitate a downward movement in economic activity.

Once this offsetting function is understood, it is not difficult to see that government, as well as business, can serve as a "spender" to offset savings, and that in the course of doing so, both government and business typically create new assets for the community.

PUBLIC AND PRIVATE ASSETS

Finally, we have seen something else that gives us a last insight into government spending. We have seen that the creation of earning assets is indispensable for business, because each asset constitutes the means by which an individual business seeks to recoup its own investment spending. But with the government, the definition of an "earning asset" can properly be much larger than with a business firm. The government does not need its assets to make money for itself directly, for the government's economic capability arises from its capacity to tax *all* incomes. So far as government is concerned, then, all that matters is that savings be turned into expenditures, and thereby into taxable incomes.

As a result, government can and should be motivated—even in a self-interested way—by a much wider view of the economic process than would be possible or proper for a single firm. Whereas a firm's assets are largely its capital goods, the assets of a nation are not only capital wealth but the whole productive capacity of its people. Thus government expenditures that redound to the health or well-being or education of its citizens are just as properly considered asset-building expenditures as are its expenditures on dams and roads.

Armament Spending

The question of the purposes for which the government spends its money finally brings us to a consideration of the military subeconomy, which we first examined in Chapter 1. How important is this subeconomy to our economic vitality? How difficult would it be to reduce? Can our economy get along without a military subsector?

The first of these questions we have already looked into, so we can review the facts briefly. At the height of the Vietnam War in 1968, more than 10 percent of our labor force was employed in defense-related work. As the Vietnam War gradually decelerated, this percentage fell to about 7.4 percent by the end of 1971. Defense expenditures, meanwhile, dropped from their peak of nearly $80 billion to a level of about $75 billion.

These global figures do not, however, give a clear picture of the strategic position of defense spending within the economy. For the problem is that war-related spending and employment are not distributed evenly across the system but are bunched in special areas and industries. In a survey made in 1967, the Defense Department found that 72 employment areas depended on war output for 12 percent or more of their employment, and that four-fifths of these areas were communities with labor forces of less than 50,000.[1] The impact of a cutback on these middle-sized communities can be devastating.

In addition, defense-employment is concentrated among special skills, as well as in a nucleus of defense-oriented companies. About one scientist or engineer out of every five in private industry is employed on a defense-related job. Thirty-eight percent of all physicists depend on war-work. Twenty-five percent of all sheet-metal workers, the same proportion of pattern-makers, and 54 percent of all airplane mechanics work on defense projects. And as we have already remarked, there is a core of companies dependent on military spending for their very existence. These are not

[1] Yarmolinsky, *The Military Establishment* (New York: Harper, 1971), p. 254.

usually the largest companies in the economy (for whom, on the average, defense receipts amount to about 10 percent of total revenues) but the second echelon of corporations: of 30 companies with assets in the $250 million to $1 billion range, 6 depended on war spending for half their incomes, and 7 depended on it for a quarter of theirs.[2]

Thus a cutback in defense spending will be felt very sharply in particular areas, where there may be no other jobs available, or among occupational groups who have no alternative employment at equivalent pay or in companies that are "captives" of the DOD. Such companies and areas naturally lobby hard for defense expenditure on which their livelihood depends. So do their representatives in Congress. It is this interweaving of economic and political interests that makes the problem of defense cutbacks so difficult.

CONVERSION POSSIBILITIES

Yet a cutback is not impossible. What is needed is a program of retraining, relocation, income support, and conversion aid that will cushion the inevitable shock of a decline in military spending. The National Urban Coalition has recently estimated that we would need to spend about $4 billion over two years to move and retrain the bulk of the personnel who would be displaced if we cut our military budget by one third (in real terms) by 1976.[3]

The sum is not large compared with the saving in national resources that would thereby be affected. *What is crucial, economically, is that the decline in war-related spending be offset by increases in peace-related spending, to be sure that the overall level of demand would remain high enough to act as a magnet, attracting the displaced workers to other jobs.* The coalition therefore proposes a broadscale attack on many social problems that would raise total (local, state, and federal) government expenditures on goods and services by over 50 percent to assure that the conversion would in fact be a smooth one.

Could such a vast conversion actually be carried out? That is a problem we will return to again in our final chapter. But at this juncture it is important to point out that there is no insuperable *economic* problem posed by conversion, whatever the political or psychological problems. After World War II, defense spending fell from 37.5 percent of GNP (compared with only 7.4 percent today) to 6.6 percent in the short space of two years. During this period 10 million men and women were demobilized from the armed forces and added to the labor force. Yet unemployment from 1947 to 1949 rose only from 3.6 percent of the labor force to 5.5 percent. Clearly the problem today is much less formidable than it was then.

---

[2] Yarmolinsky, *The Military Establishment,* p. 250.

[3] Robert S. Benson and Harold Wolman, eds., *Counterbudget: A Blueprint for Changing National Priorities, 1971-1976* (New York: Praeger, 1971), p. 274.

The difference between the two periods is that post-World War II conversion was largely the result of a huge pent-up civilian demand. Today there is no evidence of unfilled consumer needs. The Vietnam War has not imposed shortages on the American people. Thus, unless we were willing to undertake an ambitious program of public spending, along the lines proposed by the coalition, the conversion will almost certainly generate severe unemployment—and consequent political pressures to maintain military spending.

Meanwhile, it is clear that the armaments economy is not only costing us a vast sum of money, but is also weighing heavily on the Russians. The annual military expenditure of the U.S. and the U.S.S.R. together amounts to about two-thirds of the entire output of the billion peoples of Latin America, Southeast Asia, and the Near East. If we add in the arms expenditures of the rest of the world, we reach the staggering total of $200 billion of annual military spending, or more than $50 for every inhabitant of the globe. Not only is this an opportunity cost of tragically large dimensions, if we consider the uses to which those resources might otherwise be applied, but even in terms of a strictly military calculus, much of it is *total waste, since neither side has been able to gain a decisive advantage despite its enormous expenditures.*

How does such a senseless course commend itself to national governments? Needless to say, the answers lie deep in the web of political, economic, and social forces of our times. But analytical reasoning can nonetheless throw some light on the matter by unraveling a peculiar situation involving two prisoners, each of whom knows something about the other and who are being interrogated separately. If *both* prisoners remain silent, both will get very light terms, since the evidence against each is not conclusive. If one prisoner squeals on the other, he will get off scot-free as a reward for turning state's evidence, while the other prisoner gets a heavy term. But if *both* prisoners squeal, both will get severe terms, convicted by each other's testimony.

Now, if the two prisoners could confer—and more important, if they trusted each other absolutely—they would obviously agree that the strategy of shared silence was the best for each. But if the prisoners are separated or unsure of each other's trustworthiness, each will be powerfully tempted to rat on the other in order to reduce his own sentence. As a result, since the two are equally tempted, the outcome is likely to end in *both* sides ratting—and in both sides getting heavy punishment. Thus the pursuit of individual "self-interest" lures the two prisoners into a strategy that penalizes them both.

Something very like a Prisoners' Dilemma afflicts the nations of the world, especially the two superpowers, America and Russia. Although a policy of limited arms spending would clearly be to their mutual best advantage, their distrust of each other leads each to try to get ahead of the other. This state of mutual suspicion is then worsened when special interest groups in each nation deliberately play on the fears of the public. The end result is that both spend vast sums on armaments that yield them no advantage, while the world (including them) suffers an opportunity cost on an enormous scale. Only with a frank and candid exploration of shared gains and losses can both prisoners hope to get out of their dilemma. Prospects for a massive conversion of the U.S. arms economy may hinge on our understanding of this central military and political reality of our time.

KEY CONCEPTS AND KEY WORDS

Government purchases vs. government expenditures

1. The *public sector* derives its income from three main sources: indirect taxes (mainly for state and local governments), personal income and other taxes, and corporate taxes. Expenditures for *goods and services* are roughly equally divided between federal government and state and local government, but the federal government is the larger source of *transfer expenditures.*

2. Comparing 1970 with the 1920s, we find that the public sector has grown considerably as a proportion of GNP. Federal purchases have grown largely for defense purposes. Total expenditures have grown because of much larger defense spending and moderately larger spending for welfare, including such items as education, social security, and welfare assistance.

3. The critical differentiating factor between the public and the private sectors is that the public sector can be deliberately employed as an instrument of *national economic policy.*

Fiscal policy

4. The use of government spending and taxing to achieve national growth or stability is called *fiscal policy.* There are two main instruments of fiscal policy: *expenditures* can be increased or decreased, and *taxes* can be raised or cut. The former acts much as an increase or decrease in private investment; the latter is mainly used to induce or to discourage consumer spending.

Automatic stabilizers

5. *Automatic stabilizers* help implement fiscal policy by lessening the momentum of booms and cushioning the impact of recessions. The stabilizers arise from the progressive incidence of income taxation, from expenditure programs geared to unemployment, and so on.

Deficits

6. The use of the government budget as a deliberate antirecession instrument leads to *deficits.* These deficits are financed by *government borrowing* and hence lead to government debt.

Government borrowing

7. The government debt can be thought of in the same way as much private debt: as the *financial counterpart of assets.*

Government debt

8. *All debts, as long as their underlying assets are economically productive, can be maintained indefinitely* by being refunded when they come due.

Assets and debts

9. In a *progressive and growing economy, debts increase* as assets rise. Debts are only a way of financing the growth in assets.

10. National governments have the power of fiscal recapture of any money spent by them—a power not available to state governments or even to the largest businesses. Hence national governments are in a fundamentally different position regarding the safety of their domestically-held debts. This difference is expressed in the concept of *internal debts* versus *external ones*.

Internal vs. external debts

11. Domestically-held national debts do not lead to bankruptcy. They do present important and difficult problems of *monetary management,* and they can also result in the *redistribution of income.* These are *real burdens* of the debt.

12. *Repaying the debt would not lift a burden from the economy.* Taxes would decrease (because the debt need no longer be serviced), but income would also decrease (because interest would no longer be paid). Former government bondholders would have to find another acceptable financial asset.

Debt burden

13. The confusion with which the public debt is often viewed arises from a failure to understand that *the government is not a "household" but a sector,* fully comparable to the business sector in its intersectoral operations.

14. Deficits can be incurred by *tax cuts* or by *increased expenditures.* Both present problems. *Tax cuts may not put income where it is needed.* Also, tax cuts will probably not be wholly spent, but will result in some additional saving. On the other hand, *increased expenditures may take much too long* to combat a turndown efficiently.

Tax cuts vs. expenditures

15. The true problem with regard to the public sector lies in the *uses to which its activities are put,* and *the skill with which its policies are managed.* These can be very important problems, but they do not involve the propriety of fiscal policy, as such.

16. The armaments economy could be reduced if (a) a large program of peacetime expenditures were undertaken, and (b) the Prisoners' Dilemma, in which the U.S. and the U.S.S.R. find themselves, can be resolved.

Prisoners' Dilemma

Q U E S T I O N S

1. What are the main differences between the public and the private sectors? Are these differences economic or political?

2. Show in a diagram how increased government expenditure can offset a demand gap. Show also how decreased government taxation can do the same.

3. Show diagrammatically how equilibrium is the result of the interplay of two sets of forces: on the one hand, investment and public spending; on the other hand, saving and taxation.

4. What is meant by the automatic stabilizers? Give an example of how they might work if we had an increase in investment of $20 billion and the multiplier were 2; and if the increase in taxes and the decrease in public expenditure associated with the boom in investment were $3 billion and $1 billion, respectively.

5. In what ways is a government deficit comparable to business spending for investment purposes? In what way is it not?

6. What is meant by the internality of debts? Is the debt of New York State internal? The debt of a country like Israel or Egypt?

7. What relation do debts generally have to assets? Can business debts increase indefinitely? Can a family's? Can the debt of all consumers?

8. What do you consider a better way of combating a mild recession—tax cuts or higher expenditures? Why? Suppose we had a deep recession, then what would you do?

9. In what sorts of economic conditions should the government run a surplus?

10. Suppose the government cuts taxes by $10 billion and also cuts its expenditures by the same amount. Will this stimulate the economy? Suppose it raises its expenditures and also raises taxes? Would this be a good antirecession policy?

11. What are the real burdens of a national debt?

12. Trace out carefully the consequences of paying back all the national debt.

13. How would you explain to someone who is adamantly opposed to all deficit financing that it is perfectly sound policy in certain circumstances?

14. What do you think are the principal obstacles to a substantial reduction in arms expenditure?

LEARNING ABOUT STATISTICS

SAMPLING

In our last two sections, we learned what it means to correlate data. But few things are more disconcerting to someone who begins to work with such data than to be told that most of the "facts" which he correlates or uses are based on *samples*—that is, on figures derived from observing or counting not the entire set of objects in which he is interested, but only a fraction of that population, and often a very small fraction at that. How can the statistician presume to be telling us the exact story, the student asks, when he really knows only a part of it?

The question is a very important one. We should understand the answer, for it is true that most economic data *are* derived from samples. And yet it is also true that sampling can provide extraordinarily accurate information about "populations" that are not counted—or even *countable!* For example, during World War II, American and British statisticians estimated the totals for German war production by applying sampling methods to the serial numbers on captured equipment. After the war, many of their figures turned out to be just as accurate as the figures that the Germans compiled from the actual records of production itself. Moreover, the Allied figures were available sooner, since their method of counting took much less time.

The logic of sampling

What is the logic of sampling? It is based on a kind of reasoning that we use all the time. For example, we may complain that the streets in a city are dirty. Yet it is very unlikely that our complaint is based on an inspection of *all* the streets in the city or even a majority of them. Does this render our conclusion untrustworthy? It all depends. If we have seen a "fair" number of streets in all parts of the city, and all those we saw were dirty, we are quite justified in concluding that those we haven't seen would look much the same. But what is a "fair" number? What are the other criteria for selecting a sample that will enable us to generalize with a high degree of reliability about data that we have not observed?

Sample size

The first and most obvious requirement for a "fair sample" is its size. Yet, surprisingly, in making accurate statements based on samples, size turns out to be much less of a stumbling block than we might think. The U.S. Census Bureau, for example, on the basis of a sample of only about 5 percent of all families, gives a detailed and reliable description of the United States population. And if we want to study less complicated collections of data than those for the U.S. population, a sample much smaller than 5 percent will yield surprisingly good results. The

Gallup and other polls forecast election results—the whole quite accurately—on the basis of a sample of less than 1 percent of all voters.

How big a sample do we need to arrive at accurate estimates? That depends on two things: (1) how much we know about the larger "universe" of data that we are sampling, and (2) how accurate we want to be.

Suppose, for example, that we had two barrels of marbles, one filled with marbles of only two colors, white and black, and the other filled with an unknown number of colors. Obviously, the proportion of black to white marbles can be found from a much smaller sample than we would need from the second barrel, where a whole spectrum of colors and their various proportions are involved. Hence, the simpler the problem and the more clear-cut the data, the smaller the sample can be: it takes many fewer cases to establish the proportion of male to female births than to establish the pattern of average weight-to-height relation of infants at birth.

But suppose we have a "universe" that is well understood, such as our first barrel. How many marbles will we have to draw until we can make some kind of reliable statement about the *actual* proportion of black to white in the whole barrel? Here the answer depends on how accurate we want to be. Statisticians speak of "confidence intervals" to describe the fact that we can establish our own limits of reliability by increasing the size of a sample. Suppose, for example, that we know there are 100 thousand marbles in the barrel. A statistician can then tell us that on the basis of, say, 500 selections (a $\frac{1}{2}$ percent sample) we would have a 95 percent chance of being within ±5 percent of the actual proportion of white to black; that with 1,000 draws we would have a 95 percent chance of being within ±3 percent (approximately) of the actual answer, and so on.

The "correct" sample size is thus up to us, depending on our need for accuracy. If we want to be 100 percent accurate, after all, we will have to check each and every marble, thereby raising the sample to the size of the population itself.

Bias

Surprisingly, then, the problem of sample size is not so much of a difficulty as we might have thought, assuming that we know something about the characteristics of the population we are investigating. But suppose we do not. Suppose that we have traveled exclusively in the downtown streets of a city, not knowing there was a great slum just a few blocks away, and that we based our judgments of the city as a whole on the cleanliness of the business district alone? Here we have encountered a much more serious problem. *Bias* has entered our calculations. By *bias* we mean that we have not planned our sampling technique in such a way that *each and every item in the population has an equal chance of being observed.*

Bias can enter sampling in the most unexpected ways. Suppose, for example, that the white marbles in our barrel were (unknown to us) slightly heavier than the black ones, so that when we shook up the barrel to be certain the marbles were fairly mixed, we were actually causing the white marbles to move toward the bottom. If our sample were taken from the top of the barrel, it would be biased in favor of black marbles. Or suppose that we chose our city streets absolutely by chance, but that we failed to take into account that the Sanitation Department visited different parts of the city on different days. Our sample could easily be biased in one direction or another.

Perhaps the most famous example of bias was the *Literary Digest* poll of the Roosevelt-Landon election in 1936. The magazine (long since defunct) sampled

2.3 million people, most of whom said they were going to vote for Alfred Landon. On this basis, the *Digest* predicted a landslide for the Republican candidate. In fact, as we all know, the election *was* a landslide—but for the other side.

What went wrong? Obviously, the problem was that the sample, although very large, was terribly biased. It was taken from subscription lists of magazines, telephone directories, and automobile registration lists. In 1936, people who subscribed to magazines, had phones, and owned autos were highly concentrated in the upper brackets of income distribution. Furthermore, in that year income had a great deal to do with party choice. The result has been used in statistics texts ever since as the perfect example of bias.

Correcting for biases

How do we avoid biases? The answer is to strive to choose our sample as randomly as possible—that is, in such a way that every unit in the population has an equal chance of being in our sample. A purely random sample has the best chance to duplicate, in miniature, all the characteristics of the larger "universe" it represents. Clearly, the more complex that universe, the larger the random sample will have to be to give us figures that fall within respectable confidence intervals. That is why the U.S. Bureau of the Census uses a sample *as large as* 5 percent to collect information about age, sex, race, income, place of residence and many more attributes of the population as a whole.

Getting a sample that is free of bias is by no means an easy task, and statisticians spend a good deal of time devising ways to avoid the errors of bias, and in detecting unsuspected errors in the work of others. Doesn't this mean, then, that sampling is a technique we should view with considerable suspicion? In fact, doesn't it more or less cast serious doubt on a good deal of what we think are "the facts"?

As we have said before in these supplements, a healthy skepticism with regard to data is often very useful. But skepticism is not at all the same thing as a rejection of sampling as a statistical *technique*. Sampling is ultimately based on the laws of probability about which we know a good deal. Hence, far from avoiding sampling, we should use our knowledge to perfect it.

Here are three reasons why sampling is both essential and reliable:

1. *Samples may be the only way of obtaining information.*

Suppose that you are in charge of planning the development program for a nation like India and that you need to know a great many facts about the birth rate, the average size of landholdings, or average incomes. *There may be no possible way of obtaining this information except by sampling.* Or suppose you are a historian interested in reconstructing the average length of life or the average family size of some period far in the past. There may be no possible method of gaining this information except by sampling (for example, using the data on gravestones), thereafter making the best adjustment you can for the inevitable biases that have crept into your sample (the poorest people didn't get gravestones). Or suppose your doctor wants to test your blood. Would you want him to test *all* of it?

2. *Samples may be cheaper than counting.*

Even when you can count all the items in a collection, it may not be worth your while to do so. It would take an enormous expenditure of time and effort to interview each and every householder in the U.S. about every set of facts in the decennial census. It would cost a fortune to test each and every light bulb that General Electric makes. Sampling gives us accurate enough data at a vast saving in cost and time.

3. *Sampling may be more accurate than counting.*

Believe it or not, sampling is often better than taking a full count. For example, a census survey of every household would require the services of an army of census takers, most of whom could not be trained in all the pitfalls of interviewing. It is quite likely that the inaccuracies of their mass survey would be greater than those in the much smaller number of reports prepared by expert census takers who are careful to follow instructions to the letter.

Sampling, in short, has its inescapable problems. But it is an absolutely indispensable and astonishingly reliable technique with which to deal with the overwhelming mass of data in the real world.

We have almost completed our study of the determinants of gross national product, and soon we can combine the separate sectoral analyses into an over-all view of the economy. But first there is a matter that we must integrate into our discussion. This is the role that money plays in fixing or changing the level of GNP, along with the other forces that we have come to know.

Actually, we have been talking about money throughout our exposition. After all, one cannot discuss "expenditure" without assuming the existence of money. But now we must look behind this unexamined assumption and find out exactly what we mean when we speak of money. This will entail two tasks. In this chapter we shall investigate the perplexing question of what money *is*—for as we shall see, money is surely one of the most sophisticated and curious inventions of human society. Then in our next chapter, once we have come to understand what currency and gold and bank deposits are and how they come into being, we will look into the effect that money has on our economic operations.

The Supply of Money

Let us begin, then, by asking—"What is money?" The question is by no means as simple to answer as it would appear. Coin and currency are certainly money. But are checks money? Are the deposits from which we draw checks money? Are savings accounts money? Stamps? Government bonds?

The answer is a somewhat arbitrary one. From the spectrum of possible candidates, we reserve the term *money* for those items used to make *payments.* This means that we include cash in the public's possession and checking accounts, because we pay for most things by cash or check. Surprisingly, it means that we do not count savings accounts, since we have to draw "money" *out* of our savings accounts, in the form of cash or a check, if we want to use our savings account to make an expenditure. So, too, we have to sell government bonds to get money. Stamps can sometimes be used to make small payments, but they are too insignificant to matter.

Money, then, is mainly currency and checking accounts. In 1970, for example, our total money supply was $215 billion, of which $49 billion was currency in the hands of the public, and $166 billion was the total of checking accounts (or demand deposits, as they are also called).

Of the two kinds of "money," currency is the form most familiar to us. Yet there is a considerable mystery even about currency. Who determines how much currency there is? How is the supply of coins or bills regulated?

We often assume that the supply of currency is "set" by the government that "issues" it. Yet when we think about it, we realize that the government does not just hand out money, and certainly not coin or bills. When the government pays people, it is nearly always by check.

Then who does fix the amount of currency in circulation? You can answer the question by asking how you yourself determine how much currency you will carry. If you think about it, the answer is that you "cash" a check when you need more currency than you have, and you put the currency back into your checking account when you have more than you need.

What you do, everyone does. The amount of cash that the public holds at any time is no more and no less than the amount that it *wants* to hold. When it needs more—at Christmas, for instance—the public draws currency by cashing checks on its own checking accounts; and when Christmas is past, shopkeepers (who have received the public's currency) return it to their checking accounts.

Thus the amount of currency we have bears an obvious, important relation to the size of our bank accounts, for we can't write checks for cash if our accounts will not cover them.

Does this mean, then, that the banks have as much currency in their vaults as the total of our checking accounts? No, it does not. But to understand that, let us follow the course of some currency that we deposit in our bank for credit to our account.

BOOKKEEPING MONEY

When you put money into a commercial bank,* the bank does not hold that money for you as a pile of specially earmarked bills or as a bundle of checks made out to you from some payer. The bank takes notice of your deposit simply by crediting your "account," a bookkeeping page recording your present "balance." After the amount of the currency or check has been credited to you, the currency is put away with the bank's general store of vault cash and the checks are sent to the banks from which they came, where, of course, they will be charged against the accounts of the people who wrote them.

There is probably no misconception in economics harder to dispel than the idea that banks are warehouses stuffed with money. In point of fact, however, you might search as hard as you pleased in your bank, but you would find no other kind of money that was yours but a bookkeeping account in your name. This seems like a very unreal form of money, and yet, the fact that you can present a check at the teller's window and convert your bookkeeping account into cash proves that your account must nonetheless be "real."

But suppose that you and all the other depositors tried to convert your accounts into cash on the same day. You would then find something shocking. There would not be nearly enough cash in the bank's till to cover your total withdrawals. In 1970, for instance, total demand deposits in the United States amounted to about $166 billion. But the total amount of coin and currency held by the banks was only $5.3 billion!

A first blush, this seems like a highly dangerous state of affairs. But second thoughts are more reassuring. After all, most of us put money into a bank because we do *not* need it immediately, or because making payments in cash is a nuisance compared with making them by check. Yet, there is always the chance—more than that, the certainty—that some depositors *will* want their money in currency. How much currency will the banks need then? What will be a proper "reserve" for them to hold?

FEDERAL RESERVE SYSTEM

For many years, the banks themselves decided what reserve ratio constituted a safe proportion of currency to hold against their demand deposits (the technical name for checking accounts). Today, however, most large banks are members of the Federal Reserve, a central banking system established in 1913 to strengthen the banking activities of the nation. Under the

---

* A commercial bank is a bank that is empowered by law to offer checking services. It may also have savings accounts. A savings bank has only savings accounts and may not offer checking services.

Federal Reserve System, the nation is divided into twelve districts, in each of which there is a Federal Reserve Bank owned (but not really controlled) by the member banks of its district. In turn, the twelve Reserve Banks are themselves coordinated by a seven-man Federal Reserve Board in Washington. Since the members of the board are appointed for fourteen-year terms, they constitute a body that has been purposely established as an independent, nonpolitical monetary authority.*

One of the most important functions of the Federal Reserve Board is to establish reserve ratios for different categories of banks, within limits set by Congress. Historically these reserve ratios have ranged between 13 and 26 percent of demand deposits for city banks, with a somewhat smaller reserve ratio for country banks. Today, for larger banks the reserve city ratio is 17.5 percent; the country ratio 13 percent. The Federal Reserve Board also sets reserve requirements for "time" (similar to savings) deposits. These are 6 percent. Do not forget, however, that time deposits do not count—or directly serve—as "money."

Yet here is something odd! We noticed that in 1970 the total amount of deposits was $166 billion and that banks' holdings of coin and currency were only $5.3 billion. This is much less than the 17.5 percent—or even 13 percent—reserve against deposits established by the Federal Reserve Board. How can this be?

The answer is that cash is not the only reserve a bank holds against deposits. It also holds as its reserve *claims on other banks.*

What are these claims? Suppose you deposit a check from someone who has an account in Bank B in your account in Bank A. Bank A credits your account and then presents the check to Bank B for "payment." By "payment" Bank A does not mean coin and currency, however. Instead, Bank A and Bank B settle their transaction at still *another* bank where both Bank A and Bank B have their own accounts. These are the twelve Federal Reserve Banks of the country, where all banks who are members of the Federal Reserve System (and this accounts for banks holding most of the deposits in our banking system) *must* open accounts. Thus at the Federal Reserve Bank, Bank A's account will be credited and Bank B's account will be debited, in this way moving reserves from one bank to the other.†

In other words, *the Federal Reserve Banks serve their member banks in exactly the same way as the member banks serve the public.* Member banks

---

* This has resulted, on occasion, in sharp clashes of viewpoint with the Treasury Department or the Bureau of the Budget where fiscal and economic policy is formulated by each administration. There is some disagreement over whether the nation is better served by a Federal Reserve that can impede an economic policy it disagrees with or one that is bound to assist the economic aims of each incumbent administration. Generally speaking, however, there has been a harmony of views between the monetary and the fiscal authorities.

† When money is put into a bank account, the account is credited; when money is taken out, the account is debited.

automatically deposit in their Federal Reserve accounts all checks they get from other banks. As a result, banks are constantly "clearing" their checks with one another through the Federal Reserve System, because their depositors are constantly writing checks on their own banks payable to someone who banks elsewhere. Meanwhile, *the balance that each bank maintains at the Federal Reserve—that is, the claim it has on other banks—counts, equally as much as any currency, as part of its reserve against deposits.*

In 1970, therefore, when demand deposits were $166 billion and cash in the banks only $5.3 billion, we would expect the member banks to have had heavy accounts with the Federal Reserve banks. And so they did—$29 billion in all. Thus, total reserves of the banks were $34.3 billion ($5.3 billion in cash plus $29 billion in Federal Reserve accounts), enough for legal backing of all deposits.

FRACTIONAL RESERVES

Thus we see that our banks operate on what is called *a fractional reserve system.* The size of the minimum fraction is determined by the Federal Reserve, for reasons of control that we shall shortly learn about. It is *not* determined, as we might be tempted to think, to provide a "safe" backing for our bank deposits. For under *any* fractional system if *all* depositors decided to draw out their accounts in currency and coin from all banks at the same time, the banks would be unable to meet the demand for cash and would have to close. We call this a "run" on the banking system. Needless to say, runs can be terrifying and destructive economic phenomena.*

Why, then, do we court the risk of runs, however small this risk may be? What is the benefit of a fractional banking system? To answer that, let us look into our bank again.

LOANS AND INVESTMENTS

Suppose its customers have given our bank $1 million in deposits and that the Federal Reserve Board requirements are 20 percent, a simpler figure to work with than the actual one. Then we know that our bank must at all times keep $200,000, either in currency in its own till or in its demand deposit at the Federal Reserve Bank.

But having taken care of that requirement, what does the bank do with the remaining deposits? If it simply lets them sit, either as vault cash or as a deposit at the Federal Reserve, our bank will be very "liquid," but it will have no way of making an income. Unless it charges a great deal for its checking services, it will have to go out of business.

---

* A run on a *single* bank can be met by other banks lending cash. But a run on all banks far exceeds the cash resources of the community. Do not forget, however, that nowadays most accounts are insured up to $20,000 by the Federal Deposit Insurance Corporation, an agency of the federal government. This makes a run highly improbable; and even if a run should occur, it assures most depositors that they will eventually get their money back.

And yet there is an obvious way for the bank to make an income, while performing a valuable service. The bank can use all the cash and check claims it does not need for its reserve to make *loans* to businessmen or families or to make financial *investments* in corporate or government bonds. It will thereby not only earn an income, but it will assist the process of business investment and government borrowing. Thus the mechanics of the banking system lead us back to the concerns at the very center of our previous analysis.

Inside the Banking System

Fractional reserves allow banks to lend, or to invest in securities, part of the funds that have been deposited with them. But that is not the only usefulness of the fractional reserve system. It works as well to help enlarge or diminish the supply of investible or loanable funds, as the occasion demands. Let us follow how this process works. To make the mechanics of banking clear, we are going to look at the actual books of the bank—in simplified form, of course—so that we can see how the process of lending and investing appears to the banker himself.

We begin by introducing two basic elements of business accounting: *assets* and *liabilities.* Every student at some time or another has seen the balance sheet of a firm, and many have wondered how total assets always equal total liabilities. The reason is very simple. Assets are all the things or claims a business owns. Liabilities are claims against those assets—some of them the claims of creditors, some the claims of owners (called the Net Worth of the business). Since assets show everything that a business owns, and since liabilities show how claims against these selfsame things are divided between creditors and owners, it is obvious that the two sides of the balance sheet must always come to exactly the same total.

ASSETS AND LIABILITIES

Businesses show their financial condition on a *balance sheet* on which all items on the left side represent assets and all those on the right side represent liabilities. By using a simple two-column balance sheet (called a "T account" because it looks like a T), we can follow very clearly what happens to our bank as we deposit money in it or as it makes loans or investments.

We start off with the example we have just used, in which we open a brand new bank with $1 million in cash and checks on other banks. Accordingly our first entry in the T account shows the two sides of this transaction. Notice that our bank has gained an asset of $1 million, the cash

T ACCOUNTS

and checks that it now owns, and that it has simultaneously gained $1 million in liabilities, the deposits that it *owes* to its depositors (who can, after all, take their money out any time).

Assets	Liabilities
$1,000,000 (cash and checks)	$1,000,000 (money owed to depositors)
Total $1,000,000	**Total $1,000,000**

As we know, however, our bank will not keep all its newly-gained cash and checks in the till. It may hang on to some of the cash, but it will send all the checks it has received, plus any currency that it feels it does not need, to the Fed for deposit in its account there. As a result, its T account will now look like this:

Assets		Liabilities	
Vault cash	$ 100,000	Deposits	$1,000,000
Deposit at Fed	900,000		
Total	**$1,000,000***	**Total**	**$1,000,000**

* If you will examine some bank balance sheets, you will see these items listed as "Cash and due from banks." This means, of course, cash in their own vaults plus their balance at the Fed.

EXCESS RESERVES

Now we recall from our previous discussion that our bank does not want to remain in this very liquid, but very unprofitable, position. According to the law, it must retain only a certain percentage of its deposits in cash or at the Federal Reserve—20 percent in our hypothetical example. All the rest, it is free to lend or invest. As things now stand, however, it has $1 million in reserves—$800,000 more than it needs. Hence, let us suppose that it decides to put these *excess reserves* to work by lending that amount to a sound business risk. (Note that banks do not lend the excess reserves themselves. These reserves, cash and deposits at the Fed, remain right where they are. Their function is to tell the banks how much they may loan or invest.)

MAKING A LOAN

Assume now that the Smith Corporation, a well-known firm, comes in for a loan of $800,000. Our bank is happy to lend them that amount. But "making a loan" does not mean that the bank now pays the company in cash out of its vaults. Rather, *it makes a loan by opening a new checking account for the firm* and by crediting that account with $800,000. (Or if, as is likely, the Smith firm already has an account with the bank, it will simply credit the proceeds of the loan to that account.)

Assets		Liabilities	
Cash and at Fed	$1,000,000	Original deposits	$1,000,000
Loan (Smith Corp.)	800,000	New deposit (Smith Corp.)	800,000
Total	**$1,800,000**	**Total**	**$1,800,000**

Now our T account shows some interesting changes.

There are several things to note about this transaction. First, our bank's reserves (its cash and deposit at the Fed) have not yet changed. The $1 million in reserves are still there.

Second, notice that the Smith Corporation loan counts as a new asset for the bank because the bank now has a legal claim against the company for that amount. (The interest on the loan is not shown in the balance sheet; but when it is paid, it will show up as an addition to the bank's cash.)

Third, deposits have increased by $800,000. Note, however, that this $800,000 was not paid to the Smith firm out of anyone else's account in the bank. It is a new account, one that did not exist before.

THE LOAN
IS SPENT

Was it safe to open this new account for the company? Well, we might see whether our reserves are now sufficient to cover the Smith Corporation's account as well as the original deposit accounts. A glance reveals that all is well. We still have $1 million in reserves against $1.8 million in deposits. Our reserve ratio is much higher than the 20 percent required by law.

It is so much higher, in fact, that we might be tempted to make another loan to the next customer who requests one, and in that way further increase our earning capacity. But an experienced banker shakes his head. "The Smith Corporation did not take out a loan and agree to pay interest on it just for the pleasure of letting that money sit with you," he explains. "Very shortly, the company will be writing checks on its balance; and when it does, you will need every penny of the reserve you now have."

That, indeed, is the case. Within a few days we find that our bank's account at the Federal Reserve Bank has been charged with a check for $800,000 written by the Smith Corporation in favor of the Jones Corporation, which carries its account at another bank. Now we find that our T account has changed dramatically to look like this:

Assets		Liabilities	
Cash and at Fed	$ 200,000	Original deposits	$1,000,000
Loan (Smith Corp.)	800,000	Smith Corp. deposits	0
Total	**$1,000,000**	**Total**	**$1,000,000**

Let us see exactly what has happened. First, the Smith Corporation's check has been charged against our account at the Fed, and has reduced it from \$900,000 to \$100,000. Together with the \$100,000 cash in our vault, this gives us \$200,000 in reserves.

Second, the Smith Corporation's deposit is entirely gone, although its loan agreement remains with us as an asset.

Now if we refigure our reserves we find that they are just right. We are required to have \$200,000 in vault cash or in our Federal Reserve account against our \$1 million in deposits. That is exactly the amount we have left. Our bank is now fully "loaned up."

EXPANDING
THE MONEY
SUPPLY

But the banking *system* is not yet fully loaned up. So far, we have traced what happened to only our bank when the Smith Corporation spent the money in its deposit account. Now we must trace the effect of this action on the deposits and reserves of other banks.

We begin with the bank in which the Jones Corporation deposits the check it has just received from the Smith Corporation. As the following T account shows, the Jones Corporation's bank now finds itself in exactly the same position as our bank was when we opened it with \$1 million in new deposits, except that the addition to this "second generation" bank is smaller than the addition to the "first generation" bank.

Assets		Liabilities	
Cash and at Fed	\$800,000	Deposit (Jones Corp.)	\$800,000
Total	**\$800,000**	**Total**	**\$800,000**

As we can see, our second generation bank has gained \$800,000 in cash and in deposits. Since it needs only 20 percent of this for required reserves, it finds itself with \$640,000 excess reserves, which it is now free to use to make loans as investments. Suppose that it extends a loan to the Brown Company and that the Brown Company shortly thereafter spends the proceeds of that loan at the Black Company, which banks at yet a third bank. The following two T accounts show how the total deposits will now be affected.

SECOND GENERATION BANK

(after Brown Co. spends the proceeds of its loan)

Assets		Liabilities	
Cash and at Fed	\$160,000	Deposits (Jones Corp.)	\$800,000
Loan (to Brown Co.)	640,000	Deposits (Brown Co.)	0
Total	**\$800,000**	**Total**	**\$800,000**

THIRD GENERATION BANK

(after Black Co. gets the check of Brown Co.)

Assets		Liabilities	
Cash and at Fed	$640,000	Deposit (Black Co.)	$640,000
Total	**$640,000**	**Total**	**$640,000**

And as Fig. 17-1 makes clear, the process will not stop here, but can continue from one bank to the next as long as any lending power remains.

Expansion of the Money Supply

If we now look at the bottom of Fig. 17-1, we will see something very important. Every time any bank in this chain of transactions has opened an account for a new borrower, *the supply of money has increased.* Remember that the supply of money is the sum of currency outside the banking system

FIG. 17 • 1 EXPANSION OF THE MONEY SUPPLY

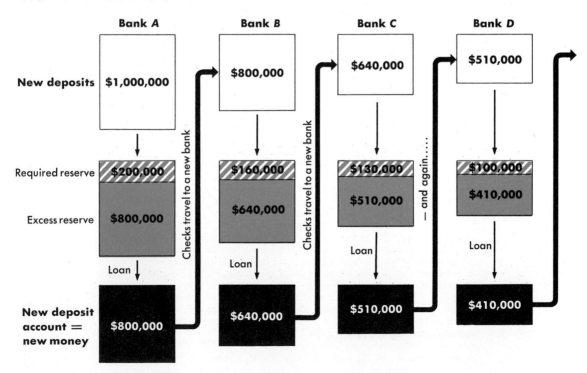

(i.e., in our own pockets) plus the total of demand deposits.* As our chain of banks kept opening new accounts, it was simultaneously expanding the total check-writing capacity of the economy. Thus, money has materialized, seemingly out of thin air.

Now how can this be? If we tell any banker in the chain that he has "created" money, he will protest vehemently. The loans he made, he will insist, were backed at the time he made them by excess reserves as large as the loan itself. Just as we had $800,000 in excess reserves when we made our initial loan to the Smith Corporation, so every subsequent loan was always backed 100 percent by unused reserves when it was made.

Our bankers are perfectly correct when they tell us that they never, never lend a penny more than they have. Money is not created in the lending process because a banker lends money he doesn't have. *It is created because you and I generally pay each other by checks that give us claims against each other's bank.* If we constantly cashed the checks we exchanged, no new money would be created. But we do not. We deposit each other's checks in our own bank accounts; and in doing so, we give our banks more reserves than they need against the deposits we have just made. These new excess reserves make it possible for our banks to lend or invest, and thereby to open still more deposit accounts, which in turn lead to new reserves.†

LIMITS ON THE EXPANSION

This all sounds a little frightening. Does it mean that the money supply can go on expanding indefinitely from a single loan? Wouldn't that be extremely dangerous?

It would of course be very dangerous, but there is no possibility that it can happen. For having understood how the supply of money can expand

---

* We can now see why only currency *outside* the banks is counted as "money." Currency in a bank's vault or till counts as part of its reserves, and reserves are not money, because we cannot write checks against them.

† All this gives us a fresh insight into the question of what money is. We said before that it is whatever we use to make payments. But what do we use? The answer is a surprising one. We use *debts*—specifically, the debts of commercial banks. Deposits are, after all, nothing but the liabilities that banks owe their customers. Furthermore, we can see that one purpose of the banking system is to buy debts from other units in the economy, such as businesses or governments, in exchange for its own debts (which are money). For when a bank opens an account for a business to which it has granted a loan or when it buys a government bond, what else is it doing but accepting a debt that is *not* usable as money, in exchange for its deposit liabilities that *are* usable as money. And why is it that banks create money when they make loans, but you or I do not, when we lend money? Because we all accept bank liabilities (deposits) as money, but we do not accept personal or business I.O.U.'s to make payments with. Someone who would like to probe deeper into the curious (and very important) problem of money and how it affects our economy could do no better than to read the lucid and sparkling analysis by Peter L. Bernstein, *A Primer on Money, Banking and Gold,* 2nd ed. (New York: Random House, 1968, paperback).

from an original increase in deposits, we may now understand equally well what keeps an expansion within bounds.

1. *Not every loan generates an increase in bank deposits.*

If our bank had opened a loan account for the Smith Corporation at the same time that another firm had paid off a similar loan, there would have been no original expansion in bank deposits. In that case, the addition of $800,000 to the Smith account would have been exactly balanced by a decline of $800,000 in someone else's account. Even if that decline would have taken place in a different bank, it would still mean that the nation's total of bank deposits would not have risen, and therefore no new money would have been created. Thus, *only net additions to loans have an expansionary effect.* We will shortly see how such net additions arise in the first place.

2. *There is a limit to the rise in money supply from a single increase in loans.*

As Fig. 17-1 shows, in the chain of deposit expansion each successive bank has a smaller increase in deposits, because each bank has to keep some of its newly gained cash or checks as reserve. Hence the amount of *excess* reserve, against which loans can be made, steadily falls.

Further, we can see that the amount of the total monetary expansion from an original net increase in loans is governed by the size of the fraction that has to be kept aside each time as reserve. *In fact, we can see that just as with the multiplier, the cumulative effect of an increase in deposits will be determined by the reciprocal of the reserve fraction.* If each bank must keep one-fifth of its increased deposits as reserves, then the cumulative effect of an original increase in deposits, when it has expanded through the system, is five times the original increase. If reserves are one-fourth, the expansion is limited to four times the original increase, and so on.

3. *The monetary expansion process can work in reverse.*

Suppose that the banking system as a whole suffers a net loss of deposits. Instead of putting $1 million into a bank, the public takes it out in cash. The bank will now have too few reserves, and it will have to cut down its loans or sell its investments to gain the reserves it needs. In turn, as borrowers pay off their loans, or as bond buyers pay for their securities, cash will drain from other banks who will now find *their* reserves too small in relation to their deposits. In turn, they will therefore have to sell more investments or curtail still other loans, and this again will squeeze still other banks and reduce their reserves, with the same consequences.

Thus, just as an original expansion in deposits can lead to a multiple expansion, so an original contraction in deposits can lead to a multiple contraction. The size of this contraction is also limited by the reciprocal of the reserve fraction. If banks have to hold a 25 percent reserve, then an original fall of $100,000 in deposits will lead to a total fall of $400,000, assuming that the system was fully "loaned up" to begin with. If they had to hold a 20 percent reserve, a fall of $100,000 could pyramid to $500,000.

4. *The expansion process may not be fully carried through.*

We have assumed that each bank in the chain always lends out an amount equal to its excess reserves, but this may not be the case. The third or fifth bank along the way may have trouble finding a credit-worthy customer and may decide—for the moment, anyway—to sit on its excess reserves. Or borrowers along the chain may take out cash from some of their new deposits and thereby reduce the banks' reserves and their lending powers. Thus the potential expansion may be only partially realized.

WHY BANKS MUST WORK TOGETHER

There is an interesting problem concealed behind this crisscrossing of deposits that leads to a slowly rising level of the money supply. Suppose that an imaginary island economy was served by a single bank (and let us forget about all complications of international trade, etc.), and suppose that this bank, which worked on a 20 percent reserve ratio, was suddenly presented with an extra million dollars worth of reserves—let us say newly mined pure gold. Our bank could, of course, increase its loans to customers. By how much? *By five million dollars!*

In other words, our island bank, all by itself, could use an increase in its reserves to create a much larger increase in the money supply. It is not difficult to understand why. Any borrower of the new five million, no matter where he spent his money on the island, would only be giving his checks to someone who also banked at the single, solitary bank. The whole five million, in other words, would stay *within* the bank as its deposits, although the identity of those depositors would, of course, shift. Indeed, there is no reason why such a bank should limit its expansion of the money supply to five million. As long as the "soundness" of the currency was unquestioned, such a bank could create as much money as it wanted through new deposits, since all of those deposits would remain in its own keeping.

The imaginary bank makes it plain why ordinary commercial banks *cannot* expand deposits beyond their excess reserves. Unlike the monopoly bank, they must expect to *lose* their deposits to other banks when their borrowers write checks on their new accounts. As a result they will also lose their reserves, and this can lead to trouble.

This situation is important enough to warrant taking a moment to examine. Suppose that in our original example we had decided to lend the Smith Corporation not $800,000 but $900,000, and suppose as before that the Smith Corporation used the proceeds of that loan to pay the Jones Corporation. Now look at the condition of our bank after the Smith payment has cleared.

Assets		Liabilities	
Cash and at Fed	$ 100,000	Original deposits	$1,000,000
Loan (Smith Corp.)	900,000	Smith Corp. deposit	0
Total	**$1,000,000**	**Total**	**$1,000,000**

Our reserves would now have dropped to 10 percent! Indeed, if we had loaned the company $1,000,000 we would be in danger of bankruptcy.

Banks are, in fact, very careful not to overlend. If they find that they have inadvertently exceeded their legal reserve requirements, they quickly take remedial action. One way that a bank may repair the situation is by borrowing reserves for a short period (paying interest of them, of course) from another bank that may have a temporary surplus at the Fed; this is called borrowing federal funds. Or a bank may quickly sell some of its government bonds and add the proceeds to its reserve account at the Fed. Or again, it may add to its reserves the proceeds of any loans that have come due and deliberately fail to replace these expired loans with new loans. Finally, a bank may borrow reserves directly from its Federal Reserve Bank, and pay interest for the loan. We shall shortly look into this method when we talk about the role of the Federal Reserve in regulating the quantity of money.

The main point is clear. A bank is safe in lending only an amount that it can afford to lose to another bank. But of course one bank's loss is another's gain. That is why, by the exchange of checks, the banking system can accomplish the same result as the island monopoly bank, whereas no individual bank can hope to do so.

If a bank uses its excess reserves to buy securities, does that lead to the same multiplication effect as a bank loan?

It can. When a bank buys government securities, it usually does so from a securities dealer, a professional trader in bonds. Its check (for $800,000 in our example) drawn on its account at the Federal Reserve will be made out to a dealer, who will deposit it in his bank. As a result, the dealer's bank suddenly finds itself with an $800,000 new deposit. It must keep 20 percent of this as required reserve, but the remainder is excess reserve against which it can make loans or investments as it wishes.

Is there a new deposit, corresponding to that of the businessman borrower? There is: the new deposit of the securities dealer. Note that in his case, as in the case of the borrower, the new deposit on the books of the bank has not been put there by the transfer of money from some other commercial bank. The $800,000 deposit has come into being through the deposit of a check from the Federal Reserve Bank, which is not a commercial bank. Thus it represents a new addition to the deposits of the private banking system.

Let us see this in the T accounts. After our first bank has bought its $800,000 in bonds (paying for them with its Federal Reserve checking account), its T account looks like this.

Assets		Liabilities	
Cash at Fed	$ 200,000	Deposits	$1,000,000
Government bonds	800,000		
Total	**$1,000,000**	**Total**	**$1,000,000**

As we can see, there are no excess reserves here. But look at the bank in which the seller of the government bond has deposited the check he has just received from our bank:

Assets		Liabilities	
Cash	$800,000	New deposit of bond seller	$800,000
Total	**$800,000**	**Total**	**$800,000**

Here there are excess reserves of $640,000 with which additional investments can be made. It is possible for such new deposits, albeit diminishing each time, to remain in the financial circuit for some time, moving from bank to bank as an active business is done in buying government bonds. But the very activity in bidding for government bonds is likely to raise their price, and thereby lower their rate of interest.

YIELDS

This is important to understand. A bond has a *fixed* rate of return and a stated face value. If it is a 4 percent, $1000 bond, this means it will pay $40 interest yearly. If the bond now sells on the marketplace for $1100, the $40 yearly interest will be less than a 4 percent return ($40 is only 3.6 percent of $1100). If the price should fall to $900, the $40 return will be more than 4 percent ($40 is 4.4 percent of $900). Thus the *yield* of a bond varies inversely—in the other direction—from its market price.

A lower rate of interest on bonds makes higher yielding loans to business look more attractive. Thus, sooner or later, excess reserves are apt to be channeled to new loans as well as new investments. Thereafter the deposit-building process follows its familiar course.

Controlling the Money Supply

We have now seen how a banking system can create money through the successive creation of excess reserves. But the key to the process is the creation of the *original* excess reserves, for without them the cumulative process will not be set in motion. We remember, for example, that a loan will not result in an increase in the money supply if it is offset by a decline in lending somewhere else in the banking system; neither will the purchase of a bond by one commercial bank if it is only buying a security sold by another. *To get a net addition to loans or investments, however, a banking system—assuming that it is fully loaned up—needs an increase in its reserves.* Where do these extra reserves come from? That is the question we must turn to next.

In our example we have already met one source of changes in reserves. When the public needs less currency, and deposits its extra holdings in the banks, reserves rise, as we have seen. Contrariwise, when the public wants more currency, it depletes the banks' holdings of currency and thereby lowers their reserves. In the latter case, the banks may find that they have insufficient reserves behind their deposits. To get more currency or claims on other banks, they will have to sell securities or reduce their loans. This might put a very severe crimp in the economy. Hence, to allow bank reserves to be regulated by the public's fluctuating demand for cash would seem to be an impossible way to run our monetary system.

But we remember that bank reserves are not mainly currency; in fact, currency is a relatively minor item. Most reserves are the accounts that member banks hold at the Federal Reserve. Hence, if these accounts could somehow be increased or decreased, we could regulate the amount of reserves—and thus the permissible total of deposits—without regard to the public's changing need for cash.

This is precisely what the Federal Reserve System is designed to do. Essentially, the system is set up to regulate the supply of money by raising or lowering the reserves of its member banks. When these reserves are raised, member banks find themselves with excess reserves and are thus in a position to make loans and investments by which the supply of money will increase further. Conversely, when the Federal Reserve lowers the reserves of its member banks, they will no longer be able to make loans and investments, or may even have to reduce loans or get rid of investments, thereby extinguishing deposit accounts and contracting the supply of money.

How does the Federal Reserve Operate? There are three ways.

1. *Changing reserve requirements.*

It was the Federal Reserve itself, we will remember, that originally determined how much in reserves its member banks should hold against their deposits. Hence by changing that reserve requirement for a given level of reserves, it can give its member banks excess reserves or can create a shortage of reserves.

In our imaginary bank we have assumed that reserves were set at 20 percent of deposits. Suppose now that the Federal Reserve determined to lower reserve requirements to 15 percent. It would thereby automatically create extra lending or investing power for our *existing* reserves. Our bank with $1 million in deposits and $200,000 in reserves could now lend or invest an additional $50,000 without any new funds coming in from depositors. On the other hand, if requirements were raised to, say, 30 percent, we would find that our original $200,000 of reserves was $100,000 short of requirements, and we would have to curtail lending or investing until we were again in line with requirements.

Changing reserve ratios is a very effective way of freeing or contracting bank credit. But it is a massive instrument that sweeps across the entire banking system in an undiscriminating fashion. It is therefore used only rarely, when the Federal Reserve Board feels that the supply of money is seriously short or dangerously excessive and needs remedy on a countrywide basis. For instance, in early 1969, the board raised reserve requirements one-half percent for all banks, partly to mop up excess reserves and partly to sound a general warning against what it considered to be a potentially dangerous inflationary state of affairs.

2. *Changing discount rates.*

A second means of control uses interest rates as the money-controlling device. Recall that member banks that are short on reserves have a special privilege, if they wish to exercise it. They can *borrow* reserve balances from the Federal Reserve Bank itself, adding them of course, to their regular reserve account at the bank. The way member banks borrow is to take the government bonds they have bought and to use these as collateral, or to take the signed loan agreements they have received from their own customers and to "re-discount" these loans—that is, to borrow on them—from their Federal Reserve Bank.

The Federal Reserve Bank, of course, charges interest for lending reserves, and this interest is called the discount rate. By raising or lowering this rate, the Federal Reserve can make it attractive or unattractive for member banks to borrow to augment reserves. Thus in contrast with changing the reserve ratio itself, changing the discount rate is a mild device that allows each bank to decide for itself whether it wishes to increase its reserves or not. In addition, changes in the discount rate tend to influence the whole structure of interest rates—either tightening or loosening money.*

3. *Open-market operations.*

Most frequently used, however, is a third technique called open-market operations. This technique permits the Federal Reserve Banks to change the supply of reserves by buying or selling U.S. government bonds on the open market.

How does this work? Let us suppose that the Federal Reserve authorities wish to increase the reserves of member banks. They will begin to buy government securities from dealers in the bond market; and to pay for these bonds, they will send Federal Reserve Bank checks in the amount of their purchases to dealers.

But notice something about these checks: *they are not drawn on any commercial bank!* They are drawn on the Federal Reserve Bank itself. The security dealer who sells the bond will, or course, deposit the Fed's check, as if it were any other check, in his own commercial bank; and his bank will send the Fed's check through for credit to its own account, as if it were any other check. *As a result, the dealer's bank will have gained reserves, although no other commercial bank has lost reserves.* On balance, then, the system has more lending and investing capacity than it had before. In fact, it now has *excess* reserves, and these as we have seen, will spread out through the system. *Thus by buying bonds, the Federal Reserve has, in fact, deposited money in the accounts of its members, thereby giving them the extra reserves that it set out to create.*

Conversely, if the authorities decide that member banks' reserves are too large, they will sell securities. Now the process works in reverse. Security dealers or other buyers of bonds will send their own checks on their own regular commercial banks to the Federal Reserve in payment for these bonds. This time the Fed will take the checks of its member banks and charge their accounts, thereby reducing their reserves. *Since these checks will not find their way into another commercial bank, the system as a whole will have suffered a diminution of its reserves.* By selling securities, in other words, the Federal Reserve authorities lower the Federal Reserve accounts of member banks, thereby diminishing their reserves.†

---

* When interest rates are high, money is called "tight." This means not only that borrowers have to pay higher rates, but that banks are stricter and more selective in judging the credit worthiness of business applications for loans. Conversely, when interest rates decline, money is called "easy," meaning that it is not only cheaper, but literally easier to borrow.

† Isn't this, some bright student will ask, really the same thing as raising or lowering the reserve ratio? If the Fed is really just putting money into member bank accounts when it buys bonds, and taking money out when it sells them, why does it bother to go through the open market? Why not just tell the member banks that their reserves are larger or smaller?

Analytically, our student is entirely right. There is, however, cogent reason for working through the bond market. It is that the open-market technique allows banks to *compete* for their share of the excess reserves that are being made available or taken away. Banks that are good at attracting depositors will thereby get extra benefit from an increase in the money supply. Thus, rather than assigning excess reserves by executive fiat, the Fed uses the open market as an allocation device. Much more about this function of the market in Part Four.

Paper Money and Gold

Here is a good place to clear up one last mystery of the monetary system—the mystery of where currency (coin and bills) actually comes from and where it goes. If we examine most of our paper currency, we will find that it has "Federal Reserve Note" on it; that is, it is paper money issued by the Federal Reserve System. We understand, by now, how the public gets these notes: it simply draws them from its checking accounts. When it does so, the commercial banks, finding their supplies of vault cash low, ask their Federal Reserve district banks to ship them as much new cash as they need.

And what does the Federal Reserve Bank do? It takes packets of $1s and $5s and $10s out of its vaults, *where these stacks of printed paper have no monetary significance at all,* charges the requisite amount against its member banks' balances, and ships the cash out by armored truck. So long as these new stacks of bills remain in the member banks' possession, they are still not money! But soon they will pass out to the public, where they will be money. Do not forget, of course, that as a result, the public will have that much *less* money left in its checking accounts.

Could this currency-issuing process go on forever? Could the Federal Reserve ship out as much money as it wanted to? Suppose that the authorities at the Fed decided to order a trillion dollars worth of bills from the Treasury mints. What would happen when those bills arrived at the Federal Reserve Banks? The answer is that they would simply gather dust in their vaults. *There would be no way for the Fed to "issue" its money unless the public wanted cash.* And the amount of cash the public could want is always limited by the amount of money it has in its checking accounts.

THE GOLD COVER

Are there no limitations on this note-issuing or reserve-creating process? Until 1967 there *were* limitations imposed by Congress, requiring the Federal Reserve to hold gold certificates equal in value to at least 25 percent of all outstanding notes. (Gold certificates are a special kind of paper money issued by the U.S. Treasury and backed 100 percent by gold bullion in Fort Knox.) Prior to 1964 there was a further requirement that the amount of gold certificates also be sufficient to give a 25 percent backing as well to the total amount of member bank deposits held by the Fed. Thus the legal obligation not to go beyond this 25 percent gold cover provided a strict ceiling on the amount of member bank reserves the Federal Reserve system could create or on the amount of notes it could ship at the request of its member banks.

All this presented no problem in, say, 1940, when the total of member bank reserves plus Federal Reserve notes came to only $20 billion, against which we held gold certificates worth almost $22 billion. Trouble began to develop, however, in the 1960s when a soaring GNP was accompanied by a steadily rising volume of both member bank reserves and Federal Reserve notes. By 1964, for example, member bank reserves had grown to $22 billion, and outstanding Reserve notes to nearly $35 billion. At the same time, for reasons that we shall learn more about in Part Five, our gold stock had declined to just over $15 billion. With $57 billion in liabilities ($22 billion in member bank reserves plus $35 billion in notes) and only $15 billion in gold certificates, the 25 percent cover requirement was clearly imperiled.

Congress thereupon removed the cover requirement from member bank reserves, leaving all our gold certificates available as "backing" for our Federal Reserve notes. But even that did not solve the problem. Currency in circulation continued to rise with a record GNP until it exceeded $40 billion in 1967. Our gold stock meanwhile continued to decline to $12 billion in that year and threatened to fall further. The handwriting on the wall indicated that the 25 percent cover could not long be maintained.

There were basically two ways out of the dilemma. One would have been to change the gold cover requirements from 25 percent to, say, 10 percent. That would have made our gold stock more than adequate to "back" our paper money (and our member bank deposits, too).*

The second way was much simpler. *It was simply to eliminate the gold cover entirely.* With very little fuss, this is what Congress did in 1967.

Does the presence or absence of a gold cover make any difference? From the economist's point of view it does not. Gold is a metal with a long and rich history of hypnotic influence, so there is undeniably a psychological usefulness in having gold "behind" a currency. But unless that currency is 100 percent convertible into gold, *any* money demands an act of faith on the part of its users. If that faith is destroyed, the money becomes valueless; so long as it is unquestioned, the money is "as good as gold."

Thus the presence or absence of a gold backing for currency is purely a psychological problem, so far as the value of a domestic currency is concerned.† Gold is, however, the accepted medium of settling accounts in international exchanges (where again, of course, its "value" is essentially psycho-

---

* Actually—as we shall see in the note on the gold standard on p. 625—the gold never really backed our currency, since no American was legally permitted to buy gold bullion.

† Some years ago a patriotic women's organization, alarmed lest the Communists had tunneled under the Atlantic, forced an inspection of the gold stock buried at Fort Knox. It proved to be all there. An interesting question arises as to the repercussions, had they found the great vault to be bare. Perhaps we might have followed the famous anthropological example of the island of Yap in the South Seas, where heavy stone cartwheels are the symbol of wealth for the leading families. One such family was particularly remarkable insofar as its cartwheel lay at the bottom of a lagoon, where it had fallen from a canoe. Although it was absolutely irretrievable and even invisible, the family's wealth was considered unimpaired, since everyone knew the stone was there. If the Kentucky depository had been empty, a patriotic declaration by the ladies that the gold really *was* in Fort Knox might have saved the day for the United States.

logical), so that the possession of a substantial gold stock has very real benefits in foreign relations, as we shall see in Part Five.

But the point is worth pursuing a little further. Suppose our currency *were* 100 percent convertible into gold—suppose, in fact, that we used only gold coins as currency. Would that improve the operation of our economy?

A moment's reflection should reveal that it would not. We would still have to cope with a very difficult problem that our bank deposit money handles rather easily. This is the problem of how we could increase the supply of money or diminish it, as the needs of the economy changed. With gold coins as money we would either have a frozen stock of money (with consequences that we shall trace in the next chapter), or our supply of money would be at the mercy of our luck in gold-mining or the currents of international trade that funneled gold into our hands or took it away. And incidentally, a gold currency would not obviate inflation, as many countries have discovered when the vagaries of international trade or a fortuitous discovery of gold mines increased their holdings of gold faster than their actual output.

MONEY
AND BELIEF

As we cautioned at the outset, money is a highly sophisticated and curious invention. At one time or another nearly everything imaginable has served as the magic symbol of money: whales' teeth, shells, feathers, bark, furs, blankets, butter, tobacco, leather, copper, silver, gold, and (in the most advanced nations) pieces of paper with pictures on them or simply numbers on a ledger page. In fact, anything is usable as money, provided that there is a natural or enforceable scarcity of it, so that men can usually come into its possession only through carefully designated ways. Behind all the symbols, however, rests the central requirement of faith. Money serves its indispensable purposes as long as we believe in it. It ceases to the moment we do not. Money has well been called "the promises men live by."

But the creation of money and the control over its supply is still only half the question. We have yet to trace how our money supply influences the flow of output itself—or to put it differently, how the elaborate institutions through which men promise to honor one another's work and property affect the amount of work they do and the amount of new wealth they accumulate. This is the subject to which our next chapter will be devoted.

KEY CONCEPTS AND KEY WORDS

Money

Deposits

Currency

1. Money is defined as whatever we use to make *payments.* As such, in modern economies, the most important constituents of money are *currency outside the banking system* and *demand deposits (checking accounts).*

2. Currency flows into, and is drawn out of, checking accounts. There is, however, much less currency in banks than the total amount of checking accounts.

3. Banks are forced, by law, to hold reserves against stated fractions of their demand deposits. For most banks these reserves can be either in *vault cash* or in *accounts* at a *Federal Reserve Bank.*

4. There are *twelve Federal Reserve Banks* that service their member banks exactly as the member banks service the public. The Reserve Banks are coordinated by a policy-making Board of Governors (Federal Reserve Board) in Washington. The Board is empowered to change reserve ratios for city or country banks, within legally established limits, and to take other actions to control the supply of money.

5. The function of the reserves established by the Federal Reserve Board is not to ensure the "safety" of the currency, but to provide a means of *controlling the supply of money.*

6. Any reserves of a commercial bank over and above those imposed by the Federal Reserve are called *excess reserves.* Commercial banks earn profits by lending or investing amounts equal to their excess reserves.

7. When a bank makes a loan, it opens an account in the name of the borrower. This account is a *net addition to total deposits and is therefore new money.* Thus bank lending can increase the supply of money. Investing in government bonds is also likely to lead to new demand deposits.

8. New deposits created by loans are typically drawn on by checks that go into other banks. Here they also give rise to excess reserves and to the possibility of *further deposit creation through more loans or investments.*

9. The total amount of new money that the banking system can create depends on the *reserve ratio.* The size of credit expansion is determined by the reciprocal of the reserve ratio.

10. It is only the banking *system* that can expand the money supply up to the limit imposed by the reciprocal of the reserve ratio. A single bank can lend only up to the amount that it is prepared to "lose". *Hence each individual bank lends only an amount that is fully covered by its excess reserves.*

11. The Federal Reserve System controls the ability of the banking system to expand the supply of money by *controlling the amount of its reserves.* It can do so in three ways:
    * By changing *reserve ratios*
    * By changing the *discount rate*
    * By *open-market operations*

12. The most commonly used method is open-market operations. This is a means of controlling the size of reserves by *purchases and sales of government bonds on the open market.* When the Federal Reserve System buys bonds, it issues in payment its own checks, which enter the commercial banks and are added to their reserves. This gives the commercial banks excess reserves and enables them to make additional loans or investments. Selling bonds brings checks from commercial bank accounts to the Federal Reserve Banks, and thereby lowers the reserve accounts of member banks. This reduces their ability to make loans or investments.

13. There is no longer any gold backing required behind member bank reserves, or behind Federal Reserve notes. The amount or percentage of gold cover is essentially arbitrary. *Gold plays only a symbolic role in a national monetary system.* The true value of money ultimately reposes in the faith men have in it.

Margin notes:

Federal Reserve Banks

Federal Reserve system

Fractional reserves

Excess reserves

Deposit creation

Loans

Reserve ratios

Excess reserves

Discount rate

Open-market operations

Monetary policy

Gold "cover"

1. Why do we not count cash in the tills of commercial banks in the money supply? Why don't we include savings accounts?

2. When you deposit currency in a commercial bank, what happens to it? Can you ask for your particular bills again? If you demanded to see "your" account, what would it be?

3. What determines how much vault cash a bank must hold against its deposits? Would you expect this proportion to change in some seasons, such as Christmas? Do you think it would be the same in worried times as in placid ones? In new countries as in old ones?

4. Is currency the main reserve of a bank? Do reserves ensure the safety of a currency? What function do they have?

5. What are excess reserves? Suppose a bank has $500,000 in deposits and that there is a reserve ratio of 30 percent imposed by law. What is its required reserve? Suppose it happens to hold $200,000 in vault cash or at its account at the Fed. What, if any, is its excess reserve?

6. If the bank above wanted to make loans or investments, how much would it be entitled to lend or invest?

7. Suppose its deposits increased by another $50,000. Could it lend or invest this entire amount? Any of it? How much?

8. If a bank lends money, it opens an account in the name of the borrower. Now suppose the borrower draws down his new account. What happens to the reserves of the lending bank? Show this in a T account.

9. Suppose the borrower sends his check for $1,000 to someone who banks at another bank. Describe what happens to the deposits of the second bank. If the reserve ratio is 20 percent, how much new lending or investing can it do?

10. If the reserve ratio is 20 percent, and the original addition to reserves is $1,000, what will be the total potential amount of new money that can be created by the banking system? If the ratio is 25 percent?

11. What is the difference between a banking system and a single competitive bank? Can a single bank create new money? Can it create more new money than an amount equal to its excess reserves? Can a banking system create more money than its excess reserves?

12. Suppose that a bank has $1 million in deposits and $100,000 in reserves, and is fully loaned up. Now suppose the Federal Reserve System lowers reserve requirements from 10 percent to 8 percent. What happens to the lending capacity of the bank?

13. If the discount rate rises from 5 percent to 6 percent, does that affect the willingness of banks to lend? How?

14. The Federal Reserve Banks buy $100 million in U.S. Treasury notes. How do they pay for these notes? What happens to the checks? Do they affect the reserves of member banks? Will buying bonds increase or decrease the money supply?

15. Now explain what happens when the Fed sells Treasury notes. Who buys them? How do they pay for them? Where do the checks go? How does payment affect the accounts of the member banks at the Federal Reserve Banks?

16. Why do you think gold has held such a place of prestige in the minds of men?

LEARNING ABOUT STATISTICS

FORECASTING   The tradition of forecasting has an ancient pedigree. The oracles of Greece or Rome predicted the future by examining the flights of birds and the entrails of animals. The astrologers of the East were indispensable consultants to its statesmen and generals (and there are people even today—hopefully not statesmen or generals—who consult the stars before deciding what to do). But now we have a newcomer to the forecasting game—the econometrician. Unlike his predecessors, however, his goal is not to practice an "art" but to perfect a science. In this supplement we will look into econometric forecasting, partly to learn something about the scientific basis on which it is indeed grounded and partly to recognize the degree to which, alas, it still remains an art.

Unlike the soothsayer, the econometric forecaster is interested only in predicting the *economic* future; that is, in predicting the future values of things such as GNP or the price level. On what does he rely for his scientific foreknowledge of these magnitudes? A vital part of his equipment, as we shall see, is the multimillion dollar computer capable of handling enormously complicated mathematical problems in very short periods of time. But behind the computer is the econometrician's basic instrument, the humble equation. When an econometrician predicts the future, essentially he is taking past relationships, reducing them to equational form, and then using these equations to indicate the probable paths of economic activity over the future.

How does our econometrician go about doing this? We know part of the answer from our introduction to econometrics. He begins by assembling as much statistical information as he can find concerning important economic relationships. Suppose, for example, that he knows from multiple regression that the demand for automobiles can be represented by an equation in which the demand for cars is related to changes in disposable income, to changes in car prices, to credit conditions, etc. This long and complicated equation will then become one element in a model of the economy that will also contain the demand for many other final products, as well as the relationships (also econometrically derived) between or among elements such as the quantity of money and the level of prices, the level of employment and consumer disposable income, and so on.

Correlation again

Thus, the predictive tool of the econometrician consists of *a series of equations which depict the simultaneous interaction of those activities that the model-builder believes to be crucial in affecting the economy.* As can be imagined, this leads to extremely complex equations and systems of equations. The famous model of the Wharton School of Business of the University of Pennsylvania, for example, has some 150 equations, most of them with strings of multiple regression elements. To solve such a system of equations by pencil and paper would be impossible—or would take so long that the future would long ago have become history. Thus the computer with its lightning speeds is an integral part of the econometrician's equipment.

But the long chain of equations that the model-builder assembles could not predict the future if *everything* in that chain depended on everything else. Hence when we examine forecasting models we find that the many variables they contain can be classified into two kinds. Many of the variables *depend* on other variables for their values; for example, automobile purchases depend on disposable income, car prices, and other variables. These are *dependent* variables in the model; that is, elements whose values will be determined by the action of the independent variables in the system.

Exogenous and endogenous variables

These *exogenous* ("outside") variables must be introduced into the system as *parameters,* or stated values that will determine or limit the values of the dependent variables. Where does the econometrician get these exogenous variables? Some of them may be known facts from which various kinds of future economic activity may be inferred by econometric analysis. For instance, the model-builder may introduce the known level of population growth as an exogenous variable on which the future level of home-building or car-buying may depend. Or exogenous variables may be based on surveys or on expected policy decisions, such as surveys of intended corporate investment or policy statements of the Federal Reserve. These and other exogenous variables are arranged along with the endogenous variables in a set of simultaneous equations that make up the econometric model and reflect the complex mechanism of the economy. The econometrician then solves the model, thus deriving values for his endogenous variables, such as consumer disposable income, automobile purchases, or GNP itself.

Here, of course, lies the central problem for econometric forecasting. We can never be certain of the accuracy of our all-important exogenous variables. We cannot predict with certainty, for instance, what the money supply will be, because we cannot know whether Federal Reserve policy will change. We cannot predict with certainty what business investment will be, because business expectations may change. To the extent that our exogenous variables are wrongly specified, the values we derive from them for dependent elements in our model will also be wrong. In 1966, for example, the Council of Economic Advisers predicted that the rate of inflation was about to slow down. Actually, it accelerated. The mistake did not lie with the reasoning of the Council or with its econometric model. It lay in the fact that the council assumed, on the basis of the data at hand, that the budget for 1967 was going to be balanced. What happened in fact was that a budgetary deficit of $9 billion was incurred to finance an expansion of the Vietnam War—a deficit that had not been included in the original budget estimates.

One way to get around such problems is to assume several sets of values for key "policy variables" and to run the model for each one. For example, a forecast put out by the Federal Reserve Bank of St. Louis has made three different predictions based on three different postulated rates of growth in the money supply. Having such a spectrum of predictions seems at first to be weaseling on the job. But actually it serves a very useful purpose. Such alternative models show us the probable *range* of our results and can therefore tell us, for instance, if the consumption of autos will be much or little affected if the money supply grows fast or slowly.

Second, because many of the key policy variables *cannot* be accurately predicted (who can foretell with certainty what next year's federal budget will be?) a spectrum of forecasts enables individuals or corporations to make their own guestimates about these critical variables and then to examine what the probable configuration of *other* economic variables are apt to look like, given these key assumptions.

Every person or firm bases his economic decisions on some kind of implicit or explicit estimate of future economic conditions. To try to improve these decisions, econometric forecasting is increasingly used by large industrial corporations, by financial institutions, and by governments. The results of the big models at the Brookings Institution or the Wharton School are even featured in news articles. Hence it is important to ask how well the econometric predictions have fared.

Performance Most econometricians would be the first to admit that their performance has been uneven. The models have worked very well—have predicted changes in the economy quite accurately—as long as things were moving along fairly steadily in one direction. But when things changed direction, *which is just when we want our models to work best,* they have not been too reliable. The influential Brookings Model, for example, did not forecast the recessions of 1957–1958 or of 1960–1961. In 1968, most econometricians predicted a recession for 1969; what actually happened was that business scored record highs through most of the year, although it did turn down in the fourth quarter.

What accounts for this disappointing performance? Part of the trouble lies in the problems of "specifying" the model correctly—that is, of overcoming the numerous problems of econometrics that we have touched on in past supplements. The fact that different econometric models use different multiple regression coefficients for the same variables attests in itself to the fact that there is more than one way to depict certain relationships.

Second is the problem that econometricians, as we have also made clear, ultimately rely on economics; and economists are by no means of one mind about the relative importance of certain key exogenous variables, such as the influence of fiscal or monetary policy on the price level or on GNP. Hence our models misperform because we are still in disagreement about economic theory itself.

And last, our models misperform because we cannot predict the course of certain critical exogenous variables that lie beyond the reach of economic reasoning itself. For example, no economic theory could have predicted the degree of escalation of the Vietnam War. Yet that event dominated macroeconomic behavior in the late Sixties.

Does this mean that econometric forecasting is doomed to failure? Not necessarily. The need is rather to understand better what our models can do for us and what they cannot. One thing they can certainly do is to clarify the nature of the interactions of many economic activities, so that important relationships within the economic system can be specified with much greater accuracy. A second very important purpose of models is to make clear the economic *requirements* to reach given targets, a task that is not quite the same as that of prediction, but that is no less important regarding the future.

THE LIMITS OF PREDICTION

Equally certainly, however, we cannot use our models to give us predictions about such things as the date of the next stock market crash or even the level of GNP ten years hence. When matters of volatile *behavior* are concerned, such as the psychology of the stock market, an econometric model has nothing to go by. By definition, such unforecastable psychological changes *alter* the very coefficients on which predictive equations are built.

In the same way, long-term predictions are made hazardous by events such as international crises, technological breakthroughs, or political upheavals, all of which also upset the parameters on which all prediction is ultimately based.

Here, in the realm of the exogenous, the *science* of econometric forecasting ends, and the art of forecasting begins. For it is here that the shrewd guess of the economist or the hunch of the econometrician will lead him—in the face of the established patterns of the past—to postulate that things have shifted or are about to shift and therefore to regard the results of his model with more than the usual degree of caution, or to recast the parameters on which his model is based. At this point the economist or the econometrician certainly does not claim access to the occult, but he humbly confesses that scientific methods, powerful as they are, still cannot give us answers as to the shape of many things to come.

In our preceding chapter, we found out something about what money is and how it comes into being. Now we must turn to the much more complicated question of how money works—of what effect changes in the supply of money have on the level of output. What happens when the banks create or destroy deposits? Can we directly raise or lower incomes by altering the quantity of money? Can we control inflation or recession by using the monetary management powers of the Federal Reserve System? These extremely important questions will be the focus of discussion in this chapter.

The Quantity Theory of Money

QUANTITY EQUATION

One relation between money and economic activity must already have occurred to us. It is that the quantity of money must have something to do with *prices*. Does it not stand to reason that if we increase the supply of money, prices will go up, and that if we decrease the amount of money, prices will fall?

Something very much like this belief lies behind one of the most famous equations in economics. The equation looks like this:

$$MV = PT$$

where
M = *quantity of money* (currency outside banks plus demand deposits)
V = *velocity of circulation,* or the number of times per period or per year that an average dollar changes hands
P = *the general level of prices,* or a price index
T = *the number of transactions made in the economy* in a year, or a measure of *physical output*

If we think about this equation, its meaning is not hard to grasp. What the quantity equation says is that *the amount of expenditure (M times V,* or the quantity of money times the frequency of its use) *equals the amount of receipts (P* times *T,* or the price of an average sale times the number of sales). What the quantity equation *seems* to say, however, is that there is a direct *causal* connection between money and prices—that if you increase the amount of money, you will increase prices, or if you decrease the supply of money you will cause prices to fall.

Is this causal relation true? Can we directly manipulate the price level by changing the size of our stock of money?

The original inventors of the quantity equation, over half a century ago, thought this was indeed the case. And of course it would be the case, if everything else in the equation held steady while we moved the quantity of money up or down. In other words, if the velocity of circulation, *V,* and the number of transactions, *T,* were assumed to be fixed, changes in *M* would have to operate directly on *P.*

Can we test the validity of this assumption? There is an easy way to do so. Figure 18-1 shows us changes in the supply of money compared with changes in the level of prices.

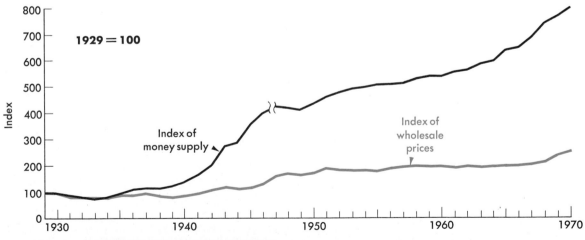

FIG. 18•1 MONEY SUPPLY AND PRICES

A glance at Fig. 18-1 answers our question. Between 1929 and 1970, the supply of money in the United States increased over *sixfold,* while prices rose only a little more than *twofold.* Clearly, something *must* have happened to V or to T to prevent the sixfold increase in M from bringing about a similar increase in P. Let us see what those changes were.

Figure 18-2 gives us a first clue as to what is wrong with a purely mechanical interpretation of the quantity theory. In it we show how many times an average dollar was used to help pay for each year's output.* We

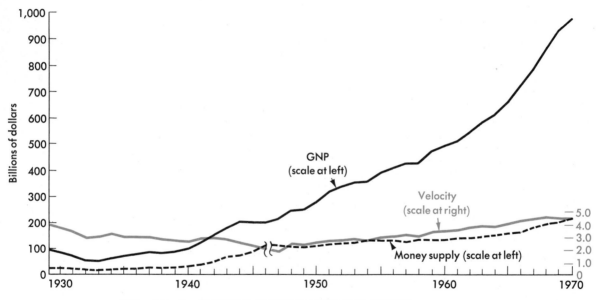

FIG. 18•2   MONEY SUPPLY AND VELOCITY

derive this number by dividing the total expenditure for each year's output (which is, of course, the familiar figure for GNP) by the actual supply of money—currency plus checking accounts—for each year. As the chart shows, the velocity of money fell by 50 percent between 1929 and 1946, only to rise again to the 1929 level over the postwar years.

We shall return later to an inquiry into why people change their rate of spending, but it is clear beyond question that they do. This has two impor-

---

* Note that final output is not quite the same as *T,* which embraces *all* transactions, including those for intermediate goods. But if we define *T* so that it includes only *transactions that enter into final output, PT* becomes a measure of gross national product. In the same way, we can count only those expenditures that enter into GNP when we calculate *MV.* It does no violence to the idea of the quantity theory to apply it only to final output, and it makes statistical computation a good deal simpler.

tant implications for our study of money. First, it gives a very cogent reason why we cannot apply the quantity theory in a mechanical way, asserting that an increase in the supply of money will *always* raise prices. For if people choose to spend the increased quantity of money more slowly, its impact on the quantity of goods may not change at all: whereas if they spend the same quantity of money more rapidly, prices can rise without any change in M.

Second and more clearly than we have seen, the variability of V reveals that money itself can be a destabilizing force—destabilizing because it enables us to do two things that would be impossible in a pure barter economy. We can:

1. *delay between receiving and expending our rewards for economic effort*

2. *spend more or less than our receipts by drawing on, or adding to, our cash balances*

The Classical economists used to speak of money as a "veil," implying that it did not itself play an active role in influencing the behavior of the economic players. But we can see that the ability of those players to vary the rate of their expenditure—to hang onto their money longer or to get rid of it more rapidly than usual—makes money much more than a veil. Money (or rather, people's wish to hold or to spend money) becomes an independent source of change in a complex economic society. To put it differently, the use of money introduces an element of uncertainty into the circular flow.*

CHANGES IN T

Now we must turn to a last and perhaps most important reason why we cannot relate the supply of money to the price level in a mechanical fashion. This reason lies in the role played by T; that is, by the volume of output.

Just as the early quantity theorists thought of V as essentially unvarying, so they thought of T as a relatively fixed term in the quantity equation. In the minds of nearly all economic theorists before the Depression, output was always assumed to be as large as the available resources and the willingness of the factors of production would permit. While everyone was aware that there might be minor variations from this state of full output, virtually no one thought they would be of sufficient importance to matter. *Hence the quantity theory implicitly assumed full employment or full output as the normal condition of the economy.* With such an assumption, it was easy to picture T as an unimportant term in the equation and to focus the full effect of changes in money or in money spending *(MV)* on P.

---

* Technically, the standard economic definition of money is that it is both a means of exchange and a store of value. It is the latter characteristic that makes money a potentially disturbing influence.

The trauma of the Great Depression effectively removed the comfortable assumption that the economy "naturally" tended to full employment and output. At the bottom of the Depression, real output had fallen by 25 percent in real terms—that is, after adjustment for changing price levels—and one-quarter of the labor force was unable to find work. Quite aside from what the Depression taught us in other ways, it made unmistakably clear that changes in the volume of output (and employment) were of crucial importance in the overall economic picture.

OUTPUT AND PRICES

How does our modern emphasis on the variability of output and employment fit into the overall question of money and prices? The answer is very simple, but very important. We have come to see that *the effect of more money on prices cannot be determined unless we also take into account its effect on the volume of transactions or output.*

It is not difficult to grasp the point. Let us picture an increase in spending, perhaps initiated by businessmen launching a new investment program, or by the government inaugurating a new public works project. These new expenditures will be received by many other entrepreneurs, as the multiplier mechanism spreads the new spending through the economy. But now we come to the key question. What will entrepreneurs do as their receipts increase?

It is at this point that the question of output enters. For if businessmen are operating factories or stores *at less than full capacity,* and if there is an *employable supply of labor available,* the result of their new receipts is almost certain to be an increase in output. That is, employers will take advantage of the rise in demand to produce and sell more goods and services. They may also try to raise prices and increase their profits further, but *if their industries are reasonably competitive,* it is doubtful that prices can be raised very much; other businessmen with idle plants will simply undercut them and take their business away. An example is provided by the period 1934 through 1940, when output increased by 50 percent while prices rose by less than 5 percent. The reason, of course, lay in the great amount of unemployed resources, making it easy to expand output without price increases.

Thus we reach a general conclusion of the greatest importance. *An increase in spending of any kind tends to result in more output and employment whenever there are considerable amounts of unemployed resources.* But this is no longer true when we reach a level of high employment or very full plant utilization. Now an increase in spending *cannot* quickly lead to an increase in output, simply because the resources for more production are lacking. The result, instead, will be a rise in prices, for no firm can lose business to competitors when competitors are unable to fill additional orders. Thus the corollary of our general conclusion is that *additional spending*—from any source—*is inflationary when it is difficult to raise output.*

Notice that our discussion has shifted its ground. We began by trying to establish the relationship between the quantity of money and the price level. Thus there is still a missing link to be added, a link that will tie the quantity of money to the volume of expenditure.

We will return to that link shortly. But the implications of our discussion about expenditure and inflation are too important to leave at this point. For we can see that the conclusion we have reached puts a capstone on our previous analysis of deficit spending. It is now possible to add a major criterion to the question of whether or not to use the public sector as a supplement to the private sector. That criterion is whether or not substantially "full" employment has been reached.*

If the economy is operating at or near the point of full employment, additional net public spending will only add more MV to a situation in which T is already at capacity and where, therefore, P will rise. But note that this conclusion attaches to more than additional *public* spending. When full employment is reached, additional spending of any kind—public or private, consumption or investment—will increase MV and, given the ceiling on T, affect P.

A different conclusion is reached when there is large-scale unemployment. Now additional public (or private) spending will result not in higher prices, but in larger output and higher employment. Thus we cannot say that public spending in itself is "inflationary." Rather, we must see that *any kind of additional spending can be inflationary in a fully employed economy, and will not be inflationary in an underemployed one.*

Full Employment vs. Underemployment

So we must distinguish between two fundamentally different situations in macroeconomics: the situation of full employment and that of underemployment. Policies that make sense when one situation obtains make no sense at all in the other. To spend more in the public or the private sector is clearly a main objective for economic well-being in an underemployed economy, for more spending will lead to more output and employment. But to spend more in a fully employed economy is only to cause economic mischief, for now more spending will lead only to higher prices and not to more goods or jobs. Similarly, to balance budgets or to run a budget surplus in the public sector makes little sense when an economy is underutilized, but it is the

* The definition of employment, as we shall see in Chapter 19, is far from simple, and "full" employment accordingly is a complex idea. Economists usually call employment "full" when about 96 percent of all job seekers are at work.

course of wisdom when there are no idle resources to absorb additional expenditures.

It is impossible to overstress the importance of this major finding of macroeconomics. One of the main differences between contemporary economic thought and that of the past is precisely this sharp division between policies that make sense in full employment and those that make sense in conditions of underemployment. It was not that the economists of the past did not recognize the tragedy of unemployment or did not wish to remedy it. It was rather that they did not see how an economy could be in *equilibrium* even though there was heavy unemployment.

The dragging years of the Great Depression taught us not only that output could fall far below the levels of full utilization, but—and perhaps this was its most intellectually unsettling feature—that an economy could be plagued with unemployed men and machines for almost a decade and yet not spontaneously generate the momentum to reabsorb them. Today we understand this condition of unemployment equilibrium, and we have devised various remedial measures to raise the equilibrium point to a satisfactory level, including, not least, additional public expenditure. But this new understanding must be balanced with a keen appreciation of its relevance to the underlying situation of employment. Remedies for an underemployed economy can be ills for a fully employed one.

MONEY AND STICKY PRICES

There is only one last point to be made, but it is an important one. All along in our discussion we have taken for granted that we need a larger supply of money in order to expand output. But why should we? Why could we not grow just as well if the quantity of money were fixed?

Theoretically, of course, we could. If we cut prices as we increased output, a given amount of money (or a given amount of expenditure) could cover an indefinitely large real output. Furthermore, as prices fell, workers would be content not to ask for higher wages (or would even accept lower wages), since in real terms they would be just as well or better off.

It is not difficult to spot the flaw in this argument. In the real world, prices of many goods cannot be cut easily. If the price of steel rose and fell as quickly and easily as prices on the stock exchange, or if wages went down without a murmur of resistance, or if rents and other contractual items could be quickly adjusted, then prices would be flexible and we would not require any enlargement of our money supply to cover a growing real output.

In fact, as we know, prices are extremely "sticky" in the downward direction. Union leaders do not look with approval on wage cuts, even when living costs fall. Contractual prices cannot be quickly adjusted. Many big firms, as we saw in Chapter 7, administer their prices and carefully avoid price competition: note, for example, that the prices of many consumer items are printed on the package months before the item will be sold.

Thus we can see that a fixed supply of money would put the economy into something of a straitjacket. As output tended to increase, businessmen would need more money to finance production, and consumers would need more money to make their larger expenditures. If businessmen could get more money from the banks, all would be well. But suppose they could not. Then the only way a businessman could get his hands on a larger supply of cash would be to persuade someone to lend it to him, and his persuasion would be in the form of a higher rate of interest. But this rising interest rate would discourage other businessmen from going ahead with their plans. Hence the would-be boom would be stopped dead in its tracks by a sheer shortage of spending power.

A flexible money supply obviates this economic suffocation. The fact that banks can create money (provided that they have excess reserves) enables them to take care of businesses that wish to make additional expenditures. The expenditures themselves put additional money into the hands of consumers. And the spending of consumers in turn sends the enlarged volume of purchasing power back to business firms to complete the great flow of expenditure and receipt.

The Problem of Inflation

Our discussion of the effect of money on prices and output has brought us to the recognition of the critical distinction between spending more in a fully employed economy and in an underemployed economy. But this distinction, so important as a basic principle, must now be somewhat blurred. For in the real world, the economy does not move from unemployment to full employment across a clear line of demarcation. On the contrary, as spending increases, general unemployment gives way at first to "tight" labor areas or to shortages in plant capacity in a few areas. Thus bottlenecks are typically the first sign that we are crossing from a condition of general unemployment to one of only partial unemployment.

These bottlenecks, however, may begin to exert their constricting effect before the economy as a whole can be considered in a condition of healthy overall employment. This is particularly the case if the bottleneck is a strategic industry, in which a price rise may lead to increases in the costs of many other industries. Bottlenecks may thus cause the beginnings of inflationary pressure *before* the economy as a whole has absorbed its unemployed.

Yet another cause of inflation, not necessarily connected with full employment, has been suggested by Professor William Baumol of Princeton. He has pointed to the fact that there is an inflationary consequence to the difference between productivity in the highly dynamic mass production industries and productivity in the much less technologically advanced ser-

BOTTLENECKS AND WAGE PRESSURES

vice areas. Wage increases in the mass production industries tend to be accompanied by increases in output per man. But high wages there also work to pull up wages in other sectors where higher pay is not matched by higher output: pay raises for teachers or firemen or office workers are not usually geared to increases in their output. As a result, the volume of total wage payments tends to rise faster than the total output of all goods and services, with the result that prices, especially in the service areas, are pushed steadily upward. For example, from 1961 through 1970, the consumer price index rose 30 percent. This mild inflationary trend, however, reflected a rise of only 16 percent in the price of manufactured goods, combined with a rise of 47 percent in the price of services.

FIG. 18·3   THE UNEMPLOYMENT-INFLATION RELATION

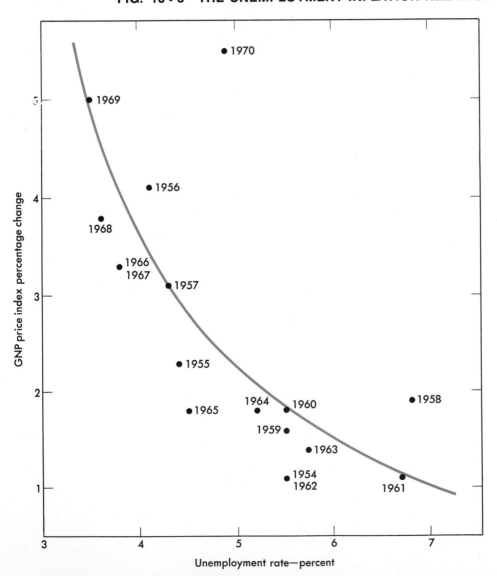

The tendency of the economy to generate bottlenecks and wage increases that run ahead of increases in productivity creates a very serious problem—that of *choosing between a degree of inflation or a degree of unemployment.* For the experience of the 1950s and 1960s makes it appear that some rise in prices is probably unavoidable if we wish the economy to operate at high levels of output and employment.

The scatter diagram (Fig. 18-3) from the 1969 *Report of the Council of Economic Advisers,* shows the relationship between the unemployment rate in recent years and the degree of "price creep." Note that the lower the unemployment, generally speaking, the higher the degree of inflation.

This relation between unemployment and inflation can be generalized in Fig. 18-4, commonly called a *Phillips curve* after the English economist A. W. Phillips, who first plotted it.

In this generalized curve we do not show the exact percent of unemployment that is associated with any particular price rise or with price stability. This percentage may vary from one country or period to another, depending, for example, on how effective are its policies of combatting unemployment (a matter we will look into at the end of our next chapter) or

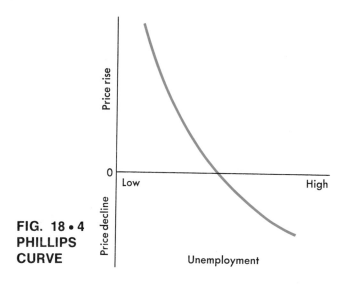

**FIG. 18 • 4
PHILLIPS
CURVE**

on how competitive is its state of industry. Note in the previous scatter diagram for the United States (Fig. 18-3), for example, that we have had *different* rates of price rises associated with the *same* rate of unemployment in a number of years.

Nevertheless the basic problem of a "trade-off" between unemployment and inflation seems to be deeply built into the structure of all industrial systems, European as well as American. In Europe or Japan, for example, where the percentage of unemployment since World War II has been less than half of ours, the rate of inflation has been roughly double our own.

INFLATION
AS A WAY
OF LIFE
Does this mean that inflation has become a chronic fact of life, uncurable except at levels of unemployment that would be socially unacceptable?

There is certainly a great deal of evidence that high employment and *some* degree of rising prices go together. What economists hope is that a middle ground can be reached, where the damage done by both inflation and unemployment can be reduced to acceptable proportions. A price rise of 1 or 2 percent per year, for example, can be fairly easily tolerated, since there is usually an increase in the *quality* of goods from year to year. Thus a small rise in prices can be accepted as reflecting a gain in the real standard of living that those improved goods provide.

Similarly, a small amount of unemployment is also tolerable, although for different reasons. There is always a percent or so of the labor force that is *voluntarily* unemployed because men have quit their jobs to look for something better. There is also a hard core of "unemployable" people whose physical disabilities or lack of education cannot be fitted into the job structure. This is a kind of unemployment that can and should be relieved through generous welfare policies. Thus, economists feel that a rate of unemployment of perhaps as much as 4 percent can be reconciled with a high level of general well-being.

It is one thing to announce such a target, however, and another to achieve it. In every industrial nation the trade-off between unemployment and inflation has provided a problem that has so far defied a perfect solution; and in every industrial nation the claims of high employment have won over those of price stability. This is a problem so important that we will return to it at the end of this chapter. Before we do so, however, we must finish our first line of inquiry.

Money and Expenditure

Starting with the simple quantity theory, we have been led, step by step, into an investigation of the significant differences between a fully employed and an unemployed economy, and from there we have gone on to learn something of the causes of inflation.

But we have not yet supplied the missing link to which we referred earlier. We know now that an increase in expenditure will be inflationary only when we have a condition of reasonably full employment. What we do not know is whether an increase in the *supply of money*—say, as a result of Federal Reserve policy—will necessarily lead to a rise in the volume of expenditure. To put it differently, we have not yet asked whether in a more sophisticated version that focused on *expenditure* rather than on prices alone, the quantity theory might not be right.

After many years of neglect, the importance of the quantity of money as a powerful economic force is again beginning to be recognized by many economists. At the base of the controversy, however, is the question, how powerful?

The most persuasive advocate of the predominant influence of money is Professor Milton Friedman of the University of Chicago, whom we have previously encountered in our chapter on consumption (p. 237 n.). Friedman insists that the quantity of money is *the* critical determinant of the volume of expenditure, and he gives some interesting and dramatic evidence in support of his views.

After the Russian Revolution of 1917, as you know, there was an enormous inflation in Russia when a new currency was introduced by the new Government and printed in large quantities. It depreciated until it became almost valueless. It was a hyper-inflation. All the time, there was some currency circulating which had been issued by the pre-revolutionary Government, by the Czarist Government. The Czarist Government was out of power; nobody expected it to return to power. Yet the value of the Czarist currency remained constant in terms of goods and rose very sharply in terms of the Bolshevik currency. Why? Because there was nobody to print any more of it. It was fixed in quantity and therefore it retained its value. Another story has to do with the American Civil War. The North overran the place in the South where the Southerners had been printing paper money to finance the war. The South had to move its headquarters. In the course of doing so, it could not print any money. As a result of this interruption, prices temporarily ceased rising. I conclude that if you want to analyse the process of inflation, "Cherchez la monnaie."[1]

Anecdotes even as striking as these do not make cases. What is the causal connection between the quantity of money and the volume of expenditure? Friedman believes it lies in a stubborn tendency of households and firms to keep their hands on cash balances that have a more or less constant real purchasing power. He believes that in the United States, for example, the public as a whole tends to hold cash balances equal to about $4\frac{1}{2}$ weeks of payrolls, household bills, and other normal expenditures. Thus, if the public finds itself, because of Federal Reserve actions, with larger balances than they feel they need, there will be a strong incentive to go out and spend them. But the result of everyone doing the same thing will only drive up prices, until these higher prices have reduced the real purchasing power of existing balances to their normal level.

By no means are all economists convinced of Friedman's hypothesis. They point out that the relationship between our cash balances, M, and our

---

[1] *Inflation, Causes and Consequences* (New York: Asia Publishing House, 1963), p. 10.

expenditure, *MV,* is really only another way of describing the velocity of circulation, *V,* and they stress that we *know* that velocity changes in response to changed economic conditions. Over the long run, as we have seen in Fig. 18-2, velocity can gradually decline—or rise. In the short run, people certainly sit on money when they *expect* prices to decline, and go on spending sprees when they expect them to rise. Although impressed by Friedman's data, the skeptics remain unpersuaded by his arguments.

MONEY AND INTEREST RATES

We shall return to this controversy at the end of our chapter. Meanwhile, however, there remains another route by which changes in the quantity of money can affect expenditure, a route that is recognized by all economists. This is the influence exerted by changes in the quantity of money on the *rate of interest,* and thereby on the rate of investment spending.

How do changes in the quantity of money affect interest rates? The easiest way to understand the connection is to trace the repercussions of an action of the Federal Reserve. Suppose the Fed wishes to encourage spending and therefore buys government bonds on the open market, or expands bank reserves by lowering the reserve ratio. As a result, banks will find themselves with extra funds that can be put to use. If they lend the funds to business, that takes care of the expenditure problem right there. But suppose banks use their excess reserves to buy bonds? The result will be a rise in bond prices, as banks bid for securities, and a *fall in bond yields.* The fall in yields is the same thing as a fall in interest rates. Money is now cheaper. As a result, we remember from our chapter on investment (p. 280), business will be encouraged to increase its rate of investment.

Liquidity and Interest Rates

FINANCIAL DEMAND FOR MONEY

Our analysis has forged an important link in the chain of our argument: more money leads to lower interest rates, which lead to more expenditure. But we are not yet quite ready to call the argument complete. Before we can claim to understand the full impact that money exerts on the economy, we have to broaden our view to take in one area of activity that has so far escaped our notice. This is the world of finance.

For not all the demand for cash balances comes from businessmen who must meet payrolls or who want to invest in capital goods or inventory or from consumers who want to make purchases of goods and services. There is also a powerful source of monetary demand from investors who want to hold larger or smaller amounts of cash as part of their *financial portfolios.*

Some of these investors will be individuals who have saved or inherited wealth and who regularly invest part of that wealth in stocks and bonds, keeping the rest in bank accounts. Other investors are institutions, such as life insurance companies or mutual funds, who are doing the same thing on a much larger scale. Still others are businesses who keep part of their liquid assets invested in short-term bonds, part in cash.

How much of our $215-odd billion in money supply belongs to this financial pool? We do not really know, *because the amount constantly varies.* Individuals and firms do not make absolutely hard and fast, unchanging decisions about how much of their wealth they will keep in cash. At certain times, for safety or to be in a position to make advantageous purchases on the securities markets, investors will want to be unusually "liquid," to hold large balances in cash. At other times, for different precautionary or speculative motives, people will be content with much smaller financial balances. So, too, when conditions in the economy demand a high rate of spending—when a boom is going on, for instance—many investors, particularly companies, will operate with as small idle bank balances as possible, because they will need their cash for transactions purposes—for payrolls and other expenditures. Again, when things are slacker, financial balances may tend to grow simply because there is less need for transactions balances.

LIQUIDITY PREFERENCE

The existence of a separate financial demand for money interests us for two reasons. As we shall shortly see, the financial demand for money complicates the task of monetary management. But in addition, the existence of financial balances plays a crucial role in determining the rate of interest itself.

Perhaps we have already intuitively sensed the connection that we are about to explore. If financial holders of cash can hold larger or smaller balances at different times, it stands to reason that one powerful inducement for them to vary the size of these balances will be the rate of interest. For when interest rates are low, the *opportunity cost* of holding cash is very slight; that is, when one can only get 2 percent on a bond he passes up the opportunity to make only $20 if he does not put $1,000 cash into that bond. But when interest rates climb and the same bond is issued at 6 percent, then it costs much more—$60—to remain liquid.

This general inverse relationship between the rate of interest and the willingness to be liquid is called *liquidity preference.* The phrase simply describes the observed fact that households and companies will generally seek to hold more cash when interest rates are low and less cash when they are high. Figure 18-5 gives us a diagrammatic view of this relationship.

Exactly how much cash will the public wish to hold if interest rates are, say, 4 percent? We cannot predict unless we know what households and

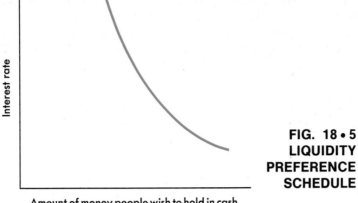

FIG. 18•5
LIQUIDITY
PREFERENCE
SCHEDULE

Amount of money people wish to hold in cash

firms expect of the future, the amount of cash they need for transactions purposes, and many other things. In other words, on two different dates, at the same interest rate, the same public might very well wish to hold two *different* amounts of cash. But we are sure that at *all* dates the public will prefer to give up liquidity when rates go up and to gain liquidity when they go down.

LIQUIDITY PREFERENCE AND INTEREST RATES

Now we must take the final step. We have seen that interest rates determine whether we wish to hold larger or smaller cash balances, given our particular preferences for liquidity. But what determines the interest rate itself? The answer is the interplay of our liquidity preferences—that is, our different desires to hold cash—and the actual amount of money that exists. To anticipate a subject we shall study in Part Four, we can think of the rate of interest as a *price* determined by the supply of money and the demand for money. The supply of money is the quantity of money as determined by the

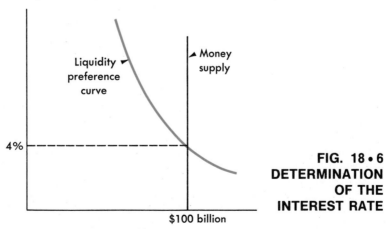

Liquidity preference curve

Money supply

4%

$100 billion

FIG. 18•6
DETERMINATION
OF THE
INTEREST RATE

Federal Reserve System. And the demand for money is nothing but the liquidity preference schedule with which we are now familiar.

A liquidity preference diagram (Fig. 18-6) will help us understand this process more clearly. In the figure, a vertical line indicates the actual supply of money (which we will call $100 billion) set by the monetary authorities. Let us also assume that the going rate of interest is 4 percent, which, as we can see, just balances the amount of money the people *want* to hold at that rate and the amount that is actually in existence.

What we see here is a market in equilibrium, in which the quantity of money that is demanded is exactly equal to the amount that is supplied. But now let us suppose that the monetary authorities want to decrease the amount of money (perhaps to stop an inflation) and that they cut member bank reserves enough to bring about a fall from $100 billion to $90 billion in the total of demand deposits. Figure 18-7 shows us the new state of affairs.

**FIG. 18 • 7
CHANGE IN
THE QUANTITY
OF MONEY**

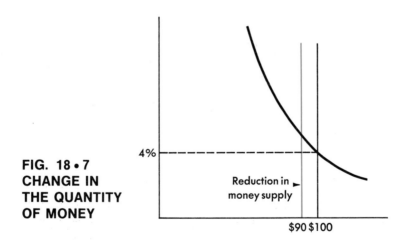

Now we no longer have a nicely balanced market, as we had before. At the going rate of 4 percent interest, people *want* to hold $100 billion in money, as our diagram shows. But there is actually only $90 billion available.

Thus households and firms want to hold more money than it is possible to hold! Of course, they do not know that. From the point of view of the public, all that has happened is that a great many investors or treasurers of firms feel that they aren't liquid enough, that their cash balances are too small. As a result, they will try to make their cash holdings bigger by selling stocks and bonds.

Now here is the important part. *Selling securities does not create a single additional dollar of money. It simply transfers money from one holder to another. But it does change the rate of interest. As the price of bonds falls, the yield on bonds rises* (see p. 370).

Now our next diagram (Fig. 18-8) shows what happens. As interest rates rise, the public is content to hold a smaller quantity of money. Hence a new interest rate, let us say 5 percent, will emerge, at which the public is *willing* to hold the $90 billion that *they have to hold*. The attempt to get more liquid ceases, and a new equilibrium interest rate prevails.

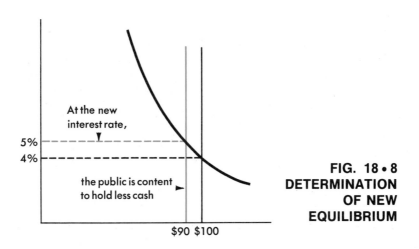

At the new
interest rate,

5%
4%

the public is content
to hold less cash

$90 $100

**FIG. 18 • 8
DETERMINATION
OF NEW
EQUILIBRIUM**

THE ARGUMENT
IN REVIEW
Now let us review once more the meaning of the process we have observed. The basic problem is to trace the way in which changes in the quantity of money can bring about changes in the rate of interest. The answer, we have seen, is that the rate of interest is determined by two elements: the position and "shape" of the liquidity preferences of the public and the quantity of money itself. By changing the quantity of money, the authorities can bring into being an amount of money larger or smaller than the public wishes to hold at the going rate of interest. Finding itself with more money (or less money) than it wishes to hold at that rate, the public will either buy bonds or other financial assets to get "out" of money, or sell bonds or other financial assets to get "into" money. In either event, the quantity of money will not change, but the price of bonds, and therefore interest rates, will.

The Art of Monetary Management

We are finally ready to put together the many pieces of the puzzle. The concept of liquidity preference has provided us with the last necessary clue to the connection between changes in the quantity of money and changes in the expenditures of the public. It remains only to consider one aspect of the money problem: the art of managing the supply of money so that the *right* increases or decreases in the supply of money will be forthcoming at the right time.

Why "art"? Is not the task of the monetary authority very clear by now? By increasing the quantity of money, it pushes down interest rates. By pushing down interest rates, it encourages investment expenditure. Hence, all it needs to do is to regulate the quantity of money so that investment expenditure proceeds at just the pace we need to keep a high, but not too high, level of employment.

SHIFTING
LIQUIDITY
PREFERENCES

Unfortunately, things are not quite that mechanical. Suppose, for example, that the Federal Reserve creates excess reserves, in the expectation that interest rates will go down and that new loans will be pumped into investment. But suppose that at the same time, the public's liquidity preferences are rising because investors feel nervous and want to be more liquid. Then the shift in the quantity of money, as shown in Fig. 18-9, will be offset by a shift in liquidity preferences, and the rate of interest will not change at all! The new money will simply wind up in larger financial cash holdings.

**FIG. 18 • 9
A SHIFT IN
LIQUIDITY
PREFERENCE**

Increase in money supply

Rise in liquidity preference

Unchanged interest rates

In other words, an attempt by the monetary authorities to drive down the rate of interest in order to encourage investment may be frustrated if the public uses all the additional funds for liquidity and not for expenditure. At the bottom of the Great Depression, for example, banks had huge excess reserves because businessmen would not risk expenditure for new capital projects. People had an insatiable desire for liquidity, and no attempted reductions of the rate of interest could persuade them to transfer money held for "security" into active expenditures.

In the same way, an attempt to raise interest rates and to halt price inflation by making credit tight may come to naught if the public reacts to higher interest rates by giving up its liquidity, thereby making funds available to others to finance increased transactions expenditure. Or take another instance: if the Fed tries to lower interest rates by increasing *M*, the effort may result in a general expectation of inflation and a movement out of bonds into stocks. In that case, interest rates, instead of falling, will go up! This actually happened in 1968.

We can see, then, that it is not easy to bring about a desired change in *expenditure*—or even in interest rates—through a change in money supply alone. For this reason, few economists today would rely solely on the power of monetary measures to move the general economy; instead, they seek a combination of monetary and fiscal policies—easy money and more government spending or tight money and a public budgetary surplus.

The Inflationary Phenomenon

Yet the last years of the 1960s and the opening years of the 1970s have proved a disconcerting period for economists. For despite fiscal and monetary measures designed to curb inflation, the rise in the price level has seemed as unstoppable as an incoming tide. Although all components do

FIG. 18 • 10   PRICE INDEX, 1965–1970

Source: Department of Labor

Council of Economic Advisers

not always rise and fall together (note the different behavior of services and food in Fig. 18-10), the price index has risen in the face of "tighter" money and efforts to curtail spending.

Before we attempt to explain this perplexing phenomenon, one important fact should be noted. It is that the American experience with inflation is by no means unique. On the contrary, as Table 18-1 shows, inflation is a worldwide disease among industrialized countries (and among the unindustrialized ones, too, although for somewhat different reasons).

TABLE 18 • 1

WORLDWIDE INFLATION

FALL IN THE VALUE OF MONEY IN INDUSTRIALIZED COUNTRIES		
Average annual percentage of decline		
1959–69	1968–69	1969–70
United States	2.2	5.1	5.7
Australia	2.4	2.8	3.1
Canada	2.4	4.3	4.0
France	3.7	5.7	5.4
Italy	3.6	2.5	3.7
Japan	5.0	4.9	7.5
Sweden	3.7	2.6	5.8
Switzerland	3.0	2.5	2.5
United Kingdom	3.4	5.1	5.3
West Germany	2.4	2.6	3.6

Source: First National City Bank, *Monthly Economic Letter* (September 1970).

What lies behind this worldwide decline in the buying power of national monetary units? Unlike a "worldwide" inflation that occurred in the sixteenth century (actually confined to a few European countries), the general rise in prices cannot be traced to discoveries of vast new quantities of gold and silver, such as those that poured into the Spanish treasuries following the conquest of Mexico and Peru. Rather, the cause of the contemporary truly worldwide inflation must be sought in *institutional changes* sufficiently great in magnitude and far-reaching in effect to have touched every nation from the largest and most powerful to the smallest and weakest.

What are these institutional changes? Looking at the developments of the postwar world, we can hazard the hypothesis that there are probably three:

1. *The concentration of economic power among both labor unions and corporations has increased.*

Before World War II, wage *cuts* were by no means an uncommon phenomenon, and corporate price wars, although waning, still exercised their sharp disciplinary effect. But since the 1950s, wages and corporate prices both have displayed a "rachet effect": both go up, but neither can come down. This is the result of the much greater power of industrial unions, coupled with the ability of oligopolistic industries to pass the costs of higher wages along through higher prices, especially in an expansionary setting.

2. *Government now plays an expansionist economic role.*

Again the contrast to pre-World War II is striking. Then, the role of government in virtually all industrialized nations was small and essentially passive. The idea of expansionary financing was unknown, and the philosophy of "guided capitalism" (see Chapter 9) was still unformulated. Today, in every industrial nation, government has assumed (or has had thrust upon it) the responsibility for maintaining reasonably full employment and fairly rapid economic growth. The result has been an expansionary atmosphere in which the economy has naturally tended to run up against the barriers of production capacity.

3. *A change in affluence and expectations.*

Last, we must notice a change in the point of view of the average person with regard to his economic security. Before World War II, few nations had Social Security, retirement pensions, family allowances, welfare, health insurance, or other government-financed forms of personal security. Since World War II, these are to be found in all industrialized nations, often on a much more liberal scale than in the United States. The result has been a rise in the economic freedom of working people—including the freedom to go on strike. The sheer pressure of need no longer operates to deter men from risking a strike for higher wages. And the atmosphere of growth—indeed the propaganda for growth—encourages men to seek to improve their living standards as rapidly as possible.

PRICE AND WAGE GUIDELINES The expectations of businessmen have also contributed to the problem. Before World War II, investment decisions were made cautiously, in the knowledge that a recession could descend at any time. Since 1946, businessmen feel that government has ruled out recessions, except as mild antidotes for too much inflation. The unpleasant fact remains, however, that real living standards cannot be increased more rapidly than the real output of goods permits; and that whenever the total disposable income received by the public rises more rapidly than the output of goods and services, inflation is virtually bound to result. Part of the inflationary dilemma in the industrialized countries is certainly traceable to this kind of "cost-push" inflation, in which—to take a particularly egregious example—the wages of construction workers may rise by 19 percent in one year (1970), while their trade unions demand further increases of 50 percent over the succeeding three years.*

Can we control the pressure by keeping the rise in incomes in pace with the rise in output? Every major government has tried to institute such a "incomes policy" since World War II—with scant results. In the United States, for example, the Kennedy Administration inaugurated the idea of "wage-price guidelines" that were intended to serve as an official index of productivity, to which it was hoped labor leaders would conform their demands. But the wage-price guidelines allowed for increases of only about 3.4 percent per year and were not very effective. Some unions whose productivity had gone up more rapidly than 3.4 percent claimed that they had the *right* to higher wages; other unions simply ignored the guidelines; and most companies only tried halfheartedly to stick by them in wage bargaining sessions because they counted on inflation itself to help them pass along any cost increases in higher prices.

Another tactic used by subsequent administrations was called "jawboning." This was simply the use of public pressure, usually through Presidential statements, to get companies (or less frequently unions) to scale down price increases. For instance in 1971, Bethlehem Steel suddenly announced that it was about to raise steel prices by 12 percent. Angry comments from the White House, coupled with stories carefully leaked to the newspapers about the possibility of relaxing steel import quotas, brought the welcome response of a much smaller (6 percent) increase from Bethlehem's main competitors. In the end, Bethlehem had to back down to the 6 percent mark.

Still, 6 percent is a stiff price increase. Hence more and more pressure has built up for the imposition of direct controls over wages and prices.†

The problem with controls is that they are administratively clumsy, hard to enforce, and almost invariably evaded in one way or another. A wage and price freeze always catches someone at a disadvantage: a union that was just about to sign an advantageous but perhaps deserved contract, a store whose prices were at "sale" levels on the day that the freeze is announced, a business whose costs increase as a result of a rise in the prices of imported goods. Thus price controls lead to endless adjustment and adjudication. Moreover, unless there is a general sentiment of patriotic "pulling together," (as during World War II or the Korean war, when controls were fairly successful in repressing inflation), controls tend to lead to black or gray markets or to downgrading the quality of the "same" goods

WAGE AND PRICE CONTROLS

---

* In all fairness we should note that construction workers are paid by the hour, and their high hourly rates do not necessarily add up to a high yearly income. A program to regularize yearly incomes of construction and other hourly workers would be a great step forward in inflation control.

† As this book goes to press, a temporary voluntary freeze has been placed on wages and prices.

that are sold at fixed prices. When we study the market mechanism in Chapter 22 we will understand more fully why a price-fixed market is hard to control, but the general problem is not difficult to understand: *unless higher taxes are imposed along with wage and price controls, spendable incomes will exceed the value of output, and the scramble for goods will either cause prices to break through controls or will require rationing.*

INFLATION AS A TAX

Permanent wage and price controls are not solutions that can be lightly imposed. Hence, the probabilities are that this country, like all industrialized nations, will try to impose milder restraints, probably leaning heavily on the willingness of major unions and companies to abide by some form of wage-price guideline. This will no doubt be accompanied by pronouncements designed to break the back of the prevailing inflationary psychology and to pave the way for a climate in which voluntary restraints and even higher taxes become acceptable, simply because they are preferred to long-lasting controls.

Given the political and psychological problems of imposing effective controls, most economists agree that some degree of inflation is likely to be endemic for a very long period of time. How serious an outlook is this? The answer depends on the relative costs we ascribe to unemployment on the one hand and to the damage done by inflation on the other. But what *is* the damage done by inflation? Essentially it consists of a forced *redistribution of income,* from those whose incomes are laggard (recipients of fixed pensions or Social Security, for example) to those whose incomes are dynamic, such as strategically located union members or profit-makers. Inflation thus becomes a kind of tax on the relatively less "aggressive" elements of society, levied by those who are in a position to demand and to get a disproportionate share of national expenditure.

This is an unpleasant, but not a necessarily disastrous price. A decline in the value of a dollar may not be nearly as destructive as unemployment is to society and to the individual's sense of personal worth. In both cases, the damage can be mitigated; for unemployment: more liberal unemployment compensation and more effective retraining policies; for inflation: efforts to keep Social Security or welfare payments (the most important sources of fixed income) at "parity." But there is also a second danger to be faced in both unemployment and inflation. It is the danger of a crisis of confidence—in the first instance leading to a massive collapse of investment, in the second to the loss of faith in the long-term stability of the currency. The second could lead to a rush into foolish investments or even a wild flight from the currency.*

* True runaway inflations, such as those that occurred in post-World War I Germany or in China or Hungary after World War II, cannot really be discussed in the same terms that we use to analyze ordinary inflations. Hyperinflations destroy public faith in the monetary unit and culminate in complete breakdowns of the monetary system and productive economic activity. The only cure for such social tragedy is the constitution of a new monetary unit in which public belief will once again reside.

For these ultimate disasters there is no remedy but firm government action—powerful intervention to offset a recession; equally powerful intervention via price and wage controls, no matter how awkward, to stop an inflationary panic. Indeed one of the services that a study of macroeconomics can render is to make important elements of the public economically sophisticated enough to understand the societal risks that both inflation and unemployment present, the difficulties of coping easily with either, and the need for bold action if the situation should threaten to get out of hand.

KEY CONCEPTS AND KEY WORDS

1. *The quantity equation, MV = PT, is actually a truism,* saying that expenditure *(MV)* equals receipts *(PT).* It was originally intended as a causal statement saying that an increase in the supply of money leads to higher prices.

   Money supply

   Quantity equation

   Quantity theory

2. This statement would be true only if *V* and *T* were fixed. In fact, *V is capable of considerable change* as businessmen and investors revise their attitudes about spending or holding cash balances.

   Velocity of circulation

3. Even more important, we find that *changes in the level of output are very marked* over the long run. This is contrary to the expectations of the early quantity theorists that the economy would always operate at full employment.

4. When a competitive economy is operating at less than full employment, an increase in the quantity of money (really in the volume of expenditure) leads to a rise in output rather than prices. *This distinction between the effects of additional expenditure, private or public, at full employment and underemployment, is one of the central conceptions of modern macroeconomics.*

   Full vs. underemployment

5. The distinction is blurred in practice because *bottlenecks and differentials in productivity that bring rising prices before full employment is reached.* The choice between high employment and a rising price level, symbolized in a Phillips curve, is one of the most difficult that monetary and fiscal authorities must face.

   Bottlenecks

   Phillips curve

6. We need a growing money supply to permit economic expansion in a world of *sticky prices.*

   Sticky prices

7. Increases or decreases in the supply of money exert their effect on *expenditures* in two different ways. One way may be through the desire of the public to hold cash balances that represent a more or less fixed amount of real purchasing power. The other way is through *the effect of changes in the quantity of money on interest rates.*

8. The quantity of money affects the rate of interest by its interaction with the *liquidity preferences* of the public. *Liquidity preference* means the willingness of firms and households to hold smaller cash balances when interest rates are high, and their desire

   Liquidity preference

to hold larger balances when rates are low. Thus, *the rate of interest is the price that balances the money holders' desire for liquidity with the opportunities for earning interest by surrendering their cash for securities.*

9. *Liquidity preferences* can complicate the job of monetary management by absorbing into financial balances cash that was intended to find its way into the transactions balances of the economy, or by supplying cash for transactions when the authorities wish to contact the availability of credit.

10. *Fiscal and monetary policy usually work side by side, each requiring the other.* Fiscal policy needs easy money to be effective in combating recessions, and tight monetary policies directed against inflation require fiscal stringency if they are to be effective.

11. The presence of *worldwide* inflation since World War II argues that institutional changes have made modern economic society more inflation-prone than it used to be. Increased *economic power,* increased individual *financial security,* and *expansionary government policies* may be the ultimate causes of this phenomenon.

12. *Wage and price guidelines or controls* are difficult to impose and administer, but they may be weapons of ultimate resort if inflation persists.

Q U E S T I O N S

1. Why is the quantity equation a truism? Why is the interpretation of the quantity equation that M affects P not a truism?

2. Suppose you are paid $140 a week and you put it in the bank. On each of the seven days of the week, you spend one-seventh of this sum. What is your average balance during the week? Now suppose that you spend the whole sum on the first day of the week. Will your average balance be the same? What is the relation between velocity of circulation and size of average balances?

3. What considerations might lead you, as a businessman, to carry higher cash balances? Could these considerations change rapidly?

4. The basic reason why the original quantity theorists thought that M affected P was their belief that V and T were fixed. Discuss the validity of this belief.

5. Why is the level of employment the critical determinant of fiscal policy?

6. If employment is "full," what will be the effects of an increase in private investment, supposing that everything else stays the same?

7. In what way can an increase in excess reserves affect V or T? Is there any certainty that an increase in reserves will lead to an increase in V or T?

8. Suppose that you had $1,000 in the bank. Would you be more willing to invest it if you could earn 2 percent or 5 percent? What factors could make you change your mind about investing all or any part at, say, 5 percent? Could you imagine conditions that would make you unwilling to invest even at 7 percent? Other conditions that would lead you to invest your whole cash balance at, say, 3 percent?

9. Suppose that the going rate of interest is 4 percent and that the monetary authorities want to curb expenditures and act to lower the quantity of money. What will the effect be in terms of the public's feeling of liquidity? What will the public do if it feels short of cash? Will it buy or sell securities? What would this do to their price? What would thereupon happen to the rate of interest? To investment expenditures?

10. Suppose that the monetary and fiscal authorities want to encourage economic expansion. What are the general measures that each should take? What problems might liquidity preference interpose?

11. If we have a price creep of 3 percent a year at 5 percent unemployment, what would you counsel as a proper economic policy?

12. Suppose the rate of inflation now rises to 8 percent a year and unemployment remains at about 5 percent. What policies would you now recommend?

13. Can you identify the social or economic groups or both who are most hurt by inflation? By unemployment?

14. What would you recommend as the criteria for a "fair" incomes policy?

We have reached a point in our investigations where we can now understand the forces that give rise to the flow of production. To that extent we have completed one long stage of our journey into macroeconomics. But our travel is not yet complete. We have concerned ourselves heretofore almost entirely with output in real or money terms, but we have somewhat thoroughly disregarded one crucial aspect of the real world: employment. In other words, we may now be able to give a general answer to the question of how GNP is determined, but we cannot as yet answer the equally important query: how is employment determined? How many people will be employed if GNP is of such-and-such a size? What are the forces that work for more or for less employment? Until we can come to grips with these problems, we have not fully answered the very questions that impelled us originally on our investigation.

Employment in Perspective

As before, let us begin by acquainting ourselves with the historical dimensions of the problem. In Figure 19-1, we see the main variables of the employment process—the total labor force and the total *civilian* labor force (members of the armed forces constituting the difference), total employment and its complement, unemployment.

Our attention is naturally drawn at first to the orange area that depicts the profile of unemployment. But we cannot discuss this aspect of the employment problem until we have looked into a more fundamental question: what determines the size of the total labor force itself, the size of the fraction of the population that is actively looking for work? For clearly, the volume of unemployment will depend, at least in part, on how many of a given population *want* to work.

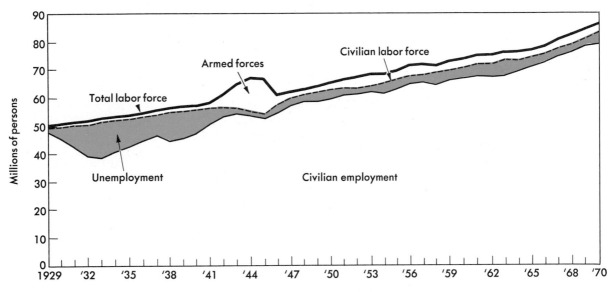

FIG. 19•1   UNITED STATES' LABOR FORCE, 1929–1970

What percent of the American population does want to work? The answer, in round numbers, is about 60 out of every 100 persons over the age of 14. In itself, this fact does not mean very much. But suppose we now ask: is this fraction of the population growing or shrinking? Do more people or fewer people seek work today than, say, in 1890 or 1900? What is the outlook for the year 2000?

Here the answer is surprising. One would expect, perhaps, that as a society grows richer and more affluent, fewer people would seek employment. But that is not the case. Looking back to 1890 or 1900, we find that only 52 out of every 100 persons over 14 sought work. Looking forward is more uncertain; but if we can extrapolate (extend) the trend of the past

PARTICIPATION IN THE LABOR FORCE

several decades to the year 2000, we can expect perhaps as many as 65 persons out of 100 to be in the labor market by that date.

How can we explain this curious upward drift of the labor force itself? The answer is to be found in an examination of the different labor participation trends of different ages and different sexes. Figure 19-2 shows this very clearly.

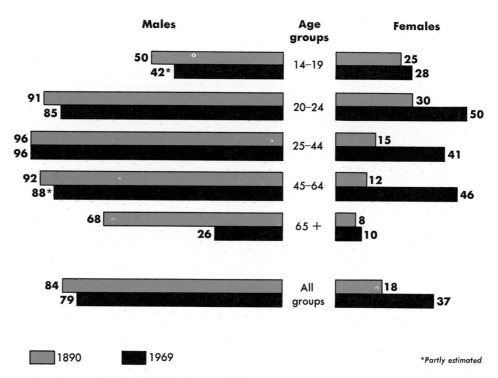

FIG. 19 • 2   PARTICIPATION RATES

Note that the overall trend toward a larger participation rate for the entire population masks a number of significant trends.

1. *Young males entering the labor force are older than those who entered in the past.*

A larger number of young men remain in high school now or go on to college, a trend that will certainly increase. Only a third of elementary school pupils now go on to college, but the ratio is steadily growing.

2. *Older males show a dramatic withdrawal from the labor force.*

The reason is the advent of Social Security and private pension plans. It is probable that the proportion of older males in the labor force will continue to fall as the retirement age is slowly reduced and as some still unprotected occupations come under Social Security or private pension arrangements.

3. *Counterbalancing this fall in male participation is a spectacular rise in total female participation. Indeed, the overall trend toward an increasing search for work within the population at large is entirely the result of the mass entrance of women into the labor force.*

This surge of women into the labor market reflects several changing factors in the American scene (many of which, incidentally, can be found abroad as well). One of these is the growth of nonmanual, as contrasted with manual, jobs. Another is the widening cultural approval of working women and working wives—it is the amazing fact that the average American girl who marries today in her early twenties and goes on to raise a family will nevertheless spend twenty-five years of her life in paid employment after her children are grown. Yet another reason for the influx of women is that technology has released them from household work. And not least is the pressure to raise living standards by having two incomes within the household.

Actually, we must view the growing number of females in the labor force as part of a very old economic phenomenon whose roots we traced back to the Middle Ages—the monetization of work. For the upward trend of female participation does not imply an increasing amount of labor performed within society. Rather, it measures a larger amount of *paid* labor. In the 1890s, many persons worked long and hard hours on a family farm or in a family enterprise, and above all within a household, *without getting paid* and, therefore, were not counted as members of the "labor force." To a very considerable extent, the rising numbers of female participants in the labor force mirror the transfer of these unpaid jobs onto the marketplace where the same labor is now performed in an economically visible way. There is every likelihood this process will continue.

These are not, of course, the only factors that bear on the fundamental question of how many persons will seek work out of a given population. The drift from country to city, the decline in the number of hours of labor per day expected of a jobholder, the general lengthening of life, the growth of general well-being—all these changes bear on the decision to work or not. Over all, what the complex trends seem to show is that we are moving in the direction of a society where employment absorbs a larger fraction of the life (but not of the day) of an average woman, and a diminishing fraction of the life and of the day of an average man.

These trends indicate the direction of persistent, albeit slow-moving, main currents within the total fraction of the population that seeks work. But when we concern ourselves with employment or unemployment on a year-to-year basis, we must also take heed of short-run shifts in and out of

SHORT-RUN
CHANGES

the active labor force. That is, while the decade-to-decade percentages reveal the gradual changes we have discussed, the proportion of the population actively seeking work from one year to the next, particularly the proportion of young people or women, may vary sharply. In Table 19-1, we can see how the labor force evidences these short-run expansions and contractions.

TABLE 19 • 1

LABOR FORCE
1964–1970

		SHORT-RUN CHANGES (IN MILLIONS)					
	1964	1965	1966	1967	1968	1969	1970
Number in civilian labor force	73.1	74.5	75.8	77.3	78.7	80.7	82.7
Civilian employment	69.3	71.1	72.9	74.4	75.9	77.9	78.6
Unemployment	3.8	3.4	2.9	3.0	2.8	2.8	4.1

Notice that between 1969 and 1970, employment and unemployment *both* rose. One would think that as employment rose, unemployment would fall! Yet the same phenomenon appeared between 1966 and 1967. How can this be?

The answer to the apparent paradox lies in the short-run responsiveness or *income-elasticity,* of the labor supply. In good times when jobs are plentiful, more youths and women will seek work. The whole labor force will then temporarily expand; and since not all of it may find work, both employment and unemployment may show increases. The reverse is true in a year of recession. What happens then is that many will be discouraged by bad times and "withdraw" from the labor force, remaining in school or in the household. As a result, the number of unemployed will then be smaller than if the larger labor force of a boom year had continued actively looking for work.

MEANING OF
UNEMPLOYMENT

The concept of a variable participation rate (or an elastic supply) for labor in the short run helps to elucidate for us a term with which we shall be much involved in this chapter: unemployment.

Clearly, unemployment is not a static condition, but one that varies with the participation rate itself. Technically, the measure of unemployment is determined by a household-to-household survey conducted each month by the Bureau of the Census among a carefully selected sample. An "unemployed" person is thereupon defined not merely as a person without a job— for perhaps such a person does not *want* a job—but as someone who is "actively" seeking work but is "unable" to find it. Since, however, the number of people who will be seeking work will rise in good times and fall in bad times, figures for any given period must be viewed with caution. A relatively low unemployment rate *may* mean only that general discouragement has driven many job seekers from the search for work. Similarly, a tendency for the unemployment rate to remain relatively steady as employment rises may testify only to an increased number of persons who have been attracted into the labor force.

These cautions by no means invalidate the concept of unemployment; but they warn us against assuming that in measuring unemployment over time, we are measuring variations in a fixed quantity. An economist first looks at the labor participation figures and then at the unemployment rates before he judges the seriousness of the situation.

Shifting Demands for Labor

What we have studied thus far are the forces that determine the supply of labor—that is, the number of persons who will be looking for a job at any time. But the problem of employment and unemployment is not decided just from the supply side. Now we must add the demand side of the equation.

From the first circular flow diagram, nine chapters ago, up to the beginning of this one, we have constantly been concerned with demand, mainly *aggregate demand* or the total demand generated by the sum of all spending in the economy. Historically, most of the social ills of unemployment can be put on the doorstep of an inadequate aggregate demand—that is, of a level of expenditure not high enough to give jobs to all who want them.

Shortly, we will discuss the relation of aggregate demand to employment. But first we must put the force of "total spending" into perspective by viewing it in the context of an economy whose pursuits are constantly changing and which therefore constantly alters the structure within which spending is generated. This brings us back to the concerns of Chapter 6, where we have already seen how the industrialization of the economy gradually but profoundly altered the location and nature of work.

A glance at Table 19-2 gives added meaning to this shift in the job

PERCENT DISTRIBUTION OF ALL EMPLOYED WORKERS		
	1900	1970
Agriculture, forests, and fisheries	38.1	4.5
Manufacturing, mining, transportation, construction, utilities	37.7	35.1
Trade, government, finance, professional and personal services*	24.2	60.4

TABLE 19•2

DISTRIBUTION OF EMPLOYMENT

Source: Calculated from *Historical Statistics*, p. 74; also from *Statistical Abstract*, 1970, pp. 213, 218.

* It is customary to include transportation and utilities among the third, or service, area of activities. In this analysis, however, we group them with goods-producing or goods-handling activities, to highlight the drift into "purely" service occupations. Since domestic servants, proprietors, and the self-employed are omitted (owing to inadequate statistics), the table under-represents the labor force in the service and trade sector.

structure, for it is apparent that a pervasive transformation has occurred in the composition of the aggregate demand of society. An economy principally concerned with wresting goods from nature and then transforming them, or transporting them, has become increasingly a society concerned with selling or administering the activities of the relatively dwindling proportion who obtain, or fashion, or carry material wealth.

What accounts for this enormous change in the nature of the productive activity of society? Mainly, we can account for it by the interaction of two factors: technology and the changing demand for goods and services.

Underlying the great migration from "primary" occupations (farming, fishing, etc.) through "secondary" ones (manufacturing, etc.) into the "tertiary" service trades lies the impelling force of technology. Without the productive capacity given us by a technology, this migration could not have taken place. In the agricultural and the manufacturing-mining-transporting-power fields we have experienced a startling increase in productivity, so that a dwindling manpower base in those fields can adequately provide the products needed by society.

Agriculture presents, of course, the most extreme example of the power of technology to enhance productivity. Between 1880 and today, for instance, the time required to harvest one acre of wheat on the Great Plains has fallen from twenty hours to three. Just between the late 1930s and the mid-1960s, the manhours required to obtain a hundredweight of milk were slashed from 3.4 to 0.9; a hundredweight of chickens, from 8.5 to 0.6. Not quite so dramatic but also far-reaching in their effect have been technological improvements in other areas. Table 19-3 shows the increase in productivity in five important activities over just two decades.

TABLE 19•3

INDEX OF OUTPUT PER MAN-HOUR FOR PRODUCTION WORKERS

Industry	1950	1968
Coal mining	100	278
Railroad transportation	100	258
Steel	100	145
Paper and pulp	100	192 (1967)
Petroleum refining	100	271 (1967)

Source: Calculated from *Statistical Abstract*, 1968, p. 230.

Finally, by way of contrast to the very great degree of technological advance in the primary and secondary occupation sectors, we must note the laggard advance in productivity in the tertiary sector of activity. Output per man-hour in trade, for instance, or in education or in the service professions such as law or medicine or, again, in domestic or personal services such as barbering or repair work or in government has not increased nearly so much as in the primary and secondary sectors.*

In the previous chapter, we noticed the inflationary consequences of this lag. Now we note the *uneven entry* of technology to be one main cause behind the overall migration of employment that we have discovered. Had we not enjoyed the enormous technical improvements in agriculture or mass production, but instead discovered vastly superior techniques of government services (in the sense of increasing the manhour output of, say, policemen or firemen or teachers), the distribution of employment might look very different. We shall return to this point when we discuss the question of automation. At the moment, we need only accept the unequal efficiencies of technology in the various sectors of economic activity as constituting one main cause for the change in employment patterns.

The differential rates of progress of technology are not, however, by themselves enough to explain the shift in employment. The fact that each farmer has become enormously more productive than his grandfather does not explain the decline of farm employment, nor does the enhancement of manufacturing and goods-handling productivity explain the stability of the employment ratios of these sectors. To account for the impact of technology on employment we must link the changes in productivity with the nature of the demand for the products emanating from these various industries and activities.

We can see this shift in demand in Table 19-4, showing the division of national income among the three main sectors and their components.†

What we see here is a shift working in a direction different from the impetus of technology. Note that as productivity has increased in agriculture, demand for the products of agriculture has *fallen* as a percent of total national expenditure. In technical language, the demand for food products was not "income-elastic"; that is, it did not rise proportionally with the rise in income. The result of this confrontation of a high-powered technology by a low-powered demand was a squeeze on employment. If the existing labor force in agriculture were equipped with the more productive techniques, the consequence would be a torrent of output that would far surpass the

INFLUENCE
OF DEMAND

---

* It is only proper to note that we cannot measure productivity of output in the service sector nearly so unambiguously as in the goods sector, and there is no doubt that the *quality* of many services has increased substantially. Compare, for example, the "productivity" of a surgeon operating for appendicitis in 1900, 1930, and 1960. On the other hand, insofar as we are interested in the effect of technology in increasing the saleable output of work, there seems little doubt of its considerable superiority in the goods-producing branches of the economy.

† The figures actually show the *income originating in these sectors.* But we know from our macroeconomic studies that this income must have been produced by the expenditures—the demand—of society as it was distributed among the sectors.

TABLE 19•4

DOMESTIC
DEMAND
FOR OUTPUT

PERCENTAGE DISTRIBUTION OF NATIONAL INCOME			
	1899–1908		1969
Primary sector (agriculture)	**16.7**		**3.1**
Secondary sector	**36.7**		**44.2**
Mining		3.1	0.9
Manufacturing		18.4	29.8
Construction		4.5	5.6
Transportation, communication, and public utilities		10.7	7.9
Tertiary sector	**46.5**		**53.6**
Trade		15.3	15.8
Miscellaneous services		9.6	12.1
Government		5.6	14.7
Finance and other		16.0	11.0

Source: *Historical Statistics,* Series F34–43; *Statistical Abstract,* 1970, p. 317. Breakdown partly estimated. Totals do not add, owing to rounding.

demand of the market. Instead, the new technology was utilized to permit a smaller labor force to fulfill demand, while the now redundant farm labor was forced to look elsewhere for employment.

Where did it go? In part, it was directed by the shift of both technology and demand to the secondary sector. Farmers, moving to factory towns, produced trucks and tractors, thereby transferring some agricultural tasks to manufacturing. Meanwhile, as incomes rose, purchasing power that was not required for food products turned to the purchase of manufactured goods, homes, power, communication, and other things. The result was that employment was steady in this sector, as Table 19-2 shows. More important, however, by way of its employment-offering effects, was the rise of the "tertiary" occupations. Here an elastic demand for services of various kinds and an absence of revolutionary labor-saving techniques permitted employment to increase very rapidly.

EVOLUTION
OF DEMAND

What we seem to be witnessing, in these shifts, is a natural "evolution" of demand in an increasingly affluent and industrialized society. Demand appears to pass from an initial concentration on the products of the earth, to and through a focus on the products of manufacture, toward a "highest" stage, where it fastens on the enjoyment of the personal services made possible by a highly productive society and on the increased need to administer the internal affairs of a complex industrial mechanism. Thus we should note that the shift in employment visible in Table 19-2, already striking enough, would be made even more so, were we to transfer the growing "service" (i.e., administration and nonproduction) component in the secondary sector to the tertiary sector. In manufacturing alone, between 1950 and 1969, the nonproduction work force grew from 18 to 27 percent of total employees.

What light does this discussion of the demand for labor shed on our original inquiry into the problem of overall employment? The conclusion points up the *importance of the shift in demand from less labor-requiring tasks to more labor-requiring tasks.* Had consumers not evinced a desire for the relatively more labor-using manufactures and highly labor-intensive services, the total labor time required to provision society would have been considerably less. We would then have become an economy that mainly produced agricultural goods very efficiently—that is, with relatively little labor input—and one that had but few "demands" for labor in other occupations.

Such a society would not necessarily suffer high unemployment. It could use its agricultural productivity, in the absence of other wants, to reduce the work week drastically; and by distributing the remaining quota of necessary work among its population, it could still give employment to all who sought it. Its standard of living, would of course, be no higher than the amount of agricultural produce it would then bring forth, but this would be a voluntarily chosen standard that accorded leisure a higher value than the nonagricultural goods and services that might have been produced.

It need hardly be said that the United States is not such a society. As our productivity in primary products has confronted the stone wall of our inelastic demand for primary products, we have shifted both our wants and our labor power into the secondary and tertiary sectors. Nonetheless, so great has been the rise in productivity in primary and secondary sectors that we have also been able to cut back our work week from sixty to forty hours. In other words, we have absorbed the employment-displacing effect of technology not only by shifting our demands, but *by substituting leisure for work.*

The conclusion, then, is that the demand for labor reflects the interplay of technology (which exerts differing leverages on different industries and occupations at different times) and of the changing demand for goods and services. Typically, the entrance of technology into industry has a twofold effect. The first is to raise the *potential* output of the industry, with its present labor force. The second is to enable the costs of the industry to decline, or its quality to improve, so that actual demand for the product will increase. But normally, the rise in demand is not great enough to enable the existing labor force to be retained along with the new techniques. Instead, some labor is displaced and must now find its employment elsewhere.

There are exceptions, of course. A great new industry, such as the automobile industry in the 1920s, will keep on expanding its labor force despite improved technology, for in such cases demand *is* sufficiently strong to absorb the output of the new technology, even with a growing labor force. Then too, there is the exception of capital-saving technology, making it possible for an industry to turn out the same product with a cheaper capital equipment, thereby making it attractive to expand production and to hire more labor.

But taking all industries and all technological changes together, the net result is unambiguous. As Table 19-5 reveals, technology has steadily increased our ability to create goods, both on the farm and on the factory floor, more rapidly than we have wished to consume them, with the result that employment in these areas has lagged behind output.

TABLE 19 • 5

OUTPUT AND EMPLOYMENT INDICES

AGRICULTURE AND MANUFACTURING: 1950 = 100		
	1950	1970
Manufacturing output	100	226
Manufacturing employment	100	116
Agricultural output	100	147 (1969)
Agricultural employment	100	50 (1969)

Note how agricultural output has increased by almost 50 percent in this period, in part because of the needs of a rapidly growing population, while

TABLE 19 • 6

NONFARM EMPLOYMENT 1950, 1970

	1950	1970	Percent increase 1950–1970
	(in millions)		
Secondary sector			
Mining, manufacturing, construction, transportation, communication, and public utilities	**22.4**	**27.9**	**25%**
Tertiary sector*			
Trade	9.4	14.8	57
Services	5.4	11.4	110
Government	6.0	12.8	113
Finance and other	1.9	3.7	95
Total tertiary sector	**22.7**	**42.7**	**94**

* Omits household and self-employed workers.

agricultural employment has shrunk by 50 percent; and notice that whereas manufacturing output has more than doubled, employment in manufacturing is up by only 16 percent.

During this same period, however, our total civilian labor force increased by 20 million. Where did these millions find employment? As we would expect, largely in the service sector.* Actual totals for employment in various parts of the economy appear in Table 19-6.

The Generation of Employment

We have seen how the long-run employment trends reflect slow-moving changes in the supply and demand for labor, and we have had a glimpse of some of the problems these forces may create. Yet all this has seemed somehow at a considerable remove from the problems of saving and investment and credit creation that have absorbed us in the earlier chapters of this book. How can we now connect the supply and demand for labor with the fluctuations in aggregate expenditure and output that have served as our focus of attention heretofore?

Let us begin, as so often before, at the simplest possible starting point, an imaginary economy uncluttered by many of the complicating factors of real life, such as changing technology or tastes. Then it is easy to trace the cause of changes in employment. They must be the result of changes in GNP—that is, of changes in expenditure. In turn, we can trace these changes to our familiar basic motive forces: fluctuations in investment spending or in government spending (or on rare occasions to spontaneous changes in consumer spending).

In point of fact, even with technology and all other complexities added

TABLE 19•7

PERCENTAGE DISTRIBUTION OF EMPLOYMENT

	Farms	Manufacturing	Services
France, 1950	35%	45%	20%
France, 1968	17	39	44
West Germany, 1950	24	48	28
West Germany, 1968	10	48	42
Britain, 1950	6	56	39
Britain, 1967	4	45	50

Source: OECD, *Basic Statistics of the Community*. Figures may not total 100, owing to rounding.

* Note that the employment shift from agriculture "through" manufacturing is by no means limited to the United States. As Table 19-7 shows, it seems to be visible in all industrialized nations.

back in, the volume of spending is *still* the single most important determinant of employment. With the exception of only the war years, with their special demands on manpower, in every year from 1929 to the present, when GNP has risen, employment has also risen; and in every year that GNP has declined, employment has followed suit.

But the impact of spending on *unemployment* is not quite so simple as this overall correlation of employment might suggest. We have already seen that short-run changes in GNP will bring about short-run changes in the labor participation rate, so that rising GNP can produce both more jobs *and* more unemployment. In the same way, a declining GNP will discourage participation and thereby "abolish" some unemployment by causing people to withdraw from the job market. During the 1960s, as we saw in Table 19-1, *unemployment and employment and GNP* all rose from 1962 to 1963 and again from 1966 to 1967.

AGE GROUPS IRREGULARLY DISTRIBUTED

Another reason why changes in spending may not be mirrored by changes in unemployment is that the age groupings of the population are not always the same. In some years there will be relatively more job seekers than in other years, with the result that a given increase in spending will leave more unemployed at some times than at others.

This has considerable relevance for the years ahead. Fifteen million workers will be added to our labor force during the decade of the 1970s, and a disproportionate amount of them will be young adults. The young job-seeker group will grow by *50 percent* in the next decade, compared with only 16 percent in the decade past. This will require a very fast-growing level of aggregate demand if we are to provide jobs for all those who will be looking for them.

NEW TECHNOLOGY

Our discussion of the supply side of employment allows us to understand why an increase in spending may not always be met by a proportional decrease in unemployment. But now we must consider an even more important reason on the demand side: technological change.

Why is technological change relevant to the demand for labor? One reason is that the introduction of new technology is usually achieved through the means of new capital investment. Hence, the steady process of investment, indispensable for the maintenance of an even flow of GNP, is a vehicle for the steady introduction of new technology into the economy. To be sure, not all investment incorporates technological change—some investment merely expands or duplicates existing facilities with very little, if any, changes in design or end use. Yet historically, investment and technology have gone hand in hand, the technology stimulating the new investment and the investment incorporating the new technology. In addition, much so-called replacement investment is actually the source of a steady upgrading of the quality of capital assets, as old and obsolete plants and parts are replaced by new and modern ones.

Thus technological change is closely allied with the ongoing flow of investment spending. But how does technological change affect the demand for labor? To answer the question, it will help us to differentiate between two kinds: demand-creating technology and cost-reducing technology.

Let us suppose that an inventor patents a new product—let us say a stove that automatically cooks things to perfection. Will such an invention create employment?

We will suppose that our inventor assembles his original models himself and peddles them in local stores, and we will ignore the small increase in spending (and perhaps in employment) due to his orders for raw materials. Instead, let us fasten our attention on the consumer who first decides to buy the new product in a store, because it has stimulated his demand.

Will the consumer's purchase result in a *net* increase in consumer spending in the economy? If this is so—and if the new product is generally liked—it is easy to see how the new product could result in sizeable additional employment.

But will it be true? Our consumer has, to be sure, bought a new item. *But unless his income has increased, there is no reason to believe that this is a net addition to his consumption expenditures.* The chances are, rather, that this unforeseen expenditure will be balanced by lessened spending for some other item. Almost surely he will not buy a regular stove. (When consumers first began buying television sets, they stopped buying as many radios and going to the movies as often.) But even where there is no direct competition, where the product is quite "new," everything that we know about the stability of the propensity to consume schedule leads us to believe that *total* consumer spending will not rise.

Thus we reach the important conclusion that new products do not automatically create *additional* spending, even though they may mobilize consumer demand for themselves. Indeed, many new products emerge onto the market every year and merely shoulder old products off. Must we then conclude that demand-creating inventions do not affect employment?

We are by no means ready to jump to that conclusion. Rather, what we have seen enables us to understand that if a new product is to create employment, it must give rise to new *investment* (and to the consumption it induces in turn). If the automatic stove is successful, it may induce the inventor to borrow money from a bank and to build a plant to mass-produce the item. If consumer demand for it continues to rise, a very large factory may have to be built to accommodate demand. As a result of the investment expenditures on the new plant, consumers' incomes *will* rise, and

NEW
DEMANDS

EMPLOYMENT
AND
INVESTMENT

more employment will be created as they spend their incomes on various consumer items.*

When we think of a new product not in terms of a household gadget but in terms of the automobile, airplane, or perhaps the transistor, we can understand how large the employment-creating potential of certain kinds of inventions can be. Originally the automobile merely resulted in consumer spending being diverted from buggies; the airplane merely cut into railroad income; the transistor, into vacuum tubes. But each of these inventions became in time the source of enormous investment expenditures. The automobile not only gave us the huge auto plants in Detroit, but indirectly brought into being multibillion dollar investment in highways, gasoline refineries, service stations, and industries whose impact on employment has been gigantic. On a smaller, but still very large, scale, the airplane gave rise not alone to huge aircraft building plants, but to airfields, radio and beacon equipment industries, and others, whose employment totals are substantial. In turn, the transistor offered entirely new design possibilities for miniaturization and thus gave many businesses an impetus for expansion.

INDUSTRY-BUILDING INVENTIONS

What sorts of inventions have this industry-building capacity? We can perhaps generalize by describing them as inventions that are of sufficient importance to become "indispensable" to the consumer or the manufacturer, and of sufficient mechanical or physical variance from the existing technical environment to necessitate the creation of a large amount of supporting capital equipment to integrate them into economic life.

Demand-creating inventions, then, can indeed create employment. *They do so indirectly, however—not by inducing new consumer spending, but by generating new investment spending.*†

Unfortunately, there is no guarantee that these highly employment-generative inventions will come along precisely when they are needed. There have been long periods when the economy has not been adequately stimulated by this type of invention and when employment has lagged as a result. We shall return to these dynamic inventions when we discuss growth, in our next chapter. But first let us consider another kind of invention that affects employment.

---

* To be sure, investment will decline in those areas that are now selling less to consumers. At most, however, this decline can affect only their replacement expenditures, which probably averaged 5 to 10 percent of the value of their capital equipment. Meanwhile, in the new industry, an entire capital structure must be built from scratch. We can expect the total amount of investment spending to increase substantially, with its usual repercussive effects.

† We should mention one effect of demand-creating inventions on consumption. It is probable that without the steady emergence of new products, the long-run propensity to consume would decline instead of remaining constant, as we have seen in Chapter 13. In this way, demand-creating technology is directly responsible for the creation of employment, by helping to keep consumer spending higher than it would be without a flow of new products.

By a cost-reducing invention, we generally mean an invention or an innovation that enables a manufacturer to turn out the *same* end product with less factor input. The factor that is saved may be, and often is, land or capital. But the type of cost-cutting invention that interests us here is probably the most common and surely the most important. These are *labor-saving* inventions or innovations, changes in technique or technology that enable an entrepreneur to turn out the same output as before, with less labor, or a larger output than before, with the same amount of labor.

COST-REDUCING INVENTIONS

Do such inventions "permanently" displace labor? Let us trace an imaginary instance and find out.

We assume in this case that an inventor has perfected a technique that makes it possible for a local shoe factory to reduce its production force from ten men to eight men, while still turning out the same number of shoes. Forgetting for the moment about the possible stimulatory effects of buying a new labor-saving machine,* let us see what happens to purchasing power and employment if the shoe manufacturer simply goes on selling the same number of shoes at the same prices as before, utilizing the new lower-cost process to increase his profits.

Suppose our manufacturer now spends his increased profits in increased consumption. Will that bring an equivalent increase in the total spending of the community? If we think twice we can see why not. For the increased spending of the manufacturer will be offset to a large extent by the decreased spending of the two displaced workers.

Exactly the same conclusion follows if our entrepreneur used his cost-cutting invention to lower the price of shoes, in the hope of snaring a larger market. Now it is *consumers* who are given an increase in purchasing power equivalent to the cut in prices. But again, their gain is exactly balanced by the lost purchasing power of the displaced workers.

INCOMES VS. EMPLOYMENT

Thus we can see that the introduction of labor-saving machinery does not necessarily imperil *incomes;* it merely shifts purchasing power from previously employed workers into the hands of consumers or into profits. But note also that *the unchanged volume of incomes is now associated with a smaller volume of employment. Thus the fact that there is no purchasing power "lost" when a labor-saving machine is introduced does not mean that there is no employment lost.*

Is this the end to our analysis of labor-displacing technology? It can be. It is possible that the introduction of labor-saving machinery will have no effect other than that of the example above: transferring consumer spending from previously employed labor to consumers or to entrepreneurs. But it is also possible that an employment-generating secondary effect may result.

* This is not an unfair assumption. The labor-saving technology might be no more than a more effective arrangement of labor within the existing plant, and thus require no new equipment; or the new equipment might be bought with regular capital replacement funds.

Our entrepreneur may be so encouraged at the higher profits from his new process that he uses his profits to invest in additional plant and equipment and thereby sets in motion, via the multiplier, a rise in total expenditure sufficient to re-employ his displaced workers. Or in our second instance, consumers may evidence such a brisk demand for shoes at lower prices that, once again, our employer is encouraged to invest in additional plant and equipment, with the same salutary results as above.*

The moral is clear. *Labor-displacing technology can offset the unemployment created by its immediate introduction only if it induces sufficient investment to increase the volume of total spending to a point where employment also rises.*

IMPACT OF AUTOMATION
It is in connection with our foregoing discussion that the much talked-of threat of *automation* becomes most meaningful. By automation, we mean technological inventions that perform increasingly complex and often self-regulatory tasks, some on the factory floor and, more significantly, some previously associated with white-collar work. In the main, automation is clearly a cost-cutting and labor-saving kind of technology, although it has important applications for new products as well.

But one aspect of automation requires our special attention. It is the fact that automation represents the belated entry of technology into an area of economic activity that until now has been largely spared the impact of technical change. This is the area of service and administrative tasks that we have previously marked as an important source of growing employment. Thus the threat inherent in the new sensory, almost humanoid, equipment is not only that it may accelerate the employment-displacing effects in the secondary (manufacturing) sector. *More sobering is that it may put an end to the traditional employment-absorptive effects of the tertiary service and administrative sector.*

What could be the implications of such a development? In simplest terms, it means that in the future, fewer people will be needed to produce the same quantity of services. The absorption of labor from agriculture and manufacturing into the ever-expanding service sector would now slow down or come to a halt, since the service sector could increase its output without hiring a proportionate increase in workers.

This *could*, of course, mean massive unemployment. But it need not. Just as our imaginary society limited its demand to agricultural goods and solved its labor problem by cutting the workweek, so a society that no longer needed to add labor as fast as its demands rose could easily solve the unemployment problem by more or less equitably sharing among its members the amount of labor it *did* require. To be sure, this raises many

---

* Do not fall into the trap of thinking that the new higher demand for shoes, will, by itself, suffice to eradicate unemployment. To be sure, shoe purchases may now increase to previous levels or even higher. But unless their incomes rise, consumer spending on other items will suffer to the exact degree that spending on shoes gains.

problems, not least among them the wage adjustments that must accompany such a reapportionment of hours.* But it makes clear that, essentially, the challenge of automation is one of finding a new balance in our attitudes toward work and leisure, and an equitable means of sharing work (and income, the reward for work) in a society where technology is beginning to invade the last precincts of human skills. The solution will assuredly not be an easy one, although it is by no means inherently impossible.

Unemployment in the U.S.

We have spoken of unemployment heretofore in a somewhat detached and analytic fashion. Now it is time to look at the actual figures in the United States and to consider how unemployment can be actively and effectively combatted.

Table 19-8 gives us the important statistics. The terrible percentages of the Great Depression need no comment. Rather, let us pay heed to the level of unemployment in the 1960s. Here the record is mixed. During the early years of the decade we were troubled with persistent levels of unemployment much too high to be healthy. In the later years, unemployment

Year	Unemployed (thousands)	Percent of civilian labor force
1929	1,550	3.2
1933	12,830	24.9
1940	8,120	14.6
1944	670	1.2
1960–65 av.	4,100	5.5
1966	2,875	3.8
1967	2,975	3.8
1968	2,817	3.6
1969	2,832	3.5
1970	4,085	4.9
1971 [prelim.]	5,033	6.0+

TABLE 19•8

UNEMPLOYMENT IN THE U.S.

* What society is trying to do in rolling back hours of work is to *share* work and incomes more equitably. This is good for those who would otherwise be unemployed, but it may not be so good for those who are lucky enough to have jobs at the time when unemployment becomes a problem. These workers will be glad to cut their workweek, but not so glad to cut their pay or to deprive themselves of increased pay in order to share incomes with their new workmates. In actuality, this source of potential conflict is softened because the process of shortening hours stretches out over fairly long periods and is often accompanied by rising productivity. As a result, hours may fall and weekly pay remain steady. But of course, if hours had not fallen, employed workers would have enjoyed a rise in pay.

declined sharply, but there is the discomfort of tracing much of this decline to an increase in war spending.

Part of our unemployment results from deliberate efforts made in 1970 by the Nixon Administration to restrain inflation by "trading off" a limited rise in joblessness for a fall in the rate of price rise. As of mid-1971, this trade-off was, unfortunately, more successful in producing unemployment than in slowing inflation.

But unemployment is not wholly a matter of fiscal and monetary policies seeking to counter inflation. The United States has experienced a fairly high level of unemployment for the past decade, as Table 19-8 shows, and as we will see at the end of this chapter when we look at the European experience. What is the cause of this "chronic" unemployment?

As with most economic problems, there is no single, simple cause. All of the possible reasons for unemployment that we have studied in our text have a relevance to the current situation. In part, our labor participation rate has been high, especially among women, thereby swelling the job-seeking labor force. In part, our total GNP has not been large enough. In part, we have experienced a considerable amount of labor-displacing invest-ment. In some industries, wages may have risen too fast. And other reasons that we have not specifically studied may be added as well, primary among them being discrimination against the Negro. For example, a larger percent-age of white, male, high school *dropouts* secure employment than do Negro males who *graduate* from high school, and the average earnings of these Negro graduates are *lower* than the earnings of white dropouts.

Thus, unemployment strikes very unequally among groups of the popu-lation and areas of the country. For example, in 1971, when the average rate of unemployment for the labor force was more than 6 percent, the rate among married men was only 3.3 percent, whereas among young workers (16 to 19 years old) it was more than 15 percent. For white workers as a whole it was 4.5 percent; for Negro and Puerto Rican workers, 8.2 percent. As we have seen in Chapter 1, among black teenagers it reached as high as 42 percent.

COMBATTING UNEMPLOYMENT

These facts suggest that combatting unemployment is a complex task that requires not one policy, but a variety of policies. Let us look into some of the major ones.

1. *Increasing demand.*

We have learned that as a general rule, anything that increases the total demand of society is apt to increase employment. This is particularly true when unemployment tends to be widespread, both in geographic location and industrial distribution. Then the expansion of GNP, whether by the stimulation of private investment or consumer spending or government expenditure or net exports should prove the single most reliable means of creating more employment.

There is, however, a problem here. Doubtless, a vast amount of employment could be created if aggregate demand were enlarged; for instance, the systematic reconstruction of our cities, a task that is becoming an increasingly pressing necessity, could by itself provide millions of jobs for decades. So could the proper care of our rapidly-growing older population, or the provision of really first-class education for large segments of the population that lack it.

The problem is that these programs require the generation of large amounts of *public demand,* and this requires the prior political approval of the electorate. If this political approval is not forthcoming, the generation of additional demand will have to be entrusted to the private sector—that is, to individual entrepreneurs in search of a profit.

Can private enterprise, without a massive public investment program, generate sufficient demand to bring about full and lasting employment? One cannot be dogmatic about such questions, but there is at least some historical reason to be uncertain. Between 1950 and 1960, for example, private enterprise accounted for only one out of every ten new jobs created in the economy.[1] All the rest were created in the public or the private not-for-profit sector (universities, hospitals, etc.). In the years since then, the private sector has been more labor-attracting; but by itself it is still far from capable of creating employment fast enough to absorb the increase in the labor force.

To this sobering trend in employment creation, we must also add the potentially serious, although as yet untested, effects of the new technology of automation, particularly as it may cut into job needs in the tertiary sector. Hence there seems to be good reason for caution in assuming that the private sector, unaided by public programs of investment, will be able to offer as much employment as the growing labor force demands. The likelihood is that a large enough aggregate demand will require the substantial use of public expenditure, whether for urban renewal and welfare services or for other ends.

2. *Wage policy.*

But suppose that a very high aggregate demand is maintained, through public or private spending. Will that in itself guarantee full employment?

The answer is that it will not if the spending creates only higher incomes for workers who are already employed, rather than new incomes for workers who are unemployed. Thus if we want to maximize the employment-creating effect of spending, whether private or public, we need to hold back wage raises at least until the unemployment has fallen to a socially acceptable level.

But if raising wages can impede the process of job creation, can cutting wages encourage it? The question is not a simple one, for lower wages set into motion contrary economic stimuli. On the one hand, lower wages cut

[1] Eli Ginzberg, *The Pluralistic Economy* (New York: McGraw-Hill, 1965), p. 144.

costs and thereby tempt employers to add to their labor force. On the other hand, lower wages after a time will result in less consumption spending, and will thus adversely affect business sales. The net effect of a wage cut thus becomes highly unpredictable. If businessmen feel the positive gains of a cut in costs before they feel the adverse effects of a cut in sales, employment may rise—and thereby obviate the fall in consumption spending. On the other hand, employers may *expect* that the wage cut will lead to lower sales, and their pessimistic expectations may lead them to refrain from adding to their labor forces, despite lower costs. In that case, of course, employment will not rise. On balance, most economists today fear the adverse effects of wage-cutting more than they welcome the possible job-creating effects.

It seems, then, that maintaining wages in the face of an economic decline and restraining wage rises in the face of an economic advance is the best way of encouraging maximum employment. It is one thing, however, to spell out such a general guideline to action and another to achieve it. To maintain wages against an undertow of falling sales requires a strong union movement. But once times improve, this same union movement is hardly likely to exercise the self-restraint needed to forego wage raises, so that additional spending can go into the pockets of the previously unemployed. This poses another dilemma for a market society in search of a rational high employment policy, and there is at this moment no solution in sight.

3. *Remedying structural unemployment.*

Not all unemployment is due to insufficient demand. Some can be traced to "structural" causes—to a lack to "fit" between the existing labor force and the existing job opportunities. For instance, men may be unemployed because they do not know of job opportunities in another city, or because they do not have the requisite skills to get, or hold, jobs that are currently being offered. Indeed, it is perfectly possible to have structural unemployment side-by-side with a lack of manpower in certain fields.

A sharp debate has raged in the United States concerning the importance of structural reasons (as contrasted with a general deficiency of demand) in accounting for the present level of unemployment. Many observers have pointed out that the unemployed are typically grouped into certain disprivileged categories: race, age, lack of training, and unfortunate geographic location. The aged and the young, the Negro and the unskilled, the displaced West Virginian coal miner or Massachusetts textile worker are not quickly pulled into employment by a general expansion of demand. The broad stream of purchasing passes most of them by and does not reintegrate them into the mainstream of the economy. Hence stress is increasingly placed on measures to assist labor mobility, so that the unemployed can move from distressed to expansive areas, and on the retraining of men for those jobs offered by a technologically fast-moving society.

Retraining is, unfortunately, much easier when it is applied to relatively few persons than when it is proposed as a general public policy affecting large numbers of unemployed. Then the question arises: for what jobs shall the unemployed be trained? Unless we very clearly know the *shape* of future demand, the risk is that a retraining program will prepare workers only for jobs that may no longer exist when the workers are ready for them. And unless the *level* of future demand is high, even a foresighted program will not effectively solve the unemployment problem.

One of the most attractive aspects of the Urban Coalition program (see p. 324) is that it combines proposals for a more effective job-finding system (a computerized national job bank), a more generous level of unemployment benefits, and a stronger emphasis on training, *together with a clear-cut program of public demand.* Based on surveys made in over 34 cities, the coalition has outlined the needs of the public sector over the next five years in education, welfare administration, environmental control, library services, police and fire protection, hospital and sanitation improvement, etc., and has estimated that these needs can provide at least a million new jobs by 1976. The existence of such a known framework of demand greatly enhances the chances of success of a job-training program.

4. *Reducing the supply of labor.*

Next, the possibility exists of attacking unemployment not from the demand side, but from the supply side, by cutting the workweek, lengthening vacations, and using similar measures. Essentially, the possibility held out by shortening the workweek is that a more or less fixed quantity of work will then be shared among a larger number of workers. This is entirely feasible and possible, provided that *the decrease in hours is not offset by an increase in hourly pay rates.* In other words, once again a rational wage policy holds the key between success and failure. Shorter hours, coupled with higher hourly wage rates, will merely raise unit costs (unless productivity rises quickly enough to compensate). This will certainly not contribute to increased employment. Shorter hours *without* increased hourly rates, on the other hand, may make it necessary for the employer to hire additional help in order to continue his established level of output.

Shortening hours of work can be a policy of despair. If people do not wish to change their working habits—the number of hours per week or the number of years in their lifetimes—then the cure for unemployment is surely to expand the demand for labor and not to diminish its supply. If private demand is inadequate to this task, then, as we have said, public demand may serve the purpose instead.

But an attack on unemployment that seeks to reduce the supply of labor, rather than to expand the demand for it, need not be a program of retreat. It can also become part of a deliberate and popularly endorsed effort to reshape the patterns and the duration of work as it now exists. Thus it may be possible to reduce the size of the labor force by measures such as subsidies that would induce younger people to remain longer in school or by raising Social Security to make it attractive for older people to retire earlier. Such policies can be useful not only in bringing down the participation rate and thus reducing "unemployment," but in affecting changes in the quality of life that would find general public approval.

5. *The government as employer of last resort.*

Finally, we can effectively limit the problem of unemployment by formally adopting the policy of using the public sector as "employer of last resort."

This proposal, first advanced by the National Commission on Technology, Automation, and Economic Progress,[1] does not mean the use of the public sector as a kind of vast "work relief" program. On the contrary, the purpose is to use public employment primarily as a positive force in establishing a higher quality of life, an objective that will require a substantial expansion of much public service activity along the lines mentioned above in the proposals of the Urban Coalition. Only as a secondary objective is "the employer of last resort" to provide jobs for those who fail to find satisfactory work in the private sector or in the career lines of public services.

THE U.S. AND EUROPEAN EXPERIENCE

As evidence of what can be done by a more vigorous attack on unemployment, using many of the above techniques, the performance of the United States in two recent fairly "low unemployment" years can be compared with that of various European nations.

TABLE 19•9

UNEMPLOYMENT RATES, SELECTED COUNTRIES*

United States	(1967)	3.8
	(1968)	3.6
West Germany	(1968)	1.2
France	(1968)	2.2
Netherlands	(1968)	1.8
United Kingdom	(1967)	2.0
Norway	(1967)	0.8
Sweden	(1967)	2.3
Denmark	(1967)	1.4

Source: *Basic Statistics of the Community*, p. 20.
*Definitions of unemployment vary slightly, as they do between the United States and European nations, but not enough to affect the basic conclusions revealed by the data.

The lesson of the table is clear. A tendency to generate unemployment may be an unavoidable consequence of a market system, *but it is not an irremediable evil.* It is possible to run a capitalist system at high levels of employment—admittedly, paying the price of a considerable degree of inflation. The problem, then, is to bring about the political changes in the

[1] *Technology and the American Economy* (Washington, 1966), p. 37.

United States that may be the prerequisite for introducing the kinds of employment programs that have proved their worth in capitalism abroad. That may involve a very difficult problem of public education and persuasion, but it is a problem different from a defeatist admission that the economic system itself cannot be made to work adequately.

KEY CONCEPTS AND KEY WORDS

1. *Participation* in the working force has slowly increased over the long run. This is the net result of three forces: the *large-scale entry of women* into the labor force after child-bearing, partly offset by the *later entry and earlier retirement of males.*

Participation rates

2. Participation in the short run mirrors economic opportunity. *The labor force is elastic* and responds to increases in job openings. As a result, *it is possible for employment and unemployment* (meaning an active, although unsuccessful, search for work) *to increase at the same time.*

Unemployment

3. The demand for labor reflects not only the total spending of the economy, but also the structure of demand of that economy. In the United States, *this pattern of demand has slowly but substantially shifted* from products of the soil to products of manufacture, and even more strikingly to services of various kinds.

4. Along with this shift in demand has come an uneven impact of technology. Machines have very greatly boosted the productivity of the primary and secondary sectors, while relatively much less affecting the output per person of the tertiary sector.

Primary, secondary, tertiary sectors

5. As a consequence of these patterns of demand and of technology, *employment has been steadily shifted out of farming into manufacturing, and even more importantly into service and administration.* It is the prospective entry of new self-regulating machinery—so-called automation—especially into the tertiary sector that now poses the greatest problems for employment.

Automation

6. Large-scale unemployment is generally caused by *inadequate total demand.* This unemployment may be aggravated, or its cure made more difficult both by changes in technology, such as the trend to automation, and by irregularities in the *population age structure*—in particular by the prospect of large numbers of youths coming onto the labor market during the next decade.

7. Technology can both displace labor and create a demand for it. *Demand-creating technology increases employment through the creation of a substantial volume of new investment.* Labor-displacing technology does not diminish incomes but can shrink employment in particular industries.

Technology

Unemployment

8. Unemployment can be combatted in several ways, of which *increasing aggregate demand* is probably the single most important way. However, because of the labor-displacing properties of modern technology, it is uncertain that private demand alone can create and maintain full employment. Public expenditure will also probably be required.

9. The creation of additional employment requires a *wage policy* that prevents increased spending from swelling the incomes of the already employed, rather than giving new income to the unemployed. *Wage-cutting,* on the other hand, *is an uncertain and possibly dangerous mode of increasing employment,* since the adverse effects of lowered consumption may more than offset the positive effects of lowered costs.

Structural unemployment

10. *Structural unemployment* requires much more specific remedies than those provided by aggregate demand. Training and education programs are the main weapon against this kind of joblessness.

11. There is a long-term trend toward *leisure* in all advanced countries, and it is probable that this trend will continue. One way of alleviating unemployment is to convert it into leisure; i.e., by lengthening the period of schooling, advancing the age of retirement, shortening the workday or week, and expanding the public sector both to improve the quality of life and to serve as an "employer of last resort." This is probably a direction in which the economy will slowly move.

12. Recent European experience proves conclusively that unemployment can be held far lower than in the United States.

Q U E S T I O N S

1. How do you account for the fact that there are more people per hundred who want to work today than there were 70 years ago, when the nation was so much poorer? How much does the monetization of labor have to do with this? How much is it a change in "life styles," especially for women? What do you expect for the very long run—say 100 years from now?

2. How can employment and unemployment *both* rise at the same time? What would you consider to be a useful definition of unemployment, one that could be easily used by interviewers in the field?

3. What do you think accounts for the shift in demand from primary to secondary and tertiary products? In particular, what do you think is the reason for the steady growth of services as a kind of output that society seems to want?

4. Suppose that technology in the 1890s had taken the following turn: a very complex development of machines and techniques for improving public and private supervisory and administrative techniques, very clever devices that performed salesmen's and clerks' services, but almost no improvement in agricultural techniques. What would the distribution of the labor force probably look like?

5. What is the relation between leisure and unemployment? Is a man who is retired before he wants to stop working "at leisure" or "unemployed"? Can one make a clear distinction between the two, or does it depend very largely on social customs, and other things?

6. Suppose that an inventor puts a wrist radio-telephone on the market. What would be the effects on consumer spending? What would ultimately determine whether the new invention were labor-attracting or labor-displacing?

7. Suppose that another new invention halved the cost of making cars. Would this create new purchasing power? What losses in income would have to be balanced against what gains in incomes? What would be the most likely way that such an invention could increase employment? Would employment increase if the demand for cars were inelastic, like the demand for farm products—that is, if people bought very few more cars despite the fall in prices?

8. Unemployment among the Negro population in many cities in the late 1960s was worse than it was during the Great Depression. What steps would you propose to remedy this situation?

9. Would raising wages, and thereby creating more consumption demand, be a good way to increase employment?

10. Do you believe that there exists general support for large public employment-generating programs? Why or why not? What sorts of programs would you propose?

11. How would you encourage private enterprise to create as many *jobs* as possible?

There remains for us to consider but one subject in our introduction to macroeconomics: the subject of growth. Actually, we have already been concerned for many pages with the main problem, if not the explicit theme, of growth. From the very beginning of our study, investment has been at the center of our focus. Up to this point, however, we have thought of investment mainly as the process by which savings were offset so that a given level of expenditure could be maintained, or in the preceding chapter, as the key to the dynamic process by which employment was sometimes created and sometimes destroyed. In all these considerations, *fluctuations* in the level of investment were all-important, a slowdown spelling recession and unemployment, an acceleration leading to the opposite.

Now we must see the process of investment in a somewhat different perspective. Whether it proceeds slowly or fast, investment consists in the addition of real wealth to the stock of wealth of the nation. Thus, so long as there is *any* net investment, our stock of capital is growing; and with a growth in our capital, there should come a growth in our capacity to produce. In this way we can see that the process of investment leads inevitably to a consideration of economic growth, and it is to this subject that we now turn.

Structural Requirements of Growth

How does growth take place? Through investment, we know. But how does investment take place? How does a society actually find the resources to devote to capital-building? In our rich, industrialized economy, such a question may seem pointless. We simply use our industrial equipment to make more industrial equipment. And for the necessary labor we simply employ the people who are already working in steel and other capital-goods industries.

But the matter-of-factness with which we answer the question hides from us the real structural significance of growth. For when we turn our gaze abroad or backward in time and ask how a poor society grows, the question is not so easy to answer. Such societies do not have steel mills waiting for orders, nor labor forces that are already deployed in capital-goods industries. How do they, then, create capital?

The process is by no means an obvious one. Suppose we have a very poor society (like an extremely underdeveloped nation) in which 80 percent of the population tills the soil, equipped with so little by way of capital—mere spades and hoes—that it produces only enough to maintain itself and the remaining 20 percent of society.

Who are the other 20 percent? In reality, of course, they might be government officials, landlords, and others, but we will simplify our model by assuming that the whole 20 percent is occupied in making the simple spades and hoes (the capital goods) with which the consumption-goods sector works. Like the farmers, the toolmakers labor from dawn to dusk; and again like the farmers, they are so unproductive that they can produce only enough capital to replace the spades and hoes that wear out each year.

Now how could such a society grow? If we look again at the capital-goods sector, we find a clue. For unlike the consumption-goods sector, we find here not one but two distinguishable kinds of economic activity going on. In the agricultural side, everyone is farming; but in the capital-goods side, not everyone is making the spades and hoes with which the agricultural laborers work. No matter how we simplify our model, we can see that *the capital-goods sector must carry out two different tasks.* It must turn out spades and hoes, to be sure. But part of the capital-goods labor force must also turn out a different kind of capital good—a very special kind that will produce not only spades and hoes, but also more of itself!

Is there such a kind of equipment? There is indeed, in a versatile group of implements known as *machine tools.* In our model economy, these may be only chisels and hammers that can be used to make spades, hoes, and more chisels and hammers. In a complex industrial system, machine tools consist of presses and borers and lathes which, when used ensemble, not only make all kinds of complicated machines but can also recreate themselves.

Thus we encounter the unexpected fact that there is a strategic branch of capital creation that lies at the core of the whole sequence of economic growth.*

How does growth now ensue? Our model enables us to see that it is not simply a matter of bringing in peasants from the fields to make more spades and thereby to increase their productivity. For they will not be able to make spades until they have laid the ground by an increase in output of this strategic branch: before spades can be made, chisels and hammers must be made. Before textile or shoemaking or food-processing or transportation equipment can be made, machine tools must be made.

Thus at the core of the growth process—whether in a very backward nation or a highly industrialized one—we can see *two* great structural shifts that must take place:

1. *A shift of effort* within *the capital sector to increase its own productive capacity.*

2. *A shift of effort from the consumption sector to the capital sector, to man the growing volume of equipment which emerges from the enlarged capital sector.*

Can we actually trace this process in real life? The shifts *within* the capital sector are not always easy to see, because there is usually some excess capacity in the machine tool branch. By running overtime, for instance, it can produce *both* more machine tools *and* more hoes and spades. Yet if we examine a society in the process of rapid industrialization, such as the U.S.S.R. (or for that matter, the United States in its periods of rapid wartime industrial buildup) we can clearly see the importance of this critical branch in setting a *ceiling* on the overall pace of industrial expansion.

When we turn to the second shift, from the consumption sector into the capital sector, the movement in real life is very apparent. Table 20-1, for instance, shows us the proportion of the population engaged in agriculture for a number of industrialized nations at an early and a late stage of their transformations.

Here we see in reality the wholesale emigration that takes place in the industrializing process (note that by 1811 Britain was already well on the road). Over the course of the nineteenth and twentieth centuries, these countries have lost two-thirds to four-fifths of their erstwhile farmers—not all to capital-building alone, of course, but to the whole industrial and commercial structure that capital-building makes possible. In this way, the process of economic growth can be seen in part as a great flow of human

---

* This raises the perplexing question of how the machine-tool industry *began,* since it needs its own output to grow. The answer is that it evolved as a special branch of industrial production during the industrial revolution when, for the first time, machinery itself began to be made by machinery instead of by hand. A key figure in the evolution of the machine-tool industry was Maudslay, whose invention of the screw-cutting lathe was "one of the decisive pieces of standardization that made the modern machine possible." (Lewis Mumford, *Technics and Civilization.* New York: Harcourt, 1963, p. 209.)

TABLE 20•1

LABOR
FORCE
IN
AGRICULTURE

PERCENT OF LABOR FORCE IN AGRICULTURE

	Early 19th century	1968
France	63% (1827)	16%
Great Britain	31 (1811)	3
Sweden	63 (1840)	10
United States	72 (1820)	5

Sources: Colin Clark, *The Conditions of Economic Progress* (London: Macmillan, 1960), pp. 512, 514, 518; B. R. Mitchell, *Abstract of British Historical Statistics* (Cambridge: Cambridge University Press, 1962), pp. 60–61; and *Basic Statistics of the Community*.

and material resources from simple consumption goods output to a hierarchy of industrial tasks—a flow that is even more dramatic in real life than we might have divined from our imaginary model.

The Historical Record: Stability and Cycles

Thus, behind the phenomenon of growth we encounter a hidden structural shift of the greatest importance. Once the shift has taken place, however— once a large capital-building sector has been established—the process of adding to the stock of capital is greatly simplified. Indeed, we now get that long process of gradually increasing output that provides us with our ordinary starting point in the study of growth. In Fig. 20-1 we see the American experience from the middle of the nineteenth century.

How regular has been our average rate of growth? The answer is: astonishingly constant, whether we take an average over the past thirty-odd years since the Great Depression, or whether we go back to the earliest reliable statistics and calculate our growth rate since the 1870s (or even 1830s). As the chart shows, the swings are almost all contained within a range of 10 percent above or below the trend. The trend itself comes to about 3.5 percent a year in real terms, or a little over 1.5 percent a year per capita.*

How do we account for this long, steady ascent? In part, the answer cites the underlying forces of propulsion that we have already discussed in

* This is a very good time to stress the dangers of intertemporal comparisons of GNP voiced in Chapter 10. In case you have forgotten, they are: (1) the *quality* of output varies greatly over a long span of time, favorably and otherwise; (2) part of GNP is *imputed* and this portion varies over time; (3) there is a long-term *monetization of household tasks* that adds a deceptive component of growth; and (4) *not all of GNP*—and different amounts in different periods—*adds to well-being*. All in all, growth statistics should be used with caution in making comparative statements about output and welfare in two widely separated periods.

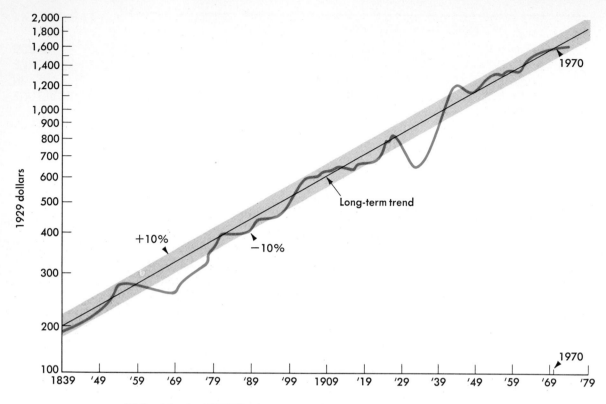

FIG. 20·1   TREND IN REAL GNP PER HEAD, 1839–1970

our historic survey on American economic development. We will not review that chapter of history now, although we will return to the forces of growth in a somewhat more analytical focus at the conclusion of this chapter.

But the second part of the answer is equally important. It is that year-by-year growth was *not* so smooth and steady as the long-term growth rates suggest. Take the years 1895 to 1905, very smooth-looking in Fig. 20-1. As Table 20-2 reveals, the advance was anything but steady.

Or examine a more recent period, not year by year, but in groups of

TABLE 20·2

**U.S. RATES
OF GROWTH
1895–1905**

1895–1896	− 2.5%	1900–1901	+11.5%
1896–1897	+ 9.4	1901–1902	+ 1.0
1897–1898	+ 2.3	1902–1903	+ 4.9
1898–1899	+ 9.1	1903–1904	− 1.2
1899–1900	+ 2.7	1904–1905	+ 7.4

Source: *Long Term Economic Growth* (U.S. Dept. of Commerce, 1966), p. 107.

years. Here is the record of the U.S. economy—or rather, the records of the U.S. economy—between 1922 and 1970. As we can see, the rate of growth has varied greatly in different periods.

FIG. 20•2 SHORT-TERM VARIATIONS IN THE RATE OF GROWTH

This extraordinary sequence of ups and downs, rushes of growth followed by doldrums, introduces us to a fascinating aspect of the subject of growth—*business cycles.* For if we inspect the profile of the long ascent carefully, we can see that its entire length is marked with irregular tremors or peaks and valleys. Indeed, the more powerful the magnifying glass we apply—which is to say, the more closely we examine year-to-year figures—the more of these tremors and deviations we discover, until the problem begins to be which of these many vibrations to consider significant and which to discard as uninteresting.

The problem of sorting out the important fluctuations in output (or in statistics of prices or employment) is a difficult one. Economists have actually detected dozens of cycles of different lengths and amplitudes, from very short rhythms of expansion and contraction that can be found, for example, in patterns of inventory accumulation and decumulation, to large background pulsations of seventeen or eighteen years in the housing industry, and possibly (the evidence is unclear) swings of forty to fifty years in the path of capitalist development as a whole.

Generally, however, when we speak of "the" business cycle we refer to a wavelike movement that lasts, on the average, about eight to ten years. In Fig. 20-3 this major oscillation of the American economy stands forth very

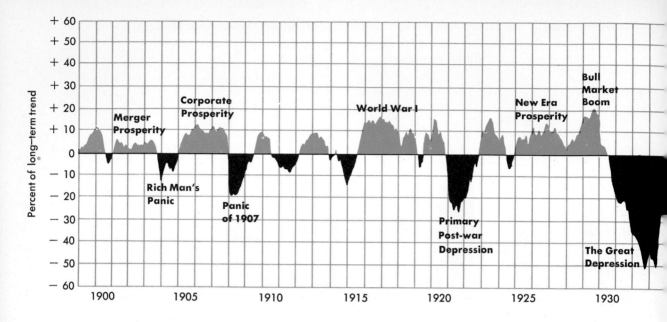

FIG. 20 • 3

clearly, for the chartist has eliminated the underlying tilt of growth so that the profile of economic performance looks like a cross section at sea level rather than a cut through a long incline.

REFERENCE CYCLES

In a general way we are all familiar with the meaning of business cycles, for the alternation of "boom and bust" or prosperity and recession (a polite name for a mild depression) is part of everyday parlance. It will help us study cycles, however, if we learn to speak of them with a standard terminology. We can do this by taking the cycles from actual history, "superimposing" them, and drawing the general profile of the so-called *reference* cycle that emerges. It looks like Fig. 20-4.

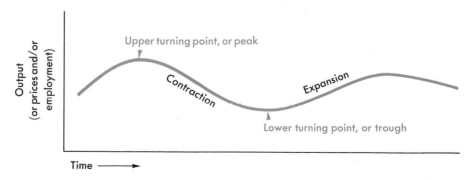

FIG. 20 • 4 THE REFERENCE CYCLE

This model of a typical cycle enables us to speak of the "length" of a business cycle as the period from one peak to the next or from trough to trough. If we fail to measure from *similar* points on two or more cycles, we can easily get a distorted picture of short-term growth—for instance, one that begins at the upper turning point of one cycle and measures to the trough of the next. Much of the political charge and countercharge about growth rates can be clarified if we examine the starting and terminating dates used by each side.

What lies behind this more or less regular alternation of good and bad times?

CAUSES OF CYCLES

Innumerable theories, none of them entirely satisfactory, have been advanced to explain the business cycle. A common business explanation is that waves of optimism in the world of affairs alternate with waves of pessimism—a statement that may be true enough, but that seems to describe the sequence of events rather than to explain it. Hence economists have tried to find the underlying cyclical mechanism in firmer stuff than an alternation of moods. One famous late-nineteenth-century economist, W. S. Jevons, for example, explained business cycles as the consequence of sunspots—perhaps not as occult a theory as it might seem, since Jevons believed that the sunspots caused weather cycles that caused crop cycles that caused business cycles. The trouble was that subsequent investigation shows that the periodicity of sunspots was sufficiently different from that of rainfall cycles to make the connection impossible.

Other economists have turned to causes closer to home: to variations in the rate of gold mining (with its effects on the money supply); to fluctuations in the rate of invention; to the regular recurrence of war; and to yet many other factors. There is no doubt that many of these events can induce a business expansion or contraction. The persistent problem, however, is that none of the so-called underlying causes itself displays an inherent cyclicality—much less one with a periodicity of eight to ten years.

Then how do we explain cycles? Economists today no longer seek a single explanation of the phenomenon in an exogenous (external) cyclical force. Rather, they tend to see cycles as our own eye first saw them on the growth curve, *as variations in the rate of growth that tend to be induced by the dynamics of the growth process itself.* As we shall see, our knowledge of macroeconomics will quickly give us the clue to the mechanism at work.

MECHANISM OF BUSINESS FLUCTUATION

Let us assume that some stimulus, such as an important industry-building invention, has begun to increase investment expenditures. We can easily see how such an initial impetus can generate a cumulative and self-feeding boom. As the multiplier and accelerator interact, the first burst of investment stimulates additional consumption, the additional consumption induces more investment, and this in turn re-invigorates consumption. Meanwhile, this process of mutual stimulation serves to lift business expectations and to encourage still further expansionary spending. Inventories are built up in anticipation of larger sales. Prices "firm up" and the stock market rises. Optimism reigns. A boom is on.

What happens to end such a boom? There are many possible reasons why it may peter out or come to an abrupt halt. It may simply be that the new industry will get built, and thereafter an important stimulus to investment will be lacking. Or even before it is completed, wages and prices may have begun to rise as full employment is neared, and the climate of expectations may thereupon become wary rather than hopeful. (Businessmen have an old adage that "what goes up must come down.") Meanwhile, perhaps tight money will choke off spending plans or make new projects appear unprofitable.

Or investment may begin to decline because consumption, although still rising, is no longer rising at the earlier *rate* (the acceleration principle in action). Previously (p. 276) we noticed that the action of the accelerator, all by itself, could give rise to wavelike movements in total expenditure. The accelerator, of course, never works "all by itself," but it can exert its upward and downward pressures within the flux of economic forces and in this way give rise to an underlying cyclical impetus.

It is impossible to know in advance what particular cause will retard spending, but it is all too easy to see how a hesitation in spending can turn into a general contraction. Perhaps warned by a falling stock market, perhaps by a slowdown in their sales or an end to rising profits, businessmen begin to cut back. Whatever their initial motivation, what follows thereafter is much like the preceding expansion, only in reverse. The multiplier mechanism now breeds smaller rather than larger incomes. Downward revisions of expectations reduce rather than enhance the attractiveness of investment projects. As consumption decreases, prices fall and unemployment begins to show up. Inventories are worked off. Bankruptcies become more common. We experience all the economic and social problems of a recession.

But just as there is a "natural" ceiling to a boom, so there is a more or less "natural" floor to recessions.* The fall in inventories, for example, will eventually come to an end: for even in the severest recessions, merchants and manufacturers must have *some* goods on their shelves and so must eventually begin stocking up. The decline in expenditures will lead to easy money, and the slack in output will tend to a lower level of costs; and both of these factors will encourage new investment projects. Meanwhile, the automatic stabilizers of government fiscal policy will slowly make their effects known. Sooner or later, in other words, expenditures will cease falling, and the economy will tend to "bottom out."

The Anatomy of Growth

Thus, business cycles appear as accelerations and decelerations to the underlying momentum of growth. But why growth? How do we know that the peak of one cycle will be higher than the peak of the previous one? What accounts for the underlying tilt to the whole cycle chart?

The essential reason is one that we are very familiar with. Even in the doldrums of recession (except for a very few severely depressed years) the economy manages to lay down a net increment of wealth in the form of investment, and this investment then adds its leverage to that of the entire stock of capital with which society works. So, too, every year, the labor force tends to grow as population increases, adding another component of potential input to the economic mechanism.

This does not mean, as we well know, that the economy will therefore *automatically* utilize its full resources. Unused men and unused machines are very well known to us in macroeconomic analysis. But the steady addition to the factors of production does mean that the *potential* of the economy will be steadily rising. *Growth is thus introduced into the system by the steady addition to its basic instruments of production, both human and material.* If we multiply the slowly rising hours of total labor input by a "productivity coefficient" that reflects, among other things, our slowly rising stock of

---

* In retrospect, the tremendous and long-lasting collapse of 1929 seems to have been caused by special circumstances having to do mainly with speculation and monetary mismanagement.

capital, we can derive a trend line of *potential GNP*. The question we then face is to see how much of this potential volume of output we will actually produce.

As Fig. 20-5 shows, all through much of the 1950s and 1960s potential output ran well ahead of the output we actually achieved. Indeed, between 1958 and 1962 the amount of lost output represented by this gap came to the staggering sum of $170 billion, or nearly $1,000 per person. Even in 1964, a very prosperous year, the President's Council of Economic Advisers reported that we could have added another $25 billion to $30 billion to GNP—more than $300 per family—if we had brought unemployment down from 5 to 4 percent and had also found jobs for the larger labor force that would have sought work in a climate of full employment.

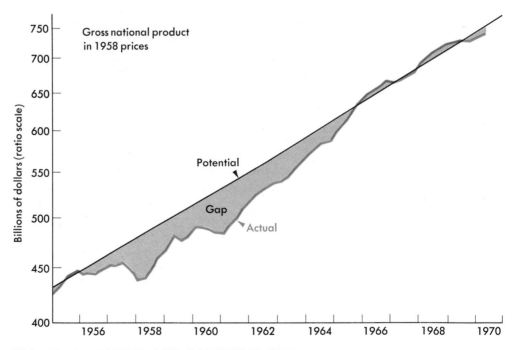

FIG. 20 • 5   ACTUAL AND POTENTIAL GNP

DEMAND VS.
CAPACITY

The problem of a potential growth rate opens an aspect of the investment process that we have not yet considered. Heretofore, we have always thought of investment primarily as an income-generating force, working through the multiplier to increase the level of expenditure. Now we begin to consider investment also as a *capacity-generating* force, working through the actual addition to our plant and equipment to increase the productive potential of the system.

No sooner do we introduce the idea of capacity, however, than a new problem arises for our consideration. If investment increases potential output as well as income, the obvious question is: will income rise fast enough to buy all this potential output? Thus at the end of our analysis of macroeconomics we revert to the question we posed at the beginning, but in a more dynamic context. At first, we asked whether an economy that saved could buy back its own output. Now we must ask whether an economy that grows can do the same.

The question brings us to consider a new relationship, unlike any we have considered before. The *marginal capital-output ratio,* as the formidable name suggests, is not a relationship that describes behavior, as the multiplier does. It describes a strictly technical or engineering or organizational relationship between an *increase in the stock of capital and the increase in output that this new capital will yield.*

Note that we are not interested in the ratio between our entire existing stock of capital (most of which is old) and the flow of total output, but only in the ratio between the *new* capital added during the period and the *new* output associated with that new capital. Thus the marginal capital-output ratio directs our attention to the *net investment* of the period and to the *change in output* of the period. If net investment was $60 billion and the change in output yielded by that investment was $20 billion, then the marginal capital-output ratio was 3.

The marginal capital-output ratio gives us a powerful new concept to bring to bear on the problem of attaining and maintaining a high, steady rate of growth, for we can now see that the problem of steady growth requires the balancing out of two different economic processes. Investment raises productive capacity. *Increases* in investment raise income and demand. What we must now do is investigate the relationship between these two different, albeit related, economic variables.

Let us begin with a familiar formula that shows how a change in investment affects a change in income. This is

$$\Delta Y = \frac{1}{\text{mps}} \times \Delta I,$$

which is nothing but the multiplier (see p. 262). For brevity, we will write it $\Delta Y = \frac{1}{s} \Delta I.$

Now we need a new formula to relate *I,* the rate of new investment (not $\Delta I,$ the *change* in new investment), and $\Delta O,$ the change in dollar output. This will require a symbol for the marginal capital-output ratio, a symbol that expresses how many dollars' worth of capital it takes to get an additional dollar's worth of output. If we use the symbol σ (sigma), we can write this formula as $\sigma = I/\Delta O$.

For example, if we have $10 of new investment, and output rises by $5, then σ (the marginal capital-output ratio) must be 2 ($10 ÷ $5). If output rises by only $3, σ is 3.3 (10 ÷ $3). Note that the *lower* the marginal capital-output ratio, the *higher* the productivity of new investment.

We now have two formulas. The first tells us by how much *income* will rise as investment grows. The second tells us the relationship between new investment and new *output*. Now, by a simple arithmetical operation, we can use our second formula to tell us the amount by which output will increase as investment increases. All we have to do is multiply both sides of the formula by ΔO and then divide both sides by σ to get $\Delta O = I/\sigma$.

This last formula tells us that if new investment is, say $10, and the marginal capital-output ratio is, say, 2.5, then the increase in output will be $4 ($10 ÷ 2.5).

We are ready to take the last and most important step. We can now discover *by how much investment must rise each year, to give us the additional income we will need to buy the addition to output that has been created by this selfsame investment.*

Our formulas enable us to answer that question very clearly. Increased income is ΔY. Increased output is ΔO. Since $\Delta Y = \dfrac{1}{s} \Delta I$ and $\Delta O = \dfrac{I}{\sigma}$ then ΔY will equal ΔO if $\dfrac{1}{s} \Delta I = \dfrac{I}{\sigma}$. This is the formula for balanced growth.

If we now multiply both sides of the equation by *s*, and then divide both sides by *I*, we get

$$\frac{\Delta I}{I} = \frac{s}{\sigma}$$

BALANCED GROWTH

What does this equation mean? It tells us what *rate of growth of investment* ($\Delta I / I$) is needed to make $\Delta Y = \Delta O$. In words, it tells us by what percentage investment spending must rise to make income payments keep pace with dollar output. That rate of growth is equal to the marginal savings ratio divided by the marginal capital-output ratio. Suppose, for instance, that the marginal savings ratio (including leakages) is ⅓ and that the marginal capital-output ratio (σ) is 3. Then s/σ is ⅓ ÷ 3 (or ⅑), which means that investment would have to grow by ⅑ to create just enough income to match the growing flow of output. If the rate of investment grew faster than that, income would move out ahead of output and we would be pushing beyond the path of balanced growth into inflation. If the rate of growth of investment were smaller than that, we would be experiencing chronic overproduction with falling prices and sagging employment.

What is the rate at which investment should rise for balanced growth in the United States? The question is difficult to answer for many reasons:

capital-output ratios present tricky statistical problems; *net* investment is not simple to calculate; and our marginal leakages do not always behave as tamely as they do in textbooks. Hence we shall sidestep the difficult *empirical* problem posed by the requirements for balanced growth and concentrate on the general insight the concept gives us. For the purpose of our analysis is not to allow us to prescribe the proper growth for investment, but to make clear the critical *relationship* between growth in income and growth in output. Our analysis shows us that we can have a "growth gap" if our leakages are too high, so that increases in investment (or for that matter, any increase in injections) do not generate enough new purchasing power; or if our marginal capital-output ratio changes, so that a given amount of investment increases our potential output (our capacity) too fast.

POLICY FOR BALANCED GROWTH

Suppose that we are not generating income fast enough to absorb our potential output. Suppose, to go back to Fig. 20-5, that we have a persistent growth gap similar to that of the late 1950s. How can we bring the economy up to its potential?

Our formula for balanced growth gives us the answer. The relationship between the growth of incomes and the growth of output depends above all on the rate at which investment *increases.* Thus, if expenditures fall short of the amount needed to absorb potential output, the answer is to raise the rate of investment or, perhaps more realistically, to raise the rate of growth of all expenditures, public and private. Conversely, of course, if we find ourselves pushing over the trend line of potential growth into inflation, as in the late 1960s, the indicated policy is to lower the rate of growth of investment (or of investment and government and consumption) to bring the flow of rising incomes back into balance with the rise of output.

Thus the critical element in balancing a growing economy is not the *amount* of investment needed to fill a given demand gap, but the *increase* in investment (or other injection-expenditure) needed to match a growing output capacity with a large enough demand.

IMPORTANCE OF GROWTH RATES

Yet, in the long run, the problem of unemployed resources may not be the most important problem we face. For when we look a few decades ahead, we begin to see that even the trajectory of full employment growth sets limits to our economic grasp. For instance, in 1960 a rather conservative Commission on National Goals established by President Eisenhower laid down a set of "goals"—from enhanced consumption through a variety of improved public and private programs—to be achieved by 1975 in some fifteen areas of national economic activity. Recently, the National Planning Association "costed out" these goals to see how many of them we were likely to reach. Its conclusion was *that even if output grew at 4 percent a year (14 percent faster than the traditional 3.5 percent rate), our GNP in 1975 would fall short by $150 billion of achieving the aspirations of the Eisenhower Com-*

Large GNP, slow growth rate

Small GNP, fast growth rate

Level of GNP

Time ⟶

**FIG. 20 • 6
THE DIFFERENCE
THAT GROWTH
RATES MAKE**

mission! GNP would then amount to $981 billion (in 1962 prices), whereas the cost of the desired goals would come to $1,127 billion. Only by raising the national growth rate to 5.5 percent (which would mean working the economy under a wartime-like forced draft) could we fulfill the program envisioned by the commission.

As this example makes clear, changes in growth rates of "only" a percentage point make very large differences in the absolute amount of output after a few years.* Indeed, if GNP grew at a 3 percent rate instead of a 4 percent rate, the shortfall to the commission's goal would increase from $150 billion to $375 billion. We might also recall that on p. 161 (Chapter 9) we indicated that at a growth rate of 4.3 percent, 40 percent of all families will have reached or surpassed an average income (in terms of 1970 dollars) of $15,000 by 1980. If growth should average only 2.5 percent, the percentage over the $15,000 line would be whittled down to 25. When we look to the future, in other words, it is not the present level of GNP that determines the outlook nearly so much as the rate at which that GNP will grow, as Fig. 20-6 illustrates.

Causes of Growth

EXTENSIVE
INVESTMENT

Thus we must think of growth not only as a means of remedying the underuse of resources, but as setting the trajectory that will define for us the scope of our realizable potential. But this changes our focus from one of merely increasing expenditures to one that asks the more fundamental question of how our capacity to produce can be increased.

* Recently, Professor Kenneth Boulding pointed out that before World War II no country sustained a growth of GNP per capita of more than 2.3 percent, whereas since World War II at least one country—Japan—has achieved and held a rate of growth of per capita GNP of 8 percent. Writes Boulding: "The difference between 2.3 percent and 8 percent may be dramatically illustrated by pointing out that [at 2.3 percent] children are twice as rich as their parents—i.e., per capita income approximately doubles every generation—while at 8 percent per annum, children are six times as rich as their parents." However, Boulding doubts that such rates of increase can be long maintained, for they would soon bring us up against absolute barriers of resources that would throttle growth back to a much slower pace. (*The Public Interest,* Fall 1966, p. 38.)

One answer to that fundamental question is obvious enough. The simplest way for an economy to raise its output is to increase its use of human and material resources—in more technical terms, *to increase factor inputs.* Indeed, total inputs *must* grow if the new members of the community are to get at least as large a share of output as the older members.

We cannot grow very successfully, however, if we try to use only the existing capital equipment for employing new members of the work force. The peasants who are born into our model underdeveloped economy, must be given spades—and this means, as we know, that there must be a prior increase in the output of hammers and chisels. In a highly developed industrial economy, an expanding labor force must be matched with new capital of all kinds (which requires additional machine-tool output). Failure to keep the capital-labor ratio constant will result in a steady falling-behind of the newer members of the labor force and a consequent diminution of growth.

Yet it is apparent that merely to match each new worker with as much equipment as his predecessors' is something like running to stay in place. This kind of *extensive* investment which "widens" the amount of capital wealth is essential if we are not to fall behind, but it does not result in our forging ahead. For that, we must *gain* output per capita—we must achieve more output for each unit of input, rather than maintain the previous level. The efficiency or *productivity* of our factors must be enhanced.

TABLE 20 • 3

REAL
OUTPUT
PER
MAN-HOUR

	1950	1969
Agriculture	100	309
Manufacturing	100	168

As we learned in the preceding chapter and as Table 20-3 reiterates, our inputs *have* been getting steadily more productive, both in industry and agriculture. On the average, during the 1950s and the 1960s, our labor productivity (our rate of output per man-hour of input) increased by a little under 2.9 percent a year, averaging industry, where it has been slower, and agriculture, where the rate has been very high. How important this increase in productivity has been in making possible our national growth is apparent in Fig. 20-7.

The chart shows that increases in productivity account for by far the larger part of our aggregate economic growth since World War II. The low labor input figure is, of course, partly the result of a rising rate of unemployment during many of these years, when we were not putting to work as

GNP (billions of 1958 dollars)

750
700
650
600
550
500
450
400
350
300
250
0

Addition to 1947 GNP attributable to increased productivity

Addition to 1947 GNP attributable to increased man-hours worked

1947 GNP

(Decline in man-hours for this year)

1947 '48 '49 '50 '51 '52 '53 '54 '55 '56 '57 '58 '59 '60 '61 '62 '63 '64 '65

Report of National Commission on Technology, 1966.

FIG. 20•7   SOURCE OF GNP INCREASES, 1947–1965

many of our increased numbers of workers as we might have. But even if 1947 rates of employment had been maintained, the role of productivity-increases would still have been predominant.

CAUSES OF IMPROVED PRODUCTIVITY

What accounts for the increase in labor productivity? Generally, we can distinguish four principal sources.

1. *Increased skills and education.*

In the short run, the dexterity, skills, and adaptability of the labor force make a tremendous difference in the amount of output obtainable from a given capital apparatus. Fiascoes of production testify to the absence of these determining influences in underdeveloped areas where modern plants must often be opened without a trained work force. In the longer run, it is not so much skills as general education that determines the output per individual worker. Contemporary studies place more and more stress on the productivity gains to be had from education, and attribute as much as one-fifth of the total U.S. growth rate to the steadily rising "stock" of education incorporated in the average worker.

2. Economies of large-scale production.

A second source of increased productivity per unit of input is the magnifying effect of mass production on output. Typically, when the organization of production reaches a certain critical size, especially in manufacturing, so-called "economies of scale" become possible. Many of these are based on the possibility of dividing complex operations into a series of simpler ones, each performed at high speed by a worker aided by specially designed equipment. It is difficult to estimate the degree of growth attributable to these economies of size. Certainly during the era of railroad-building and of the introduction of mass production, they contributed heavily to growth rate. In a careful study of the contemporary sources of U.S. growth, Edward F. Denison estimates that new economies of large-scale production add only about 10 percent to our annual rate of productivity increase.*

3. Deepening of capital.

We have talked of the "widening" of capital, as each new worker was given the necessary equipment to put him on a productive par with his fellows. Now we must add the concept of the "deepening" of capital, or increasing amount of capital with which each worker is equipped. Clearly, if we give each worker more machinery and other types of capital goods to work with, we should expect him to be able to increase his output for each hour's work. Over the long course of economic growth, increased productivity has required the slow accumulation of very large capital stocks per working individual. Thus investment that increases capital per worker is, and will probably continue to be, one of the most effective levers for steadily raising output per worker. But unlike the steady widening of capital, the deepening of capital is not a regular process. Between 1929 and 1947 there was no additional capital added per worker! This was, of course, a time of severe depression and thereafter of enforced wartime stringencies. Since 1947, the value of our stock of capital per worker has been growing at about 2.7 percent a year. As we shall see, immediately following, however, the *size* of this additional stock of capital is of less crucial importance than the *productivity* of that capital—that is, its technological character.

4. Technology.

We have just mentioned the fourth and last main source of increases in productivity—technology. During the past half century, GNP has consistently grown faster than can be accounted for by increases in the work force or the size of the capital stock. (Even during the 1929-1947 era, for instance, when capital stock per worker remained fixed, the output of GNP per

---

* *The Sources of Economic Growth in the United States* (New York: Committee for Economic Development, 1962).

worker grew by 1.5 percent a year.) Part of this "unexplained" increase can be attributed to some of the sources of growth we have itemized above—mainly education and training, and economies of scale. But contemporary economic investigation increasingly attributes the bulk of the "bonus" rate of growth to the impact of new technology.

The term is, admittedly, somewhat vague. By "new technology" we mean new inventions of the demand-creating kind we have talked about, innovations of a labor-displacing (but productivity-enhancing) kind, the growth of knowledge in the form of research and development, changes in business organization or in techniques of management, and many other activities. What is increasingly apparent, however, is that the search for new products and processes is the main force behind much productivity-enhancing investment. Thus while investment has become less important for growth simply as a means of adding sheer quantities of capital to the labor force (although that is still a very important function, particularly in construction), it remains the strategic variable as the carrier of technological change.

CHANGING
PATTERNS
OF GROWTH

It is time to sum up what we have covered. We have seen that long-term growth proceeds from two sources: *more* input and more *productive* input, and we have been concerned with studying some of the main facets of both kinds of growth. Perhaps we can summarize our findings in Fig. 20-8, comparing the sources of growth in two eras of our past.

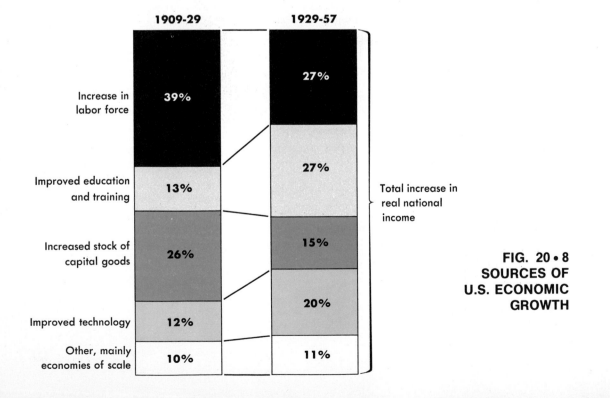

FIG. 20 • 8
SOURCES OF
U.S. ECONOMIC
GROWTH

Note the declining importance played by increases in numbers of workers or sheer dollar value of capital, and the increasing importance of the "intangibles" of education and technology. To a number of observers, this shift implies that we have been slowly moving into a new phase of industrial organization in which productivity will more and more reflect the application of scientific knowledge, rather than the brute leverage of mechanical strength and power. Whether this "post-industrial" society will grow at a faster or slower rate than in the past is a question that we will not be able to answer for many years.

But will we want to grow as fast as possible in the future? Until very recent years, economists talked as if growth were a self-evident goal, an activity that justified itself. And indeed, if growth unfailingly brought better living conditions to most Americans, we could make that assumption. But within the last decade we have come to recognize that for some segments of our society, uncontrolled growth may actually bring disbenefits that outweigh its gains for others.

Two reasons underlie this increasing skepticism with regard to the "self-evident" benefits of growth. The first we have already looked into in Chapter 10, where we warned that we *measure* growth by the concept of GNP, that great catch-all, which includes pointless or even harmful as well as socially useful production (Kenneth Boulding's Gross National Cost, again). As long as GNP counts armaments and junk and the cleaning bills imposed by dirty smokestacks, along with food, clothing, and shelter, we are only deluding ourselves that a growth in GNP can be *automatically* equated with genuine social betterment.

But there is a second reason. Even if all production *were* socially useful, we have come to realize that output always and invariably includes more than the goods and services we consume or accumulate. *Integrally connected with the production of goods and services is the production of residuals, wastes, and effluents.* After a good has been "consumed" by a household or "used up" by a business enterprise, it is still there, either as scrap or garbage or in physically and chemically changed form as gas or liquid or solid waste or dissipated heat.

Thus growth—indeed, production itself, even without growth—unavoidably involves us in an interference with the environment, first as we extract materials from their natural settings, then as we "process" them (creating physical and chemical by-products while so doing), and finally as we throw them away after we have finished with them.

Until recent years, we have largely ignored most of this environmental disruption, although we have been concerned from time to time with particularly dangerous or obnoxious by-products such as the smells from slaughterhouses or the poisonous smokes from certain chemical manufacturing processes. In the main, however, we have regarded these aspects of production as unimportant, primarily because the environment seemed to provide an immense dumping ground into which we could throw away the by-products and unwanted end-products of production without thought or concern.

Now, however, as our first glimpse into the pollution problem in Chapter 1 made clear (and as we will see again in Chapter 28 when we look into the matter of controlling pollution), we no longer have that comfortable assurance. It is clear that the absorptive capacity of the environment is not limitless. Hence the question arises as to whether we can *permit* growth, taking the risk that it may become a danger to survival. Must not the objective of a rational economic policy be stability and ecological balance rather than a mindless accumulation of wealth that may end by smothering us all?

THE STATIONARY STATE AND ECOLOGICAL BALANCE

Is zero growth the answer to the ecological problem? Or in the terminology introduced by John Stuart Mill in 1848, should the goal of a rational society be a "stationary" state?

Here it is helpful to disentangle two quite separate ideas. A *stationary* state essentially means a society in which *output per capita remains stable* (and in which population growth has come to an end, so that there is need for only replacement investment). Such a society no longer "grows," *but that does not mean it no longer pollutes.* A society that has no growth in per capita output can still be pouring wastes into the environment; and if those wastes are greater than the environment can absorb, its real standard of living will decline.

The second idea is that of a society in ecological "balance." By this we mean a society that has controlled its rate of pollution so that the environment is not significantly affected. It may have strictly regulated the allowable output of smoke or the means of garbage disposal, or it may have greatly encouraged the use of waste materials as new inputs into the system (so-called recycling). Such a society will have rationally controlled its relationship with the environment,* but it need not be a stationary state!

There is no reason, for example, why the per capita production of nonpolluting output, such as personal services, could not increase indefinitely; so, too, with the output of goods that do not impose environmental ill effects. For example, if we learn to grow more crops with fertilizers that do not damage the soil, there is no reason why an ecologically-minded society

---

* There are certain adverse environmental effects that are unavoidable—one being the generation of heat, the other the gradual depletion of nonrenewable resources, such as fossil fuels and ores. An ecologically advanced society can plan its rate of heat generation and resource depletion to minimize the problems that each imposes, but it cannot avoid either problem entirely.

should not seek to increase its agricultural output if it so desired. To the extent that it could harvest its wastes by recycling them, its standard of living could also increase.

In the short run, then, the pollution problem imposes a new series of costs on production. Pollution control will require the expenditure of large sums to minimize the environmental disruption caused by rising production; but pollution does not in and of itself dictate an end to growth as a meaningful social goal. Rather, it cautions us that we shall have to learn to distinguish between growth that harms the environment and growth that does not, and to beware of "growth" that is present in the statistics of GNP but not in real life. For example, the very expenditures needed to control pollution will themselves be included in GNP (Gross National Cost, again), but these "defensive" expenditures will serve only to maintain, not to improve, the well-being associated with our "growing" output.

THE SHORT AND THE LONG RUN

In the long run, the problem is more complex and demanding. When the underdeveloped nations finally create high-productivity economies, in which each individual will enjoy the use of more than the miserably inadequate fraction of the earth's resources that he now has at his disposal, a new imperative is likely to emerge. For the sum total of demands on the earth's agricultural, mineral, or energy resources may then exceed the rate at which those resources can be made available. Moreover, the effluents from a global rate of production carried on at U.S. or European levels might constitute an overload on the earth's total absorptive capacity unless we become more and more adroit at recycling. If we do not, a ceiling on global production may be imposed by nature if not by man, and in all likelihood such a ceiling would entail a considerable diminution of the standard of living of the industrialized nations.

We will refer to this problem again in Chapter 34 when we study the underdeveloped nations. But it is clear that in a long-run perspective the issue of ecological balance takes on an aspect different from that in the short run. For in the long run there is no alternative to viewing the earth itself as a spaceship (in Kenneth Boulding's phrase) to whose ultimately finite carrying capacity its passengers must adjust their ways. From this point of view, production itself suddenly appears as a "throughput," beginning with the raw material of the environment and ending with the converted material of the production process, which is returned to the environment by way of emissions, residuals, and so on. In managing this throughput, the task of producers is not to maximize "growth," but to do as little damage to the environment as possible during the inescapable process of transformation by which man lives. If "growth" enters man's calculations in this period of rationally controlled production, it can be only insofar as he can extract more and more "utility" from less and less material input; that is, as he learns to economize on the use of the environment by recycling his wastes and by avoiding the disturbance of delicate ecological systems.

Such a spaceship economy is probably still some distance off, although by no means so far away that our children or grandchildren may not encounter its problems. Much depends on the rate at which the backward countries grow in population and productivity, and on the technological means of lessening pollution in the advanced countries. Much depends also on the development of means to prevent the dumping of pollutants across national boundaries, such as the gases from West Germany that blow into Sweden. Not least, a true spaceship earth would require a feeling of international amity sufficiently great so that the industrialized peoples of the world would willingly acquiesce in global production ceilings that penalized them much more severely than their poorer sister nations.

These longer perspectives begin to make us aware of the extent of the ecology problem. Growth is desperately needed by a world that is, in most nations, still desperately poor. Pollution is already beginning to threaten a world that is running out of "environment." If growth inevitably brings pollution, we shall be faced with a cruel choice indeed. Today we have only begun to recognize the problems of pollution-generating growth, and we are engaged in devising remedies for these problems on a national basis. Ahead lies the much more formidable problem of a world in which growth may encounter ecological barriers on a worldwide scale, bringing the need for new political and economic arrangements for which we have no precedent. The true Age of Spaceship Earth is still some distance in the future, but for the first time the passengers on the craft are aware of its limitations.

KEY CONCEPTS AND KEY WORDS

1. **Growth in output derives from *investment that adds to our stock of capital wealth.* In an industrialized society, this investment is achieved by utilizing an existing capital-goods sector. But in a poor society, the process is much more difficult.**

Capital-goods sector

2. **In such a poor society, we can see that the *capital-goods sector consists of two subsectors:* one producing capital goods that, in turn, make the equipment used in the consumption-goods sector; and the other making machine tools, capital goods that can create more capital goods.**

3. ***Thus growth requires two shifts:* (1) the machine-tool capacity of the capital-goods sector must be enlarged and (2) resources must be shifted from the consumption sector to the capital goods sector.**

Growth rates

4. **United States growth has been shown a *persistently steady rate* of 3.5 percent—1.5 percent per capita—for well over a century. From *year to year,* however, the *rate of growth is very uneven.***

Business cycles

5. **We can discern *many cyclical patterns* in the year-to-year variations. The most important is "the" *8 to 10 year business cycle.* We designate its main features as upper and lower turning points (or peak and trough), expansion and contraction.**

6. Many causes have been suggested to explain the business cycle, but none has been wholly satisfactory in accounting for its *cyclicality* or in explaining why its *periodicity* is 8 to 10 years.

7. Economists today explain the cycle as *variations in the rate of expansion.* The interaction of the multiplier and the accelerator explain the expansive and contractive phases. Upper turning points are usually caused by one or more of the many economic strains induced by the expansion itself; lower turning points tend to come about from the "bottoming out" of the contractive spiral.

Multiplier-
accelerator
interaction

8. Actual growth often falls behind *potential growth* or full employment growth. The wastage in output is best avoided by maintaining a high rate of aggregate demand.

9. The goal of a high steady rate of growth leads us to investigate the problem of matching our increase in capacity, or potential output, with a sufficient increase in purchasing power, or income. Increases in capacity depend on the *marginal capital-output ratio,* which describes the relationship between an increase in capital stock and the increased flow of output from that new stock. Increases in demand result from the multiplier, which magnifies the income-effect of a *rise* in investment (or of any injection). Balanced growth will occur when the income effect is just equal to the capacity effect.

Marginal
capital-output ratio

Balanced growth

10. If growth falls below the potential of the economy, the remedy lies in increasing the rate of growth of expenditures in the economy, both private and public. If we exceed our potential, the remedy is to cut the rate of growth of these expenditures.

Potential growth

Productivity

11. Potential growth depends on deeper causes. One of these is the *amount of labor input and the extensive investment* needed to maintain labor/capital ratios. A second and more important cause is *improved productivity.*

Economies of scale

12. Productivity, in turn, results from many sources. Among the most important are: *increased skills and education, economies of large-scale production, deepening of capital equipment,* and *technological advance.* Increasingly, growth has resulted from enhanced education and technology rather than from more inputs of labor or capital.

Extensive investment

Deepening
of capital

13. Growth has many advantages, but it is far from costless. We are increasingly conscious that the process of production itself inevitably creates wastes, effluents, scrap, and other unwanted by-products. Growth thus poses the prospect of environmental damage that may more than offset any addition to output.

Pollution

14. Is zero growth the answer? We must distinguish between a *stationary state,* which can still be pouring effluents into the environment, and an *ecologically "balanced" state,* in which environmental disruption is minimized but where growth may still occur.

Stationary state

15. In the short run we must seek to curb *harmful* growth. In the long run, it is possible that we may have to impose global ceilings on some forms of material outputs. This vast problem constitutes a major political and economic challenge to the future.

Ecological
balance

Q U E S T I O N S

1. Describe carefully the shifts in labor needed to begin the process of growth in a very simple economy. Are such shifts visible in an advanced economy?

2. What is the special property of machine tools? Is there a very simple article of output that is also capable of the dual uses of machine tools? How about the seed corn held back by a farmer?

3. How do you explain the fact that the year-to-year growth of the United States is so much more irregular than the long-term growth?

4. Describe the course of events in a "typical" business cycle. How does such a cycle get started? How does it build up? What is likely to bring it to an end? How does the decline come about? What stops it?

5. Do you think that the policies needed to minimize the fluctuations of the business cycle are the same as those needed to accelerate long-term growth? Discuss what you would do to improve stability and to augment potential output.

6. What is meant by the marginal capital-output ratio? How is it different from the multiplier?

7. Write the formula for changes in *capacity* and for changes in *income*. Show algebraically how an increase in income can match an increase in output. *Explain* what the formula of balanced growth means.

8. What is different between a demand gap, in our original analysis, and a growth gap? Explain how the remedy in one case is a given amount of investment, and in the other, a rate of growth of investment.

9. What is extensive investment? What is intensive investment? Which is more conducive to growth?

10. Why is productivity so important in achieving growth? What are its main sources? What would you recommend as a long-term program to raise American productivity?

11. What do you think are the main purposes to which growth should be directed? How would you arrange for growth to be directed to these ends?

12. Suppose that the discovery of a hitherto unsuspected poisonous effluent made it necessary to impose zero growth on the *material* output of the U.S. economy. Can you think of ways in which the same volume of material production could be used to yield higher aggregate well-being? Could you devise a plan for growth that would avoid increasing material production?

13. Do you think that *global* "growth-control" is a realistic goal? If not, what do you foresee as the long-term "scenario" of world economics and politics?

Microeconomics

anatomy

of a

market

system

Thus far we have looked at the economic panorama from two very different perspectives. In the first part of our text we surveyed the scene from an historical vantage point that gave us a sense of the evolution of things, a feeling for the direction in which our own world was drifting. Then, in the second part, we took another look at the economy, this time not from a position that highlighted long-term currents of change, but from one that illumined the problems of its day-to-day operation as a vast mechanism for producing an aggregate flow of goods and services.

Now we pass to a third, and in some ways most basic, view of economic society—one that brings us *within* the economy to a degree that we have not as yet experienced. Put differently, we know a good deal about the operation of "the system" as a whole, but very little about the activities of the individuals who, in their various roles, make the system behave as it does. The study of microeconomics will introduce us to this essential aspect of the economic process.

MICRO- AND MACRO- ECONOMICS

How is it that we have been able to study so much about the workings of the system without learning about the basic role of the individual? The answer is that we already *have* touched on microeconomic problems, without, however, stopping to examine them in detail. Throughout macroeconomies, for example, we have referred to supply and demand, but until now we have neither looked very carefully into the meaning of those words nor sought to make clear how these "forces" in the market system originated in the specific behavior of buyers and sellers. So, too, we have talked of investment or employment or consumption without pausing to examine these economic processes in terms of their behavioral roots—that is, without looking into the *individual decisions* to expand production or to hire or fire a worker or to buy a commodity, out of which the aggregative phenomena themselves arose.

Yet all these large-scale economic processes necessarily have their origins in the behavior patterns of individuals or firms. Inflation and deflation, the operations of the multiplier or the workings of the credit system, all take place through changes in the market actions of households or businesses.

The point leads to a conclusion of importance: *Every macroeconomic process has its microeconomic base.* All the problems we have studied as aggregative economic movements can be resolved under the microscope of economic inquiry into the motions of large numbers of individual market participants. Macro- and microeconomics are thus not two separate fields of economics, but only two approaches to the selfsame processes and problems.

Why the two perspectives? The answer is that one approach by itself fails to illumine the whole range of economic concerns. Macroeconomics is not very pertinent, for instance, if we are interested in the effect of monopoly on prices—a problem that microtheory lights up brilliantly. Microtheory, on the other hand, is of relatively little use when we investigate the level of output as a whole, a problem that lies at the very center of macroeconomics. Perhaps some day a new approach to economics will combine the broad scope of macrotheory with the finer scrutiny of microtheory, but until that time, someone who wants to understand how a market system works has no choice but to supplement his macro perspective with a view of economics at the micro level.

What do we see when we approach the economy from this new angle of vision? Our first impression is totally unlike that of macroeconomics. Perhaps we remember looking down from our initial flight over the economy on the broad and impressive landscape of our national wealth. Nothing so orderly greets our eye as the aircraft alights and we take our first glimpse of the economy at close range.

We seem to have landed in a scene of considerable confusion. The patterns so clearly distinguishable from above have disappeared; where there was order there is now a seeming chaos. Land, labor, and capital, for instance—those factors of production whose interaction we followed so easily from the air—turn out at ground level to be nothing but thousands of

SYSTEM IN MICRO PERSPECTIVE

men and women bustling around in search of someone to hire their services; it is hard to see a man as a "factor of production" when he is sitting in an employment office or in a brokerage office, and still more difficult to think of his actions—taking a job or not, buying a stock or selling it—as part of a large-scale social process. So, too, consumption and investment—those majestic rivers of expenditure on which depend the aggregate flow of output—now appear as nothing more than the activities of housewives in supermarkets, or the decisions of the supermarket operator as to whether or not to add another checkout counter. Even the price level disappears; there is no "level" at close quarters, but only a thousand different prices, some in motion, some not.

Our overriding first impression of the microeconomy is no longer one of orderly and clearly distinguishable patterns of behavior, but of the most highly individualistic, uncoordinated, perhaps even disorderly behavior. We seem no longer to be observing an economy, but to be watching a bazaar. And our first impression is largely correct. We have landed in the market.

THE MARKET AS A SYSTEM

The market is not, of course, a bazaar; it is a system. The confusion of shoppers, job seekers, prices is not confined to a single locale but is diffused throughout every part of the society to which our eyes now turn. The buying and selling that we see are not merely casual activities, but somehow bind the whole system together, providing not alone the dynamic impulse but the guiding hand to a process that, when viewed from above, seemed to take place without any individual motivation at all.

How does the market system exert its controlling as well as its impelling force? The question reminds us again of the consternation expressed by the delegation from an underdeveloped country to whom we talked in Chapter 2. The representatives of a traditional society found it hard to believe that a community of unrestrained buyers and sellers could hang together and solve its economic problems. Now that we are face to face with the market in reality it is not so easy for us, either, to be certain that it can.

The Tasks of the Market

Perhaps it will help if we refresh our memory of what the market system is supposed to do. We remember from our early introduction to the market society that all economic systems had to solve the twin tasks of production and distribution—of determining *what* goods to produce and *how* to produce them, and of deciding *to whom* to give them. In our first approach we stressed the social aspect of these questions—that is, the problem of devising social institutions that would be capable of mobilizing men and securing their assent to some division of their output. But whereas that emphasis was necessary as a prelude to learning how the market society itself evolved, it is less useful when we can now take such a society for granted and inquire into its economic mechanism.

Let us therefore look at the tasks of the market once again, in a somewhat different light. Suppose we have an island where we can make only two kinds of output. We can use our land, labor, and capital to grow grain or we can use them to raise cattle for milk. Now suppose that we used all of our resources for grain production for one year and found that we could grow 1,000 tons of grain. The following year, we put our whole effort into dairy farming and discovered that we netted 500 gallons of milk. We would now have discovered two extreme production possibilities for the allocation of our social effort.

But the chances are that we would prefer to have a mixture of grain and milk, rather than all of one and none of the other. Hence we would have to find out, by experimenting, what combinations of grain and milk we could enjoy by using some of our resources for each occupation. Fig. 21-1 shows us what kind of *production-possibility curve* we might in fact have.

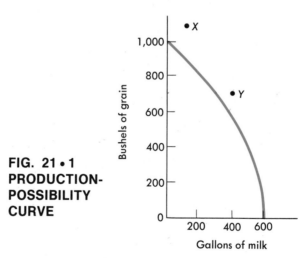

FIG. 21•1 PRODUCTION-POSSIBILITY CURVE

The production-possibility curve shows us a number of things. First it makes vivid the material meaning of the word *scarcity*. Any point outside the frontier of the curve is unattainable for our island community, given its present resources. This is obviously true of point X. But look at point Y. This is an output that represents roughly 700 bushels of grain and 400 gallons of milk. Either one of these goals, taken separately, lies well within the production possibilities of the island. What the curve shows us is that *we cannot have both at the same time.* If we want 700 bushels of grain, we must be content with less than 400 gallons of milk: and if we want 400 gallons of milk we will have to settle for about 600 bushels of grain. Thus we see that *at the core of the production problem lies the necessity for choice.* This unavoidable choice is imposed, of course, by the existing resources and our technical knowledge. But the frontier of possibilities is not static. As capital and knowledge grow, the frontier can advance, so that what was impossible in the past becomes attainable in the future. For instance, the invention of a new cattle fodder might raise the production-possibility of milk on our island. Then our production-possibility curve would look like Fig. 21-2.

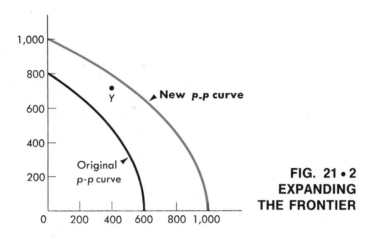

FIG. 21 • 2
EXPANDING
THE FRONTIER

We could now easily produce 700 bushels of grain and 400 gallons of milk—in fact, more of either or more of both. But the location of point *Y* in Fig. 21-2 makes clear another meaning of the *p-p* curve. The curve shows our production possibilities *when we use our resources fully.* If we fail to employ all our land, labor, and capital (or if we use them ineffectively) we will end up with a collection of goods, such as *Y*, that falls short of our potential. From our study of macroeconomics, we know that this is all too often the case.

MORE PRODUCTION POSSIBILITIES

The production-possibility curve illumines for us more than the choice we may have to make between alternative goods such as grain and milk. We can use the concept to illustrate as well the choice between consumption and investment for a fully employed society, or between the division of output into public or private use. In fact, with a little imagination we can construct a three-dimensional production-possibility *surface* that will show us the limits imposed by scarcity on a society that divides its output among three uses, such as consumption, investment, and government. Figure 21-3 shows what such a diagram looks like.

Note how the production-possibility surface swells out from the origin like a wind-filled spinnaker sail. Any place on the sail represents some combination of consumption, investment, and government spending that is within the reach of the community. Any place "behind" the surface represents a failure of the economy to employ all its resources. It is a graphic depiction of unemployment of men or materials.

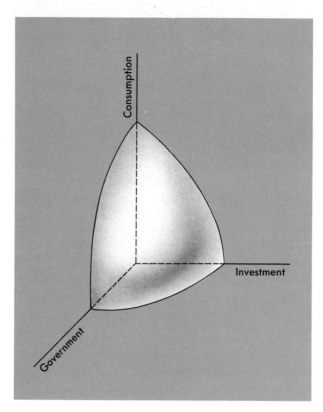

FIG. 21 • 3
A PRODUCTION-
POSSIBILITY
SURFACE

One last point deserves clarification before we move on. The alert student may have noticed that all the production-possibility curves have bowed shapes. The reason for this lies in the *changing efficiency* of our resources as we shift them from one use to another. When we are concentrating all our resources on grain, for example, we have to use some land, labor, and capital that would be much better suited to producing milk. Hence the initial transfer of some resources out of grain and into milk gives us a relatively larger gain in milk than our loss in grain—which is why the curve at this end of the graph slopes "milkward" rather that "grainward." At the other end of the curve, just the opposite considerations prevail. Now we have to cram into milk production the last units of resources that must be withdrawn from the grain production to which they are better suited. Hence, here the gain in milk output is proportionately much less than at the

THE LAW OF
INCREASING
COST

other end of the scale, and the loss in grain output proportionately much more. Therefore the curve now slopes more sharply in the direction of grain than milk.

We call this changing efficiency, represented by the bowed curve, the *law of increasing costs*. Note that it is a law imposed by nature, rather than behavior. For what would it mean if the curve connecting the two points of all-out grain or milk production were a straight line? It would mean that as we shifted resources from one use to the other, we would always get exactly the same results: the last man and the last acre put into milk would give us exactly as much milk, at the loss of exactly as much grain, as the first man and the first acre.

This *could* be the case, of course, but it implies that there is absolutely no difference from one man, or acre, to another, or that it made no difference as to the *proportions* in which factors, even if they were homogenous, were combined. That is a very unrealistic assumption. Men and land (and any other resource) *are* different and different products *do* utilize them in different proportions. Hence, as we shift them from one use to another, assuming that we always choose the resources best suited for the job, society's efficiency changes. At first we enjoy a very low cost in terms of what we must give up for what we get; thereafter, an increasing cost. Although the shapes of production-possibility curves may have considerably different contours, the unevenness of nature's gifts make most of them bowed, or concave from below. We will study more about the limitations imposed by nature when we come to the law of diminishing returns in Chapter 25.

FROM PRODUCTION POSSIBILITIES TO MARKET ACTUALITIES

The production-possibility curve gives a fresh meaning to the tasks of the market, in particular to the questions of what goods to produce and how to produce them. It makes us see that economics is basically concerned with choices and decisions that result in different levels and assortments of output.

But there is something of a puzzle in the contrast between the production-possibility diagram with its clear-cut outline of economic choice and the milling confusion of the marketplace. We turned to the production-possibility curve to clarify the tasks that the market as a system was to perform. But we have yet to understand how a particular point X or Y on the diagram is brought into being. Who decides whether society will use its resources for milk or grain, or public or private use or what combination of them? Who determines whether society operates on the frontier of its potential or suffers the consequences of a less than-full use of resources?

The answer, of course, is the interaction of individuals and firms we call the market system. Thus we study the market mechanism to learn about not only the potentialities of a system, but about its actualities, for microeconomics will teach us how the financial exchanges of buyers and sellers bring about the actual level and composition and disposition of output in our society.

How does the market, with its immense confusion of individuals and firms, determine the allocation of society's resources? If we are to answer this question we will have to disentangle the market's activities and discover in its flux some pattern that will allow us to grasp how it works.

Is there such a pattern? Indeed, there is—and what is more, exactly the same pattern that originally illumined the economy from the perspective of macroeconomics. There, we recall, we first understood the structure of the macro system as a great circular flow that linked together the expenditures of the sectors and the receipts of the various firms, and then the expenditures of firms and the receipts of the sectors. Now if we look carefully into the market we can find the selfsame circular flow, only reduced from its vast national dimensions to the tiny circuits that bind together individual households and individual firms. We can see the circular flow in Fig. 21-4. Note that the units of the microeconomic world, households (or individuals) and firms, interact in two ways, just as they do in the macro process. Each household, acting as a consumer, buys goods from individual firms who act as sellers. And each household, now acting as a factor of production, sells its

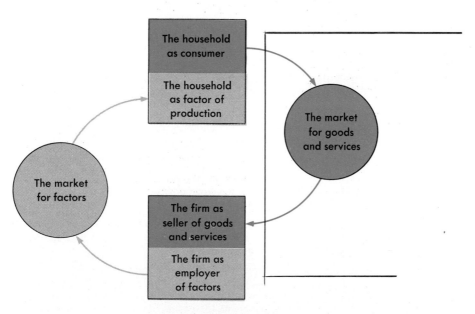

FIG. 21 • 4 CIRCULAR FLOW IN MICROVIEW

services to firms who now become buyers. Thus, as before, a flow of spending from households to firms, and a return flow from firms to households, binds the system together.

<table>
<tr><td>

THE
TWO
MARKETS
</td><td>

But why bother to retrace a circular flow that is already familiar to us? The answer is that an examination of the flow gives us a clue to *where* the transactions of the marketplace exert their pushes and pulls on the allocation of goods and resources that we examined in the production-possibility curve. For looking at the circular flow, we notice that it passes through two markets. One of these, the *market for goods and services,* is certainly a key location for the allocation of goods to various uses. Equally important, we can see, is the *market for factors* through which the flow of expenditure returns to the household where it originated: here is certainly where the distribution of incomes (and therefore of shares in the total output) must be determined. Last, there is the firm itself, where the services of the factors are combined to yield a flow of output. This must be where the system determines in what way output shall be produced.

Hence we begin to see how the complicated flux of the market system can be untangled. One by one we must study the market for goods and then that for factors and then the internal operations of the firm, to find out how the system decides *what goods* to produce and *to whom* to give them and *how to produce them.* It will take us several chapters before the links can be joined and the system as a whole set into motion. But by then we will have learned a good deal about what the economy looks like at the micro level.
</td></tr>
</table>

KEY CONCEPTS AND KEY WORDS

<table>
<tr><td>

Microeconomics
</td><td>

1. Microeconomics *is an approach* to economics that begins with the actions of *individuals and firms* in the market process.

2. *Every macroeconomic process has its roots in microeconomic behavior.*
</td></tr>
<tr><td>

Production-
possibility curves
</td><td>

3. The market is a system for the solution of the basic economic problems of *production* and *distribution.* We can visualize the basic production tasks of the market by means of a *production-possibility diagram.*

4. The production-possibility curve makes clear the limiting fact of scarcity and the consequent need for *choice.* It also indicates clearly the difference between the full use of resources and their inefficient or partial use.
</td></tr>
<tr><td>

Increasing costs
</td><td>

5. The bowed shape of production-possibility curves reflects the *law of increasing costs.* This basic economic relationship describes the fact that our efficiency changes as we shift resources from one use to another, and that typically we experience a decreasing efficiency (with the consequence of increasing costs) as we move more and more resources into the production of any given item.
</td></tr>
</table>

6. The market brings about the dispositions of the real economy through a *network of transactions.* We can simplify this network into a *circular flow,* similar to that in the macroeconomy.

Circular flow

7. The circular flow reveals the critical points at which the market performs its tasks—*the market for goods and services, the market for factors, and the internal workings of the firm.* Here is where society faces the three critical questions: what to produce, how to produce it, and to whom to distribute it.

What, how, to whom

Q U E S T I O N S

1. What is meant by the microeconomic roots of behavior? What is the microeconomic base of the following macrophenomena: inflation, depression, economic growth, the demand gap? Is there such a thing as macroeconomic *behavior?*

2. What is meant by the market as a *system?*

3. Describe the circular flow as it appears from the micro viewpoint. What relation does it bear to the circular flow from the macro viewpoint?

4. What is the difference between the market for goods and that for factor services? On which market is the household a seller? The firm a seller? Can household and firm both be on the same side of the same market?

5. What would a production-possibility curve look like for a society that could produce either a million cars per year or 100,000 buildings? Now suppose that technical advances made it possible to build 200,000 buildings, but only the same number of cars. In what way would the curve shift? Mark a point *x* to show where a fully employed society might locate its production, to yield both cars and buildings (in whatever proportions you wish). Mark another point *y* to show the consequence of unemployment for such a society. Mark still another point *z* to show a point that is beyond the production capacity of the society, even though it represents fewer cars and fewer buildings than the economy could produce if it concentrated on either one of those alone.

The market for goods is the part of the market system with which we are all most familiar, for we constantly enter it as purchasers of commodities.* Now we must scrutinize this market to learn how it actually works—to discover not only how prices are formed by transactions of individuals and firms, but also how these prices, once formed, help carry out the allocatory tasks of the market system as a whole.

Everyone knows, whether or not he has taken a course in economics, that prices in the market reflect "supply and demand." When the price of milk goes up, we all say that the demand for milk must have risen for some reason or other, or that the supply of milk must have been cut. But this very general appreciation of the "forces" at work only begins to explain how prices are actually determined, and tells us nothing about how these prices in turn affect our own behavior.

BEHAVIOR AND PRICES

What is the meaning of supply and demand? Our acquaintance with the rise of market society tells us a good deal about the kind of behavior the terms describe. We remember that the emergence of the market system forced individuals to shift for themselves in a harsh world where private transactions determined both their incomes and their expenses. In such a world, sheer self-preservation dictated that buyers and sellers had to follow the arrow of price advantage if they were going to survive, much less prosper. Hence buying as cheaply as possible and selling as dearly as possible became the cardinal rule of behavior for both individuals and firms in a market setting. Added to this was the growing acceptance of economic

---

* For many years, the late E. H. Chamberlain used to enliven his famous course at Harvard on the workings of the market by dividing his students into "sellers" and "buyers," giving to each person secret instructions about the price range he was allowed to operate within. Thereafter the students were loosed into a free-for-all, each to make bargains with the other side as best he could. As each buyer and seller reached accord, their agreed-upon price was shown to Professor Chamberlain. At the end of the session, the average of the prices reached in the classroom was compared with the average of the price options given out. Chamberlain noted that the class result was regularly *under* the true average of buying and selling options, and he hypothesized that this was due to the superior skill his students had already accumulated as buyers, and their relative unfamiliarity with the role of seller.

gain as a primary goal of economic life, and the rule of Buy Cheap and Sell Dear was given a second social sanction.

These historic motives of self-preservation and economic gain have changed considerably as the extreme pressures of early capitalism have given way to the far more sheltered setting of contemporary capitalism. Yet, albeit in the pursuit of somewhat altered objectives, we still usually behave as buyers by trying to spend as little as possible for the goods we want, and as sellers by trying to get as much as we can for the goods and services we have to offer.

This clearly makes *the prices of goods* very important as stimuli that guide our behavior. Comparative prices enable us to make choices that will improve our economic position. But prices do more than this. *Prices also become signals that direct our behavior.* In fact, it is through our reaction to prices that self-interest becomes a "force" on the market-place.

But since buyers and sellers have conflicting self-interests, how can this be? The answer is that the same price signal gives rise to *different* behavior, depending on which side of the market we are. A rising price will usually look bad for buyers but good for sellers. Falling prices will generally be in the self-interest of buyers (who can now satisfy their wants for less money), but against the self-interest of sellers (who will now get less return for their efforts). Thus we begin to see that the price mechanism may be the way of satisfying divergent interests, of bringing together parties whose economic gains lie in opposing directions. That is why microeconomics is sometimes called *price theory.*

Conditions of Supply and Demand

Let us explore this idea by looking more carefully into the actual considerations that guide me as a buyer or seller.

When I enter the market for goods, which I do virtually every time I walk along a street, two factors determine whether or not I will actually become a buyer and not just a window-shopper. The first factor is the *tastes and desires* that decide whether I am willing to spend my money on the things I see. The windows of shops are crammed with many things that I could afford to buy if I wanted to, but which I simply do not wish to own. Perhaps if they were very cheap, I might wish to buy them; or possibly I would not even want them if they were free. For such goods, for which my desires are too weak to motivate me, my demand is zero.

On the other hand, my tastes and desires alone by no means suffice to make me a buyer. The shop windows are also full of goods that I would very much like to own but that I cannot afford to buy because they are too expensive: my demand for Rolls Royces is also zero. Thus demand hinges on the *ability*—the possession of sufficient wealth or income—as well as on the *willingness* of the buyer. If it did not, the poor, whose wants are always very large, would constitute the greatest source of demand.

Note that my demand for goods depends on both my willingness and my ability to buy them *at their going price.* From this it follows that the amount of goods I will demand will change as their prices change. If I see a sports car for $10,000 I am likely to be neither willing nor able to make the purchase, whereas the same car at $5,000 would find me both a great deal more willing and much more able; and at $2,000, it might set me to wondering if perhaps I should not buy two.

In the same way, willingness and ability both enter the market force of supply. Many suppliers of goods would be *willing* to offer certain commodities or services at certain prices, but are unable to do so because they lack the skills or the access to certain materials. Other suppliers may be perfectly *able* to offer the commodity at that price but may be unwilling to do so because they would incur a loss by doing so, or because of some other disinclination. Once again, price enters into the middle of this decision. At $10,000 many enterprisers would be willing (although not all might be able) to produce sports cars; at $5,000 the willingness and ability would be much reduced; and at $2,000 no one might be prepared to supply a single car.

This simple dissection of the considerations behind buying and selling tells us a good deal: supply and demand are terms that indicate our willingness and ability to sell or buy certain quantities of goods at certain prices. *Supply and demand are thus concepts that link our market behavior with price.*

MARGINAL
UTILITY

There is a point to be cleared up here before we go on. We have no difficulty in understanding why our ability to buy a commodity should decline as the price rises or increase as the price falls—our wealth simply stretches further or less far. But why should our willingness be related to price?

Economists answer this question by postulating that as we increase the quantities that we own of any good (within a given time period), the pleasures and benefits derived from successive units of that good will decline.

Hence we will be less and less willing to go on buying more and more of the same good, because its *marginal utility*—the increment of satisfaction we derive from each additional unit—will diminish.

Suppose for example that a man were dying of thirst on the Sahara. The marginal utility to him of a pint of water per day would be immense, and he would pay a vast sum for just one pint. So too, perhaps, for the second or third pint. But after a certain number of pints per day, the utility of the next pint begins to fall. If such a man has 40 or 50 pints of drinking water a day, the marginal utility of the 41st or the 51st may be next to nothing. This does not mean that the *total* utility he enjoys is less than that of a man who is desperately short of water; just the opposite. But the *addition* to his utility of still another pint will have fallen so low that he will be willing to pay only very little for it.

The notion of diminishing marginal utility also clears up another puzzle of economic life. This is why we are willing to pay so little for bread, which is a necessity for life, and so much for diamonds, which are not. The answer is that we have so much bread that the marginal utility of any loaf we are thinking of buying is very little, whereas we have so few diamonds that each carat has a very high marginal utility. If we were locked inside Tiffany's over a long holiday, the prices we would pay for bread and diamonds, after a few days, would be very different from those we would have paid when we entered.*

This relationship between price and quantity yields a conception of demand and supply that is different from the one that we ordinarily carry about in our heads. We are used to thinking about demand, for instance, as denoting a single purchase at a single price; or supply as referring to the readiness of a storekeeper to sell a certain good at a given price.

But that is not the idea of supply and demand as these words describe the behavior that drives the market system. *Demand and supply in their proper economic sense refer to various quantities of goods or services that we are willing and able to buy (or sell) at various prices at a given time.*

In other words, demand and supply both refer to *functional* relationships, or to the interdependence of price and quantity. This is a condition of

* By the way, it is the assumption of the diminishing marginal utility of money-income that provides the rationale for a progressive income tax. Presumably, the millionaire receives less utility from his millionth dollar than from his first dollar. From this we make the daring leap to the assumption that the millionaire receives less utility from his millionth dollar than you or I do from our ten-thousandth. This involves us in the very shaky business of making intersubjective comparisons with outcomes that are always suspect. Maybe the millionaire gets *more* utility from his top dollar than you or I get from ours. However shaky the logic, most of us do assume that millionaires should pay a larger *proportion* of their incomes (as well as a larger absolute amount), because we think this imposes a more nearly equal "real" burden of taxation. If we believed that the marginal utility of a millionaire's last dollar was no smaller than that of your thousandth, there would be no reason to assume that a 10 percent tax across the board would not impose as great a proportional loss of *utilities* to him as to you.

which we do not often become conscious, but an imaginary situation may bring out the essential point. Suppose that you went into a clothing store to buy shirts and were waited on by an inexperienced clerk. Having found some shirts you liked, you asked the price and were told they were five dollars. "Very well," you say, having consulted your state of mind and your pocketbook, "I'll take three of them."

The salesman is about to write up the order when he stops in embarrassment. "I'm sorry, sir," he says, "I'm afraid I got the price wrong. It should be six dollars."

At six dollars you may be able to buy the shirts, but we will assume that you are no longer willing to—they are "too expensive." But just as you are about to leave the clerk reappears. "I'm wrong about the price again," he admits. "These are six dollar shirts, all right, but they're on sale, reduced to $4.50."

At the new price, you make another mental calculation. "Very well," you say, "I'll take four."

Our example is meant to illustrate an aspect of demand that we do not ordinarily encounter in real life, when prices rarely change so rapidly. This is the fact that our "demand" covers a whole range of different quantities that we are willing and able to buy at different prices at a given time, and not just one quantity that we do buy (or do not buy) at a given price.*

The same functional relationship is of course visible between price and the quantity we are willing and able to sell, but now the relationship goes the other way. A tailor, for example, might be willing to make ten shirts a day if he could sell them for $6 each, whereas if the price dropped to $5 he would make only 3, using his time to make other garments; and at $4.50 he would make none.

If we make a tabulation of the amounts of a commodity that will be bid for and offered at different prices, we present a *schedule* of demand and supply. For the example of shirts, it would look like Table 22-1.

TABLE 22 • 1

Price	Quantity demanded	Quantity supplied
$6.00	0	10
5.00	3	3
4.50	4	0

* Just for the sake of completeness, we ought to note that there is a class of so-called *luxury goods* for which the quantity demanded rises as their prices go up. The reason is that part of the utility of these goods is their price. It is not for nothing that Joy perfume advertises itself as "the most expensive perfume in the world." Its sales would probably fall sharply if it dropped its price and announced itself as "the second most expensive perfume in the world."

From here it is only a step to graphs representing these schedules in the very convenient form of *demand and supply curves.* The schedules for shirts are plotted in Fig. 22-1.

FIG. 22 • 1   DEMAND AND SUPPLY CURVES

Perhaps we have already grasped the next step of our analysis. The fact that supply and demand schedules (or curves) show *contrary functional relationships* between prices and quantities suggests that from the interplay of these different market forces an equilibrium might be reached—a point at which price will balance the force of demand against that of supply. In the case below, this equilibrium price is obviously $5, since I will be willing and able to buy three shirts at that price and the tailor is willing and able to make them for me.

Now we must add one last word before we continue our study of supply and demand. Thus far we have considered only the factors that make a single individual more willing and able to buy as prices fall, or less willing and able to sell. But generally when we speak of supply and demand we mean markets in which each side is composed of many suppliers and demanders. That gives us an additional reason for the slope of each curve. If we assume that most individuals have somewhat different willingnesses and abilities to buy, because their incomes and their marginal utilities are different; or that they have unequal willingnesses or abilities to sell, then we can see that *a change in price will bring into the market new buyers or sellers.* As price falls, for instance, it will trigger off the willingness or ability to buy of one person after another, thereby adding to the quantity of the good that will be purchased at that price; and conversely, as prices rise, the entry of sellers into the market will increase, and the quantity of goods they offer will rise accordingly.

BALANCING SUPPLY AND DEMAND

Let us investigate a case of collective demand and collective supply by examining the supply and demand schedules for shoes for a small city over a period of a year. Suppose we discover that the price-quantity relationships look like Table 22-2.*

TABLE 22 • 2

Price	$50	$45	$40	$35	$30	$25	$20	$15	$10	$5
Quantity (thousand prs.)										
Demanded	1	5	10	20	25	30	40	50	75	100
Supplied	125	90	70	50	35	30	20	10	5	0

As before, the schedules tell us that buyers and sellers react differently to prices. At high prices, buyers are either not willing or unable to purchase more than small quantities of shoes, whereas sellers would be only too willing and able to flood the city with them; at very low prices, the quantity of shoes demanded would be very great, but few shoe manufacturers would be willing or able to gratify buyers at such low prices.

But if we now look at *both* schedules at *each* price level, we discover an interesting thing. *There is one price—$25 in our example—at which the quantity demanded is exactly the same as the quantity supplied.* At every other price, either one schedule or the other is larger, but at $25 the amounts in both columns are the same—30,000 pairs of shoes. We call this balancing price the *equilibrium price*, and we shall soon see that it *is* the price that emerges spontaneously in an actual market where supply and demand contend.†

* Do these price-quantity relations have to be orderly and logical—that is, as the price falls by $5 increments, should demand or supply change in some regular fashion? The answer could be yes or no. In some markets, the relationship of demand or supply to price may be a very regular one; in others it is possible that reactions will be irregular and "illogical." This is a complicated subject, but it is well to be aware that demand and supply curves do not have to be as straight or smooth as they always appear in textbooks.

† Of course we have made up our schedules so that the quantities demanded and supplied would be equal at $25. The price that actually brought about such a balancing of supply and demand might be some odd number such as $25.01.

Emergence of the Equilibrium Price

How do we know that an equilibrium price will be brought about by the interaction of supply and demand? The process is one of the most important and fundamental in all of economics, so we should understand it very clearly.

Suppose in our example above that for some reason or other the shoe retailers in our city put a price tag on their shoes not of $25 but of $45. What would happen? Our schedules show us that at this price shoe manufacturers will be pouring out shoes at the rate of 90,000 pairs a year, whereas customers would be buying them at the rate of only 5,000 pairs a year. Shortly, the shoe factories would be clogged with unsold merchandise. It is plain what the outcome of this situation must be. In order to realize some revenue, shoe manufacturers will begin to unload their unsold stocks of shoes at lower prices.

As they do so, the situation will begin to improve. At a price of $40, demand picks up from 5,000 pairs to 10,000, while at the same time the slightly lower price discourages producers enough so that output falls from 90,000 pairs to 70,000. Shoe manufacturers are still turning out more shoes than the market can absorb at the going prices, but the difference between the quantities supplied and the quantities demanded is now smaller than it was before.

Let us suppose that the competitive pressure continues to reduce prices so that shoes soon sell at $30. Now a much more satisfactory state of affairs exists. Producers will be turning out 35,000 pairs of shoes, and consumers will be buying them at a rate of 25,000 a year. But still there is an imbalance, and some shoes will still be piling up, unsold, at the factory. Prices will therefore continue to fall. Eventually they reach $25. At this point, the quantity of shoes supplied by the manufacturers—30,000 pairs—is exactly that demanded by customers. There is no longer a surplus of unsold shoes hanging over the market and acting to press prices down. *The market clears.*

Now let us quickly trace the interplay of supply and demand from the other direction. Suppose that prices were originally $5. Our schedules tell us that customers would be standing in line at the shoe stores, but that producers would be largely shut down, unwilling or unable to make shoes at those prices. We can easily imagine that customers, many of whom would gladly pay more than $5, let it be known that they would welcome a supply of shoes at $10 or even more. If enough customers bid $10, a trickle of shoe output begins. But the quantity of shoes demanded at $10 far exceeds the available supply. Customers snap up the few pairs around, and shoe stores tell suppliers they could easily get $20 a pair. Prices rise accordingly. Now we are getting closer to a balance of quantities offered and bid for. At $20 there will be a demand for 40,000 pairs of shoes and output will have risen to 20,000 pairs. But still the pressure of unsatisfied demand raises prices further. Finally a price of $25 is tried. Now, once again, the quantities supplied and demanded are exactly in balance. There is no further pressure from unsatisfied customers to force the price up further, because at $25 no customer who can afford the price will remain unsatisfied.

FUNCTION OF EQUILIBRIUM PRICES

Thus we can see how *the interaction of supply and demand brings about the establishment of a price at which both suppliers and demanders are willing and able to sell or buy the same quantity of goods.* We can visualize the equilibrating process more easily if we now transfer our supply and demand schedules to graph paper. Figure 22-2 is the representation of the shoe market we have been dealing with.

FIG. 22·2 DETERMINATION OF AN EQUILIBRIUM PRICE

The graph shows us at a glance the situation we have analyzed in detail. At the price of $25, the quantities demanded and supplied are equal—30,000 pairs of shoes. But the graph also shows more vividly than the schedules why this is an *equilibrium* price.

Suppose that the price were temporarily lifted above $25. If you will draw a horizontal pencil line from any point on the vertical axis above the $25 mark to represent this price, you will find that it intersects the demand curve before it reaches the supply curve. In other words, *the quantity demanded is less than the quantity supplied at any price above the equilibrium price, and the excess of the quantity supplied means that there will be a downward pressure on prices, back toward the equilibrium point.*

The situation is exactly reversed if prices should fall below the equilibrium point. Now the quantity demanded is greater than that supplied, and the pressure of buyers will push the price up to the equilibrium point.

Thus equilibrium prices have two important characteristics:

1. *They are the prices that will spontaneously establish themselves through the free play of the forces of supply and demand.*

2. *Once established, they will persist unless the forces of supply and demand themselves change.*

There is one last thing carefully to be noted about equilibrium prices. *They are the prices that bring about an equality in the quantities demanded and the quantities supplied.* They are not the prices that bring about an equality of "supply and demand." Probably the commonest beginning mistake in economics is to say that supply and demand are equal when prices are in equilibrium. But if we remember that both supply and demand mean the *relationships* between quantities and prices, we can see that this would mean that the demand schedule and the supply schedule for a commodity were alike, so that the curves would lie one on top of the other. In turn, this would mean that at a price of $50, buyers of shoes would be willing and able to buy the same number of shoes that suppliers would be willing to offer at that price, and the same for buyers at $5. If such were the case, prices would be wholly indeterminate and could race high and low with no tension of opposing interests to bring them to a stable resting place.

Hence we must take care to use the words *supply* or *demand* to refer only to relationships or schedules, and to use the longer phrase *quantity demanded* or *quantity supplied* when we want to speak of the effect of a particular price on our willingness or ability either to buy or sell.

We have seen how stable, lasting prices spontaneously emerge from the flux of the marketplace. But we have silently passed over a basic condition for the formation of these prices. This is the role played by competition in the operation of the market mechanism.

How does competition fit into the process of establishing equilibrium prices? The answer is that it provides the regulator that "supervises" the orderly working of the market. It does so because economic competition, unlike the competition for prizes outside economic life, is not a single contest, but a *continuing process*—a race in which the runners never win but

THE ROLE OF COMPETITION

must go on endlessly trying to stay in front to avoid the penalties of falling behind.

Second, unlike the contests of ordinary life, economic *competition involves not just a single struggle among rivals, but two struggles,* one of them between the two sides of the markets and the other among the marketers on each side. For the competitive marketplace is not only where the clash of interest between buyer and seller is worked out by the opposition of supply and demand, but also where buyers contend against buyers and sellers against sellers.

It is this double aspect of the competitive process that accounts for its usefulness. A market in which buyers and sellers had no conflict of interest would not be competitive, for prices could then be arranged at some level convenient for both sides, instead of representing a compromise between the divergent interests of the two. And a market that was no more than a place where opposing forces contended would be only a tug of war, a bargaining contest with an outcome about which we could say nothing unless we knew the respective strengths and cunning of the two sides.

It is the fact that each side of the price contest is also contesting against itself—the fact that vying takes place not merely *between* those who want high prices and those who want low ones, but on each side of this divide *among* marketers whose self-interest urges them to meet the demands of the other side—that makes a competition a process that drives buyers and sellers to a meeting point. If some of our unsatisfied shoe buyers, for example—although preferring low prices to high ones—were not pushed into offering a little higher price than the prevailing one by their desire to get shoes, and if some unsatisfied sellers, although hoping for high prices, were not driven by self-interest to offer a price a little below that of their rivals, the price would not move to that balancing point where the two sides arrived at the best possible settlement.

Thus competition is a key condition for the operation of a market system. What are we to make, then, of the fact that we know that monopolistic and oligopolistic elements are to be found in many markets in the real economy? We shall have to wait until Chapter 27 before we can fully analyze the effect that these market inperfections have on the solutions to market problems; but suffice it to say now that for all the departures they will introduce from the competitive model, the basic relevance of that model will still apply. Moreover, until we have understood how a competitive market works, we will not be able to understand the differences that monopoly or oligopoly introduce.

Hence, during the next several chapters we will be proceeding under the assumption of "pure" competition. In due course we will examine very carefully exactly what we mean by this kind of competition and the extent to which economic reasoning built on it is applicable to the real world. But there is a good deal to learn before we add these finishing touches to our microeconomic knowledge.

Prices and Allocation

We have already cleared up a good deal of the mystery about how prices are formed in a market system. Although we have not really looked into supply curves (and we cannot until we probe the operations of the firm) we understand in general that prices for most goods on the marketplace reflect the interplay of the demand schedules of consumers and the supply schedules of producers. In our next chapter we will see how changes in demand affect prices and how various characteristics of demand exert different influences on the price structure.

But before we turn to the dynamics of supply and demand, there is a further illumination that our understanding of the price mechanism can shed on the problems of microeconomics. It begins to explain to us how the market system solves the problems of allocation with which it is entrusted. In particular it clears up the puzzle of how the market system *rations* goods among claimants.

In one form or another, rationing—or the allocation of goods among claimants—is a disagreeable but inescapable task that every economic system must carry out; for in all societies, the prevailing reality of life has been the inadequacy of output to fill the needs of the people. In traditional economies, we will remember, rationing is performed by a general adherence to rigidly established rules that determine the rights of various individuals to share in the social product, whether by caste or class or finally position or whatever. In command societies, the division of the social product is carried out in a more explicitly directed fashion, as the authorities— lords, priests, kings, commissars—determine the rights of various groups or persons to share in the fruits of society.

A market society, as we know, dispenses with the heavy hand of tradition or the arbitrary one of command, but it too must impose some system of rationing to prevent what would otherwise be an impossibly destructive struggle among its citizens. This critical allocative task is also accomplished by the price mechanism. *For one of the prime functions of a market is to determine who shall be allowed to acquire goods and who shall not.*

Imagine a market in which we have ten buyers, each willing and able to buy one unit of a commodity, but each having a different price that is agreeable to him, and ten suppliers, each also willing and able to put one unit of supply on the market, again each at a different price. Such a market might look like Table 22-3.

As we can see, the equilibrium price will lie at $6, for at this price there will be five suppliers of one unit each and five purchasers of one each. Now let us make a graph in which each bar stands for a single individual, and where the height of the bar tells us how much that individual will be willing to pay for the unit of the commodity or how much he would sell it for. If

TABLE 22 • 3

Price	$11	$10	$9	$8	$7	$6	$5	$4	$3	$2	$1
Number willing and able, at above price, to											
buy one unit	0	1	2	3	4	5	6	7	8	9	10
sell one unit	10	9	8	7	6	5	4	3	2	1	0

we line up our marketers in order of their demand and supply capabilities, our market will look like Fig. 22-3.

FIG. 22 • 3 HOW THE MARKET RATIONS

What we have drawn is in fact nothing but a standard supply and demand diagram. But look what it shows us. All the buyers who can afford and are willing to pay the equilibrium price (or more) will get the goods they want. All those who cannot, will not. So, too, all the sellers who are willing and able to supply the commodity at its equilibrium price or less will be able to consummate sales. All those who cannot, will not.

Thus the market, in establishing an equilibrium price, has in effect allocated the goods among some buyers and withheld it from others, and permitted some sellers to do business and denied that privilege to others. In our previous case, anyone who could pay $25 or more got a pair of shoes, and all those who could not were unable to get shoes; while all producers who could turn out shoes for $25 or less were able to do business, and those who could not meet that price were unable to make any sales at all.

Note that the market is in this way a means of excluding certain people from economic activity—namely, customers with too little money or with too weak desires, or suppliers unwilling or unable to operate at a certain price.

The rationing system of the market is both its triumph and its trouble. At the outset of our book we briefly surveyed the problems of nonmarket control mechanisms. In the case of tradition, we remember, the problem is the profound inertia that comes from a static arrangement of economic duties and rewards. In the case of command economies, the problem lies in the difficulty of administering a system without resort to bureaucratic inefficiency on the one hand or dictatorial intervention on the other.

Against these very grave difficulties of other systems, the price system has two great advantages: (1) *it is highly dynamic,* and (2) *it is self-enforcing.* That is, on the one hand it provides an easy avenue for change to enter the system, while on the other, it permits economic activity to take place without anyone "overseeing" the system.

The second (self-regulating) attribute of the market is especially useful with regard to the rationing function. In place of ration tickets with their almost inevitable black markets or cumbersome inspectorates or queues of customers trying to be first in line, *the price system operates without any kind of visible administration apparatus or side effect.* The energies that must go into planning, or the frictions that come out of it, are alike rendered unnecessary by the self-policing market mechanism.

On the other hand, the system has the defects of its virtues. If it is efficient and dynamic, it is also devoid of values: it recognizes no priorities of claim to the goods and services of society except those of wealth and income. In a society in which all shared alike, or in which incomes were distributed in accordance with some universally approved principle, this neutrality of the market would be perfectly acceptable, for then each would enter the market on equal terms or at least with advantages and disadvantages that bore the stamp of social approval.* But in a society in which inheritance still perpetuates large fortunes made in the past, and where unemployment or old age can bring extreme deprivation, the rationing results of the market often affront our sense of dignity.

Therefore every market society interferes to some extent with the "natural" outcome of the price rationing system. In times of emergency, such as

---

* Suppose incomes were distributed absolutely evenly among all families. What would happen to prices? Since tastes are different among different individuals, there would no doubt be a rush to buy some commodities, the prices of which would soar, and a disinclination to buy others, the prices of which would sink. In the end (forgetting about costs for the moment), relative prices would reflect the relative marginal utilities of different goods to the population, and the people who would consume the more expensive goods would be those whose tastes made them willing to spend their money on them.

war, it issues special permits that take precedence over money and thereby prevent the richer members of society from buying up all the supplies of scarce and valuable items, such as gasoline. In depressed areas, it may distribute basic food or clothing to those who have no money to buy them. And to an ever-increasing extent it uses its taxes and transfer payments to redistribute the ration tickets of money in accordance with the prevailing sense of justice and right.

SHORTAGES

Our view of the price system as a rationing mechanism helps to clarify the meaning of two words we often hear as a result of intervention into the market-rationing process: *shortage* and *surplus.*

What do we mean when we say there is a *shortage* of housing for low income groups? The everyday meaning is that people with low incomes cannot find enough housing. Yet in every market there are always some buyers who are unsatisfied. We have just noted, for instance, that in our shoe market, all buyers who could not or would not pay $25 had to go without shoes. Does this mean there was a shoe "shortage"?

Certainly no one uses that word to describe the outcome of a normal market, even though there are always buyers and sellers who are excluded from that market because they cannot meet the going price. Then what does a "shortage" mean? *We can see now that it usually refers to a situation in which the price has been fixed by some nonmarket agency, such as the government, below the equilibrium price.*

Figure 22-4 shows us such a situation. Note that at the price established by the government, the quantity demanded is much greater than the quantity supplied. If this were a free market, the price would soon rise to the equilibrium point, and we would hear no more about a shortage. But so long as the price is fixed at ceiling level, this equilibrating process cannot take place. Thus the quantity demanded will remain larger than the quan-

FIG. 22•4 SHORTAGES

tity supplied, and some buyers will go unsatisfied *even though they are willing and able to pay the going price.*

This bears directly on the problem of wage-and-price controls that we discussed in Chapter 18. The problem with such controls is that they tend to fix prices that are below the level that would be established in a free (inflationary) market. As a result, some buyers who would ordinarily have been "priced out" of the market remain *in* the market, although there are not enough goods offered to satisfy their demands. The result tends to be queues in stores to buy things before they are gone; under-the-counter deals to get on a "preferred list"; or black or gray markets, in which goods are sold illegally at higher prices than are officially sanctioned.

The opposite takes place with a surplus. Here, in Fig. 22-5, we see a price floor fixed above the equilibrium price, as when the government supports crops above their free market price.

**FIG. 22•5
SURPLUSES**

Now we have a situation in which the quantity supplied is greater than that demanded (note that we do not say that "supply" is greater than "demand"). In a free market the price would fall until the two quantities were equal. But if the government continues to support the commodity, then more will be produced than the amount for which there will be private buyers. The unsold amounts will be a "surplus."

Thus the words shortage *and* surplus *mean situations in which there are sellers and buyers who are willing and able to enter the market at the going price but who remain active and unsatisfied because the price mechanism has not eliminated them.* This is very different from a free market where there are unsatisfied buyers and sellers *who cannot meet the going price* and who are therefore not taken into account. Poor people have no demand for fresh caviar at $40 per pound and therefore do not complain of a caviar shortage, but if the price of fresh caviar were set by government decree at $1 a pound, there would soon be a colossal "shortage."

What about the situation with low cost housing? Essentially what we mean when we talk of a shortage of inexpensive housing is that we view the outcome of this particular market situation with noneconomic eyes and pronounce the result distasteful. By the standards of the market, the poor who cannot afford to buy housing are simply buyers at the extreme lower right end of the demand curve, and their elimination from the market for housing is only one more example of the rationing process that takes place in *every* market. When we single out certain goods or services (such as doctor's care or higher education) as being in "short supply," we imply that we do not approve of the price mechanism as the appropriate means of allocating scarce resources in these particular instances. This is not because the market is not as efficient a distributor as ever. It is because in these instances we feel that the underlying distribution (or maldistribution) of income causes the outcome of the market rationing process to clash with other standards of the public interest that we value even more highly than the standard of efficiency.

KEY CONCEPTS AND KEY WORDS

Price theory

1. In the market system, prices give *stimuli* or *signals* telling us how to act to *increase our pecuniary advantage.* Microeconomics is therefore often called *price theory.*

2. *Price stimuli give rise to different economic reactions depending on what side of the market we are located*—that is, whether we are buyers or sellers.

Willingness and ability

3. The actions of both buyers and sellers reflect both their *willingness* and their *ability* to purchase or sell. Thus the words *demand* and *supply* tell us what *quantities* will be bought and sold *at different prices.*

4. Our willingness to buy larger quantities at lower prices is explained by the hypothesis that the *marginal utility of goods diminishes* as we possess more and more of them (within a fixed period of time). Note that this is not the same as saying that *total* utility declines.

Quantities demanded and supplied

5. *Demand and supply are both functional relationships* that describe our behavior at different prices.

6. In a competitive market, prices will be determined by the interaction of buyers and sellers. *At low prices the quantities demanded will exceed the quantities supplied, and vice versa at high prices. The prices at which the quantities demanded and supplied are equal is called the equilibrium price.* (Note that "demand" and "supply" are *not* equal at this price.)

Demand; supply

Equilibrium price

7. *At equilibrium prices the market clears.* Because quantities demanded and supplied are identical, there are no unsatisfied buyers or sellers able and willing to enter the market and therefore to alter its quantities offered or sought.

8. Equilibrium prices will *spontaneously establish themselves* in competitive markets and will *persist* until the forces of supply or demand change.

9. Markets depend not only on *self-interest,* but on the force of *competition.* This is the outcome of *two struggles*—one across the market and another on either side of the market.

10. Prices perform an *allocatory function, rationing goods* among those buyers and sellers who are willing and able to enter the market at the going price. This rationing system is *highly dynamic* and is *self-enforcing.* At the same time, it recognizes no distributive principles or values except those of wealth.

11. *Shortages and surpluses* refer to situations in which prices have been imposed on a market and are below or above the equilibrium price. We do not count as victims of shortage or surplus the unsatisfied buyers or sellers we encounter in an equilibrium market. When we do label a situation as "shortage" or "surplus," it means that we do not approve of the market system as an appropriate rationing device for that good or service.

Allocatory
function

Rationing

Self-enforcing

Shortage

Surplus

Q U E S T I O N S

1. Why is microeconomics called price theory? What different things does the same price signal mean to buyers and sellers? Do sellers and buyers, for example, both like falling prices?

2. What is meant by saying that demand is a function of price? Does this mean that we will buy more of a good when its price goes up? What are the motivational roots of "demand"? Why is not our ability to buy—our income—enough to give us a demand schedule?

3. Why would the marginal utility of bread and diamonds change if you were locked in Tiffany's over the weekend? Why are so many necessities of life so inexpensive, when they are indispensable?

4. Draw up a hypothetical demand schedule for yourself for one year's purchases of books, assuming that the average price of books changed from $10 through $1.

5. Draw up a supply schedule for your local bookstore, assuming that book prices ranged from $1 to $10.

6. What is the equilibrium price of books in your examples above? Exactly what do you mean by equilibrium price? What is special about the quantities demanded and supplied at this price?

7. What is the difference between "supply and demand" and "quantity supplied" and "quantity demanded"?

8. What do we mean when we say that there are two aspects to competition? What are they? Why is any one not enough?

9. What is meant by allocation? How do prices allocate goods among buyers?

10. What is meant by a surplus? A shortage? Draw diagrams to illustrate each.

11. Because the market is such an efficient distributive mechanism, it has been proposed as the means by which a country might achieve Zero Population Growth, assuming that this were the declared national policy. Since a sizeable minority (probably about 15 percent) of all families voluntarily choose to have no children or only one, a country could achieve ZPG if the *average* family had 2.2 children; that is, if 100 families have 220 children. The question is how to decide which families should be allowed to have the extra children? Professor Boulding has ventured an answer that leans heavily on the market mechanism. He proposes that each girl and boy at adolescence be given 110 green stamps, of which 100 are required if a woman is to have a legal child. (The penalty for having an illegal child would be very severe, possibly even sterilization.) Unwanted or surplus stamps would then be sold in a market organized for that purpose. It can be seen that the total number of stamps would permit the population as a whole to have 2.2 children per family—the ZPG rate. The market would therefore serve to ration the extra stamps, making them available to those with higher incomes or a greater desire for children. "As an incidental benefit," writes Boulding, tongue in cheek, "the rich will have loads of children and become poor, and the poor will have few children and become rich."

When this scheme was first published, it provoked a storm of criticism. Commenting on its reception, Boulding observes: "This modest and humane proposal, so much more humane than that of Swift, who proposed that we eat the surplus babies, has been received with so many cries of anguish and horror that it illustrates the extraordinary difficulty of applying rational principles to processes involving human genera-tion."[1] What do you think of the idea?

[1]Kenneth E. Boulding, *Economics as a Science* (New York: McGraw-Hill, 1970), p. 39.

We have learned how equilibrium prices emerge "mysteriously and marvellously" from the wholly unsupervised interaction of competing buyers and sellers; and we have seen how those prices, once formed, silently and efficiently perform the necessary social task of allocating goods among buyers and sellers. Yet our analysis is still too static to resemble the actual play of the marketplace. For one of the attributes of an equilibrium price, we remember, is its lasting quality, its persistence. But the prices around us in the real world are often in movement. How can we introduce this element of change into our analysis of microeconomic relations?

The answer is that the word *equilibrium* in micro analysis no more implies changelessness than it did in macro analysis. Equilibrium prices are indeed lasting—so long as the forces that produce them do not change, but just as shifts in saving and investment continuously reset the point of equilibrium for GNP, so changes in supply and demand constantly alter the resting point of individual prices.

Shifts in Demand and Supply

But what makes supply and demand change? If we recall the definition of those words, we are asking *what might change our willingness or ability to buy or sell something at any given price?* The basic reasons are not difficult to discover. Suppose, for instance, that in the course of our previous adventure in shirt buying, we had taken out our wallet and found that we had less money in it than we imagined. Such a change in our financial circumstances would be very likely to alter the quantity of merchandise we were willing and able to acquire. The discovery of more money would affect our demand in the opposite direction.

A similar change in financial circumstances would also alter the willingness and ability of the supplier to make various quantities of shirts at various prices. If the cost of shirt material fell sharply, our tailor might be perfectly willing and able to make shirts at $4.50 (whereas formerly he could not afford to); and might find it profitable to make more shirts than he did previously, at higher prices.

Psychological changes in our condition as buyers or sellers can alter our willingness and ability to buy or sell equally as much as financial changes. A change in our tastes, induced by advertising or whatever, can make us more or less willing to spend our money for a given commodity, even though its price remains the same. A change in our attitudes toward work may make us more or less willing to undertake a given job at a given price: our tailor may decide to give up tailoring altogether or to make his fame as a designer of shirts. Either would change the quantity of shirts he would produce at various prices.

Thus changes in taste or attitudes, or in income or wealth will shift our whole demand schedule, and the same changes, plus any change in costs, will shift our whole supply schedule. Note that this is very different from a change in the quantity we buy or sell when *prices* change. In the first case, as our willingness and ability to buy or sell is increased or diminished, *the whole demand and supply schedule (or curve) shifts bodily.* In the second place, when our basic willingness and ability is unchanged, but prices change, our schedule (or curve) is unchanged, but *we move back or forth along it.*

Here are the two cases to be studied carefully in Fig. 23-1. Note that when our demand schedule shifts, we will buy a *different amount at the same price.* If our willingness and ability to buy is enhanced, we will buy a larger amount; if they are diminished, a smaller amount. Similarly, the quantity a seller will offer will vary as his willingness and ability are altered. Thus demand and supply curves can shift about, rightward and leftward, up and down, as the economic circumstances they represent change. In reality, these schedules are continuously in change, since tastes and incomes and attitudes and technical capabilities (which affect costs and therefore sellers' actions) are also continuously in flux.

CHANGES IN QUANTITIES DEMANDED OR SUPPLIED vs. ·················· CHANGES IN DEMAND OR SUPPLY

A change in price alone changes the QUANTITY we demand or supply

A change in our willingness or ability changes our whole DEMAND SCHEDULE

FIG. 23·1   CHANGES IN QUANTITIES DEMANDED OR SUPPLIED VS. CHANGES IN DEMAND OR SUPPLY

PRICE
CHANGES

How do changes in supply and demand affect prices? We have already seen the underlying process at work in the case of shoes. Changes in supply or demand will alter the *quantities* that will be sought or offered on the market at a given price—an increase in demand, for instance, will raise the quantity sought. Since there are not enough goods offered to match this quantity, price will be bid up by unsatisfied buyers to a new level at which quantities offered and sought again balance. Similarly, if supply shifts, there will be too much or too little put on the market in relation to the existing quantity of demand, and competition among sellers will push prices up or down to a new level at which quantities sought and offered again clear.

In Fig. 23-2, we show what happens to the equilibrium price in two cases—first, when demand increases (perhaps due to a sudden craze for the good in question); second, when demand decreases (when the craze is over).

FIG. 23 • 2   SHIFTS IN DEMAND CHANGE EQUILIBRIUM PRICES

Quite obviously, a rise in demand—other things being equal—will cause prices to rise; a fall will cause them to fall.

We can depict the same process from the supply side. In Fig. 23-3, we show the impact on price of a sudden rise in supply and of a fall. Again the diagram makes clear what is intuitively obvious: an increased supply (given an unchanging demand) leads to lower prices; a decreased supply to higher prices.

FIG. 23 • 3   SHIFTS IN SUPPLY CHANGE EQUILIBRIUM PRICES

And if supply and demand *both* change? Then the result will be higher or lower prices, depending on the shapes and new positions of the two curves—that is, depending on the relative changes in the willingness and ability of both sides. Figure 23-4 shows a few possibilities.

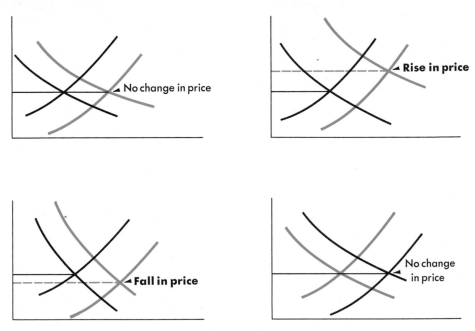

FIG. 23•4 HOW SHIFTS IN BOTH SUPPLY AND DEMAND AFFECT PRICES

LONG AND SHORT RUN

There is one point we should add to conclude our discussion of supply and demand. Students often wonder which "really" sets the price—supply or demand. Alfred Marshall, the great late nineteenth century economist, gave the right answer: *both do,* just as both blades of a scissors do the cutting.

Yet, whereas prices are always determined by the intersection of supply and demand schedules, we can differentiate between the *short run* when demand tends to be the more dynamic force, and the *long run,* when supply is the more important force. In Fig. 23-5 we see a case (on the left) in which short-run supply is fixed, as in the instance of fishermen bringing a catch to a dock. Since the size of the catch cannot be changed, the supply curve is totally inelastic, and the demand curve is the only possible dynamic influence. As can be seen by the broken lines, changes in demand alone will set the price.

But now let us shift to the long run, and draw a horizontal supply curve, representing the average cost of production of fish (and thus the supply price of fish) in "the long run." Fluctuations in demand now have no effect on price, whereas a change in fishing costs that would raise or lower the supply curve would immediately affect the price.

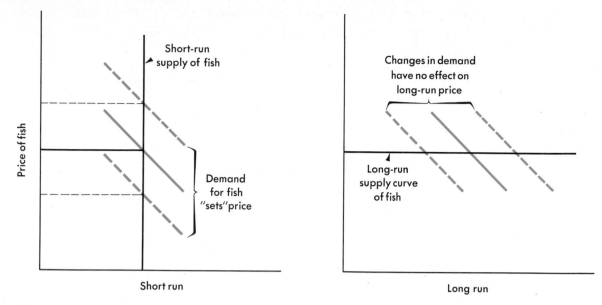

Short-run supply of fish

Price of fish

Demand for fish "sets" price

Short run

Changes in demand have no effect on long-run price

Long-run supply curve of fish

Long run

FIG. 23 • 5

Quantity of fish

In both cases, do not forget, *both* demand and supply enter into the formation of price. But in the short run, as a rule, changes in demand are more likely to affect changes in prices, whereas in the long run, changes in supply are apt to be the predominant cause of changes in price.

Elasticity

We have seen how shifts in demand or supply affect price. But *how much* do they affect price? Suppose, for example, that demand schedules have increased by 10 percent. Do we know how large an effect this change will have on price?

These questions lead us to a still deeper scrutiny of the nature of supply and demand, by way of a new concept called *elasticity* or, more properly, *price elasticity*. Elasticities describe the shapes of supply and demand curves, and thereby tell us a good deal as to whether a given change in demand or supply will have a small or large effect on price. Figure 23-6 illustrates the case with two supply curves. Our diagrams show two commodities selling at the same equilibrium prices and facing identical demand schedules. Note, however, that the two commodities have very different supply curves. In both cases demand now increases by the same amount. Notice how much greater is the price increase in the case of the good with the inelastic supply curve.

FIG. 23•6 HOW ELASTICITY OF SUPPLY CURVE AFFECTS PRICE

Similarly, the price change that would be associated with a change in supply will be greater for a commodity with an inelastic demand curve than for one with an elastic demand curve. Figure 23-7 shows two identical supply curves matched against very different demand curves. Note how much greater is the fall in price of the commodity for which demand is inelastic.

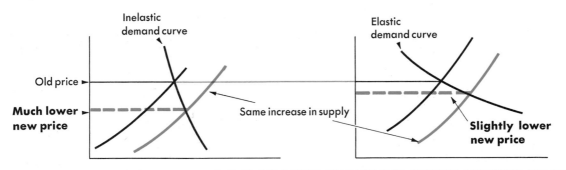

FIG. 23•7 HOW ELASTICITY OF DEMAND CURVE AFFECTS PRICE

Clearly, elasticities are powerful factors in explaining price movements.* This is because the word "elasticity" refers to our sensitivity of response to price changes. What we mean by an elastic demand (or supply) is that, as buyers or sellers, our willingness or ability to buy or sell is

---

* We should notice that we can use another term—*income elasticity*—to describe the response of our willingness and ability to buy and sell, not to a change in price, but to a change in our incomes. There are some goods—cigarettes are evidently one—in which the quantities we buy seem to be more influenced by changes in income than by normal fluctuations in price. For other goods, such as coffee, it has been estimated that housewives' purchases are more influenced by changes in price than by fluctuations in income. In the real world, price and income elasticities are inextricably mixed, but we will confine our attention here to the simpler case of price elasticity alone.

TOTALLY INELASTIC DEMAND OR SUPPLY. The quantity offered or sought is unchanged despite a change in price. Examples: Within normal price ranges there is probably no change at all in the quantity of table salt bought. Similarly, a fisherman landing a catch of fish will have to sell it all at any price within reason.

Demand for table salt

Supply of fish (catch)

INELASTIC DEMAND OR SUPPLY. Quantity offered or sought changes proportionately less than price. Examples: We probably do not double bread purchases if the price of bread halves. On the supply side, the price of wheat may double, but farmers are unable (at least for a long time) to offer twice as much wheat for sale.

Demand for bread

Supply of wheat

UNIT ELASTICITY. This is a special case in which quantities demanded or supplied respond in exact proportion to price changes. (Note the shape of the demand curve.) Examples: Many goods may fit this description, but it is impossible flatly to state that any one good does so.

Note that the demand curve of unit elasticity is not a straight line

The supply curve is straight

ELASTIC DEMAND OR SUPPLY. Price changes induce proportionally larger changes in quantity. Examples: Many luxury goods increase dramatically in sales volume when their price is lowered. On the supply side, elastic demand usually affects items that are easy to produce, so that a small price rise induces a rush for expanded output.

Demand for color TV sets

Supply of plastic toys

TOTALLY ELASTIC DEMAND OR SUPPLY. The quantity supplied or demanded at the going price is "infinite." Examples: This seemingly odd case turns out to be of great importance in describing the market outlook of the typical small competitive firm. Merely as a hint: For an individual farmer, the demand curve for his output at the going price looks horizontal because he can sell all the grain he can possibly raise at that price. A grain dealer can also buy all he wants at that price.

Demand for one farmer's output

Supply of all farm output to one dealer

FIG. 23 • 8

strongly affected by changes in price, whereas when our schedules are inelastic, the effect is small. In more precise terms, *an elastic demand (or supply) is one in which a given percentage change in prices brings about a larger percentage change in the quantity demanded (or supplied).* An inelastic schedule or curve is one in which the response in the quantities we are willing and able to buy or sell is proportionally less than the change in price.†

It helps if we see what elasticities of different kinds look like. Figure 23-8 is a family of supply and demand curves that illustrates the range of buying and selling responses associated with a change in prices.

ELASTICITIES, EXPENDITURES, AND RECEIPTS

Elasticities not only affect the determination of market prices, they also have a very great effect on the fortunes of buyers and sellers in the marketplace. That is, it makes a great deal of difference to a buyer whether the supply curve of a commodity he wants is elastic or not, for that will affect very drastically the amount he will have to spend on that particular commodity if its price changes; and it makes an equal amount of difference to a seller whether the demand curve for his output is elastic or not, for that will determine what happens to his total revenues as prices change.

Here is an instance in point. Table 23-1 shoes three demand schedules: elastic, inelastic, and of unit elasticity. Let us see how these three differently constituted schedules would affect the fortunes of a seller who had to cater to the demand represented by each.

TABLE 23•1

DEMAND SCHEDULES FOR THREE GOODS

		QUANTITIES DEMANDED	
Price	Inelastic demand	Unit elasticity	Elastic demand
$10	100	100	100
9	101	111 1/9	120
8	102	125	150
7	103	143	200
6	104	166 2/5	300
5	105	200	450
4	106	250	650
3	107	333 1/3	900
2	108	500	1,400
1	109	1,000	3,000

† Notice that elasticity is a *quantitative* notion—that it is measured by changes in quantities bought or sold compared with changes in price. This caution is needed because it is possible to make demand or supply curves "look" elastic or inelastic by changing the calibration of the horizontal or vertical axes on a diagram. For simplicity's sake we will continue to rely on the visual "look" of elasticity and inelasticity, but the student should remember that the real test is provided by the proportional changes in quantities, not by the possibly misleading shapes he sees. There is more about elasticity in Professor Hannaford's *Student's Guide*, Chapter 23.

Now a very interesting result follows from these different schedules. *The total amount spent for each commodity (and thus the total amount received by a firm) will be very different over the indicated range of prices.* In Table 23-2 are the amounts spent (price times quantity).

TABLE 23 • 2

TOTAL EXPENDITURES (or receipts)

Price	Good with inelastic demand	Good with unit elasticity demand	Good with elastic demand
$10	1,000	1,000	1,000
9	909	1,000	1,080
8	816	1,000	1,200
7	717	1,000	1,400
6	612	1,000	1,800
5	525	1,000	2,250
4	424	1,000	2,600
3	321	1,000	2,700
2	216	1,000	2,800
1	109	1,000	3,000

We can see that it makes a lot of difference to a seller whether he is supplying goods for which the demand is elastic or not. *If demand is elastic and he cuts his price, he will take in more revenue.* If his demand is inelastic and he cuts his price, he will take in *less* revenue. (This has typically been the case with farm products, as we recall from our history.)

Conversely, a businessman who raises his price will be lucky if the demand for his product is inelastic, for then his receipts will actually increase. Compare the fortunes of the two businessmen depicted in Fig. 23-9. Note that by blocking in the change in price times the change in quantity, we can show the change in receipts. (Because we have ignored changes in costs, we cannot show changes in profits.)

FIG. 23 • 9 HOW ELASTICITIES AFFECT RECEIPTS WHEN PRICES CHANGE

Our figure shows something else. Notice that if we reverse the direction of the price change, our businessmen's fortunes take a sharp change. A demand curve that is elastic spells bad news for a businessman who seeks to raise his price, but the same demand curve brings good fortune to a businessman who intends to cut prices. Just the opposite is the case with an inelastic demand curve: now the condition of demand is favorable for a price rise, since the seller will hold most of his sales even at the higher price, but inelastic demand is bad for someone who cuts prices, since he will gain few additional customers (or his old ones will increase their purchases only slightly) when prices fall.

Obviously, what every businessman would like to have is a demand for his product that was inelastic in an upward direction and elastic at lower than existing prices, so that he stood to gain whether he raised or lowered prices. As we shall see when we study pricing under oligopoly, just the opposite is apt to be the case.

BEHIND ELASTICITIES OF DEMAND

Because elasticities are so important in accounting for the behavior of prices, we must press our investigation further. However, we must leave the supply side of elasticity to be studied in our next chapter when we look into the behavior of factors and for later chapters when we will study the operation of firms. Here we will ask why are demand curves shaped the way they are? Why is our price (or income) sensitivity for some commodities so great and for others so slight?

If we think of a good or service for which our demand might be very inelastic—say eyeglasses (assuming we need them)—and compare it with another for which our demand is apt to be highly elastic—say, a trip to Europe—the difference is not difficult to grasp. One thing is a necessity; the other is a luxury. But what do we mean by *necessity* and *luxury?* If we think more carefully about the terms, we can define them still more clearly in terms of the case with which we can *substitute* other goods or services in their place.

A necessity is a good for which it is hard to find substitutes. If we need eyeglasses, we will spend a great deal of money, if need be, to acquire a pair. Hence such a necessity has a very inelastic demand curve.

MARGINAL UTILITY AGAIN

Necessities are never absolute in the sense that nothing can be substituted for the commodity in question. High enough prices will drive buyers to *some* substitute, however imperfect.* Just when will the buyer be driven

---

* What *would* be the substitute for eyeglasses? For a very nearsighted person, the demand for one pair of glasses would be absolutely inelastic over a considerable price range. But when glasses got to be, say, $500 a pair, substitutes would begin to appear. At those prices, one could hire someone to guide him around or to read aloud. Admittedly this is less satisfactory than having glasses; but if the choice is between spending a very large amount on glasses and on personal help, the latter might seem preferable.

to the "next-best thing"? Traditionally, economists describe the decision as determined by a comparison of the marginal utility derived from a dollar's worth of the high-priced item with that derived from the lower-priced substitute. As the price of champagne goes up and up, there comes a point when we would rather spend our next dollar for a substantial amount of beer, rather than for a sip of champagne.

We can describe *all* consumer purchasing as following this pattern of maximizing marginal satisfactions. Presumably we always buy the thing that gives us the highest marginal utility for the dollar we are spending at any particular moment. As we buy more of the "best" thing, its marginal utility to us diminishes. When the marginal utility of another unit of the "best thing" has finally fallen below the marginal utility of the "next-best thing," we switch over. That is, when we have drunk so much champagne that the marginal utility of another dollar's worth is now less than the marginal utility of a dollar's worth of beer, we spend our next dollar on beer, since our enjoyment will be maximized by doing so.

In fact, we always face an immense choice of goods on which we could spend our next dollar. As a result, we end up with a situation in which the marginal utility of a dollar spent by us for *any* good brings in the same amount of satisfaction. We say "presumably," since marginal utility cannot actually be measured. A number of economists have correctly pointed out that there can be no *proof* that we equalize marginal utilities by our actions. Nonetheless, the concept of maximizing our marginal utilities by "comparison shopping" seems to offer a plausible description of the motives that guide us as buyers.

We have seen that necessities have inelastic demand curves, so that we stick to them as prices rise. But what about when they fall? Won't we rush to buy necessities, just because they *are* necessities? Won't that make their demand curves elastic?

Surprisingly, the answer is that we do not rush to buy necessities when their prices fall. Why? The answer is that necessities are the things we buy *first,* just because they are necessities. Having bought what we needed before the fall in price, we are not tempted to buy much more, if any more, after the fall. Bread, as we commented before, is a great deal more valuable for life than diamonds are, but we ordinarily have enough bread, so that the marginal utility of another loaf is no greater than that of an equivalent expenditure on any other good. Thus, as the price of bread drops, the quantity we seek expands only slightly. So, too, with eyeglasses.

Compare the case with a luxury, such as a trip to Europe. There are many substitutes for such a trip—trips out West, trips South, or some other kind of vacation. As a result, if the price of a European trip goes up, we are easily persuaded to switch to some alternative plan. Conversely, when the price of a European trip gets cheaper, we are quick to substitute *it* for other possible vacation alternatives and our demand accordingly displays its elastic properties.

Do not make the mistake, however, of thinking that elasticity is purely a function of whether items are "expensive" or not. Studies have shown that the demand for subway transportation in New York City is price-elastic, which hardly means that riding in the subway is the prerogative of millionaires. The point, rather, is that the demand for subway rides is closely affected by the comparative prices of substitutes—bus fares and taxis. Thus *it is the ease or difficulty of substitution that always lies behind the various elasticities of demand schedules.*

Other Influences on Demand

IMPORTANCE OF TIME

Time also plays an important role in shaping our demand curves. Suppose, for example, that the price of orange juice suddenly soared, owing to a crop failure. Would the demand for orange juice be elastic or inelastic?

In the short run, it would generally be more inelastic than in the longer run. Lovers of orange juice would likely be willing to pay a higher price for their favorite juice because (they would believe) there was really no other juice quite as good. But as the weeks went by they might be tempted to try other breakfast juices, and no doubt some of these experiments would "take." Substitutes would be found, after all.

The point is that it takes time and information for patterns of demand to change. Thus demand curves generally become more elastic as time goes on, and the range of discovered substitutes becomes larger.*

SUBSTITUTION AND DEMAND

There is a last point we should make before we leave the subject of substitution. We have seen that the substitutability of one product for another is the underlying cause of elasticity. Indeed, more and more we are led to see "products" themselves as bundles of utilities surrounded with

---

* To be sure, the search for substitutes is a complicated process that can lead to equally complicated supply-and-demand reactions. Just after a taxi strike in New York City, when fares went up 50 percent, people switched to substitutes (they rode buses, subways, or walked), and the taxi business suffered severely. Then after the shock of the increase wore off, business revived. People got used to higher fares; that is, they discovered that the marginal utility of a high-priced taxi ride was still greater than the marginal utility of the money they saved with other transportation, plus the marginal utility of the time they wasted or the business they lost because they weren't taking taxis. In other words, the substitutes weren't satisfactory. Gradually, people began taking more cab rides, and taxi receipts were higher than before the fare hike. The quantity of taxi service consumed was down somewhat, but not by as much as the original drop. In this case, demand proved to be more *inelastic* over time than it was in the very short run.

other competing bundles that offer a whole range of alternatives for a buyer's satisfaction.

What is it that ultimately determines how close the substitutes come to the commodity in question? As with all questions in economics that are pursued to the end, the answer lies in two aspects of reality before which economic inquiry comes to a halt. One of these is the human being himself, with his tastes and drives and wants. One man's substitute will not be another's.

The other ultimate basing point for economics is the technical and physical nature of the world that forces certain relationships of ends and means upon us. Cotton may be a substitute for wool because they both have the properties of fibers, but diamonds are not a substitute for the same end-use because they lack the requisite physical properties. Diamonds, as finery, may be a substitute for clothes made out of cotton, but until we learn how to spin diamonds, they will not be a substitute for the cloth itself.

Because substitutes form a vast chain of alternatives for buyers, changes in the prices of substitutes change the positions of demand curves. Here is a new idea to be thought about carefully. Our existing demand curve for bread or diamonds has the shape (elasticity) it does because substitutes exist at various prices. But when the prices of those substitutes *change,* the original commodity suddenly looks "cheaper" or "more expensive." If the price of subway rides rises from 20 cents to 25 cents, while the price of taxi rides remains the same, we will be tempted to switch part of our transportation from subways to taxis. If subway rides went to 50 cents, there would be a mass exodus to taxis. Thus we should add changes in the prices of substitutes to changes in taste and in income when we consider the possible causes of a shift in demand. If the price of a substitute commodity rises, the demand for the original commodity will rise; and as the price of substitutes falls, demand for the original commodity will fall. This may, of course, bring changes in the price of the original commodity.

COMPLEMENTS

There is another connection between commodities besides that of substitution—the relationship of *complementarity*. Complementarity means that some commodities are technically linked, so that you cannot very well use one without using the other, even though they are sold separately. Automobiles and gasoline are examples of such complementary goods, as are cameras and film.

Here is another instance in which changes in the price of one good actually affects the position of the demand curve for the other. If the price of film goes up, it becomes more expensive to operate cameras. Hence the demand for cameras is apt to drop. Note that the price of cameras has not changed in the first instance. Rather, when the price of the complementary good—the film—goes up, the whole demand curve for cameras shifts to the left. Thereafter, the price of cameras is apt to fall as well.

We are almost ready to take our first overview of the whole market system, but there is still a missing link in our analysis chain. We have dealt thus far largely in terms of individual demand and supply schedules and curves—that is, in terms of the motivation between one person's willingness and ability to buy or sell. All through our macroeconomic studies, however, we spoke of demand and supply in collective or sectoral or national terms. How do we connect the two?

When we speak of the national demand for, or supply of, a good or service, we are really doing no more than adding up all the demand schedules of the individuals concerned. Thus the national demand for automobiles is a schedule whose shape and position reflects the sum of the tastes, incomes, preferences, etc., of all persons willing and able to buy cars.

The situation is more complicated, however, when we speak of demand on a still larger scale—for instance, the demand for all consumption goods, or the demand for GNP itself. Some of the relationships we have discovered in this chapter continue to hold. We have already spoken of the effect of a change in income on total consumption demand when we discussed the propensity to consume schedule. We can now see this schedule as a demand curve that relates our willingness and ability to buy all consumption goods at different levels of aggregate income. On the other hand, some attributes of demand at the micro level disappear when we magnify them to macro size. For example, problems of changing tastes, or of substitutes and complements, are usually unimportant in analyzing macroeconomic phenomena, for they represent shifts *within* the sphere of consumption and do not affect the *total* of consumption spending.

More complex is the matter of price and total spending. Can we speak of a price elasticity of total consumption demand? Will consumption spending fall, as a percentage of disposable personal income, if all prices rise? The trouble in answering this question from the perspective of microeconomics is that we have to balance two contradictory effects. Higher prices throughout the economy will mean higher incomes for some people and therefore increased consumer demand. For others however, higher prices will bear against fixed incomes and may well cause a contraction in total expenditures. (Then, just to complicate matters further, higher prices will mean both higher revenues and higher costs to producers, thereby involving us in the supply side of the situation.)

It is easier to deal with questions such as this by going over to the macroeconomic perspective and coping directly with statistical aggregates, such as the marginal propensity to consume, than by trying to calculate the positive income elasticities of millions of consumers against the negative price elasticities of others. Nonetheless, the illustration reminds us that the macro effects we deal with are made up, in fact, of innumerable small micro reactions which constitute the fundamental source of all private economic activity.

The Market as a
Self-Correcting Mechanism

We have begun to see how the market for goods and services operates as a dynamic, constantly altering—and yet self-adjusting—mechanism. From the interplay of supply and demand schedules for goods emerge equilibrium prices of those goods. Yet these prices are rarely at rest. As the incomes and tastes of the throngs of goods-seekers change—or as the conditions of supply change—the prices of goods are continuously seeking new levels that will equate, if only for a moment, the quantities offered and sought. Moreover, as the prices of goods change, new ripples of disturbance are set into motion, for each good is a substitute for (or perhaps a complement of) others, and thus as each price changes, it will induce shifts in the demand curves that affect other prices. Meanwhile, the ever-shifting pattern of prices is silently carrying out its task of allocating the products on the market among the throng seeking them, distributing goods and permitting sales to those who meet the test of going prices, and quietly but uncompromisingly refusing them to those who do not.

How is order maintained in this extraordinary flux of activity? We have learned a good deal about some of the basic principles that keep the process smoothly and continuously working. One of these, we have seen, is the pressure of self-interest that drives buyer and seller to seek their respective economic advantages—the buyer searching for the cheapest market for the good or service he wants, the seller looking for the highest price for the commodity he wants to sell. The other is the continuous pressure of competition that serves to bring buyer and seller together at a point acceptable to both.

Do self-interest and competition alone guarantee the orderly working of the market? As we shall see, they do not. But to understand why not, we must investigate what we mean by an "orderly" market, in the first place.

We have already seen one meaning for the word *orderly* in the extraordinary ability of a market situation to produce equilibrium prices that serve to bring together buyers and sellers in a stable situation of exchange, despite the different directions in which their self-interests propel them.

STABILITY AND INSTABILITY

But we cannot confine orderliness to such a static solution. What happens when things change? Suppose, for example, that the demand curve for shoes shifts because the number of people in town has increased. The first effect of this, we know, will be a new, higher equilibrium price for shoes, as Fig. 23-10 shows. Notice also that at the new higher price, the quantity of shoes supplied will also be larger than it was before.

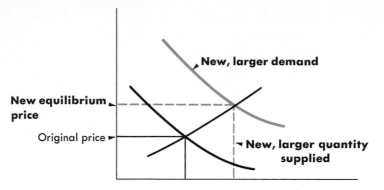

FIG. 23•10   SHORT-RUN CHANGE IN EQUILIBRIUM PRICE

For the short run, this provides an orderly solution to the problem of change. There is now a new level of prices as stable as before, and a new equally stable level of output. (To be sure, there have been shifts in patterns of spending and in incomes that may exert pressures elsewhere on the economy, but we will ignore that for the moment. As far as the market for shoes is concerned, the problem of change has been met in an orderly way.)

In the long run, however, the process of adjustment is apt to be more complicated.* At higher shoe prices, entrepreneurs in other lines are apt to move into the industry, with the result that the whole supply curve of shoes shifts to the right. As a result, shoe prices will again fall (although we cannot tell by how much unless we know more about the costs of the industry). This solution would look like Fig. 23-11.

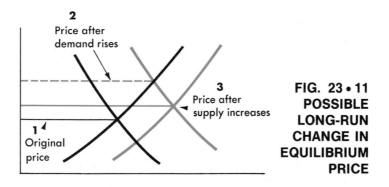

FIG. 23•11 POSSIBLE LONG-RUN CHANGE IN EQUILIBRIUM PRICE

Here are two orderly outcomes to a disturbing change. What would be workable outcomes for a *fall* in demand? In the simplest short-run case, a new lower price and a smaller output. A longer-run solution might entail an

---

* The "long run" is not just a vague figure of speech. It means, in cases like this, the time necessary for producers to build new plant and equipment. Conversely, in the "short run," producers are limited to adjusting their supplies as best as they can from their given plant and equipment.

exodus of suppliers and of capital equipment from the industry, so that the supply curve moved leftward and prices again recovered from their initial drop. Whichever the solution, *in the end we would again have stable prices and outputs.*

Now look at a less reassuring case. This time let us suppose that it takes a considerable time before a larger or smaller demand for a product can be met by a larger or smaller output. Since it takes many months between planting and harvesting, we will choose Christmas trees as the commodity to illustrate this situation for us.

In Fig. 23-12, we show the supply and demand curves for Christmas trees and imagine that the quantity supplied is initially indicated by point *A* on the supply schedule.

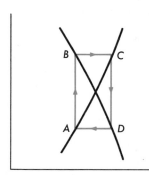

**FIG. 23 • 12
THE COBWEB**

We can see that quantity *A* will sell at price *B*. Figuring that this will be next year's price, tree growers now plant the amount they are willing and able to offer at price *B*—quantity *C*. Alas, when the harvest comes, it is found that quantity *C* will fetch only price *D*. Now the process goes into reverse. Growers will figure that next year's price will be *D*, and they plant amount *A*, since at price *D* the quantity they wish to supply is no more than that. Thereupon, next harvest time, the price goes back to *B*—and around we go. If the supply and demand schedules were differently sloped, we *could* have a so-called cobweb that converged toward equilibrium as we show on the left of Fig. 23-13; and we could also have one that "exploded"—as we can see on the right.

Cobwebs show us that markets need not necessarily produce equilibrium prices. Why, then, do most markets tend toward a resting point and not gyrate or explode like our examples? The answer is that, unlike the cobweb assumptions, most changes in supply are *gradual* and *continuous,* so that prices steadily fall as supplies augment, or rise as they dwindle, thus guiding buyer and seller to the appropriate adjustments.

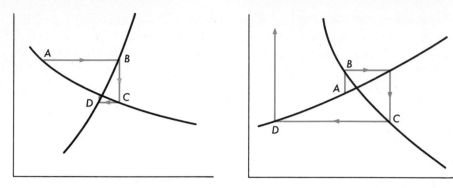

FIG. 23 • 13   STABILIZING AND EXPLOSIVE COBWEBS

Cobwebs are something of an anomaly in the market, although they illustrate an important point. But there is another cause of instability that is far from a rarity in the market process. This is the potentially disturbing effect of changes in *expectations* on prices and outputs.

We have already encountered expectations as a central agency of economic change when we looked into the motives behind business investment. But investment, for an ordinary business firm, is not an activity undertaken daily. Hence expectations play their role only when a decision must be made whether to expand operations or not.

Not so, in the marketplace. There expectations affect the decisions of marketers virtually every time a purchase or sale is contemplated. More than that, *as expectations change, the motive of self-interest will drive buyers and sellers in directions that imperil the orderly adjustment of the market process.*

To understand this very important point, you must put yourself in the shoes of a buyer or seller who suddenly faces a change—let us say a fall—in prices. What must *you* do to make the market react to that fall in an orderly way, by reaching a new stable equilibrium price?

The answer is that you must behave as our now familiar diagrams say you will behave. As a buyer, you must respond to the fall in price, by buying a larger quantity. As a seller, you must respond by offering somewhat less to the market. In this way, a new stable point of rest will be reached, either further down the demand curve, or—if some suppliers leave the field after a time—perhaps at a higher price along a new supply curve.

But what will make you behave this way? The answer is that your self-interest will, *if you expect that the price fall will go no further or eventually turn around.* Then as a buyer, it will pay you to take advantage of lower prices, and as a seller it will cut your losses if you now offer less for sale.

Now suppose, however—and here is the case to be thought about carefully—*that you expect prices to keep on falling.* Then what will your self-interest guide you to do? As a buyer, you will *not* buy more, because you figure, quite correctly, that if you hold off, you will get things still cheaper tomorrow. So too, as a seller, you will *not* offer less, because you fear that if you do not sell as much as you can immediately, you will get even worse prices tomorrow. Thus, in place of the stabilizing reactions that bring a halt to price changes or that may even initiate price reversals, *when expectations themselves are based on runaway price changes, they bring about behavior that creates the very situation they fear.* For in these cases, as buyers hold back and sellers rush forward, the imbalance between quantities supplied and demanded will worsen, and prices will fall further.

The same expectational problem can upset a situation with rising prices. Again, an orderly market requires that the price rise be limited or in time turned around. This requires buyers to demand smaller quantities and sellers to offer larger ones. Both will do exactly that if they anticipate that prices will not rise further. But if expectations become "destabilizing," buyers will react to rising prices by *increasing* the quantities they demand, in order to get them at a better price today than tomorrow; and sellers will hold *back their* supplies, hoping to sell them at higher levels tomorrow. As a result, quantities demanded will increase and supplies offered will fall, and the price rise will accelerate rather than come to a halt.

How are such instabilities handled? What effect do they have on the market? In the nature of things, usually they are short-lived affairs that result in wild splurges and busts that disrupt particular markets but do not derange the system as a whole. Sometimes, though, destabilizing reactions can become generalized throughout the whole goods market, as they do when buyers and sellers generally expect an inflation or a depression, and proceed to rush in or hold back in a way that aggravates the very thing they dread. In these cases, destabilizing reactions can be of the gravest importance and must be countered by public policies or public pronouncements aimed at changing peoples' anticipations of the future, so that self-interest will again move them in the direction that brings order rather than disorder.

The narrow line that separates order from disorder, and stability from instability, brings us at the end of this chapter to a final perspective on the subject we are studying. This is the relation of microtheory to the reality of the markets and market behavior in the real world.

Most of us study microtheory in the expectation that it will describe the way markets really are, and therefore serve us in a *predictive* way. And so it will, in a great many cases. When Macy's wants to increase its sales, it lowers its prices in the confident expectation that microeconomics is right when it says that the quantity demanded at lower prices is greater than that at higher ones. Microtheory does describe actual behavior in all "ordinary" cases, and we can and do predict successfully according to its logic.

But sometimes—and these times may be very important—the market does not behave in the way that microtheory describes as the normal case.

As we have just seen, this is when expectations turn the normal price-quantity relationships upside down. Yet even in these cases, microeconomics has a special relevance. For it then tells us what behavior would restore normality, and therefore serves as our guidebook when we seek to bring that behavior about. When it is used in this way, price theory is *normative* rather than predictive; that is, it tells us how to achieve a desired state of affairs, rather than what will be the outcome of the existing state, left to itself. Both uses are important, one for understanding how the market system is ordinarily capable of producing an orderly solution to the tasks it performs despite the incredibly complicated stimuli that beat upon it; the other for giving us the necessary knowledge to reintroduce order into the system when, under the influence of wild expectations, it threatens to break down.*

KEY CONCEPTS AND KEY WORDS

Demand and
supply schedules

1. Equilibrium prices change when *supply or demand schedules change.* In turn these schedules change when our willingness or ability to buy or sell is altered.

2. *Changes in taste or income* lie behind shifts in demand schedules; behind changes in supply lie *changes in attitudes or costs.*

Shifts of curves
and shifts
along curves

3. A change in demand (or supply) means a shift of the whole *schedule.* This must be contrasted with changes in the *quantity demanded* (or supplied) which refers to movements *along given curves.*

4. Shifts in demand or supply mean that *different quantities* will be sought or offered *at the same price.*

Elastic

5. Price elasticities measure the proportionate change in quantities offered or sought when prices change. *Elastic demand* (or supply) means that the *percentage change in quantities demanded* (or supplied) *will be larger than the percentage change in price;* inelastic demand (or supply) means that the percentage quantity change is smaller than the percentage price change.

Inelastic

6. Price elasticities very greatly affect price changes. Price changes will be larger when demand and supply curves are inelastic than when they are elastic. *Elasticities also affect the receipts of the seller or the expenditures of the buyer.*

Substitutes

7. Elasticities reflect the ease or difficulty of *substitution.* Hence, elasticities typically increase over time, as new substitutes are found or as information about them spreads. The *ease of substitution* is an important concept that helps us define what a "commodity" is.

8. Substitutes are commodities for which the demand rises when the price of the original commodity rises, and for which demand falls when the price of the original commodity falls.

Complements

9. *Complements* are commodities that are technically linked to one another. The demand for one of them therefore falls when the price of the linked commodity rises and rises when the price of the linked commodity falls. This case is just the opposite from that of substitutes.

* For the fullest discussion of these problems, see Adolph Lowe, *On Economic Knowledge* (Harper & Row, 1965).

10. The market is ordinarily a self-correcting and orderly mechanism. By *"orderly"* we mean that *changes in supply or demand produce new, stable prices and outputs.*

Orderly markets

11. In some instances, the outcome of the market is not orderly. One of these is the cobweb situation, where the reaction of supply to demand is not continuous. More important is the case *when expectations are not "stabilizing."*

Destabilizing expectations

12. Orderly markets depend on buyers responding to price falls by buying more, and on sellers responding to price falls by offering less. *When either side expects the price fall to continue, these orderly reactions will not be forthcoming.* The result can be a runaway price situation. (The same effect can occur when price rises are not met by the orderly behavior of decreased buying and increased offering.)

13. Microtheory has two uses. It *predicts* the outcome of market situations when behavior is orderly and normal. When behavior is not orderly, it informs us as to *what kind of behavior is needed to restore stability and order to the market.*

Q U E S T I O N S

1. What changes in your economic condition would increase your demand for clothes? Draw a diagram to illustrate such a change. Show on it whether you would buy more or less clothes at the prices you formerly paid. If you wanted to buy the same quantity as before, would you be willing and able to pay prices different from those you paid earlier?

2. Suppose that you are a seller of costume jewelry. What changes in your economic condition would decrease your supply curve? Suppose that costs dropped. If demand were unchanged, what would happen to the price in a competitive market?

3. Draw the following: an elastic demand curve and an inelastic supply curve; an inelastic demand curve and an elastic supply curve; a demand curve of infinite elasticity and a totally inelastic supply curve. Now give examples of commodities that each one of these curves might represent.

4. Show on a diagram why elasticity is so important in determining price changes. (Refer back to the diagrams on p. 470 to be sure that you are right.)

5. Draw a diagram that shows what we mean by an increase in the quantity supplied; another diagram to show what is meant by an increase in supply. Now do the same for a decrease in quantity supplied and in supply. (Warning: it is very easy to get these wrong. Check yourself by seeing if the decreased supply curve shows the seller offering less goods at the same prices.) Now do the same exercise for demand.

6. How does substitution affect elasticity? If there are many substitutes for a product, is demand for it elastic or inelastic? Why?

7. Show on a diagram (or with figures) why you would rather be the seller of a good for which demand was elastic, if you were in a market with falling prices. Suppose prices were rising—would you still be glad about the elasticity of demand?

8. By and large, are luxuries apt to enjoy elastic or inelastic demands? Has this anything to do with their price? Can high-priced goods have inelastic demands?

9. Why is demand more apt to become elastic over time?

10. The price of pipe tobacco rises. What is apt to be the effect on the demand for pipes? On the demand for cigars?

11. What is meant by an orderly market? If prices fall, how should you behave as a buyer to insure an orderly market? As a seller? What might make you behave differently?

12. If we faced the prospect of a runaway inflation, what public statement would you advise the President to make?

When we now look around at the hum of transactions on the marketplace, a great deal has become clear to us. We understand how prices are formed for the goods and services that are traded there, why and how those prices change, and the way in which changes are normally kept within bounds so that the system can maintain an orderly flow of output. We understand, as well, how those very same prices serve as rationing agencies for the society, distributing the output of the economy among those who are capable of paying for it.

But who *is* capable of paying for it? Through the market pass men and women in all walks of life, in all occupations, in all degrees of property ownership. Some are rich, some poor; some are very well treated by the market, some pushed aside by its operation. Does microeconomics shed light on this side of the market mechanism? Does it explain the causes of individual riches and poverty?

DISTRIBUTION OF INCOME

Anyone who first looks at the realities of income distribution recognizes that there are some aspects of it that microeconomics has little to say about. At one end of the scale of income distribution are the 20 million to 25 million individuals who, as families, have less than $60 a week; or as single individuals, less than $30; at the other end are the few hundred individuals whose incomes from property alone are over a million dollars each. Microeconomics does not enlighten us much concerning the root causes of these extremes of income. If we want to understand the reasons for poverty (particularly the poverty of the slums and of racially disprivileged groups), it is sociology and psychology and political science to which we must turn rather than to price theory, while the presence of vast private fortunes requires us to learn about economic history and the workings of the tax laws quite as much as about the operations of the market for factors.

Microeconomics, in other words, will not help us understand the origin or nature of incomes that have relatively little to do with the operation of the market mechanism. Those who are outside the market framework in the enclaves of the slums, or those whose incomes represent the inheritance of great sums won in the past do not fall mainly within the microeconomic examination of the factor market. Yet, about the 85 percent of the population that lies above the poverty line and that enters the market regularly to earn its income, microtheory will tell us a good deal. If it cannot explain for any single individual exactly why his income is what it is, it will at least tell us what kinds of forces bear on his earning capacity, and therefore how changes in the market are likely to affect his economic future.

LAND, LABOR, AND CAPITAL

In a very general way we already know the answer to the problem of individual earnings. Men make what they make because they sell their services in the market for the factors of production and receive as their reward whatever price the market puts on their contribution.

This general explanation serves only to orient us to the more interesting and difficult aspects of the problem, but even the first view makes one important thing clear. It is that the market for factors is essentially one in which *productive services* are bought and sold. When a firm buys Labor, it does not (except in a slave economy) buy an actual human being. It hires him, which is a very different thing, for it means that it buys his labor only, and not the physical asset (his body) in which it is contained.

The same differentiation between productive services and assets must be noticed in the markets for Land and Capital. When a farmer buys land, what he is willing to pay for are the powers of fertility contained in the soil. True, in order to get the use of those powers, he may want to, or have to, buy the real estate itself. In that case, however, the price of the asset will depend entirely on the *yield* that the land is expected to produce. Suppose our farmer is hoping that land values themselves will rise. Then he is acting as a speculator rather than as a farmer and is betting that the value of the *future services* of that land (where perhaps he hopes one day a factory will stand) will be so much higher than the value of its present services, that values will increase. (If he is wrong in his guess, he will be saddled with very high-priced land for farming—a thought that explains a good deal of the ill-fortunes that have beset the American farmer from time to time.)

Does a manufacturer also buy the services of capital? Indeed he does. As we saw in the section on the Marginal Efficiency of Capital (p. 279), when a businessman buys a machine, his demand for it will depend on his estimate of the present and future returns the machine will bring, so that the price he will offer derives directly from the value of the machine's services. Suppose he acquires money—that is, suppose he borrows funds from someone else? In that case the price he will pay for the temporary use of these funds—the *interest* cost—will certainly be governed by the present and prospective profits he expects to derive from using the money he has borrowed.*

Thus, when we speak of the market for factors we are actually talking about the value of their *services*. Clearly, there is a relation between the value of those services and the so-called capitalized value of the assets themselves, much like the relationship between the rate of interest and bond prices (see p. 346).

The Supply Curves of Factors

What do we know about the willingness and ability of the owners of land, labor, and capital to offer their services on the marketplace at varying prices for these services?

Except for the important case of labor (about which more in a moment), we really do not know too much about the shapes of the individual supply curves of land and capital. Will a man with a certain capital sum be willing to lend more of it when interest goes up—or will he lend more when interest declines, so that he can get as much income as before? In the same way, will a typical landowner increase or decrease the amount he rents out as rentals rise and fall?

These questions are difficult to answer for the individual. For the community, however, they are simpler to deal with. A rising price of land tempts many owners of real estate who were not previously "in the market" to rent out their land or their rooms or their houses. So, too, a rising price of interest attracts savings from people who were formerly not interested in saving, or brings about switches of money from checking accounts into interest-bearing accounts or securities.

---

* Is money itself a factor of production? Not in the technical sense of the term. Money can buy factors of production—land, labor, or capital goods—but it does not in itself contribute to output.

Hence we assume that aggregate supply curves of land and capital have the normal upward rising and rightward sloping shapes. The individual *labor supply curve* is an interesting exception, however. As Fig. 24-1 shows us, it has a curious shape. Up to wage level *OA,* we have no trouble explaining things. The curve simply tells us that normally we will not be willing and able to work longer hours (i.e., to offer more of our labor services within a given time period) unless we are paid more per hour. Economists speak of the *increasing marginal disutility* of labor, meaning by this that the bother and toil of work mounts after a time, so that we will not labor long hours unless the reward per hour rises enough to compensate us for our added pains.

**FIG. 24 • 1
THE
BACKWARD-
BENDING
SUPPLY CURVE
OF LABOR**

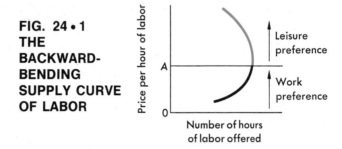

How then do we explain the "backward-bending" portion of the rising curve above wage level *OA?* The answer lies in adding to the rising marginal disutility of labor the falling marginal utility of *income* itself, on the assumption that an extra dollar of income to a man who is making $10,000 is worth less than the utility of an additional dollar when he was making only $5,000.

Together, these two forces explain very clearly why the supply curve of labor bends backward above a certain level. Take a man who has been tempted to work 70 hours a week by wage raises that have finally reached $5 an hour. Now suppose that wages go up another 10 percent. It is possible of course, that the marginal utility of the additional income may outweigh the marginal disutility of these long hours, so that our man stays on the job or even works longer hours. If, however, his marginal utility of income has reached a low enough point and his marginal disutility of work a high enough point, the raise may bring a new possibility: he may work *fewer* hours and enjoy the same (or a somewhat higher) income as well as additional leisure. For example, as his pay goes up 10 percent, he may reduce his workweek by 5 percent.

Backward bending supply curves help explain the long secular trend toward reducing the workweek. Over the last century, weekly hours have decreased by about 40 percent. Although many factors have converged to bring about this result, one of them has certainly been the desire of individual men and women to exchange the marginal utility of potential income for that of increased leisure.

ELASTICITIES AND MOBILITY

These psychological considerations behind supply curves are the counterpart of the tastes and desires behind our demand curves. Yet, when we discussed demand, we found technical reasons, such as substitution and complementarity, as well as psychological ones, for the differing positions and shapes of demand curves. Are there technical reasons to be looked for also in explaining the nature of the supply curve of factors?

One such comes immediately to mind: the potential *geographic mobility* of factors. Suppose there is a sudden rise in the demand for labor in a particular locality. We would expect to witness a rise in the price of labor, at least for a while. But then the higher price of labor should serve to attract this factor of production from other areas, and in this way bring about a compensating increase in supply to mitigate or reverse the price rise.

Mobility is thus an enormously important technical condition affecting the shape and position of the labor supply curve. More than a million American families change addresses in a typical year, so that over a decade the normal mobility of the labor force may transport 15 to 20 million people (including wives and children) from one part of the country to another. Without this potential influx of labor, we would expect wages to shoot up steeply whenever an industry in a particular locality expanded, with the result that further profitable expansion might then become impossible.

We also speak of mobility of labor in a vertical sense, referring to the movement from occupation to occupation. Here the barriers to mobility are not usually geographical but institutional (for instance, trade union restrictions on membership) or social (discrimination against the upward mobility of Negroes) or economic (the lack of sufficient income to gain a needed amount of education). Despite these obstacles, occupational mobility is also very impressive from generation to generation, as the astounding changes in the structure of the U.S. labor force (see p. 105) have demonstrated.

Here again the upward streaming of the population in response to the inducement of better incomes makes the long-run elasticities of supply of favored professions much more elastic than they are in the short run. This is a force tending to reduce the differences between income extremes, since the mobility of labor will not only shift the supply curve to the right in the favored places to which it moves (thereby exerting a downward pressure on incomes), but will move the supply curve to the left in those industries it leaves, bringing an upward impetus to incomes. Figure 24-2 shows how this process works.

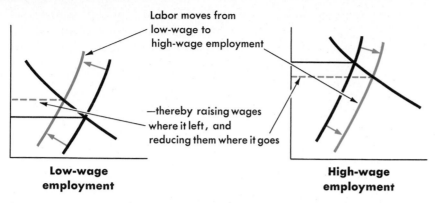

Labor moves from
low-wage to
high-wage employment

—thereby raising wages
where it left, and
reducing them where it goes

**Low-wage
employment**

**High-wage
employment**

FIG. 24•2   EFFECT OF LABOR MOBILITY ON RELATIVE WAGES

Mobility is by no means an attribute of labor alone. Take that seemingly least mobile of factors, land. In the very short run, the supply curve of land to any one industry is likely to be very inelastic. For example, if the orangegrowers of Florida want to increase their crop acreage within a year, they may find that it is very difficult to do so. But over a stretch of years, it is surprising how "mobile" the supply of land can become. Acres formerly devoted to other crops can be put into oranges. If the price of oranges goes high enough, it may even pay to reclaim land from urban or industrial use. To be sure, in the long run, the amount of land suitable for orangegrowing is limited, so that at some point the supply curve becomes totally inelastic. But over a very long intermediate range, land is in elastic supply. A graph of the short- and long-run supply curve of land for a given purpose would look like Fig. 24-3.

Short run ►   ◄ Long run

**FIG. 24•3
SHORT-RUN
AND LONG-RUN
SUPPLY OF LAND**

The example of land makes clear that it is not only geographic mobility but *technical specificity* that determines the responsiveness of a factor to changes in price. This helps explain why *time* plays such an important role in the elasticity of factor supply. Supply curves, like demand curves, are much more elastic over time because the process of redeploying factors from one use to another typically requires efforts that cannot be quickly brought to bear.

Suppose, for instance, that there is a sudden increase in the demand for steel products in the South and a simultaneous fall in the demand for lumber. In the short run there is not very much mobility that can be expected of the capital in these two industries. Lumber mills cannot be used to make steel. Hence the supply of steel mill services would be steeply inelastic. Over a period of time, however, the supply of capital, like land and labor, gains mobility. The lumber mills will eventually become depreciated or will be sold, and funds may thereupon be directed into steel. Or new mills will be built by funds supplied by other parts of the country. In other words, capital goods are usually limited in their flexibility of use, but money capital is tremendously mobile. In this way, the flow of money capital from one industry to another serves the same purpose as the flow of labor between employments, increasing the quantities of the factor where its price is rising, and diminishing it where it is not, in this way acting to keep the discrepancies between industries at a minimum.

Rents and Incomes

The importance of time in bringing about increases in factor supplies alerts us to a very important reason for the existence of very large incomes (and very large disparities of incomes) in the short run. This is the phenomenon of *quasi rent* (sometimes also called *economic rent*).

QUASI RENTS

Quasi rents, or economic rents, are not the same as the rent on land, and the unfortunate fact that the terminology is so close has justifiably aggravated a good many generations of students. Hence let us begin by making a clear distinction between the two. *Rent is the payment we make to induce the owner of land to offer the services on the market.* If we cease to pay rent or pay less rent, the amount of land offered on the market will fall. If we pay more, it will rise. Thus rent is both a payment made to a factor of production to compensate its owner for its services, and an element of cost that must enter into the calculation of selling prices. If a farmer must pay $100 rent to get an additional field he needs, that $100 will clearly be part of the cost of producing his new crop.

Quasi rents or economic rents are different from this. *First, the term applies to all resources—land, labor, or capital goods. Second, it is not a return earned by the factor, in that the payment has nothing to do with inducing the factor to enter the market. Third, quasi rents are not a cost that helps to determine selling price, but they are earnings that are determined by selling price.* Let us see what these differences mean.

An illustration may help clarify the problem. Figure 24-4 shows the supply curve for first-class office space in New York City. Note that over a considerable range there is an unchanging price for space—evidently there is all the space anyone can want up to quantity OX at a price (determined, let us say, by given costs) OA. The receipts of landlords—OA times OX—are real rent in the sense of being a necessary payment for the resources used. If no rent were paid, no space would be offered; as more is paid, more is forthcoming.

**FIG. 24 • 4
QUASI RENT
AND REAL RENT**

But now suppose that the demand for office space increases from DD to D_1D_1. The supply of space is now stretching thin, and additional first-class offices are hard to get, or expenditures are required to upgrade "second-class" space. The price rises accordingly from OA to OA_1.

Now we must differentiate carefully between rent and quasi rent. As the price rises, the quantity of space increases from OX to OX_1. Hence, for each unit of *additional* space the higher price was needed in order to bring that particular unit onto the market. But the higher price A_1 of space will not just apply to these new units. All "first-class office space" will go up in price. As a result, all the space represented by OX_1 will now receive a rental of OA_1, instead of OA. *But this increase in rental served no purpose in bringing these original units* (OX) *into the market. The additional revenue comes to them solely because the supply curve of which they are a part has become upward sloping. Thus economic rent or quasi rent is a return that accrues to factors by virtue of their scarcity.*

Note also that the amount of quasi rent is determined by the selling price. At the margin of the supply curve, where supply and demand meet, the last unit of supply earns its full return (for it would not appear on the market for less). Therefore the rent necessary to induce this last unit to come onto the market is *price-determining*. That is, it is part of the costs of production of that last unit of output.

Not so, however, with the previous units. They are all beneficiaries of a situation of scarcity in which the price received by the last unit has no influence whatsoever on their own entrance into production. The quasi rents

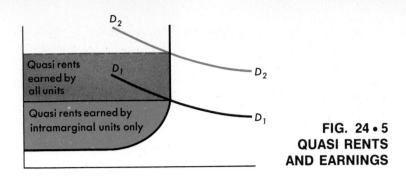

FIG. 24 • 5
QUASI RENTS
AND EARNINGS

they receive are thus *price-determined*. Note that if we run out of first-class office space entirely, and the supply curve therefore becomes totally inelastic, quasi rents will be received by *all* units, including the marginal ones (see Fig. 24-5).

QUASI RENTS AND PRICES

An important point is that these quasi rents, although determined by the *total* demand for the factor in question, in turn determine the individual costs of people who use these factors in production. To take the example of office space again, we have seen that the total amount of quasi rent is determined by the price paid for the last unit of space. For someone who rents an office, however, rent is simply a cost of production, which will enter into the selling price of his output. Thus the price-*determined* quasi rents become part of the price-*determining* costs of production of the individuals who use these rents.

Note carefully that the concept of quasi rent or economic rent is not limited to land. Take car rentals, for instance. Let us suppose that there is a going rate for cars, and that we can rent all the car transportation we need at that price. Suddenly there is a jump in demand, and the rentable car fleet is too small. Rentals will rise. If no additional cars come into the market, the fleet owners will simply enjoy economic rents on all their cars. But quite possibly the rising rental will bring new cars into the supply curve: fleet owners will expand their fleets; or private owners may rent cars on their own. These marginal cars will be earning no more than the return required for their addition to the supply curve, so that we cannot call their earnings an economic rent. But the previous cars, all of which will enjoy the rise in rates, are the sources of quasi rents for their owners.

QUASI RENTS AND INCOMES

In the same way the earnings of actors or authors or of the owners of any scarce talent or skill are likely to be partly economic rents. An actress might be perfectly content to offer her services for a fine movie role of $50,000, but she may be able to get $100,000 for the part because of her "name." The first $50,000, without which she would not work, is her wage;

the rest is an economic rent. So, too, a plumber who would be willing to work for standard wages, but who gets double because he is the only plumber in town, earns economic rents. And as we shall see in our next chapter, economic rent also helps to explain part of business profits.*

The concept of economic rent gives us a much-needed insight into the cause of income differentials. Anything that inhibits the mobility of factors—anything that impedes their pursuit of self-interest by moving from lower to higher-paid occupations or localities—creates or perpetuates economic rents. *Barriers of race and wealth, of patents and initiation fees, of geography and social custom—all give rise to shelters behind which economic rents flourish.* Some of these barriers cannot be helped in the short run, and others may simply reflect the occasional virtuosity of a few performers: baseball stars and great painters both earn rents, not because they are the beneficiaries of factor immobility, but simply because they are unique performers whose output (supply curve) is fixed, and who therefore enjoy the rewards of a high demand. Many other rents, however, are the creations of artificial scarcity and can be remedied by removing these man-made barriers.

Economic rents are clearly a source of waste for society, for they reward factors more generously than is necessary for their services. Why do we not remove them, therefore, by price controls? The answer is that price controls would create a situation of "shortage" such as we discussed on p. 460. For instance, a price ceiling to prevent rented cars from earning quasi rents would force us to adopt some rationing system other than price, to determine who would get the available cars. Thus economic rents still serve a purpose in aiding the allocation tasks of the market.

Can we not remove economic rents by taxation? We can indeed, insofar as we are able to tax the *original* receiver of such a rent—for example, the movie actress or the original fleet owner. In the case of the car owner, however, his fleet may be sold to a second owner. In that case, the price of the cars when sold will reflect their higher earnings; and the second owner, although presumably making normal profits, will no longer make a quasi rent. Hence economic rents are capturable by taxation only when the taxes affect the original beneficiary.

---

* A good deal of the very high incomes of corporate managers is also probably economic rent. In 1962, according to Robert Averitt (*The Dual Economy,* Norton, 1968, p. 178) the salaries and bonuses paid to the fifty-six officers and directors of General Motors exceeded the combined remuneration received by the President of the United States, the Vice-President, 100 senators and 435 representatives, 9 Supreme Court Justices, 10 cabinet members, and the governors of 50 states. How could we ascertain whether the incomes of the General Motors executives (or for that matter, of the officials of government) contained economic rent? The answer is simple: we would have to reduce their incomes and observe whether they reduced their output of work. Presumably that is what the income tax tries to do, and as far as we can see, the payment of a portion of income to the government does not seem to affect the supply curve of labor for executive skill. The presumption, then, is that a good part of their income *is* an economic rent, which the income tax siphons off in part.

Inelasticities of supply (and economic rents) help us to explain how some of the price adjustments we studied in the last chapter actually take place on the market.

Take the case of the increase in the demand for eggs. Suppose that housewives, for whatever reason, begin to buy larger quantities of eggs from their grocers. Most grocers will not raise prices, the way we have assumed that they will. Many small businesses price on a "mark-up" basis—adding a fixed percentage to the price charged them by their own suppliers. Hence when the demand for eggs rises, grocers will notice it only because their egg stocks run out, and their response will be only to order more eggs from their wholesale suppliers. Since wholesalers are prepared for such emergencies and have extra stock on hand, the higher demand of housewives can be accommodated without any increase in price, as Fig. 24-6 shows.

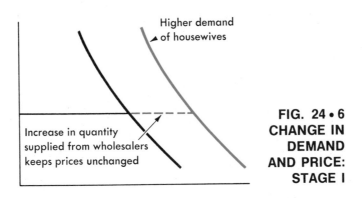

Higher demand of housewives

Increase in quantity supplied from wholesalers keeps prices unchanged

**FIG. 24 • 6
CHANGE IN
DEMAND
AND PRICE:
STAGE I**

But now suppose that the higher demand of housewives persists for a week. Grocers keep renewing their larger egg orders, and wholesalers soon find themselves out of stock. They begin to place larger orders with the egg farmers who supply them. Here we encounter a situation with an *inelastic* supply. Presumably the egg farms are already shipping all their eggs, so that orders for additional quantities have no (or very little) effect on production, at least in the short run. Instead, egg prices on the farm will now go up, and egg farmers will earn economic rents on their chickens. We can see this in Fig. 24-7.

Note further that once egg prices have been raised by the farmer, costs go up to wholesalers, who must now raise the price of eggs to grocers, who in turn will pass along the boost to consumers. If the housewife then asks the grocer why egg prices are higher, the grocer will answer perfectly correctly that "costs are up." And so they are—because demand is up. The cause of the whole change in prices has been the increased demand of the

New price ►
Economic rent
Old price ►

Increased demand of wholesalers

Totally inelastic supply curve of farmers

FIG. 24 • 7   CHANGE IN DEMAND AND PRICE: STAGE II

housewife, but the mechanism for raising prices has involved a series of markets, with the kingpin market that in which supplies were inelastic.*

Income Differences

We have come to understand something of the complex forces at work in the factor market, where the incomes are generated that will buy the wares in the goods market. But our explanation is obviously incomplete until we have looked into the demand for factors as well as their supply.

DIRECT
DEMAND
FOR FACTORS

In part, we already understand the demand for factors from our previous chapters. A portion of the labor force, or of land, or capital is demanded directly by consumers for their own personal enjoyment, exactly the same as a good or service. This kind of demand for factors of production takes the guise of the demand for lawyers and barbers and servants, or the demand for plots of land for personal dwellings, or the demand for cars and washing machines and the like that consumers hold as personal capital goods. To the extent that factors are demanded directly for such consumer purposes, there is nothing that differs in analyzing the price they receive from the price of any good.

Take the price of dental services, for example, which obviously determines much of the income of dentists. We can draw a demand curve for dentists' services which will certainly slope downward (and will probably be

---

* I have adapted this example from Armen A. Alchian and William R. Allen, *University Economics,* 2nd. ed. (Belmont, Calif.: Wadsworth, 1967), p. 105f., one of the best expositions of the market mechanism I have seen.

Short-run supply curve
of dentists' services

Prevailing price ►
per hour of
dental service

◄ Demand for
dental services

Quantity of hours

FIG. 24 • 8 DEMAND AND SUPPLY FOR LABOR CONSUMED
AS A SERVICE

highly income- and price-elastic), and we can draw a supply curve of dentists' services which, in the short run anyway, will probably be fairly inelastic and perhaps backward sloping. Figure 24-8 then shows us how much a typical dentist makes.

COMPARATIVE
EARNINGS

Now suppose that we compare the prices per hour of a number of occupations in which demand stems directly from the consumer, and that we find the result to look like Table 24-1.

How can we explain the differentials we find? Part of the answer lies in the differently shaped and located demand curves for these different services. What we must know, in other words, is the amount of money a consumer of a given income level is willing to spend for different quantities of the services of lawyers, dentists, barbers, and baby-sitters, and also the elasticities of his demand curves for these various services.

TABLE 24 • 1

	Lawyers	Dentists	Barbers	Baby-sitters
Prices per hour	$10	$8	$4	$1

But a knowledge of the pattern of demand only sets the stage. We also need to know why the supply curve of different occupations is differently located and why each has the shape it does. And here we must look in particular for reasons that make some supply curves more inelastic that others over the long run—that is, reasons that prevent labor from moving out of low-paid occupations such as baby-sitting or barbering into high paid ones like dentistry and the legal profession.

We are alert to the role that institutional and social barriers can play in creating economic rents. The other side of this story is that other sets of barriers constitute sources of *discrimination* that lower the earnings of those who are discriminated against. Blacks, for example, typically earn only two-thirds to three-quarters of white incomes. Some, perhaps much, of this differential is the result of the lack of education of the black labor force (the deficiency itself being a result of discrimination), but part of it is simply a kind of tacit conspiracy not to pay Negroes the same wages as whites *for the same work.* A striking confirmation of this is that a black college graduate, over his lifetime, earns only about as much as does a white high school graduate!

A second instance of discrimination lies in the pay differentials between men and women. As Table 24-2 shows, women typically earn substantially less than men for similar occupations. A portion of this may be the result of women withdrawing from the labor force to have children and to nurture them in their early years, but there is no doubt that these "economic" reasons for pay differentials do not begin to account for the full differences we observe.

Occupation	Women	Men
Scientists	$10,000	$13,200
Professional, technical	6,691	10,151
Proprietors, managers	5,635	10,340
Clerical workers	4,789	7,351
Sales workers	3,461	8,549
Craftsmen	4,625	7,978
Factory workers	3,991	6,738
Service workers	3,332	6,058

TABLE 24 • 2

MEDIAN ANNUAL EARNINGS OF FULL-TIME WORKERS IN 1968

Statistics comparing men and women at age 35 show that the average *single* woman will be on her job another 31 years—which will be longer than her male counterpart will work—and the average *married* woman will work another 24 years. Second, the facts show that married women are *less* likely to leave one employer for another than men are (only 8.6 percent of employed women changed employers in a year compared with 11 percent of men). And finally, U.S. Public Health data reveal that on the average, women are absent from work only 5.3 days per year, a fractionally *better* record than men's.

Discrimination against blacks and women is beginning to melt away. The most recent census survey showed that among northern black families with both wife and husband present, incomes averaged 91 percent of similar white families, compared with 62 percent in 1960. This represents only a minority of black families, however; among the less fortunate majority, income differentials have not significantly narrowed during the 1960s. Meanwhile the Women's Liberation movement has won important court battles to establish the right of equal pay for equal work, as well as equal rights to jobs, regardless of sex. Just by way of comment on our unconscious "sexist" attitudes, we might bear in mind that the United States has been unusually slow in admitting women to a full range of professional and occupational tasks. Only about 7 percent of our doctors are women, for example, whereas in West Germany 20 percent, and in the U.S.S.R. 70 percent, are women. Perhaps even more surprising, in Sweden 70 percent of overhead crane operators are women, an occupation virtually unknown to women in the U.S.[1] These surprising percentages at both ends of the "social" scale leave little doubt that women *could* earn a great deal more than they do, if the barriers of discrimination were removed.

"DIRTY WORK"

Discrimination results in an economic disadvantage, but it springs from a "noneconomic" cause. Other kinds of income differentials fit more readily within the framework of rational, utility- or profit-maximizing behavior. For example, part of the difference in the pay of two occupations may also reflect *different estimates of its marginal disutility*. Thus dangerous work typically pays a premium over safe work, because the higher disutility of dangerous work requires an additional incentive to attract labor to it. It is interesting to reflect that in a world without any barriers to occupational mobility at all, dangerous and dirty work would command the highest remuneration in the society, and easy and pleasant work the lowest. In such a world coal miners would make much more than lawyers, for there would be a flood of labor into law and a general exodus of labor from coal mining, with the expected effects on the market price of each. That is why one effect of prosperity is to raise the relative wages of "dirty work," since good times tend to improve mobility and thereby enable workers in low-grade occupations to move laterally or vertically to better ones.

HUMAN CAPITAL

There is still another ingredient in determining the differential of incomes. This is the *investment that different occupations require*. It takes very little training to be a baby-sitter; a fair amount to be a barber; a lot to be a dentist or lawyer. The investment expenditures for these different occupations take the form, mainly, of education—which is one reason why it seems odd to classify education as a consumers' good in the national income accounts (see p. 213n). The point is that the money that has been poured

[1] National Industrial Conference Board *Record,* February 1971, p. 10.

into a long education must be expected to earn a return: therefore, part of the higher incomes of trained people consists really of interest on the capital sums invested in their careers. Here, of course, is where the underlying distribution of wealth affects the distribution of income, for the sons of the rich have better chances than those of the poor in investing in their own futures.

Finally there is the plain fact of *the differences in human abilities.* Here there is an interesting bit of corroborative evidence. We believe that the distribution of abilities for nearly all skills follows the well-known "bell curve," with a few people at the very low and the very talented ends of the scale and with most people grouped evenly around a middle point, as Fig. 24-9 shows.

ABILITIES

FIG. 24 • 9 NORMAL BELL CURVE

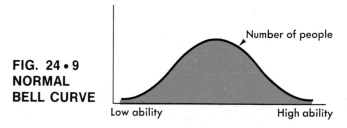

Number of people

Low ability   High ability

Yet when we study the distribution of incomes within a given trade, we usually find that the distribution is "skewed," with most of the individuals clustered at the low end of the scale as shown in Fig. 24-10. (See definition of *skewness* on p. 227.)

FIG. 24 • 10 "SKEWED" CURVE OF WAGE DISTRIBUTION

Number of people

Low pay   High pay

This would seem to deny the validity of the effect of ability on earnings—until we make an adjustment in the scale on which we plot earnings. Instead of measuring them on a regular arithmetic scale, we must plot them on a *proportional* (logarithmic) scale which gives equal emphasis to equal percentages of changes, as shown in Fig. 24-11. Then we discover that the

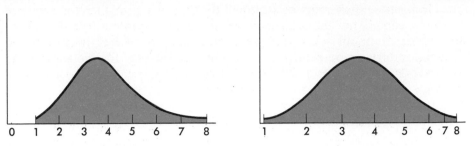

FIG. 24•11 ARITHMETIC SCALE (LEFT) LOGARITHMIC SCALE (RIGHT)

distribution of earnings does indeed show a bell configuration that reflects the distribution of underlying abilities.[2]

CAUSES OF INCOME DISPARITY

What conclusion can we then reach about the reasons for disparities of incomes, at least in those occupations in which demand stems directly from the consumer? We have seen that these disparities stem from two sets of causes, one transient and one not.

The transient—but very powerful—reasons involve all those social barriers that hinder the movement of factors from low-paid to high-paid employments and uses. Wealth on the one hand, prejudice and discrimination on the other are probably the main roots of differences in the capacity to move vertically or geographically or occupationally. Insofar as these impediments are social, however, they are capable of being by-passed or leveled, and indeed, the history of Western society is marked by a slow but gradual demolition of traditional or hereditary barriers and of a gradual opening of achievement to all talents.

There are, however, still more deep-seated reasons for variations in earnings in the differing marginal disutilities in which the spectrum of occupations is held, and in the differing "innate" abilities of men. We must conclude that in a world where the social barriers of privilege had been finally dismantled, differences would still be observed in the levels of reward, although they would probably be very unlike those we see today.

PROPERTY INCOME

We will return to a further analysis of income differences, and especially of poverty, in Chapter 29. But before we leave the subject of income differences, we should note that our explanations in this chapter have so far involved only labor, in all its range of skills, and that they have not touched on the question of why incomes derived from labor are different from those derived from capital or land.

[2] See E. H. Phelps Brown, *The Economics of Labor* (New Haven: Yale University Press, 1962), pp. 154, 156.

Here microtheory has relatively little to say. It can tell us why the return to capital in one industry is higher than in another (there may be difficulties of various sorts that prevent the flow of capital into the high-earnings industry), or it can tell us why land brings different prices in different localities or times. But it cannot compare the income of a landowner or that of a capitalist with an income earned purely from work. This is because the ownership of assets in a market system is not realistically to be pictured as the result of a race for wealth that each generation conducts anew from an impartial starting line, but reflects to a large degree inequalities of private property formed in the past and perpetuated by inheritance.

For example, the Board of Governors of the Federal Reserve System studied 57.9 million household units and reported on the distribution of wealth among them in 1962 (Table 24-3).

Size of asset holdings	Percent of households
$ 0 to $ 999	25.8%
1,000 to 4,900	18.0%
5,000 to 9,999	16.0%
10,000 to 24,999	23.0%
25,000 to 49,999	11.0%
50,000 to 99,999	5.0%
100,000 and over	1.2%

TABLE 24 • 3

DISTRIBUTION OF WEALTH AMONG HOUSEHOLD UNITS, 1962

Effectively, one-quarter of the population owned no assets (other than its household goods, the depreciated value of its automobile, and its small bank balance, if any), and another 18 percent owned little more than the value of its house. At the other end of the scale, however, are the 1 percent of the most favorably situated households who, according to a study by National Bureau of Economic Research, own at least one-third of all privately owned wealth and up to three-quarters of all corporation stock.[3] It is possible, furthermore, that this concentration of wealth (not income) at the very summit may be increasing.

Such figures make it impossible to hold current market activity responsible for the distribution of the ownership of capital assets. Instead we are forced to return to the perspective of economic history to evaluate the sources of this wealth and its probable distribution in the future. Certainly there can be no doubt that American capitalism (as indeed, capitalism

[3] See *Survey of Financial Characteristics of Consumers,* Board of Governors of the Federal Reserve System, Washington D.C., 1963, p. 151; Robert Lampman, *Changes in the Share of Wealth Held by Top Wealth Holders,* 1922–1956, National Bureau of Economic Research, 1960; and F. Lundberg, *The Rich and the Super-Rich* (New York: Lyle Stuart, 1968), p. 19.

everywhere) is characterized by a very small class of extremely wealthy persons whose assets are largely invested in the stocks and bonds of the nation's big corporations. Whether or not they "control" those corporations is difficult to say, but certainly they benefit disproportionately from their operations.

One reflection in this regard is interesting and germane, however. When we trace the overall division of the social product between the share going to property and that going to labor (of all skills), we find the property share to have fallen slightly since the beginning of the twentieth century. In the decade 1900-1909, business profits and all interest and rent took 21.4 percent of national income; in the 1960s and in 1970, this has slipped to under 19 percent. These measures are far from exact, but they suggest that the rewards to property are certainly not growing.

DERIVED DEMAND

There remains only the last, but most important aspect of factor pricing—the case in which demand arises not from a consumer but from a firm. What is the difference? It is that when a consumer hires a factor, he does so because of the personal enjoyments—the utilities—he will gain from doing so. No such consideration affects the entrepreneur's decision to buy factor services. When a businessman enters the factor markets, he does so not because land, labor, or capital will afford him increased utilities, but because using those factors will bring profits to his firm. Thus, unlike the direct demand of a consumer, the firm's demand for factors is a *derived demand.*

How much will a businessman pay for a factor's services? We can see that the answer must have something to do with how much the factor is worth to him and that, in turn, this will involve the productivity of the factor—its contribution to output. But these questions bring us to the last of the processes by which the market system is knit together. We are finally ready to invade the precincts of the firm.

KEY CONCEPTS AND KEY WORDS

Services of land, labor, capital

1. The rewards to land, labor, and capital are paid for the *services* that each offers on the market.

2. The supply curves of individual landowners and capitalists are indeterminate. But the supply curve for land or for capital in the aggregate is probably upward sloping, since a rise in price attracts new land and capital into the market.

Marginal disutility

3. The labor supply curve is typically *backward bending* above a certain price. This reflects the *increasing marginal disutility of work* and the *diminishing marginal utility of income.*

Mobility of factors

4. The elasticity of factor supply curves depends in large part on the *mobility of factors.* This is affected by geographical considerations, although more importantly by social and technical barriers and by the unequal distribution of wealth.

5. *Quasi rents* are an important constituent of earnings in all cases in which mobility is impaired. Quasi rents must be differentiated from *rents* in that they have nothing to do with increasing the supply of a factor on the market. Quasi rents can be found in many labor, land, and capital earnings. *Quasi rents are determined by price,* rather than helping to determine the price, as is the case with true rent.

Rent and
quasi-rent

6. Insofar as the demand for factors issues directly from consumers, we can explain factor earnings (incomes) by simple supply and demand analysis. In this case, however, we must note the following causes for differentials in incomes:

Causes of
income
differentials

   * *Discrimination* on account of race or sex
   * *Different marginal disutilities* of different employments
   * The different *amounts of investment* required for different occupations
   * Underlying differences in *abilities*

7. *Property incomes* cannot be compared directly with factor incomes. There is some evidence that property incomes are slowly declining as a claimant on national income.

8. Entrepreneurial demand for labor, unlike that of consumers, is *derived demand.* It depends on the expected profitability of hiring labor, not on the utilities to be enjoyed from it.

Derived demand

Q U E S T I O N S

1. When a suburban homeowner buys "land," what services is he actually buying? When he hires domestic help, what services is he buying? When he borrows money from a bank?

2. Suppose you had $10,000 and that you had invested half of it at 6 percent. If the rate of interest went up to 7 percent would you be tempted to invest more? Or the same? Or might you think that it would be wise to invest a little less, since your income was now higher? Are there reasonable arguments for all three?

3. What do you think the supply curve of executive labor looks like? Is it backward bending? Would you expect it to be more or less backward bending than the supply curve of common labor? Why?

4. What do you think are the main impediments to factor mobility in the labor market? Location? Education? Discrimination? Wealth? How would you lessen these barriers?

5. How technically "specific" is a printing press? A lathe? In the long run, how can the capital in a printing press be moved from one use to another?

6. Exactly what is meant by rent? Does rent have something to do with the quantity of land offered on the market? What is quasi rent? If quasi rents go up, does this mean that more of a good is being offered?

7. What is meant by saying that rent is price-determining and that quasi rent is price-determined? Show the answer in a diagram.

8. Trace the consequences of a rise in the demand for beef on the price of beef. What have the various elasticities of supply of different stages in beef production to do with the eventual effect of a rise in demand on price?

9. Draw a supply and demand diagram for domestic help. What changes in demand or supply might affect domestics' wages? To what extent would you explain the relatively low level of domestics' wages in terms of marginal disutility? Lack of wealth? Investment?

10. In your own experience do you know of an instance of discrimination in economic rewards (remember, this means unequal pay for *equal ability and work)?* How do you think discrimination can best be combatted?

11. In a world without any disparities in inherited wealth, what trends would you expect to find in the occupational differences in income? Would any income differences remain among occupations? Within occupations? What would each be traceable to?

From our survey of economic history we already know something of the variety of businesses that make up the American economic scene, and in particular of the predominating importance of the great corporation. But in this first look into the workings of the firm we shall be dealing with a kind of enterprise very different from that giant corporation whose powers and whose relative exemption from price competition interested us so much in Part Two. Here we shall concern ourselves with the other end of the business scale, learning how very small businesses with little or no power manage to survive, exposed to the full blast of competition.

There are good reasons for this initial limitation of our investigation. First, the kind of small, highly competitive firm we will describe exists as an important reality on the business scene, and we must understand how such firms do in fact survive and what role they play. Second, even the biggest and most monopolistic firms bear certain family resemblances to small competitive ones, so that our study will lay the groundwork for a later analysis of very big business. And last, until we have grasped how the market mechanism works with small competitive firms, we will not be in a position to understand and to measure the difference that large firms and imperfect competition add to the system.

In addition to limiting our scrutiny to markets made up of small, competitive firms, we will add two assumptions about the behavior of these firms—one of them realistic and one perhaps not. The unrealistic assumption is that our firm acts *intelligently and rationally* in the pursuit of its goals. Since the world is littered with the bankruptcies that result from mistaken calculations and foolish decisions, this assumption may strain our credulity, but at least it will do no violence to understanding the *principles* of the market system.

Second, we will assume that our firm is motivated by a desire to *maximize its profits in the short run*—that is, day by day. Later, when we study the operations of very large firms we shall have to ask whether this maximizing assumption makes much sense in their case. But when we deal with the "atomistic" competition of small firms, the assumption stands up very well *because as we shall see, it is only by trying to maximize short-term profits that small firms manage to survive at all.* This gives to microtheory the same two-sided relevance that we noted in the case of its description of the competitive market. Microtheory tells us how small firms actually do behave—and thereby enables us to make predictions about the way the market system works—and it also serves as a goal-oriented description of how small business firms *should* conduct their affairs if they hope to survive.

Economics of the Firm

What are the problems and pressures that beset the small firm in its fight for survival? They will become gradually clear to us as we move along. But at the outset one problem attracts our attention not only because it is unresolved from our last chapter, but because it bears directly on the ability of the firm to make profits. This is how a firm decides how many factors to hire and in what proportions to combine them.

Suppose, for example, that we are considering opening a bookstore. The first question that we will have to answer is how much land, labor, and capital we will need in the form of space that we rent, help that we hire (including ourselves), and equipment or inventories of books that we must have. No matter what business we are in, there will be some minimum size below which we know we cannot operate profitably. A bookstore may be very small, but it has to have *some* reasonable number of books on the premises, and it must have at least one person around to sell them. If we were in a somewhat more technical line of work—say, manufacturing plastic parts—we would base the minimum size of our plant on the machinery that would be essential for our operation. If we were in a highly complex mass assembly business, such as typewriters, the *smallest* efficient plant might run

THE PROBLEM OF SCALE

into an investment of millions of dollars and would require a work force of thousands of people. But that would take us well out of the world of atomistic competition to which we are still devoting our attention.

In other words, the first decision about the hiring of factors involves the choice of *scale,* and that choice, it can be seen, is basically determined by the prevailing technology. In every kind of business there is usually a minimum size of establishment below which it is impossible to operate competitively because one of the factors would not be present in large enough quantity to allow certain technical efficiencies to be realized. This fact, in turn, arises because factors are not infinitely divisible for all uses— there is always a minimum amount of one factor that must be applied if a certain output is to be secured. In agriculture, for example, this minimum may be established by requirements of acreage; in manufacturing it is likely to be set by the irreducible requirements of the needed capital equipment. It is simply not possible to build an efficient automobile plant that will fit into a cigar store or to raise cattle profitably in a suburban back yard.

FACTOR MIX
But once the minimum size of our enterprise has been established, we know the amount of only *one* factor we will have to hire if we are to open shop. Suppose that the limiting factor is land and that we decide that the smallest profitable bookstore would have to have at least 500 square feet of space. There is still the question of how much of the other factors we are to add to the predetermined factor of land. Assuming that we had $10,000 to spend, where should we put our money—into a large inventory of books and a small sales and office force (perhaps only ourselves), or into two or more salespeople working with a smaller inventory of books?

This question involves us not in a determination of the scale of the enterprise, but of the *mix of factors* that will be most profitable within a given scale. To go back to our plastics manufacturer for a moment, assume that he decides what the minimum investment in machinery will be for a profitable operation. He will then have to decide whether to spend relatively more money on land or on labor. Perhaps he has a choice of building his plant in two areas—one in which land is expensive but labor abundant, another where land is very cheap but labor is dearer. Which should he choose?

The answer to these problems takes us back to consider an attribute of the factors of production that we have been able to overlook until now, because we were considering their output as if it were a consumers' good to be directly enjoyed. *When a factor is being hired by a firm, the firm considers the usefulness of that factor as a means to an end*—the end being the output of its own product, be that the sale of books or plastics. Therefore it is the *profitability of the factor* that interests the businessman who is considering which factor to hire. If land will produce more business for him than labor, he will hire land. If a sales clerk will sell more books for us than having a larger inventory of books, we will hire a sales clerk. The question is, how do we know which factor will be the better buy?

Law of Variable Proportions

As we shall see, this is by no means a simple question to answer, for many considerations bear on the decision to hire a factor or not, or on the choice of one factor over another. But in the center of any businessman's calculations lies one extremely important fact to which we must now pay close attention. This is the physical productivity of different factors—their capacity to increase his output—and more than that, *the changing physical productivity that results from combining different amounts of one factor with fixed amounts of the others.*

Let us begin with a case that is very simple to imagine. Suppose we have a farmer who has a farm of 100 acres and a certain amount of equipment, and no labor at all. Now let us picture our farmer first hiring one man, then a second man of the same abilities, then a third, and so on. Obviously, the output of the farm would grow. What we want to find out, however, is whether it will grow in some clearly defined pattern that we can attribute to the changing amounts of the factor that is being added.

What would such a curve of productivity look like? Assume that one man, working the 100 acres alone as best he can, produces 1,000 bushels of grain. A second man, helping the first, should be enormously valuable, because two men can begin to specialize and divide the work, each doing the jobs he is better at and saving the time formerly wasted by moving from one job to the next. As a consequence, output may jump to 3,000 bushels. Since the *difference* in output is 2,000 bushels, we speak of the *marginal productivity* of labor, when two men are working, as 2,000 bushels. Note that we should not (although in carelessness we sometimes do) speak of the marginal productivity of the second *man*. Alone, his efforts are no more productive than those of the first man: if we fired the first man, worker number 2 would only produce 1,000 bushels. What makes the difference is the jump in the combined productivity of the *two* men, once specialization can be introduced. Hence we should speak of the changing marginal productivity of *labor,* not of the individual.

It is not difficult to imagine an increasing specialization taking place with the third, fourth, and fifth man, so that the addition of another unit of labor input in each case brings about an output larger than was realized by the average of all the previous men. Remember that this does not mean the individual factor units themselves are more productive. *It means that as we add units of one factor, the total mix of these units plus the fixed amounts of other factors, forms an increasingly efficient technical combination.**

We call the range of factor inputs, over which average productivity rises, a range of *increasing average returns.* It is, of course, a stage of production that is highly favorable for the producer. Every time he adds a factor, efficiency rises. (As a result, as we shall see in our next chapter, costs per unit of output fall). The rate of increase will not be the same, for the initial large marginal leaps in productivity will give way to smaller ones—that is, *marginal* output is actually falling. But the overall trend of productivity, whether we measure it by looking at *total* output or at *average* output per man, will still be up. And all this keeps on happening, of course, because the factor we are adding has not yet reached its point of maximum technical efficiency with the given amount of other factors.

DIMINISHING
RETURNS

Then our farmer notices a disconcerting phenomenon. At a certain point, average productivity no longer rises when he adds another man. Total output will still be rising with the addition of more men, but a quick calculation reveals that the last man on the team has added so little to the productivity of the farm that *average* output per man has actually fallen.†

What has happened has been that we have overshot the point of maximum technical efficiency, and that labor is now beginning to "crowd" the land or the equipment. Opportunities for further specialization have become nonexistent—worse yet, additional labor is forced to perform so inefficiently that the *average* output of the whole labor force is pulled down. We *call this state of falling average performance a condition of decreasing average returns.* As the words suggest, we are getting back less and less as we add the critical factor—not only from the "marginal" man, but from the average efforts of all the men. (Now, of course, costs will be rising per unit.) If we went on foolishly adding men, eventually the addition of another worker would add nothing to total output. In fact, the next worker might then so disrupt the factor mix that *total* output would actually fall and we would be in a condition of negative returns.

This changing profile of physical productivity is one of the most impor-

---

* With each additional man, the proportions of land, labor, and capital are altered, so that the change in the level of output should rightfully be ascribed to new levels of efficiency resulting from the interaction of *all three factors.* But since labor is the factor whose input we are varying, it has become customary to call the change in output the result of a change in "labor productivity." If we were altering land or capital alone, we would call the change the result of changes in their productivities, even though, as with labor, the real cause is the changing efficiency of *all* factors in different mixes.

† It is also possible to speak of the onset of diminishing returns as soon as *marginal* product begins to fall, even though average productivity is rising. Usage varies; the underlying relationships do not.

tant generalizations that economics makes about the real world. It will help us to think it through if we now study the relationships of marginal and average productivity and of total output in Table 25-1.

TABLE 25 • 1

Number of men	Total output	Marginal productivity (change in output)	Average productivity (total output ÷ no. of men)
1	1,000	1,000	1,000
2	3,000	2,000	1,500
3	5,500	2,500	1,833
4	7,800	2,300	1,950
5	9,800	2,000	1,960
6	11,600	1,800	1,930
7	13,100	1,500	1,871
8	14,300	1,200	1,790

TOTAL, AVERAGE, AND MARGINAL PRODUCT

All three columns are integrally related to one another, and it is important to understand the exact nature of their relationships. The column for marginal productivity shows the *change* in output as we add each man; it is therefore derived by subtracting the total output at one level of employment (say the 7,800 bushels reaped by 4 men) from the output of the previous level of 5,500 bushels. Or if we wish, we can think of the total output column being obtained by adding up the successive marginal increments that come with additional personnel. The average productivity column is, of course, simply the total output divided by the number of men.

One thing must be carefully studied in this example. Note that marginal productivity begins to diminish with the fourth man, who adds only 2,300 bushels to output, and not 2,500 as did his predecessor. Average productivity, however, rises until we hire the sixth man, because the fifth man, although producing less than the fourth, is still more productive than the average output of all four men. *Thus marginal productivity can be falling while average productivity is still rising.*

The three curves in Fig. 25-1 actually all show the same thing, only in different ways. The top curve shows us that as we add men to our farm, output at first rises very rapidly, then slowly, then actually declines. The marginal productivity curve shows us *why* this is happening to total output: as we add men, the contribution they can make to output changes markedly, at first each man adding so much that average output grows rapidly; thereafter marginal output falling but average output still rising; finally each man adding so little that he actually pulls down the average that obtained before his hiring. And the average curve, as we have just indicated, merely

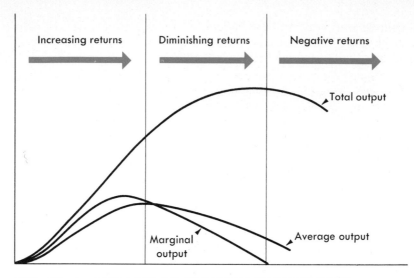

FIG. 25•1   THE LAW OF VARIABLE PROPORTIONS

sums up the overall output in an arithmetical way by showing us what the average person contributes to it.

Put into the form of a generalization, we can say that *as we add successive units of one factor to fixed amounts of others, the average output of the units of the variable factor will at first rise and then decline. We call this the law of variable proportions or the law of diminishing returns, or we can simply talk about it as the physical productivity curve.*

THE LAW REVIEWED

The generalizations of the law of variable proportions constitute one of the key insights that a study of microeconomics gives us into the workings of the real world. Hence let us be certain that we understand exactly what the law says and implies.

1. The law of variable proportions describes what happens to physical productivity when we add units of one factor and *hold the others constant.* As we added labor in the example above, we did not also add land or capital. Had we done so, there would have been no way of ascribing changes in output to the addition of one factor rather than the other.

2. The law applies to the additions of *any* factor to fixed quantities of the others. Suppose that we had started with a fixed amount of labor and capital and had added successive acres of land. The first acre would not have been very productive, for we would have had to squeeze too much labor and capital into its area. The second acre would have permitted a better utilization of all three factors, and so "its" marginal productivity would have been much higher. But in time the addition of successive units of land would pass the point of optimum mix, until another acre would add so little yield that the average production of all acres

would be pulled down. And the same pattern of increase, diminution, and final decrease would of course attend the addition of doses of capital—say successive bags of fertilizer or additional tractors—to a fixed amount of land and labor.

3. Unlike many other "laws" in economics, the law of variable proportions has nothing to do with behavior. The actions of men on the marketplace, or the impulses or restraints of utility and disutility, play no role in diminishing returns. *Essentially, the law expresses a constraint imposed by the laws of nature.* If there were no such constraint, we could grow all the food required by the world in a single acre, or even in a flowerpot, simply by adding more and more labor and capital.

Economics, as we have said before, is the study of how men seek to provision themselves, of how society solves the universal problem of production and distribution. Through most of this book we have been concerned with the *social* aspects of this problem—with the difficulties in arranging the institutional and behavioral requirements for survival and growth. It is well to bear in mind that nature also imposes its conditions on man, and nowhere more visibly than in the diminishing returns that ultimately hamper all his efforts.

This technological or physical reason behind the law of diminishing returns is related to that behind the law of increasing costs that we met on p. 442. Here we are interested in learning why the marginal output of a given good decreases as a single factor is added to given quantities of other factors; previously, we wanted to know why the marginal output of a given good decreased as we shifted *all factors* from other uses to produce that good. In both cases the critical element lies in the fact that technology or nature decrees a certain "mix" as the optimal resource combination for making any good. When we move factors from one use to another, sooner or later we encounter one factor that will become scarce relative to the others. From that point on, additional units of the other factors cannot be employed at maximal efficiency, and marginal output must fall.

Marginal Revenue and Marginal Cost

But now we must get back to our point of interest—the firm seeking to hire factors to its own best advantage. Is a knowledge of factor productivity all a businessman needs? To revert to our first illustration, suppose we knew that a single salesperson in our bookstore had a productivity of (i.e., could sell) 5 books a day. Would that alone tell us if we should hire him?

The question answers itself. Before we can hire the clerk or any other factor, we have to know two other things: (1) *we have to know what the unit of the factor will cost*, and (2) *we have to know how much revenue our firm will get as a result of hiring that unit of the factor.*

For instance, if the price of a salesperson is $6,000 and if we think his activity as a salesperson will add 5 books a day to our sales, at an average price per book of $5, then if he works for 250 days, he will bring in revenues of $6,250 (5 × $5 × 250). Obviously it will pay to hire him.* On the other hand, if his productivity were less—if he sold only 4 books per day—then the revenues from hiring him would be only $5,000 (4 × $5 × 250), or $1,000 less than his wage. He would be a dead loss.

Our illustration enables us to see the general process by which entrepreneurs make their hiring decisions, and also enables us to see how productivity fits into those decisions. Whenever we are considering hiring any factor, we compare in our minds two sums. On the one hand, any increase in the units of the factor we hire will raise our cost. On the other hand, that same increased use of one factor should increase our output, and therefore our revenue. The conclusion is very simple. *If the marginal revenue expected from the addition of a unit of a factor is greater than the marginal cost of a unit of the factor, it pays to hire it. If the marginal cost is greater than the marginal revenue, it does not.* (Furthermore, it may even raise our profits if we fire factors, provided that in each case we reduce our costs by more than we reduce our revenues.)

Just where does productivity fit into this picture? The answer is that productivity tells us how much additional physical output we can get from hiring additional units of a factor. Thus, if we know what the unit of the factor will cost and what the sales price of our output will be, it is productivity that determines whether a factor will be worth its hire or not.

Let us see how this actually works in practice. In the schedules below we go back to our farm, this time armed with two new pieces of information. We know that labor costs $4500 per man and that a bushel of wheat sells for $2.50. (Later we will look into *how* we know these things, but now we can take them for granted.) Our farm schedule of marginal cost and marginal revenue therefore looks like Table 25-2.

What does our table tell us? Our first man seems to be very unprofitable, for he costs us $4,500 and brings in only $2,500. We suspect, however, that he is so inefficient because he is trying to spread his one unit of labor over the whole farm. The addition of a second man confirms our suspicions. He also costs us $4,500, but brings in $5,000. (Remember it is not the second man himself who does so, but the two men working together who give rise to an increase in revenues of that amount.) The third and fourth and fifth men also show profits, but when we reach the sixth man, the law of diminishing returns brings its decisive force to bear. The sixth man is unable to increase the productivity of the team by more than $4,500, which is just his hire. It is not worthwhile to engage him.

---

* For simplicity's sake, we assume that the bookstore gets its books free. We will take up the problem of business costs in our next chapter.

TABLE 25 • 2

Number of men	Marginal cost per man @ $4,500	Marginal output per man (from Table 25-1)	Marginal revenue per man (output × $2.50)	Marginal profit or loss per man
1	$4,500	1,000	$2,500	−2,000
2	4,500	2,000	5,000	500
3	4,500	2,500	6,250	1,750
4	4,500	2,300	5,750	1,250
5	4,500	2,000	5,000	500
6	4,500	1,800	4,500	0
7	4,500	1,500	3,750	− 750
8	4,500	1,200	3,000	−1,500

Are we certain that hiring five men will really maximize the profits of the farm? We can find out by adding up our *total* costs and our *total* revenues and figuring our profit at each level of operation.* (We get the totals by adding each marginal increment to the preceding sum of costs or revenues.)

TABLE 25 • 3

Number of men	Total cost of men	Total revenue	Profit (total revenue less cost)
1	$ 4,500	$ 2,500	− $2,000
2	9,000	7,500	− 1,500
3	13,500	13,750	250
4	18,000	19,500	1,500
5	22,500	24,500	2,000
6	27,000	29,000	2,000
7	31,500	32,750	1,250
8	35,000	35,750	750

As we can see, our best profit comes with the hire of 5 men. The addition of a sixth does us no good. A seventh lowers our net income—not for any lack of skill or effort on his part, but because with seven men the mix of labor and the fixed amounts of other factors is no longer so efficient as before.

---

* We are really fooling ourselves when we "check" on our former calculations about marginal changes by looking at the totals. For the totals are themselves nothing but the sum of the marginal changes! As long as each man brings *some* addition to revenue, large or small (that is, so long as marginal revenue is larger than marginal cost when that man is hired), then the total of all revenues must be growing larger too. When we add up the marginal contributions, we measure each different-sized contribution. We should not consider it surprising that the whole contains the sum of what we put into it.

We can also see now how neatly the physical productivity curve ties together marginal cost and marginal revenue. For three things would entice us to hire the sixth or even the seventh man.

1. *A fall in cost.* If wages dropped to any figure under $4,500, our sixth man will immediately pay his way. By how much would they have to drop to make it worthwhile to hire the seventh man? Marginal revenue when seven men are working is only $3,750. The wage level would have to drop below that point to bring a profit from seven men.

2. *A rise in the price of output.* If the demand for grain increased, and the price of grain went to $3, our calculations would change again. Now the sixth man is certainly profitable: adding him now brings a marginal revenue of 1,800 bushels × $3 or $5,400, far above his wage. Is the seventh man profitable? His physical productivity is 1,500 bushels. At $3 per bushel he is not quite worth hiring. At $3.01 he would be.

3. *An increase in productivity.* If a change in skills or techniques raises the physical output of each man, this will also change the margin of profitable factor use. Any small increase will lead to the employment of the sixth man.*

CHOICE AMONG FACTORS

We have talked, so far, as if an entrepreneur had only one "scarce" factor, and as if his only task were to decide how much of that factor to add. But that is not quite the problem faced by the businessman. He has to make up his mind not only *whether* to add to his output at all, but *which* factor to hire in order to do so.

How does a businessman make such a choice? How would we choose between adding a salesclerk to our bookstore or adding inventory, or how would our farmer decide between hiring labor or spending the same sum on capital or land? Suppose that our farmer has already hired four men to work for him and has also rented a certain amount of land and used a certain amount of capital. Now when he thinks about expanding output he needs to know not only how much the addition of another man will yield him, but *what the alternatives are.*

They might look like this:

1. He can hire a fifth worker for $4,500 who will, as we know, bring about an increase of $5,000 in revenues.

2. He could spend the same amount on land, renting, let us say, 10 acres that would increase his output by 2,100 bushels, worth (@ $2.50) $5,250.

3. For the same outlay he could engage the services of a tractor that would add 2,200 bushels a year to his output, worth $5,500.

---

* We can see that an increase in productivity leads to an increase in employment in the case of an individual firm. But we cannot generalize that an increase in the productivity of *all* workers will lead to increase in total employment. That depends on what happens to aggregate demand or to the structure of employment. This is a problem we studied in macroeconomics (see p. 389f.)

The problem is not difficult. If the farmer compares marginal costs and marginal revenues of his three alternatives, he will find his course.

Factor	Marginal cost	Marginal revenue	Profit
Additional man	$4,500	$5,000	$ 500
Additional land	4,500	5,250	750
Additional capital	4,500	5,500	1,000

Obviously, the tractor is the best buy, and he should spend his money on tractors, not on land or labor, as long as the relative prices and productivities of the three factors remain unchanged.*

But will factor prices remain unchanged? The question brings us back to the answered query of our last chapter: how are factor prices determined when firms, rather than consumers, provide the demand? We have taken a long detour into productivity because we could see that productivity was inextricably entangled in the firm's calculations as it bid for factors. But it was just this, the outcome of this bidding process, that we wanted to track down in the first place. Now we should be in a position to do so. We must begin by examining a critical supposition about factor pricing that we have already introduced very quietly. You will remember we assumed that the farmer was able to bid for additional land, or for any other factor, *without thereby affecting its price.*

Why were we able to make this assumption? The answer follows from the premise of atomistic firms from which we started. The amount of land or labor or capital that such a small firm can add to its operations is so insignificant a portion of the total supply of that factor that the individual firm's demand does not affect the price of the factor at all. If there are 100,000 young women looking for sales work in New York City, the addition of a few salespeople in any single business will not change the going price for salespeople at all. Neither will a small farmer's demand, by itself, alter the rent of land, nor will one firm's demand for capital change the rate of interest.

For one small firm, the supply curve of any factor looks like a horizontal line. It is infinitely elastic, because a firm can engage all of the factor it requires at the going price without affecting the price of that factor at all.

But this is not the case when many small firms all begin to demand the same factor. If all stores are looking for sales help, the salaries of salespeople will rise. If many farmers seek land or capital, rentals or interest rates (or

---

* Ideally, an economist would wish to compare the marginal productivities of much smaller amounts of these three factors; i.e., an hour's worth of labor or a very small parcel of land or a day's use of a tractor. We have dealt in big chunks because factors often do come in indivisible units, and because this is the way the problem usually looks in the business world.

the prices of capital goods) will go up. As a result, each individual firm will find that the going price for the factor in general demand has a mysterious tendency to rise, as Fig. 25-2 shows.*

Supply and demand sets the prices of factors, just as it does when consumers buy them, but now the demand is exercised by a whole cluster of firms or by an industry. The individual firm has no impact on the market and no choice but to accept its price as given.

**FIG. 25 • 2 SUPPLY CURVE TO ALL FIRMS
VS. SUPPLY CURVE TO ONE FIRM**

**FACTOR
PRICING**

We can now finish our whole analysis of the pricing of factors. We remember that in our last example it was profitable for farmers to buy tractors, rather than land or labor. Now we must suppose that many farmers, finding themselves in the same situation, all bid for tractors. The result, of course, is that tractor prices will rise. The consequence of this, plainly, is that tractors become less profitable to the farmer, compared with land or labor, than they were originally. Suppose, for example, that the price of tractor hire goes up to $5,000; so that for an outlay of $4,500 a farmer can now afford to get a tractor on his place only four days out of the week instead of five (or if he buys a tractor, he has to get a smaller model). Since the expenditure of $4,500 will now buy fewer tractor inputs, the tractor's addition to output will also decrease. Let us imagine that tractor output falls by almost one-fifth with the cut in tractor hours. Then $4,500 of expenditure will bring an increase in output of 1,800 bushels instead of 2,200. At $2.50 per bushel, the marginal revenue from using a tractor now amounts to only $4,500. There is no net profit in using tractors at all!

Actually things will work out in less dramatic fashion than this. As tractor prices rise (and as the marginal productivity of tractors falls, owing to their more intensive use), the profit advantage between tractors and land will narrow. At a certain point land will be just as attractive to farmers as

* The diagram does not emphasize a very important difference in *scale.* One inch along the horizontal axis of the industry diagram on the left may represent 100,000 units. The same inch along the firm's horizontal axis would then stand for only a few hundred units.

tractors. Thereafter, since both land and tractors are still better buys than labor, the price of *both* land and tractors will continue to rise. Again as a result, the profit difference between them and labor will narrow until the same profit will be derived from an equal expenditure on any of the three factors. Now, finally, the prices of *all three* factors may rise if there is still a profit obtainable from using them. Only when rising prices and falling marginal productivities make it no longer profitable to seek any more factors at all will the bidding stop and factor prices stabilize.

Now perhaps we can stand back and review the process.

1. *An entrepreneur who makes a profit in a competitive market will seek to expand his output to increase that profit. This will require hiring additional factors.*

2. *When deciding which factor to hire, an entrepreneur will compare the dollar return he will get from an equal dollar outlay on different factors. The size of these relative returns will depend on the relative costs of the various factors and on their different physical productivities.*

3. *All entrepreneurs in a given industry will normally discover that one factor is more profitable than any other, at a given time, and all will concentrate their demand on that factor. As a result, the price of that factor will rise; and as more of it is used, its marginal productivity will decline. Hence its profit advantage over the other factors declines.*

4. *As the result of continuously bidding for the most profitable factor, the profitability of all factors will be equalized. There will then be no advantage to spending a given sum on land instead of labor, or on capital instead of land, and so on. Instead, all factors will now be equally sought.*

5. *Finally, all factors will be bid up in price until there is no longer any profit to be had from using any more of any of them. At that point the expansion of the industry stops, and the prices of factors remain steady.*

The Market Solution
to Distribution

Perhaps we can already see, from this brief capsule of the factor-hiring process, the remarkable nature of the market solution to the problem of distribution. For our bidding process has not only eliminated any advantages of profit enjoyed by one factor over another, but it also has led to three striking results.

1. *It has eliminated exploitation.*

We have seen that as long as the marginal revenue from the employment of any factor exceeds its marginal cost, firms will bid for that factor. As a result, its price will rise (and its productivity may fall) until marginal revenue and marginal cost are equal. Suppose, for example, that the value of labor's marginal product was $6,000 but that labor was paid only $5,000. The possibility of making $1,000 profit per worker would lead to a general demand for labor, and the increased use of labor would lead to a fall in its marginal product. Together, competitive bidding and falling marginal productivity would bring a new price for labor—let us say $5,800—at which MC and MR would be equal. Labor would thereupon be paid a wage equal to the value of its marginal product.

Two observations must be made about this result. First, it is important to stress that the elimination of exploitation depends on the existence of a perfect market. Prejudice, ignorance, inequalities of starting point, or other barriers will prevent the auction for factors from taking its full effect. Hence, in the real world, pockets of exploitation certainly exist despite the existence of the market. Second, a world in which labor is paid the full value of its marginal product may not necessarily be a world that accords with our sense of moral equity. At the end of this chapter, we shall look more carefully into the question of whether the outcome of the market process is to be judged as "just."

2. *At the end of the bidding process, all factors will be priced so that their relative rewards will mirror their relative marginal productivities.*

This is easiest to see by means of an illustration. Let us suppose that we have two grades of labor—skilled and unskilled—and that skilled labor produces twice as much per hour as unskilled labor in a given industry. Further, we will suppose that unskilled labor is paid $1 per hour, whereas skilled labor is paid $3 per hour.

Which would an entrepreneur hire, assuming that he could freely substitute one kind of labor for the other in his plant? For $1 outlay on unskilled labor he gets, let us say, 10 units of output. For $3 outlay on skilled labor he gets twice that, or twenty units. Thus a unit of output produced by unskilled labor costs 10¢ and a unit produced by skilled labor costs 15¢.

Of course our employer will use unskilled labor. So will all employers. The price of unskilled labor will accordingly rise. At $1.50 an hour, its ten units of output will now cost 15¢ each, the same as skilled labor. At this point, employers no longer prefer unskilled labor. Its price will now settle down. Notice, however, that the price of the two grades of labor is now exactly proportional to their marginal productivities:

$$\frac{\$1.50}{10 \text{ units}} = \frac{\$3.00}{20 \text{ units}}$$

Unskilled labor   *Skilled labor*

As we have seen, precisely the same bidding process, with precisely the same result, has taken place between land and labor, or labor and capital, and so on. Thus we can generalize the outcome of the competitive auction:

$$\frac{\text{Price of Factor A}}{\text{Marginal productivity of Factor A}} = \frac{\text{Price of Factor B}}{\text{Marginal productivity of Factor B}}$$

Thus, in a settled competitive market, if one unit (say an acre) of land rents for $500 and a unit of capital (say a machine) can be hired for $1,000, and a unit of labor (say a man-year) costs $5,000, then we know that the marginal productivity of an acre of land is only half that of a machine, and one-tenth that of a man. Once again, let us caution that these results assume that the market will be perfectly competitive.

3. *As firms seek to equalize factor yields, they will also be maximizing efficiency.*

We have left until last what is perhaps the most important effect of the competitive bidding process we have been investigating. It is that the search for the most profitable factor requires that an entrepreneur always hires the factor that makes the *largest physical contribution to output for a given expenditure.* In our previous example, as long as tractors were the best buy for farmers, it meant that a dollar's expenditure on tractor services yielded more output than a dollar's expenditure on any other factor; and when all factors were ultimately sought for equally, it was because the physical contribution of a dollar's worth of each was the same.

Thus the process of competitive bidding for factors steers the system in the direction of maximizing efficiency; that is, toward getting the largest possible physical return from any given expenditure on factors. As we shall have reason to see when we turn to the study of planned economies in Chapter 33, this built-in impetus toward the efficient utilization of resources is one of the most powerful sources of economic advantage for market economies.

Our analysis has begun to reveal the extraordinary attributes of the market system as a distributive mechanism. But it also reveals this disturbing fact: attempts to interfere with the market mechanism for pricing factors may bring unexpected and unwanted effects. Take for example the problem of low-priced labor. Suppose the government decided tomorrow to eliminate all low-paid work by legislating a minimum wage of $100 a week (or that trade unions accomplished the same thing through bargaining).

What would be the result? As the price of low-paid labor rises, the differential in pay that compensated for its lower productivity is removed. The unavoidable consequence is that entrepreneurs will swing their factor demand toward other factors—land, capital, or high-priced labor—because a dollar of expenditure will now bring them a larger return from these factors. Hence the result of the minimum wage is very likely to bring unemployment to the very persons it was designed to help!

MINIMUM WAGES

How *much* unemployment depends on how "substitutable" is the factor in question. Suppose the new minimum wage affects the pay of grocery boys. Grocers will try to use trucks to make deliveries wherever possible instead of sending boys on bicycles, or they will simply eliminate some deliveries. If it is possible to persuade customers to carry their own groceries, or if it is not too expensive to deliver groceries by truck, many delivery boys will be let go. In the latter case, in more technical terms, if capital can be substituted for labor, a slight rise in the price of labor will mean a considerable swing from labor-using to relatively capital-using techniques. In that case, delivery boys' aggregate incomes are likely to suffer.

If, on the other hand, grocers find that they can't replace the delivery boy, they will be forced to retain most of the boys and to pay them higher wages. As a result, grocery prices will rise somewhat, and the quantity of groceries demanded will decrease—how much or little depending on the price-elasticity of demand for groceries. If demand is very elastic, sales will fall off sharply, and many delivery boys will be fired because there is no need for them. If enough are fired, the income of the whole group may even fall. On the other hand, if demand is inelastic, grocery sales will remain relatively unchanged, few delivery boys will be let go, and their incomes as a whole will rise.

Thus the effect of setting floors under factor prices is difficult to predict insofar as its effect on *incomes* is concerned. Here everything depends on the technical ease of substituting other factors in place of the one whose price has been pushed up, and on the elasticities of demand for the final good or service itself. But the effect on *employment* must almost always be adverse, although again its extent will hinge on substitutability and elasticities of demand for final products.

Hence the efforts of government authorities or of trade unions to raise wages can backfire and actually reduce the incomes as well as the employment of those affected. To point this out is not to preach against such efforts. There are powerful arguments of social justice that favor some interventions into the market process. But one must not overlook the fact that interventions to "remedy" the rewards of the market will invariably bring their side effects. A thoughtful social policy will anticipate these effects and will not intervene into the market without plans for coping with the repercussions that are apt to ensue.

MARGINAL PRODUCTIVITY AND SOCIAL JUSTICE

But why interfere in the market process at all? Is not the market's solution to the problem of distribution a just and equitable one? If A is twice as productive as B, should he not be paid twice as much?

There are two important caveats before we accept this deceptively attractive proposition. First, as we have repeatedly warned, the market will not price factors according to their marginal productivities if there are impediments to the free movement of factors within society. The same barriers that we discovered in our last chapter, where demand originated with consumers rather than with business firms, distort the entrepreneurial determination of income as they do the direct pricing factors. Tariffs or union barriers or patent restrictions, immobilities due to geographical location or lack of education—all impair the achievement of the solution that microtheory promises. When a worker in Detroit does not know of a job at higher pay that he could fill in Chicago, or if he knows of the job but does not have the spare cash to move there, or if he has the cash but cannot find a house or apartment, then the market will not play its equilibrating, evening role. In some nations, such as Sweden, an elaborate system of labor exchanges seeks to avoid this kind of imperfection by making available to unemployed workers information about possible jobs and by subsidizing their movement to new localities when necessary.

In addition, in the real world, where firms are by no means always the small competitive units we have dealt with, the buyer of factors may be able to pay them less than their marginal productivity warrants, because there are no competitive firms to bid factors away. Hence, as was the case previously, we must not make the serious error of confusing the distribution of incomes in the real world with that of an ideal market, or commit the error of defending those incomes on the basis of theoretical premises that may not fit the case.

Second, even if all factors were remunerated in proportion to their productivities, it does not follow that the resulting levels of compensation would be "just." Even if one man is twice as productive as another, there is no inherent reason why he "should" be compensated twice as highly. Should a young worker, who is unmarried, make more money than an older one with a large family? Nor is there any inherent reason that, because a dollar's worth of land or capital makes a larger contribution to output than a dollar's worth of labor, the *owners* of those resources should therefore receive a compensation as large as the marginal revenue product of "their" resources. As John Stuart Mill wrote in a famous passage in his *Principles of Economics* in 1848:

The things are there; mankind individually or collectively can do with them as they please. They can place them at the disposal of whomsoever they please, and on whatever terms. The distribution of wealth ... depends on the laws and customs of society. The rules by which it is determined are what the opinions and feelings of the ruling portion of the community make them, and are very different in different ages and countries, and might be still more different, if mankind so chose.

Thus the market solution must be judged on its *efficacy,* not on its "intrinsic" merits. The rewards meted out by the market serve a purpose—to maintain the efficiency of the market system—but we should not confuse their functional merits with their moral worth. This is particularly pertinent to a society of considerable affluence in which the sheer necessity for efficiency of output becomes a matter of less pressing moment and in which, accordingly, other noneconomic standards can be allowed to play a more prominent role in the establishment of the community's goals.

KEY CONCEPTS AND KEY WORDS

Maximization

1. The study of the firm concentrates initially on the small enterprise. It assumes that such enterprises act intelligently and rationally and that they *try to maximize their profits in the short run.*

Scale

2. In all enterprises there is a *minimum size* or scale necessary for effective competition. This size is essentially determined by technology.

Marginal productivity

3. The choice of the amounts of the remaining factors to be added will be determined by their *profitability.*

Increasing returns

Diminishing returns

4. Their profitability in turn will depend to an important degree on their *productivity.* This leads to the discovery that as we add any factor to a fixed supply of other factors *its marginal productivity changes.* Initially it rises, and we enjoy increasing average returns. Subsequently it begins to decline, and the average drops. At this point we enter the stage of diminishing average returns.

Law of variable proportions

5. The *law of diminishing returns* (or *variable proportions*) applies to any factor, provided that we hold the amounts of the other factors fixed. It is entirely a natural phenomenon, not a behavioral one.

6. Marginal productivity is a critical element in determining the *marginal revenue* we can expect from hiring a factor. This marginal revenue will then be compared with marginal cost, to determine whether the unit of the factor is profitable.

Marginal revenue

7. The addition of factors is made by *comparing the returns from alternative factor mixes.* The factor yielding the highest return per dollar will be the factor that is hired.

Equal returns at the margin

8. *The process of many entrepreneurs bidding for the most profitable factor will raise its price.* Any single entrepreneur can bid for a factor without affecting its price; but when all firms bid for the same factor, its price rises.

Factor prices proportional to marginal productivities

9. This bidding process will eventually *equalize the return* to be had among all factors. The result is threefold:
   • *All factors will be sought as long as their marginal cost is less than their marginal revenue:* i.e., there will be no exploitation.
   • *All factors will be priced relative to one another in proportion to their marginal productivities.*
   • *Factors will be combined in the most efficient possible way.*

Efficiency

10. *If any factor price is "artificially" raised, its employment must be reduced* because other factors will now be relatively cheaper. Whether or not the more expensive factor suffers a fall in income depends on the technical possibilities of substitution and on the elasticity of demand for the end product.

11. The pricing of factors according to their respective marginal productivities is an *efficient but not necessarily "just" solution* to the problem of distribution.

1. Suppose that you were about to open a small business—say a drugstore. What do you think would be the factor that was critical in determining the scale of your operation? Name businesses in which land, labor, and capital, respectively, would play this limiting role.

2. Once you had decided on your scale, what consideration would be uppermost in your mind when you were deciding how much of the other two factors to hire? What is the cardinal rule you would have to bear in mind in deciding if a unit of a factor would or would not pay its way?

3. One thing that would affect your decision to hire or not to hire a factor would be the amount of physical increase in output it would yield. What is the generalization we make about the change in output associated with combining more and more of one factor to a fixed combination of others? Is this generalization based on behavior? State the law of variable proportions as carefully as you can.

4. What is meant by marginal productivity? What is its relation to average productivity? Suppose that you were considering the increase in your drug sales that would result from adding square feet of space. Draw up a schedule showing that the addition of square footage (in units of 100 sq ft) would at first yield increasing returns (dollars of sales) and then diminishing returns.

5. Suppose that a manufacturer had the following information for a given plant and number of men:

Number of machines	1	2	3	4	5	6	7	8
Total output (units)	100	250	450	600	710	750	775	780

What would be the marginal productivity of each successive machine? The average productivity from using additional machines? When would diminishing *marginal* productivity set in? Diminishing *average* productivity?

6. Why must we hold the other factors constant to derive the law of variable proportions?

7. Suppose that each machine in our example above cost $1,000 and that each unit of output sold for $10. How many machines would it be most profitable to hire? (Figure out the marginal revenue and marginal cost for each machine added.)

8. What would be the most profitable number to have if the cost of the machine rose to $1,500? If the price per unit of sales fell to $9?

9. Suppose that our manufacturer found he had the following alternatives:

   • He could spend $1,000 on a machine that would add 115 units to sales (each unit selling at $10).
   • He could spend $5,000 to hire a new man who would increase output by 510 units.
   • He could rent new space for $10,000 that would make possible an increase in output of 1,100 units.

   How would he know which was the best factor to hire? Would he have to begin by asking what is his dollar return per dollar of cost in each case? What is this in the case of the machine? The new man? The land? Which is the best buy?

10. If one manufacturer in a competitive market adds to his factor inputs, will that affect their price? What happens when all manufacturers bid for the same factor? In the example above, which factor will be bid for? What will happen to its price? What will then be the "best buy"? What will happen to *its* price? What will be the final output of the bidding?

11. In the end, what will be the relation between the prices of factors? Will it be proportional to their costs? To their average outputs? To their marginal productivities? Explain carefully which is correct.

12. How do we know that there will be no "exploitation" of factors in a competitive market?

13. Suppose that the manufacturers of a certain kind of machinery got together (illegally) and agreed to keep its price above the level that would be set in a competitive market. What would happen to the number of machines they sold? What would we have to know before we could predict the effect on their total incomes?

14. By and large, do you think the market is a just allocator of incomes? If not, why not; and what would you suggest to improve it?

We have reached the last step in our analysis of the circular flow in the marketplace. We have learned how households create a demand for goods and services by spending their incomes in the market, and we have had a glimpse of the supply of goods and services coming to meet their demand. Then we have followed those selfsame householders in their role as factors of production, and we have discovered how the incomes they had spent were earned by selling their services to other individuals and to firms.

Now it remains only to close the circuit. We must complete the circular flow inside the firm itself: watch the enterprise receive revenues from the market and transfer them to the pockets of its factors of production. At the same time, we can complete our picture of how the firm, which is the active pump of the circular flow, serves both as an agency of the market system and as an organization in search of its own private ends.

Inside the Firm:
Fixed and Variable Cost

This will require us once again to put ourselves in the shoes of an imaginary entrepreneur. Since we have already become familiar with the firm's calculations in regard to buying factor services, let us begin our inquiry into the firm by extending our knowledge into a full appreciation of what the cost problem looks like to the entrepreneur.

We know that a firm's total costs must rise as it hires additional factors. Yet if we put ourselves in a businessman's position, we can see that our total costs are unlikely to rise as fast as our additional factor costs, because there are some costs of production that will not be affected by an increase in factor input. Real estate taxes, for example, will remain unchanged if we hire one man or 100—so long as we do not acquire additional land. The depreciation cost of machinery will not be affected by additions to land or labor. Rent will be unchanged, unless the premises are expanded. The cost of electric light will not vary appreciably despite additions to labor or machinery. Neither will the salary of the president. *Thus some costs, determined by legal contract or by usage or by the unchanging use of one factor, do not vary with output. We call these fixed costs.*

In sharp contrast with fixed costs is another kind of cost that does vary directly with output. Here are most factor costs, for generally we vary inputs of labor and capital (and sometimes land) every time we seek a new level of production. To increase output almost always requires the payment of more wages and the employment of more capital (if only in the form of inventories) and sometimes the rental of more space. *We call all costs that vary with output variable costs.*

This important dichotomy between fixed and variable costs also requires us to shift our view a little within the business enterprise. We have been mainly concerned with calculating the costs of *inputs* in relation to their marginal productivities, but fixed costs do not lend themselves to this kind of treatment. Hence we must now turn around and begin to think about costs in relation to *output.*

In particular, we have to learn to think in terms of *cost per unit of output.* As we have seen, when a manufacturer (or a farmer or a storekeeper) expands his output, his total costs usually rise because his variable costs are going up, but total costs do not rise as fast as variable costs, because his fixed costs are set. But it is not easy to work with this upward rising curve of total costs. Hence businessmen and economists usually convert the figures for total cost into *unit costs* by dividing the total cost by the number of units of goods produced. This results, of course, in a figure for the *average cost per unit of output.* We shall see that this gives us a very useful way of figuring what happens to costs as output expands.

PER UNIT COST

There is certainly no difficulty in picturing what happens to fixed costs per unit of output as output rises. By definition, they must fall. Suppose a manufacturer has fixed costs (rent, certain indirect taxes, depreciation, and overhead) of $10,000 a year. If he produces 5,000 units of his product per year, each unit will have to bear $2 of fixed costs as its share. If output rises to 10,000 units, the unit share of fixed costs will shrink to $1. At 100,000 units it would be a dime. Thus a curve of fixed costs per unit of output would look like Fig. 26-1.

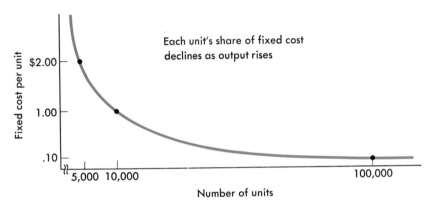

FIG. 26 • 1 PROFILE OF FIXED COSTS PER UNIT

What about variable costs per unit? Here the situation is more complex, for it depends directly on the analysis of the productivity curve we discussed in our last chapter. Hence, let us first set up a schedule of output for our manufacturer (Table 26-1), showing how the total numbers of units he produces will rise at first rapidly, then more slowly, as he adds labor input to his plant.

TABLE 26 • 1

Number of men	Total output (units)	Marginal product
1	5,000	5,000
2	13,000	8,000
3	23,000	10,000
4	32,000	9,000
5	39,000	7,000
6	44,000	5,000
7	47,000	3,000
8	49,000	2,000

To convert this schedule of physical productivity into a unit cost figure, we must do two things:

1. *We must calculate total variable cost for each level of output.*
2. *We must then divide the total variable cost by the number of units, to get average variable cost per unit of output.*

Here are the figures (assuming that the going wage is $5,000).

TABLE 26 • 2

Number of men	Total variable cost @ $5,000 per man	Total output (units)	Average variable cost per unit of output
1	$ 5,000	5,000	$1.00
2	10,000	13,000	.77
3	15,000	23,000	.65
4	20,000	32,000	.63
5	25,000	39,000	.64
6	30,000	44,000	.68
7	35,000	47,000	.74
8	40,000	49,000	.82

Notice that average variable costs per unit decline at first and thereafter rise. The reason is by now clear enough. Variable cost increases by a set amount—$5,000 per man—as factors are added. Output, however, obeys the law of variable proportions, increasing rapidly at first and then displaying diminishing returns. It stands to reason, then, that the variable cost *per unit* of output will be falling as long as output is growing faster than costs, and that it will begin to rise as soon as additions to output start to get smaller.

If we graph the typical variable cost curve per unit of output, it will be the dish-shaped or U-shaped profile that Fig. 26-2 shows.

FIG. 26 • 2 PROFILE OF CHANGING VARIABLE COSTS PER UNIT

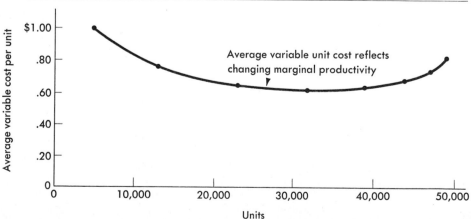

Average variable unit cost reflects changing marginal productivity

We can now set up a complete cost schedule for our enterprise by combining fixed and variable costs, as in Table 26-3. Notice how marginal costs begin to turn up *before* average costs.

TABLE 26 • 3

Number of men	Total cost ($10,000 fixed cost + $5,000 per man)	Output (units)	COST PER UNIT OF OUTPUT	
			Average (total cost ÷ output)	**Marginal** (change in cost ÷ change in output)*
1	$15,000	5,000	$3.00	$ —
2	20,000	13,000	1.54	.63
3	25,000	23,000	1.09	.50
4	30,000	32,000	.94	.55
5	35,000	39,000	.90	.71
6	40,000	44,000	.91	1.00
7	45,000	47,000	.96	1.67
8	50,000	49,000	1.02	2.50

*Ideally, we should like to show how marginal cost changes with *each* additional unit of output. Here our data show the change in costs associated with considerable jumps in output as we add each man. Hence we estimate the marginal cost per unit by taking the *change in total costs* and dividing this by the *change in total output*. The result is really an "average" marginal cost, since each individual item costs actually a tiny fraction less than, or more than, its predecessor. We have shown the data this way since it is much closer to the way businessmen figure.

If we graph the last two columns of figures—average and marginal cost per unit—we get the very important diagram in Fig. 26-3.

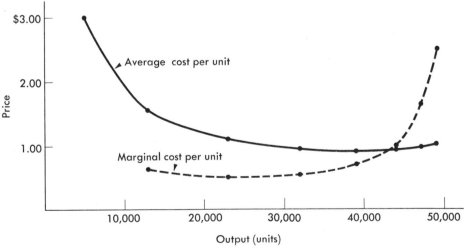

FIG. 26 • 3

We have reached the end of our cost calculations, and it will help to take stock of what we have done. Actually, despite all the figures and diagrams, the procedure has been quite simple.

1. We began by seeing what would happen to our *fixed costs* per unit as we expanded output. Since fixed costs, by their nature, do not increase as production increases, the amount of fixed cost that had to be charged to each unit of output fell sharply as output rose.

2. Next we calculated the *variable costs* that would have to be borne by each unit as output increased. Here the critical process at work was the law of variable proportions. As the marginal productivity of factors increased, variable cost per unit fell. But when the inevitable stage of diminishing returns set in, variable costs per unit had to rise.

3. Adding together fixed and variable costs, we obtained the *total unit cost* of output. Like the variable cost curve, average total unit costs are dish-shaped, reflecting the diminishing marginal productivity of factors as output grows.

4. Finally, we show the changing *marginal cost per unit*—the increase in total costs divided by the increase in output. As before, it is the changing marginal costs that the entrepreneur actually experiences when he alters output. It is the increase at the margin that changes his total cost, and which therefore determines his average cost.

Actually, the cost profile that we have worked out would be known by any businessman whether he had ever studied microeconomics or not. Whenever a firm starts producing, its average cost per unit of output is very high. A General Motors plant turning out only a few hundred cars a year would have astronomical costs per automobile.

But as output increases, unit costs come down steadily, partly because overhead (fixed costs) is now spread over more units, partly because the factors are used at much greater efficiency. Finally, after some point of maximum factor efficiency, average unit costs begin to mount. Even though overhead continues to decline, it is now so small a fraction of cost per unit that its further decline does not count for much, while the rising inefficiency of factors pushes up variable cost per unit steadily. If General Motors tries to jam more cars through a plant than it is designed to take, the cost per auto will again begin to soar.

So much for the average cost per unit. By directing our attention to the *changes* that occur in total cost and total output every time we alter the number of factors we engage, the marginal cost curve per unit simply tells us why all this is happening. In other words, as our plant first moves into high gear, the cars we add to the line (the marginal output) will cost considerably less than the average of all cars processed previously; later, when diminishing returns begin to work against us, we would expect the added (marginal) cars to be high-cost cars, higher in cost than the average of all cars built so far.

Since the cost of marginal output always "leads" the cost of average output in this way, we can understand an important relationship that the marginal and average curves always bear to one another. *The marginal cost curve always cuts the average cost curve at the lowest point of the latter.*

Why? Because as long as the additional cars are cheaper than the average of all cars, their production must be *reducing* average cost—that is, as long as the marginal cost curve is lower than the average cost curve, the average cost curve must be falling. Conversely, as soon as additional output is more expensive than the average for all previous output, that additional production must *raise* average costs—again, (look at the previous diagram) as soon as marginal cost is above average cost, average cost must begin to rise. Hence it follows that the *MC* (marginal cost) curve must cross the *AC* (average cost) curve at the minimum point of the latter. This relationship has nothing to do with economics, as such, but with simple logic, as Fig. 26-4 may elucidate.

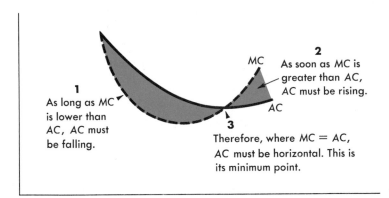

1
As long as MC is lower than AC, AC must be falling.

MC

2
As soon as MC is greater than AC, AC must be rising.

AC

3
Therefore, where MC = AC, AC must be horizontal. This is its minimum point.

**FIG. 26 • 4
RELATION OF
MARGINAL AND
AVERAGE COST
PER UNIT**

From Cost to Revenue

The cost profile gives us a clear picture of what happens to unit costs as our firm hires additional factors. But that is only half the information we need to understand how a firm operates with one foot in the factor market and the other in the market for goods. Now we need a comparable profile of what happens to revenues as the firm sells the output its factors have made for it.

**FROM SUPPLY
TO DEMAND**

This brings us over from supply to demand—from dealing with factors who are selling their services, back to householders who are buying goods. What the entrepreneur wants to know is whether "the market" will buy his goods and if so, at just what price it will buy them. In other words, he wants to know the demand curve for his particular output. If he knows that, he can easily figure what his revenues will be.

What does the demand curve look like for a small competitive firm? Let us take the case of our manufacturer, with whose costs we are now familiar, and assume that the "units" he is making are simple metal stampings of which several million are sold each year. Our manufacturer knows two things about the market for those stampings. First, he knows that there is a "going" price for stampings (which we will say is $1.50) that is established by "the market." Second, he knows that he can personally sell all the stampings he can make at the going price without altering that price by so much as a penny—that "the market" will not be affected whether he closes down his shop entirely or whether he sells every last stamping he can afford to make at the price the market offers.

What our manufacturer knows in his bones, we can translate into economics. The price of any commodity is set in the goods market by the interplay of supply and demand. Our firm is one of the many suppliers whose willingness and ability to sell at different prices (which are, of course, largely determined by their costs) makes up the supply curve. The demand curve for the commodity is familiar to us as the expression of the consumers' willingness and ability to buy.

But now we can also see that as far as the output of any *one* small firm is concerned, the demand for *its* output is a horizontal line—that there is an "infinite" willingness to buy its product, provided it can be supplied at the going price. The output of any one seller, in other words, is too small to affect the equilibrium price for the market as a whole. Why, then, cannot an ambitious firm make an "infinite" profit by expanding its sales to match demand? The shape of its cost curve gives the answer. As factor productivity declines, marginal costs soon rise above selling price.

Thus the competitive firm operates between two horizontal curves. On the supply side it faces a perfectly elastic supply of factors, meaning that it can hire all the factors it wishes without changing prices an iota in the factor market. On the demand side it also faces a perfectly elastic curve, meaning that it can sell as much as it can produce without any perceptible price effect here, either. The firm is thus squeezed between two forces that it is powerless to change. As a result, it must devote all its energies to those parts of the market process that are in its control—the efficient combining of factors to minimize its costs, and the selection of the most profitable scale and line of output.

Facing a known demand curve, our manufacturer can now calculate his revenues. He will take in an amount determined by his total unit output multiplied by the price of each unit. And since, with a horizontal demand curve, the price of each unit will be exactly the same price as the previous

AVERAGE AND MARGINAL REVENUE

TABLE 26 • 4

Output (units)	Price per unit	Marginal revenue per unit	Total revenue	Average revenue per unit
5,000	$1.50	$1.50	$ 7,500	$1.50
10,000	1.50	1.50	15,000	1.50
20,000	1.50	1.50	30,000	1.50
40,000	1.50	1.50	60,000	1.50

one, the marginal revenue of each unit sold—that is the additional amount it will bring in—will be unchanged no matter how much is sold by the firm. If the selling price is $1.50, then the marginal revenue per unit will be $1.50. As a result, average revenue per unit will also be $1.50. The schedules of revenue will look like Table 26-4. We can see that a graph of the average and marginal costs curves for this (or any) small, highly competitive firm would be horizontal as in Fig. 26-5.

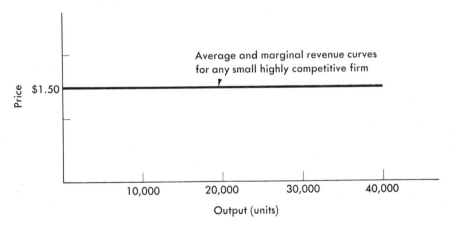

FIG. 26 • 5

MARGINAL REVENUE AND MARGINAL COST

Now we have all the information we want. We have a cost profile that tells us what happens to unit costs as we hire or fire factors. We have a revenue profile that tells us what happens to unit revenues as we do the same. It remains only to put the two together to discover just how much output the firm should make to maximize its profits.

We can do this very simply by superimposing the revenue diagram on top of the cost diagram. The point where the marginal revenue and the marginal cost curves meet should indicate exactly what the most profitable output will be. As we can see in Fig. 26-6, it is just about at 45,000 units.

FIG. 26•6 THE POINT OF OPTIMUM OUTPUT

Why is this the point of best possible output? Because another unit of output—as we can see by looking at the two curves—will cost more than it brings in, while a unit less of output would deprive us of the additional net revenue that another unit of output could bring.

What is the total amount of profit our firm makes at this level of output? That is very difficult to tell from the diagram above, since it is hard to figure out what total cost is. But with the addition of our familiar curve of average costs per unit, we can tell at a glance. Average costs, as we know, are nothing but total costs reduced to a per-unit basis. Average revenues are also on a per-unit basis. Hence, *if we compare the average unit revenue and cost curves at any point, they will tell us at a glance what total revenues and costs look like at that point.*

Figure 26-7 reveals what our situation is at the point of optimum output. (This time we generalize the diagram rather than putting it into the specific terms of our illustrative firm.)

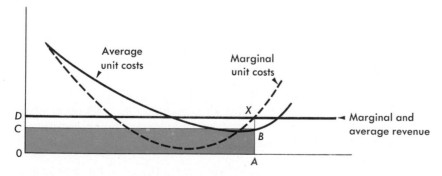

FIG. 26•7 THE FIRM IN EQUILIBRIUM WITH PROFITS

The diagram shows several things. First, as before, it indicates our most profitable output as the amount OA — the output indicated by the point X, where the marginal revenue and marginal cost curves meet. Second, it shows us that at output OA, our *average cost* is OC ($=AB$) and our *average revenue* is OD ($=AX$), the same as our marginal revenue, since the demand curve for the firm is horizontal. Our profit on the *average* unit of output must therefore be CD ($=BX$), the difference between average costs and average revenues at this point. The *total* profit is therefore the rectangle $CDXB$, which is the average profit per unit (CD) times the number of units.

We can translate this in terms of our firm. At the point where $MC = MR$, it is making about 45,000 stampings, as Fig. 26-6 shows, at an average cost that we will estimate at 92¢ per unit. (Table 26-3 does not show us the exact cost at 45,000 units, but we will assume it is 1¢ more than the 91¢ cost of making 44,000 units). Since the selling price is $1.50, we are now taking in a total of $1.50 x 45,000 units, or $67,500, while our total cost is 92¢ x 45,000 units or $41,400. Our profit is the difference between total revenues and total costs, or $26,100.

Note that at an output of 44,000 units our revenues would have been $1.50 x 44,000 or $66,000, and our total costs 91¢ x 44,000 or $40,040, with the result that our profit would have been slightly smaller ($25,960). If we sold a larger quantity, 46,000 units, at a cost of, say, 94¢ per unit, our revenues would have come to $69,000 and our costs to $43,240, with a profit of the difference, or $25,760, also less than the $26,100 we made at an output of 45,000 units. Thus, given our cost figures and our selling price, an output of 45,000 is the optimal level for our firm. It gives us the maximum profit obtainable.*

However satisfactory from the point of view of the firm, this is not yet a satisfactory stopping point from the point of view of the system as a whole. If our firm is typical of the metal stamping industry, then small firms throughout this line of business are making profits comparable to ours. Unhappily for them, there are numerous businesses in other lines of endeavor that do not make $21,500 of clear profit. *Hence entrepreneurs in these lines will now begin to move into our profitable industry.*

ENTRY AND EXIT

Perhaps we can anticipate what will now happen. Our firm is now going to experience the same "mysterious" change in prices that we have already witnessed in the factor market, when many firms altered their demands for land or labor or capital and the prices of these factor services changed accordingly. Only this time, it is the price of goods that will change, not that of factors. For the influx of entrepreneurs from other areas will move the industry supply curve to the right and thereby reduce the going price. As it falls, our own business will experience a disconcerting fall

---

* We will have more to say about profit later. At this juncture, it should be said only that profit is what is left *after* all factors have been paid, including management's salaries.

Increased supply as
new firms move in

Former
price

New
price

MC   AC

Firm suffers fall in
price and profits

FIG. 26•8   THE INDUSTRY IN ADJUSTMENT TO PROFITS

in the price for its goods which it is powerless to stop. We can see the
process in Fig. 26-8.

How long will this influx of firms continue? Suppose that it continues
until price falls *below* the average cost curve of our representative firm. Now
its position looks like Fig. 26-9. Output will still be set where $MC = MR$,
but now the average cost curve is above the average revenue curve at this
point. The unavoidable result is a loss for the firm, as the diagram shows.

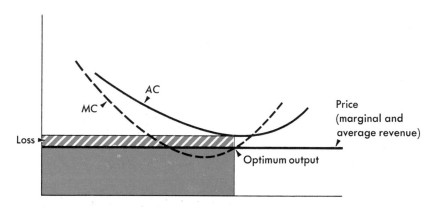

AC

MC

Price
(marginal and
average revenue)

Loss

Optimum output

FIG. 26•9   THE FIRM SUFFERING A LOSS

What will happen? Clearly, we need a reverse adjustment process—an
exodus of firms into greener pastures, so that the supply curve for our
industry can move to the left, bringing higher prices for all producers. This
may not be a rapid process, but eventually depreciation and the withdrawal
of producers should bring about the necessary adjustment, shown in Fig. 26-
10.*

* There is an interesting reason for this slowness. A firm can suffer losses for quite a while, as long
as its revenues are high enough to pay its variable costs and a little more. In that case, it can meet
some of its fixed costs from its operating income. If it shut down entirely, *its fixed costs would
continue.* Thus it will lose less money if it continues to produce—provided always that its revenues
meet its variable costs in full and cover part, if not all, of its fixed expenses. Eventually, of course,
such a firm will go bankrupt, for it will be spending more than it is taking in. But it will go
bankrupt more quickly if it stops producing altogether, for then it could pay none of its fixed costs!
Hence it will go on producing, thereby delaying the needed market adjustment.

Supply shrinks
as firms leave

New
price ►

Former ►
price

MC   AC

Firm's losses are
reduced as
price rises

FIG. 26•10   INDUSTRY ADJUSTMENT TO LOSSES

**LONG-RUN
EQUILIBRIUM**

Finally we reach a point of equilibrium both for the firm and the industry (or the system as a whole). It looks, of course, like Fig. 26-11.

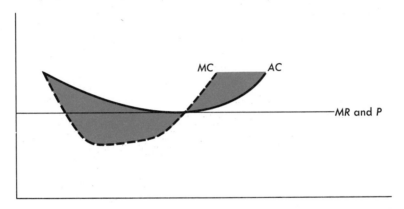

MC   AC

MR and P

FIG. 26•11   THE MARGINAL FIRM IN EQUILIBRIUM WITH NO PROFIT

Note that this position of equilibrium has two characteristics.

1. *Marginal cost equals marginal revenue,* so there is no incentive for the individual entrepreneur to alter his own output.

2. *Average cost equals average revenue* (or price), so there is no incentive for firms to enter or leave the industry.

Thus we can state the conditions for the equilibrium resting point of our firm and industry as being a four-way equality:

$$MC \quad = \quad MR \quad = \quad AC \quad = \quad P$$

Marginal = Marginal = Average = Price
cost   revenue   cost   (average
                                       revenue)

**PROFITS AND
EQUILIBRIUM**

We have reached an equilibrium both for the firm and for the industry, but it is certainly an uncomfortable one for ourselves as typical manufacturers. For in the final resting point of the firm, it is clear that *profits have been totally eliminated*. Is this a realistic assumption?

The question forces us to confront the slippery question of what "profits" are. By definition, they are not returns to factors, for these payments have already been made by the firm—including all payments made to entrepreneurs for the full value of their contribution to output.

To put it differently, we do not include in the term *profit* any revenues the firm *must* have to stay in business. An accountant, examining the books of a marginal firm in an industry, might find that there was a small bookkeeping profit. But an economist, looking at these revenues, would not call this sum a true economic profit if it were necessary to maintain the firm (or its entrepreneur) in operation. We should note as well that profits are usually figured as a return on the capital invested in a firm, not as a return on each unit sold. It is simpler for our purposes, however (and it does no violence to the argument) to talk of profits in relation to output (= sales) rather than as a return on investment.

What are profits, then? There have been numerous attempts to define them as the return for risk, or for innovation, and so on. But however we describe them, we are driven to the conclusion that in a "perfect" competitive market, the forces of competition would indeed press toward zero the returns of the *marginal* firms in all industries, so that the cost and revenue profile of the last firms able to remain alive in each industry would look like our diagram.

Note, however, that these are marginal firms. Here is a clue to how profits can exist even in a highly competitive situation. In Fig. 26-12, we show the supply curve of an industry, broken down into the individual supply curves of its constituent firms. Some of these firms, by virtue of superior location, or access to supplies, or managerial skills will be lower-cost producers than others. When the industry price is finally established, they will be the beneficiaries of the difference between the going price (which reduces the profits of the marginal firm to zero) and the lower unit costs attributable to their superior efficiency.

FIG. 26 • 12 INTRAMARGINAL PROFITS

Really, these intramarginal profits are *quasi rents*. That is, they result from scarcities—of location, or managerial talents, or whatever—that earn a high return. If, through a fall in price, any one of these firms were suddenly put at the margin of production, it would continue to produce, fully covering its costs, but earning no profits. Even without a fall in price, we would expect intramarginal rents to diminish over time, owing to factor mobility. Badly located firms will pick up and move, or newcomers will locate favorably and thereby displace a firm at the margin. Managerial skills will be learned elsewhere or hired. Thus in the long run, we must expect the *tendency* in a fully competitive market to be a constant pressure toward lower prices, and thus toward the elimination of quasi rents.

Long Run and Short Run

We have seen how the market makes it necessary for firms to produce goods at the lowest points along their average unit cost curves and to sell those goods at prices that will yield no profit to the least efficient firm in the industry. Yet there is one last adjustment process to consider. In all our investigations into the firm's operations, we have hitherto taken for granted that the *scale of output* would remain unchanged. As a result, all of our adjustments have involved us in moving back and forth along a cost curve that was basically set in place by one or more limiting factors.

This may be accurate enough in the short run, when most firms are circumscribed by a given size of plant, but it certainly does not describe the long run. *For in the long run, all costs are variable.* A firm can usually enlarge its scale of plant; and as the scale increases, it is often possible to realize additional savings in cost, as a result of still finer specialization of the production process. If our expanding firm confines its growth to a single plant, the cost curves of these succesive scales of output are apt to look like Fig. 26-13.

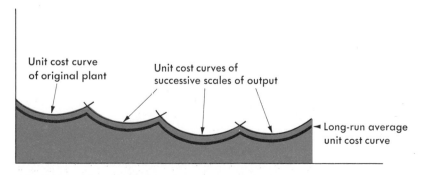

Unit cost curve of original plant

Unit cost curves of successive scales of output

Long-run average unit cost curve

FIG. 26•13 LONG-RUN COST CURVE

If we connect the successive short-run cost curves attributable to various scales of output, we get a *long run average unit cost curve* shown in the heavy line below. We have already explained that its initial downward slope is due to savings that size continues to bring in the utilization of factors. The extent to which a firm will be able to realize these so-called *economies of scale* depends mainly on the technological possibilities in its industry. In Chapter 6 we saw how the development of mass production in the late nineteenth century brought about a change in many industries from atomistic competition to the domination of a few, very large-scale producers.

Our diagram shows, however, that economies of scale do not go on forever. At some point—again determined by technology—the limits of efficient plant operation are reached. A sprawling enterprise begins to stretch too thin the coordinating powers of management. *Diseconomies of scale* enter, and the long-run unit cost curve again begins to mount.

Note, however, that these long-run cost curves apply to individual *plants*. What about a firm that pushes each plant to its optimum size and then adds a new plant, or a firm that diversifies its efforts among many different kinds of businesses, like the conglomerates? Does it also face a long-run, upward sloping cost curve, owing perhaps to eventual diseconomies of management? We really do not know the answer. To hazard an unsubstantiated guess, it may well be that the new technology of information retrieval has so increased the efficiency of management that the economically effective size of multiplants or diversified plants is today extremely large. For all practical purposes, the long-run cost curve is probably horizontal or perhaps even falling.*

There is still, however, another way in which our firm's long-run costs can be altered. Together with all of its competitors it may be subject to *increasing or decreasing costs for the industry as a whole.*

The source of these changes in cost do not lie within the firm, in the relative efficiency of various factor mixes. Rather, they are changes thrust upon the firm—for better or worse—by the interaction of the growing industry of which it is a part and the economy as a whole. A new industry, for example, by its very expansion may bring into being satellite firms that provide some of its necessary inputs; and as the main new industry grows, the satellites also expand and thereby realize economies of scale that will benefit the main industry itself. The automobile industry was surely an instance of such long-run falling costs (for a long period, at least) resulting from the economies of scale enjoyed by makers of tires, makers of batteries, and other equipment. In turn, the rise of low-cost trucking brought "external economies" to many other industries.

---

* For an interesting discussion of this point, see Robert T. Averitt, *The Dual Economy,* pp. 105-9.

Industries may also experience long-run rising costs if their expansion pushes them up against factor scarcity of a stubbornly inelastic kind. Extractive industries, for example, may be forced to use progressively less-accessible mineral deposits; or agricultural industries may be forced to use progressively less-fertile or less-conveniently-located land. Such industries would experience a gradual rise in unit costs as their output increased.

Are most industries the beneficiaries of decreasing cost or the victims of increasing cost? Empirical studies seem to suggest that save for youthful, growing industries, and for the special case of extractive ones, most industries enjoy a middle position of roughly constant long-run unit costs, at least over a considerable period of time. That is, for most industries it is probably accurate to state that the so-called *external economies* or *diseconomies* are much less important than internal economies or diseconomies.

The Competitive Environment

Our consideration of the forces bearing on long-run costs brings our discussion of the firm to an end. We have seen how the firm has closed the circular flow by transforming its receipts from householders into payments to its factors, and we have simultaneously watched as it performed its social function of combining factors as efficiently as possible in the course of pursuing its short-run profits.

Now we must ask a question that has surely occurred to the reader. Does the world really behave as microtheory has portrayed it? Do firms really equate marginal costs and revenues or balance the advantages of one factor versus another with the fine precision that our model has indicated? That is not a question we can fully answer until our next chapter. But we already know one condition that must be fulfilled if firms are to behave as we have pictured them. This is the condition of "pure" competition to which we have already referred as the environment we would take for granted during our initial microeconomic investigations. Now is the time to look carefully into exactly what the term means.

PURE COMPETITION DEFINED

In general, when economists use the term *pure competition*, they imply three necessary attributes of the market situation:

1. *Large numbers of marketers.*

Unless there are numerous buyers and sellers facing one another across the market and jostling one another on each side of it, the competitive process will not fully work itself out. When the number of marketers is few (whether as buyers or sellers) the vying among them that gives competition its resistless force is apt to be muted or even lacking entirely. As the extreme case of this we have outright *collusion,* in which a few buyers or sellers agree to bid only at one low price or to offer only at one high price. But even when collusion is absent, fewness of buyers or sellers will lead, as we shall see in our next chapter, to results that are considerably at variance with those of the competitive process we have assumed.

How many buyers or sellers does it take to make a fully competitive market? There is no clear-cut answer. The critical number is reached when no firm, by varying its scale of output, is able to affect the price of the factors it buys or the product it sells. We have pictured this condition in terms of the horizontal factor supply and market demand curves that present the purely competitive firm with the unalterable data of factor and goods prices to which it must accommodate itself. *Thus under conditions of pure competition, the only thing the firm can control is its scale of output and the mix of factors it uses; all prices are beyond its power to influence.*

2. *Ease of entry into, and exit out of, industries.*

A second prerequisite for so-called pure competition is a condition that we have already relied upon frequently in discussing the operation of the market. *This is the ability of firms and factors to move freely and easily from one industry to another in search of the highest possible return.* Only in this way can supply and demand schedules move rightwards and leftwards, bringing about the needed adjustments of quantities and prices.

We have seen as well that this is by no means an easy set of conditions to achieve. With firms, as previously with factors, it rules out all legal barriers to interindustry movement, such as restrictive patents. But beyond this it implies that industries in which the initial scale of manufacture is very large cannot be considered as meeting the requirements for pure competition. In automobile or steel manufacturing, for example, in which the minimum size of plant entails an investment of millions of dollars, the degree of competitive pressure from "outside" entrepreneurs is obviously much less than in the stationery store business, where a newcomer can enter for an investment of a few thousand dollars.

Ease of exit is a no less necessary and equally demanding requirement. The competitive process will not shift about supply curves if some producers cannot withdraw their investments in land or capital and move them to alternative uses. Yet, as we have seen, this inability to move out can indeed retard adjustments of supply, particularly in industries with large fixed investments that are highly "specific" in their use. Such industries may go on producing even if they cannot cover their full costs, as long as their revenues bring in enough to nibble away at fixed expenses (see p. 537n). Thus the problems of securing easy entry and exit further restrict the environment of pure competition to industries in which no large or technically specific investments are required.

3. *Nondifferentiated goods.*

But even these strict conditions still do not define the state of competition we have implicitly assumed. It is possible for a market to consist of many small buyers and sellers, each operating with relatively simple equipment, and yet these firms may not compete fully against one another. This is the case when each firm sells a product that is *differentiated* (or distinguishable) from that of its competitors. For if there is a difference, however slight, between one man's product and another's, the demand curve for the product of each will be sloping rather than horizontal, even if the slope is very small. As a result, product differentiation will enable a seller to hold onto *some* of his trade even if his price is a trifle higher than his competitor's, whereas in a purely competitive market where goods and services are indistinguishable from one another, no marketer can depart in the slightest degree from the prevailing price.

There are markets in which perfectly anonymous undifferentiated commodities are sold—for example, the market for grain or for coal or for common labor, in which no seller can ask even a penny more for his product or services than the going price. In the great bulk of retail and wholesale markets, however, such totally undifferentiated products are the exception rather than the rule.

Why must commodities be exactly alike for a state of pure competition to exist? The answer is that *only identical commodities compete solely on the basis of price.* Much of what we call "competition" in the impure markets of the real world consists in differentiating products through style, design, services, etc., so that they will *not* have to compete just on price. We shall look into this very common case of "imperfect competition" in our next chapter. But we must rule it out as a permissible form of competition to bring about the exact results of our market analysis thus far. The essential rule for a purely competitive market is that the word "competition" must mean *price competition only.*

COMPETITION IN FACT AND THEORY

Obviously, pure competition is an extremely demanding state of affairs. It requires small and numerous firms selling identical products in a highly mobile and fluid environment. Does such a market in fact exist?

It has been customary to claim that farming constitutes a perfect example of pure competition, since its units are very numerous and its main products undifferentiated. But farming lacks one qualification. It has proved to be a very difficult occupation to move out of when prices fall. Of the roughly 2.9 million farms in the United States, perhaps nearly a million sell less than $5,000 worth of farm products a year and are, by any definition, uneconomical operations. Yet submarginal farmers are reluctant to leave an occupation that gives them at least a minimal security, for the frightening insecurity (and perhaps even worse economic luck) of the city.

The world of retailing qualifies much more readily in terms of easy entry and exit, and it is characterized by many small firms. But retailing loses out on the question of differentiation. The very essence of most retail establishments, even if they sell exactly the same wares as the competitor down the street (in fact, especially if they do), is to try to be "different."

Hence the search for perfect examples of pure competition is apt to end with very few cases. Why, then, do we spend so much time analyzing it?

The answer is twofold. In part it lies in the fact that as much as 40 or 50 percent of the output of the nation comes from sectors that *resemble*—even though they do not exactly qualify for—pure competition. The service trades, the wholesale markets, much retailing, some raw material production are near enough to being "pure" in their competitive structures, so that we can apply the reasoning of price theory very closely in understanding the market results we see in those industries.

But there is a second reason as well. Even in those sectors or industries where pure competition obviously does not apply—in the monopolistic or oligopolistic situations with which our next chapter will be concerned—the mechanism of the market will still be clearly discernible. Supply and demand, factor productivities, marginal revenue and marginal cost will continue to be the prevailing guidelines. Hence we must understand the basic elements of microeconomics because most of them will still apply. And unless we know to what results these elements lead us in the ideal environment of pure competition, we will hardly be in a position to know what a difference monopoly or oligopoly make to the workings of the market system.

KEY CONCEPTS AND KEY WORDS

1. We divide costs within the firm into *fixed and variable costs.* Variable costs change with the addition or discharge of factors. Fixed costs are contractual costs or costs that are associated with the unchanged use of one factor. They do not vary with output.

   Fixed and variable costs

2. Both fixed and variable (and total) costs are usually calculated *per unit of output. Fixed costs decline per unit of output as total output increases.*

3. *Variable costs first decline and then rise,* reflecting the increasing and then deminishing marginal productivity of the factors. The typical shape of the variable unit cost curve is *U-shaped* or *dish-shaped.*

   U-shaped unit cost curve

4. Adding together fixed and variable costs we get a *dish-shaped unit cost curve for the firm.*

5. The marginal cost curve shows us the actual operative factor at work. The relation of marginal and average figures to one another is such that the *marginal unit cost curve always cuts the average unit cost curve at the lowest point of the latter.*

   Marginal and average unit cost curve

6. *The competitive firm operates between two horizontal curves: The demand curve for its product is infinitely elastic. The supply curve of factors to itself is also infinitely elastic.*

Maximum profit	7. *The point of maximum profit is that output where marginal revenue just equals marginal cost.* In a competitive market for a single firm, marginal revenue and average revenue are both equal to price. Therefore it pushes its output until the marginal cost of the last unit just equals price. Any output more than this would incur losses, and any output less than this would fail to gain all potential profit.
$MC = MR$	8. If a competitive firm enjoys profits in this position of $MC = MR,$ it will experience an *influx of firms from other areas.* This will cause industry supply to increase and prices to fall. Conversely, if it experiences a loss, there will be a gradual *exodus of firms* until supply for the industry falls and prices rise.
Equilibrium = $MC = MR = AC = P$	9. The *equilibrium point for the competitive firm is reached when marginal revenue equals marginal cost, and average cost equals price.* At this point there is no incentive for the entrepreneur to alter his scale of output or for firms to leave or enter the industry.
Intramarginal firm	10. In a competitive market, the *marginal* firm enjoys no profit. Intramarginal firms may have quasi rents.
Economies of scale	11. In addition to changes in cost from moving along a fixed unit cost curve, firms can enjoy *economies of scale,* provided that the technology of the industry leads to these. At some point, economies of scale cease and the long-run cost curve again turns up.
External economies	12. In addition, *external economies or diseconomies* can affect the cost curves of all firms within an industry. For most industries a condition of roughly *constant* long-term costs seems to prevail.
Pure competition	13. The environment of the firm is assumed at first to be that of pure competition. By this we mean a market in which there are:
Large numbers	• *Large numbers of marketers.* As a result, each faces a market situation, both with regard to factors and goods, in which his own actions are powerless to affect prices. Only the factor mix is under the control of the competitive entrepreneur.
Exit and entry	• *Ease of exit and entry.* This requires the absence of all barriers to mobility, including that of size and technical specificity.
Nondifferentiated products	• *Nondifferentiated products.* This insures the restriction of competition to price alone.
	14. Pure competition is obviously rarely found in actuality. But it does describe the actions of some markets tolerably well and it provides a bench mark from which to measure the degree of competition that we find in the real world.

That is, it can sell all it can profitably make without disturbing the market price, and it can hire or fire all the factors it wishes without disturbing their price. The only process under its control is the combination of factors to secure maximum efficiency.

Q U E S T I O N S

1. If you were a retail grocer, what kinds of costs would be fixed for you? Variable? If you were a manufacturer who owned a large computer, would its maintenance be a fixed cost? If you *rented* the computer, would it be?

2. Assume that your fixed costs are $500 a week and that your output can vary from 100 to 1,000 units, given the scale of your enterprise. Graph what happens to fixed costs per unit.

3. Assume that your plant hires 6 men successively, and that output changes as follows:

Number of men	1	2	3	4	5	6
Total units of output per week	100	300	550	700	750	800

What is the marginal productivity of each man? If each worker costs you $100 per week, what is the variable cost per unit as you add men?

4. If you add fixed costs at $500 per week to the variable cost you have just ascertained, what is the average cost per unit? What is the marginal cost per unit? (Remember, this is figured by dividing the *change in total cost by the change in total output.)*

5. Graph the curve of average total unit costs and marginal unit costs. Why does the marginal unit cost curve cross the average unit cost curve at its lowest point?

6. What does average revenue mean and what is its relation to price? What is meant by marginal revenue? Why is marginal revenue the same as average revenue for a competitive firm?

7. Explain carefully why a competitive firm operates between two horizontal curves, one on the demand side and one on the factor supply side.

8. Suppose that the price per unit at which you sell the output of your firm (in the example above) is $1.35. Draw in such a marginal revenue curve. Now very carefully indicate where the *MR* and *MC* curves meet. Show on the diagram the output corresponding to this point. What is the approximate average cost at this output? Is there a profit here? Indicate by letters the rectangle that shows the profit per unit of output and the number of units.

9. What will be the result, in a competitive industry, of such a profit? Draw a diagram showing how an influx of firms can change the ruling market price. Will it be higher or lower?

10. Draw a diagram showing how price could drop below the lowest point on the average total unit cost curve, and indicate the loss the firm would suffer.

11. Carefully draw a diagram showing the equilibrium position for the firm. What is the relation of *MC, MR,* and *P* at this point? If *MC* = *MR,* does this mean that the entrepreneur is now motivated to alter his output? If *AC* = *P,* what does this mean as to the movement of firms into or out of the industry?

12. Suppose that you are a druggist, and you know that the least efficient druggist in town makes virtually no profit at all. Assuming that you sell in the same market as he does at the same prices and that you hire factors at the same prices also, what causes could bring about a profit to your enterprise? What would you expect to be the trend of these profits?

13. Would you expect economies of scale from greatly enlarging your drugstore? Why or why not?

14. Do you think as the entire drugstore business expands it enjoys external economies or suffers from external diseconomies? How about the goldmining business?

15. Is the drugstore business an example of pure competition? Explain carefully in what ways it might qualify and in what ways it might not.

Monopoly (and nowadays oligopoly) are bad words to most people, just as competition is a good word. But not everyone can specify exactly what is good or bad about them. Often we get the impression that the aims of the monopolist are evil and grasping, while those of the competitor are wholesome and altruistic, and therefore the essential difference between a world of pure competition and one of very impure competition is one of motives and drives—of well-meaning competitors and ill-intentioned monopolists.

The truth is that *exactly the same motives drive the monopoly and the competitive firm.* Both seek to maximize their profits. Indeed, the competitive firm, placed in a situation in which it must keep careful track of costs and revenues in order to survive is apt to be, if anything, *more* penny-pinching and more intensely profit-oriented than the monopolist who (as we shall see) can afford to take a less hungry attitude toward profits. The lesson to be learned—and it is an important one—is that motives have nothing to do with the problem of less-than-pure competition. *The difference between a monopoly, an oligopoly, and a situation of pure competition is entirely one of market structure*—that is, of the number of firms, ease of entry or exit, and the degree of differentiation among their goods.

Monopoly

We have already noted a very precise distinction between the competitive situation, with its numerous firms and undifferentiated goods, and markets in which the number of sellers is few or in which goods are highly differentiated. In the competitive case, as we have seen, each firm caters to so small a section of the market that the demand curve for its product is, for all intents and purposes, horizontal. By way of contrast, in a monopolistic or oligopolistic market structure there are so few firms that each one faces a distinctly sloping demand curve. That means that each firm, by varying its ouput, can affect the price for its product.

Another way of describing this difference is to call purely competitive firms, who have no control over their price, *price-takers* and to label monopolies or oligopolies or any firm that can affect the price of its product, *price-searchers.*

By examining the economic problems faced by a "pure" monopoly, let us see how such a price-searcher operates. Why do we place the word "pure" in quotes? Because a monopoly is not as easy to define as one might think. Essentially, the word means that there is only *one* seller of a particular good or service. The trouble comes in defining the "particular" good or service. In a sense, any seller of a differentiated good is a monopolist, for no one else dispenses *quite* the same utilities as he does: each shoeshine boy has his "own" customers, some of whom would probably continue to patronize his stand even if he charged slightly more than his competition.

Thus at one end of the difficulty is the fact that there is an element of monopoly in many seemingly competitive goods—a complication we shall come back to later. At the other end of the problem is that even where there is only one seller of a commodity—say the telephone company—there are still *substitutes* for its service. We can send a telegram or write a letter if telephoning becomes too expensive. Hence, before we can draw conclusions from the mere fact that a company provides the "only" service of a kind, we need to know how easy or difficult it is to switch into other products or services.

Evidently the problem of defining a "pure" monopoly is not easily resolved.* Let us, however, assume that we will all agree to call the local

"PURE" MONOPOLIES

LIMITS OF MONOPOLY

* How do we recognize a monopoly? Because of the problem of substitutes, there is no very clear sign, except in a few cases such as the "natural" monopolies discussed above. Usually when we speak of "monopolies" we mean (a) very large businesses, (b) with much higher than competitive profits, and (c) with relatively little direct product competition. Not many firms satisfy all three conditions. GM or Standard Oil is a monopoly by criteria *a* and *b*, but not by *c*; Polaroid by *b* and *c* but not *a*. Note, furthermore, that even small businesses can be monopolies, such as "the only gambling house in town" famed in all Westerns.

**FIG. 27 • 1
DEMAND CURVE
FOR A
MONOPOLY**

Amount of gas and light sold

power company a monopoly, because no one else sells gas and electricity to the community. In Fig. 27-1 we show what the demand curve of such a monopoly looks like.

One point is immediately clear. *The monopolistic firm faces the same kind of demand curve that the competitive industry faces.* That is because it caters to *all* the demand for that particular product, just as does the industrial group of competitive firms. A corollary follows. The monopolist faces a fundamental limitation on his power to control the market imposed by the demand curve itself. Suppose a monopolist is selling quantity *OX* at price *OA* as shown in Fig. 27-2. He would like to sell quantity *OY* at price *OA*, but *he cannot.* He has no way of forcing the market to take a larger quantity of his product—unless he lowers the price to *OB.**

The situation is very similar (on the seller's side) with a *union.* A union can raise the price of labor, since it controls the supply of labor, but it cannot force employers to hire more labor than they want. Hence the question "Can unions raise wages?" must be answered "Yes," insofar as those who continued to be hired are concerned. But until we know the

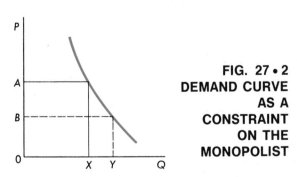

**FIG. 27 • 2
DEMAND CURVE
AS A
CONSTRAINT
ON THE
MONOPOLIST**

*What would be the *most* profitable course for the monopolist to follow? It would be to sell his goods at *varying* prices, charging more when the buyer is willing and able to pay a high price. (One could imagine an auction, for example, in which a monopolist doled out his product in this manner.) We call this *discriminatory pricing.* Why does the monopolist not follow it? (1) In some industries it is illegal. (2) It is extremely difficult to carry out, because someone with a low personal demand could buy more than he himself wanted of a good, in order to resell it to someone higher up on the demand curve. If this trading among customers goes on, the final average price will be exactly that established by the demand curve and the supply schedule. Nevertheless, discriminatory pricing is not uncommon in certain fields: antiques, used cars, pawnshops—and perhaps some professional fees.

elasticity of the demand for labor, we cannot say if unions can raise the total amount of labor's revenues. (Recall our analysis, pp. 521f).

There is one thing a monopolist can do, however, that neither a union nor a purely competitive firm can. He can advertise and thus seek to move the demand curve for his product to the right. Advertising does not "pay" for a purely competitive firm selling undifferentiated goods, for such a firm has no way of being sure that *its* goods—and not a competitor's—will benefit: imagine a single farmer advertising "Buy wheat!" But advertising *can* pay for a monopolist who will get all the demand he can conjure up. We can think of advertising as an attempt to sell larger quantities of a good or service without reducing prices, by shifting the demand curve itself. Figure 27-3 shows us this important effect.

FIG. 27 • 3
ADVERTISING
AND
DEMAND

Demand curve after advertising

Additional quantity sold at same price, as a result of advertising.

COST CURVES FOR THE MONOPOLIST

We have seen in what way the shape of the demand curves faced by monopolists differs from those faced by competitive firms. Are cost curves similarly different?

In general, they are not. We can take the cost profile of a monopoly as being exactly the same as that of a competitive firm. The monopoly, like the competitive firm, buys factors and exerts no control over their prices. A.T.&T. does not affect the level of wages or the price of land or capital by its decisions to expand production or not.* The monopolist, like the competitive entrepreneur, experiences the effects of changing productivity as he hires additional factors, and again like the competitive firm, he shops for the best buy in the factor markets. Thus the same U-shaped average cost curve and the same more steeply sloped marginal cost curve will describe the cost changes experienced by a monopolist quite as well as those of a competitive firm.

---

* There is a special situation in which there is only one *buyer,* that we call "monopsony." A large employer who is the only substantial buyer of labor in a small town may be a monopsonist, and his decisions to hire labor or land or capital *will* affect their prices. For the monopsonist, the marginal cost curve is affected not only by the changing productivity of a factor but by its varying price, as more and more of the factor is hired. Because this is a situation infrequently found in the marketplace, we shall not analyze it further here. The principles involved are in no way different from those of monopoly.

It is when we come to the revenue side of the picture that we meet the critical distinction of monopoly. Unlike a competitive firm, *a monopoly has a marginal revenue curve that is different from its average revenue curve.* The difference arises because each time a monopolist sells more output, he must reduce his price, whereas a competitive firm sells its larger output at the same price. Therefore, the revenue yielded to the monopolist by each additional unit will be less than that of the preceding higher-priced unit.

A table may make this clear. Let us suppose we have a monopoly that is faced with an average revenue or price schedule as in Table 27-1.

TABLE 27 • 1

Price	Quantity sold	Total revenue	Marginal revenue
$20	1	$20	$20
19	2	38	18
18	3	54	16
17	4	68	14
16	5	80	12
15	6	90	10

The graph of such a marginal revenue curve looks like Fig. 27-4.

FIG. 27 • 4 AVERAGE AND MARGINAL REVENUE FOR A MONOPOLIST

What determines the shape of the marginal revenue curve? Obviously, the change in demand that will be brought about by a drop in price. In turn, this reflects—as we remember from our discussion in Chapter 3—the elasticity of demand which, in turn, hinges on our tastes, the availability of substitutes, and so on.

The next step is obvious enough. We must superimpose the cost profile and the revenue profile to determine the equilibrium position for the monopolist. We can see it in Fig. 27-5.

What will be the equilibrium position? *The monopolist who seeks to maximize profit is guided by exactly the same rule as the competitive firm: he*

FIG. 27•5 EQUILIBRIUM FOR THE MONOPOLIST

adds factors so long as the marginal revenue they bring in is greater than their marginal cost. Hence we look for the intersection of the *MC* and *MR* curves on Fig. 27-5. Now if we extend a vertical line down to the horizontal axis, we will discover how much output will be produced (*OX*) at what price (*OA*). (See Fig. 27-6.)

And what will the profit be? As before, profit is the difference between *average* cost and *average* revenue. The intersection of the *MC* and *MR* curves determines in the first place what our output will be; and now, knowing that, we can tell what our average cost and price, or average revenue, will be. Hence we can easily block in the profit of the enterprise. We do this in Fig. 27-6.

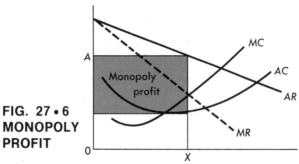

FIG. 27•6 MONOPOLY PROFIT

MONOPOLY VS. COMPETITIVE PRICES

What is the difference between this price and that of a purely competitive market? We remember the formula for the equilibrium price of such a market: $MC = MR = AC =$ Price. In the monopoly situation MC still equals MR (this is always the profit-maximizing guide), but price certainly does not equal AC. Whereas the competitive firm is forced to price its goods at the lowest point on its cost curve, the monopolist sells at a price far above cost. Then, too, there is no pressure from "outside" forcing the monopolist to reduce costs. Hence his entire cost curve may well lie above that of a competitive industry producing the same product. It is interesting to note that when hard pressed, some big auto firms (not even monopolies) have reduced overhead expenses by as much as a third. But most of the time, monopolies are not hard pressed.

If this were the case in a competitive market, we know what the remedy would be. An influx of firms would move the supply curve to the right; and as a result, prices would fall until excess profits had been wiped out. But in a monopoly situation, by the very definition of a monopoly, there is no entry into the market. Hence the monopolist is able to restrict his output to the amount that will bring in the high price he enjoys.

Monopoly thus imposes two burdens on society. It sells wares at a *higher price* than that of the competitive firm, and its *output is smaller* than would be the case under competitive conditions. The consumer gets less and pays more for it.

This is not, as we have had occasion to remark before, a full accounting of the "social cost" of monopoly. It is a description of the *economic* difference between the market solution of a competitive and a monopolistic firm. It ignores entirely such matters as power or influence, which may make monopoly politically undesirable, and it omits as well any consideration of the possible usefulness of some monopolies (like the phone company) in providing a unified service or considerable economies of large-scale production.

Finally, we should note that most "natural" monopolies, such as the utility companies or water supply companies or the telephone company, are regulated by public authorities. By imposing price ceilings on these monopolies (usually calculated to allow the companies to earn a "fair return" on their invested capital), the regulating commissions seek to approximate the results of a competitive environment. As Fig. 27-7 shows, its *MR* will be horizontal along the price ceiling, just like that of a competitive firm, and therefore its output will expand.

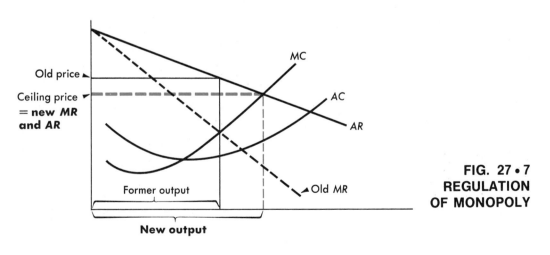

FIG. 27 • 7
**REGULATION
OF MONOPOLY**

Oligopoly

Monopoly in its "pure" form is a rarity, and unregulated monopoly is rarer still. From our previous study of the American economy, we know that the market structure in which most big corporations operate is not that of pure monopoly, but rather that of oligopoly. In an oligopolistic market situation, a *few* sellers divide the market and typically compete with one another by means of advertising, product differentiation, service, etc., rather than by the classic competitive means of price (see pp. 126-28).

What does a typical oligopoly look like under the lens of price theory? On the cost side, it is much the same as a monopolist or a perfect competitor. There is, however, an essential difference between the demand curve of a monopolist and that of an oligopolist. The demand curve for a monopolist, since it comprises the entire demand for the commodity, is the downward sloping curve of the kind with which we are familiar. But the demand curve for an oligopolist, although it is also downward sloping, has a shape that is new to us and quite unusual.

Suppose that you were the president of a large company that, along with three other very similar companies, sold roughly 80 percent of a certain commodity. Suppose also that a price had been established for your commodity. It yielded you and your competitors a "reasonable" profit, but you and your fellow officers were considering how that profit might be increased.

One possibility that would certainly be discussed would be to raise the price of your product and hope that your customers would continue to be loyal to you. But your company economists might point out that their analyses showed a very elastic demand for your product *if you raised your price, but your competitors did not.* That is, at the higher price, many of your "loyal" customers would switch to a competitive brand, so that your revenues would fall sharply and your profits decline.

Suppose, then, you took the other tack and gambled on that very elasticity of demand by cutting your prices. Would not other firms' customers switch to you and thereby raise your revenues and profits? This time your advisors might point out that if you cut your price, your competitors would almost certainly do the same, to prevent you from taking a portion of "their" market. As a result, with prices cut all around, you would probably find demand highly *inelastic,* and your revenues not larger but smaller.

As Fig. 27-8 shows, you are facing a *kinked* demand curve. In the situation, you might well be tempted to sit tight and do nothing.

For a very interesting thing happens to the marginal revenue curve that is derived from a kinked demand curve. As Fig. 27-9 shows, we now get two marginal revenue curves: one applicable to the upper, elastic section of the demand curve, and the other to the lower, inelastic section. At the point of the kink, the marginal revenue curve is discontinuous, dropping vertically from the end of one slope to the beginning of the next. *As a result, there is*

**FIG. 27 • 8
THE KINKED
DEMAND CURVE**

Your demand curve if you raise prices but your competitors do not.

Existing price

Your demand curve if you cut prices and your competitors follow.

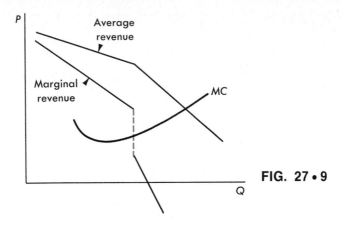

FIG. 27 • 9

no single point of intersection of the marginal revenue and marginal cost curves. This means that an oligopolist's costs can change considerably before he is forced to alter his optimum volume of output or selling price.

The kinked demand curve helps explain why oligopoly prices are often so unvarying even without collusion among firms, but it does not really explain how the existing price is arrived at. For once cost or demand conditions have changed enough to overcome oligopolistic inertia, a new "kink" will again appear around the changed price. The kinked curve thus shows what forces affect *changes* in the oligopolistic situation, rather than how supply and demand originally determine the going price.

Price theory, as such, does not shed as much light on how the price of steel or cars or tires or tin cans is arrived at, as it does in a fully competitive industry. But why should this be so? We know in general what the demand curves look like for oligopolistic commodities, and we have a general idea of their supply behavior. Does it not follow therefore that price will be set by the standard supply-and-demand interplay?

THE MAXIMIZING ASSUMPTION

The answer—or rather, the lack of a clear-cut answer—causes us to examine another underpinning of classical price theory. We have already looked into the assumptions of pure competition—indeed, in this chapter we are tracing the consequences of failing to meet those assumptions. But the oligopoly problem forces us to confront a second fundamental premise of microeconomic theory. This is the assumption that firms maximize short-run profits.

Under pure competition, as we have seen, such profit maximization has a powerful motive working for it, quite above that of an entrepreneur's desire to get rich. This is the motive of *self-preservation.* Firms that do not constantly equate marginal cost and marginal revenue—the iron rule of maximizing—will simply fail to survive the competitive test. Hence, in the classical model, we can accept short-run profit maximizing as a fair description of reality, as well as a valid guideline for a well-working market system.

Not so, however, with oligopoly or monopoly. To be sure, a great corporation that failed to make any profits for many years would eventually fail, but there is little danger that a large company will go under if it does not make the last dollar—or even the last ten million dollars—of possible profits in any one year or even over two or three years running.

Do the great oligopolistic concerns try to equate marginal cost and marginal revenue, and thus maximize their income?

This is a question that is difficult to answer, by virtue of the very indeterminacy of the oligopolistic equilibrium resting point. We have just seen that a kinked demand curve makes likely a very high degree of oligopolistic inertia. The classic route to higher profits—beating one's competitor on price—tends to be shunned. What we find instead of the single-minded pursuit of gain is a strategic pursuit of long-run growth and strength that may very well lead to short-run decisions *not* to make as much money as possible.

Two factors in particular make the oligopolist's day-by-day behavior difficult to predict in theory. The first is his limited but not insignificant ability to influence the demand curve for his own product. Oligopolies are typically the largest advertisers, for one way in which competition *can* be carried out without disturbing the price structure is by inducing customers to switch brands at the same price.* Thus a considerable degree of oligopolistic success depends not on pursuing the traditional course of profit-maximizing, but on pursuing a successful strategy of sale-enlargement.

Second, the *long-term* considerations that guide the behavior of oligopolies introduces a new element into the profit-maximizing picture that is missing in the competitive case. The entrepreneur of the small firm lives in a world in which his costs and his demand curve are both subject to change without notice. He must do the best he can, at each moment, to obtain the highest income for himself. The oligopolist, on the other hand, has a considerable degree of control over his future. Since his overhead costs are usually high, he is able to make stringent economies if the need arises. And since he lives in a market situation where he is reasonably sure of not having to face price competition, he plans for the future in terms of improving or changing his product or his advertising or both.

This necessarily introduces into his plans a *time dimension* of much greater depth than in the case of classic competition. And in turn, the ability—not to say necessity—to plan several years in advance gives greater latitude to whatever decisions may be in the best immediate interests of the firm. *Thus profit-maximizing, however valid as a description of the state of mind or aim of the oligopolist, no longer serves, as it does in the competitive*

* Thus we find a new kind of cost in oligopolistic firms—*selling* cost, or cost incurred, not to hire factors of production and thereby directly to increase output, but to move the demand curve and thereby to increase sales. A competitive firm has no selling costs, because its product is indistinguishable from that of anyone else.

case, to describe the exact price and output decisions that we can expect firms to undertake in the face of market pressures. Oligopolies are, within broad limits, free to follow whatever course—aggressive or defensive—their managements decide is best, and competing oligopolies have often followed *different* courses. Hence microtheory can say relatively little about how the market will impinge on the oligopolistic firm, since its economic pressures are much less imperious than they are in pure competition.

Imperfect Competition

We shall return once more to an assessment of the market under the conditions of oligopoly, but we must first finish our review of the marketplace in reality, rather than theory. For oligopoly, although perhaps the most striking departure from the ideal of pure competition, is not the most common departure. Once we pass from the manufacturing to the retail or service sectors where competition is still intense and "atomistic" (i.e., characterized by numerous small units), we encounter a new kind of market situation, equally strange to the pages of a text on pure competition. This is a situation in which there are many firms, with relatively easy entrance and exit, but in which *each firm sells a product slightly differentiated from that of every other.* Here is the world of the average store or the small competitive manufacturer of a brand-name product—indeed, of every seller who can "identify" his product to the public and who must face the competition of many other makers of similar but not exactly identical products.

Economists call this market situation in which there is a tinge of monopoly *imperfect competition* or *monopolistic competition.* How does it differ from pure competition? Once again, there is no difference on the cost side, which is exactly the same for both a perfectly competitive and an imperfectly competitive firm. The difference, again, comes in the nature of the demand curve.

We recall that the special attribute of the demand curve facing a firm in a purely competitive situation is its horizontal character. By way of contrast, *in a market of imperfect competition, the demand curve facing each seller slopes gently downward.* As we have already seen, this is because his good or service is not exactly like that of his competitors, and because he therefore has some ability to raise price without losing all his business.

EQUILIBRIUM IN MONOPOLISTIC COMPETITION

What is the equilibrium position of such an imperfectly competitive firm—say a dress manufacturer? In Fig. 27-10, we show, on the left, an imperfect competitor who is obviously making substantial profits. Note that his best position where $MR = MC$ is *exactly* like that of a monopolist.

But our firm is not a monopolist, and its profits are therefore not immune to erasure by entry into its field. In Fig. 27-10, we show the same firm after *other entrepreneurs have moved into the industry* (with additional

FIG. 27 • 10

| Before other firms enter | After other firms enter |

similar, although not identical, products) and thereby taken away some of our firm's market and moved its demand curve to the left.

Note that our final position for the marginal dress firm has no more profit than that of a purely competitive seller. On the other hand, because his demand curve slopes, the equilibrium point cannot be at the lowest point on the average cost curve, nor will output have reached optimum size. (Of course, intramarginal firms can be more profitable than the marginal case we have graphed.)

This outcome clearly dissipates economic well-being. The fact that firms are forced to operate to the left of the optimums on their cost curves means that *they have not been able to combine factors to yield their greatest efficiency*— a failure that penalizes factors, once when they are paid too little because their potential marginal productivity has not been reached, and again as consumers when they are forced to pay too much for products that have not been produced at lowest possible cost. In addition, wastage is incurred because the attempt to differentiate products leads in many instances to too many small units—for example, the famous (and all too common) case of four gas stations at one intersection.

Inefficient though it may be, just as in a purely competitive industry, monopolistic competition yields the marginal firm in an industry no profit. The entrepreneur therefore feels fully as hard-pressed as would the producer of an undifferentiated commodity. The difference is that a monopolistic competitive businessman has the possibility of *further differentiating* his product, hoping thereby to tilt his demand curve in a more inelastic position. In turn, this might allow him to raise his prices slightly and to squeeze out a tiny "pure monopoly" profit. The result is that we find a tremendous variety of goods in industries in which monopolistic competition is typical—the ladies garment industry being a prime example.*

---

* Oligopolists as well as monopolistic competitors march to the drums of competition through product differentiation. In the fields of cigarettes, soaps, and breakfast cereals, the market is pretty much made up of three firms, and thirty or forty years ago most grocery stores stocked only about three or four brands of each. But today the shelves holding these products have been expanded again and again as each of the three firms came forward with a new differentiation or one to match a new, highly successful brand of one of its competitors.

How much of the whole market system is imperfect in one sense or another?

Let us begin with pure monopolies. We have seen how difficult it is to define what such a monopoly is, but if we are not too careful about looking for product substitutes, then perhaps we can classify 10 to 20 percent of output as monopolistic. Nearly all of it is the output of public utilities, regulated by public agencies, or consists of the output of the public sector (for the government is certainly a monopoly, although not a profit-maximizing one).

Oligopolies constitute a more significant category. As we know, they are the predominant form of market structure in important areas of the economy, particularly manufacturing. Yet the degree of oligopoly varies greatly from one industry to another. Within the industrial sector as a whole, about half of the manufactured products sold nationally are produced by industries in which the top eight firms do at least a third of the business. But this very mild degree of concentration is an average of some industries (bottled soft drinks, sawmills, printing) where the top twenty companies produce only a third of all output, and other industries (autos, cans, cigarettes) where the top *four* companies do up to 90 percent of the business.

In addition, the problem of measuring or even defining oligopoly is complicated by the question of the market division of sales. For example, the top eight beer and ale companies sell only 28 percent of the nation's total consumption of beer; but because these drinks are usually produced and marketed within a limited region, the concentration of sales among a few brewers is much greater in any one area, such as New York or Chicago, than it is in the nation as a whole. Concentration ratios are generally higher when we consider regions or localities than when we measure sales in the nation's market as a whole. For instance, the ice cream and frozen dessert industry is only mildly concentrated if we measure the percentage of business going to the top four firms on a national basis—37 percent—but when we descend to the level of localities, we find that the average proportion of a local market claimed by the top four firms in *that* locality rises to 70 percent. (Of course, the top four firms are not the same in every locality.)

It is worth noting the difference between concentration within market areas, however defined, and the over-all concentration of industry discussed in Chapter 7. The emergence of the giant conglomerate corporation has not yet noticeably raised the concentration ratios within most markets, although it is possible that this may happen if the conglomerate movement continues much longer. Hence the growth of the giant multiproduct company poses problems of a political nature, or perhaps of financial speculation, rather than problems related directly to the degree of competition. As of 1970, the texture of the marketplace had not been significantly changed by the emergence of the conglomerate giant, although the structure of American capitalism as a whole had certainly been affected by it.

It is much more difficult, and perhaps even impossible, to measure the extent of monopolistic competition. As we have already discussed, very few industries fully meet the qualifications of pure competition; and even if we remove the proviso of easy entry and exit, not much of America's output is both undifferentiated in character and produced by many firms. Only agriculture, fisheries, and a few other industries comprising perhaps 10 to 15 percent of national output could then be called purely competitive. Another 30 to 40 percent resembles pure competition in its numerous firms, but is characterized by differentiated output. Perhaps the same percentage of output is produced in more or less oligopolistic markets.

These estimates should not be taken as more than very rough orders of magnitude. What is important is that market *imperfection*, in one form or another, is the prevailing reality in the micro system of the United States (or any other industrial nation). What significance does this fact have for the effectiveness of that system or for the relevance of the theory that seeks to describe it? These are the culminating questions to which we must now seek to provide some answers.

The Cost of Market Imperfection

WASTE

The first effect of market imperfection is clear. It represents a departure from the standards of extreme efficiency promised by pure competition. No longer is every firm producing at the lowest point on its cost curve. No longer are profits held to a minimum. No longer is the consumer the undisputed sovereign of the marketplace. *In various forms and guises, waste—useless effort or useless expenditure—is introduced into the system.*

ADVERTISING

One form of waste is the enormous proliferation of advertising in an imperfect market society. State and local governments are in fiscal crisis caused largely by the costs of education, but today we spend two-thirds as much to persuade buyers to choose this or that brand as we spend for all primary and secondary education—indeed, advertising expenditures can be thought of as a vast campaign to educate individuals to be "good" consumers. As we have already pointed out in Chapter 7, some of this expenditure may be necessary to stabilize and solidify consumer demand in an affluent society, and some of it certainly has an important informational function or even an enjoyable aspect. After all, if there were no advertising it would be exceedingly difficult for genuine improvements or for new products to make their way into most households. It is probably fair to state that without the possibility of advertising products, the system would lose a great deal of its dynamism.

Yet not all advertising, by any manner of means, conveys information that is genuinely useful to the consumer or introduces new products. It is difficult to contemplate the battles of aspirins, airlines, soaps (up to 10 percent of the price of soap is accounted for by selling expense), cars, and cigarettes, without recognizing that much of this represents a wastage of scarce resources, including the resources of very gifted and clever people whose efforts are largely directed toward annulling the work of their counterparts in a different advertising agency.

PRODUCT DIFFERENTIATION

Waste appears, too, in product differentiation. It has been calculated that the cost to the consumer of annual style changes in cars runs to $5 billion a year or some $700 per car. What the corresponding figures are for other "style" goods, such as the ever-new models of dishwashers and refrigerators, detergents and cosmetics, we do not know. But certainly the prices of many goods could be greatly reduced if a single model were decided on, and all improvements poured into cost reduction. So, too, the resources that must now be spread among competing establishments—the case we mentioned before of "four gas stations"—would be much more efficiently employed in one.

GAINS FROM ADVERTISING AND DIFFERENTIATION

Yet, there are counterarguments. The elimination of brands that assuredly sell the same thing in different packages would leave the question of what policing force would then be left to regulate the one remaining brand. And where product differentiation results in variations in the product itself—and not just in its "image"—one must ask whether the aim of an affluent society is to produce the largest possible quantity of a standardized product at the cheapest possible cost or to offer an array of differing products that please our palates, admittedly at somewhat higher costs. Few consumers in a rich society would prefer an inexpensive uniform to more expensive but highly individualized clothes. From this point of view, even the wasteful parade of car styles has a certain rationale.

Thus, as with advertising, *some* production differentiation plays a useful and utility-increasing function. The question is how much? This is a matter on which it is difficult to form a purely objective judgment, for even if the amount of "useless" product differentiation is relatively small, its impact on the public taste may be disproportionately large. The problem is perhaps particularly acute insofar as much of our "taste" for style seems to be the product of the deliberate advertising efforts of manufacturers. No doubt there is a real aesthetic pleasure in variety, but one doubts that it would take the form of a yearning for "this year's model" without a good deal of external stimulation. Product differentiation thus becomes in part an effort to maximize the public's utilities; but it is also in part an effort to create those "utilities" in order to maximize the producers' profits.

Last, *the wastes of an imperfect market system lie in its inability to push all resources to their point of highest return (and lowest cost).* Every monopoly, large or small, represents a shelter behind which factors are used in lesser quantities than would be the case if the shelter did not exist. Indeed, the whole problem of monopoly is that it prevents the inrush of land, labor, and capital that would take place if there were no barriers to entry.

How serious is the resulting misallocation of resources? Estimates for 1954 give a surprisingly small answer in terms of the aggregate for resources that is blocked out of its point of natural gravitation—perhaps no more than $5 billion—and the effect of transferring this amount of resources would have only a slight effect on the general level of prices. On the other hand, it is also true that profits in monopolistic industries are 50 to 100 percent higher than those in highly competitive industries: in 1962, for example, the ten largest manufacturing corporations enjoyed profits of 8.7¢ on the sales dollar, whereas the half million corporations doing less than $50,000 of sales each averaged profits of but 3.5¢ per dollar of sales.

MONOPOLY AND INEFFICIENCY

Are the higher profits of big business pure waste, like all economic rents? They certainly imply that some prices could be materially reduced. Yet it is difficult to maintain that the high profits of the monopolistic sector have no social utility whatsoever. The handsome factories and offices, the generally more relaxed and generous attitudes toward employees, the growth of fringe benefits and amenities, the prospective transformation of the blue-collar worker into a white-collar salaried employee—all these important evolutionary changes in our economy must also be related to the easier pace and larger earnings of a monopolistic system, rather than to the frenzied pace and pennypinching attitudes necessitated by a system of full price competition.

More important still, the development of large-scale technologies of low-cost mass production requiring the investment of vast sums, the cultivation of research that cannot possibly "pay off" for years, the restless search for new products that continuously redynamizes the macroeconomy—these attributes of modern capitalism are also byproducts of its oligopolistic character and would be impossible to achieve in a regime of atomistic producers.

GAINS FROM MONOPOLY

Thus, the economic argument of waste is not a simple issue to assess. The gains and losses are difficult to measure and cannot easily be weighed on the same scale. Perhaps it is more useful to ask whether the presence of waste has seriously impeded the operation of the market as a *system.* And here the answer can be given with more assurance. For the forces of the marketplace, although more slowly and sluggishly, continue to press in the *direction* of pure competition.

WASTE AND THE MARKET'S OPERATION

The pattern of demand, for example, although clearly to some extent the creature of advertising, still retains an independence (if only in the choice of the advertising it believes) that imposes an ultimate authority over the imperfect market. No firm, however large, feels secure in the "possession" of its customers. In the same way, the mobility of firms and factors is badly impeded by market imperfections, but there is nonetheless visible a long-term circulation of land, labor, and capital both among industries and regions: witness the rise of the computer industry, or the decline of rail transportation before the onslaughts of trucking and air travel. And whereas product competition is much less stringent than price competition, it also exerts a slow winnowing effect, certainly on the product, if not always on its maker.

SIZE AND INSTABILITY

Thus the forces of self-interest and of a muted competition still prod the economy in the general direction spelled out by microtheory. But the viscosity of the market in the real world, compared with its extreme fluidity in theory, brings further problems in its wake. Specifically, it endangers the capacity of the market for *self-correction.*

We remember that one of the ways in which the market system assured the orderly provisioning of society was through a complicated chain of price signals and quantity responses—a chain that, as we have seen, brought about larger supplies when prices and profits rose, thereby pressing *against* a further price rise or even rolling prices back; and vice versa when prices fell.

These self-correcting market responses were automatically forthcoming in an environment of small competitive firms who "read" price and profit signals in terms of tomorrow's prospects, but they are by no means so reliable in an environment of giant firms who may ignore price changes entirely (for reasons of sheer bureaucratic inertia) or who may interpret them in a perspective of long-run market strategy. American steel firms, for example, were extremely reluctant to add to steel capacity all through the early postwar period, despite urgent price signals to do so, since they figured (erroneously, as it turned out) that the demand for steel would soon be saturated. As a result, we had a steel "shortage," since the industry neither raised its prices to the equilibrium point (for fear of political repercussions) nor produced enough steel to satisfy the quantity demanded at going prices.

Similarly, the self-correcting market of microtheory takes for granted a flexibility of prices as well as outputs. But big firms and big unions are not eager to allow their prices to fluctuate in response to every change in demand—especially not downward. As a result, market imperfections give us the phenomenon of "sticky" prices, whose difficulties we have already encountered in Part Three in dealing with the problem of money supply and general inflation. Thus monopoly elements in the market introduce problems into not only microeconomics but also macroeconomics, by complicating the problem of clearing the market for all goods—that is, making it more difficult to equate the supply of gross national output *at going prices* to the demand for gross national output, without either "gaps" or excesses of demand.

In Chapter 29 we will return to the ultimate problem posed by monopoly and oligopoly: the problem of how to exercise effective control over the giant corporation. But our discussion has begun to veer in a new direction which we should pursue further. The issue of instability raises questions of a kind different from those of the strictly "micro" consequences of bigness. In a curious way we have returned to a macro view of the economy, although still from a micro viewpoint. Let us extend this investigation by looking next into a question that we touched on at the end of our macro section, when we considered the relation of growth to the environment. We looked at the ecological problem then from a macro point of view. Now we must investigate this critically important issue again—not as a consequence of heedless growth, but as a problem of the market mechanism itself.

KEY CONCEPTS AND KEY WORDS

1. The motives of monopoly and oligopoly are exactly those of competition. What is different is the *structure of the market* in which these motives give rise to action.

   Monopoly

2. The monopoly or oligopoly faces a sloping rather than a horizontal demand curve. It is a *price-searcher rather than a price-taker.*

   Price-searcher

3. A monopoly is difficult to define narrowly because of the existence of *substitutes* for all commodities. The monopolistic *firm* enjoys the same demand curve as does the competitive *industry,* and is forced to obey the limitations imposed by its demand curve. It can, however, attempt to *shift the curve to the right by advertising.*

   Price-taker

4. The cost curves of monopolists and oligopolists are shaped the same as those of competitive firms. However, monopolists face *marginal revenue curves that are not identical with their average revenue curves.* The difference arises because the monopolist must lower his price to increase his sales. Therefore, each additional unit brings in a smaller addition to total revenues than the previous unit brought.

   Marginal
   revenue

5. Equilibrium for the monopoly (as for the competitive firm) is that output where $MR = MC$. This the point of maximum profit. AC will not equal P, however, for there is no influx of firms to push prices down to this point.

   Equilibrium
   for monopoly

6. The result of monopoly is twofold: prices will be higher than in competitive firms, and output will be smaller.

7. Oligopoly is a more common market structure than monopoly. It is characterized by a few sellers, rather than one.

   Oligopoly

8. The oligopolist's *demand curve is typically kinked.* This shape reflects the difficulty of holding his market share if he raises prices alone, and the difficulty of maintaining his price advantage if he cuts price, which will be quickly followed by his fellow oligopolists.

   Kinked
   demand curve

9. Oligopolies often need not obey the dictates of *short-run* profit maximizing. On the contrary, they can plan considerable distances into the future. As a result, *profit-maximizing,* however accurate a description of their goal, *does not lead to the exactly predictable behavior that it does in the case of the competitive firm.*

Monopolistic competition

10. Imperfect or monopolistic competition is used to describe markets in which there are *many sellers selling differentiated products.* The point of difference is the existence of a slightly sloping demand curve.

Differentiation

11. Imperfect competition leads to two main results. First, output *does not reach the point of lowest cost* and greatest efficiency, thereby penalizing both consumers and factors. Second, there is a tendency for *differentiation to increase* in the hope of gaining a small profit.

Waste

12. The bulk of all markets in industrial countries are *imperfect to some degree.* Pure competition is perhaps as rare as "pure" monopoly. There are several main consequences of this imperfect market. One is *waste.* We see waste, in part, in advertising, some of which is merely economic effort to nullify other economic effort. Waste is also visible in *product differentiation,* in particular when the "demand" for differentiation is deliberately created. Finally, waste lies in the *failure of the system to push resources to their point of highest return,* because of monopolistic elements in the system.

13. There are some compensating gains from the wasteful elements. Advertising brings *information,* production differentiation brings *variety,* size brings *efficiency* and a more relaxed pace of economic life. And the slow currents of the change that make a market system work are still visible in a reduced but nonetheless effective competitiveness and mobility.

Problems of market imperfection

14. Another problem created by imperfection in the market is that of a *lessened capacity of the market for self-correction.* This can result in a failure of the market to clear, in the generation of "surpluses" or "shortages," and in the *sticky prices* that complicate monetary problems.

Q U E S T I O N S

1. In what way, if any, do the motives of a monopolist differ from those of a perfect competitor? In what way does the time span of his decision-making differ? Can this affect his behavior (as contrasted to his motivation)?

2. How would you define a monopoly? Are monopolies necessarily large? What constraints does a demand curve put on the behavior of a monopoly?

3. Suppose that you were the only seller of a certain kind of machinery in the nation. Suppose further that you discovered that your demand curve looked like this:

Price	$100	$90	$80	$70
Quantity of machines sold	1	2	3	4

What is the average revenue at each price? What is the marginal revenue at each price? Draw a diagram showing the marginal and average revenue.

4. Now superimpose on this diagram a hypothetical cost profile for your business. Where is the point of equilibrium for the monopolist? Is this the same, in terms of *MC* and *MR,* as the point for the competitive firm? Now show the equilibrium output and price.

5. Does the equilibrium output of the monopolist yield a profit? What are the relevant costs for figuring profit, average costs per unit, or marginal costs? Show on your diagram the difference between average cost and selling price.

6. Why will a monopolist's selling price not be pushed to the lowest point on the cost curve?

7. What is the difference between monopoly and oligopoly? Between oligopoly and pure competition? Between pure competition and monopolistic (or imperfect) competition? Between the latter and oligopoly?

8. What is meant by the kinked demand curve of an oligopolist? How do you explain the kink?

9. Why does the profit-maximizing assumption lead to such clear-cut results when we speak of pure competition, and to such indeterminate ones for oligopolies? Does the answer have something to do with the time over which the consequences of actions can be calculated?

10. What is a differentiated commodity? Give examples. Draw the demand curve for a farmer selling wheat and that for a toy manufacturer selling his own brand of dolls. What will happen if the doll manufacturer makes a large profit? What will his final point of equilibrium look like if he has many competitors?

11. Compare on two diagrams the equilibrium of the purely competitive firm and of the imperfectly competitive one. Show, by a dotted line, what the demand curve would look like for the imperfectly competitive firm if its product differentiation were removed. Where would its output now be located? What would be its selling price? Would the consumer gain from this?

12. Make a careful list of all the institutional changes you can think of that would be needed if we were to institute a system of perfect competition.

13. What kinds of advertisements are informational? What kinds are "taste-forming"? Do you think that if there were no ads for cigarettes, smoking would decrease?

14. How much product differentiation do you consider useful? Dress styles? Car models? Laundry soaps?

We have had an introduction to the problem of ecology, both in Chapter 1, when we glanced at some of its more horrifying aspects, and in Chapter 20, when we looked into the connection between environmental disturbance and economic growth. What we lacked in our earlier investigations, however, was a set of concepts and tools that our micro-investigations have now given us. We did not see the market as a *system*—a system for allocating goods and services and, therefore, also for misallocating them. We had no basic yardstick by which to measure economic performance.

As we will soon discover, we do have such a yardstick now. But before we begin to apply it to the problem of the environment, this is a good place to solidify our understanding of the ecological problem as a whole.

BEHIND THE ECOLOGICAL CRISIS

The first question we should clarify in our minds is a very important one. It is why the ecological "crisis" has seemingly burst upon us suddenly. What lies behind our sense of urgency about the environment?

Basically there are three answers to this question:

1. *Population growth.*

Part of the ecological crisis is caused by the sheer pressure of numbers of individuals on the environment itself. In the underdeveloped world this takes the form of an actual race between population and food, into which we shall look when we study underdevelopment (Chapter 34). But even in the most productive and advanced countries, the steady growth of population has given rise to a series of pollution problems with roots in population density. We can call these problems of *congestion.*

This is not to say that we are running out of space in America. Population per square mile in the U.S. is less than 70 today; compare Switzerland, with 387; U.K., with 590; Japan, with 710; Netherlands, with 985. But population densities in some *parts* of the United States are serious enough to lead to severe environmental problems. The city of Akron, for example, is denser in population than Japan; Anaheim-Santa Ana is more than double the density of Akron (1,612 persons per square mile); Chicago reaches a density of 1,832; Detroit, 2,114; New York, 5,327; Jersey City, 13,087!

At these densities, very grave problems of pollution begin to occur as a result of congestion. Moreover, these problems affect the population with an intensity that goes up as the *square* of the number of individuals. William Baumol has explained the reason for this in an important article in the June 1967 *American Economic Review*. Consider the illustrative diagram, Fig. 28-1. The two circles represent two equal-sized cities, in which the dots stand for numbers of people (in thousands or millions) and the crosses for numbers of (smoky) chimneys, also in some suitable multiple. Suppose that the number of chimneys is primarily determined by the number of people, say as the number of private houses grows. Then, as the different shadings of the two circles suggest, the absolute amount of smoke pollution per unit/area (say, per block) within the two cities will be determined directly by the numbers of their respective populations.

But the matter does not stop there. Take the city on the right, in which population and the number of chimneys has increased from two to six. The absolute amount of smoke over the city has now tripled—*but this tripled density of smoke is now inflicted on three times as many people.* Thus the impact of pollution has gone up not three times, but nine!*

Smoke pollution is not the only form of environmental damage that goes up by the square of the population. Noise pollution is another environ

FIG. 20-1

* We can put the matter into simple algebra. The "annoyance" (or damage) of pollution is the product of the *amount* of pollution per unit/area times the *number* of people who are affected by it. Thus we can write:

(1) Pollution annoyance = $P \cdot n$

where P stands for the amount of pollution per unit/area and n for population. But since P is itself *caused* by the number of people, we can also write:

(2) $P = f(n)$

or the amount of pollution is some function of population. Substituting equation (2) into (1) we get:

(3) Pollution annoyance = $f(n) \cdot n$, or $f(n^2)$

mental hazard that may be directly produced by population density and that feeds back in turn across the whole population. Perhaps the "damage" caused by the sheer ugliness of crowded neighborhoods is another. Certainly the number of manhours spent fuming in traffic jams is on the list, a fact that may add understanding, if not consolation, the next time you are trapped on a clogged freeway.

2. The cumulative effects of industrialization.

Growing population density thus constitutes one cause for the emergence of the ecological crisis, particularly in urban areas. But a second reason operates quite independently of population growth. It is the *cumulative addition of pollutants* to the air and water and land, to the point at which they threaten to overload the absorptive or chemical cleansing powers of the environment.

Although population growth accelerates this cumulative overloading, the sheer addition of indissoluble poisons, such as mercury or long-lasting chemical agents like those in DDT, becomes a source of environmental danger, even without the pollution caused by additional production to meet the needs of additional people. And of course, when we add population growth to the growth in production per head of population, the cumulative effect is greatly intensified. As Kenneth Boulding has very aptly put it, we have moved from a cowboy economy, where the great open spaces were endless, to a spaceship economy in which we are acutely aware of the cramped confines of our collective living space.

There is an economic side to this "running out of environment." It is linked to a category of inputs into the productive process that we have heretofore overlooked. These inputs are called *free goods*—the air, the water, the empty space of the environment itself, into which we throw things away. Old-fashioned textbooks used to begin their discussion of economics by mentioning free goods, then forgetting about them, since they never entered the economic calculus. Now free goods again become important, because although they remain "free"—that is, there is no charge for using them—they have become *scarce*.

3. New technology and externalities.

We will return in a moment to the problem of scarce free goods, but first we should note the third cause for the environmental crisis. This is the swift emergence of *new technologies* of extraordinary environmental impact: pesticides, radiation, jet planes, and many more.

These ecology-disturbing new commodities are really only particularly dramatic examples of an economic effect we have not formerly noted. This effect is the so-called *externalities* of production or consumption. By *externali-*

ties we mean effects exerted by the process of producing or consuming goods that bypass the price system. For example, ordinarily when we consider the price of a good—say an automobile—we assume that this price fully reflects all its costs of manufacturing. But suppose that the auto factory emits smoke that lowers local real estate values or multiplies local cleaning bills. These are costs that are not included in the price of autos. Or suppose that the *use* of automobiles requires the installation of traffic lights or expensive throughways. These are consumption externalities that will impose costs (taxes) on users and nonusers alike. Or suppose the consumption or production of a product has *beneficial* externalities, such as the construction of a new school that greatly improves the value of a neighborhood. One would think that these benefits would be credited against the cost of the school, but they are not.

We used to believe that externalities were mere curiosities of the economic process—that the prices of a perfectly competitive market system fully reflected *all* costs of outputs or *all* benefits that buyers expected to obtain from them. But we have begun to recognize that *externalities are a pervasive and inescapable attribute of nearly all economic processes, and that one of the problems of even a perfect market system is that it fails to take into account their benefits or costs.* Thus the new, environment-threatening technologies constitute a special cause of the ecological crisis only because they point up more sharply the failure of the market system to deal with a well-nigh universal, but previously ignored problem.

The point is so important it is worth repeating. In back of the conception of the marketplace as an *efficient* allocator of goods and incomes (recall our discussion on pp. 520-21), was the assumption that all the inputs going into the process were owned by some individual and that all the outputs were bought by some person or firm or agency. Presumably, then, the price at which commodities were offered would include all the costs that were incurred in the process; and presumably also, the price that would be offered would reflect all the prospective benefits accruing to the buyer. In other words, prices established in the marketplace were supposed to take into account all the disutilities involved in the process of production, such as the fatigue or unpleasantness of work, and all the utilities ultimately gained by the final consumer of those goods.

What the ecological crisis has brought home is that the *market is not a means for effectively registering a great many of these costs and benefits.* The examples of the damage wrought by smoke that is not charged against the factory or of a neighborhood nuisance such as a bar or a hideous advertising sign are instances of economic activities in which *private costs are less than social* costs. Contrariwise, when a person spends money to educate himself, he benefits not only himself but also the community, partly because he becomes a more productive citizen and partly because he presumably becomes a more responsible one. Thus the *social benefits* of some expenditures may be greater than their *private benefits.*

EQUATING SOCIAL AND PRIVATE MARGINAL COSTS AND BENEFITS

But suppose that the social and private gains and losses do not coincide. How does that reflect on the efficiency of the market process?

The answer is very plain. If we are interested ultimately in maximizing everyone's well-being, we want the price system to act as a guide to firms and factors and consumers, urging them to buy more or produce more of socially useful goods and to make or buy fewer socially deleterious ones. (As the saying now goes, we want an economy that produces more goods and less "bads".) But under a pricing system that takes no account of the externalities wrought by consumption and production, the economy will produce too many bads and too few goods. Because no charge for smoke is levied on the factory owner, there is no economic incentive to economize on smoke, perhaps by switching to more expensive but less smoky fuel. If there is no reduction in the price of education, it will be bought only to the point at which the marginal dollar spent on education by a consumer is equal to the marginal *private* gain he hopes to get from that dollar; whereas if the community's benefit were calculated in the price, education would be subsidized so that the consumer would be tempted to buy more of it for himself, at the same time creating external benefits for the society.*

COST-BENEFIT ANALYSIS

How are we to estimate what the proper allocation of resources should be, if we *do* take into account the externalities that production (or consumption) may impose? By how much, in other words, should we try to reduce the smoke flowing from factory stacks or the waste pouring from a pulp mill? "By whatever degree our technology makes possible," answers the antipollution engineer. "No, by whatever amount equates marginal costs and marginal benefits," answers the antipollution economist. The difference yields important insights into how an economist approaches certain social problems.

Let us first familiarize ourselves with Fig. 28-2, a diagram that shows the costs of, and the benefits from, reducing pollution, say from a factory. The cost and benefit of each unit of pollution reduction are the vertical axis. Along the horizontal axis we show the amount of pollution reduction, beginning at point *O* with no reduction and proceeding toward point *B*, where we reach complete pollution elimination.

---

* It is precisely because society recognizes that education does bring benign externalities that we *do* subsidize education; for example, by scholarships.

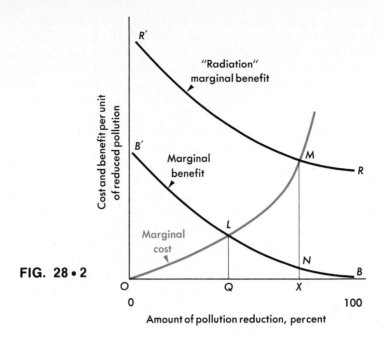

FIG. 28 • 2

Amount of pollution reduction, percent

On the diagram we have two curves. The dashed curve, rising from point *O* up to (and beyond) point *M* is a curve showing us the cost of bringing pollution closer and closer to zero. Note that by the time we have reduced pollution by an amount *OX,* the marginal cost curve is very steep, meaning that it will cost a great deal to achieve a relatively small amount of additional control beyond this point.

The marginal benefit curve, *B'B,* slopes in the opposite direction. At zero pollution control, the benefit from even a small amount of reduction is very high *(OB');* but as more and more smoke is prevented from reaching the air, the benefit from an additional unit of improvement steadily falls. If we ever get to point *B,* where pollution is completely eliminated, the marginal benefit at that point would also be zero.

Now, how much should we spend for pollution control? The engineer, studying the technical possibilities, might conclude that our target should be a reduction by *OX.* But the economist notes that at *OX,* the cost of controlling the last unit of smoke has reached *MX,* whereas the benefits enjoyed from the reduction of the last unit have fallen to *NX.* Thus his solution is to cut pollution by only *OQ,* at which the benefits from eliminating this last unit of smoke are just equal to the costs of doing so.

Doesn't this mean that the economist knowingly allows some pollution to occur, even though it could be eliminated? In this case, that is true—the engineer's solution is cleaner than the economist's by an amount *QX.* But it

**ECONOMICS
VS.
ENGINEERING**

need not be so. Suppose that the smoke from the factory were radioactive. In that case the benefit curve would shift upwards, because each unit of pollution reduction would be worth a great deal more than it was when mere soot was the problem. As a result, the cost-benefit solution could well be the same as that of the engineer's (see $R'R$, the "radiation" marginal benefit curve on the diagram). On the other hand, if the pollution were no more than an annoyance, the benefit curve would be lower (as in our first case), and the economist would indeed suggest a target that would be less than the greatest possible engineering capability.*

Thus the economist tends to think not only in terms of technological possibilities, but also in terms of relative plusses and minuses, gains and losses, opportunities won and lost. Needless to say, the computation of these benefits and costs is an exceedingly complicated task. Smoke over a city not only adds to cleaning bills and causes ill health, but defaces buildings, delays air traffic, and irritates people (who then move to the suburbs). Putting dollars and cents values on these effects is inevitably a somewhat arbitrary procedure, often little better than an educated guess. Nonetheless, the economist's view of things alerts us to the fact that the task of rational environmental control is not always to push for the most advanced possible engineering solution, but to look for a solution that, in the best informed opinion, balances the marginal cost of making a better environment and the marginal benefits to be had from it.

THE SOCIAL RATE OF DISCOUNT

Putting figures on the marginal (or even the total) costs and benefits of environmental improvement or deterioration is one difficulty in applying the calculus of economics to ecology. A second is the perplexing problem of what *social rate of discount to apply*.

What is a social rate of discount? The term describes the fact that we all tend to value present benefits more highly than future ones—a phenomenon we discussed when we defined the marginal efficiency of investment (p. 279). A businessman cannot make a rational decision about whether the expected return on an investment "pays" or not, until he compares the discounted value of its expected stream of earnings with the cost of the investment. Similarly, an environmentalist cannot determine whether a proposed environmental improvement is "worth it," until he has determined some rate of discount by which to calculate the present value of the expected future benefits.

But what rate of discount? The problem is not easy to solve because we often have no way of putting firm values on the benefits that an environmental project will bring. What should we estimate to be the value of an unspoiled lake—the amount that bathers and fishermen would be willing to

---

* Of course, the cost curve might also shift in the case of radioactive waste. For simplicity of exposition, we have assumed it remains unchanged.

pay for its use? That may be very much less than we instinctively feel that an unspoiled bit of wilderness is "worth."

Not only do we have problems assigning values to the benefits of environmental projects, but we also have difficulties deciding what rate of return is socially desirable, once we *have* assigned the values. Suppose, after due consideration, that we have arrived at a money value to be attributed to a conservation program. Should that now show a "return" as large as if the cost of the program were invested in manufacturing? Or should some lower rate of return be deemed adequate for social projects?

There are no "correct" answers to these genuine problems. We raise them, rather, to emphasize that there *are* problems, and that expenditures designed to correct environmental disturbances are apt to seem profligate or stingy depending on the estimated social benefits or the social discount rate that we consciously or unconsciously apply. If we take the view that the unpriceable "output" of public expenditures is very high, or that very low discount rates should be applied to the estimated benefits, we may end up approving costly and highly inefficient projects exemplified by some work of the army's Corps of Engineers. If we take the tightfisted point of view, we end up with the severe shortage of public facilities typical of most American communities. All that an economist can do is to alert the community to the fact that a decision has to be made with regard to benefits and social discount rate; and that such a decision should reflect, as best it can, the thoughtful judgment of the concerned and educated public.

CONTROLLING EXTERNALITIES

So far we have pointed out how a market system generates externalities and how difficult it is to decide what to spend on reducing pollution or improving the environment. Now let us turn to another, equally important matter: the problem of choosing among various ways of lessening harmful production or consumption activity.

Basically, there are three main ways in which we can control external costs.

1. We can *regulate* the activity which creates it.

2. We can *tax* the activity that creates it.

3. We can *subsidize* the polluter to stop (or lessen) his activity.

REGULATION

Faced with the ugly view of smoke belching from a factory chimney, sludge pouring from a mill into a lake, automobiles choking a city, or persons being injured by contaminants, most ecologically concerned persons cry for regulation. Pass a law to forbid smoky chimneys or sulferous coal; pass a law to make mills dispose of their wastes elsewhere or purify them; pass a law against automobiles in the central city; pass a law against DDT.

Sometimes regulation *is* the cheapest and easiest and most effective means of bringing pollution to a halt. If the pollution is extremely dangerous (as in the case of radiation damage or mercury poisoning or DDT), then outright prohibition may be the proper solution. Strict laws against just such abuses have recently been passed by most states and by the federal government; still stricter ones may follow.

But regulation is not always the indicated solution. In some cases (smoke from trash fires or from private chimneys, private garbage disposal, littering, etc.) the regulations may be too expensive or too difficult to enforce. A law that is semi-enforced is often worse than no law at all, since it encourages an attitude of deliberate law-evasion. In other cases, severe regulation may bring results that are not in the best social interests of the community. The only way to stop *all* smoke from a particular factory may be to discontinue production in that factory. With that drastic step, society would gain well-being from the absence of smoke, but *it would lose the well-being derived from goods and services the factory produced.* Hence, as in our earlier diagram, when the aim of social policy is not to eliminate all pollution, but to hold it to socially acceptable levels (levels at which marginal costs and benefits are equal), regulation may not be the instrumentality best adapted to the purpose.

TAXATION

Then what about taxation? An alternative to regulating a polluter, whether an industry or individual, is to allow him to pollute all he pleases but to make him pay for each "unit" of pollution he creates. For instance, we can powerfully discourage factories from burning high sulfur content fuel if we tax them for each unit they buy; or we can discourage the abandonment of old cars by charging a considerable sum (say $100) as a special "environment tax" payable on the purchase of a new car, which is returnable to the purchaser if he trades in his car or disposes of it to certified automobile disposal yards, but which he forfeits if he simply abandons his car. Very high deposits on beer cans and bottles would also serve as a "tax" to deter throwing these objects away.

As we have mentioned, taxes cannot be used as a means of pollution control when the pollutant is very dangerous, since the antipollution tax, by its very intent, is a license to permit pollution activity but to make it more expensive. Hence it is important to understand the reasoning behind the use of taxes as an antipollution measure.

Pollution taxes are an effort to impose a cost where previously none was levied. Thus *taxes, by making a free good no longer free, attempt to "internalize" externalities;* that is, to force the firm (or person) who creates a negative externality to pay for it himself (or have his customers pay for it) instead of foisting the charges upon the community. If the tax is appropriately figured, it should raise the marginal private costs of carrying on the activity to equal the social costs that the activity imposes on the community.

The use of a tax graduated by degrees of pollution has much to recommend it where it is technically and administratively possible. Such a tax permits the polluting companies to increase their profits by focusing their technology on the elimination of pollution—a most effective incentive. Ideally, in other words, we can use the tax mechanism to allow the market itself to include *all* costs and thus to allocate resources in the public interest, with the efficiency inherent in the pricing mechanism.

SUBSIDIES

But taxes, like regulation, are *not* always effective. For example, taxes on fumes or unpleasant smells coming from a factory or an effluent from a mill require that we have accurate devices for monitoring the amount of pollutant. Moreover, since the pollution damage may vary from still days to windy ones, ideally the tax should be steeper on some days (or hours) than on others—a difficult arrangement for technical reasons. When municipalities are sources of pollution (from city incinerators or sewage systems), who is going to tax the city? Here the solution lies either in state or federal regulation or in state or federal subsidies to help municipalities bear the cost of environmental improvement. Where effective taxation is technically difficult (and where outright regulation may not be effective either), a solution to the problem may be to *pay* the polluter to install antipollution equipment. That is, we might offer him an outright payment or subsidy to stop polluting.

The problem with subsidies is that the public may resent paying taxes to induce someone to stop doing something it feels he shouldn't be doing in the first place. But there are times when subsidy may nonetheless be the easiest way of bringing about a desired result. For example, it may be very difficult to suppress the emission of dangerous but invisible fumes from car exhausts either by regulation (which will take care of new cars, but not old ones) or by taxation (who can tell which car is polluting?). But it might be possible to reduce this dangerous form of pollution by installing the necessary equipment *free*, along with a windshield sticker. This would of course be a subsidy, but it might also be the best means of dealing with a difficult problem.*

THE UBIQUITY OF EXTERNALITIES

Our discussion of the control over externalities has barely scratched the surface of a broad and complex problem. But it is not our purpose here to explore that problem fully, so much as to relate the subject of environmental damage and repair to the market system itself. For we will remember that we began to look into the problem of externalities as part of our first overview of the market. Now it is time to come to a few preliminary judgments.

---

* If we charged for the sticker, to cover the cost of the installed device, we would be using a combination of regulation and *tax* instead of a subsidy.

1. *The market is a very poor allocator of resources for which there is no price tag attached.* That is, the market allows "free goods" to slip through its meshes entirely unnoticed. Hence there is a tendency for marketers—firms and individuals—to overuse free goods, even when in fact these goods have become scarce.

2. *The market is not equipped to take into account the social as well as the private costs and benefits of economic activity.* Hence a market allocation of activity typically leads to too much production of "bads" and not enough of "goods"; that is, to the production of goods or services to the point at which *social cost* is greater than the social benefit (even though the *private* cost may be just equal to the private benefit). For example, a factory may be making money in a fully competitive market, but only because the wastes it pours into the rivers are not charged to it as a cost.

3. *Externalities*—that is, costs and benefits for which no allowance is made in the prices of goods or services—*are virtually omnipresent.* The employee in a pleasant office treats his family well and adds well-being to the community; the employee in an unpleasant establishment gets drunk, beats his wife and children, and imposes additional police costs on the town. One man builds a beautiful house and embellishes the neighborhood; another builds an eyesore, runs the neighborhood down, and sends his sensitive neighbors fleeing.

4. *Through taxation and subsidy, it is possible to "internalize" a considerable amount of the externalities of a market system;* that is, to impose costs on (or to allot benefits to) those who would not otherwise be fully charged or recompensed for the social results of their activity through the marketplace alone. When taxes or subsidies cannot be used, regulation (provided it can be enforced) can reduce pollution or control other externalities.

5. *Control over pollution and improvement of the environment are matters to which an economic calculus applies.* Indeed, the more conscious we become of the ubiquity of the ecological problem and the vast amounts that must eventually be spent to improve our environment, the more important it becomes to think in terms of balancing marginal costs and benefits, as best we can figure them, and to make intelligent use of such ideas as the social discount rate.

KEY CONCEPTS AND KEY WORDS

Ecology

1. The causes of the ecological crisis are three: (1) *population density*, which creates special problems of congestion; (2) *cumulative effects of industrialization*, which overload the environment with pollutants; and (3) *new technologies*, which create unduly striking or hazardous externalities.

Externalities

2. By *externalities* we mean *effects of production or consumption that are not reflected in the price mechanism.* One such effect is the damage of smoke imposed upon the consumer but not included in the costs of the smoke producer. Externalities may also be positive instead of negative, as they are when a handsome building creates economic and esthetic values for a neighborhood.

3. Externalities are important because they are instances in which the market price of a good does not accurately reflect all the disutilities or utilities involved in producing or consuming that good; that is, the *private costs of the good may be greater than or less than its social costs,* and the social benefits of consuming the good may also be different from its private benefits.

4. As a result of this divergence of social and private marginal cost and benefit, society will tend to produce too many "bads" (goods with less social value than private value) and too few "goods" (whose social benefits are greater than their private ones).

5. In estimating the degree to which we should seek to control externalities, such as pollution or other environmental damage, *we try to equate the marginal costs and benefits* of doing so. This leads to an economic solution that may be less thorough-going than an engineering solution, but that is more economic; that is, focused upon opportunity costs.

6. Cost-benefit analysis involves us in the estimation of many intangible costs and benefits and is at best a guide to, rather than a rigid set of rules for, pollution control. Not least of its problems is what *social discount rate* is appropriate for environmental improvement.

7. There are three basic ways of controlling externalities:
   - *Regulation* best used when easy to administer or when the danger of pollution is very great.
   - *Taxation* best used when pollution can be tolerated to some degree and when we wish to use the market mechanism itself to internalize the externality.
   - *Subsidy* best used when regulation or taxation are administratively awkward or impossible.

8. As a ubiquitous feature of all economic systems, externalities pose a severe problem for the effective operation of a market economy. *To the extent that the costs of benefits of externalities can be "internalized"—that is, picked up by taxes or other fees or subsidies, so that they are included within the price of the commodity—the market itself can be used as an administrative device for controlling the effects of externalities.*

Q U E S T I O N S

1. Of the ecological problems that most disturb you, which do you attribute to density, which to environmental overload, which to new technologies?

2. Can you think of an externality imposed by a producer on a consumer? (That's easy.) Of one imposed by a producer on another producer? (How about the effect on work efficiency caused by the noise of erecting a building?) Of an externality imposed by a consumer on another consumer? Of one imposed by consumers on producers?

3. How would you go about systematically trying to reduce the many externalities imposed by traffic in a big city? How would you figure marginal costs and benefits? Could you arrange a schedule of fees or taxes or tolls that might reduce the net burden of congestion? Suppose you decided to ban traffic from downtown during certain hours. How would you estimate the costs and benefits involved?

4. Explain carefully why a perfectly competitive market will turn out an assortment of goods in which the sum of the private costs and benefits imposed by, or enjoyed from, those goods will be different from the sum of the social costs and benefits associated with those goods.

5. What do you think would be the best way to control the following externalities? (1) a smoke-producing utility company, (2) roadside littering, (3) overfishing in a stream, (4) noise from a jetport, (5) radiation hazards in a hospital, (6) billboards, (7) pornography, (8) overcutting of forests. In each case discuss the relative merits of taxation, subsidy, or outright regulation.

In our last chapter we began to ask questions about the functioning of the market system from a vantage point of social welfare. Now it is time to attempt a still broader appraisal of the market with regard to two of the major problems of America Today: poverty and power. What relationship does poverty have to the market mechanism? And what of the giant corporation whose presence we emphasized in our survey of economic history, but whose role has been somehow lost to sight in our discussion of the microeconomic process? In this chapter let us come back to these central social and political issues with whatever insights our study of economic theory affords us.

The Problem of Poverty

MACRO AND MICRO ASPECTS

Poverty, we can now see, has two aspects: one is primarily concerned with macroeconomics, and one is more closely related to microeconomics. The macroeconomic side of poverty directs our attention to the overall size of GNP, which determines how much income there is to be divided up. The micro side, which interests us now, concentrates on how the existing flow of income is divided up; not how much there is, but who gets it.

We have more than once discussed the distribution of income in America (see Chapters 9 and 24), and have called attention to some of the factors affecting the skewness we find among occupations and social classes. But we have not really approached the question of poverty itself as a market phenomenon. *To what extent is poverty the result of market forces?* To what extent can we blame the market mechanism, rather than the overall level of output, for the poverty we find in America today?

WAGE LEVELS IN THE MARKET SYSTEM

Let us begin to answer this question by examining the spectrum of earnings of male workers in various occupations. Table 29-1 shows us a breakdown of earnings by broad categories.

Professional and technical	$10,542	**TABLE 29•1**
Managers, officials, proprietors	9,794	
Sales workers	8,292	**MEDIAN**
Craftsmen, foremen, etc.	7,858	**EARNINGS OF**
Clerical workers	7,324	**YEAR-ROUND**
Semiskilled workers	6,773	**FULL-TIME**
Service workers	5,898	**MALE WORKERS,**
Laborers (nonfarm)	5,606	**1968**
Farmers	3,353	
Farm laborers	2,870	

Note that this table shows the earnings of *full-time* workers; the figures would be lower if part-time earners were included. Note also that it does *not* show family income. We know from Chapter 19 that a very large number of married women work. Thus median family incomes for each occupation would be higher than shown on the table. (For the United States as a whole in 1968, median family income amounted to $8,632.)

With all its deficiencies, Table 29-1 nevertheless reveals two important facts. The first is that *the market provides incomes that are certainly well above the poverty line for the great majority of American workers. The second is that for some classes of workers the market mechanism clearly does not provide an adequate income;* for example, the income of a nonfarm laborer (and certainly of a farm laborer), unless augmented by substantial earnings of his wife or children, would be too little to bring an urban family of five above the official poverty line of 1968. Thus a great deal of poverty is certainly rooted in low wages. Indeed, according to a survey by Anthony Downs, *one quarter of all poor persons in metropolitan areas suffered poverty because of low earnings.* Further, in the nation as a whole, roughly half the heads of poor families worked full time in 1968.[1]

---

[1] Downs, *Who Are the Urban Poor?* pp. 3-4; *Statistical Abstract,* p. 330.

POVERTY AND MARGINAL PRODUCTIVITY

Is the market "responsible" for this low-wage poverty? Much depends on what we mean by responsible. If the word implies that workers receive low incomes because they are severely exploited on the marketplace, most economists would deny the implication. While they would concede the existence of pockets of exploitation, where poor workers are paid much less than their marginal productivity entitles them to, most economists would maintain that the reason why considerable numbers of working Americans are poor is that *their marginal productivity is low.* The migrant worker or the kitchen hand may be meanly treated and taken advantage of, but basically he is not in a position to fight back, because his productivity is so low that his employer could not pay him substantially more without incurring a loss.

With considerable allowances for the imperfections of the labor market, and for efforts to prevent unionization in many low-wage occupations, this answer is correct as far as it goes. But the answer does not really go far enough. For it leads logically to the question: *why is the marginal productivity of certain groups so low?* Why do some groups fail to gain the skills and education and attitudes that are the keys to higher incomes? The answers to that question bring us back to the institutional barriers that make it very hard for certain disprivileged groups in our society to acquire the training that is within the reach and capabilities of others. It is difficult or impossible for the son of a migrant farm worker to gain the education that will raise him to a level of professional skill. It is next to impossible for a black to gain admission to certain craft unions. The "culture of poverty" is not one in which Horatio Alger heroes retain their enthusiasm very long.

POVERTY AND THE MARKET

Is the market system, then, responsible for low-wage poverty? The answer is complex. Insofar as the market mechanism generally tends to push economic society in the direction of efficiency and high productivity, the answer is *No.* After all, most Americans are *not* poor, because the market mechanism has worked to their advantage.

But insofar as the market mechanism faithfully reflects the low productivity of those groups who have been left behind in the general advance of society, the answer is *Yes.* Yet, even here one must distinguish between the blind workings of the market system and the institutional realities whose advantages or handicaps the system reveals. In a society where the overall level of productivity is high enough to provide a decent living for the majority, it is not the market system that must be blamed for the persistence of low wages, but the failure of the larger society to help disprivileged groups break out of situations in which they cannot improve their productivity.

But there is a further problem. If *low* productivity is the immediate cause of much poverty in America, a still larger portion of poverty can be explained by *no* productivity. Anthony Downs, in the report referred to above, tells us that 42.2 percent of all the metropolitan poor were *children*, most of them not even of working age; that 18.3 percent were elderly persons retired from work; that 4.5 percent were disabled persons who could not work. A very important survey conducted by the Department of Health, Education and Welfare in 1968 showed that *of some 8.4 million people on welfare, fewer than 80,000 were employable males.*[2] For the majority of these poor Americans, poverty was not caused by the "workings" of the market, but by its nonworkings. For them, poverty was the result of a system of income distribution that made no provision for those who failed to adapt to the market. The market did not "produce" this poverty; it simply ignored it.

Thus by virtue of its very emphasis on work and productivity, the market system is also an inadvertent cause of some of the most crippling poverty in America. Poverty *within* the market system can be alleviated by tearing down the institutions that prevent workers from bettering their productivity, but the poverty that exists outside the market system has no such remedy. For the old, the crippled, the heads of families who cannot work, and above all for their children, poverty exists because there is no other way than employment to receive a decent income.

Should there be another way? For someone who is physically qualified to work, perhaps not. But for the unemployable, the absence of an adequate transfer mechanism simply means that poverty is a condition from which there is no escape. Hence more and more economists have concluded that the most effective cure for such poverty is a program of *income support*, in which below-poverty incomes are brought up to minimum levels by direct cash payments.

Three main income-support plans have been put forward.

1. *The negative income tax.*

The negative income tax would provide cash "refunds" to all families (or single individuals) who reported incomes below a certain level. For example, if $4,000 were defined as the minimum income level for a family of four, any family of this size that reported an income of only $3,000 would receive an income tax refund of $1,000. This would, of course, help low-wage earners as much as no-wage earners.

---

[2] Downs, *Who Are the Urban Poor?* pp. 3–4; Carolyn Bell, *The Economics of the Ghetto,* p. 84.

2. *Family allowances.*

Some economists object to discriminating between the poor and the non-poor. They propose paying a fixed sum per child to all families, regardless of income. Since 44 percent of all poor children are in families with 5 or more children, this would in fact help poor families more than nonpoor ones. In addition, because the allowances would be taxable, nonpoor families would return (via taxes) a considerable portion of the aid they received, whereas poor families, who pay little or no income tax, would keep all their aid.

3. *Family assistance.*

A third plan is something of a mixture of the above two. It would offer cash payments to *all* families, the payments varying with family size and income. As a family's income rose, its assistance receipts would gradually fall until—at a level of income adequacy—they would cease altogether.

WELFARE

Why not simply continue the present welfare system? There are two very different, but equally compelling, reasons. (1) The present system places its burdens largely on the cities and states who are very hard pressed to finance welfare. All the systems above would transfer the main cost to the federal government, whose taxing powers are vastly greater than those of the state and localities. (2) The present welfare system discourages welfare recipients from working. Usually welfare payments are reduced by an amount equal to any earnings that a welfare recipient may make. Hence there is actually a 100 percent tax on earnings! All the plans above supplement, rather than supplant, earned income.

COST OF A POVERTYLESS SOCIETY

How much would these programs cost?

A rock-bottom program designed only to bring the 24 million Americans who today live *below subsistence* to the levels required for healthful existence would cost roughly $10 billion per year (in addition to what they are now receiving in transfer payments) or about 1 percent of GNP. A program of family assistance aimed at bringing all families to a level at least 25 percent above the present official poverty line would cost about $30 billion per year, or 3 percent of today's GNP. A program designed to pay $600 for each child in America would cost some $43 billion (although much of this would be recaptured by taxes), or about 4.3 percent of GNP.

These are certainly not large sums for a society whose gross national product has crossed the trillion-dollar mark. And in fact, these sums *overstate* the cost of eliminating poverty, for they fail to take into account the lightening of other costs that poverty imposes on society. Not all, but some crime; not all, but many ghetto riots; not all, but a considerable amount of government bureaucracies would go if poverty went. To this must be added the additional production and, more important, the additional sheer human well-being that would be gained if the poor, especially the young, were brought back into the mainstream of American life. By any rational calculation, the benefits to be had from eliminating poverty vastly outweigh the costs of not doing so.

Won't poverty go away, if we just keep on growing? It is true that each year the percentage of families below the "poverty line" has fallen—the number of officially poor families is down from 13.2 million in 1959 to under 10 million in 1968. The problem is that poverty diminishes very slowly and unevenly. Among certain groups, as we have noted, it is even increasing—in particular among black central-city children. Finally, do not forget how low the official poverty line is: an income of $3,553 for an urban family of *four* in 1968. Estimates of the numbers of Americans who are "near-poor" (a family of four with less than $5,948) doubles the number of families in trouble. Just by way of reference, the Bureau of Labor Statistics estimated that the income needed for a "moderate" standard of living in 1968 for four persons was $9,600.

Then why do we not undertake a program to abolish poverty? The hope is that we will. The danger is that we will not. But that brings us to a consideration of issues of American society that we have promised to examine in our final chapter and that we should not go into yet. Suffice it to say that the cost of the most expensive income-support program is well within the range of transfer payments already in operation in many European nations. The challenge for the American economy is thus not to break new ground but only to catch up with what has already been done in more socially advanced market economies elsewhere.

The Problem of Power

We have discovered that much poverty in our society is a consequence of a lack of market power. Low productivity or the inability to work deprives one of economic power in a society where income accrues to successful marketers. Now, however, we must turn our attention to the other end of the power spectrum. What about the problems that result from being powerful? This is an issue into which we looked in Chapter 7 and again briefly in our study of monopoly and oligopoly. Now it is time to combine our historical and analytical findings.

In our formal study of microeconomics, the problem of power has been conspicuous largely by its absence. Why is this? The answer is that in *a*

CONSUMER SOVEREIGNTY

world of pure competition power tends to disappear.* The direction of society's activities becomes fragmented into the innumerable decision-making atoms of "the public," acting as consumers of products and as suppliers of services. In such a world, the public becomes the repository of most of the economic power that rules the marketplace. This diffusion of power is often called *consumer sovereignty,* and the ideal of consumer sovereignty is frequently cited as providing a basic rationale for the market system itself.

Does consumer sovereignty exist? In a diluted form, it certainly does. As we have seen in Chapter 27, even the most formidable corporations cannot brook the indifference of the consumer to the products they offer; and despite the fortunes spent on advertising, it is uncertain to what extent corporations can actually create or alter consumer demand. Yet few would claim that the ideal of a power-fragmented marketplace represents the reality of the marketplace in action today.† On the contrary, as our study of economic history has shown, the technological drive of modern society has given rise to large organizations in every aspect of economic life—in business, labor, and government—and with these huge organizations has come the unavoidable concomitant of mixed political, social, and economic power.

As a result, the market is no longer a field in which power disappears, but a setting in which business, labor, and the government establish bases of operation for the exercise of their power. Because the market itself is constantly changing, these bases shift, and power structures built on it are never wholly secure, as we see in the slow turnover of the corporate giants or the rise and fall of union strength in different industrial areas or in the shift of government power from one regulatory agency to another. In all cases, however, the market itself becomes a field to be organized, administered, regulated, and controlled, whether in the name of business, labor, or government, rather than a force before which all economic actors are wholly without defenses, as we picture them to be in the theory of pure competition.

POWER AND RESPONSIBILITY

What can be done about the fortresses of power that have emerged in modern capitalism? Is there a way of imposing public responsibility on the labor union, the government office, the big corporation? As we shall see, the question is exceedingly difficult. Let us discover this for ourselves by examin-

---

* Power is actually always present in the institutional framework that legitimates private property itself. Capitalism, like socialism or precapitalist societies, is ultimately a system of legitimated power. But formal economics does not discuss these institutions; it discusses their *consequences.* So-called radical economics is interested in bringing the institutions themselves back into the center of focus.

† Remember, however, that we had no basis for measuring the social losses caused by the self-serving exercise of market power until we had developed rigorously the ideal of the perfectly competitive market system.

ing four frequently encountered proposals for increasing the social responsibility of the giant corporation.

1. *Profit as social responsibility.*

The first suggestion is most prominently associated with the name of Professor Milton Friedman, whose views we have previously encountered in our study of inflation. Professor Friedman is a philosophic conservative whose response to the question of what a corporation should do to discharge its social responsibility is very simple: *make money.*

The function of a business organization in society, argues Friedman, is to serve as an efficient agent of production, not as a locus of social improvement. It serves that productive function best by striving after profit—conforming, while doing so, to the basic rules and ethical norms of society. It is not up to business to "do good"; it is up to government to prevent it from doing bad.

Moreover, as soon as a businessman tries to apply any rules other than money-making, he takes into his own hands powers that rightfully belong to other parts of society, such as its political authorities. Friedman would even forbid corporations to give money to charities or universities. Their business, their responsibility to society, he insists, is *production.* Let the dividend-receivers give away the money the corporations pay them, but do not let corporations become the active social welfare agencies of society.[3]

The counterarguments to Friedman's position are not difficult to frame. They are two:

1. Friedman assumes that stockholders have a superior moral claim to the earnings of the vast semimonopolies they "own" than do the consumers or workers from whose pockets these profits are plucked. This is at least a debatable point: since the stockholders are *not* active entrepreneurs, they make little or no contribution to the profits of the corporation. Why, then, should their claim exceed a reasonable compensation for the risk of their money?

2. Friedman assumes that the government, whose purpose is to set the rules and oversee the operations of business, acts *independently* of the corporations they regulate. But many studies show that the so-called regulatory agencies of the government usually act on *behalf of the big corporations* they "regulate," rather than on behalf of the consumer. For example, the Food

---

[3] Friedman, *Capitalism and Freedom,* Chap. 8. Professor Frank Knight, a distinguished predecessor of Friedman's at the University of Chicago, would agree with the proposal and carry it even further: force corporations, he urges, to pay out to stockholders *all* their earnings every year! That would deprive them of the market power that stems from the very large "retained earnings" they do not distribute as dividends. Under Knight's proposal, a corporation would be under constant economic scrutiny from its stockholders who would have to be persuaded to reinvest their earnings with the company if it were to grow.

and Drug Administration banned cyclamates as a dangerous food additive in 1969, *nineteen years* after the first warnings of their dangerous effects had been brought to its attention! In the long interim, it failed to act, largely because of its reluctance to incur the wrath (and political counterattack) of the industry it was supposedly "regulating."[4]

2. *The corporation as social arbiter.*

Quite a different approach to the problem of social responsibility has been widely espoused by many concerned corporate executives. This view recognizes that the corporation, by virtue of its immense size and strength, has power thrust upon it, whether it wishes to have it or not. The solution to this problem, as these men see it, is for corporate executives to act "professionally" as the arbiters of this power, doing their best to adjudicate equitably among the claims of the many constituencies to which they are responsible: labor, stockholders, customers, and the public at large. The executive of one of the largest enterprises in the nation said, two decades ago, "The manager is becoming a professional in the sense that like all professional men he has a responsibility to society as a whole."[5]

There is no doubt that many top corporate executives think of themselves as the referees among contending groups, and no doubt many of them use caution and forethought in exercising the power of decision. But the weaknesses of this argument are also not difficult to see. Unlike other professions, there are neither criteria for "qualifying" as a corporate executive nor penalties for failing to accept social responsibilities. The executive of a corporation who fails to act responsibly may incur the opprobrium of the public, but the public has no way of removing him from office or reducing his salary.

Nor is there any clear guideline, even for the most scrupulous executive, defining the manner in which he is *supposed* to exercise his responsibility. Is his concern for the prevention of pollution to take precedence over his concern for turning in a good profit statement at the end of the year or giving wage increases or reducing the price of his product? Is the contribution of "his" company to charity or education supposed to represent *his* preferences or those of his customers or workers? Has Xerox a right to help the cause of public broadcasting; Standard Oil of New Jersey, to help finance Harlem Academy (a private school aimed at assisting Harlem youths to go on to college); the makers of firearms, to help support the National Rifle Association?

[4] See James S. Turner, "The Chemical Feast," in *The Report on the Food and Drug Administration,* eds. Ralph Nader and Summer Study Group (New York: Grossman, 1970), pp. 5–30. See also John C. Esposito, "Vanishing Air," in *The Ralph Nader Study Group Report on Air Pollution* (New York: Grossman, 1970); and Grant McConnell, *Private Power and American Democracy* (New York: Knopf, 1966).

[5] R. W. Davenport and *Fortune* editors, *U.S.A.: The Permanent Revolution* (Englewood Cliffs, N.J.: Prentice-Hall, 1951), p. 79. (The executive is Frank Abrams of Standard Oil, N.J.)

These are questions to which there are no answers. But they begin to indicate the complexity of the issue of "social responsibility" and the problems implicit in allowing these extremely important *social* decisions to be made by private individuals who are in no way publicly accountable for their actions.

3. *Dissolution of monopoly.*

A third approach to the problem of responsibility takes yet another tack. It suggests that the power of big business be curbed dividing large corporations into several much smaller units. A number of studies have shown that the largest *plant* size needed for industrial efficiency is far smaller (in terms of financial assets) than the giant firms typical of the *Fortune* list of the top 500 industrial corporations (or for that matter of the next 500). Hence a number of economists have suggested that a very strict application of antitrust legislation should be applied, not only to prohibit mergers but to separate a huge enterprise such as General Motors into its natural constituent units: a Buick Company, an Oldsmobile Company, a Chevrolet Company, and so on.

One major problem stands in the way of this frontal attack on corporate power. It is that size and social responsibility are by no means clearly correlated. Perhaps we recall Professor Galbraith's wry remark (see p. 131) with regard to the fact that the largest firms are the very ones that *exemplify* certain kinds of social responsibility. The other side of that coin is that small competitive industry is typically beset by low research and development programs, antilabor practices, and a general absence of the kinds of amenities we associate with "big business."

Moreover, there is no reason to believe that smaller firms would be more pollution-conscious (indeed, owing to competitive pressures, they might be less inclined to minimize pollution) or that they would be more conscientious in advertising, racial nondiscrimination, and other practices. In other words, the loss of *political* power, which might well accompany the fractioning of the largest firms, is apt to be offset by a rise in certain forms of economic ruthlessness or even antisocial behavior.

Competition, it has been remarked more than once, is a social condition to which all parties in an enterprise economy pay homage, but which only economists take seriously. Business and labor both spend much of their energies trying to avoid competition or to minimize it, and the attempt to intensify competition by breaking up large firms into smaller ones might bring about worse problems than it alleviates.

4. *Nationalization.*

Then why not nationalize the large firms? The thought comes as rank heresy to a nation that has been accustomed to equating nationalization with socialism. Yet Germany, France, England, Sweden, Italy, and a host of other capitalistic nations have nationalized industries ranging from oil refineries to airlines, from automobile production to the output of coal and electricity. Hence, Professor Galbraith has suggested that we should nationalize the giant armaments producers who are wholly dependent on the Pentagon, in order to bring such firms under public control.

But would nationalization achieve its purpose of assuring social responsibility? We have seen the Pentagon prevent one of its "ward" companies, Lockheed Aircraft, from suffering the fate of an ordinary inefficient firm by rescuing it from bankruptcy with special contracts and "loans." Outright nationalization would only cement this union of political and economic power, by making Lockheed a part of the Pentagon and thus making it even more difficult to put pressure on it to perform responsibly.

Or take the Tennessee Valley Authority, perhaps the most famous American public enterprise: it is currently being sued for the environmental devastation it has wrought by its strip-mining operations. So, too, the Atomic Energy Commission, which operates "nationalized" plants, has been severely criticized for its careless supervision of radioactive processes, and the Post Office has been converted into a semi-autonomous agency, having proved a disaster as a "nationalized" industry.

The problem is that nationalization not only removes the affected enterprise *entirely* from the pressures of the market, but almost inevitably brings it under the political shelter of the government, which further removes the venture from any effective criticism. Experience in the socialist world (to which we will turn in Chapter 33) as well as in Europe, where a number of industries have been nationalized, suggests that nationalization may be a necessary step to rescue a sick industry, but that it is no guarantee of the good operation of a potentially healthy one.

REMAINING
POSSIBILITIES

All these difficulties make it clear that the problem of social responsibility will not be easy to solve (or for that matter, even to *define*), no matter what step we choose, from Professor Friedman's laissez faire to Galbraith's nationalization. And for each of these problems with regard to the corporation, we could easily construct counterparts that have to do with the control over labor unions or over the government itself.

What, then, is to be done? A number of lines of action suggest themselves. One is the widening of the *legal responsibility* of the corporation to include areas of responsibility for which it now has little or no accountability. Environmental damage is one of these; consumer protection is another. (The suits filed against the Chevron Oil Company for its oil spills and against the producers of the thalidomide sleeping pills are important first steps in this direction.) Ralph Nader has further suggested that a top corporate official be legally charged with seeing to it that his company complies with the law in full, and that the top officers of noncomplying companies be suspended, as is the case in certain violations of SEC regulations. He also strongly advocates the federal, rather than state, incorporation of big companies—a step that would greatly facilitate the establishment of tough national standards of corporate responsibility.

A second step would be a widening of *public accountability through disclosure*—the so-called fishbowl method of regulation. Corporations could be required to report to public agencies their expenditures for pollution control, for political lobbying, and so on. Corporate tax returns could be opened to public scrutiny. Unions and corporations both could be required to make public disclosure of their race practices, with regard to hiring or admission, advancement, and rates of pay. Public responsibility for advertising, with formal proofs submitted to back all claims, is yet another means of securing better accountability to the public.

Still another course of action would be to appoint *public members* to boards of directors of large companies or to executive organs of large unions and to charge these members with protecting the consumers' interest and with reporting behavior that seemed contrary to the public interest. Worker-members of boards of directors might also serve such a useful purpose (there are such members in Germany). The mobilization of the votes of concerned stockholders (nonprofit institutions own $26 billion of corporate securities) is still another way of bringing social pressure to bear.

Finally, there is the corrective action of dedicated private individuals such as Ralph Nader, who rose to fame on his exposé of the safety practices of the auto industry, and who has since turned his guns on pollution, and other irresponsibilities of big business, and on poor performance in the federal bureaucracy. Such public pressure is necessarily sporadic and usually short-lived, but it has been a powerful source of social change.

It would be a mistake to conclude this recital with the implication that corporate (or union or government) power can be easily brought under control through a few legal remedies or by the power of public opinion. Certainly, many abuses can be curbed, and much better levels of social performance achieved.

POWER: THE UNRESOLVED PROBLEM

But it is a sober fact that mass organizations seem an inescapable concomitant of our age of high technology and increasing social interdependence. The roots of this fact were discussed earlier, and its broader consequences will be seen later. Here we should note that, depending on our interests, we stress different aspects of this universal phenomenon. To some, who fear the continued growth of very large-scale business, the most significant aspect is that we have not managed to control business power. To others, concerned over the emergence of large labor unions, it is labor power that most dangerously eludes effective control. And to still others who are most worried by the growth of big government, it is the growth of public power that is the main problem.

What is common among these concerns is the awareness that very large, only half-controlled organizations have come to dominate much of the market system. But the problem is bigger than that. For if we look to the nonmarket systems, we see the growth of socialist ministries of production and administration that display much the same bureaucratic indifference and mixed political and economic power as do our corporations, unions, and government agencies, together with the same uncertainty about how to reconcile their power with their conception of the public good.

This is a problem that we will examine in Chapter 35. But there we will also see that the market system, for all its problems, has certain advantages that go a long way toward redressing the balance in historical perspective. For it must be clear, if we reflect back on our exploration of microeconomics, that the market system has huge strengths in bringing about the *efficient operation* of an economic society, and that these strengths may be more important *at certain stages of historical development* than the weaknesses into which we have been looking.

In other words, in a final appraisal of the market system—and of capitalist society that depends on a market mechanism—it is a historical perspective that we require more than any narrow calculus of pluses and minuses. Before we proceed to that last perspective, however, there is one more section of theoretical teaching that we must add. We cannot follow the larger trajectory of the market system until we have come to understand a whole chapter of economics that we have heretofore ignored: the relation of the American economy to the world about it. Hence, we turn next to a subject that will expand our focus from the problems of a self-contained economy to those of an economy forced to cope with the economic stresses of other economies. We must now learn something about the very important—though to most Americans very unfamiliar—subject of foreign trade. Having traced the rise of the market society and analyzed in some detail how its economic machinery works, we must extend our view to the operation of the market system among nations, and then trace the trajectory of that system as far into the future as we can see.

KEY CONCEPTS AND KEY WORDS

Poverty and productivity

1. Poverty has two aspects: the macroeconomic aspect of *the volume of total output (per capita)* and the microeconomic aspect of *how a given output is divided among the population.*

Income support programs

2. The market is the source of two kinds of poverty. First, the market distributes inadequate incomes to those whose productivity is low. *The market is not the cause of this low productivity, but the instrument by which low productivity is translated into low income.* Second, the market is also the cause of poverty for those who cannot make a contribution to output. In a market society, *transfer mechanisms must take care of those who cannot seek gainful employment.*

3. Because the bulk of American poverty consists of this second category of poverty, many economists today espouse *income support programs* to bring the income of nonearners up to some socially acceptable level. These plans generally take one of three forms: (1) negative income tax "refunds"; (2) children's allowances; (3) assistance to all families below some specified income line.
   The cost of these transfer schemes is generally below 4 percent of GNP, and this cost would be further reduced by the decrease in social costs imposed by poverty.

   Negative income tax

   Family assistance

4. Power is a difficult problem of modern society. A market system finds an important rationale in the idea of *consumer sovereignty,* in which power is fragmented into the households who constitute the sources of demand (and of factor supply). But it is clear that in modern society, huge units of business, labor, and government have greatly reduced, although not entirely eliminated, consumer sovereignty.

   Power

   Consumer sovereignty

5. A number of proposals have been advanced for assuring the responsible social conduct of large corporations. These include: (1) strict attention to *profit-making only;* (2) *"professional" standards* of conduct and self-conscious attention to social needs; (3) *break-up of big business;* and (4) *nationalization.*

   Corporate responsibility

6. Each of these proposals has its weaknesses. (1) The abdication of social responsibility by business assumes that stockholders have a "right" to profits and that government will in fact supervise, and not protect, big business. (2) The professionalization of corporate management ignores the absence of any professional standards for management and the essential arbitrariness of corporate decisions in the social area. (3) The breakup of big business assumes that smaller, more competitive business is also more socially responsible, which is doubtful; and (4) nationalization ignores the sorry record of many state-owned enterprises.

7. There remain as means of improving corporate (or union or government) performance the development of new *legal responsibilities* for business and labor, new areas of *public accountability, public representation* on executive boards, and the important power of *private investigation and publicity.*

8. The overall problem of power remains recalcitrant, not only in a market society but in all societies. This is a problem to which we will return in our subsequent investigation of the historical trajectory of the market system itself.

Q U E S T I O N S

1. What is the difference between poverty in India and in the United States? Which do you consider a macro problem, which a micro problem? Is your decision changed by the fact that the inequality of income is *greater* in India than in the U.S.?

2. Max Weber, a great sociologist, spoke of "life chances" as describing the different positions of different social classes. Do you think the "life chances" of a black child born in Harlem are significantly different from those of a white child born in Beverly Hills? Can you spell out exactly what those differences might be? How would you change life chances in Harlem?

3. A Ph.D. candidate, defending a dissertation on poverty, was asked what he thought was the single most important reason among the many causes that could be shown to "produce" poverty. After some thought he replied, "Lack of education." He was then asked what he thought was the single greatest cause of the lack of education among certain groups. After some more thought he replied, "Poverty." Was he saying that poverty was the cause of poverty? Was he right?

4. How would you go about estimating the social cost of poverty in the United States? How much of this cost do you think would disappear with the adoption of a significant anti-poverty program?

5. Which income-support program do you prefer? Why?

6. Do you consider yourself to be a "sovereign" consumer? Do you think you are influenced by advertising? If you could imagine a nonadvertising society, do you think you would change your life style?

7. Do you think businessmen should be more socially responsible? How would you go about achieving a higher level of social responsibility in the following areas: (1) truth in advertising, (2) absence of political interference with government, (3) colorblind hiring and promotion, (4) high levels of antipollution performance? What measures would you propose for numbers 2 and 3 with regard to labor unions? How would you bring government agencies to a higher level of social responsibility?

8. Do you think corporations have a right to back right-wing groups? Left-wing groups? Center-wing groups? Modern art? Old-fashioned art? Universities? Sports groups? Political parties? How do you justify your answers?

9. Do you think it would help to nationalize the big arms companies? Could you imagine a situation in which you would favor the nationalization of any company? How about the railroads, if they were about to go bankrupt and leave the nation stranded? How about GM if it defied a government regulation with regard to producing a pollution-free vehicle? How about a textile company that admitted to racial discrimination in its advancement policies?

10. What relation do you see between the growth of power in all areas of the society and the development of modern technology? Discuss with relation to the automobile, the airplane, nuclear power, the computer.

The economics

of international

gain and loss

Americans have had the fortune to be extraordinarily sheltered from the currents of international economics that wash against other shores. British students are brought up knowing about exports and imports because a quarter of their national income derives from foreign trade. A Canadian knows about international economics because one Canadian dollar in five is earned or spent beyond Canadian borders. Any educated person in the underdeveloped world will tell you that the future of his country is critically affected by the exports it sells to the developed world and the capital it brings in from that world. Only the United States, among the nations of the West, is generally unconcerned and uneducated about foreign trade, for the general opinion is that we are relatively self-sufficient and could, if we had to, let the rest of the world go hang.

Could we? It is true that only about 6 percent of our gross national product is sold overseas and only 4 or 5 percent of the value of GNP is bought overseas. Yet it is worth considering what would happen to our own economy if some mischance severed our ties with the rest of the world.

We would feel the impact first in highly selective, but all too noticeable, changes we would have to make in our diet. Coffee and tea, the very mainstays of civilized existence, would no longer be available. Chocolate, the favorite flavor of a hundred million Americans, would be unobtainable. There would be no bananas in the morning, no pepper at supper, no Scotch whiskey at night. Substitutes could be developed for some of these commodities, but judging from our experience in World War II, we might find that they do not taste very good.

More serious would be the loss of certain other products of the world. In the earlier years of the country, we were inclined to treat our natural resources as inexhaustible, but the astounding rate of our consumption of industrial raw materials has disabused us of that notion. Today the major fractions of our iron ore, our copper, and our wood products come to us from abroad. Ninety percent of the bauxite from which we make aluminum is imported. Ninety-four percent of the manganese needed for high-tempered steels, all our chrome, virtually all our cobalt, the great bulk of our nickel, tin, platinum, asbestos is foreign-bought. Many of these metals are so strategically important that we stockpile them against temporary disruption, but in a few years the stockpiles would be used up and we should be forced radically to change some of our technology.

Then there would be other losses, less statistically impressive but no less irksome to consumers and industry: the loss of Japanese cameras, of British tweeds, of French perfume, of Italian movies, of Rolls Royce engines, Volkswagen cars, Danish silver, Indian jute and madras. Clearly, shutting down the flow of the imports into America, however relatively self-sufficient we may be, would deal us a considerable blow. One can imagine what it would mean in the case of, say, Holland, where foreign products account for as much as 45 percent of all goods sold in that country.

But we have still not fully investigated the effects of international trade on the United States, for we have failed to consider the impact of a collapse of our exports. The farm country would feel such a collapse immediately of course, for a fifth of our cotton, almost a quarter of our grains, and more than a quarter of our tobacco go overseas. Mining country would feel it because a fifth of our coal and a third of our sulphur are sold abroad. Manufacturing enterprises in cities scattered all over the nation would feel the blow, as a seventh of our auto production, a quarter of our metalworking machinery and of our textile machinery, a third of our construction and mining machinery could no longer be sold overseas—not to speak of another thirty to forty industries in which at least a fifth of output is regularly sold to foreign buyers. In all, some three to four million jobs, three-quarters of them in manufacturing or commerce, would cease to exist if our foreign markets should suddenly disappear.

Now to be sure, many of those jobs would be replaced by new industries that would be encouraged if our overseas markets and sources of supply vanished. If we could not buy watches or watch parts in Switzerland, we would make more of them here. If we could not sell automobiles to the world, we would no doubt try to use our unemployed skills to make some product or service that could be marketed at home—perhaps one of the items we no longer imported. With considerable effort (especially in the case of strategic materials) we *could* readjust. Hence the question: Why don't we? What is the purpose of international trade? Why do we not seek to improve our relative self-sufficiency by making it complete?

THIRTY

No sooner do we ask the question of the aims of international trade than we encounter an obstacle that will present the single greatest difficulty in learning about international economies. This is the bias of nationalism—the curious fact that relationships and propositions that are perfectly self-evident in the context of "ordinary" economics suddenly appear suspect, not to say downright wrong, in the context of international economics.

For example, suppose that the governor of an eastern state—let us say New Jersey—wanted to raise the incomes of his constituents and decided that the best way to do so was to encourage some new industry to move there. Suppose furthermore that his wife was very fond of grapefruit and suggested to him one morning that grapefruit growing would be an excellent addition to New Jersey's products.

The governor might object that grapefruit needed a milder climate than New Jersey had to offer. "That's no problem," his wife might answer. "We could protect our grapefruit by growing them in hothouses. That way, in addition to the income from the crop, we would benefit the state from the incomes earned by the glaziers and electricians who would be needed."

The governor might murmur something about hothouse grapefruit costing more than ordinary grapefruit, so that New Jersey could not sell its crop on the competitive market. "Nonsense," his wife would reply. "We can subsidize the grapefruit growers out of the proceeds of a general sales tax. Or we could pass a law requiring restaurants in this state to serve state grapefruit only. Or you could bar out-of-state grapefruit from New Jersey entirely."

"Now, my dear," the governor would return, "in the first place, that's unconstitutional. Second, even if it weren't, we would be making people in this state give up part of their incomes through the sales tax to benefit farmers, and that would never be politically acceptable. And third, the whole scheme is so inefficient it's just downright ridiculous."

But if we now shift our attention to a similar scene played between the prime minister of Nova Jersia and his wife, we find some interesting differences. Like her counterpart in New Jersey, the wife of the prime minister recommends the growing of hothouse grapefruit in Nova Jersia's chilly climate. Admittedly, that would make the crop considerably dearer than that for sale on the international markets. "But that's all right," she tells her husband. "We can put a tariff on foreign grapefruit, so none of the cheap fruit from abroad will be able to undersell ours."

"My dear," says the prime minister after carefully considering the matter, "I think you are right. It is true that grapefruit in Nova Jersia will be more expensive as a result of the tariff, but there is no doubt that a tariff looks like a tax on them and not on us, and therefore no one will object to it. It is also true that our hothouse grapefruit may not taste as good as theirs, but we will have the immense satisfaction of eating our *own* grapefruit, which will make it taste better. Finally, there may be a few economists who will tell us that this is not the most efficient use of our resources, but I can tell them that the money we pay for hothouse grapefruit—even if it is a little more than it would be otherwise—stays in our own pockets and doesn't go to enrich foreigners. In addition to which, I would point out in my television appearances that the reason foreign grapefruit are so cheap is that foreign labor is so badly paid. We certainly don't want to drag down the price of our labor by making it compete with the cheap labor of other nations. All in all, hothouse grapefruit seems to me an eminently sensible proposal, and one that is certain to be politically popular."

Is it a sensible proposal? Of course not, although it will take some careful thinking to expose all of its fallacies. Will it be politically popular? It may very well be, for economic policies that would be laughed out of court at home get a serious hearing when they crop up in the international arena. Here are some of the things that most of us tend to believe:

SOURCE OF THE DIFFICULTY

Trade between two nations usually harms one side or the other.

Rich countries can't compete with poor countries.

Cheap foreign labor is a threat to a prosperous nation.

There is always the danger that a country may sell, but refuse to buy.

Are these fears true? One way of testing their validity is to see how they ring in our ears when we rid them of our unconscious national bias by recasting them as propositions in ordinary economics:

Is it true that trade between businesses or persons usually harms one side or the other?

Is it true that rich companies can't compete with poor ones?

Is it true that cheap labor is a threat to a successful firm?

Is it true that one company might only sell, but never buy—not even the services of factors of production?

What is the source of this curious prejudice against international trade? It is not, as we might think, an excess of patriotism that leads us to recommend courses of action that will help our own country, regardless of the effect on others. For, curiously, the policies of the economic superpatriot, if put into practice, would demonstrably injure the economic interests of his own land. The trouble, then, springs from a root deeper than mere national interest. It lies in the peculiarly deceptive problems posed by international trade. What is deceptive about them, however, is not that they involve principles that apply only to relations between nations. *All the economic arguments that elucidate international trade apply equally well to domestic trade.* The deception arises, rather, for two reasons:

1. International trade requires an understanding of how two countries, each dealing

in its own currency, manage to buy and sell from each other in a world in which there is no such thing as international money.

2. International trade requires a very thorough understanding of the advantages of and arguments for trade itself.

Gains from Trade

In a general way, of course, we are all aware of the importance of trade, although we have hardly mentioned it since the opening pages of our book. *It is trade that makes possible the division and specialization of labor on which our productivity is so largely based.* If we could not exchange the products of our specialized labor, each of us would have to be wholly self-supporting, and our standard of living would thereupon fall to that of subsistence farmers. Thus trade (international or domestic) is actually a means of *increasing productivity,* quite as much as investment or technological progress.

GAINS FROM SPECIALIZATION   The importance of trade in making possible specialization is so great that we should take a moment to make it crystal clear. Let us consider two towns, each of which produces two goods, wool and cotton; but Wooltown has good grazing lands and poor growing lands, while Cottontown's grazing is poor but growing is good. Suppose, moreover, that the two towns had equal populations and that each town employed half its people in cotton and half in wool. The results might look like Table 30-1.

TABLE 30 • 1

	Wooltown	Cottontown
Wool production (lbs)	5,000	2,000
Cotton production (lbs)	10,000	20,000

As we can see, the same number of grazers in Wooltown turn out two-and-one-half times as much wool as they do in Cottontown, whereas the same number of cotton farmers in Cottontown produce double the amount of cotton that they do in Wooltown. One does not have to be an economist to see that both towns are losing by this arrangement. If Cottontown would shift its woolworkers into cotton, and Wooltown would shift its cotton farmers into wool, the output of the two towns would look like Table 30-2 (assuming constant returns to scale).

TABLE 30 • 2

	Wooltown	Cottontown
Wool output	10,000	0
Cotton output	0	40,000

Now, if we compare total production of the two towns (see Table 30-3) we can see the gains from specialization.

TABLE 30 • 3

	TWO TOWNS' PRODUCTION		
	Mixed	Specialized	Gain from specialization
Wool output	7,000	10,000	3,000
Cotton output	30,000	40,000	10,000

In other words, specialization followed by trade makes it possible for both towns to have more of both commodities than before. No matter how the gains from trade are distributed—and this will depend on many factors, such as the relative elasticities of demand for the two products—both towns will gain, even if one gains more than the other.

If all the world were divided into nations, like Wooltown and Cottontown, each producing for trade only a single item in which it has a clear advantage over all others, international trade would be a simple matter to understand. It would still present problems of international payment, and it might still inspire its prime ministers of Nova Jersias to forego the gains from trade for political reasons that we will examine at the end of this chapter. But the essential rationale of trade would be simple to understand.

Unfortunately for the economics student as well as for the world at large, this is not the way international resources are distributed. Instead of giving each nation at least one commodity in which it has a clear advantage, many nations do not have such an advantage in a single product. How can trade possibly take place under such inauspicious circumstances?

To unravel the mystery, let us turn again to Cottontown and Wooltown, but this time call them Supraville and Infraville, to designate an important change in their respective abilities. Although both towns still enjoy equal populations, which are again divided equally between cotton and wool production, in this example Supraville is a more efficient producer than Infraville in *both* cotton and wool, as Table 30-4 shows.

TABLE 30 • 4

	Supraville	Infraville
Wool output	5,000	3,000
Cotton production	20,000	10,000

Is it possible for trade to benefit these two towns when one of them is so manifestly superior to the other in every product? It would seem out of the question. But let us nonetheless test the case by supposing that each town began to specialize.

But how to decide which trade each town should follow? A look at Fig. 30-1 may give us a clue. The production-possibility diagrams are familiar to us from Chapter 21, where we used them to clarify the nature of scarcity and economic choice. Here we put them to use to let us see the results of trade.

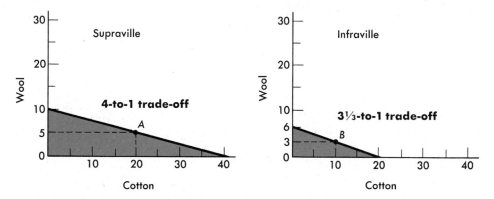

FIG. 30·1 PRODUCTION POSSIBILITIES IN THE TWO TOWNS BEFORE TRADE

What do the diagrams show? First, they establish the limits that each town could produce if it devoted all its efforts to one product. Since we have assumed that the labor force is divided, this means that each town could double the amount of cotton or wool it enjoys when it divides its workers fifty-fifty. Next, a line between these points shows the production frontier that both towns face.* We see that Supraville is located at point *A* where it has 5,000 lbs of wool and 20,000 lbs of cotton, and that Infraville is at *B*, where it has 3,000 lbs of wool and 10,000 lbs of cotton.

But the diagrams (and the figures in the preceding table, on which they are based) also show us something else. It is that each town has a different "trade-off" relationship between its two branches of production. When either town specializes in one branch, it must, of course, give up the output of the other. *But each town swaps one kind of output for the other in different proportions,* as the differing slopes of the two *p-p* curves show. Supraville, for example, can make only an extra pound of wool by giving up 4 pounds of cotton. That is, it gets its maximum potential output of 10,000 lbs of wool only by surrendering 40,000 lbs of cotton. Infraville can reach its production maximum of 6,000 lbs of wool at a loss of only 20,000 lbs of cotton. *Rather than having to give up 4 lbs of cotton to get one of wool, it gives up only 3.3 lbs.* Thus, in terms of how much cotton it must surrender, wool is actually cheaper in Infraville than in Supraville!

_____

* Why are these lines drawn straight, not bowed as in Chapter 21? As we know, the bowing reflects the law of increasing cost, which makes the gains from a shift in resource allocation less and less favorable as we move from one extreme of allocation to another. Here we ignore this complication for simplicity of exposition. We have also ignored the problem of diminishing returns when we assumed that each town could double its output of cotton or wool by doubling its labor force.

Not so the other way round, of course. As we would expect, cotton costs Supraville less in terms of wool than it costs Infraville. In Supraville, we get 40,000 lbs of cotton by relinquishing only 10,000 lbs of wool—a loss of a quarter of a pound of wool for a pound of the other. In Infraville, we can get the maximum output of 20,000 lbs of cotton only by a surrender of 6,000 lbs of wool—a loss of $\frac{1}{3}$ lb of wool rather than $\frac{1}{4}$ lb of wool for each unit of cotton.

COMPARATIVE
ADVANTAGE

Perhaps the light is beginning to dawn. Despite the fact that Supraville is more productive in terms of output per man than Infraville in both cotton and wool, it is *relatively* more productive in cotton than in wool. And despite the fact that Infraville is absolutely less productive, man for man, in both cotton and wool than Supraville, it is *relatively* more productive in wool. To repeat, it requires a smaller sacrifice of wool to get another pound of cotton in Infraville than in Supraville.

We call this kind of relative superiority *comparative advantage*. It is a concept that is often difficult to grasp at first but that is central to the reason for trade itself. When we speak of *comparative* advantage, we mean, as in the case of Supraville, that among *various* advantages of one producer or locale over another, there is one that is better than any other. *Comparatively* speaking, this is where its optimal returns lie. But just because it must abandon some lesser opportunity, its trading partner can now advantageously devote itself in that direction, where its comparative disadvantage is least.

This is a relationship of logic, not economics. Take the example of the banker who is also the best carpenter in town. Will it pay him to build his own house? Clearly it will not, for he will make more money by devoting all his hours to banking, even though he then has to employ and pay for a carpenter less skillful than himself. True, he could save that expense by building his own house. But he would then have to give up the much more lucrative hours he could be spending at the bank!

Now let us return to the matter of trade. We have seen that wool is *relatively* cheaper in Infraville, where each additional pound cost only 3.3 lbs of cotton, rather than 4 lbs as in Supraville; and that cotton is *relatively* cheaper in Supraville, where an additional pound costs but $\frac{1}{4}$ lb of wool, instead of $\frac{1}{3}$ lb across the way in Infraville. Now let us suppose that each side begins to specialize in the trade in which it has the comparative advantage. Suppose that Supraville took half its labor force now in wool and put it into cotton. Its output would change as in Table 30-5.

	Before the shift	After the shift
Wool production	5,000	2,500
Cotton production	20,000	30,000

TABLE 30 • 5

SUPRAVILLE

Supraville has lost 2,500 lbs of wool but gained 10,000 lbs of cotton. Now let us see if it can trade its cotton for Infraville's wool. In Infraville, where productivity is so much less, the entire labor force has shifted to wool output, where its greatly inferior productivity can be put to best use. Hence its production pattern now looks like Table 30-6.

TABLE 30•6

INFRAVILLE

	Before the shift	After the shift
Wool	3,000	6,000
Cotton	10,000	—

Infraville finds itself lacking 10,000 lbs of cotton, but it has 3,000 *additional* lbs of wool. Clearly, it can acquire the 10,000 lbs of cotton it needs from Supraville by giving Supraville *more* than the 2,500 lbs of wool it seeks. As a result, both Infraville and Supraville will have the same cotton consumption as before, but there will a surplus of 500 lbs of wool to be shared between them. As Fig. 30-2 shows, *both towns will have gained by the exchange, for both will have moved beyond their former production frontiers* (from *A* to *A'* and from *B* to *B'*).

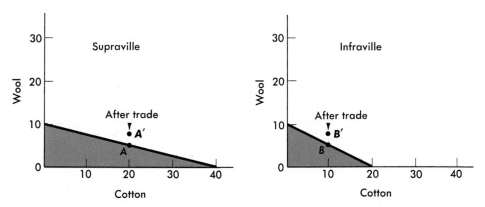

FIG. 30•2 PRODUCTION POSSIBILITIES IN THE TWO TOWNS AFTER TRADE

This last point is the crucial one. If we remember the nature of production-possibility curves from our discussion of them in Chapter 21, any point lying outside the production frontier is simply unattainable by that society. In Fig. 30-2, points *A* and *B* do lie beyond the pre-trade *p-p* curves of the two towns, and yet trade has made it possible for both communities to enjoy what was formerly impossible.

OPPORTUNITY COST

Comparative advantage gives us an important insight into all exchange relationships, for it reveals again a fundamental economic truth that we have mentioned more than once before. It is that *cost, in economics, means opportunities that must be foregone.* The real cost of wool in Supraville is the cotton that cannot be made because men are engaged in wool production, just as the real cost of cotton is the wool that must be gone without. In fact, we can see that the basic reason for comparative advantage lies in the fact that opportunity costs vary, so that it "pays" (it costs less) for different parties to engage in different activities.

If opportunity costs for two producers are the same, then it follows that there cannot be any comparative advantage for either; and if there is no comparative advantage, there is nothing to be gained by specializing or trading. Suppose Supraville has a two-to-one edge over Infraville in *both* cotton and wool. Then, if either town specializes, neither will gain. Supraville may still gain 10,000 lbs of cotton for 2,500 lbs of wool, as before, but Infraville will gain only 2,500 lbs of wool (not 3,000) from its shift away from cotton. Thus, the key to trade lies in the existence of *different* opportunity costs.

Are opportunity costs usually different from country to country or from region to region? For most commodities they are. As we move from one part of the world to another—sometimes even short distances—climate, resources, skills, transportation costs, capital scarcity, or abundance all change; and as they change, so do opportunity costs. That is why trade is more likely to occur between dissimilar producers than between similar ones. There is every possibility for rich countries to trade with poor ones, precisely because their opportunity costs are certain to differ.

But we have not yet fully understood one last important aspect of trade—the *prices* at which goods will exchange. Suppose that Supraville and Infraville do specialize, each in the product in which it enjoys a comparative advantage. Does that mean they can swap their goods at any prices?

A quick series of calculations reveals otherwise. We remember that Supraville needed at least 2,500 lbs of wool for which it was going to offer some of its extra production of cotton in exchange. But how much? What price should it offer for its needed wool, in terms of cotton?

Suppose it offered 7,500 lbs of cotton. Would Infraville sell the wool? No, it would not. At home it can make its own 7,500 lbs of cotton at a "cost" of only 2,273 lbs of wool, for we recall that Infraville traded off one pound of wool for 3.3 lbs of cotton (7,500 ÷ 3.3 = 2,273).

Suppose, then, that Infraville counter-offered to sell Supraville 2,500 lbs of wool for a price of 12,000 lbs of cotton. Would Supraville accept? Of course not. This would mean the equivalent of 4.8 lbs of cotton for a pound of wool. Supraville can do better than that by growing her own wool at her own trade-off ratio of only 4 lbs to one.

We begin to see, in other words, that the price of wool must lie between the trade-off ratios of Infraville and Supraville. Infraville wants to import cotton. If it did not trade with Supraville, it could make its own cotton at the cost of one pound of wool for every 3.3 lbs of cotton. Hence, for trade to be advantageous, Infraville seeks to get *more* cotton than that, per pound of wool.

Supraville is in the opposite situation. It seeks to export cotton and to import wool. It could make its own wool at the sacrifice of 4 lbs of cotton per pound of wool. Thus it seeks to gain wool for a *lower* price than that, in terms of cotton. Clearly, any ratio between 3.3 and 4.0 lbs of cotton per pound of wool will profit both sides.

THE ROLE OF PRICES

Let us put this into ordinary price terms. Suppose that cotton sells for 30¢ per pound. Then wool would have to sell between 99¢ and $1.20 (30¢ × 3.3 and × 4) to make trade worthwhile.* Let us say that supply and demand established a price of $1.10 for wool. Supraville can then sell its 10,000 lbs of extra cotton production at 30¢, which will net it $3,000. How much wool can it buy for this sum? At the going price of $1.10 per lb, 2,727 lbs. Therefore Supraville will end up with the same amount of cotton (20,000 lbs) as it had before specialization and trade, and with 227 *more* lbs of wool than before (2,500 lbs produced at home plus 2,727 lbs imported from Infraville—a total of 5,227 lbs). It has gained by trade an amount equal to the price of this extra wool, or $249.70.

How has Infraville fared? It has 3,273 lbs of wool left after exporting 2,727 lbs to Supraville from its production of 6,000 lbs, and it also has 10,000 lbs of cotton which it imported from Supraville in exchange for its wool exports. Thus it, too, has a gain from trade—the 273 lbs of wool (worth $300.30) over the amount of 3,000 lbs that it would have produced without specialization and trade.† In brief, *both* sides have profited from the exchange.

The Case for Free Trade

Would the prime minister of Nova Jersia be convinced by these arguments? Would his wife? They might be weakened in their support for hothouse

---

* Needless to say, these prices are used for illustrative purposes only.

† Gains need not be distributed so evenly between the trading partners. If the price of wool had been $1.00, trade still would have been worthwhile, but Supraville would have gained almost all of it. Had the price of wool been $1.19, both sides again would have come out ahead, but now Infraville would have been the larger beneficiary by far. The actual price at which wool would sell would be determined by the supply and demand schedule for it in both communities.

grapefruit, but some arguments would still linger in their minds. Let us consider them.

1. *"Our workers cannot compete with low-wage workers overseas."*

This is an argument one hears not only in Nova Jersia but also in the United States where the competition of sweatshop labor in Hong Kong is often cited at tariff hearings. And indeed, labor in Hong Kong is paid only a fifth of what it is paid here. Will not American labor be seriously injured if we import goods made under these conditions?

There is, of course, no doubt that an American textile worker who loses his job because of low-priced imports *will* be hurt. We shall come back to him later. But note that he would also be hurt if he lost his job because of regular domestic competition. Why do we feel so threatened when that competition comes from abroad?

Because, the answer goes, foreign competition isn't based on American efficiency. It is based on exploited labor. Hence it pulls down the standards of American labor to its own low level.

There is an easy reply to this argument. The reason Hong Kong textile labor is paid so much less than American textile labor is that the *average* wage in Hong Kong is so much lower than the *average* wage in America. Why is that? Because productivity in Hong Kong industry is so much lower than that in American industry. Thus *it is not the low wage of the Hong Kong tailor that makes it difficult for the American garment worker to compete, but the high wage of American workers in other more efficient American industries.*

To put it differently, the reason that American wages are high is that we use our workers in industries where their productivity is very high. If Hong Kong, with its very low productivity can undersell us in textiles, then this is a clear signal that we must move our factors of production out of textiles into other areas where their contribution will be greater; for example, in the production of machinery. It is no coincidence that machinery—one of the highest wage industries in America—is one of our leading exports, or that more than 75 percent of our manufactured exports are produced by industries in which the hourly wage rates are above the national average for all manufacturing industries. In fact, all nations tend to export the goods in which their local wages are highest, not lowest! Why? Because those are the industries in which their labor is most effectively employed.

This fact opens our eyes to another. Why is it that the American garment industry is worried about competition from Hong Kong, but not the American auto industry or the electrical machinery industry or the farm equipment industry? After all, the manufacturers of those products would also avail themselves of low wages in Hong Kong.

The answer is that American manufacturers can make these products at much lower cost in America. Why? Because capital is much more abundant in America than in Hong Kong, and capital is needed in large amounts for these manufacturers. Thus, if Hong Kong has a comparative advantage over us in the garment trade, we have a comparative advantage over her in many other areas.*

But suppose Hong Kong accumulated large amounts of capital and became a center for the manufacture of heavy equipment, so that it sold *both* garments and electrical generators more cheaply than we. We are back to Supraville and Infraville. There would still be a *comparative* advantage in one or more of these products in which we would be wise to specialize, afterward trading with Hong Kong for our supplies of the other good.

2. *"Tariffs are painless taxes because they are borne by foreigners."*

This is a convincing-sounding argument advanced by the prime minister of Nova Jersia (and by some other prime ministers in their time). But is it true? Let us take the case of hothouse grapefruit which can be produced in Nova Jersia only at a cost of fifty cents each, whereas foreign grapefruit (no doubt produced by sweated labor) can be unloaded at its ports at twenty-five cents. To prevent his home industry from being destroyed, the prime minister imposes a tariff of twenty-five cents on each grapefruit—which, he tells the newspapers, will be entirely paid by foreigners.

This is not, however, the way his political opponent (who has had a course in economics) sees it. "Without the tariff," he tells his constituency, "you could buy grapefruit for twenty-five cents. Now you have to pay fifty cents for it. Who is paying the extra twenty-five cents—the foreign grower, or you? Even if not a single grapefruit entered the country, you would still be paying twenty-five cents more than you have to. In fact, *you are being asked to subsidize an inefficient domestic industry.* Not only that, but the tariff wall means they won't ever become efficient because there is no pressure of competition on them."

Whether or not our economic candidate will win the electoral battle, he surely has the better of the argument. Or does he? For the prime minister, stung by these unkind remarks, replies:

3. *"But at least the tariff keeps spending power at home. Our own grapefruit growers, not foreigners, have our money."*

In our next chapter we will look into the soundness of this argument. There we will see that the money we pay to foreigners does not leave the country, but ends up in bank accounts in our own banks. A number of things can then happen to these foreign-owned bank accounts, as we shall see, but the single largest use of them must be obvious. Foreigners use them to buy goods from us.

---

* Newspapers in Southeast Asia carry editorials seeking protection from American imports because, they say, we do not use labor in our production and it is unfair to ask their citizens to compete with our machines that do not have to be paid wages.

Then there is a second very important consideration. When tariffs prevent inexpensive foreign goods from entering a country, they are depriving the efficient industries of that country from receiving their full share of consumer spending. If American consumers are prevented by tariff from buying inexpensive suits from Hong Kong, they will have to spend more money for suits (whether bought from high-cost American producers or from Hong Kong makers who have paid the tariff), and *they will therefore have that much less left over to spend for efficiently produced American products that do not need tariff protection.*

Are there no arguments at all for tariffs? As we shall see, there are some important cases in which tariffs make sense—or can at least be justified rationally. But the basic case stands. Economists have always advocated the widest and freest possible trade—not for doctrinaire reasons, but because *trade makes possible maximum production.* Free trade must be considered a means of increasing GNP, not essentially different from technological improvement in its effect on output and growth.

Then, why is the case for free trade so difficult to present when industries are threatened? Again our national bias beclouds our judgment. It was never more charmingly or effectively presented than in this argument by Frédéric Bastiat, a delightful exponent of mid-nineteenth-century classical economic ideals, in a little book entitled *Social Fallacies.*[1]

In Bastiat's book, Robinson Crusoe inhabits an island with Friday. In the morning, Crusoe and Friday hunt for six hours and bring home four baskets of game. In the evening they garden for six hours and get four baskets of vegetables. But now let Bastiat take over:

One day a canoe touched at the island. A good-looking foreigner landed, and was admitted to the table of our two recluses. He tasted and commended very much the produce of the garden, and before taking leave of his entertainers, spoke as follows: "Generous islanders, I inhabit a country where game is much more plentiful than here, but where horticulture is quite unknown. It would be an easy matter to bring you every evening four baskets of game, if you will give me in exchange two baskets of vegetables."

At these words Robinson and Friday retired to consult, and the debate that took place is too interesting not be be reported in extenso.

FRIDAY: What do you think of it?
ROBINSON: If we close with the proposal, we are ruined.
FRIDAY: Are you sure of that? Let us consider.
ROBINSON: The case is clear. Crushed by competition, our hunting as a branch of industry is annihilated.
FRIDAY: What matters it, if we have the game?

[1] Translated by Frederick James Sterling (Santa Ana, Calif.: Register Publishing, 1944), p. 203f.

ROBINSON: Theory! It will no longer be the product of our labour.

FRIDAY: I beg your pardon sir; for in order to have game we must part with vegetables.

ROBINSON: Then, what shall we gain?

FRIDAY: The four baskets of game cost us six hours' work. The foreigner gives us them in exchange for two baskets of vegetables, which cost us only three hours' work. This places three hours at our disposal. . . .

ROBINSON: You lose yourself in generalities! What should we make of these three hours?

FRIDAY: We would do something else.

ROBINSON: Ah! I understand you. You cannot come to particulars. Something else, something else—that is easily said.

FRIDAY: We can fish, we can ornament our cottage, we can read the Bible.

ROBINSON: Utopia! Is there any certainty we should do either the one or the other? . . . . Moreover there are political reasons for rejecting the interested offers of the perfidious foreigner.

FRIDAY: Political reasons!

ROBINSON: Yes, he only makes us these offers because they are advantageous to him.

FRIDAY: So much the better, since they are for our advantage likewise. . . .

ROBINSON: Suppose the foreigner learns to cultivate a garden and that his island should prove more fertile than ours. Do you see the consequences?

FRIDAY: Yes; our relations with the foreigner would cease. He would take from us no more vegetables, since he could have them at home with less labour. He would bring us no more game, since we should have nothing to give him in exchange, and we should then be in precisely the situation that you wish us in now. . . .

The debate was prolonged, and, as often happens, each remained wedded to his own opinion. But Robinson possessing a great influence over Friday, his opinion prevailed, and when the foreigner arrived to demand a reply, Robinson said to him: "Stranger, in order to induce us to accept your proposal, we must be assured of two things: the first is, that your island is no better stocked with game than ours, for we want to fight only with equal weapons. The second is, that you will lose by the bargain. For, as in every exchange there is necessarily a gaining and a losing party, we should be dupes, if you were not the loser. What have you got to say?"

"Nothing," replied the foreigner; and, bursting out laughing, he regained his canoe.

The Case for Tariffs

Is Crusoe as much of a fool as he appears? Not quite, although his arguments are poorly taken, and Bastiat had little trouble in demolishing them. But in fact Crusoe is groping with ideas that are very important in weighing the gains from trade—interregional as well as international.

MOBILITY   *The first concerns the problem of mobility.* Explicit in Bastiat's case is the ease with which Crusoe and Friday move back and forth between hunting and gardening. Implicit in the case of Supraville and Infraville is the possibility of shifting men and resources from cotton to wool production. But in fact it is sometimes exceedingly difficult to move resources from one industry to another.

Thus when Hong Kong textiles press hard against the garment worker in New York, it is scant comfort to him to point to the higher wages in the auto factories in Detroit. He has a lifetime of skills and a long established home in New York, and he does not want to move to another city where he will be a stranger, and to a new trade in which he would be only an unskilled beginner. He certainly does not want to move to Hong Kong! Hence, the impact of foreign trade often brings serious dislocations that result in persistent local unemployment, rather than in a flow of resources from a relatively disadvantaged to a relatively advantaged one. If Crusoe had suggested that it was very difficult (perhaps because of the noonday sun) to work in the gardens in the morning when they usually went hunting, Friday would have been harder pressed for a reply.

There is, it should be noted, an answer to this argument—an answer, at any rate, that applies to industrial nations. It is that a government intent on increasing its national productivity should itself bear the costs of relocation and retraining, rather than asking the worker or businessman to shoulder them himself. To the extent that we assist factors in making a transition from a less to a more effective use, we incur a one-time cost in exchange for a lasting benefit. (Incidentally, this argument applies equally well to dislocations originating in domestic adjustments.)

Second, *the argument for free trade rests on the very important assumption that there will be substantially full employment.*

In the days of the mid-nineteenth century when the free trade argument was first fully formulated, the idea of an underemployment equilibrium would have been considered absurd. When Crusoe asks what use they should make of their free time, Friday has no trouble replying that they should work or enjoy their leisure. But in a highly interdependent society, work may not be available, and leisure may be only a pseudonym for an inability to find work. In an economy of large enterprises and "sticky" wages and prices, we know that unemployment is a real and continuous object of concern for national policy.

Thus, it makes little sense to advocate policies to expand production via trade unless we are certain that the level of aggregate demand will be large enough to absorb that production. *Full employment policy therefore becomes an indispensable arm of trade policy.* Trade gives us the potential for maximizing production, but there is no point in laying the groundwork for the highest possible output, unless fiscal and monetary policy are also geared to bringing about a level of aggregate demand large enough to support that output.

Last, *there is the argument of nationalism pure and simple.* This argument does not impute spurious economic gains to tariffs. Rather it says that free trade undoubtedly encourages production, but it does so at a certain cost. This is the cost of the vulnerability that comes from extensive and extreme specialization. This vulnerability is all very well within a nation where we assume that law and order will prevail, but it cannot be so easily justified among nations where the realistic assumption is just the other way. Tariffs, in other words, are defensible because they enable nations to attain a certain *self-sufficiency*—admittedly at some economic cost.

When Crusoe made the argument on his island economy, Friday properly scoffed. But the argument is much more valid for an economy of complex industrial processes and specialized know-how that cannot be quickly duplicated if trade is disrupted. In a world in which the threat of war is always present, self-sufficiency has a value that may properly override considerations of ideal economic efficiency. The problem is to hold the arguments for "national defense" down to proper proportions. When tariffs are periodically adjusted in international conferences, an astonishing variety of industries (in all countries) find it possible to claim protection from foreign competition in the name of national "indispensability."

Equally interesting is the nationalist argument for tariffs advanced by so-called "infant" industries, particularly in developing nations. These newly-formed or prospective enterprises claim that they cannot possibly compete with the giants in developed countries while they are small; but that if they are protected by a tariff, they will in time become large and efficient enough no longer to need a tariff. In addition, they claim, they will provide a more diversified spectrum of employments for their own people, as well as aiding in the national transition toward a more modern economy.

The argument is a valid one, if it is applied to industries that have a fair chance of achieving a comparative advantage once grown up (otherwise one will be supporting them in infancy, maturity, and senility).* Certainly it is an argument that was propounded by the youthful industries of the United States in the early nineteenth century, and that was sufficiently persuasive to bring them a moderate degree of protection (although it is inconclusive as to how much their growth was ultimately dependent on tariff help). And it is being listened to today by the underdeveloped nations who feel that their only chance of escaping from poverty is to develop a nucleus of industrial employments at almost any cost.

---

* If every industry must have a comparative advantage in one country or another, how can there be steel industries (or any other) in more than one country? The answer, quite aside from considerations of nationalism, lies in *transportation costs* which compensate for lower production costs in many products and thereby allow a relatively inefficient industry to supply a home market.

Thus there are arguments for tariffs, or at least rational counterarguments against an extreme free trade position. Workers *are* hurt by international competition; and in the default of proper domestic plans for cushioning these blows, modest tariffs can buffer the pains of redeployment. Free trade *does* require a level of high employment; and when unemployment is already a national problem, tariffs may protect additional workers from losing their jobs. Strategic industries and development-stimulating industries *are* sometimes essential and may require protection from world competition. All these arguments are but qualifications to the basic proposition on which the economist rests his case for the freest *possible* trade, but they help to define "possible" in a realistic way.

Nonetheless it may help if we sum up the classical argument, for there is always a danger that the qualifications will take precedence over the main argument.

1. *Free trade brings about the most efficient possible use of resources, and any interference with free trade lessens that efficiency.*

   Note that international trade is in no wise different from interregional domestic trade in this regard. We recognize that we would suffer a loss in higher costs or smaller output by imposing restrictions on the exchange of goods between New York and Chicago. We suffer the same loss when we interfere with the exchange between New York and Hong Kong, whether by tariffs, quotas, or other means.

2. *When international trade brings problems of a frictional kind, such as unemployment in an industry that cannot meet foreign competition, the answer is not to block the imports but to cure the unemployment by finding better uses for our inefficiently used resources.*

   Once again, international trade is no different in this regard from domestic trade. When low-price textiles from the South cause unemployment in New England, we do not prevent the sale of southern goods. We try to find new jobs for New Englanders, in occupations in which they have a comparative advantage over the South.

3. *The purpose of all trade is to improve the well-being of the consumer by giving him the best and cheapest goods and services possible. Thus imports, not exports, represent the gains from trade.*

   The whole point of trade is to exchange things that we make efficiently for other things in which our efficiency is less. Anything that diminishes imports will reduce our standard of living, just as anything that blocks a return flow of goods from Chicago to New York will obviously reduce the benefit to New Yorkers of trade with Chicago.

In our last section when we turn to the rise of modern European capitalism and to the troubles of the underdeveloped world, we will see these arguments—and the cost of ignoring them—illustrated not in textbook example, but in reality. However, it is encouraging that since 1948 the total value of world exports has risen from $54 billion to over $250 billion, and that the volume of world trade increased at the rate of 6 percent a year all during the 1960s.*

1. **Imports and exports constitute small but strategic branches of economic activity for the United States.** Precisely *the same arguments of economic rationality apply to them as to all purely domestic economic exchanges.* It is mainly the bias of nationalism that hinders us from applying the same reasoning in both cases.

Gains from trade

2. The gains from trade essentially arise *from the specialization and division of labor that trade makes possible.* Trade is a means of *increasing productivity.*

Comparative advantage

3. Trade is obviously advantageous when each of the two trading partners had a clear superiority in the production of one item. It can also be advantageous whenever a *comparative advantage exists*—that is, whenever one partner, although superior to the other in the production of all products, is relatively superior in some. By the logic of the case, the inferior partner must be relatively superior in the production of the others, and output will be increased if each devotes its energies to its favored products.

Trade-offs

Opportunity cost

4. We can tell which product is relatively favored for each trading partner by calculating the *trade-off relationship* represented by the productivity curve. This shows us the *opportunity cost* of producing each product in terms of the output of other products that must be foregone.

5. Products must exchange *at prices that lie between the ratios established by the trade off possibilities.* Neither country will accept in exchange a product on terms (that is, at prices) that are less favorable than the terms it has available by devoting its own resources to the production of the item in question.

6. The arguments against free trade often stress the dangers of low-wage competition. This argument overlooks the fact that *low wages are a symptom of low productivity.* Generally it is high-wage (i.e., high-productivity) items that are exported. It also ignores the fact that low-wage countries are generally deficient in capital and have trouble competing with capital-using products from nations in which capital is abundant.

Tariff

7. *Tariffs are taxes that are borne by domestic consumers.* They constitute a subsidy to a domestic industry that cannot meet competition from abroad.

---

* A considerable part of the impetus to the growth of world trade must be credited to the spread of more rational—i.e., lower and fewer—tariff barriers. The General Agreement on Tariffs and Trade (GATT), an international body formed in 1947 to work for wider world trade, has succeeded in steadily reducing tariff levels and in dismantling import quotas. It is pleasant to record that the United States initially played a major role in this movement. During the 1930s we had the unenviable reputation of being one of the most restrictive trading nations in the world, but our tariff wall has been far reduced since those irresponsible days. Today our average level of duties on dutiable imports is roughly 10 percent, compared with 53 percent in 1930; and in addition, a third of all our imports are admitted duty-free. On the negative side, however, it must be noted that we continue to discriminate against imports that affect our manufacturing interests. For example, coffee comes in free, but not instant coffee, so that the underdeveloped nations who would like to process coffee within their own economies are gravely disadvantaged. Moreover, in recent years there has been a revival of U.S. protectionism, resulting in "voluntary" agreements on the part of foreign producers to restrict certain kinds of exports, such as textiles, to us, and in quotas on oil imports. The lessons of free trade continue to persuade economists more than businessmen.

8. One avoidable cost of free trade is the necessity for *factor mobility*. Government can help bear relocation and retraining costs in cases where free trade imposes severe strains of readjustment.

9. Free trade *assumes the existence of full employment, and a policy of encouraging free trade must be accompanied by one encouraging maximum output.*

10. *National self-sufficiency* and the encouragement of *infant industries* during their early years provide rational arguments for tariffs, although it is not easy to prevent these arguments from being indiscriminately applied.

11. The basic argument for free trade is that it brings about the *most efficient use of resources*. The purpose of all trade is to improve the well-being of the consumer. *Thus, imports, not exports, represent the gain from trade.*

Q U E S T I O N S

1. Is it true that a colossal nation like the United States can trade with a tiny one like Honduras to the benefit of both? Can it also trade with an industrial, small nation, like Holland? What products do we buy from and sell to each?

2. What do we mean when we say that trade is "indirect production"?

3. Suppose that two towns, Coaltown and Irontown, have equal populations but differing resources. If Coaltown applies its whole population to coal production, it will produce 10,000 tons of coal; if it applies them to iron production, it will produce 5,000 tons of iron. If Irontown concentrates on iron, it will turn out 18,000 tons of iron; if it shifts to coal, it will produce 12,000 tons of coal. Is trade possible between these towns? Would it be possible if Irontown could produce 24,000 tons of iron? Why is there a comparative advantage in one case and not in the other?

4. In which product does Coaltown have a comparative advantage? How many tons of iron does a ton of coal cost her? How many does it cost Irontown? What is the cost of iron in Coaltown and Irontown?

5. Draw a production-possibility diagram for each town. Show where the frontier lies before and after trade.

6. If iron sells for $10 a ton, what must be the price range of coal? Show that trade cannot be profitable if coal sells on either side of this range.

7. What is the opportunity cost of coal to Irontown? Of iron to Irontown?

8. Is it true that American watchmakers face unfair competition from Swiss watchmakers because wages are lower in Switzerland? If American watch workers are rendered unemployed by the low-paid Swiss, what might be done to help them—impose a tariff?

9. Is it true that mass-produced, low-cost American watches are a source of unfair competition for Switzerland? If Swiss watchmakers are unemployed as a result, what could be done to help them—impose a tariff? Is it possible that a mutually profitable trade in watches might take place between the two countries? What kinds of watches would each probably produce?

10. Are the duties on French wines borne by foreigners or by domestic consumers? Both? What, if any, is the rationale for these duties?

11. Do you believe that there should be a tariff on steel products because steel is essential for national defense? Should we refuse to buy low-cost, Russian turbo-generators because the domestic industry needs support?

12. Why do imports represent the gains from trade and not exports?

We have learned something about one of the sources of confusion that surrounds international trade—the curiously concealed gains from trade itself. Yet our examples of trade have thus far not touched on another source of confusion—the fact that international trade is conducted in two (or sometimes more) currencies. After all, Infraville and Supraville both trade in dollars. But suppose Infraville were Japan and Supraville America. Then how would things work out?

Foreign Exchange

The best way to find out would be to price the various items in Japan and America (assuming that Japan produces both wool and cotton, which she does not). Suppose the result looked like this:

TABLE 31 • 1

	United States	Japan
Price of wool (lb)	$1.10	¥300
Price of cotton (lb)	.30	¥100

What would this tell us about the cheapness or dearness of Japanese products compared with those of the U.S.? Nothing, unless we knew one further fact: *the rate at which we could exchange dollars and yen.*

Suppose you could buy 400 yen for a dollar. Then a pound of Japanese wool imported into America (forgetting about shipping costs) would cost 75¢ (¥ 300 ÷ 400) and a pound of Japanese cotton in America would cost $0.25. Assuming that these are the only products that either country makes for export, here we have a case in which Japan can seemingly undersell America in everything.

But now suppose the rate of exchange were not 400 to one but 250 to one. In that event a pound of Japanese wool landed in America would cost $1.20 (¥300 ÷ 250); and a pound of cotton, $0.40. At this rate of exchange everything in Japan is more expensive than the same products produced in the United States.

The point is clear. *We cannot decide whether foreign products are cheaper or dearer than our own until we know the rate of exchange,* the number of units of their currency we get for ours.

MECHANISM OF EXCHANGE

What determines the rate of exchange? The simplest way to understand it is to follow through a single act of international exchange from start to finish. Suppose, for example, that we decide to buy a Japanese camera directly from a Tokyo manufacturer. The price of the camera as advertised in the catalog is ¥20,000, and to buy the camera we must therefore arrange for the Japanese manufacturer to get that many *yen.* Obviously, we can't write him a check in that currency, since our own money is in dollars; and equally obviously we can't send him a check for dollars, since he can't use dollars in Tokyo any more than we could use a check from him in yen.

Therefore, we go to our bank and ask if it can arrange to sell us yen to be delivered to the Tokyo manufacturer. Yes, our bank would be delighted to oblige. How can it do so? The answer is that our bank (or if not ours, another bank with whom it does business) keeps a regular checking account in its own name in a so-called correspondent bank in Tokyo. As we might expect, the bank in Tokyo also keeps a checking account in dollars in *its* own name at our bank. If our banker has enough yen in his Tokyo account, he can sell them to us himself. If not, he can buy yen (which he will then have available in Japan) from his correspondent bank in exchange for dollars which he will put into their account here.

Notice that two currencies change hands—not just one. Notice also that our American banker will not be able to buy yen unless the Japanese banker is willing to acquire dollars. And above all, note that banks are the intermediaries of the foreign exchange mechanism because they hold deposits in foreign banks.

When we go to our bank to buy ¥20,000, the bank officer looks up the current exchange rate on yen. Suppose it is 385. He then tells us that it will cost us $51.95 (20,000 ÷ 385) to purchase the yen, plus a bank commission for his services. We write the check, which is deducted from our bank balance and added to the balance of the Tokyo bank's account in this country. Meanwhile, the manufacturer has been notified that if he goes to the Tokyo bank in which our bank keeps its deposits of yen, he will receive a check for ¥20,000. In other words, the Tokyo bank, having received dollars in the United States, will now pay out yen in Japan.

Thus the mechanism of foreign exchange involves the more or less simultaneous (or anyway, closely linked) operations of two banks in different countries. One bank accepts money in one national denomination, the other pays out money in another denomination. Both are able to do so because each needs the other's currency, and each maintains accounts in the other country. *Note that when payments are made in international trade, money does not physically leave the country.* It travels back or forth between American-owned and foreign-owned bank accounts *in America.* The same is true in foreign nations, where their money will travel between an American-owned account there and the account of one of their nationals. Taken collectively, these foreign-owned accounts (including our own overseas) are called "foreign exchange." They constitute the main pool of moneys available to finance foreign trade.

Supply of, and Demand for, Foreign Exchange

But what determines the *rate* at which banks sell the foreign exchange they own? The answer is in no way different from that of all economic analysis of prices. *It depends on the supply of, and the demand for, the commodity in question—in this case, foreign exchange.*

MERCHANDISE

We have already seen how imports give rise to a demand for yen and to a supply (a sale) of dollars, and how the end result of the transaction is an increase in foreign-owned bank deposits in this country. Exactly the opposite is true in the case of exports. Suppose that we were manufacturers of chemicals and that we sold a $1,000 order to Tokyo. In Japan, the importer of chemicals would go to his bank to find out how many yen that would cost. If the rate were 385, it would cost him ¥385,000, which he would then pay to the Japanese bank. The bank would charge his account and credit the yen to the Tokyo account of an American bank with which it did business, meantime advising the bank here that the transaction had taken place. When the appropriate papers arrived from Japan, our U.S. bank would then take note of its increased holdings of yen and pay the equivalent amount in dollars into our account.

Thus, buying and selling goods abroad generates a need for foreign exchange. The same demand for foreign currency (and the same sale or supply of our own) arises when we import *services,* such as transportation or insurance. Every time we fly on Air France, for example, we move dollars from our private bank accounts to the bank accounts of Air France in the United States. These dollars will then be sold for francs. As a result, dollars will go into the American account of a correspondent French bank, while in France, francs will be paid by the French bank to Air France's home office.

NON-MERCHANDISE ITEMS

In the same way, of course, every time a foreigner flies on an American plane or ships cargo on an American ship or buys insurance from an American company, United States holdings of foreign currency rise abroad, while in this country, banks will take note of their increased foreign deposits and issue dollar checks to the American sellers.

In addition to goods and services, we should note three other regular sources of supply and demand for foreign exchange. The first of these is *travel.* When we travel in a foreign country we need to pay our expenses in its currency, and therefore we have to sell dollars for pounds or pesos or whatever currency we need. When a foreigner travels here, he must, of course, sell his money to get dollars.

Second, we often send gifts of money to friends or relatives in another country or mail pensions to individuals living overseas. These *remittances* supply dollars in exchange for foreign money, just as remittances coming from abroad demand dollars in exchange for foreign money.

Last, we also send and receive large sums of money to transfer dividends or interest or other *income on investments* between countries. When IBM in Italy wishes to transfer part of its profits to the IBM parent company in the United States, lira will move in Italy from its account to the account of an American bank; and in New York, IBM will be able to draw dollars from the local branch of that bank. By way of turnabout, when a dividend on an American security is sent to a foreign holder, dollars will have to travel from America to that country (which is to say, from American-owned bank accounts into foreign-owned bank accounts in America).

The items we have so far discussed are by no means all the transactions that give rise to a demand for, or a supply of, foreign exchange, but they form a group of activities that we call *transactions on current account.* They are, that is to say, part of the everyday business of international exchange, giving rise regularly to a need for foreign exchange both for us and for other countries.

BALANCE OF PAYMENTS ON CURRENT ACCOUNT

TABLE 31•2

U.S.
BALANCE OF
PAYMENTS
ON PRIVATE
CURRENT
ACCOUNT
(1970)

BILLIONS OF DOLLARS*

Activities that supplied exchange to the U.S. (Transactions that moved foreign currencies from foreign hands into American bank accounts)		Activities that demanded exchange from the U.S. (Transactions that moved dollars from American bank accounts into foreign-owned bank accounts)	
Export of merchandise on private account†	$39.2	Imports of merchandise	$39.4
Foreign purchases of U.S. transportation, insurance, and other private services†	4.7	U.S. purchases of foreign transportation, insurance, and other private services	4.8
		Private remittances	0.9
Foreign travel in the U.S.	2.3	U.S. travel abroad	3.9
U.S. income from private investments abroad	10.2	Foreign income from private investments in the U.S.	4.3
Total	**$56.4**	**Total**	**$53.3**
Net balance	3.1		

* First three quarters at annual rates.

† Excludes military and foreign aid and all other items financed by government. See quarterly "Survey Current Business" balance of payments reports, Table 1, lines 3–6–9, minus Table 5, lines 27, 28.

Table 31-2 shows what these actual transactions looked like in 1970.

The table, which shows us the flows of dollar payments to and from foreigners (by which we really mean, never forget, the flows of dollar payments into and out of foreign-owned bank accounts in America), reveals the forces of supply and demand that rise from the basic transactions of international trade. It is called the *balance of payments on current account*. We will shortly see that there are other balances of payments as well. It should be noted that we include under *exports* only those shipments of goods that were sent abroad through the normal channels of private trade. Exports that were sent as part of foreign aid or military aid are not included here, for reasons that we shall subsequently discuss.

Usually we show only the net figure in the balance of payments, preceded by a plus sign (or with no sign) if the balance is "favorable" to us—that is, if it brings in a net flow of dollars—and with a minus sign if it is unfavorable. The balance of payments of all the items above for the years 1960–1970 is shown in Fig. 31-1.

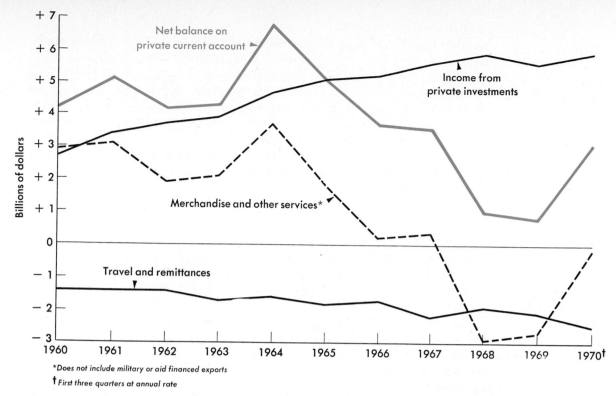

FIG. 31•1 U.S. BALANCE OF PAYMENTS ON CURRENT
PRIVATE ACCOUNT, 1960–1970

It is clear from the graph which way the balance of supply and demand on current account tips. Through most of the 1960s, and indeed for many years before that, foreigners have been spending more dollars within the United States than we have been spending abroad.

It is worth a moment to take note of exactly how this "favorable" balance of current account comes about. In normal years, Europe and the rest of the world are strong net buyers of American goods, although as we can see, this "merchandise balance of payments" has been negative in recent years, as European productive capacity has enlarged.* At the same time, however, our expenditure of dollars for foreign travel and remittances has grown steadily larger, so that we are considerable net spenders of dollars for these purposes, especially for travel in Europe and Canada. Finally, we note the mounting stream of net income from private investments—the dividends and royalties earned on America's vast investments overseas. This tips the total balance on current account decisively in our favor.

Thus the international flows of exchange on current private account are very reassuring. Our expenditures in most years have been outweighed by a

* Our graph lumps payments for transportation and insurance together with merchandise. Merchandise is overwhelmingly the largest item of the three.

healthy surplus of expenditures by foreigners. But is the surplus really healthy? Indeed, does not the positive balance of current account mean that the United States is in danger of doing the very thing that so often frightens us: selling or earning so much more than we buy or pay out that we threaten to drain all the money from the rest of the world?

**RATE OF
EXCHANGE
AND BALANCE
OF PAYMENTS**

The answer to this question—it is a question that has worried many foreigners—hinges on the relation between the rate of exchange and the balance of payments. We have already seen that the rate of exchange establishes the general relation between international price levels. We have seen that the balance of payments reveals the supply and demand for foreign exchange. Now let us put the two together.

Let us suppose, as a first approach to the problem, that goods and services like those above are the only activities that require international exchange (we will soon see that they are not), and let us assume that the rate of exchange, like any other price, is free to move. Then it is not difficult to see that a situation such as we have depicted would soon lead to a new *rate of exchange that would change the level of prices in the U.S. in terms of the prices of other countries.*

For what our figures show is that foreigners will be paying dollars out of their U.S. bank accounts a great deal faster than Americans will be making payments into those foreign accounts. (Similarly, foreigners abroad will be making payments in their own money into the U.S.-owned accounts of their money faster than Americans will be making payments out of those accounts.) The result will soon be a shortage of dollars in the American bank accounts of foreigners and a very large supply of foreign currencies in bank accounts abroad owned by Americans.

**APPRECIATION
AND
DEPRECIATION
OF FOREIGN
EXCHANGE**

At this point, suppose that a Japanese importer wants to buy another $1,000 worth of American chemicals. He goes to his bank to find out what dollar exchange costs—and has an unpleasant surprise. His banker tells him that exchange is very "tight" at the moment, meaning by this that his own dollar balances in the United States are very low, and that American balances of yen are very high. As a result, the Japanese banker can no longer buy dollars for 385 yen. The bank in this country is now insisting on 390 or 395 or perhaps even 400. Because of supply and demand, the yen had cheapened or *depreciated* in value vis-à-vis the dollar, and the dollar has, of course, risen or *appreciated* vis-à-vis the yen.

Now our importer makes a quick calculation. At 400 yen to the dollar, the $1,000 worth of chemicals costs him ¥400,000 instead of ¥385,000. That is too expensive for the Japanese market. He decides not to place the order.

Exactly the opposite situation would confront an American importer of Japanese goods. Suppose we wanted to buy another camera for ¥20,000. When we went to our bank in this country, we would find our banker very eager to get rid of the yen piling up in his account in Tokyo. Faced with the competition from the bank across the street (which is also trying to get rid of its yen), he will offer us the 20,000 yen not at $51.95 (which is what it cost at 385 yen to the dollar) but for only $51.50 or $51 or even $50, which is what it would cost if the yen slipped to 400 to the dollar.

Faced with this change in exchange rates, our own calculations have to be refigured, especially if we are dealers in cameras. Clearly, the more yen we can get for a dollar, the cheaper will Japanese cameras be, once we price them in American dollars. Thus, just as the depreciation of the yen discouraged the sale of American goods to Japan, it acts to encourage the sale of Japanese goods to America.

The principle is very clear. Movements in exchange rates *always* change the relative price levels of two countries. As a result, one country *always* finds its exports stimulated and its imports made more expensive, while the other country *always* experiences exactly the opposite effect—its exports are discouraged, while its imports are given a boost.

Now let us go back to clear up the business of trade between Infraville and Supraville, once and for all—this time with Japan and the United States again taking the leading roles.

As at the beginning of this chapter, we assume that the prices in the two countries are as shown in Table 31-3.

TABLE 31 • 3

	U.S.	Japan
Wool (lb)	$1.10	¥300
Cotton (lb)	.30	¥100

What happens next?

The first part of the answer depends on exchange rates. We suppose that they are 400 to 1, a rate at which the prices of both iron and wool are *below* the prices of those products in America. As a result, Japan will begin by selling both cotton and wool to us, whereas we will be able to sell nothing to her.

This is however only the beginning of the process. If exchange rates are flexible, they will immediately reflect the fact that the demand for yen is so much greater than the supply. The yen will rise to, say, 300 to 1. At this exchange rate, Japanese wool is now $1.00 in American money (¥300 ÷ 300) but Japanese cotton has gone up to 33⅓¢ (¥100 ÷ 300). Suddenly cotton is *more* expensive than the same product in America. In other words, the pressure of supply and demand on foreign exchange has pushed the exchange rate within the trading range offered by the differentials in opportunity cost of the two countries.

Could the exchange rate continue to rise until the yen was much dearer—say 250 to 1? If it did, not only would Japanese cotton be very much more expensive than American, but even Japanese wool would now be a shade over the U.S. price (¥3,000 ÷ 250 = $1.20). If the exchange rate swung this far, it would be America that threatened to undersell Japan in everything. But again the very imbalance between the supply and demand for foreign exchange would prevent the threat from happening.

Thus we can see that under the conditions of a freely moving exchange rate, fluctuations in the rate of exchange serve to balance out flows of payments between countries, and in turn these flows tend to stabilize the exchange rate. *Under these conditions no country can ever be only a seller (or only a buyer).* Even if it is a land of sweatshop labor, it cannot undersell the world, for the very glut of its exports would raise the international value of its money and in this way set a limit to its exports.

Fixed vs. Flexible Exchange Rates

The method of establishing international price levels that we have just described is called that of *flexible, or freely fluctuating, exchange rates.* It is the easiest of all means of establishing international prices for the student to understand—but alas for him, it is not the means that is actually used to establish exchange rates between nations.

PROBLEMS OF FLEXIBLE EXCHANGE RATES

Why not? The reasons are not difficult to understand. One of them involves the fact that most international transactions are not concluded immediately across a counter, but extend over weeks or even months between the time that a sale is agreed upon and the time when the goods arrive and payment is due. If exchange rates changed during this period, either the importer or the exporter could be severely penalized. If I agreed to buy a camera for Y20,000, thinking it would cost $50, and when the camera arrived I found that yen had advanced in price to 300 to 1, so that the camera cost me $67, I would hardly be pleased. And although it is possible to insure oneself to some extent against exchange variations by buying "forward exchange," most traders would rather not deal in exchange rates that are likely to alter over the course of a transaction. More important, international investors who put money overseas for long periods have no way of protecting themselves against changes in rates and are even more concerned about the risks of flexible exchange.

In addition, most monetary authorities fear that fluctuating rates would lead to speculative purchases and sales of foreign currencies just for the purpose of making a profit on swings in their price—and that these speculative "raids" would have the effect of still further aggravating those swings.

There are counterarguments to these fears, and it should be noted that a growing number of economists strongly favor flexible or freely fluctuating exchange rates as the best way to arrange international transactions. It will be a happy day for the students of international finance when their recommendations are accepted, for much of the difficulties of learning about international finance will then disappear. It is possible that flexible exchange rates may replace the present system of fixed exchange rates, at least to a limited extent, if the international monetary situation deteriorates. But we will learn about that in due course. First, let us study the problems of international finance under a system of fixed rates.

How are exchange rates determined if they are not set by supply and demand? The answer is that exchange rates have been "fixed" in relation to one another by declarations of the governments of all nations. At the center of this fixed relationship is an announced value of one ounce of gold as being worth 35 United States dollars, a price set by the Treasury in 1933. All other countries have declared the value of their currencies in terms of this relationship, so that there is a definite number of francs or pounds or marks that can be bought for a dollar (or for an ounce of gold). *Hence the world operates with rates of exchange that do not fluctuate with supply and demand, but that remain more or less stationary, or change only infrequently.*

Under this system of fixed exchange rates, the U.S. Treasury stands willing to buy all gold offered to it, from foreigners or domestic suppliers, at $35 an ounce. More important, it agrees as well to *sell* gold at $35 an ounce to any foreign government (or the central bank of any foreign government).* Thus all dollar balances held by foreign governments are potentially convertible into gold—a fact that gives rise to many problems, as we shall quickly see.

---

* Under the *gold exchange standard* the Treasury will not sell gold to *American* holders or to foreign *nongovernment* holders of dollars. The "convertibility" of dollars (like that of most other currencies) into gold is thus limited strictly to balances held by foreign central banks or intergovernmental agencies such as the World Bank.

This limitation on the availability of gold differentiates the so-called gold exchange standard from the old-fashioned gold standard. Under the gold exchange standard, a nation's gold is entirely reserved for the official settlement of international obligations. Under the old gold standard, a nation's gold was available at any time to any citizen who wished to exchange his bank balance for gold coins or gold bullion. This led to two problems. One was the risk of a "run" on gold in times of panic: it was this that provided the rationale for the gold "backing" of currency, which, as we have seen, was originally enjoined on the Federal Reserve system by Congress.

The second problem was that anyone could at any time convert his dollars into gold and then ship the gold abroad to buy francs or pounds, or any other currency if that was profitable. This international private shipment of gold posed a serious difficulty for any government that sought to launch an expansionary program, if the rest of the world was experiencing a recession. For as soon as a nation's program began to work, and its prices began to rise, citizens found it profitable to turn their currencies into gold and ship the gold to depressed economies whose currencies were cheap. This drained gold from the expanding economy and rapidly brought its expansion to a halt.

By denying private citizens access to national reserves of gold, the modern gold exchange standard permits a much greater degree of international independence for economic policies than did the "lock-step" of the old gold standard. But as we shall see, even under the gold exchange standard, a government must temper its economic independence to some extent to preserve a viable balance of payments.

Now suppose, as before, that the United States runs a surplus in its balance of payments on current account—in other words, that its excess of exports over imports is steadily depleting the dollar accounts of foreign banks. And suppose that the exchange rate could not fluctuate as we have previously imagined. What could then happen?

There are but three possibilities.

One is that trade would simply come to a halt. If the United States undersold the rest of the world on everything, and if the rate of exchange were fixed and there was no way for the world to get U.S. dollars, no one would be able to buy any more American merchandise, whether it was "cheaper" or not. For how could he pay the American seller?

Second, it might be possible to alter the rate of exchange by government decree. If we could make foreign currencies less expensive in relation to American dollars, we could make foreign goods cheaper than American goods. In that way, we could tempt Americans to buy abroad, and thereby make it possible for foreigners once again to buy American goods. We shall look into this possibility later.

Third, we have already hinted above that *currencies might be made available in ways other than current transactions.* This is the very important subject that we must now look into.

One such transaction may have already occurred to the reader. Not all the exchanges between nations take place between individuals or firms. Governments also need foreign exchange to maintain their diplomatic establishments in other nations or for participation in foreign affairs, foreign aid, debt service, and other such purposes. Much more important, war and military assistance use up large sums of exchange. The United States, for instance, maintains armies in many nations where U.S. soldiers must be fed and supplied with locally bought produce and labor. All these activities, peaceful and otherwise, cost foreign exchange.

Figure 31-2 shows us the net result of our government transactions divided into two major flows of payments. The first flow, net military expenditures, reveals the drain on the dollar that arises from our overseas military activity. It is "net" because it arises *after* earnings of about a billion dollars per annum from sales of American military equipment to foreign governments. The second flow, "other government," shows us the net result of our foreign aid, our normal diplomatic and other expenditures, and of payments and repayments of government loans.

This second flow must be scrutinized more carefully. We have said that it included foreign aid expenditures, which are gifts of American dollars to other countries. These expenditures have averaged $2 billion to $3 billion per year during the last decade. One would think, then, that the "other

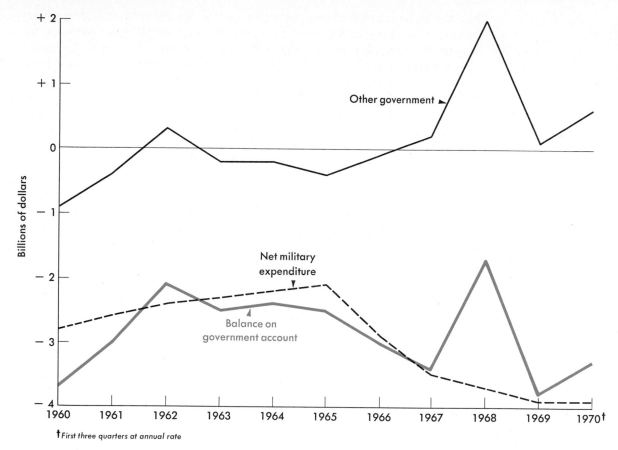

**FIG. 31·2   U.S. BALANCE OF PAYMENTS
ON GOVERNMENT ACCOUNT**

† *First three quarters at annual rate*

government" account would show a very substantial outflow of dollars over these years. Instead it shows, in most years, a modest inflow. How can this be?

The answer is that the overwhelming bulk of our foreign aid expenditures does not constitute a dollar drain. Between 80 to 90 percent of all foreign aid extended by the United States consists of grants or loans *tied to the purchase of American goods.* This means that we are giving away goods for the purpose of economic development by transferring dollars into the bank accounts of foreign governments *on the condition that those dollars be spent in this country.* Hence these expenditures do not in any way affect our balance of payments.

A small portion of U.S. foreign aid is untied, and this portion—10 to 20 percent of our total aid expenditures—is indeed spent in other nations. This small dollar outflow is included in the "other government" account and would make that account a deficit were it the only item included therein.

But the most important component of the "other government" flow comes from other governments steadily paying back their various debts to the United States, and this has resulted in an inflow of dollars on "other government" account.*

CAPITAL MOVEMENTS

Thus, net government expenditures overseas for military and other purposes provide us with one explanation of how dollars can be provided to foreign nations to supplement the dollars earned by their direct sales to us. But there is still another very important means of replenishing their dollar accounts. *This is by the movement of capital from the United States to other lands.*

Capital is sent abroad (or can be received from abroad) in several forms. It may travel as additions to American plants in foreign nations, or as additions to their physical assets here. This does not mean that it travels as the actual steel, for example. When investors add to their plant and equipment abroad, what they send is the money. Thus, in order to "export" capital, we must acquire foreign exchange—that is, put dollars into foreign bank accounts here in order to release foreign money abroad (or vice versa if foreigners are exporting capital to us).†

We call this overseas expenditure of American investment funds a shipment of *long-term capital.* We might note that such overseas investment is a normal attribute of a wealthy nation. It was by exports of capital from Britain to the United States that much of our nineteenth-century railroad network was originally financed. By way of turnabout, a good deal of the growth of many European nations since World War II owes its source to American capital invested there. By 1970 the value of American investments in plant and equipment and real estate around the world totaled over $70 billion, whereas foreigners owned some $12 billion of assets in the U.S. From this capital, both American and foreign, interest and dividends flowed in both directions across the oceans. It is because our capital assets are so

---

* Note that the "official" U.S. balance of payments accounts *include* foreign-aid financed exports in the total of *merchandise* exports. This gives the erroneous impression that these exports earn us dollars, which they do not. In the official balance of payments figures, these "exports" are then offset by an entry for foreign aid that looks as though all foreign aid costs us foreign exchange, which we have seen is not true. In the end, the *net* dollar drain of foreign aid is the same on our basis of accounting as on the official methods, but the false impression of foreign aid "exports" and foreign aid "dollar cost" is avoided. I am indebted to Professor Robert W. Stevens for assistance in preparing these figures. This presentation follows the lines of his article in the *Harvard Business Review,* Nov.-Dec., 1966.

† There is an all-too-easy source of confusion in the terminology with which we speak of capital movements. Capital going abroad from the U.S. is called a capital "export." This sounds as if it earned dollars for us, like a merchandise export. But we have seen, it does not—*we have to give up dollars to send capital abroad.* Similarly capital coming into the U.S. is called a capital "import" although it increases our supply of foreign currencies. It helps clear up the confusion to think of a capital "export" as actually being the *import of a claim* to foreign assets (which is indeed the reality behind the financial transaction), and to think of capital "imports" as *exporting* claims to American assets.

much larger than those of foreigners that the income from investments in our current accounts showed as a large net source of dollar payments to the United States.

Still another form of long-term capital consists of *financial investments*— purchases by Americans of bonds or stocks from foreigners. In the same way, when foreigners buy American securities, foreign exchange is also involved. In early 1968, American citizens owned roughly $23 billion in foreign securities, and foreigners owned approximately $17 billion of ours.

Last, money also moves from nation to nation as *short-term capital*. This is capital invested by individuals or firms in very liquid foreign securities such as short-term government bonds, or merely held in banks to earn interest. There are several billions of such capital that moves from nation to nation in search of the highest possible return, or as part of the pool of foreign exchange from which international payments are financed. Fig. 31-3 shows us these flows over the last decade.

As we can see, there has been a steady drainage of capital from the United States abroad, some of it going into new plant and equipment—a phenomenon we will study when we take up the multinational corporation in Chapter 32; some of it going into foreign short-term bonds or bank

FIG. 31 • 3   U.S. BALANCE OF PAYMENTS ON CAPITAL ACCOUNT

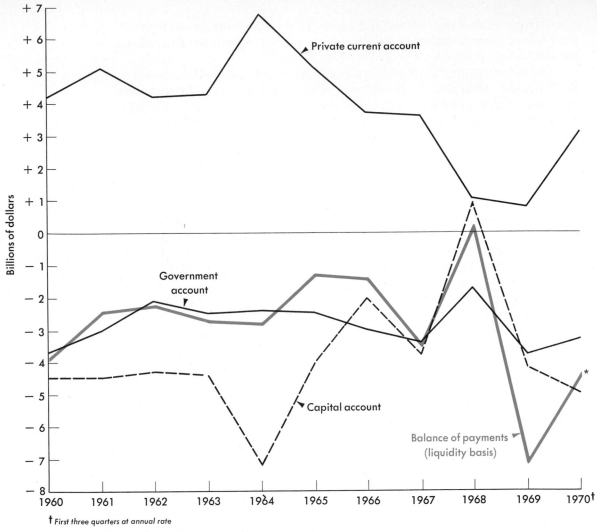

FIG. 31•4 U.S. BALANCE OF PAYMENTS

accounts, in search of interest rates higher than those available here.* (The surprising "plus" figure for 1968 is the result of a government appeal to corporations not to send capital abroad, because of critical balance of payments problems in that year. More about that shortly.)

* The reader will notice a line called "Errors and omissions" in Fig. 31-3. This term is actually a "balancing item," compiled at the end of the balance of payments calculations to assure the bookkeeping equality of debits and credits (see p. 633f.). The need for the item arises because some kinds of transactions do not get recorded, and thereby throw the totals of payments and receipts out of balance. Smuggling is one such kind of transaction. More important are perfectly legal activities such as the deposit of money by American or foreign travelers in banks in the nations they are visiting. Such items are really transfers of short term capital, and in fact *Errors and omissions* can be thought of as mainly composed of just such short-term capital movements.

If we now add our balance of payments on capital account to those we have learned about earlier on current private and government account, we see the overall picture represented by Fig. 31-4.

What we see in Fig. 31-4 is quite different from what we saw at first. Our balance of payments on current private account generates a steady overdemand for dollars, but our balances on government and capital account give rise to an even larger demand for foreign currency. Thus America does not have a "surplus" but a "deficit" in its balance of payments with the rest of the world.

What is the result of this? If the exchange rate were free to move, we know what would happen. The dollar would now be overabundant, as the U.S. bank balances of foreigners increased. Hence its price would fall. With this fall would come a stimulus for American exports and a deterrent to imports from abroad.* The deficit would thus soon be eliminated.

But under the system of exchange rates tied to gold, this means of adjustment is ruled out. What then?

Gold and Reserves

The answer brings us finally to consider the role of gold in international finance. We have already encountered gold in our study of the domestic monetary system where we discovered that it now played no role whatsoever in relation to our national money (pp. 350-52). But gold plays a very large role as a medium for the settlement of international deficits.

What happens when dollars pile up in the American accounts of foreign central banks because of an excess of dollar payments over dollar withdrawals? *The answer is that these banks will normally use their large dollar balances to buy gold from the U.S. Treasury, which will be added to their national reserves.*† Such a purchase of gold counts as an international

---

* Note that it would also be more expensive for an American company to build abroad, since it would cost more dollars to amass the necessary francs, pounds, or whatever. Similarly, investors in foreign securities would find it dearer to send money abroad. Conversely, foreigners would find American investments cheaper. This would set up a corrective tendency in the flow of international capital. Only the government account (which is chiefly determined by political considerations) would be largely unaffected by the changed exchange rate.

† The gold is *not* usually shipped abroad, as one might think. Instead it is trucked to a vault many feet below the street surface in the Federal Reserve Bank of New York, where it is stacked in dull yellow bricks about the shape (but half the thickness) of a building brick. It is possible to visit this vault which now holds some $13 billion of foreign gold, neatly separated into bins assigned to different countries. To see this modern equivalent of Montezuma's treasure is an astonishing sight. Gold may well be, as many have said, a kind of international psychosis, but its power over the imagination, no doubt the result of its traditional association with riches, is still remarkable. It is amusing to note that the Federal Reserve Bank, as custodian of this foreign gold, once suggested to its binholders that they might save a considerable sum if, instead of actually weighing the bricks and moving them from bin to bin whenever gold was bought and sold, both parties agreed to move the gold just on the books, the way bank balances are moved about. All governments demurred. They wanted the actual gold bricks in their bins. Hence, when gold moves from nation to nation to help settle up accounts, it is still actually pushed across the floor of the Fed's vault and carefully piled in the proper bin.

transaction like any export, and thus establishes a formal offset to our deficit. At the same time, it reduces the oversupply of dollars and thus takes the "pressure" off the dollar.

A second way of offsetting the deficit is to borrow from the International Monetary Fund, an international institution into which nearly all the nations of the world have deposited both gold and national currencies. Under certain conditions, nations can borrow currencies of which they are short—or gold—and can use these acquired reserves to settle their international deficits.

DOLLAR RESERVES

A third way of meeting the deficit does not require either gold or IMF borrowing. It consists in the willingness of foreign banks to allow their dollar balances to accumulate without converting them into gold. These rising balances count as an inflow of short-term capital.

We have seen that the meaning of a deficit in the balance of payments is that we make more payments to foreigners for goods, government services, and capital purposes than they make to us, and that this results in steadily growing amounts of dollars in their U.S. bank balances. Ordinarily, these extra-large balances would be skimmed off by using them to buy gold. It is possible, however, for foreign central banks and other official institutions to hold (or invest) their dollars here and to count these dollar balances—all of which *can* be converted into gold—as part of their *reserves*.

Why would foreign countries wish to do that? The answer is that it is profitable. Gold is, after all, an asset that yields a negative return—it costs money to hold it and protect it. Dollar balances, on the contrary, yield positive returns of interest and dividends. By permitting their reserves to remain in dollars, European countries are using American banks as "financial intermediaries," much as individual savers use mutual funds or savings banks as their profit-making depositaries.

In this way the dollar has become an important *reserve currency* for many nations, who count their holdings of dollars much as we count our holdings of gold. In much the same way, within the British Commonwealth, the pound sterling serves as a reserve currency for many Commonwealth members.

BALANCING THE BALANCE OF PAYMENTS

When we add the transfers of gold and IMF reserves and the increased official holdings of dollars, our balance of payments deficit disappears, as we can see in Table 31-4.

Does this mean that there is no balance of payments problem after all? Indeed, it does not. By now we must realize that what we mean by the balance of payments is the relationship between the demand for, and the supply of, dollars for *certain purposes*. That is why we can speak of a balance of payments on current account, government account, capital account, and so on. Each account summarizes our receipts and expenditures for certain categories of international transactions.

TABLE 31 • 4

FINANCING THE U.S. BALANCE OF PAYMENTS (billions of dollars)

Year	Balance of payments	Financed by:	
		Decrease (−) in gold, convertible currencies and claims on IMF (including Special Drawing Rights) held by U.S.	Increase (−) in liquid assets held by foreigners
1960	$−3.9	$−2.1	$−1.8
1961	−2.4	−0.6	−1.8
1962	−2.2	−1.5	−0.7
1963	−2.7	−0.4	−2.3
1964	−2.8	−0.2	−2.6
1965	−1.3	−1.2	−0.1
1966	−1.4	−0.6	−0.8
1967	−3.5	−0.1	−3.5
1968	+0.2	+0.9	−0.7
1969	−7.2	+1.2	−8.4
1970+	−4.4	−2.2	−2.2

Totals may not add, due to rounding.
+First three quarters at annual rates.

When we speak of our "overall" deficit in the balance of payments, we mean that all dollar payments coming to us from "normal" international transactions are not large enough to cover our dollar outlays for all "normal" purposes. Where did the extra dollars come from? They were received from gold sales or from IMF borrowings or from the willingness of foreigners to accept dollars without being reimbursed in their own currencies or in gold.

This means that it is possible to define our deficit in a number of different ways, depending on what we count as a "normal" international transaction. Suppose, for example, that we want to know how we finance our current and government account and our flows of long-term capital. Then we "draw the line" under those three items, giving us what is called the *"basic"* balance of payments. If we want to know how we financed all these items, plus flows of short-term capital, we draw it in the manner we have done, to reveal what is called the balance on a *"liquidity* basis." And there are still other ways of striking meaningful subtotals of our foreign transactions.*

Which is the "correct" way? Which is the "true" deficit? The answer depends entirely on the information that we are interested in procuring. The basic balance is useless if we want to see how we finance our short-term

MEANING OF
BALANCE
OF PAYMENTS
DEFICIT

* An interested student should consult *The Survey of Current Business,* June, 1971, pp. 24 f.

capital movements. And the liquidity balance tells us nothing if we want to know the manner in which we finance our long-term capital expenditures abroad.

But suppose we wanted to know how *everything* balanced—not only current and government account and long- and short-term capital, but movements of gold and changes in foreign-held dollars? Then we would draw the line at the very bottom of the table of international transactions—where the net balance is always exactly zero!

Why zero? Because the total balance of payments only shows us *how* all purchases (or sales) were financed. Suppose for example that the sole U.S. transaction were the purchase of one Japanese camera. Our balance of payments would look like this:

Merchandise	−$50
Short-term capital	+$50
Balance	0

The merchandise item of −$50 represents, as we know, the import of a good. And what is the balancing item of +$50? That is the increase in a Japanese-owned bank account in the U.S. that resulted from our payment for the camera. It is listed as a "+" because it really stands for the export of a *claim* on U.S. production, and exports are listed under the + column. (See †footnote, p. 628.) Suppose now that the following year we cleared out the Japanese account by sending them gold. If that were the only transaction that year, the Balance of Payments would look like this:

Short-term capital	−$50
Gold	+$50
Balance	0

Here we would have reduced the claim of the Japanese against our production (whence the minus $50), and this would have been offset by the export—always a plus—of $50 in gold. Once again the total of all payments must be zero.

In other words, our overall balance of payments always balances. But depending on where we draw the line, we can see how we financed (or how foreigners financed) the particular categories of international exchange in which we are interested.

THE GOLD
PROBLEM

The United States has been running a deficit in both its basic and liquidity balances of payment for over a decade. As a result, we are not too surprised at Fig. 31-5.

As we can see, we have lost half our gold stock in fifteen years. But there is something even more serious than that. The dollar reserves of foreign banks and governments are now larger than the remaining gold

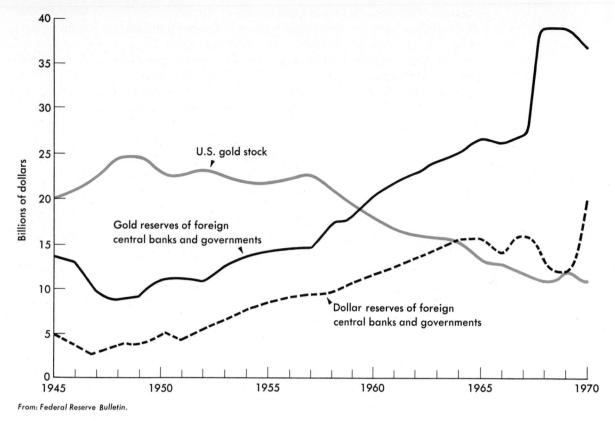

From: Federal Reserve Bulletin.

FIG. 31·5 THE CHANGING U.S. GOLD STOCK

stock! If those reserves were even converted *en masse* into gold, our gold supply would be wiped out. In fact, we could not even honor all the existing claims for gold.

It need hardly be pointed out that this would be a major economic catastrophe—not because we would have no gold "behind" our currency, but because we would have cheated foreign nations out of hundreds of millions or billions worth of purchasing power. For if the gold supply ran out, foreigners could no longer repatriate their dollar holdings at a known exchange rate. Instead, their dollar holdings would now have to find their own price vis-à-vis their own currencies; and since dollars are held in very large quantities, this price might be very low.

Take, for example, a Netherlands bank that had allowed $1 million to remain in America, because it was confident that it could always get 28,571 ounces of gold for it (at $35 per ounce) *with which it could then purchase other currencies whose value in gold was also firmly fixed.* Suddenly it would find that its million-dollar deposit would be worth only as many ounces of gold as the market decreed—very possibly much less than the quantity it thought it owned. In turn, the amounts of other currencies available to the Netherlands bank would also fall, since it would have less gold to buy them with.* *Thus countries that had cooperated with us by allowing their dollars to remain here would be penalized.* They would never again allow dollars to pile up in U.S. banks.

Not less important is the likelihood that a world trading slump of violent proportions would probably follow from the sudden inconvertibility of the dollar. Since World War II, the dollar has been *the* unit for settling balances among nations, and its general acceptability has provided a payment means that has helped to sustain the swift rise in world trade since the war. The loss of confidence in the dollar would undo at one stroke the long process of establishing a means of payment that would be as "good" in Europe or Asia as in Latin America or the United States, and it might be a long while before another international unit of payment took its place. In the meantime, many nations would refuse to do business unless they were paid in gold—and since the volume of gold is much smaller than that of internationally held dollars plus gold, the amount of world trade would suffer a terrible collapse.

THE GOLD RUSH OF 1968

Now, just because the consequences of a "run" on gold would be so disastrous, it is exceedingly unlikely that the central banks of foreign nations would take such a suicidal course of action as to demand their dollar balances in gold. This is not to say, however, that *private* speculators abroad might not take their holdings of dollars and convert them into gold. For many years there has been a perfectly legal market in gold in London and elsewhere, where private individuals could exchange their holdings of dollars or other currencies for gold bullion. The gold they bought was sold to them at the fixed price of $35 an ounce by an international gold pool comprised of the main gold-holding nations. In the pool, the United States, as the largest holder of gold in the world, was committed to providing 59 percent of all bullion supplied to the market.

In March, 1968, the gold pool suddenly faced a crisis. Alarmed at the shrinkage of U.S. gold reserves, private speculators converged on the London market to convert their dollars into bullion. On the first day of that month, the pool, which had normally sold 3 to 4 tons of gold per day, suddenly found itself obliged to sell 40 tons. A week later the demand had risen to 75 tons. On March 13, it was 100 tons; the next day, 200 tons.

At this rate of drainage, the United States Treasury was being forced to put $1 million of gold into the pool every two to three minutes. Officials in

---

* We can now see that this possibility of capital loss provides another strong argument against flexible exchange rates. Private investors would be severely penalized if they found their dividends and interest—or the repayment of their capital—depreciated in value because of a change in exchange rates. Of course, there is also the chance of a profit from fluctuating rates. But most investors are first concerned about the *safety* of their investment.

Washington nervously figured that if the gold hemorrhage were not checked, the nation's entire gold reserves would be used up in a few weeks. To prevent such a crisis, the world's central bankers hurriedly convened in Washington, and after a weekend of continuous conferences, announced that the gold pool was to be discontinued and that a new "two-price" system would immediately begin. All *official* holders of dollars (i.e., governments and central banks) would still be able to buy gold at $35 an ounce from the Treasury. But there would no longer be any effort to maintain the price of gold at an "official" level in the private market by supplying whatever gold was needed there at that price. Instead, there would be no sales from any national reserve of gold into the private market, and "private" gold would be allowed to find its own price.*

The system worked fairly well for a while. But the continuing imbalance of American accounts made it clear that such a means of avoiding an international currency crisis was at best a stopgap.

We shall shortly see what further measures were required. Meanwhile, the gold crisis teaches us three things:

LESSONS OF 1968

1. *The balance of payments is subject to very rapid improvement or deterioration.*

As we have seen, between 1968 and 1969, the United States balance of payments was capable of changes of $7 billion in a single year. This sensitivity is due to the fact that a strong influence on the balance of payments is exerted by flows of short-term capital that can move very rapidly—such as the European money that flowed into the U.S. stock markets—or by large-scale, but also very fast-moving transactions among governments. The balance, of course, may swing dramatically the other way in another year.

2. *The deterioration in our merchandise balance of payments suggests that we are moving to a new relationship vis-à-vis the rest of the world.*

Part of the tremendous rise in imports in 1968 and 1969 was due to special factors: a long domestic copper strike that boosted copper imports, for example, and heavy U.S. buying of foreign steel in anticipation of a U.S.

---

* To work, such a system depends on the willingness of central bankers to "play the game." Otherwise they could convert their official holdings of dollars into gold at $35 per ounce, sell the gold in Europe at a higher price in the free market, use the dollars they received once again to buy at $35 an ounce, and so on *ad infinitum,* or at least until the forces of supply and demand had brought the two markets together. A great deal of international monetary cooperation depends on "playing the game." For a scholarly but very readable account of international monetary cooperation, see Henry Aubrey, *Atlantic Economic Cooperation* (Council on Foreign Relations, 1967); and for a very lively and perceptive popular account see John Brooks, "In Defense of Sterling," in *Business Adventures* (New York: Weybright and Talley, 1969).

strike. But there is no doubt of an underlying trend, visible if we look back to Fig. 31-1, that suggests a gradual deterioration in the merchandise component of our balance on current account.

Such a trend is actually long overdue. Much of the American export surplus of the 1950s and earlier 1960s was due to Europe's inability to meet heavy production demands, a condition that has now been remedied. In addition, the growth of American *production* overseas—a development into which we will look in our next chapter—has further weakened our flow of exports.

But there is a reason even more fundamental than that. We should expect that a nation such as ours, with large amounts of capital invested overseas and a rising inflow of dividends and royalties, would *properly* run a negative merchandise balance on current account. After all, in the normal course of world affairs we know that there must be some rough equating of the inflows and outflows of foreign exchange among countries. If we are to enjoy a steady net inflow of profits and earnings from our capital, we stand in exactly the same danger that we have discussed at various times in other contexts: the danger of "draining" all the foreign exchange of other nations. The only normal way to return this surplus foreign exchange is to buy more than we sell. Thus, as a so-called mature creditor nation, we should expect our normal trade relationship, over the long run, to have a net import balance on goods and services.

3. *The American balance of payments problem is by no means yet solved.*

We have already emphasized how rapidly flows of capital can move in an adverse direction as well as in a favorable one, and now we have added that the likelihood is that our balance of payments on goods and services is apt to worsen. This means that as long as our balance on government account continues to run a large negative figure, we can by no means count ourselves out of the woods. One of the main objectives of our foreign policy over the coming years must be to establish a viable economic relationship between America and the rest of the world.

Curing the
Balance of Payments Deficit

But it is one thing to say that we must find a viable economic relationship with the rest of the world, and another thing to find the means to establish such a relationship. How shall we deal with the tendency to spend more foreign currencies than we acquire? Or to put it differently, how can we cut down the surplus of dollars that foreigners acquire, over and beyond the amount of dollars they spend?

Basically, there are four possibilities.

1. *The classical medicine.*

One of the remedies one hears is that we must take the bitter purge of the "classical remedy" for balance of payments problems. What is the remedy? Specifically it consists of a stiff application of higher interest rates and a strict diet as far as government spending is concerned. In terms of its objective, it aims to cure the balance of payments problem by *deflating* the economy: forcing down our price level until our exports look more attractive to foreign buyers and until foreign goods become much more expensive for us to buy.

Thus the classical medicine essentially seeks to cure the deficit by boosting exports and cutting imports. Will it work? It may, when a nation is losing out in international markets and must re-establish its competitive position overseas. In a situation such as that of the United States, however, where a balance of payments deficit has persisted despite a very favorable showing on current account, it may do little to remedy the situation. For all the much talked-about inflation in postwar America, prices have risen here less rapidly than in the dozen major trading nations of the world, so that our prices have actually *declined* relative to world prices. This hardly seems an appropriate situation in which to apply the classical medicine.

And then there is another chastening thought. The classical remedy works, as we have seen, by deflating the economy. But there is always the danger that a would-be deflation of costs will tip over into a general contraction of expenditures. In that case, deflation becomes recession, and the "cure" for our balance of payments difficulties consists of unemployment and a slowdown in our real rate of growth. Few Americans are likely to want to pay that price for international equilibrium.

2. *Restraints on capital.*

Still, the problem is there. In some way or other, the excess of dollar payments *must* be reduced. Hence a number of suggestions have been made to reduce the imbalance not by an overall deflation, but by measures that will serve to discourage American spending abroad on capital account. One of these is the imposition of a tax on the purchase of foreign securities. Another is a general plea to business to defer inessential plans for overseas expansion. A third is the deliberate raising of short-term interest rates at home to attract foreign short-term capital here.

All these measures (which we have taken) aim at restraining the net outflow of American capital. In the short run, there is no doubt that they can help alleviate our deficit on international account. The problem arises when we ask if this is a wise *long-run* policy or not. For there is a useful purpose served when American capital goes overseas—useful not only to the nations to which it brings wealth, but to us as well. Our capital exports soon earn income which returns to us as a "plus" item on current account. In a normal year this investment income from abroad is larger than our capital exports abroad. Thus if we stifle capital exports to save dollars today, we jeopardize a larger flow of dollars to ourselves tomorrow.

3. *Correcting the government overseas deficit.*

The difficulties of taking more than short-term action in the capital market bring us to the next obvious candidate for paring down: the heavy overseas deficit incurred on government account. For the past decade, this government balance has cost us a net deficit of between $2 billion and $3 billion. Here, it seems is a likely cure for the balance of payments problem. What can be done about it?

We have already looked into one often suggested area of "remedy"—reducing our foreign aid expenditures. But we have discovered that the overwhelming bulk of these expenditures does not constitute any dollar drain. If we cut back our foreign aid expenditures, we would cut back on the considerable volume of American production that is transferred to the underdeveloped world, but we would hardly improve our dollar drain at all. The suggestion that the richest nation on earth curtail its aid to the poorest and most miserable for the sake of saving the few hundred millions of dollar drain that is the net "foreign exchange cost" of foreign aid seems like the last and not the first measure to be taken in curing the balance of payments.

What of reducing our military expenditures abroad? That would be a much clearer net saving of dollars, for there is much less linkage between the dollars we spend to sustain troops or bases or actual fighting abroad and the *sale* of American goods to those areas. To the extent that we are able to reduce our overseas commitments, not only in Vietnam but in Europe where we still maintain a large and expensive armed presence, we will certainly contribute greatly to the solution of our payments problem. The problem, however, is not an economic one—although it has profound economic consequences. The flexibility of our military budget is based on political considerations about which the economist, whatever his private views, has no professional competence.

4. *Semiflexible exchange rates.*

Finally, might it not be possible to avoid the problem of the deficit altogether by going part way toward flexible exchange rates? We will remember that if exchange rates could move freely there would never be a "deficit" in the first place, since the price of exchange, like any price, would always clear the market. (Indeed, we can now see that a fixed exchange rate creates a problem of "surpluses" and "shortages" exactly the way an arbitrary price floor or ceiling does in a market for goods. See pp. 460-62.)

The difficulty with a freely moving exchange rate, we also recall, was that it posed formidable difficulties for the smooth flow of trade and capital. But suppose we tried to take the best of both worlds by permitting the prices of currencies to fluctuate freely *within fixed limits,* perhaps 5 percent above or below their "official" rate. That way the normal imbalances of supply and demand could be worked out without requiring a flow of gold, and the instability of the exchange rate would nevertheless be held within reasonably narrow boundaries.

Two problems present themselves for this attractive proposal. The first is that the price of the dollar (or any other currency) would rapidly fall to the floor if it came under speculative attack. At that point we would be back in the same difficulties we are in now. The second problem is that even a small fluctuation of 5 percent might be sufficient to unsettle world trade. Suppose, for example, that in one year the dollar was 5 percent below "par" and the German mark was 5 percent above. In the following year conditions changed, and each currency went the full 5 percent in the opposite direction. What seems like a movement of only 10 percent for each currency, considered separately, becomes a swing of 20 percent when the prices of the two currencies are considered against each other. This might indeed be enough to interfere with the optimum flow of trade or investments.

Thus there is the risk that semiflexible exchanges will prove to be satisfactory only so long as speculative raids or wide swings in exchange rates do not trouble the international scene. But *any* system will work well when things are in basic equilibrium. The trick is to find the means that will work when things are in basic disequilibrium, as in the case of the United States balance of payments deficit.

Whatever cure we apply—and over the next decade we will have to apply *some* remedy—all of our proposals so far assume that we can undo the chronic deficit that has plagued our nation. But suppose we cannot? Suppose that we find it impossible to increase our balance on merchandise account, and impossible (or unwise) to restrict the flow of long-term capital abroad, and impolitic to cut back our government overseas spending? What could we do then?

DEVALUATION

One course of action must be apparent. It is to change the relationship of the dollar to gold, so that the Treasury would ask not $35 for an ounce of gold, but $45 or $75 or any other large sum. Instantly this new exchange rate would make American prices cheaper abroad—it would be the classical medicine painlessly taken. But better yet: with devaluation, our remaining gold stock would immediately be worth a great many more dollars. There-fore, any deficit on the balance of payments could be easily settled by shipping a much smaller quantity of gold. The crisis would be over.

Or would it? We have already seen the problems that would ensue if the United States were unable to meet its obligations in gold at all. But devaluing would in fact be tantamount to very much such a state of affairs. Countries that had held their dollar balances secure in the conviction that they would always be worth so much in gold (and thereby in other currencies), would now find themselves shortchanged by the amount of the devaluation.

The problem, in other words, is that devaluation is a very difficult course for a country to take when its own currency serves many other nations as part of their international reserves. For then, devaluation does not merely affect the value of *our* reserves, but of *theirs* too. Our gold stock is worth more; their dollars are worth less.

But this is not the only difficulty with devaluation. Changing the price of one's currency by fiat is always a two-edged sword. A nation devalues, among other reasons, to increase its exports and to discourage imports. But other nations may not take kindly to this prospect of increased international competition. Hence they may devalue also, leaving international price relationships just where they were.* The era of the 1930s saw a number of such competitive devaluations that brought little in their train but international friction.

Last, we must take into account an effect of devaluation that applies less cogently to us than to nations that are heavily dependent on foreign commerce. It is that *devaluation raises the costs of imports to countries that have devalued.* If the dollar now buys fewer yen, Japanese cameras will cost more. If imports are an important part of that country's standard of living, this means that devaluation will raise domestic prices.

Thus devaluation looks much more attractive superficially than it does on careful examination. This does not mean that it is therefore never useful. There are occasions when it is plain that a nation's exchange rate is hopelessly out of line with other countries, and that none of the milder medicines will suffice to restore a balance of payments. In that case there is a choice to be made. Either trade must be allowed to wither away and fall to the level that the overpriced country can afford, or the difficult step of devaluation must be made, once again putting the country on a competitive footing. Great Britain, for example, after World War II, devalued its prewar pound which was obviously far out of line with postwar realities from $4.00 to $2.80 and then, when it was unable to cure a persistent balance of payments gap that was draining away its reserves, had to devalue again in 1967, from $2.80 to $2.40. Underdeveloped nations on numerous occasions have devalued to bring their inflated price levels back to some sort of parity with world market levels.

FLOATING THE DOLLAR

For many years, the United States resisted the temptation to cope with its balance of payments problem by devaluation. But in the late summer of 1971, the pressures on the dollar again worsened, especially after it became known that the United States would probably incur a sizeable adverse

---

* A multilateral devaluation does leave *some* countries ahead of the game—the gold-producers, who now sell their gold for more units of currency of the other nations. Thus multilateral devaluation would in fact make a vast gift to the major gold-producing nations: the Republic of South Africa and the Union of Soviet Socialist Republics.

balance of trade on its merchandise account, long a net dollar earner, as we have seen. To prevent what might have been an intolerable strain on the fragile international machinery for maintaining the $35 price of gold, the Nixon administration stunned the world by announcing that it was refusing to sell anymore gold and that the price of the dollar would be "temporarily determined," much as it would under a flexible exchange system.

By "floating" the dollar, rather than declaring a new higher price of gold, the administration avoided an outright devaluation. Immediately after the announcement, however, the price of the dollar cheapened in relation to other currencies, so that, in fact, the dollar was devalued. Further, the administration declared its intention of repegging the dollar to gold as soon as a more realistic international value for our monetary unit had been found.

THE IMF
AND SDR'S

But why repeg the dollar to gold at all? Why not allow it to continue to float, accepting the problems of a flexible exchange rate in place of those of an inflexible one?

The answer seems to lie mainly in the fact that international bankers and investors, not having studied their economics hard enough, continue stubbornly to believe that gold is in some way intrinsically more "valuable" than dollars or marks or francs. Particularly in times of crisis, there is a general rush to buy gold as the "safest" investment. Hence it seems likely that gold will continue to play a central role in international finance for some time to come.

We may, however, be seeing the first step away from what has been called "the international psychosis of gold" in the creation of a *new international reserve currency* by the International Monetary Fund (IMF). Today the IMF operates as a kind of board of international financial adjustment. Its member nations have all subscribed both gold and national currency to the fund and have the privilege of borrowing gold or other currencies from the fund. In turn, the fund serves as a monitor of exchange adjustments, since it will not lend reserves unless it approves the exchange rates and policies of its would-be borrowers.

At the end of the Sixties, the IMF took a very important step beyond these functions, by persuading its members to accept a new monetary unit as an addition to their reserves. Called SDR's (Special Drawing Rights), the new units are, in fact, reserves created out of thin air and credited to members' IMF accounts. Because they have the backing of the fund, these SDR's are just as "good" as gold and are already used by nations as a means of settling their international debts.

To date, however, the SDR's amount to only a very small proportion of total international banking reserves. They point the way, nevertheless, to a means of avoiding future crises of the kind we have experienced. Very slowly and hesitantly, the international community seems to be moving toward a more direct and purposive control over international finance, rather than an acquiescence in its "automatic" workings. In this process, the abandonment by the Nixon administration of the dogma of a "sacred" gold content of the dollar was a very important step. The decade of the 1970s may bring a degree of control into international finance comparable to the control over domestic financial affairs that accompanied the introduction of central banking in the first quarter of this century.

International vs. Interregional Trade

Why does the world have to operate under any of these bothersome and difficult international monetary arrangements?

We may better understand the matter if we go back to our initial paradigm and compare the case of New Jersey with that of Nova Jersia. Suppose that New Jersey had an adverse balance of payments with its sister states—that people in New Jersey were buying many products made outside New Jersey, but producing and selling little in exchange. The immediate effects would be severe. New Jersey checks would constantly be leaving the state, but an equal value of outside checks would not be entering it. Hence bank deposits would fall in New Jersey and rise elsewhere. As a result, money would be relatively scarce in New Jersey and interest rates would rise there. At the same time, because expenditures would be discouraged in New Jersey, wage rates there would fall and unemployment increase.

But correctives would soon appear. Men would leave New Jersey to seek work in New York or Pennsylvania. Money would flow back to New Jersey banks, attracted by higher interest rates. Cheaper wages and prices in New Jersey would serve to tempt capital back into the state. The market mechanism, in other words, would work (although perhaps only slowly) to bring New Jersey back into line with the prevailing price and employment and production levels of the region. To put it differently, New Jersey would tend "naturally" to share in the general economic well-being of its surrounding states.

Why does not this automatic mechanism work as well with Nova Jersia and its sister nations? In part, the answer is that nations, unlike states, are entitled to place *barriers in the way of international movements of labor and capital,* so that an easy shifting back and forth of the factors of production is difficult to achieve. Remember that one of the articles of the Constitution forbids the states from interfering with the movement of commerce across their borders. We have yet to achieve this degree of cooperation in the world. And even if we did, labor and capital are both shy of venturing abroad under different laws and regulations.

The second reason is that Nova Jersia, unlike New Jersey, insists on having *its own currency.* Given that prerogative of sovereignty, the question then arises as to how comparisons of price are to be made at all between countries that have different units of measurement for their commodities.

Thus it is essentially the stubborn reality of nationalism, with its fierce insistence on the separation rather than the joining together of human communities, that imposes the special difficulties of international economics. The world, from an economist's view, is a single vast human community in which he would like to see the powerful agency of the market bring the same salutary results as it does in smaller regions. But his hope is thwarted by the suspicions and jealousies and considerations of national pride and place. And nowhere do we find this tension between the "economic" and the "natural" view more clearly displayed than in the rise of a startling new development in international economics—the emergence of the multinational corporation. But that will have to be the subject of our next chapter.

KEY CONCEPTS AND KEY WORDS

1. We cannot compare international prices until we know the *exchange rates* of nations' currencies. These are basically determined by the supply and demand for *foreign exchange.*

Exchange rates

2. Foreign exchange arises from international transactions. In these transactions importers pay money to banks in their own nations, where this money is transferred to the local accounts of foreign banks. The home office of the foreign bank in turn pays the exporter in the money of his country. *The total of foreign-owned bank accounts in all nations is the sum of foreign exchange.*

Foreign exchange

3. The transactions that give rise to foreign exchange are of three basic kinds. One is transactions in *current private account* (imports and exports of merchandise, services, travel, remittances, and income on foreign investments). A second is *payments on government account* (regular government expenditures, foreign aid, military). A third is transactions involving *capital account* (long-term and short-term).

Current private, capital, and government accounts

4. *A freely moving exchange rate would reflect the supply and demand from these transactions.* If a country tended to spend more abroad than it received from abroad, it would soon run short of foreign exchange, whereas other nations would hold large amounts of its money. As a result its currency would fall in price relative to other currencies. In turn, this would make its imports more expensive and its exports cheaper. The change in prices would then tend to correct the imbalance of supply and demand. (A surplus of receipts over expenditures would work in just the other direction.)

Fixed vs. free exchange rates

5. *Under freely fluctuating exchange there can be no balance of payments problem;* however, there are other difficulties involving the *risk of trading or investing loss* or of *speculative raids.*

6. *Fixed exchange rates* are established through the commitment of nations to exchange their currencies for gold on the demand of official holders of foreign balances. The Treasury has agreed to buy and sell gold at $35 an ounce, and nearly all other nations have announced either gold or dollar values for their currencies.

Semiflexible exchange rates

7. Under fixed exchange rates, a disequilibrium in the supply and demand for foreign exchange cannot be remedied by a change in the price of foreign exchange. It must be settled either by the *shipment of gold* or by the *agreement of one country not to demand payment in gold from another but to hold its currency instead.* Foreign nations now hold larger balances in the U.S. than our entire gold stock. Thus the *dollar has become a world reserve currency.*

Balance of payments

8. *The overall balance of payments must always balance*—that is, every transaction must be paid for in one way or another. What we mean by the "balance" of payments is the aggregate of receipts and expenditures for normal international transactions—current private, government, and capital accounts. What our balance of payments shows is *how any difference in receipts and expenditures has been settled*—whether by gold flows or by a rise in foreign-held accounts.

9. A continuation of the gold drain from the United States would pose serious consequences both for trade and for the international economic position of the U.S. The means of remedying the imbalance, however, are not simple. There are six basic ways of doing so.

"Classical medicine"

- The *"classical medicine,"* or price deflation, carries the risk of recession. In addition the U.S. usually has a very favorable balance on merchandise account.
- The *deliberate curtailment of capital outflows* penalizes both the world (which needs U.S. capital) and the United States (which will lose the income from its potential foreign investments).
- A curtailment of U.S. military spending abroad necessitates a political decision to alter U.S. foreign policy.
- *Semiflexible exchange rates* are an attractive possibility—provided that heavy speculation or wide swings of rates do not occur.

Devaluation

- *Devaluation,* while useful as a means of redressing the trade balance of a small nation, is very difficult for a nation whose currency occupies a reserve status.

IMF

- *Strengthening of the IMF* will be a slow and tentative process.

Although none is without its difficulties, one or more of these remedies (or new remedies altogether) will have to be applied during the coming years.

10. The basic reason why a smooth-working international finance is so much more difficult to achieve than interregional finance is that factors cannot move freely across national borders and that nations insist on having independent currencies. In the end it is the *political barrier of nationalism* that poses the special problems of international currency.

Q U E S T I O N S

1. If you wanted to buy a Swiss watch and discovered that it cost 200 francs, what would you need to know to discover if it were cheaper or more expensive than a comparable American watch? Suppose that the price of francs was 20¢ and the American watch $50? What if the price of francs rose to 30¢?

2. If you now bought the watch, to be sent to you, how would you pay for it? What would happen to your bank check? How would the Swiss watchmaker be paid?

3. Suppose that the Swiss, in turn, now decided to buy an American radio that cost $40. He finds the rate of exchange is 5 Swiss francs to the dollar. Explain how he makes payment.

4. Now suppose that the rate of exchange rises for the Swiss, so that he has to pay 6 francs for a dollar. What happens to the price of the radio in Swiss terms? Suppose the rate cheapens, so that he pays only 4 francs? Now what is the price of the radio to him?

5. What are the main categories of the total balance of payments? Why do we divide them into the groups we do?

6. Suppose that the U.S. sold abroad only one product—machines—and that at the going rate of exchange, our machines were more expensive than those of other nations. What would happen if exchange rates were free to move?

7. Suppose exchange rates were fixed. Then what might happen? Could trade simply stop? Might the U.S. devalue (forgetting about its special responsibilities for international payments)? What would be the effect of devaluation on the price of the U.S. machines?

8. What are the difficulties of adjusting the government balance of payments? The balance on capital account?

9. Why is it important to retain our gold supplies for international use rather than using them to back the U.S. money supply?

10. What is actually meant by the balance of payments? Is it possible for the total flows of all international expenditures and receipts to be different? Then why is the balance of payments considered to be a problem?

11. Describe the consequences of a sudden announcement that the U.S. has gone off gold. What would happen at first to the international value of the dollar? Do you think that after a time the dollar might recover its strength? Why?

12. What is there to prevent a country from deliberately subsidizing all its export industries, so that they can undersell the whole world on everything? Assume that the United States tried this policy. Describe carefully what would happen to the balance of payments. What would be the final outcome of the policy?

We have looked fairly carefully into the advantages and disadvantages of free trade as a means of organizing the economic intercourse of nations, and we shall have something more to say about it when we study the problems of the underdeveloped world. But in this chapter we must add a new dimension to our picture of international economics. Everything we have heretofore learned has had to do with the international *exchange* of goods and services. What we must now consider is a revolutionary development in international economics, based not on exchange, but on the *international production* of goods and services. To understand what this means we must learn about a new institution that has sprung up as the most important agency for international production: the multinational corporation.

THE MULTINATIONAL CORPORATION

What is a multinational corporation? Essentially, we mean a corporation that has producing branches or subsidiaries located in more than one nation. Take PepsiCo, for example. PepsiCo does not ship its famous product around the world from bottling plants in the United States. It *produces* Pepsi Cola in 512 plants located in 114 countries. When you buy a Pepsi in Mexico or the Philippines or Israel or Denmark, you are buying an American product that was manufactured in that country.

PepsiCo is a far-flung, but not a particularly large multinational corporation: in 1969 it was only the 119th largest industry. More impressive by far is the Ford Motor Company, a multinational that consists of a network of 60 subsidiary corporations, 40 of them foreign-based. Of the corporation's total assets of $8 billion, 36 percent are invested in 27 foreign nations; and of its 388,000 employees (as of 1966) 150,000 were employed outside the U.S. And, if we studied the corporate structures of GM or IBM or the great oil companies, we would find that they, too, are *international* companies— not only because they export their goods (or import their materials), but also because they all have substantial portions of their total wealth invested in productive facilities outside the United States.

Indeed, if we broaden our view to include the top 100 American firms, we find that 62 have such production facilities in at least 6 nations. Moreover, the value of output that is produced overseas by the largest corporations by far exceeds the value of the goods they still export from the United States. In 1968, sales of manufacturing foreign affiliates of U.S. firms (which means their wholly or partially owned overseas branches) came to over $59 billion.[1] In the same year, our total exports of manufactures amounted to $24 billion, only 40 percent as much as American firms produced abroad. Indeed, *all* U.S. exports, including agricultural and other nonmanufactures, amounted to $9 billion less than our manufacturing output abroad.[2]

But that is still only a part of the picture. The $59 billion refers only to *manufacturing* abroad. If we add the sale of all goods and services produced abroad (which brings oil into the picture, as well as U.S. trade and retail activities abroad) our total foreign-produced flow of output probably amounted to over $110 billion in 1968.[3] One estimate for 1970 places the value of all U.S. overseas output at a staggering $200 billion.[4]

Another way of establishing the spectacular rise of international production is to trace the increase in the value of U.S. foreign direct investment; that is, the value of foreign-located, U.S.-owned plant and equipment (*not* U.S.-owned foreign bonds and stocks). In 1950 the value of U.S. foreign direct investment was $11 billion. In 1970 it was over $70 billion. Moreover, this figure, too, needs an upward adjustment, because it includes only the value of American dollars invested abroad and not the additional value of foreign capital that may be controlled by those dollars. For example, if a U.S. company has invested $10 million in a foreign enterprise whose total

INTERNATIONAL DIRECT INVESTMENT

---

[1] *Survey of Current Business,* October 1970, p. 20; *Statistical Abstract,* p. 696.

[2] *Ibid.*

[3] Estimate by Emile Benoit in *World Business,* Courtney Brown, ed. (New York: Macmillan, 1970), p. 19.

[4] Estimate by Judd Polk before the Subcommittee for Economic Policy of the Joint Economic Committee, July 27, 1970.

net worth is $20 million, the U.S. official figures for our foreign investment take note only of the $10 million of American equity (ownership) and not of the $20 million of wealth that our equity actually controls. If we include the capital controlled by our foreign direct investment as a whole, the value of American overseas productive assets almost certainly exceeds $120 billion and may be as large as $200 billion.[5] In general, something between a quarter and a half of the real assets of our biggest corporations are located abroad.

<table>
<tr><td>THE
"AMERICAN
CHALLENGE"</td><td>

The stunning expansion of American corporate production overseas, especially in Europe, has given rise to what has been called *The American Challenge.* In a book with that title, Jean-Jacques Servan-Schreiber describes the "take over" of French markets by dynamic American firms that have seized 50 percent of Europe's semiconductor market, 80 percent of its computer market, and 95 percent of its integrated circuit production. Servan-Schreiber fears that the American Challenge portends the Americanization of Europe's fastest growing industries. "Fifteen years from now," he writes, "it is quite possible that the world's third greatest industrial power, just after the United States and Russia, will not be Europe, but American industry in Europe."[6]
</td></tr>
</table>

Servan-Schreiber argues that Europe must fend off this American threat by the formation of equally efficient, large pan-European corporations. But he fails to see that the movement toward the internationalization of production is not a strictly American but a truly multinational phenomenon. If the American multinationals are the most imposing (of the world's biggest 500 corporations, 306 are American), they are closely challenged by non-American multinationals. Philips Lamp Works, for example, is a huge Dutch multinational company with operations in 68 countries. Of its 225,000 employees, 167,000 work in nations other than the Netherlands "home" nation. Royal Dutch/Shell is another vast multinational, whose "home" is somewhere between the Netherlands and the United Kingdom (it is jointly owned by nationals of both countries): Shell *in the United States* ranks among our top 20 biggest companies. Another is Nestlé Chocolate, a Swiss firm, 97 percent of whose $2 billion revenues originate outside Switzerland.

Thus if we look at the world picture of production, we find that European (and Japanese) firms have been expanding their production overseas just as rapidly as, or even more rapidly than, American firms; and although American companies have been growing very rapidly in Europe, thereby scaring the daylights out of their European competition, non-American firms have been growing even faster in other parts of the world market,

---

[5] Estimate by Kenneth Waltz in Brown, *World Business,* p. 219; also Louis Turner, *Invisible Empires* (New York: Harcourt, 1971), p. 71; and Polk testimony, *op. cit.*

[6] J.-J. Servan-Schreiber, *The American Challenge* (New York: Atheneum, 1968), pp. 3, 13.

including America itself.[7] (Think, for example, of the invasion of the American automobile market within the last 15 years by Volkswagen, Toyota, and a host of British and French makes.)

The point is that the change in international economic relations is truly worldwide. If we take the ten leading capital-exporting nations together (including the United States), we find that in 1967 their combined exports came to over $130 billion, but their combined overseas production amounted to well over $240 billion. For 1970, Judd Polk, economist for the International Chamber of Commerce, estimates that total international production—U.S. production abroad, foreign production here, and foreign production in other foreign countries—may account for as much as *one-sixth* of the total value of all world output, and a much higher fraction of the world output of industrial commodities.[8]

Because we do not have complete statistics on many aspects of international production, the full extent of this new form of economic relationship is still uncertain. But a number of economists have made projections based on the continuance of the rapid growth of international production. Professor Harold Perlmutter, for example, predicts that by 1988 most noncommunist trade will be dominated by 300 large corporations, of which 200 will be American, and that these corporations will account for roughly half of total world industrial output.[9] Perhaps the reader will recall Professor Berle's remark (p. 132) that some corporations "can be thought of only in somewhat the way we have heretofore thought of nations." A glance at Table 32-1,

TABLE 32 • 1

GNP OF VARIOUS COUNTRIES COMPARED WITH SALES OF SELECTED
MULTINATIONAL CORPORATIONS (billions of current dollars, 1967)

Netherlands	$26.6	Norway	$8.3
General Motors	**20.0**	**General Electric**	**7.7**
Belgium	19.7	Greece	7.1
Switzerland	15.9	**Chrysler**	**6.2**
Standard Oil (N.J.)	**13.3**	**Mobil**	**5.7**
Denmark	12.2	**Unilever**	**5.6**
Austria	10.6	**IBM**	**5.3**
Ford	**10.5**	Portugal	4.6
Royal Dutch/Shell	**8.4**		

Source: Louis Turner, *Invisible Empires* (New York: Harcourt, (1970), pp. 135–36.

[7] See Robert Rowthorn and Stephen Hymer, *International Big Business* (New York: Cambridge University Press, 1971), pp. 84–85.

[8] Polk testimony, *op. cit.*

[9] Turner, *Invisible Empires*, p. 191.

comparing the GNPs of various countries with the sales of selected multinational corporations, shows that Berle's statement was not just rhetoric.

Cautionary note: Corporate sales are not the equivalent of GNPs. The table vastly overstates the relative importance of corporations with respect to manpower: Portugal, for instance, has a population of 9 million, whereas GM employs less than 1 million. On the other hand, the table understates the economic strength of corporations: GM can borrow a great deal more easily than Portugal; and it controls *all* of its receipts, whereas Portugal gets only the taxes from its GNP. Nonetheless, the table makes it clear that Berle's comparison was not a wholly fanciful one.

EMERGENCE OF MULTINATIONAL PRODUCTION

Why has the multinational phenomenon arisen? The question is not altogether simple to answer. After all, it is cheaper to export goods or to license production abroad than to establish a branch in a faraway nation and encounter troubles and risks, which we will look into. Why, then, has production itself leaped overseas?

The initial reason arises from a characteristic of the firm, to which we have heretofore paid only passing attention. This is the drive for expansion that we find in nearly all capitalist enterprises. In our overview of the rise of American big business, we saw the emergence of giant enterprise as a consequence of the pull of markets and the push of a mass production.* Much the same logic has driven firms, from early times, to expand their market overseas. Samuel Colt, the inventor of the first "assembly line" revolver, opened a foreign branch in London in the mid-1850s (and promptly failed). But in those same years American entrepreneurs were already successfully pushing a railway line to completion across the Panama isthmus, and by the 1870s the Singer Sewing Machine was gaining half its revenues from overseas production and exports.

But what drives a firm to *produce* overseas, rather than just to sell overseas? The answers are many. One of them may be that transport costs become too large, once a certain volume of exports is reached, and simple economics dictates overseas production instead. Another may be a desire to locate a factory behind the tariff walls that a country may have erected in the hope of keeping out imports of the very goods the factory will produce. Another is simply the growth of the "horizon" of the giant companies, so that it becomes a matter of as great importance for IBM to win a commanding share of production overseas as it is to gain dominance at home. At some point in their expansion many companies make the transition from the

---

* Alfred Chandler has shown in a brilliant book, *Strategy and Structure* (Cambridge, Mass.: M.I.T. Press, 1962), that the typical domestic firm went through a series of "logical" changes in organization, growing from the single-product, single-plant firm (in which every operation was supervised personally by the founder-owner) to the multidivisional, multiproduct enterprise in which a tiered organizational structure became necessary to superintend the strategic requirements of national geographic scope and increasing technical complexity.

viewpoint of a "national" enterprise to that of a genuinely international one, whose markets are now worldwide in extent and whose production facilities must be located wherever these global markets are served most efficiently.* This is a matter we will return to when we consider the problem of imperialism.

What economic changes have followed from the startling rise of international production? One clear answer is that the growth of the multinational enterprise has dramatically changed the *geographic location* and the *technological character* of international economic activity.

ECONOMICS OF
MULTINATIONAL
PRODUCTION

The shift away from exports and imports to international production has introduced two changes into the international economic scene. One change is a movement of foreign investment away from its original concentration in the underdeveloped areas of the world toward the richer markets of the developed areas. Fifty years ago, in the era of high imperialism, most of the capital leaving one country for another flowed from rich to poor lands. Thus foreign investment in the late nineteenth and early twentieth centuries was largely associated with the creation of vast plantations, the building of railways through jungles, and the development of mineral resources.

But the growth of the multinational enterprise has coincided with a decisive shift away from investment in the underdeveloped world to investment in the industrial world. In 1897, 59 percent of American foreign direct investment was in agriculture, mining, or railways, mainly in the underdeveloped world. By the end of the 1960s, our investment in agriculture, mining, and railways, as a proportion of our total overseas assets, had fallen to about 20 percent; and its geographical location in the backward world came to only 36 percent of all our overseas direct investments. More striking, almost three-quarters of our huge rise in direct investment during the decade of the 1960s had been in the developed world; and the vast bulk of it has been in manufacturing (and oil) rather than in plantations, railroads, or ores.[10] *Thus the multinational companies are investing in each others' territories rather than invading the territories of the underdeveloped world.* This is not to say that they do not wield great power in the backward regions, as we shall see, but their thrust of expansion has been in other industrial lands, not in the unindustrialized ones.

The second economic change is really implicit in the first. It is a shift away from "heavy technology" to "high technology" industries—away from

---

* The internal dynamics that send some firms overseas, but not others, are by no means wholly understood. The internationalization of production is much more widely spread in some industries, such as glass, than in others, such as steel. Drugs are widely produced on an international basis; machine tools are not.

[10] See Mira Wilkins, *The Emergence of Multinational Enterprise* (Cambridge: Harvard University Press, 1970), p. 110; also *Survey of Current Business*, October 1970, pp. 28-29.

enterprises in which often vast sums of capital were associated with large, unskilled labor forces, as in the building of railways or plantations—toward industries in which capital is perhaps less strategic than research and development, skilled technical manpower, and sophisticated management techniques typical of computer, petrochemical, and other new industries.

Table 32-2 sums up the overall shift.

TABLE 32 • 2

SIZE AND DISTRIBUTION OF U.S. FOREIGN DIRECT INVESTMENT			
	1929	1950	1969
Total (millions)	$7,528	$11,788	$70,763
Percent distribution, by market			
Canada	27	30	30
Europe	18	14	30
Latin America	47	41	20
Asia, Africa, other	8	15	18
Percentage distribution, by industrial sector			
Manufacturing	24	31	42
Petroleum	15	29	29
Transport and utilities	21	12	4
Mining	15	9	8
Trade	5	7	8
Agriculture	12	5	} 9
Other	8	6	

Sources: *Historical Statistics of the U.S.*, p. 566; *Survey of Current Business*, October 1970, pp. 29, 31.

Note the dramatic shift away from Latin America and away from transport, mining, and agriculture into Europe and manufacturing, a shift that would be even more accentuated if we were not still dependent on oil as a major source of the world's energy. If nuclear power or the fuel cell displace oil within the next two decades, we can expect a still more rapid decline in investment in the backward areas (especially in the Near East), and a proportionately still larger concentration of foreign direct investment in manufacturing.

POLITICAL
ECONOMICS OF
MULTINATIONAL
ENTERPRISE

Thus the international corporations have served as vehicles for the redirection of the world's international allocation of capital investment. But the economic effects of the multinationals are perhaps less important than their political effects, for international production has a political factor that makes international economic relationships sharply different from those of pre-multinational days.

As we have seen, the "classical" conception of international trade was based on the familiar model of a competitive world in which factors of production were free to move about to find their points of highest return *within* their own national territories. The result, as our discussion of Infraville and Supraville revealed, was a final equilibrium in which each nation discovered the best allocation of resources both with regard to its own resources and to the advantageous exchanges it could make with other nations. In this final equilibrium, political considerations might enter in the form of tariffs or other trade barriers, but these were always considered by economists as the product of national nearsightedness, so that in theory— and to some extent in practice—it was possible to use the notion of *an equilibrium determined entirely by economic considerations.*

Not so, under the peculiar conditions of international production. For now the unit of economic activity is no longer the tiny "factor of production" subject to market forces, but a giant corporation capable of the maneuvers, tactics, and strategies characteristic of oligopolistic, rather than competitive, economic units. *Within* a given country, as we have seen, oligopolies tend to "settle down" to a more or less steady division-of-the-market, usually by tacit agreement not to engage in price warfare. But this division-of-the-market becomes rudely disturbed when a newcomer from the "outside" establishes his production unit within the home market of another nation. Moreover, the new division-of-the-market between the invader and the established giants will not be determined solely by the economic growth potentials of the various contestants. *There is an inescapable political element that will also play an important, perhaps determinative, role.*

This political element has two aspects. On the one hand, it depends on the ability of smaller nations, such as those we find in Europe, to relinquish their feelings of national pride sufficiently to allow the creation of big enough pan-European enterprises to challenge the (American) invader successfully. (Here is Servan-Schreiber's problem in a nutshell.) The cost of IBM's research and development, for example, is more than the entire sales earnings of its largest British competitor. To stand up against IBM, therefore, it may be necessary for British companies to merge with French or German ones, to form a competitor with the economies of scale, the ability to generate finance, the command over technical talent that will put it in a league with IBM. But that will require a *political* decision on the part of England or France or Germany to give up exclusive national control over "their" biggest computer companies.

A few such genuinely international companies have come into existence. Royal Dutch/Shell and Unilever are truly bi-national enterprises run by boards of directors that represent both Dutch and English directors and an effort is being made to create more such genuinely "European" enterprises. Whether or not this effort will be successful, it is too early to tell. But surely the critical element in the final division of the market among the multinationals will depend fully as much on the politics of international merger as on the economics of market tactics.

There is, moreover, a second political element that enters into the new multinational thrust. This is the question of the extent to which foreign governments will *permit* "foreign" corporations to operate within their borders.

This problem has its counterpart in the political decision on how much to tax (by tariffs) the goods that foreign companies sell to a given nation. But the problem of permitting the entry of a foreign-owned production unit is much more important—and much more difficult to resolve—because this may be the only way that a nation can "import" the *technology* and the *productivity* that the multinational invader will bring with it.

For example, the French government has been extremely uneasy over the virtual preemption of its high technology computer industries by American firms. Thus when General Electric sought to buy a 20 percent interest in Machines Bull, a leading French manufacturer of computer and desk machinery, the French government balked at the "Americanization" of the firm and forbade the transaction. That was in 1962. Within a very few years it became apparent that without an infusion of American technology, Machines Bull could not stand up to the competition of IBM, and the French government unhappily acquiesced in the American "takeover." But then it *was* a takeover, for G.E. demanded (and got) 50 percent control of Machines Bull.*

Thus, the pan-national thrust of economic activity unavoidably hinges on political decisions concerning the national independence of the economies into which the multinationals seek to move. Canadians, for example, have recently awakened to the fact that they own only *15* percent of their "own" industry. All the rest is foreign owned. Americans alone control 46 percent of Canadian manufacturing, 58 percent of its oil and gas, and almost 100 percent of its auto industry. The next biggest slice is owned by various European, mainly British, interests. Canada is thus a minority stockholder in its own economy, a situation that has led to strong sentiments to block further foreign ownership. But there would, of course, be a real economic price—a diminished rate of growth—for such a blockage.

HOST AND HOSTAGE

This conflict between the jealous claims of nation-states who seek to retain national control over productive activity within their own borders and the powerful thrust of pan-national corporations for new markets in foreign territories introduces profound tensions into the political economics of multinational production. On the one hand, the multinational is in a position to

* An investment that did not work out very successfully, by the way, for G.E.

win hard bargains from the "host" country into which it seeks to enter (as in the case of France and G.E.), because the corporation *is* the main bearer of new technologies and management techniques that every nation seeks. Therefore, if one country—say France—refuses to give a would-be entrant the right to come in (and possibly to cause financial losses to its established firms), the multinational may well place its plants, with their precious economic cargo of productivity, in another country, leaving the recalcitrant nation the loser in the race for international growth.

On the other hand, the power is by no means entirely one-sided; for once a multinational *has* entered a foreign nation, it becomes a *hostage* of the host country. It is now bound by the laws of that country and may find itself forced to undertake activities that are "foreign." For example, in Japan it is an unwritten law that workers engaged by giant corporations are *never* fired, but become permanent employees. Japan has been extremely reluctant to allow foreign capital to establish manufacturing operations on Japanese soil, to the great annoyance of foreign companies. But if, as now seems likely, Japan is opened to American and European capital, we can be sure that American or European corporations will be expected to behave in the Japanese way with their employees. This will not be an easy course to follow, since these corporations are not likely to receive the special support that the Japanese government gives to its own big firms.

Or take the problem of a multinational that is forced by a fall in demand to cut back the volume of its output. A decision made along strictly economic lines would lead it to close its least profitable plant. But this may bring very serious economic repercussions in the particular nation in which that plant is located—so serious that the government will threaten to take "action" if the plant is closed. What dictates shall the multinational then follow: those of standard business accounting or those of political accounting?

Or consider the multinational seeking to expand or to alter its operations in an underdeveloped country. This, too, may lead to friction, for as former Undersecretary George Ball has candidly asked: "How can a national government make an economic plan with any confidence if a board of directors meeting 5,000 miles away can, by altering its pattern of purchasing and production, affect in a major way the country's economic life?"[11]

As we have seen in Peru, Bolivia, and Chile (*before* the victory of the socialist party there in 1970), this incompatibility of aims may become so great that the underdeveloped country eventually seizes and nationalizes the assets of the multinational.

Is there an "answer" to this conflict between the business rationality of the multinational corporation and the political priorities of the nation-state? At this stage in the development of both institutions, none is in sight. The

MULTINATIONALS AND WORLD ORDER

[11] Brown, *World Business*, p. 334.

very idea of pan-national production is itself so new that we lack even a conceptual model of how to deal with its problems, much less a set of practical rules and regulations to follow. Take something so simple—but so important—as the location of the "head office" of the corporation to which a nation would make representations if the action of an international corporation were contrary to national interest. From one nation to another the legal definition of the *head office* differs: in the U.S. and the U.K., it is the place where the company is formally incorporated; in Morocco it is the location of the "registered" home office; in France, Germany, and Belgium, it is the main center of management; in Italy and Egypt it is the place of principal business activity. Which of these will respond when a country in search of legal redress calls out: "Will the real head office please stand up?"

Or take the question of the patriotic accountability of the multinational enterprise. Suppose a company wishes to move its profits from country A to country B, but that country A has balance-of-payments difficulties. Is the company bound to obey the wishes of A? Suppose the government in B also has balance-of-payments difficulties and desires the company to import capital? What should the corporation do? In 1966, for example, the United States government asked corporations not to export capital, lest our precarious balance of payments be worsened. But the Ford Motor Company decided that its long-term interests required the purchase of British Ford, so that despite objections of the U.S. government, Ford exported $600 million of capital to make the purchase. Was Ford "unpatriotic," if its actions were in the long-term interests of the company? Was it similarly "unpatriotic" (from a British point of view) for a group of English investors to export British capital to finance the building of the Pan Am skyscraper in New York?

Or suppose a multinational company, in one of its foreign plants, undertakes work that is integral to the defense of that nation; and that the foreign policy of the nation in question brings its military strength to bear against another country in which the multinational is also located? Is the company supposed to "take sides"?

UNRESOLVED QUESTIONS

There are no answers to such questions, only speculations.[12] Here are some of them.

Speculation 1. Will the conglomerate serve as a means of mediating between the demands of business production efficiency and political "national" control? For example, why didn't Ford build the Pan Am building, and why didn't the British investors put their pounds into autos? Both sides would have told you (in 1966) that they weren't "in the business" of real estate or cars, as the case may be. But the rise of the conglomerates (see pp. 123-24)

---

[12] For a searching commentary see Detlev F. Vagts, "The Multinational Enterprise: A New Challenge for Transnational Law," *Harvard Law Review*, February 1970.

opens new possibilities in this direction. If, in the future, the controlling center of Ford becomes (as I.T.&T. has already become) a capital-allocation office rather than the headquarters of an auto firm, it is possible that Ford *will* build buildings and that British realtors *will* build automobiles. In that case, the big corporation may surrender some of its multinationality in exchange for multi-industrial coverage.

Speculation 2. Will the multinationals, if they continue their growth, constitute the skeleton of a new form of world order? Some economists and businessmen see the rise of a pan-national system of oligopolies controlled by boards of directors that represent many nations (rather than mainly one, as is now the case), whose operations will pave the way for a much more pragmatic, down-to-earth, effective system of world production and distribution than the present competition of hostile, suspicious, and dangerous nation-states. Such an international rationalization of production, they believe, could bring a "businessman's peace," in which the big companies serve to accelerate world growth, to introduce efficiency into the backward areas, and to assert the logic of economic performance over the outmoded rivalries of jealous nation-states.

Speculation 3. Will the multinationals, on the contrary, serve to heighten the tension of a world which, for better or worse, must continue to use the powerful appeal of nationhood? How can giant corporations, necessarily dedicated to profit-making, adjust their operations to the often unprofitable needs of national development? How can corporations, jockeying for market position, provide the basis for a stable world economic system? The opponents of the multinationals see in them not a force for progress but only a means of imposing a calculus of profits on a world whose needs at the moment often demand an entirely different set of fundamental values.

AN UNWRITTEN ENDING

It is much too early to determine which of these arguments will eventually be proven correct. Perhaps the safest guess is that all will be, at least in our lifetimes. The big corporations are likely to continue to go in both multinational and conglomerate directions. To some extent they will be the international carriers of efficiency and development, especially in the high technology areas for which they seem to be the most effective form of organization. But if the power of the nation-state will be challenged by these international production units, it is not likely to be humbled by them. There are many things a nation can do that a corporation cannot, including, above all, the creation of the spirit of sacrifice necessary both for good purposes such as development and for evil ones such as war.

Perhaps all we can say at this stage of human development is that both nation-states and huge corporations are necessary, in that they seem to be the only ways in which we can organize mankind to perform the arduous and sustained labor without which humanity itself would rapidly perish. Perhaps after the long age of capital accumulation has finally come to an end and sufficient capital is available to all peoples, we may be able to think seriously about dismantling the giant enterprise and the nation-state, both of which overpower the individual with their massive organized strength. However desirable that ultimate goal may be, in our time both state and corporation promise to be with us, and the tension between them will be part of the evolutionary drama of our period of history.

KEY CONCEPTS AND KEY WORDS

Multinational corporations

1. The basic conception of international trade has entered a new stage marked by *international production carried on by the multinational corporation.*

2. The natural impetus of the drive for growth has pushed most large U.S. corporations into multinational operations. As a result, our exports of manufactures are today only 40 percent of our overseas production of manufactured commodities. In fact, *overseas production is now considerably larger than the exports of all U.S. goods.*

Foreign direct investment

3. As a result of the thrust of the multinationals, U.S. foreign direct investment has risen to approximately $70 billion of foreign direct American investment and may be much larger than that if the value of foreign capital controlled by American equity is included.

4. The rise of the American multinational in Europe has been very rapid and has led to a European fear of an "American challenge." However justified in Europe, this fear masks the fact that *European (and Japanese) foreign investment is rising as rapidly as American—and much of it in America.*

Internationalization of production

5. *The prospect is for a genuine internationalization of production within the next few decades.* A few hundred large firms, of which the majority will probably be American, are apt to control a very large fraction of the production of industrial commodities on a worldwide basis.

6. *The rise of multinational production has resulted in striking shifts in the geographic location and technological character of international investment.* The trend has been away from investment in underdeveloped nations to investment in the markets of high-consumption countries; and away from low-skilled labor-intensive or capital-intensive industries to high skill-intensive industries.

High technology

7. The *incursion of the multinationals across national boundaries has raised sharp new problems of political economics.* An equilibrium in international production will depend on political decisions as well as economic forces. These are:
   - The ability of smaller nations to abandon national prerogatives in order to form effective international corporations to challenge American or other companies.
   - The willingness of countries to allow foreign companies to dominate industries that they may consider vital to their national interests.
   - The ability of most nations to import new high technology if they deny entry to the multinationals.

8. Equally perplexing problems are posed for the multinationals themselves. *If they are often in a position to drive hard bargains before entrance, once they have committed themselves, they are "hostages."* To which of the many countries where they may be located do they owe allegiance if the interests of those countries clash? To what extent should the dictates of profit determine their international allocations of manpower and capital? To what extent can a multinational "defy," and to what extent must it "bow before," the demands of a host country?

9. There are no answers to the questions above. *We still have no established rules or procedures or laws to cover this new mode of organizing the world's production.* Nor do we know if the growth of multinational enterprise will serve as a force for order and rationality or for friction and tension.

Q U E S T I O N S

1. How many products produced in America can you identify as "foreign"? (You might start with the detergents and soaps produced by Lever Brothers, the office machinery produced by Olivetti-Underwood, the gas and oil refined by Shell.)

2. Can you suggest a hypothesis that might be testable as to why certain industries seem to go "overseas" more rapidly than others? Why autos and tractors but not washing machines? Why plate glass but not sheet steel? (Little is known about this, so you might become famous if you come up with an idea that tests out.)

3. Do you think a nation is right to exclude a foreign company from producing in certain areas? Would you wish to exclude from the U.S. Japanese production of, say, high-speed computers if *this were the only way we could get high-speed computers?*

4. What do you think is the duty of a company that is active in nations A, B, and C, when all have balance-of-payments problems and request domestic corporations not to make unnecessary international payments? Suppose the headquarters of the company is in A and the stockholders want the profits from B and C repatriated?

5. Can you draw up a plan for a company that would be privately owned and managed but not officially "headquartered" in any one nation? From whom would it receive its charter? Under what laws will it operate so far as the top management is concerned?

6. Do you think that the rise of multinational production opens the way for a more rational world or a more divided one?

The challenge

to the

market system

Many chapters back, we focused our narrative of economic history on the rise of modern capitalism in America: and then, to understand better what we had described, we undertook a long theoretical journey, first through macro- and microeconomics and then through foreign trade. But our initial narrative is not yet complete. For the central subject of our early pages was not just the rise of American capitalism, but the emergence of the market system itself, and in describing its development in America we have by no means described it everywhere. That will be our task in this final section of our book. We must follow the fortunes of the market first in Europe and Russia, and then in the underdeveloped world. Then we will hazard a concluding generalization about the market system in the long evolution of economic society.

TRIALS OF CAPITALISM ABROAD

One thing is immediately apparent when we direct our eyes away from America to the continents of the East, West, and South. It is that the trajectory of economic evolution there has been utterly different from that in the United States. No doubt we recall that when we left the European scene in the early 1800s capitalism was fast becoming the dominant form of economic society. England was the very cradle of industrial capitalism itself; elsewhere on the Continent, if capitalism was not already established, it was clearly waiting in the wings for the last remnants of feudalism to disappear. Moreover, had we looked abroad from America at any time in the nineteenth century, our expectations would have been fully justified. By then, all of Europe was unquestionably capitalist in orientation. And not only Europe. By the end of the nineteenth century, capitalism had reached out to touch most of the other continents of the world. In Asia and Africa, the main European nations had established colonies or spheres of influence that projected the imprint of capitalism into these societies, many of which had barely awakened from an age-long slumber of ancient ways. In South America, as well, capitalism was clearly the main fertilizing influence. Even in reactionary Russia—the last of the great European powers to abolish the legal fetters of feudalism—by the early 1900s, capitalism had succeeded in creating a small but active nucleus from which further growth seemed assured.

Yet what do we find today? To our astonishment, the seemingly unopposed evolution of the world into a capitalist market system has not taken place. In Europe, its original birthplace, capitalism continues to be the dominant economic system; and yet we find that socialist parties either hold power or constitute the main opposition in England, France, Belgium, Netherlands, Italy, Sweden, Norway, Denmark, Germany, and Austria. In Russia, the nucleus of capitalism has been entirely swept away by a communist society. In the huge continents of East and South—in Asia and Africa and South America—we find that the original organizing impetus of capitalism has given way, in many of the most important nations, to a noncapitalist framework of economic organization. China is more communist than communist Russia. India proclaims herself a socialist state. So do Burma, Ceylon, Egypt, Guinea, Syria. Only in South America do we find socialism largely absent from the official ideologies of political economy; and even there, the examples of Cuba and the rumblings elsewhere hardly make it possible to anticipate the kind of capitalist development that we would have expected fifty years ago.

What happened outside America to abort the seemingly assured development of capitalism? A full answer to such a question would require much more than a book in itself, but we can begin to grasp the main picture of evolutionary trends if we follow, first, the factors that caused capitalism in Europe to take on a form different from that in America. From Europe it is not so long a jump, geographically or historically, to Russia; and from Russia we can turn with increased understanding to the so-called underdeveloped world.

What are the reasons behind the turn of events in Europe? They must be sought, to begin with, not in the economic tendencies of European capitalism but in the social and political background whence those tendencies emerged.

Certainly the social background was significantly different from that of America. In the New World, capitalism developed with a population that had, to a large degree, spiritually and physically shed the feudal encumbrances of the Old World; but in that Old World, many of the social

EUROPEAN CAPITALISM: FEUDAL HERITAGE AND NATIONAL RIVALRY

outlooks and habitudes of the past lingered on. An awareness of class position—and more than that, an explicit recognition of class hostility—was as conspicuous by its presence in Europe as by its absence in America. In Vienna, in 1847, writes one social historian:

At the top were the nobles who considered themselves the only group worth noticing. The human race starts with barons, said one of them. Then there were the big businessmen who wanted to buy their way into the human race; the little businessmen; the proud but poor intellectuals; the students who were still poorer and still prouder; and the workers who were poor and had always been very, very humble.[1]

The result was a totally different climate for the development of an economic society. Capitalism in America, building on a new and vigorous foundation, was, from the beginning, a system of social consensus. Capitalism in Europe, building on a feudal base, was deeply tinged with class conflict. It was without effort that American capitalism secured the loyal support of its "lower orders"; but in Europe, by the time of the revolutions of 1848, those lower orders had already turned their backs on capitalism as a vehicle for their hopes and beliefs.

Second and no less important in explaining the divergence of American and European economic evolution was the profound difference between the political complexion of the two continents. In America, save only for the terrible crisis of the Civil War, a single national purpose fused the continent; in Europe, a historic division of languages, customs, and mutually suspicious nationalities again and again prevented just such a fusion.

Accordingly, American capitalism came of age in an environment in which political unity permitted the unhindered growth of an enormous unobstructed market, while in Europe a jigsaw puzzle of national boundaries forced industrial growth to take place in cramped quarters and in an atmosphere of continued national rivalry. It is curious to note that whereas Europe was considered "wealthier" than America all through the nineteenth century, American productivity in many fields began to outstrip that of Europe from at least the 1850s, and perhaps much earlier. For instance, at the Paris Exposition of 1854, an American threshing machine was twice as productive as its nearest (English) rival and eleven times as productive as its least (Belgian) competitive model.[2]

These advantages of geographic space, richness of resources, and political unity were widened by subsequent developments in European industry. Not surprisingly, European producers, like those in America, sought to limit the destructive impact of industrial competition, and for this purpose they turned to *cartels*—contractual (rather than merely voluntary) agreements to share markets or fix prices. Unlike the case in America, however, this self-

[1] Priscilla Robertson, *Revolutions of 1848* (New York: Harper, Torchbooks, 1960), p. 194.
[2] Thomas Cochran and William Miller, *The Age of Enterprise*, rev. ed. (New York: Harper, Torchbooks, 1961), p. 58.

protective movement received the blessing, overt or tacit, of European governments. Although "anticartel" laws existed in many European countries, these laws were almost never enforced: by 1914 there were more than 100 international cartels, representing the most varied industries, in which most European nations participated.*

Cartelization was undoubtedly good for the profit statements of the cartelized firms, but it was hardly conducive to growth—either for those firms or new ones. By establishing carefully delineated and protected "preserves," the cartel system rewarded unaggressive behavior rather than economic daring; and together with the ever-present problem of cramping national frontiers, it drove European producers into a typical high-cost, high profit-margin, low-volume pattern rather than into the American pattern of very large plants with very high efficiencies. The difference in economic scale is dramatically illustrated by steel. In 1885, Great Britain led the world in the production of steel; fourteen years later her entire output was less than that of the Carnegie Steel Company alone.

As a result, by the early twentieth century, European productivity lagged very seriously behind American. A study by Professor Taussig in 1918 showed that the daily output of coal per underground worker was 4.68 tons in the United States, as contrasted with 1.9 tons in Great Britain, 1.4 tons in Prussia, and 0.91 tons in France. In 1905, the output of bricks per person employed was 141,000 in the United States and 40,000 in Germany; U.S. pig iron production was 84.5 tons per worker in 1909, compared with only 39 tons in Great Britain in 1907.[3] Parts of these differences were attributable to geological differentials, but these, too, were made worse by restrictive business practices. The result was a steady falling-behind in Europe as the twentieth century went on.

The divergence was strikingly noticeable in per capita incomes. In 1911, for example, when per capita income in the United States was $368, the corresponding figure for Great Britain was $250, for Germany $178, for France $161, for Italy $108. By 1928, American per capita income was $541 (in unchanged dollar values), while that of the United Kingdom was only $293; of Germany, $199; of France, $188; and of Italy, $96.[4] While American per capita incomes had grown by nearly 46 percent, English and French per capita incomes had increased only one-third as rapidly. German incomes rose only about one-quarter as fast, and Italian per capita incomes had actually declined.†

---

* In 1939 an estimated 109 cartels also had American participation, since American companies were not prohibited by antitrust laws from joining international restrictive agreements.

[3] Heinrich E. Friedlaender and Jacob Oser, *Economic History of Modern Europe* (Englewood Cliffs, N.J.: Prentice-Hall, 1953), p. 224.

[4] *Ibid.,* p. 522.

† We must be wary of placing too much faith in the translation of one income—say £500—into its "equivalent"—$1,200. Until we know the price levels, the living standards and customs of the nations we are comparing, we make such translations strictly at our own risk. But changes *within* a country, from year to year, are, of course, as meaningful in one currency as in another.

Still another consequence followed from the division of European industry and agriculture into national compartments. To a far greater extent than in America, it made the development of European capitalism subject to the expansion of international trade.

For the division of the European Continent into many national units made international trade a continuous and critical preoccupation of economic life abroad. For instance, a study has shown that in 1913, when manufactured imports provided but 3.6 percent of United States' consumption of manufactured goods, they provided 9 percent of Germany's, 14 percent of England's, 21 percent of Sweden's.[5] Perhaps even more striking is the degree to which some nations in Europe depended on international trade for the foodstuffs on which they lived: in the five years preceding World War I, for instance, England produced less than 20 percent of the wheat she consumed and barely over 55 percent of the meat.[6] We find the same dependence on foreign trade in the export side of the picture. Whereas the United States in 1913 exported a mere fifteenth of its national product, France and Germany exported a fifth, and Britain nearly a quarter of theirs.

Thus, to a far greater degree than America, Europe lived by foreign trade. Here we clearly see the advantage to America of its enormous unbroken market over the fragmented national markets of Europe. All the gains from trade with which we became familiar in Chapter 30 were realized in the swift rise of American productivity; whereas these same gains were denied to Europe. To put it differently, in America, the division of labor was permitted to attain whatever degree of efficiency technology made possible, for in the end virtually all products entered into a single vast market where they could be exchanged against one another. In Europe, where the need for, and the potential benefits of, a far-reaching division of labor were no less pressing, a tangle of national barriers prevented the optimal specialization of effort from taking place.

Instead, what was visible in Europe was a struggle between the need for international trade as a primary means for advancing productivity, and the retarding hand of national suspicions, rivalries, and distrust. A striking example was provided as recently as the early 1950s by the great cluster of European steel and coal industry near the German-Belgian-Luxembourg borders. Here, in a triangle, 250 miles on a side, was gathered 90 percent of European steelmaking capacity in a kind of European Pittsburgh. But this natural geographic division of labor had to contend with political barriers which largely vitiated its physical productivity. Typically, German coal mines in the Ruhr sold their output to French steelmakers at prices 30 percent higher than to German plants; while, in turn, French iron-ore producers charged far higher prices in Germany than at home. As a result,

---

[5] *Der Deutsche Aussenhandel* (Berlin: 1932), II, 23.

[6] Friedlaender and Oser, *Economic History of Modern Europe,* p. 206.

while American steel production soared 300 percent between 1913 and 1950, the output of Europe's steel triangle rose but 3 percent during the same period.

Our example, itself, poses a question, however. Prior to 1913, as we have seen, something like a great international division of labor did, in fact, characterize the European market, albeit to nothing like the extent seen in America. By 1913, we will remember, a very considerable flow of international trade was enhancing European productivity, despite the hindrances of cartels and national divisiveness. It was only the beginning of a truly free and unhampered international market, but at least it *was* a beginning.

What brought this promising achievement to an end? Initially, it was the shock of World War I, with its violent sundering of European trade channels and its no less destructive aftermath of punitive reparations, war debts, and monetary troubles. In a sense, Europe never recovered from its World War I experience. The slow drift toward national economic separatism, at the expense of international economic cooperation, now accelerated fatefully. Tariffs and quotas multiplied to place new handicaps before the growth of international trade.

Then came the Depression of 1929 as the final blow. As the Depression spread contagiously, nation after nation sought to quarantine itself by erecting still further barriers against economic contacts with other countries. Starting in 1929, an ever-tightening contraction of trade began to strangle economic life around the world. For 53 grim months following January 1929, the volume of world trade was lower each month than in the preceding month. Between the late 1920s and the mid-1930s, manufactured imports (in constant prices) fell by a third in Germany, by nearly 40 percent in Italy, by almost 50 percent in France. As international trade collapsed, so did Europe's chance for economic growth. For two long decades there followed a period of stagnation which earned for Europe the name of the "tired continent."

Against this background of economic malfunction it is easier to understand the growing insecurity that afflicted European capitalism. During the 1930s serious rumblings were already heard. In England the Socialist Labour Party had clearly displaced the middle-class Liberals as the Opposition. In France, a mildly socialist "Popular Front" government came to the fore, albeit insecurely. Even in Italy and Germany, the fascist dictators repeatedly declared their sympathy with "socialist" objectives—and whereas their declarations may have been no more than a sop to the masses, it was certainly indicative of the sentiments the masses wanted to hear.

Note that the socialist movements were not communist—that is, they were pledged strongly to democratic political principles and envisaged a "takeover" through education and persuasion rather than by revolution and coercion. In addition, the socialists sought to convert only the strategic centers of production into public enterprises, rather than to "socialize" all of industry and agriculture. Thus socialism was always a much more evolutionary program than communism. Nevertheless, to the European conservatives of the 1930s, the Socialist leaders appeared every bit as dangerous as did the Socialists' bitterest enemies, the Communists.

By the end of World War II, socialist ideas were clearly ascendant throughout most of Europe. Even before the war was concluded, the Labour Party swept into office in England and rapidly nationalized the Bank of England, the coal and electricity industries, much of the transportation and communications industry, and finally steel. As the first postwar governments were formed, it was evident that a socialist spectrum extended across Europe from Scandinavia through the Lowlands and France to Italy (where the communists came within an ace of gaining power). To many observers, it seemed as if capitalism in Europe had come to the end of its rope.

RECOVERY OF EUROPEAN CAPITALISM

Yet, European capitalism did not come to an end. Instead, beginning in the late 1940s and early 1950s, it embarked on what is unquestionably its period of strongest economic growth. Indeed, a comparison not only with the past but with United States performance during the same period shows the remarkable change that had come over the Continent.

TABLE 33 • 1

COMPARATIVE GROWTH RATES

AVERAGE ANNUAL RATES OF PER CAPITA INCREASE					
	France	Germany	Italy	U.K.	U.S.
Pre-World War I (1870–1913)	1.4	1.8	0.7	1.3	2.2
Post-World War II (1948–1962)	3.4	6.8	5.6	2.4	1.8 (1950–64)

Source: M. M. Postan, *An Economic History of Western Europe* (London: Methuen, 1967), p. 17.

Note that the nations of Europe not only doubled and tripled their pre-World War I rates of per capita growth, but actually outstripped the contemporary performance of the United States economy by a margin almost as large.

To bring about such results, important changes obviously must have taken place in these economic societies. One of them, it is hardly surprising to learn, was political. The postwar socialist governments quickly showed that they were not revolutionary but reform-minded administrations. Once in power they quickly instituted a number of welfare and social planning measures, such as public health facilities, family benefits and allowances, improved social security, and the like; but they did not engage in sweeping changes. Hence, when many of the socialist governments, facing the exigencies of the postwar period, were voted out again, they bequeathed to the conservatives the framework of a welfare state *which the conservatives accepted.* Harking back to one of the traditional weaknesses of European capitalism, we can say that this represented a conservative attempt to create a social service state which would mend the historic antagonism of the lower classes. As a result, we find today that in most European states, welfare expenditures form a considerably higher proportion of government expenditures than they do in the United States.

The second reason was even more important. This was the rise of a movement within the conservative ranks to overcome a still more dangerous heritage of the past—the national division of markets. This great step toward creating a full-scale Continental market for European producers is called the European Community—or more usually, the Common Market.

To some extent, the Common Market was born out of the vital impetus given to postwar European production by the so-called Marshall plan, under which Europe received some $12 billion in direct grants and loans from the United States to rebuild its war-shattered industry. Despite Marshall aid, it soon became apparent that Europe's upward climb would necessarily be limited if production were once again restrained by cartels and national protectionism. To forestall a return to the stagnation of the prewar period, a few farsighted and courageous statesmen, primary among them Jean Monnet and Robert Schuman, proposed a truly daring plan for the abolition of Europe's traditional economic barriers.

THE COMMON MARKET

The plan as it took shape called for the creation of a *supranational* (not merely an international) organization to integrate the steel and coal production of France, Germany, Italy, Belgium, Luxembourg, and the Netherlands. The new Coal and Steel Community was to have a High Authority with power to eliminate all customs duties on coal and steel products among members of the Community, to outlaw all discriminatory pricing and trade practices, to approve or disapprove all mergers, to order the dissolution of cartels, and to provide social and welfare services for all Community miners and steelworkers. The Authority was to be given direct power to inspect books, levy fines, and enforce its decrees—and still more remarkable, it was to be responsible not to any single member government but to a multinational Parliament and a multinational Court, both to be created as part of the Community. A Council of Ministers was to act as a *national* advisory and permissory body, but even here action could be taken by majority vote, so that no single nation (or even two nations) could block a decision desired by the Community as a whole.

By the fall of 1952, the Coal and Steel Community was a reality, and it lost no time going about its business. At mid-1954, customs duties and discriminatory pricing within the coal and steel "triangle" had been virtually eliminated, and roughly 40 percent more coal and steel was being shipped across national boundaries than had been shipped prior to the establishment of the Community. Cartels and secret agreements still remain, but the restrictive influence on production was much less than it was formerly.

The success of the Coal and Steel Community led, in 1957, to the next two organizations: Euratom, a supranational atomic power agency, and the Common Market itself, an organization that was to do for commodities in general what the Coal and Steel Community had done for its products. Under the Common Market treaty, a definite schedule of tariff cuts was laid down, envisaging within slightly more than a decade an entirely unimpeded Continental market for Common Market members, with a single "external" tariff vis-à-vis the world. In addition, there were to be a single agricultural policy and, perhaps most imaginative, full freedom for the intermember mobility of both capital and labor.

The Common Market is still in the process of achieving some of these goals, although it is well ahead of its timetable.* Already, however, it has led to a remarkable increase in European trade and production. Trade among member countries has grown from $6.8 billion in 1958 to $28.4 billion in 1968. As a result, the Community's rate of growth has surged ahead, as Table 33-2 shows.

TABLE 33·2

PERCENT AVERAGE ANNUAL GROWTH IN REAL GNP

	1950–1960	1958–1968
Common Market	5.9%	5.3%
Rest of Europe	3.1	3.8
United States	3.2	4.7

Source OECD; *Basic Statistics of the Community*, p. 24.

Notice that during the decade of the 1950s, the Common Market's growth was almost twice that of the United States; and although the pace of expansion has slowed somewhat abroad and quickened at home in recent years, it is clear that the doldrums of the European past are well behind us.

The figures, of course, only point to the real changes that have occurred. For the first time the style of life and level of consumption of the European working and middle classes have begun to resemble that of America. The number of autos in use has been growing at the rate of 12

* The first agreements have now been signed for the introduction of a single currency throughout the Community, although this will take many years to work out fully.

percent a year; the number of TV sets, at 30 percent. Not less important, the boom in European trade has led to an even greater boom in world trade.

There is much in these prosperous statistics that reminds us of the general course of affairs in the United States. After its time of trial, European capitalism, like American capitalism, seems to have achieved a high degree of economic success. It is true that socialist parties continue to constitute a strong political movement in Europe, but the thrust of these programs is no longer directed mainly toward nationalization or other fundamental economic changes, but aims instead at correcting social privileges or at buttressing still further the welfare arrangements that we find in every European country. Equality—social as well as economic—is the present main objective of European socialism, and although equality requires adjustments in the existing distribution of rewards, the socialists do not see it as requiring the destruction of the system by which those rewards are determined.

Yet if socialism has made its peace with modern capitalism in Europe, there is a deeper reason than a mere change of mind on the part of Europe's socialists. The reason is that capitalism in Europe has borrowed a central idea of socialism and adapted it to conservative uses—the idea of *national economic planning*.

For all through Europe we see a reliance on planning that is both greater and more outspoken than anything we have encountered in the United States. In our country, we recall from Chapter 9, we have arrived at a consensus as to fiscal and monetary policy as the proper implements for achieving a stable and satisfactory rate of growth. But in most European nations, there is visible a further commitment to planning as a means of achieving publicly determined patterns of resource allocation as well as adequate rates of growth.

In France, for example, a central planning agency, working in consultation with Parliament and with representatives of industry, agriculture, labor, and other groups, sets a general plan for French growth—a plan that not only establishes a desired rate of expansion, but determines whether or not, for example, the provincial cities should expand faster or slower than the nation as a whole, or where the bulk of new housing is to be located, or to what degree social services are to be increased. Once decided, the plan is then divided into the various production targets needed for its fulfillment, and their practicality is discussed with management and labor groups in each industry concerned.

From these discussions arise two results. First, the plan is often amended to conform with the wishes or advice of those who must carry it out. Second, the general targets of the plan become part of the business expectations of the industries that have helped to formulate them. To be sure, the government has substantial investment powers that can nudge the economy along whatever path has been finally determined. But in the main, French "indicative" planning works as a *self-fulfilling prophecy*—the very act of establishing its objectives setting into motion the behavior needed to realize them.

In England, Germany, the Netherlands, Italy, and Scandinavia, we see other forms of government planning, none so elaborately worked out as the French system, but all also injecting a powerful element of public guidance into the growth and disposition of the resources of their economies.

The plans have not been wholly successful. As we have noted (p. 377), inflation has been the curse of Europe to an even greater degree than it has here; and nothing like a successful "incomes policy" has been worked out in any nation. But considerable success has been attained in the allocation of resources for public purposes through planning, and in the shaping of the general contours of national development.

What is beyond dispute is that a basic commitment to planning seems to have become an integral part of modern European capitalism. *Note, however, that all these planning systems utilize the mechanism of the market as a means for achieving their ends.* The act of planning itself is not, of course, a market activity; but the realization of the various desired production tasks for industry is entrusted largely to the pull of demand acting on independent enterprises. Thus the market has been utilized as an instrument of social policy.*

EUROPE AND AMERICA

How do we account for the fact that in Europe the evolution into a guided capitalism has evidently progressed much further than in America? In part, the reason is no doubt ascribable to the problems that have racked Europe and have forced upon it a much greater degree of necessary government intervention for survival. The Common Market, for example, would never have been brought into being had Europe not suffered from the effects of economic fragmentation, and the Common Market in turn stimulated and supported the development of purely national planning efforts.

To some extent the difference may be due, as well, to the survival in Europe of those "feudal" (or at least monarchical) attitudes that contrast so sharply with the democratic climate in America. Europeans are used to, and accept, a larger role for public authority in the economic direction of affairs; whereas Americans have traditionally tended to resist and reject such a role. Hence the movement toward planning in Europe has not encountered the fierce ideological opposition it has met in America, where the very word still

---

* Anyone who wishes to learn more about the important subject of European planning should read Andrew Shonfield, *Modern Capitalism* (New York: Oxford University Press, 1965).

conjures up fearsome "socialistic" visions to some people. This is a matter we will discuss again in our last chapter. But we cannot put these questions into focus until we have looked into another significant drift—in the opposite direction. But to see that striking development we must now examine the rise of a totally different economic structure: the socialist economy of the Soviet Union.

We cannot here recount in detail the history of Soviet socialism. Let us, rather, begin by noting the extraordinarily difficult problem that faced the revolutionary leaders who had secured the victory of "socialism" in Russia in 1917. In the first place, Russia was a semifeudal society in which capitalism was restricted to a small industrial and commercial sector. Second, both production and distribution were highly disorganized in the chaotic situation following the civil war.

Finally, there was little guidance in the official literature of the Communist movement as to how a socialist society should be run. Marx's *Das Kapital*, the seminal work of communism, was entirely devoted to a study of capitalism; and in those few essays in which Marx looked to the future, his gaze rarely traveled beyond the watershed of the revolutionary act itself. With the achievement of the revolution, Marx thought, a temporary regime known as "the dictatorship of the proletariat" would take over the transition from capitalism to socialism, and thereafter a "planned socialist economy" would emerge as the first step towards a still less specified "communism."* In the latter state—the final terminus of economic evolution according to Marx—there were hints that the necessary but humdrum tasks of production and distribution would take place by the voluntary cooperation of all citizens and that society would turn its serious attention to matters of cultural and humanistic importance.

In reality, the Revolution presented Lenin, Trotsky, and the other leaders of the new Soviet Union with problems far more complex than this utopian long-term design. Shortly after the initial success of the Revolution, Lenin nationalized the banks, the major factories, the railways, and canals. In the meantime, the peasants themselves had taken over the large landed estates on which they had been tenants, and they had carved them up into individual holdings. The central authorities then attempted for several years to run the economy by requisitioning food from the farms and allocating it

---

* What is the difference between *socialism* and *communism?* We have already noted one difference in the West, where socialism implies an adherence to democratic political mechanisms, whereas communism does not. But within the socialist bloc there is another interesting difference of definition. Socialism there represents a stage of development in which it is still necessary to use "bourgeois" incentives in order to make the economy function; that is, people must be paid in proportion to the "value" of their work. Under communism, a new form of human society will presumably have been achieved in which these selfish incentives will no longer be needed. Then will come the time when society will be able to put into effect Karl Marx's famous description of communism: "From each according to his ability; to each according to his need."

to factory workers, while controlling the flow of output from the factories themselves by a system of direct controls from above.

This initial attempt to run the economy was a disastrous failure. Under inept management (and often cavalier disregard of "bourgeois" concerns with factory management), industrial output declined precipitously: by 1920 it had fallen to *14 percent* of prewar levels. As goods available to the peasants became scarcer, the peasants, themselves, were less and less willing to acquiesce in giving up food to the cities. The result was a wild inflation followed by a degeneration into an economy of semibarter. For a while, toward the end of 1920, the system threatened to break down completely.

To forestall the impending collapse, in 1921 Lenin instituted a New Economic Policy, the so-called NEP. This was a return toward a market system and a partial reconstitution of actual capitalism. Retail trade, for instance, was opened again to private ownership and operation. Small-scale industry also reverted to private direction. Most important, the farms were no longer requisitioned but operated as profit-making units. Only the "commanding heights" of industry and finance were retained in government hands.

There ensued for several years a bitter debate about the course of action to follow next. While the basic aim of the Soviet government was still to industrialize and to socialize (i.e., to replace the private ownership of the means of production by state ownership), the question was how fast to move ahead—and, indeed, *how* to move ahead. The pace of industrialization hinged critically on one highly uncertain factor: the willingness of the large, private peasant sector to deliver food with which the city workers could be sustained in their tasks. To what extent, therefore, should the need for additional capital goods be sacrificed in order to turn out the consumption goods that could be used as an inducement for peasant cooperation?

**THE DRIVE
TO TOTAL
PLANNING**

The student of Russian history—or, for that matter, of economic history—will find the record of that debate an engrossing subject.[7] But the argument was never truly resolved. In 1927, Stalin moved into command, and the difficult question of how much to appease the unwilling peasant disappeared. Stalin simply made the ruthless decision to appease him not at all, but to *coerce* him by collectivizing his holdings.

The collectivization process solved in one swoop the problem of securing the essential transfer of food from the farm to the city, but it did so at a frightful social (and economic) cost. Many peasants slaughtered their livestock rather than hand it over to the new collective farms; others waged outright war or practiced sabotage. In reprisal, the authorities acted with brutal force. An estimated five million "kulaks" (rich peasants) were executed or put in labor camps, while in the cities an equally relentless policy

[7] See Alexander Erlich, *The Soviet Industrialization Debate: 1924–1928* (Cambridge: Harvard University Press, 1960).

showed itself vis-a-vis labor. Workers were summarily ordered to the tasks required by the central authorities. The right to strike was forbidden, and the trade unions were reduced to impotence. Speed-ups were widely applied, and living conditions were allowed to deteriorate to very low levels.

The history of this period of forced industrialization is ugly and repellent, and it has left abiding scars on Russian society. It is well for us, nonetheless, to attempt to view it with some objectivity. If the extremes to which the Stalinist authorities went were extraordinary, often unpardonable, and perhaps self-defeating, we must bear in mind that industrialization on the grand scale has always been wrenching, always accompanied by economic sacrifice, and always carried out by the more or less authoritarian use of power. We have already seen what happened in the West at the time of the industrial revolution with its heavy-handed exploitation of labor; and without "excusing" these acts, we have seen their function in paving the way for capital accumulation.

In much the same fashion, when the Soviet leaders deliberately held down consumption, regimented and transferred their labor forces into the new raw industrial centers, and ruthlessly collected the foodstuffs to feed their capital-building workers, they were, in fact, only enforcing the basic process of industrialization. What was new about the Soviet program was that totalitarian control over the citizenry enabled the planners to carry out this transformation at a much faster tempo than would have been possible had protests been permitted. Under Stalin's iron will, the planners did not scruple to exercise their industrializing power to the hilt.

Without seeking to justify the Russian effort, it is worth pondering one last question. Can rapid industrialization, with its inescapable price of low consumption, ever be a "popular" policy? Will poor people willingly vote for an economic transformation which will not "pay out" for twenty or forty years?* Does rapid and large-scale industrialization *necessitate* a large degree of authoritarian political control? We will return to these problems when we turn to underdevelopment, but we might well begin to think about them now.

A massive industrialization drive requires a determined effort to hold consumption to a minimum and to transfer resources to capital-building, an effort greatly facilitated, as we have seen, by the totalitarian political apparatus. But there is still another question to be considered. How are the freed resources to find their proper destination in an integrated and workable industrial sector?

THE PLANNING MECHANISM

---

* We might note in passing that universal male suffrage was not gained in England until the late 1860s and 1870s. Aneurin Bevan has written: "It is highly doubtful whether the achievements of the Industrial Revolution would have been permitted if the franchise had been universal. It is very doubtful because a great deal of the capital aggregations that we are at present enjoying are the results of the wages that our fathers went without." (From Gunnar Myrdal, *Rich Lands and Poor.* New York: Harper, 1957, p. 46.)

Let us remind ourselves again of how this is done under a market economy. There, the signal of profitability serves as the lure for the allocation of resources and labor. Entrepreneurs, anticipating or following demand, risk private funds in the construction of the facilities which they hope the future will require. Meanwhile, as these industrial salients grow, smaller satellite industries grow along with them to cater to their needs.

The flow of materials is thus regulated in every sector by the forces of private demand, making themselves known by the signal of rising or falling prices. At every moment there emanates from the growing industries a magnetic pull of demand on secondary industries, while, in turn, the growth salients themselves are guided, spurred, or slowed down by the pressure of demand from the ultimate buying public. And all the while, counterposed to these pulls of demand, are the obduracies of supply—the cost schedules of the producers themselves. In the cross fire of demand and supply exists a marvelously sensitive social instrument for the integration of the overall economic effort of expansion.

And in the absence of a market? Clearly, the mechanism must be supplied by the direct orders of a central controlling and planning agency. *In a growing industrial economy, a planning agency must act as a substitute for the market.* Let us reflect for a moment what this entails.

To begin with, it means that the planning agency must provide a substitute for the forward-looking operations of the great entrepreneurs in a market economy. In place of a Carnegie or a Ford, building their plants in anticipation of, or response to, an insistent demand for their products, the planning body must itself set overall goals and objectives for economic growth. Not the consumer but the planners' own judgment and desires determine the force of "demand."*

Establishing the overall objectives is, however, only the first and perhaps the easiest part of the planning mechanism. It is not enough to set broad goals and then assume that they will be fulfilled by themselves. We must remember that planning in a totalitarian economy is not superimposed on a market structure in which individuals take care of the "details" of production according to the incentives of price and profit. In a totally planned economy, each and every item which goes into the final plan must also be planned. Schedules of production are needed for steel, coal, coke,

---

* In the case of the Soviet Union, the planning authority has typically set its demand goals in terms of Five-Year Plans. The first of these, from 1928 to 1932, had as its basic objective the intensification of industrialization in heavy industry, with special emphasis on electrification; the second took as its main goal the development of transportation and the beginning of agricultural planning; the third plan (1938-1942) was essentially occupied with producing the needs for a war economy; the fourth, from 1946 to 1950, was mainly a plan of reconstruction from wartime damage, with continuing emphasis on heavy industry; a fifth plan, 1951-1955, emphasized a steep increase in output with some stress being given (for the first time) to consumer goods. A sixth plan was scrapped in midcourse; a seventh (1959-1965) aimed to increase industrial output by 80 percent, agricultural output by 70 percent, and to bring significant increases in housing (a sector long neglected in the interests of industrialization) and in consumer goods, generally. We know that many of these objectives were not met, but there is no doubt of growing emphasis on consumer goods and housing.

lumber, on down to nails and paper clips, for there is no "automatic" device by which these items will be forthcoming without a planning directive. Supplies of labor must also be planned; or if labor is free to move where it wishes, wage rates must be planned in order to draw labor where it is wanted.

Thus supplementing and completing the master objective of the overall plan must be a whole hierarchy of subplans, the aggregate of which must bring about the necessary final result. And here is a genuine difficulty. For an error in planning, small in itself, if it affects a strategic link in the chain of production, can seriously distort—or even render impossible—the fulfillment of the total plan.

THE PLAN IN ACTION

How is this infinitely complicated planning system carried out in the Soviet Union? It is begun by breaking down the overall, long-term plan into shorter one-year plans. These one-year plans, specifying the output of major sectors of industry, are then transmitted to various government ministries concerned with, for example, steel production, transportation, lumbering, and so forth. In turn, the Ministries refer the one-year plans further down the line to the heads of large industrial plants, to experts and advisers, and so on. At each stage, the overall plan is thus unraveled into its subsidiary components, until finally the threads have been traced as far back as feasible along the productive process—typically, to the officials in charge of actual factory operations. The factory manager of, for instance, a coking operation is given a planned objective for the next year, specifying the output needed from his plant. He confers with his production engineers, considers the condition of his machinery, the availability of his labor force, and then transmits his requirements for meeting the objective back upward along the hierarchy. In this way, just as "demand" is transmitted downward along the chain of command, the exigencies of "supply" flow back upward, culminating ultimately in the top command of the planning authority (the Gosplan) itself.[8]

From this description of the tasks of planning, it is obvious that planning is an enormously complex task. Indeed, the very complexity of the task is such that more than one economist in the first days of chaos following the Russian Revolution declared socialism—meaning by this, centralized decision-making—to be "impossible."

PLANNING AND EFFICIENCY

Central planning is not impossible for certain kinds of economic tasks: for "forcing" growth, in particular, it may be more effective than any other means of bringing about the needed allocation of resources. The most recent investigation into Soviet economic performance, for example, indicates that over the period 1929 to 1961, Soviet output rose between 5.2 and 7.2

[8] For an excellent description of Soviet planning, see Robert W. Campbell, *Soviet Economic Power*, 2nd ed. (Boston: Houghton Mifflin, 1966).

percent per annum—roughly twice as fast as the United States' growth over these years.[9] Part of this extraordinary record, to which must be credited Russia's passage from a peasant society to an industrial one, is certainly due to the ability of central planning to bring about tremendously high levels of investment: measured in 1937 prices, investment was pushed from 8.4 percent of GNP in 1928 to 30.6 percent in 1961.

The trouble comes when we look to the planning system for its *efficiency* in allocating resources, rather than to its success in forcing total volumes of output. An economy may be very successful in producing larger and larger quantities of steel and electric power, but it may be very unsuccessful in producing the right kinds of steel or in locating its electric power plants effectively or in producing its goods at the lowest possible cost. Sooner or later, such inefficiency will interfere with the rate of growth, and that is exactly what we see in the case of the U.S.S.R. From many indications it appears that the Soviet rate of expansion has been declining in recent years and that the economy is increasingly plagued with difficulties arising from a failure to produce the right goods at the best possible prices. The result is a system that has operated more and more unevenly and awkwardly, as first one and then another of the gears in the great machine jammed.

In 1962, for example, an observer reports:

The Byelorussian Tractor Factory, which has 227 suppliers, had its production line stopped 19 times ... because of the lack of rubber parts, 18 times because of ball bearings, and 8 times because of transmission components. The pattern of breakdowns continued in 1963. During the first quarter of 1963 only about one-half of the plant's ball bearing and rubber needs were satisfied, and only half of the required batteries were available. One supplier shipped 19,000 less wheels than called for in the contract. In total, they were short of 27 items.[10]

Stories such as these abound in any book describing the Soviet economic system. They should not be taken to mean that Russian planning is a "failure" or that it is on the point of collapse. Taken as a whole, the system continues to produce at good rates. But the bottlenecks do point to deep-seated troubles in running the economy smoothly, even now when industrial needs are still relatively simple and consumers are not yet highly critical. These troubles are apt to exact a higher price as the Soviet economy turns its attention to the more complex and demanding problems of a highly integrated industrial process and a much more demanding citizenry.

What is at the root of the inefficiency of central planning? *Essentially the problem is to find a means of guiding the production of individual firms.* Do not forget that a Russian factory manager has very little leeway in what he

[9] Richard Moorsteen and Raymond P. Powell, *The Soviet Capital Stock, 1928-1962* (Homewood, Ill.: Irwin, 1966).

[10] Barry Richman, *Soviet Management* (Englewood Cliffs, N.J.: Prentice-Hall, 1965), p. 123.

produces or the combination of factors that he uses for production. Both his inputs and his outputs are carefully specified for him in his plan. What the manager *is* supposed to do is to beat the plan, by "overproducing" the items that have been assigned to his plant. Indeed, from 30 to 50 percent of a manager's pay will depend on bonuses tied directly to his "overfulfillment" of the plan, so that he has a very great personal incentive to exceed the output "norms" set for him.

All this seems sensible enough. Trouble comes, however, because the manager's drive to exceed his factory's quota tends to distort the productive effort from the receivers' point of view. For example, if the target for a textile factory is set in terms of yards of cloth, there is every temptation to weave the cloth as narrowly as possible, to get the maximum yardage out of a given amount of thread. Or if the plan merely calls for tonnages of output, there is every incentive to skimp on design or finish or quality, in order to concentrate on sheer weight. A cartoon in the Russian satirical magazine *Krokodil* shows a nail factory proudly displaying its record output: one gigantic nail suspended from an immense gantry crane. (On the other hand, if a nail factory has its output specified in terms of the *numbers* of nails it produces, its incentive to overfulfill this "success indicator" is apt to result in the production of very small or thin nails.)

What is the way out of this kind of dilemma? A few years ago, a widely held opinion among the Russian planners was that more detailed and better integrated planning performed on a battery of computers would solve the problem. Few still cling to this belief. The demands of planning have grown far faster than the ability to meet them; indeed, one Soviet mathematician has predicted that at the current rate of growth of the planning bureaucracy, planning alone would require the services of the entire Russian population by 1980. Even with the most complete computerization, it seems a hopeless task to attempt to beat the problem of efficiency by increasing the "fineness" of the planning mechanism.[11]

Rather, the wind for reform in the Soviet Union is now blowing from quite another quarter. Led by economist E. G. Liberman, there is a growing demand that the misleading plan directives of weight, length, etc., be subordinated to a new "success indicator" that will, all by itself, guide the manager to results that will make sense from the overall point of view. And what is that overriding indicator? It is the *profit* that a factory manager can make for his enterprise!

Note several things about this profit. To begin with, it is not envisaged that it can arise from price manipulations. Factory managers will continue to operate with the prices established by the planners; but they will now

[11] For an interesting glimpse into the Russian change of mind, see *Planning, Profit and Incentives in the U.S.S.R.*, Myron E. Sharpe, ed. (White Plains, N.Y.: International Arts and Sciences Press, 1966).

have to *sell* their output and *buy* their inputs, rather than merely deliver or accept them. This means that each factory will have to be responsive to the particular needs of its customers if it wishes to dispose of its output. In the same way, of course, its own suppliers will now have to be responsive to the factory's needs if the suppliers are to get the factory's business.

Second, the profit will belong not to the factory or its managers, but to the State. A portion of the profit will indeed be allocated for bonuses and other rewards, so that there is a direct incentive to run the plant efficiently, but the bulk of the earnings will be transferred to the State.

Thus, profits are to be used as an efficiency-maximizing indicator, just as we saw them used in our study of microeconomics (see p. 521). Indeed, to view the change even more broadly, we can see that the reintroduction of the use of profits implies a deliberate return to the use of the *market mechanism* as a means of achieving economic efficiency. Not only profits but also interest charges—a capitalist term that would have been heresy to mention in the days of Stalin—are being introduced into the planning mechanism to allow factory managers to determine for themselves what is the most efficient thing to do, both for their enterprises and for the economy as a whole.

The drift toward the market mechanism is still new in the Soviet Union, and we do not know how far it will ultimately progress. The objectives of the 1971–1975 Plan call for a much greater emphasis on consumer goods, but speak of "an extensive use of economic-mathematical methods," which implies something of a return to the computer rather than a rapid movement in the direction of freer trade. Nonetheless, there seems to be no doubt from which quarter the winds blow most steadily. As Soviet economist A. Birman has put it: "Only three years ago, no one would have thought that there would be anything but the direct physical allocation of goods. Now economists talk of *torgovat* (trading) instead of *snabzhat* (allocating)."[12] Furthermore, the government has warmly endorsed the idea of "production associations,"—groups of geographically separate plants that coordinate their marketing, purchasing, research, and management, just like corporations. The market idea of economies of large-scale production has triumphed over the political idea of production organized by locality.

Meanwhile, the trend toward the market has proceeded much further in a large part of Eastern Europe, and above all in Yugoslavia. There, the market rules very nearly as supreme as it does in Western capitalist countries. Yet the Yugoslavs certainly consider themselves a socialist economy. As in the U.S.S.R., enterprise profits do not go to the "owners" of the business but are distributed as incentive bonuses or used for investment or other purposes under the overall guidance of the State. And again as in

[12] From Marshall I. Goldman, *The Soviet Economy: Myth and Reality* (Englewood Cliffs, N.J.: Prentice-Hall, 1968), p. 129.

the U.S.S.R., the market is used as a deliberate instrument of social control, rather than as an institution that is above question. Thus, the main determination of investment, the direction of development of consumers' goods, the basic distribution of income—all continue to be matters established at the center as part of a planned economy. More and more, however, this central plan is allowed to realize itself through the profit-seeking operations of highly autonomous firms, rather than through being imposed in full detail upon the economy.*

How far will this drift toward the market proceed? That is a question to which we will return in our penultimate chapter. What is important to recognize at this juncture is that there has been a visible movement toward the market mechanism in every *European* communist nation (we will see shortly why it is only in these nations). One consequence is that we find the same ideological alarm being expressed in these nations as in the United States, as each sees itself in danger of being subverted by the introduction of some elements of the other system: indeed, one of the reasons behind the Soviet invasion of Czechoslovakia was its concern that Czech economic (as well as political) liberalization had gone too far.

This convergent tendency of different systems is clearly of great importance in the perspective of economic history. But we cannot deal with it properly until we have surveyed one last type of economic situation that differs as much from Russian socialism as from American capitalism. This is the situation of economic underdevelopment, to which we next turn.

---

* One of the most interesting aspects of Yugoslav socialism is its effort to introduce worker-run enterprises. At least in theory, the top authority in most enterprises is a Worker's Council, which has the right to *fire* the boss of the plant, and which also determines wage and bonus payments, plant investments, and so on. We do not yet know whether this economic democracy exists in fact as well as on paper. If it does, it may prove to be one of the important social developments of our time. See Paul Blumberg, *Industrial Democracy* (New York: Schocken Books, 1969).

1. The development of European capitalism was considerably hampered by a number of factors absent from the American scene. Among these were a *feudal heritage* that brought serious political problems and *severe national rivalry* that prevented economic unification. As a result, productivity in Europe lagged behind that of the United States. Compounding the problem of slow growth was the *breakdown of international trade* following World War I.

National planning

2. Capitalism in Europe was seriously threatened by the rise of a *socialist opposition.* However following World War II, conservative parties generally accepted the reformist ideas of socialism and backed large programs of *social welfare and a commitment to*

European Community

national economic planning.

Common Market

3. Equally, or more, important was the creation of the *European Community* with its *Common Market,* a successful attempt to revive inter-European trade.

Indicative planning

4. Among the many European planning mechanisms, the most elaborate is the French system of *"indicative planning."* A centrally formulated plan is discussed among representatives of industry, labor, and other groups, and in the process of discussion and amendment becomes part of the general expectations of these groups. This leads to the requisite investment needed to bring the plan about. Thus the system works as a *self-fulfilling prophecy.*

5. All the European planning systems *rely on the market mechanism.* While the commitment of the European nations to a guided economy is in most cases greater than our own, a similar drift toward planning is visible in American capitalism as well.

Central planning

6. The U.S.S.R. has followed a totally different course. Following the Revolution of 1917, a system of *central planning* was initiated, but it early collapsed. Thereafter a semimarket system was introduced as a rescue measure.

Collectivization

7. Following long debates about how to secure agricultural production to feed workers engaged in industrial projects, Russia under Stalin began a *total collectivization* that used naked force to solve the food transfer problem and the industrialization program.

Success
indicators

8. The planning mechanism by which Russia carries out its industrial growth requires the formulation of *highly detailed and accurately interlocked subplans,* any one of which, if wrongly designed or unmet, can wreck the larger one. *Inefficiency* has been the plague of the central planning system, although the system did succeed in achieving its larger objectives. The problem has been that "success indicators" have led to misallocation of resources.

9. As a result, we see the *introduction of the market mechanism,* using profit as *the* success indicator, into the European communist economics. *The market is being introduced into socialism just as planning is being introduced into capitalism.*

QUESTIONS

1. Discuss how the fragmentation of a continent can affect the gains from trade. Does the experience of Europe illustrate that the bias of nationalism constitutes the main source of international economic difficulties?

2. In what ways is communism different from socialism? Are these differences merely economic?

3. What is the difference between indicative planning, as we find it in France, and the kind of planning we find in the U.S.S.R.?

4. What is a "self-fulfilling prophecy"? If you were a bank president and said in a speech that you thought your bank would fail, might that provoke behavior that would make your prediction true? Can you think of another example?

5. Imagine that you were in charge of automobile production in Russia. How would you decide how many cars to make? How expensive to make them? What materials to order? What prices to pay for various grades of labor? How to mix land, labor, and capital?

6. How is the transfer of food from country to city accomplished under capitalism? Why was the problem so acute under early Soviet rule? Do you think a program of rapid industrialization can be managed without recourse to coercion of some sort?

7. Do you think that profit-seeking enterprise is compatible with a planned economy? What kind of planning could utilize such enterprises? What kinds could not?

THE UNDERDEVELOPED

We must begin this very important chapter with a sobering realization. It is that our account of the long sweep of Western economic advance has simply ignored the economic existence of four out of five human beings on earth. Mere parochialism was not, however, the reason for this concentration on Western progress. Rather, it was the shocking fact that, taken in the large, *there was no economic progress in the rest of the world.*

This is not to say that tides of fortune and misfortune did not mark these areas, that great cultural heights were not achieved, and that the political or social histories of these regions do not warrant interest and study. Yet the fact remains that the mounting tide of *economic* advance that has engaged our attention was a phenomenon limited to the West. It is no doubt something of an oversimplification, but it is basically true to claim that in Asia, Africa, South America, or the Near East, economic existence was not materially improved for the average inhabitant from the twelfth— and, in some cases, the second—to the beginning of the twentieth century. Indeed, for many of them it was worsened. A long graph of non-Western material well-being would depict irregular rises and falls but an almost total absence of cumulative betterment.

The near end of such a graph would show the standard of living of three-quarters of the human race who inhabit the so-called underdeveloped areas today. Most of this mass of humanity exists in conditions of poverty that are difficult for a Westerner to comprehend. When we sum up the plight of the underdeveloped nations by saying that a billion human beings have a standard of living of "less than $100 a year," and that another, more fortunate, billion people enjoy in a year one-quarter to one-half the income a typical American family spends in a single *month,* we give only a pale statistical meaning to a reality that we can scarcely grasp.*

* In Iran, for instance, in years of famine, the children of the poor examine the droppings of horses to extract morsels of undigested oats. In Calcutta, 250,000 people have no home whatsoever and live in the streets. In Hong Kong, large numbers of families of four or more live in one bed-space in a squalid dormitory. In Cali, Colombia, when the river rises, the city's sewers run through the homes of the poor. In Hyderabad, Pakistan, child labor employed in sealing the ends of bangles over a kerosene flame is paid eight cents—per *gross* of bangles.

CHAPTER

Why are the underdeveloped nations so pitiably poor? Only a half-century ago it was common to attribute their backwardness to geographic or climatic causes. The underdeveloped nations were poor, it was thought, either because the climate was too debilitating or because natural resources were lacking. Sometimes it was just said that the natives were too childlike or racially too inferior to improve their lot.

Bad climates may have had adverse effects. Yet, many hot areas have shown a capacity for sustained economic growth (for example, the Queensland areas of Australia), and we have come to recognize that a number of underdeveloped areas, such as Argentina and Korea, have completely temperate climates. So, too, we now regard the lack of resources in many areas more as a *symptom* of underdevelopment than a cause—which is to say that in many underdeveloped areas, resources have not yet been *looked for.* Libya, for instance, which used to be written off as a totally barren nation, has been discovered to be a huge reservoir of oil. Finally, little is heard today about native childishness or inherent inferiority. (Perhaps we remember how the wealthy classes similarly characterized the poor in Europe not too many centuries ago.) Climate and geography and cultural unpreparedness unquestionably constitute obstacles to rapid economic growth—and in some areas of the globe, very serious obstacles—but there are few economists who would look to these disadvantages as the main causes of economic backwardness.

Why then are these societies so poor?

The answer takes us back to an early chapter of our book. These are poor societies because they are *traditional* societies—that is, societies which have developed neither the mechanisms of command nor of the market by which they might launch into a sustained process of economic growth. Indeed, as we examine them further we will have the feeling that we are encountering in the present the anachronistic counterparts of the static societies of antiquity.

Why did they remain traditional societies? Why, for instance, did Byzantium, which was economically so advanced in contrast with the Crusaders' Europe, fall into decline? Why did China, with so many natural advantages, not develop into a dynamic economic society? There are no simple, or even fully satisfactory, answers. Perhaps the absence of economic progress elsewhere on the globe forces us to look upon our Western experience not as the paradigm and standard for historic development, but as a very special case in which various activating factors met in an environment peculiarly favorable for the emergence of a new economic style in history. The problem is one into which we cannot go more deeply in this book. At any rate, it is today an academic question. The dominant reality of our times is that the backward areas are now striving desperately to enter the mainstream of economic progress of the West. Let us examine further their chances for doing so.

CONDITIONS OF BACKWARDNESS

Every people, to exist, must first feed itself; there is a rough sequence to the order of demands in human society. But to go beyond existence, it must achieve a certain level of efficiency in agriculture, so that its efforts can be turned in other directions. What is tragically characteristic of the underdeveloped areas is that this first corner of economic progress has not yet been turned.

Consider the situation only a few years ago in that all-important crop of the East, rice. Table 34-1 shows the difference between the productivity of rice fields in the main Asiatic countries and those of the United States and Australia as of the later 1950s.

What is true of rice can be duplicated in most other crops.* It is a disconcerting fact that the backward peasant nations which depend desperate-

TABLE 34•1

RICE PRODUCTION

(100 kilograms per hectare)	
U.S.	34.3
Australia	45.9
Burma	14.8
China (1954)	24.7
India	12.6
Indonesia	16.5
Thailand	14.3
Philippines	11.9

Source: Benjamin Higgins, *Economic Development* (New York: Norton, 1959), p. 16.

* Table 34-1 shows only the productive differentials of equal *areas* of land. When we consider that a single American farmer tends up to a hundred times as large an acreage as a peasant in an underdeveloped area, the difference in output *per man* would be much more striking. The "Green Revolution" (see p. 700) has improved the situation, but we do not yet have the data we need to determine outputs for the new rice strains. Despite the improvement, a vast gulf still separates U.S. agricultural productivity from that of the underdeveloped nations.

ly on their capacity to grow food cannot even compete in these main products with the advanced countries: U.S. Louisiana rice undersells Philippine rice, California oranges are not only better but cheaper than Indonesian oranges.

Why is agriculture so unproductive? One apparent reason is that the typical unit of agricultural production in the underdeveloped lands is far too small to permit efficient farming. What has been called "postage stamp cultivation" marks the pattern of farming throughout most of Asia and a good deal of Africa and South America. John Gunther, reporting the situation in India thirty years ago, described it vividly. It has not changed since that time.

There is no primogeniture in India as a rule, and when the peasant dies his land is subdivided among all his sons with the result that most holdings are infinitesimally small. In one district in the Punjab, following fragmentation through generations, 584 owners cultivate no less than 16,000 fields; in another, 12,800 acres are split into actually 63,000 holdings. Three-quarters of the holdings in India as a whole are under ten acres. In many parts of India the average holding is less than an acre.[1]

In part, this terrible situation is the result of divisive inheritance practices which Gunther mentions. In part, it is due to landlord systems in which peasants cannot legally own or accumulate their own land; in part, to the pressure of too many people on too little soil. There are many causes, with one result: agriculture suffers from a devastatingly low productivity brought about by grotesque man/land ratios.

These are, however, only the first links in a chain of causes for low agricultural productivity. Another consequence of these tiny plots is an inability to apply sufficient capital to the land. Mechanical binders and reapers, tractors and trucks are not only impossible to use efficiently in such tiny spaces, but they are costly beyond the reach of the subsistence farmer. Even fertilizer is too expensive: in much of Asia, animal dung is used to provide "free" fuel rather than returned to the soil to enrich it.

This paralyzing lack of capital is by no means confined to agriculture. It pervades the entire range of an underdeveloped economy. The whole industrial landscape of a Western economy is missing: no factories, no power lines, no machines, no paved roads meet the eye for mile upon mile as one travels through an underdeveloped continent. Indeed, to a pitiable extent, an underdeveloped land is one in which human and animal muscle power provide the energy with which production is carried on. In India in 1953, for instance, 65 percent of the total amount of productive energy in the nation was the product of straining man and beast.[2] The amount of usable electrical power generated in all of India would not have sufficed to light up New York City.

[1] *Inside Asia* (New York: Harper, 1939), p. 385.
[2] Daniel Wit and Alfred B. Clubok, "Atomic Power Development in India," *Social Research*, Autumn 1958, p. 290.

A lack of agricultural and industrial capital is not the only reason for low productivity. As we would expect in traditional societies, an endemic cause of low per capita output lies in prevailing social attitudes. Typically, the people of an underdeveloped economy have not *learned* the "economic" attitudes that foster rapid industrialization. Instead of technology-conscious farmers, they are tradition-bound peasants. Instead of disciplined workers, they are reluctant and untrained laborers. Instead of production-minded businessmen, they are trading-oriented merchants.

For example, Alvin Hansen reports from his observations in India:

Agricultural practices are controlled by custom and tradition. A villager is fearful of science. For many villagers, insecticide is taboo because all life is sacred. A new and improved seed is suspect. To try it is a gamble. Fertilizers, for example, are indeed a risk. . . . To adopt these untried methods might be to risk failure. And failure could mean starvation.[3]

In similar vein, a UNESCO report tells us:

In the least developed areas, the worker's attitude toward labour may entirely lack time perspective, let alone the concept of productive investment. For example, the day labourer in a rural area on his way to work, who finds a fish in the net he placed in the river the night before, is observed to return home, his needs being met. . . .[4]

An equally crippling attitude is evinced by the upper classes, who look with scorn or disdain upon business or production-oriented careers. UNESCO also reports that of the many students from the underdeveloped lands studying in the United States—the majority of whom come from the more privileged classes—only 4 percent were studying a problem fundamental to all their nations: agriculture.[5]

All these attitudes give rise to a *social inertia* that poses a tremendous hurdle to economic development. A suspicious peasantry, fearful of change that might jeopardize the slim margin yielding them life, a work force unresponsive to monetary incentive, a privileged class not interested in production—all these are part of the obdurate handicaps to be overcome by an underdeveloped nation.

Many of these problems, as we anticipated, remind us of the premarket economies of antiquity. But in addition, the underdeveloped lands face an obstacle with which the economies of antiquity did *not* have to cope: a crushing rate of population increase threatens to nullify their efforts to emerge from backward conditions.

[3] *Economic Issues of the 1960s* (New York: McGraw-Hill, 1960), pp. 157-58.
[4] *Report on the World Social Situation,* UNESCO, March 9, 1961, p. 79.
[5] *Ibid.,* p. 81.

Only a few figures are needed to make the point. Let us begin with our southern neighbor, Mexico. Today, Mexico has a population equal to that of New York State, Pennsylvania, New Jersey, and Connecticut. Thirty years from now, if Mexico's present rate of population increase continues, it will have as many people as the present population of these four states *plus* the rest of New England, *plus* the entire South Atlantic seaboard, *plus* the entire West Coast, *plus* Ohio, Indiana, Illinois, Michigan, and Wisconsin. Or take the Caribbean and Central American area. That small part of the globe has a population of around 70 million. In some thirty years, at present growth rates, its population will outnumber by 30 million the entire population of the United States today. South America, now 20 percent less populous than we, will be 200 percent larger than our present population. India will then very likely number a billion souls. China will probably number 1.6 billion.

We have already seen one result of the relentless proliferation of people in the fragmentation of landholdings. But the problem goes beyond mere fragmentation. Eugene Black, formerly president of the International Bank for Reconstruction and Development (the World Bank) tells us that in India a population equivalent to that of all Great Britain has been squeezed out of any landholding whatsoever—even though it still dwells in rural areas.[6] Consequently, population pressure generates massive and widespread rural poverty, pushing inhabitants from the countryside into the already over-crowded cities. Five hundred families a day move into Jakarta from the surrounding Javanese countryside where population has reached the fantastic figure of 1,100 per square mile.

Even these tragic repercussions of population growth are but side effects. The main problem is that population growth adds more mouths almost as fast as the underdeveloped nations manage to add more food. They cancel out much economic progress by literally eating up the small surpluses which might serve as a springboard for faster future growth.

Ironically, this population "explosion" in the underdeveloped countries is a fairly recent phenomenon, attributable largely to the incursion of Western medicine and public health into the low income areas. Prior to World War II, the poorer countries held their population growth in check because death rates were nearly as high as birth rates. With DDT and penicillin, death rates have plunged dramatically. In Ceylon, for example, death rates dropped 40 percent in one year following the adoption of malaria control and other health measures. As death rates dropped in the underdeveloped areas, birth rates, for many reasons, continued high, despite efforts to introduce birth control. In the backward lands, children are not only a source of prestige and of household labor for the peasant family, but also the only possible source of "social security" for old age. The childless older

[6] Eugene R. Black, *The Diplomacy of Economic Development* (Cambridge: Harvard University Press, 1960), p. 9.

couple could very well starve; as parents or grandparents they are at least assured of a roof over their heads.

Is there a solution for this grim question? Until very recent years, any candid expert could have answered only with a discouraged shake of the head. In the long run there was always the hope that industrialization would eventually bring the lower birth rates characteristic of all urban societies. But the problem was how to reach the long run against the overwhelming tides of population increase.

Today there is some hope. New techniques of birth control—especially the IUD (for *intra-uterine device*)—have shown promising results in those areas—mainly Taiwan and South Korea—where they have been introduced. There seems now to be a chance, if the underdeveloped countries apply their full efforts with the assistance of Western *expertise*, that the floodtide can be stemmed, perhaps within another generation or two. That still leaves the prospect of a Niagara of births to come. But there is new hope that the human torrent can be dammed before it has washed away all possibility of progress.

NINETEENTH-CENTURY IMPERIALISM

This gives us a brief introduction to underdevelopment as it exists today. Before we turn to the problem of how this condition can be remedied, we must inquire into one more question. Why did not the market society, with all its economic dynamism, spread into the backward areas?

The answer is that the active economies of the European and American worlds *did* make contact with the underdeveloped regions, beginning with the great exploratory and commercial voyages of the fifteenth and sixteenth centuries. Until the nineteenth century, unfortunately, that contact was little more than mere adventure and plunder. And then, starting in the first half of that century and gaining momentum until World War I, came that scramble for territory we call the Age of Imperialism.

What was this imperialism? It was, in retrospect, a compound of many things: militarism, jingoism, a search for markets and for sources of cheap raw materials to feed growing industrial enterprises. Insofar as the colonial areas were concerned, however, the first impact of imperialism was not solely that of exploitation. On the contrary, the incursion of Western empires into the backward areas brought some advantages. It injected the first heavy dose of industrial capital: rail lines, mines, plantation equipment. It brought law and order, often into areas in which the most despotic personal rule had previously been the order of the day. It introduced the ideas of the West, including, most importantly, the idea of freedom, which was eventually to rouse the backward nations against the invading West itself.

Yet if imperialism brought these positive and stimulating influences, it also exerted a peculiarly deforming impulse to the underdeveloped—indeed, then, totally undeveloped—economies of the East and South. In the eyes of the imperialist nations, the colonies were viewed not as areas to be brought along in balanced development, but essentially as immense supply dumps to be attached to the mother countries' industrial economies. Malaya became a vast tin mine; Indonesia, a huge tea and rubber plantation; Arabia, an oil field. In other words, the direction of economic development was steadily pushed in the direction that most benefited the imperial owner, not the colonial peoples themselves.

The result today is that the typical underdeveloped nation has a badly lopsided economy, unable to supply itself with a wide variety of goods. It is thereby thrust into the international market with its one basic commodity. For instance, in South America we find that Venezuela is dependent on oil for some 90 percent of its exports; Colombia, on coffee for three-quarters of its exports; Chile, on copper for two-thirds of its foreign earnings; Honduras, on bananas for half of its foreign earnings. On the surface, this looks like a healthy specialization of trade. We shall shortly see why it is not.

Economic lopsidedness was one unhappy consequence of imperialism. No less important for the future course of development in the colonial areas was a second decisive influence of the West: its failure to achieve political and psychological relationships of mutual respect with its colonial peoples. In part, this was no doubt traceable to an often frankly exploitative economic attitude, in which the colonials were relegated to second-class jobs with third-class pay, while a handful of Western whites formed an insulated and highly paid managerial clique. But it ran deeper than that. A terrible color line, a callous indifference to colonial aspirations, a patronizing and sometimes contemptuous view of "the natives" runs all through the history of imperialism. It has left as a bitter heritage not only an identification of capitalism with its worst practices, but a political and social wariness toward the West which deeply affects the general orientation of the developing areas.

IMPERIALISM TODAY

What about imperialism today? Certainly it has changed. The naked power grabs are in the past, when imperialism often meant only the acquisition of territory that would look good on a map. In the past, also, are the seizures of raw materials on the unfair terms characteristic of mineral empires built in the late nineteenth century. Gone as well are attitudes of racial "superiority" so infuriating to peoples whose culture was often of far greater delicacy and discrimination than that of the West.

Yet that is not the whole story. For there is also no doubt that some Western capitalist nations continue to exercise a mixed political and economic hegemony over "independent" governments: Portugal over Angola, England over portions of Africa, and above all, the United States over South and Central America and Southeast Asia.

The nature of this imperialism is now changing, partly under the pressures exerted by a restive Third World, partly as a result of developments within the advanced nations themselves. The rise of the so-called multinational corporation, for example, puts the problem of the economic relationship of advanced and backward countries in a new light. The backward nations are extremely wary of the power inherent in a giant U.S. or European corporation. Yet they also need the big companies. Big multinationals pay higher wages, keep more honest books, provide better working conditions and fancier career opportunities, and bring in more technological expertise than do the domestic enterprises of the "host" nation.

The result is that the problem of imperialism in our day, at least so far as the United States is concerned, has taken an unexpected turn. On the economic side of the question, the *danger now is as much that the big companies will bypass the backward nations as that they will dominate them.*

Meanwhile, the political element of imperialism seems to be diminishing. The erstwhile capitalist empires of Germany, Belgium, Netherlands, England (with a few exceptions), have disappeared. Portugal, for all its ruthless domination of Angola, is an archaic remnant of the past, not an entering wedge of the future. What is left is a strong effort on the part of the United States to preserve its ideological and political influence, particularly in Latin America and Southeast Asia, but the election of a Marxist president in Chile and the debacle of the American Vietnam policy indicate that the prospects for a "successful" imperialism of this kind are limited, at best.

The Engineering of Development

Up to this point we have concentrated our attention mainly on the background of underdevelopment. Now we must ask a more forward-looking, more technically "economic" question: How can an underdeveloped nation emerge from its poverty?

From what we have learned, we know the basic answer to this question. The prerequisite for economic progress for the underdeveloped countries today is not essentially different from what it was in Great Britain at the time of the industrial revolution, or what it was in Russia in 1917. To grow, an underdeveloped economy must build capital.

How is a starving country able to build capital? When 80 percent of a country is scrabbling on the land for a bare subsistence, how can it divert its energies to building dams and roads, ditches and houses, railroad embankments and factories which, however indispensable for progress tomorrow, cannot be eaten today? If our postage-stamp farmers were to halt work on their tiny unproductive plots and go to work on a great project like, say, the Aswan Dam, who would feed them? Whence would come the necessary food to sustain these capital workers?

Here is our grim "model" of a peasant economy from Chapter 20 come to life, and we will remember from that model that when consumption could not be cut, growth could not ensue. Still, when we look again at the underdeveloped lands, the prospect is not quite so bleak as that. In the first place, these economies *do* have unemployed factors. In the second place, we find that a large number of the peasants who till the fields are not feeding themselves. They are, also, in a sense, taking food from one another's mouths.

As we have seen, the crowding of peasants on the land in these areas has resulted in a diminution of agricultural productivity far below that of the advanced countries. Hence the abundance of peasants working in the fields obscures the fact that *a smaller number of peasants, with little more equipment—perhaps even with no more equipment—could raise a total output just as large.* One observer has written: "An experiment carried out near Cairo by the American College seems to suggest that the present output, or something closely approaching it, could be produced by about half the present rural population of Egypt."[7] Here is an extreme case, but it can be found to apply, to some degree, to nearly every underdeveloped land.

Now we begin to see an answer to the predicament of the underdeveloped societies. In nearly all of these societies, there exists a disguised and hidden surplus of labor which, if it were taken off the land, could be used to build capital. Most emphatically, this does not mean that the rural population should be literally moved, en masse, to the cities where there is already a hideous lump of indigestible unemployment. It means, rather, that the inefficient scale of agriculture conceals a reservoir of both labor and the food to feed that labor if it were elsewhere employed. By raising the productivity of the tillers of the soil, a work force can be made available for the building of roads and dams, while this "transfer" to capital building need not result in a diminution of agricultural output.

This rationalization of agriculture is not the only requirement for growth. When agricultural productivity is enhanced by the creation of larger farms (or by improved techniques on existing farms), *part of the ensuing larger output per man must be saved.* In other words, the peasant who remains on the soil cannot enjoy his enhanced productivity by raising his standard of living and eating up all his larger crop. Instead, the gain in output per cultivator must be siphoned off the farm. It must be "saved" by the peasant cultivator and shared with his formerly unproductive cousins, nephews, sons, and daughters who are now at work on capital-building projects. We do not expect a hungry peasant to do this voluntarily. Rather, by taxation or exaction, the government of an underdeveloped land must arrange for this indispensable transfer. Thus in the early stages of a *successful* development program there is apt to be no visible rise in the individual peasant's food *consumption,* although there must be a rise in his food *production.* What is apt to be visible is a more or less efficient—and sometimes harsh—mechanism for assuring that some portion of this newly added productivity is not consumed on the farm but is made available to support the capital-building worker. We see here the problem that caused the Russian planners such trouble in the early days of Soviet industrialization.

[7] Ragnar Nurkse, *Problems of Capital Formation in the Underdeveloped Countries* (New York: Oxford University Press, 1958), p. 35, fn. 2.

What we have just outlined is not, let us repeat, a formula for immediate action. In many underdeveloped lands, as we have seen, the countryside already crawls with unemployment, and to create, overnight, a large and efficient farming operation would create an intolerable social situation. We should think of the process we have just outlined as a long-term blueprint which covers the course of development over many years. It shows us—as did our earlier model—that the process of development takes the form of a huge internal migration from agricultural pursuits, where labor is wasted, to industrial and other pursuits, where it can yield a net contribution to the nation's progress.

PROBLEM OF EQUIPMENT

Our model also showed us that capital-building is not just a matter of freeing hands and food. Peasant labor may construct roads, but it cannot, with its bare hands, build the trucks to run over them. It may throw up dams, but it cannot fashion the generators and power lines through which a dam can produce energy. In other words, what is needed to engineer the great ascent is not just a pool of labor. It is also a vast array of industrial equipment.*

How is this equipment obtained? In our model, by expanding the machine-tool—that is, the capital-equipment-building—subsector. But an underdeveloped economy does not have a capital-equipment-building sector. Consequently, *in the first stages of industrialization, before the nucleus of a self-contained industrial sector has been laid down, a backward nation must obtain its equipment from abroad.*

This it can do in one of three ways. (1) It can buy the equipment from an industrialized nation by the normal process of *foreign trade*. Libya, for example, can sell its oil and use the foreign currency it receives to purchase abroad the tractors, lathes, and industrial equipment it needs. (2) It can receive the equipment by *foreign investment* when a corporation in an advanced nation chooses to build in a backward area. This is the route by which the United States got much of its capital from Britain during the nineteenth century, and it is the means by which the underdeveloped nations themselves received capital during their colonial days. (3) It may receive the foreign exchange needed to buy industrial equipment as a result

---

* An allied problem of no less importance arises from the lack of technical training on which industrialization critically depends. At the lowest level, this is evidenced by appalling rates of illiteracy (up to 80 or 90 percent) which make it impossible, for instance, to print instructions on a machine or a product and expect them to be followed. And at a more advanced level, the lack of expert training becomes an even more pinching bottleneck. Before its catastrophic civil war, United Nations economists figured that Nigeria alone would need some 20,000 top-level administrators, executives, technicians, etc., over the next ten years and twice as many subordinates. On a worldwide scale, this implies a need for at least 700,000 top-level personnel and 1,400,000 second-level assistants. Not 1 percent of these skilled personnel exists today, and to "produce" them will be a task of staggering difficulty. Yet, without them it is often impossible to translate development plans into actuality.

of a grant or a loan from another nation or from a United Nations agency such as the World Bank. That is, it can buy industrial equipment with *foreign aid.*

Of these three avenues of industrialization, the most important is foreign trade. In all, the underdeveloped nations earn from $30 to $40 billion a year from foreign trade. Not all of this, by any manner of means, however, is available for *new* industrial capital. A lion's share of export earnings, unfortunately, must go to pay for indispensable imports—replacements of old equipment, or even food—or to pay interest on loans contracted with the industrialized world.

In addition, another problem plagues the underdeveloped nations in foreign trade. We have seen how international trade is the means by which a great international division of labor can be achieved—that is, by which productivity can be enhanced in all trading countries, by enabling each to concentrate on those products in which it is most efficient.

With the underdeveloped nations, however, this international division of labor has worked badly. First, as we have seen, their structural backwardness has prevented them from developing their productivities even in their main occupational tasks. Second, most of them suffer from another problem. As sellers of raw commodities—usually only one raw commodity—typically, they face a highly inelastic demand for their goods. Like the American farmer, when they produce a bumper crop, prices tend to fall precipitously, and demand does not rise proportionately. At the same time, the industrial materials they buy in exchange tend to be firm or to rise in price over the years. Thus the "terms of trade"—the actual *quid pro quo* of goods received against goods offered—are likely to move against the poorer nations, who must give more and more coffee for the same amount of machinery.* In 1957 and 1958, when commodity prices took a particularly bad tumble, the poor nations actually lost more in purchasing power than the total amount of all foreign aid they received. In effect they subsidized the advanced nations! As another example, it has been estimated that falling prices have cost the African nations more, in the two decades since World War II, than all foreign funds given, loaned, or invested there.[8]

That is why all the underdeveloped nations are seeking commodity stabilization agreements (not altogether dissimilar from the support programs that stabilize American farm incomes). Recently, the advanced nations of the West have come to recognize the need for some such device if the underdeveloped nations are to be able to plan ahead with any assurance of

---

* It should be noted that not everyone agrees with this argument which has been advanced mainly by Dr. Raul Prebisch, a famous Chilean economist. The argument on the other side claims that the quality of machinery and industrial products is constantly improving, whereas the quality of raw commodities is not, so that the higher prices of industrial goods are offset by their greater productivity when put to use.

[8] Reginald H. Green and Ann Seidman, *Unity or Poverty* (Baltimore: Penguin, 1968), p. 400.

stability, and agreements have been signed for the international stabilization of coffee prices.

Another possibility lies in the prospect of encouraging diversified exports from the underdeveloped nations—handicrafts, light manufactures, and others. The difficulty here is that these exports may compete with the domestic industry of the advanced nations: witness the problems of the American textile industry in the face of textile shipments from Hong Kong. No doubt, a large source of potential earnings lies along this path, but it is unlikely to rise rapidly as long as the advanced nations refuse to allow the backward ones equal access to their own markets.

LIMITATIONS
ON PRIVATE
FOREIGN
INVESTMENT

A second main avenue of capital accumulation for the backward nations is foreign investment. Indeed, before World War II, this was *the* source of their industrial wealth. Today, however, it is a much diminished avenue of assistance for reasons we have learned in our exploration of the multinational corporation. On the one hand, the former capital-exporting nations are no longer eager to invest private funds in areas over which they have lost control and in which they fear to lose any new investments they might make. On the other hand, many of the poorer nations, for reasons that we have discussed, view Western capitalism with ambivalence. On the one hand, they need capital, technology, expertise. On the other, they see in the arrival of a branch of a powerful corporation run by faraway "headquarters" another form of the domination they have just escaped. As a result, foreign investment is often hampered by restrictive legislation in the underdeveloped nations, even though it is badly needed. Consequently, not much more than $3 billion to $4 billion a year from all the advanced nations goes overseas as foreign investment into the underdeveloped world.

Another difficulty is that Western corporations partially offset the growth-producing effects of their investments by draining profits out of the country. In the period 1950-1965, for example, the flow of income remitted from Latin America to the United States was $11.3 billion, three times larger than the flow of new capital into Latin America. From 1968 to 1969, income of $3.2 billion was transmitted to the United States, and only $0.7 billion was sent back to Latin America. This pattern of economic flows should not be misinterpreted as implying that foreign investment is a "negative" influence: the plant and equipment that the West has sent abroad remains in the underdeveloped world, where it continues to enhance the productivity of labor. But the *earnings* on this capital are not typically plowed back into still more capital goods, so that their potential growth-producing effect is far from realized.

THE CRUCIAL
AVENUE
OF AID

These considerations enable us to understand the special importance that attaches to the third channel of capital accumulation: foreign aid. Surprisingly, perhaps, in the light of the attention it attracts, foreign aid is not a very large figure. International assistance, from *all* individual nations and from the UN and its agencies, has run at a rate of about $6 billion to $7 billion per year through the 1960s and is now *diminishing*. This is an insignificant contribution to the gross output of the noncommunist underdeveloped world.

It is, however, a substantial fraction—perhaps as much as 15 percent—of the *gross investment* of that world. Thus, foreign aid makes possible the accumulation of industrial capital much faster than could be accomplished solely as a result of the backward lands' export efforts or their ability to attract foreign private capital.* To be sure, an increase in foreign earnings or in private capital imports would have equally powerful effects on growth. But we have seen the difficulties in the way of rapidly increasing the receipts from these sources. For the near future, foreign aid represents the most effective channel for *quickly* raising the amount of industrial capital which the underdeveloped nations must obtain.

Foreign aid, particularly from UN sources, is also an extremely important source of *technical assistance* which enables the backward regions to overcome the handicaps imposed by their lack of skilled and trained personnel. For the near term, this may be even more important than the acquisition of the industrial capital itself in promoting growth. Largely because of this bottleneck of skills, it is estimated that the underdeveloped countries could absorb at best $8 billion to $10 billion a year in foreign aid during this decade.

Against these handicaps, can the underdeveloped nations grow? Can the terrible conditions of poverty be relegated to the past? Economic analysis allows us to ask these questions systematically. For growth depends on the interplay of three variables.

1. *The rate of investment that an underdeveloped nation can generate.*

As we know, this depends on the proportion of its current effort that it can devote to capital-creating activity. In turn, the rate of saving, the success in attracting foreign capital, the volume of foreign aid—all add to this critical fraction of effort on which growth hinges.

2. *The productivity of the new capital.*

The saving that goes into new capital eventually results in higher output. But not all capital boosts output by an equal amount. A million-dollar steel mill, for example, will have an impact on GNP very different from that of a

---

* Note "makes possible." There is some disturbing evidence that foreign aid may displace domestic saving, that an underdeveloped country receiving aid may relax its own efforts to generate capital. Much depends on the political will of the recipient country. (See K. B. Griffin and J. L. Enos, "Foreign Assistance: Objectives and Consequences," *Economic Development and Cultural Change*, April, 1970.)

million-dollar investment in schools. In the short run, the mill may yield a higher return of output per unit of capital investment; in the long run, the school may. But in any event, the effect on output will depend not merely on the amount of investment, but on the marginal capital-output ratio of the particular form of investment chosen.

3. *Population growth.*

Here, as we know, is the negative factor. If growth is to be achieved, output must rise faster than population. Otherwise, per capita output will be falling or static, despite seemingly large rates of overall growth.

THE CRITICAL BALANCE

With these basic variables, is growth a possibility for the backward lands? We can see that if investment were 10 percent of GNP and if each dollar of new investment gave rise to a third of a dollar of additional output,* then a 10 percent rate of capital formation would yield a 3.3 percent rate of growth (10 percent × one-third). This is about equal to population growth rates in the nations with the highest rates of population income.

The trouble is that most of the backward nations have investment rates that are closer to 5 percent than 10 percent of GNP. In that case, even with a marginal capital-output ratio of one-half, growth rates would not be enough to begin a sustained climb against a population growth of 2.5 percent (5 percent × $\frac{1}{2}$ = 2.5 percent). And this gloomy calculation is made gloomier still when we confront the fact that the labor force is rising faster than the population as a whole, as vast numbers of children become vast numbers of workers. In 1960 in Latin America it was estimated that at least *25 percent* of the working-age population was unemployed. In the decade since then, unemployment as a percent of the labor force seems to have increased in virtually every country.[9]

ECONOMIC PROSPECTS: THE "GREEN REVOLUTION"

Nobody can confront these economic realities and make optimistic forecasts for the developing countries. Yet the situation is not hopeless. For many nations, an increase in their capital formation rates of 50 or 100 percent—a difficult but by no means impossible task—should bring them to the point of cumulative growth. What is then needed is a program of encouragement to small industry, to absorb the flood of unemployed while the essential industrial core is being built, and an all-out effort to bring

* This seems to be *roughly* what the marginal capital-output ratio of new investment in the underdeveloped areas may be.

[9] See William Thiesenhausen, "Latin America's Employment Problem," *Science,* March 1971; also H. Oshima in *Economic Development and Cultural Change,* January 1971.

about manageable rates of population growth through the IUD and other means. These are also difficult, but again not impossible, undertakings.

Meanwhile a vitally important breakthrough has been scored on the agricultural front with the development of new crops that can literally double and triple yields. This so-called Green Revolution, in effect in parts of India, has almost certainly removed the spectre of mass famine, which haunted the food officials of the world during the 1960s when they looked ahead to the 1970s. The Green Revolution will require vast amounts of fertilizer, huge irrigation projects, and much administration; so it is far from a simple "solution" to the development problem, but it offers vital time for a critical effort to stop the juggernaut of population growth and to institute an all-out developmental effort.

Thus it is possible, not only in theory but in actuality, to foresee a long, slow developmental climb. But this is not the end of our analysis, for it is impossible to think of development only in terms of economics. As we have seen in the case of Western growth, *economic development is nothing less than the modernization of an entire society.* When we talk of building capital or redirecting agriculture, we must not imagine that this entails only the addition of machines and farm equipment to a peasant society. In entails the conversion of a peasant society into an industrial one. It means a change in the whole tenor of life, in the expectations and motivations, the environment of daily existence itself.

We have already noted some of the changes that economic development imposes on a society. Illiterate peasants must be made into literate farmers. Dispirited urban slum-dwellers must be made into disciplined factory workers. Old and powerful social classes, who have for generations derived their wealth from feudal land tenure, must be deprived of their vested rights and oriented toward often despised business pursuits. Above all, the profligate generation of life, conceived in dark huts as the only solace available to a crushed humanity, must give way to a responsible and deliberate creation of children as the chosen heirs to a better future.

These changes will *in time* be facilitated by the realization of development itself. A growing industrial environment breeds industrial ways. The gradual realization of economic improvement brings about attitudes that will themselves accelerate economic growth. A slowly rising standard of living is likely to quicken the spread of birth control, as it did in the West.

All these changes, as we have said, may take place in time. But it is time itself that is so critically lacking. The changes must begin to take place now—today—so that the process of development can gain an initial momentum. The transition from a backward, tradition-bound way of life to a modern and dynamic one cannot be allowed to mature at its own slow pace. Only an enormous effort can inaugurate, much less shorten, the transition from the past into the future.

These sobering considerations converge in one main direction. They alert us to the fact that *in the great transformation of the underdeveloped areas, the market mechanism is apt to play a much smaller role than in the comparable transformation of the West during the industrial revolution.*

We will recall how lengthy and arduous was the period of apprenticeship through which the West had to pass in order for the ideas and attitudes, the social institutions and legal prerequisites of the market system to be hammered out. When the industrial revolution came into being, it exploded within a historic situation in which market institutions, actions, customs had already become the dominant form of economic organization.

None of this is true in the underdeveloped nations today. Rather than having their transition to a market society behind them, many of those nations must leap overnight from essentially tradition-bound and archaic relationships to commercialized and industrialized ones. Many of them are not even fully monetized economies. None of them have the network of institutions—and behind that, the network of "economic" motivations—on which a market society is built.

Hence it is not difficult to foresee that the guiding force of development is apt to be tilted in the direction of central planning. Regardless of the importance of private enterprise in carrying out the individual projects of development, the driving and organizing force of economic growth will have to be principally lodged with the government.

But the outlook indicates more than a growth of economic command. Implicit also in the harsh demands of industrialization is the need for strong political leadership, not only to initiate and guide the course of development, but to *make it stick*. For it is not only wrong, but dangerously wrong, to picture economic development as a long, invigorating climb from achievement to achievement. On the contrary, it is better imagined as a gigantic social and political earthquake. Eugene Black, ex-president of the World Bank, soberly pointed out that we delude ourselves with buoyant phrases such as "the revolution of rising expectations" when we describe the process—rather than the prospect—of development.[10] To many of the people involved in the bewildering transformations of development, the revolution is apt to be marked by a loss of traditional expectations, by a new awareness of deprivation, a new experience of frustration. For decades, perhaps generations, a developing nation must plow back its surplus into the ugly and unenjoyable shapes of lathes and drills, conveyor belts and factory smokestacks. Some change toward betterment is not ruled out, particularly in health, basic diet, and education; but beyond this first great step, material improvement in everyday living will not—cannot—materialize quickly.

[10] *The Diplomacy of Economic Development*, p. 9.

As a consequence, many of the policies and programs required for development, rather than being eagerly accepted by all levels of society, are apt to be resisted. Tax reform, land reform, the curtailment of luxury consumption are virtually certain to be opposed by the old order. In addition, as the long march begins, latent resentments of the poorer classes are likely to become mobilized; the underdog wakens to his lowly position. Even if his lot improves, he may well feel a new fury if his *relative* well-being is impaired. The late anthropologist Oscar Lewis warned:

The political stability of Mexico is grim testimony to the great capacity for misery and suffering of the ordinary Mexican. But even the Mexican capacity for suffering has its limits, and unless ways are found to achieve a more equitable distribution of the growing national wealth and a greater equality of sacrifice during the difficult period of industrialization, we may expect social upheavals, sooner or later.[11]

These considerations enable us to understand how, along with a rise in economic standards can come a *rise* in social tensions, and this prospect, in turn, enables us to appreciate the fearful demands placed upon political leadership, which must provide the impetus, the inspiration—and, if necessary, the discipline—to keep the great ascent in motion. The strains of the early industrial revolution in England, with its widening chasm between the proletariat and capitalist, are not to be forgotten when we project the likely course of affairs in the developing nations.

In the politically immature and labile areas of the underdeveloped world, this exercise of leadership typically assumes the form of "strong man" government. In large part, this is only the perpetuation of age-old tendencies in these areas, but in the special environment of development, a new source of encouragement for dictatorial government arises from the exigencies of the economic process itself. Powerful, even ruthless, government may be needed, not only to begin the development process, but to cope with the strains of a *successful* development program.

It is not surprising, then, that the political map reveals the presence of authoritarian governments in many developing nations today. The communist areas aside, we find more or less authoritarian rule in Egypt, Pakistan, Burma, South Korea, Indonesia, and the succession of South American junta governments. From country to country, the severity and ideological coloring of these governments varies. Yet in all of them we find that the problems of economic development provide a large rationale for the tightening of political control. At least in the arduous early stages of growth, some form of political command seems as integral to economic development as the accumulation of capital itself.

[11] *The Children of Sanchez* (New York: Random House, 1961), pp. xxx-xxxi.

THE ECOLOGICAL PROBLEM

To this endless list of problems one last one must now be added. It is the fact that the sheer resources of the earth may be insufficient, at least with modern technology, to make possible a "Western" standard of living for all the peoples of the world. Paul and Anne Ehrlich, of Stanford University, write:

> To raise all the 3.6 billion people of the world of 1970 to the American standard of living would require the extraction of almost 30 billion tons of iron, more than 500 million tons of copper and lead, more than 300 million tons of zinc, about 50 million tons of tin, as well as enormous quantities of other minerals. That means the extraction of some 75 times as much iron as is now extracted annually, 100 times as much copper, 200 times as much lead, 75 times as much zinc and 250 times as much tin. The needed iron is theoretically available, and might be extracted by tremendous efforts over long periods of time, but ... needed quantities of the other materials far exceed *all* known or inferred reserves. Of course, to raise the standard of living of the projected world population of the year 2000 would require doubling all of the above figures.[12]

The solution to this problem reinforces the political argument above. For it is clear that the free play of market forces, *insofar as these are permitted to develop along the lines of traditional capitalism,* would lead rapidly to an ecological impasse. Instead, the development of the backward nations, once an initial momentum has been attained, will have to be planned to economize on materials and production to a degree unknown in the West. The absurd waste of resources involved in providing transportation through the proliferation of private automobiles instead of public conveyances; the encouragement of individual ownership of washing machines and television sets and domestic conveniences—the very center of the Western ideal of a "high standard of living"—will be impossible to duplicate on a global scale.

What will be required in their place is a new pattern of *public consumption,* new ideals of stable rather than ever-rising standards of material achievement, perhaps even a wholly new conception of what is meant by an advanced society. All this will be required not as a matter of ideological preference, but as one of long-run necessity. The ecological barriers of resource availability and the absorption capacity of the earth thus pose truly staggering problems for the underdeveloped nations, once they manage to escape from the stagnation that still characterizes most of them. No one knows how these obdurate limitations of nature will be translated into the realities of social life, but it is certain that the relatively laissez-faire attitudes of Western capitalism will be hopelessly inadequate to the task.

[12] *Population, Resources, Environment* (San Francisco: Freeman, 1970), pp. 61-62.

Does this imply that the underdeveloped nations are apt to follow the route of communism?

It is a possibility. For its political and social ugliness notwithstanding, communism—or perhaps we should say, *revolutionary socialism*—offers a means of achieving the Great Ascent. There is no secret about this means. A communist nation, like a capitalist one, must transfer its workers from traditional pursuits to modern ones, must rationalize its agriculture, must build an industrial center, and must relentlessly plow back its increments of output, at least in the initial stages of the Ascent, into more capital, more capital, ever more capital. The difference is that communism or revolutionary socialism does the job without the handicaps of a free society. Where land is needed, it is simply taken; where workers are required, they are moved; where opposition is encountered, it is suppressed.

As was the case with Russia, all this is likely to be accomplished at a fearful social cost and with huge waste. In communist China, large numbers of people have been put to death for opposing the regime, and life is regimented to a chilling degree. Even in Cuba, where an initial great burst of enthusiasm carried the revolution forward with a minimum of repressiveness, a creeping militarization now seems to be entering the economy, as enthusiasm wanes and the economy staggers under the burdens of forced and inefficiently planned growth. One of the bitterest facts of the present era is that even with all the will of a revolutionary party, growth has been painful and excruciatingly slow, so that the chances for a tolerant and mild socialist regime in the backward areas are not good. All the more will this be true if environmental restrictions make it plain that the dazzling (if wasteful) achievements of the West are doomed to remain forever beyond duplication on a mass scale.

Yet it would be wrong to concentrate wholly on the negative side of revolutionary socialism. Oppression weighs less heavily on a people if it believes that a regime imposes it not for personal gain, but on behalf of children who would otherwise be born to lives of misery and want. This last point is crucial. It must not be forgotten that for all its cruel errors, Russia is still the only peasant nation that has escaped from poverty in the twentieth century; and that for all their turmoil and disappointments, China and Cuba are making an unparalleled effort to escape from poverty. Communism or iron collectivism *is* a way out of underdevelopment, at least in the beginning, and to see it in any less serious—and in this regard, respectful—light is to underestimate its challenge.

It would be fatuous to pretend that somewhere, concealed in this picture, is an answer which will solve all problems happily. Rather, the likelihood is very great that the West, quite as much as the underdeveloped areas themselves, will have to make bitter choices and to follow unwelcome paths for many years. Yet, the fact that many alternatives are closed does not mean that none remain. There are degrees of command, political as well as economic, which result in a very different tenor of existence for those who must bear the burden of development and which offer very different possibilities for the future. Nothing could be more disastrous for the West than to overlook these differences and to brand all nonmarket economies or all nondemocratic governments as constituting a single undesirable species. In the mold of economic development is being cast the shape of much of world civilization for the long-term future. On the capacity of the West to overcome its stereotyped conception of other societies, on its capacity to discriminate between mere oppression and purposeful social direction, on its capacity to persevere in the encouragement of development despite inevitable disappointments and failures will depend much of the outcome of this central process of historic change in our time.

KEY CONCEPTS AND KEY WORDS

Underdevelopment

1. *Underdevelopment* constitutes the economic environment for the vast majority of mankind. It is ascribable in part, perhaps, to bad climates or inadequate resources, but in the main it springs from the inability of traditional societies to mount sustained programs of investment and change.

Population explosion

2. The main attributes of underdevelopment are *very low levels of productivity,* especially in agriculture where man/land ratios often impose highly inefficient scales of production. No less important, and more difficult to correct, are deep-seated *attitudes of inertia* on the part of the population. And constituting a main obstacle to a development effort are very high rates of *population growth.* (Here the new birth control techniques now offer some hope for the future.)

Industrialization

3. The development effort requires a *shift from consumption* to *investment activity.* This necessitates a prior increase in agricultural productivity, accompanied by measures that will transfer the food surplus from the peasant cultivator to workers on capital projects. This is an exceedingly difficult task to carry out.

4. In addition to shifting resources from agriculture to capital building tasks, a nucleus of *industrial equipment* must be brought in. This can be done by *international trade,* by *foreign investment,* or by *foreign aid.*

Imperialism

5. The channel of international trade is a difficult one for many backward nations, as a consequence of *imperialism.* Many underdeveloped nations have *"lopsided" economies* that sell one raw commodity in markets where demand is typically inelastic. Foreign investment has not produced much capital for the backward nations, partly because of their own suspicions of Western nations, partly because the West has not reinvested its earnings there. *Foreign aid* thus becomes a small but crucial avenue for the transfer of funds and skills. It should be noted that skill is often essential to acquire before funds can be absorbed.

Foreign aid

Rate of investment

6. Development hinges on three economic variables: the *rate of investment,* the *capital-output ratio* (the size of additional output yielded by net investment) and the *rate of population growth.* Given a 10 percent net investment rate and a one-third capital output ratio it should be possible to begin growth even against a 3 percent population increase.

7. The problem is that the economic effort is not detachable from the whole array of *social and political problems.* To mount a development program requires that many traditional institutions and ways be discarded for new and untried ones. This process of change occurred over several centuries in the West, but the exigencies of the population crisis make it necessary to compress it within a few generations today.

Marginal capital-output ratio

8. Constraints imposed by resource limitations impose ceilings on the material attainments open to the underdeveloped nations. At least in the long run, they will be forced to develop resource allocation patterns very different from ours. *Planned economies* are not a matter of choice, but necessity, for their futures.

Ecological constraints

9. The result is that the modernization of the backward areas is very likely to require *authoritarian measures,* both political and economic. The strains of maintaining a successful development program, no less than the initial problems of mounting one, are apt to lead to "strong-man" government and collectivist economic measures. In this light *we can see communism as a technique for attempting to bring about the deep-seated changes required for rapid modernization.*

Collectivism

Modernization

Q U E S T I O N S

1. In what ways do you think underdeveloped countries are different from the American Colonies in the mid-1600s? Think of literacy, attitudes toward work and thrift, and other such factors. What about the relationship to more advanced nations in each case?

2. Why do you think it is so difficult to change social attitudes at the lowest levels of society? At the upper levels? Are there different reasons for social inertia at different stations in society?

3. Does the United States have a population problem? Will population growth here affect economic or social aspects of life more? Do you think we should adopt an American population control policy? What sort of policy?

4. Review your acquaintance with the model of a peasant economy in Chapter 20. Is this model applicable to China today? Was it applicable to the American Colonies? What differences do population pressure and social inertia impart to the solutions implied by the model?

5. Many economists have suggested that all advanced nations should give about 1 percent of their GNP for foreign aid. In the U.S., that would mean a foreign aid appropriation of about $10 billion. Actually we appropriate about $2 billion. Do you think it would be practicable to suggest a 1 percent levy? How would the country feel about such a program?

6. What are the main variables in determining whether or not growth will be self-sustaining? If net investment were 8 percent of GNP and the capital output ratio were $\frac{1}{4}$, could a nation grow if its rate of population increase were $2\frac{1}{4}$ percent? What changes could initiate growth?

7. What do you think is the likelihood of the appearance of strong-arm governments and collectivist economies in the underdeveloped world? For the appearance of effective democratic governments? For capitalist economies? Socialist ones? Is it possible to make predictions or judgments in these matters that do not accord with your personal preferences?

8. If you had to plan the 50-year development of a nation like India, and if you knew that it would be essential to economize on the production and consumption of minerals, how would you suggest that patterns of consumption be changed to effect major resource savings? To what extent would such changes impose further changes in the pattern of social life?

With this somber look at the underdeveloped areas we bring to a conclusion our overview of general economic history. Throughout the pages behind us we followed a majestic theme of economic development in the West; and now in the twentieth century, this same long process is stirring in the East and South. Thus, from our vantage point, we can see the beginning of worldwide economic development as a genuine watershed in human history. An active and dynamic form of economic life, until recently the distinctive characteristic of the industrial West, is about to be generalized over the face of the globe. The process of diffusion will take generations, but it marks a profound, irreversible, and truly historic alteration in the economic condition of man.

Yet, if the process of economic growth is henceforth to be carried out on a global scale, it is also clear that there will be significant change in the auspices under which this process is likely to unfold. As we have seen, it is command rather than the market system which is in the ascendant as the driving force in the underdeveloped regions. And when we combine the geographic extent of these regions with those in which communism has become firmly entrenched, it seems that command now bids fair to become *the* dominant means of organizing economic activity on this planet, as tradition was not very long ago.

But again there is a difference. During the centuries in which tradition held sway over most of the world, the economies run by the market system were the locus of progress and motion. Today and in the future, one cannot with assurance say the same. For a pre-eminent motive of the rising economies of command is to *displace* the market societies as the source of the world's economic vitality.

Does this mean that economic history now writes finis to the market system? Does it mean that the market, as a means of solving the economic problem, is about to be relegated to the museum of economic antiquities, or at best limited to the confines of North America and Western Europe? The question brings to a focus our continuing concern with the market system through history. Let us attempt in these last pages to give an appraisal of its prospects.

Stages of Economic Development

We might well begin such an appraisal by taking a last survey of the array of economic systems which marks our times. It is, at first glance, an extraordinary assortment: we find, in these mid-years of the twentieth century, a spectrum of economic organization that represents virtually every stage in economic history from the earliest and most primitive. But at second look, a significant pattern can be seen within this seemingly disordered assemblage. The few remaining wholly traditional economies, such as those of the Near East or tribal Africa, have not yet begun to move into the mainstream of economic development. A much larger group of underdeveloped nations, in which institutions of economic command are now rising amid a still traditional environment, have just commenced their development efforts and are now coping with the initial problems preparatory to eventual all-out industrialization. Going yet further along we find the economies of iron command, such as China and to a much lesser extent Russia; here we find national communities that are (or recently were) wrestling with the gigantic task of rapid massive modernization. Finally, we pass to the market economies of the West, to encounter societies with their developmental days behind them, now concerned with the operation of high-consumption economic systems.*

The categorization suggests a very important general conclusion. *The economic structures of nations today bear an integral relation with their stage of economic development.* Acts of foreign intervention aside, the choice of command or market systems is not just the outcome of political considerations, or ideologies and preferences. It is also, and perhaps primarily, the result of functional requirements which are very different at different levels of economic achievement.

* A glance at the back end papers reveals a map keyed to these economic differences. Needless to say, the map gives no more than a subjective interpretation of the extent of Tradition, Command, and Market in the various countries of the world.

We have already noted this connection in our discussion of the under-developed areas. Now, however, we can place what we have learned into a wider frame of reference. For if we compare the trend of events in the underdeveloped economies with the "equivalent" stage of development in Western history, we see a significant point of resemblance between the two. The emergence of command in the development-minded countries today has a parallel in the mercantile era, when the Western nation also received a powerful impetus toward industrialization under the organizing influence of the "industry-minded" governments of that period.

Thereafter, to be sure, the resemblance ceases. In the West, following the first push of mercantilism, it was the market mechanism that provided the main directive force for growth; in the underdeveloped lands, as we have seen, this influence is likely to be preempted to a much larger extent by political and economic command.

Three main reasons lie behind this divergence of paths. *First, the underdeveloped areas today start from a lower level of preparedness* than did the West in the seventeenth and eighteenth centuries. Not only have the actual institutions of the market not yet appeared in many backward lands, but the whole process of acculturation has failed to duplicate that of the West. In many ways—not all of them economic—the West was "ready" for economic development, as Chapter 4 sought to make clear. A similar readiness is not in evidence in the majority of the backward lands today, with the result that development, far from evincing itself as a spontaneous process, comes about as the result of enforced and imposed change.

Second, the *West was able to mount its development effort in leisurely tempo.* This is not to say that its rate of growth was slow or that strong pressures did not weigh upon many Western countries, arousing within them feelings of dissatisfaction with their progress. Yet the situation was unlike that of the backward areas today. Here immense pressures, both of population growth and of political impatience, create an overwhelming need and desire for speed. As a result, the process of growth is not allowed to mature quietly in the background of history, as it did for much of the West, but has been placed at the very center of political and social attention.

Finally, the underdeveloped countries, who suffer from so many handicaps in comparison with the developmental days of the West, enjoy one not inconsiderable advantage. Because they are in the rear guard rather than the vanguard of history, they know where they are going. *In a manner denied to the West, they can see ahead of them the goal they seek to reach.* They do not wish to reach this goal, however, by retreading the painful and laborious path marked out by the West. Rather, they intend to shortcut it, to move directly to their destination by utilizing the mechanisms of command to bring about the great alterations that must be made.

Can economic command significantly compress and accelerate the growth process? The remarkable performance of the Soviet Union suggests that it can. In 1920 Russia was but a minor figure in the economic councils of the world. Today it is second only—though still a far second—to the United States. If Soviet production continues to gain on American production at the rate of the last ten years, in little more than another generation its industrial output (although not its per capita output) will be larger than our own. Not less important, Chinese growth, until the great famine disaster of 1959-1960, was two or three times faster than India's; and despite political turmoil, China's economic advantage over India still seems substantial.[1]

It is no doubt wise not to exaggerate the advantages of a command system. If it holds the potential for an all-out attack on backwardness, it also contains the possibilities for substantial failure, as in the very badly planned Cuban economy.[2] The mere existence of a will to plan is no guarantee that the plans will be well drawn, or well carried out, or reasonably well obeyed. Nonetheless, these caveats must be set against the dismal record of economies that continue to wallow in the doldrums of tradition, or that undertake the arduous transition into modernity under the inadequate stimulus of halfhearted regimes and half-formed market systems. In this comparison of alternatives, the advantage seems strongly on the side of those backward societies that are capable of mustering a strong central economic authority.

ECONOMIES IN MID-DEVELOPMENT

Once the development process is well under way, however, the relative functional merits of the market and the command mechanisms begin to change. After planning has done its massive tasks—enforcing economic and social change, creating an industrial sector, rationalizing agriculture—another problem begins to assume ever more importance. This is the problem of efficiency, of dovetailing the innumerable productive efforts of society into a single coherent and smoothly functioning whole.

In the flush period of middevelopment, the market mechanism easily outperforms the command apparatus as a means of carrying out this complex coordinating task. Every profit-seeking entrepreneur, every industrial salesman, every cost-conscious purchasing agent becomes in effect part of a gigantic and continuously alert planning system within the market economy. Command systems do not easily duplicate their efforts. Bottlenecks, unusable output, shortages, waste, and a cumbersome hierarchy of bureaucratic forms and officials typically interfere with the maximum efficiency of the planned economy in midgrowth.

[1] See Alexander Eckstein, *Communist China's Economic Growth and Foreign Trade* (New York: McGraw-Hill, 1966), pp. 45f. For problems of interpreting Russian statistics, see Alec Nove, *Communist Economic Strategy* (Washington, D.C.: National Planning Association, 1959), pp. 38-42.

[2] For a remarkable account of Cuban problems with planning, see the speech by Fidel Castro in the *New York Review of Books,* September 24, 1970.

What we see here is not just a passing problem, easily ironed out. One of the critical lessons of the twentieth century is that the word *planning* is exceedingly easy to pronounce and exceedingly difficult to execute. When targets are still relatively simple, and the priorities of action beyond dispute—as in the case of a nation wrenching itself from the stagnation of an ineffective regime—planning can produce miracles. But when the economy reaches a certain degree of complexity, in which the coordination of ten activities gives way to the coordination of ten thousand, innumerable problems arise, *because planned economies enjoy no "natural" congruence between private action and public necessity.*

Here is where the market comes into its own. As we know from our study of microtheory, each firm must combine its factors of production with one eye on their relative costs and the other on their respective productivities, finally bringing about a mix in which each factor is used as effectively as possible, given its cost. Thus in seeking only to maximize their own profits, the units in a market system inadvertently tend also to maximize the efficiency of the system as a whole.

Even more remarkable, one operating rule alone suffices to bring about this extraordinary conjunction of private aims and public goals. *That single rule is to maximize profits.* By concentrating on that one criterion of success and not by trying to maximize output in physical terms or by trying to live by a complicated book of regulations, entrepreneurs in a competitive environment do in fact bring the system to a peak of operating efficiency. In other words, *profits are not only a source of privileged income, but also an enormously versatile and useful "success indicator" for a system that is trying to squeeze as much output as possible from its given inputs.*

Furthermore, the market mechanism solves the economic problem *with a minimum of social and political controls.* Impelled by the drives inherent in a market society, the individual marketer fulfills his public economic function without constant attention from the authorities. In contradistinction to his counterpart in a centralized command society, who is often prodded, cajoled, or even threatened to act in ways that do not appeal to his self-interest, the classical marketer obeys the peremptory demands of the market as a voluntary exercise of his own economic "freedom."

Thus it is not surprising that we find many of the motivating principles of the market being introduced into command societies. For as these societies settle into more or less established routines, they too can utilize the pressure of want and the pull of pecuniary desire to facilitate the fulfillment of their basic plans.

Economic freedom, as we know it in the West, is not yet a reality, or even an official objective, in any of these countries. The right to strike, for example, is not recognized, and nothing like the fluid consumer-responsive market system is allowed to exert its unimpeded influence on the general direction of economic development. But the introduction of more and more discretion at the factory level argues strongly that the principles of the market society are apt to find their place in planned societies at an appropriate stage of economic development.

Thus our survey of successive stages of development brings us to a consideration of Western economic society—that is, to the advanced economies which have progressed beyond the need for forced industrialization and now enter the stage of high consumption.

From our foregoing discussion, it is clear that the market mechanism finds its most natural application in this fortunate period of economic evolution. Insofar as the advanced Western societies have reached a stage in which the consumer is not only permitted but encouraged to impose his wants on the direction of economic activity, there is little doubt that the market mechanism fulfills the prevailing social purpose more effectively than any other.

Nonetheless, as we noted in Chapters 28 and 29, the market is not without its own grave problems, even in this regard. For one thing, *it is an inefficient instrument for provisioning societies—even rich societies—with those goods and services for which no "price tag" exists,* such as education or local government services or public health facilities.

A market society "buys" such public goods by allocating a certain amount of taxes for these purposes. Its citizens, however, tend to feel these taxes as an exaction in contrast with the items they voluntarily buy. Typically, therefore, a market society underallocates resources to education, city government, public health or recreation, since it has no means of "bidding" funds into these areas, in competition with the powerful means of bidding them into autos or clothes or personal insurance.

A second and perhaps even deeper-seated failing of the market system is its application of a strictly economic calculus to the satisfaction of human wants and needs. As we said before, the market is an assiduous servant of the wealthy, but an indifferent servant of the poor. Thus it presents us with the anomaly of a surplus of luxury housing existing side-by-side with a shortage of inexpensive housing, although the social need for the latter is incontestably greater than the former. Or it pours energy and resources into the multiplication of luxuries for which the wealthier classes offer a market, while allowing more basic needs of the poor to go unheeded and unmet.

Finally, these shortcomings are aggravated by *the inability of the market system to cope with the externalities that, as we have seen, are inextricable from the workings of the market system.* But there is no need to spell out further the deficiencies of the market. In one form or another, all are indicative of a central weakness of the market mechanism: *its inability to formulate effective stimuli or restraints other than those that arise from the marketplace itself.*

So long as the public need roughly coincides with the sum of the private interests to which the market automatically attends, this failing of the market system is a minor one. But in an advanced economic society, it tends to become ever more important. As primary wants become satisfied, the public aim turns toward stability and security, objectives not attainable without a degree of public control. As technological organization becomes more complex and massive, again a public need arises to contain the new agglomerations of economic power. So, too, as wealth increases, pressure for education, urban improvement, welfare and the like, comes to the fore, not only as an indication of the public conscience, but as a functioning requirement of a mature society. And finally, the public stimulus and management of continued growth take on increased political urgency as the ecological problems of industrial societies multiply.

We have already paid much attention to the rise of planning in the advanced market societies as a corrective force to deal with just such problems. Now we can go so far as to generalize the economic meaning of this trend. *Planning arises in the advanced market societies to offset their inherent goal-setting weaknesses, just as the market mechanism arises in advanced command societies to offset their inherent motivational weaknesses.* In other words, planning and market mechanisms, in those societies which have begun to enter the stage of high consumption, are not mutually incompatible. On the contrary, they powerfully supplement and support one another.

CONVERGENCE OF SYSTEMS

What seems to impend at the moment, then, is a *convergence of economic mechanisms* for the more advanced societies. In the planned economies the market is being introduced to facilitate the smoother achievement of established objectives, while in the market economies, a degree of planning is increasingly relied upon to give order, stability, and social direction to the outcome of private activity.

This does not imply that the two major systems today are about to become indistinguishable. The convergence of economic mechanisms may blur but not obliterate the basic distinctions between them. Nor does the convergence of mechanisms in itself portend profound changes in the larger social structures of socialism and capitalism. A gradual rapprochement of the economic mechanisms should not lead us to hasty conclusions about the rebirth of "capitalism" in the Soviet Union or the advent of "socialism" in the United States. This is a matter into which we will look more deeply in our last chapter.

COMMON PROBLEMS

There is another way in which the phenomenon of convergence reveals itself, in addition to that of a coming together of economic mechanisms. *It is the appearance of similar problems in advanced industrial societies.* When we examine capitalism and socialism, we will pay special attention to the problems that separate and distinguish these two kinds of societies. Here it is important to realize that they are also bound together by certain common difficulties.

What is the nature of these overarching problems? As we would expect, they stem from the very technical capability and social organization that bring similar economic mechanisms into being. Three problems in particular seem of major importance:

1. *The control over technology.*

One of the most important attributes of modern history is lodged in a striking difference between two kinds of knowledge: the knowledge we acquire in physics, chemistry, engineering, and other sciences, and that which we gain in the sphere of social or political or moral activity. The difference is that knowledge in some sciences is cumulative and builds on itself, whereas knowledge in the social sphere does not. The merest beginner in biology soon knows more than the greatest biologists of a century ago. By way of contrast, the veteran student (or practitioner) of government, of social relations, of moral philosophy is aware of his modest stature in comparison with the great social and moral philosophers of the past.

The result is that all modern societies tend to find that their technological capabilities are constantly increasing, while the social and political and moral institutions by which those capabilities are controlled cannot match the challenges with which they are faced. Television, for example, is an immense force for cultural homogenization; medical technology changes the composition of society by altering its age groups and life expectancy; rapid transportation vastly increases mobility and social horizons; and the obliterative power of nuclear arms casts a pervasive anxiety over all of life. All these technologically-rooted developments fundamentally alter the conditions and problems of life, but we do not know what social, political, and moral responses are appropriate to them. *As a result, all modern societies— socialistic and capitalistic—experience the feeling of being at the mercy of a technological and scientific impetus that shapes the lives of their citizens in ways that cannot be accurately foreseen nor adequately controlled.*

2. *The problem of participation.*

The second problem derives from the first. Because advanced societies are characterized by high levels of technology, they are necessarily marked by a high degree of organization. The technology of our era depends on the cooperation of vast masses of men, some at the levels of production, some at the levels of administration. The common undergirding of all advanced industrial or "postindustrial" societies lies not alone in their gigantic instrumentalities of production, but in their equally essential and vast instrumentalities of administration, whether these be called corporations, production ministries, or government agencies.

The problem is then how the citizen is to find a place for his individuality in the midst of so much organization; how he is to express his voice in the direction of affairs, when so much bureaucratic management is inescapable; how he is to "participate" in a world whose technological structure calls for ever more order and coordination. This is a matter which, like the sweeping imperative of technology, affects both capitalism and socialism. In both kinds of societies, individuals feel overwhelmed by the impersonality of the work process, impotent before the power of huge enterprises—above all, the state itself—and frustrated at an inability to participate in decisions that seem more and more beyond any possibility of personal influence.

No doubt much can be done to increase the feeling of individual participation in the making of the future, especially in those nations that still deny elementary political freedoms. *But there remains a recalcitrant problem of how the quest for increased individual decision making and participation can be reconciled with the organizational demands imposed by the technology on which all advanced societies depend.* This is a problem that is likely to trouble societies—capitalist or socialist—as long as technology itself rests on integrated processes of production and requires centralized organs of administration and control.

3. *The problem of work.*

Finally, we must raise a problem that has just begun to appear in the advanced countries of the West but that seems virtually certain soon to make its appearance in the advanced socialist nations as well. It is the problem of work, or rather the gradually diminishing need for work, and the rising question of what will take the place of work as the great object of human energy.

Work has always been considered the curse of man; and in most societies, where work is long and onerous, boring and monotonous, it fully deserves its bad reputation. Hence for most people, the vista of a society in which the need to work is progressively reduced—indeed, in which leisure rather than work is the central feature of every day—appears to be much more of a paradise than a problem.

For the great majority of humankind, who are born into societies from which there will be no escape from work for decades, that vista can remain an unquestioned dream. But for a growing number of advanced societies, socialist as well as capitalist, the dream has to be questioned more seriously. Under the combined influences of the labor-saving potential of automation, the braking force exerted by the environment, and perhaps a deep-rooted "antimaterialistic" change of life-style, the rich societies of the world may well be standing on the theshold of a substantial reduction in the number of work hours expected of an average citizen.

In the United States we are witnessing the beginning of a four-day week in certain industries. If the trend of the past century continues, a three-day week, possibly even a two-day week, will be the stint expected of our grandchildren. Will this explosive expansion of leisure come as a welcome release of creativity, or will it be only a stultifying bore? History gives us scant guidance, for if we look to the manner in which the leisured classes of the past have made use of their release from work, we find such extremes as the exquisite mandarin culture of China or the warlords of feudal Europe; the indolent nobility of Rome or the amateur scientists of the eighteenth-century British aristocracy.

All we can say is that leisure is a condition that can lead to destructive as well as constructive activities, and that its enlargement, on a hitherto unimagined scale, will present to all wealthy societies a mixed promise and problem of vast proportions. Along with the problem of controlling the onrush of technology or of securing democratic participation in a technocratic society, the challenge of coping with the vacuum left by the diminishing need to work bids fair to constitute another point of convergence between rich societies, socialist and capitalist.

CONVERGENCE AND HISTORY

In a larger sense, then, "convergence" brings us beyond economics to the common human adventure in which economic systems are only alternate routes conducting humanity toward much the same general direction and destination. Perhaps it is well that we end our survey of economic history with the recognition that the long trajectory of the market system does not bring us to a terminus of social history, but only to a state in which some kinds of problems—the pitifully simple problems of producing and distributing goods—begin to be solved, only to reveal vastly larger problems in the very technology and organization that prepared the means for solving them.

But those are problems for the future. Meanwhile it is the present that absorbs us, for it is in the present that we have our personal encounter with history. And so we cannot end our study of economics until we have considered a question that we posed many hundreds of pages back, but which has waited until now for a full scrutiny. This is the question of America Today, and of its prospects and problems. Many of these we have dealt with in the course of our text, but a central question remains. What of capitalism itself? To this last stage of our inquiry we are finally ready to turn.

Stages of
development

1. The spectrum of economic systems in the world corresponds generally to their *stages of economic development.*

Mercantilism

2. The inception of growth seems to require a political stimulus. In the West, this was provided by *mercantilism,* after which the market took over the task of growth. The West was favored over the present underdeveloped areas by its ability to mount a *leisurely development,* and by its *vanguard position* vis-à-vis the rest of the world.

3. Today, *command economies* are attempting to push their societies off dead center and to initiate the process of growth. For these tasks, command seems a more appropriate system than the market.

Mid-development

4. *Economies in mid-development,* such as the Soviet Union, are characterized by mixtures of command and market systems. Command is best suited for massive economic and social reallocations, but not to the problems of running a smoothly integrated high-output economy. Bureaucratic inefficiency, and the absence of a congruence between private interest and public requirement, introduce many difficulties into the planning mechanism. Here the market begins to achieve a new relevance.

High consumption
economies

5. *High consumption economies* are naturally suited to market guidance. However, these economies now suffer from the inability of the market to formulate public needs. *Thus, planning arises in market systems to offset their inherent goal-setting weaknesses, just as the market arises in command systems to offset their inherent motivational weaknesses.*

Market and goals

Convergence

6. Thus we see a *convergence of systems* in the more advanced nations. However, a convergence of economic systems does not mean that "capitalism" and "socialism" are becoming indistinguishable.

Cumulative vs.
noncumulative

7. Convergence seems to mean, also, that all advanced industrial societies share certain overarching problems: (1) a noncumulative social or political or moral understanding trying to control the effects of a cumulative technology; (2) finding a place for the individual who wants to participate in a system that demands large-scale, coordinated processes of production and administration; and (3) coping with the promise or problems of an unprecedented rise in leisure. These problems manifest themselves differently in capitalism and socialism, but in neither does a solution seem to be in sight.

Participation

Leisure

1. How do you account for the simultaneous existence in the world of such radically different economic systems?

2. In what ways was the early growth experience of the West unlike the present growth prospects of the backward world? Do you think these differences will have a substantial effect on the choice of economic systems for the backward countries?

3. Discuss the difference in social goals and priorities between a nation that is just beginning its development and one in mid-development. Between one in mid-development and one at a stage of high mass consumption. What is the relevance of planning techniques for each of these stages of development? Would you expect the techniques of planning to be similar in all stages? What differences would you look for?

4. What is meant by the congruence of self-interest and public requirement in a market system? Is this what we mean by the "invisible hand"? How can this congruence be reconciled with the fact that the market has no means of establishing public priorities?

5. What are the advantages of the market system for economic freedom? Do you think the market system is also productive of political freedom? Draw a scatter diagram showing on one axis the degree of planning and on the other axis your estimate of relative political freedoms for the following nations: Sweden, England, U.S., France, South Africa. Is there much, if any, relationship between the two variables?

6. Do you think there can be a convergence of economic systems without a convergence of social and political systems?

7. What specific technological processes seem to defy social control? How about the effect of television? Urbanization? The arms race? Can you think of others?

8. Why do you think that knowledge accumulates more easily in science than it does in the areas of morality or politics or social activities?

9. Do you think that bureaucracy is an avoidable aspect of industrial society? If so, how? If not, what problems does it pose?

10. Do you think that the freedom to choose one's profession, to go to graduate school "to see how you like it," to become a hippie, etc., makes life easier or more difficult? Do you think your parents would agree?

At this final stage in our inquiry, as in its first stage, let me again speak in the first person, because what I have to say should not be given the authority that rightly or wrongly seems to adhere to statements made in the impersonal third person of textbook prose. What follows is no more than the fruit of personal reflection, offered not to settle matters, but only to make explicit my own convictions and to give student and instructor an opportunity to discuss the most important social issue with which economics is ultimately concerned. As the title of this chapter indicates, that ultimate problem is capitalism itself, and the extent to which it must be held responsible for the troubles of our country.

DEFINITIONS: WHAT IS CAPITALISM? SOCIALISM?

We had better begin with definitions. If we are now to ask whether America's troubles are due to capitalism, we should know what we mean by that crucial word.

It is surprisingly difficult to find a succinct definition of capitalism.[1] But I think that all shades of opinion, from right to left, would agree that its essential characteristics are these:

1. *The legal right to private ownership of the means of production.*

Under capitalism, the capital equipment of society is owned by a minority of individuals (capitalists) who have the right to use this property for private gain.

2. *The market determination of distribution.*

Capitalism relies primarily on the market system, not only to allocate its

---

[1] One of the few clear-cut definitions is in Max Weber's *General Economic History* (New York: The Free Press, 1950), Chapters 22 and 30. The Marxian definition is more diffuse, referring at different times to an *economic system,* to the *bourgeois society* built on that system, and occasionally to a *stage of Western civilization.* See George Lichtheim, *Marxism* (New York: Praeger, 1961), p. 164, note 4.

resources among various uses, but also to establish the levels of income (such as wages, rents, profits) of different social classes.

What is the corresponding definition of socialism? As we might expect, it is something of a mirror image of capitalism. "In its primary usage," writes Paul M. Sweezy, a leading Socialist theoretican, "the term 'socialism' means a social system which is differentiated from other social systems by the character of its property relations. . . . Capitalism recognizes a relatively unrestricted right of private ownership in the means of production, while socialism denies this right and reserves such ownership to public bodies."[2]

Thus Sweezy, like most socialists, makes the crucial distinction between capitalism and socialism the question of *property ownership*—to which I think most socialists would also add that socialism, unlike capitalism, depends primarily on *planning*, rather than on the market, both for its overall allocation of resources and for its distribution of income.

These definitions are what the sociologist Max Weber called "ideal types." They are meant to summarize and abstract out of the enormous variety of actual institutions and historical experiences those essential elements that make up a pure model of the institution or activity in which we are interested. We dealt with such an ideal type when we studied the operation of a "market" under pure competition, knowing full well that no market was in fact ever free of all imperfections. In the same fashion, the emphasis on public vs. private property, and on market vs. planned distribution serves to sharpen our conception of the "irreducible" elements of capitalism and socialism that are to be discovered behind their many variations in actual history.

IDEAL TYPES VS. REAL CASES

But no sooner do we create these ideal types than we find ourselves in something of a quandary. For the question then arises as to what practical

[2] Paul M. Sweezy, *Socialism* (New York: McGraw-Hill, 1948), p. 3.

function these models of capitalism and socialism serve. For example, if one asks a dedicated humanitarian socialist if "socialism" is better than "capitalism," he will unhesitatingly tell you that it is, basing his reply on the superiority of public over private ownership and on the preference to be accorded to planning over the market. But the same humanitarian socialist recoils in horror at the repressiveness of Russia and looks with approval on the humaneness of (capitalist) Denmark. How does he reconcile this contradiction? By telling you that Russia is not "really" socialist, but only a grim travesty of socialism; and that Denmark is not "really" capitalist but a modified socialist version of capitalism. Yet, unquestionably, the Soviet Union has public ownership of property and a thorough-going system of planning, and Denmark has private ownership of property and a general market determination of incomes and outputs.

The point of this disconcerting confrontation is clear. It is that the elements that all agree are decisive in defining capitalism and socialism as "ideal types" do not tell us very much about the societies that display those characteristic elements. As a matter of fact, thinking about the differences among capitalist nations—compare Sweden and the Union of South Africa—or among socialist countries—contrast Russia and China—we begin to wonder if the words *capitalism* and *socialism* mean anything at all.

CAPITALISM AND SOCIALISM AS ECONOMIC SYSTEMS

I think the answer is that the terms *do* mean something, although perhaps less than we often assume. As we shall see, there are crucial areas of life to which they add little if any understanding. But there are other areas where they add a good deal, and it is to these that we now direct our attention.

The first such area should be obvious. It is that of economics proper. *Capitalism and socialism as ideal types identify for us a series of economic problems that we find among all members of each type.*

What are these problems? For capitalism, we have but to refer to the micro and macro sections of this text. Disequilibrium, instability, misallocation of resources, and inequality of incomes are results of the economic process in *every* society in which there is private ownership of property and a market determination of prices. Whether we look to Japan or Sweden, the Union of South Africa or the United States, we see similar tendencies toward too much or too little growth, inflation or unemployment, a struggle between the private and the public sector, and a highly uneven division of incomes between the property-owning and the working classes. These are problems as specific to capitalism as the problems of guild life were specific to feudalism.

Can we apply the same general finding to socialism? To a certain extent our comparison is muddied by the fact that so many socialist systems are still in (or only very recently out of) a period of forced economic growth. Hence we do not really have "mature" socialisms to compare with mature capitalisms.

Nonetheless, there seems to be a set of common economic problems that is built into socialism in much the same fashion as the problems that are intrinsically part of the capitalist mechanism. As we would expect, these are problems of public ownership and planning—in particular, the problem of controlling unwieldy state bureaucracies and avoiding inefficient production and distribution directives. Indeed, one of the most brilliant socialist economic theoreticians, the late Oskar Lange, wrote presciently in 1938: *"The real danger of socialism is that of the bureaucratization of economic life...."*[3]

We shall return to a consideration of what these deep-rooted problems imply for capitalism and socialism.* But first let us ask if we find a parallel to the economic attributes of the two systems in their political characteristics. Some eminent political economists, Milton Friedman prominent among them, believe that we do. Friedman believes that the *existence of a market mechanism separate from the state provides the necessary basis for a free political life.* He does not insist that every capitalist society is therefore a free one—indeed, he specifically singles out Fascist Italy and Nazi Germany and Spain and Tsarist Russia as societies in which capitalist economic structures did *not* provide political freedom. But he is firm in his conviction that the existence of capitalism is a *necessary,* even if not a sufficient, condition for political freedom.

Friedman spells out his argument forcefully:

One feature of a free society is surely the freedom of individuals to advocate and propagandize openly for a radical change in the structure of society. ... It is a mark of the political freedom of a capitalist society that men can openly advocate and work for socialism. ... How could the freedom to advocate capitalism be preserved and protected in a socialist society?

In order for men to advocate anything, they must in the first place be able to earn a living. This already raises a problem in a socialist society, since all jobs are under the direct control of political authorities. It would take an act of self-denial whose difficulty is underlined by experience in the United States after World War II with the problem of "security" among Federal employees, for a socialist government to permit its employees to advocate policies directly contrary to official doctrine.

But let us suppose this act of self-denial to be achieved. For advocacy of capitalism to mean anything, the proponents must be able to finance their cause—to hold public meetings, publish pamphlets, buy radio time, issue newspapers and magazines and so on. How could they raise the funds?[4]

---

[3] Oskar Lange and Fred M. Taylor, *On the Economic Theory of Socialism* (New York: McGraw-Hill, 1956), p. 109.

* It is equally obvious that the phenomenon of convergence in the economic mechanisms of the two systems tends to bring the problems of one system into the other.

[4] *Capitalism and Freedom,* pp. 10, 16–18.

Does Friedman's logic establish a second fundamental dividing line between capitalism and socialism? It may. There *is* a certain refuge for the dissident individual in the free-for-all of the market that may be missing in socialism for the very reasons that Friedman suggests. Indeed, as M. A. Adelman has written, one main objection to socialist society is that it too much resembles the company town under capitalism, in which one employer has power over everyone within his jurisdiction.[5]

Yet I do not think that the issue has the clarity of the economic differences between capitalist and socialist societies. Certainly it weakens Friedman's position that among capitalist societies—that is, in the spectrum of systems relying on private property and the market system—*there seems to be no correlation whatsoever between the degree of political freedom and the use of "socialistic" limitations of property rights or the market mechanism.* Indeed, the most "socialistic" capitalisms, such as the Scandinavian bloc, England, or New Zealand, are probably the world's freest political societies.

Second, it should be pointed out that in the provision of a *guaranteed income* to all citizens, there is available a protection against the very kind of political vulnerability Friedman warns us about. As we have seen, the United States seems to be moving slowly toward such a system, and there is no reason why a socialist system could not adopt one very easily. A guaranteed income under socialism would free the dissident citizen from political pressure, just as private employment offers him this freedom under capitalism.

To be sure, such a system also requires that a socialist state value political liberty so highly that it would not cut off the income of an agitator for capitalism. Certainly no socialist state today displays any such easy tolerance—just as very few capitalist states allow complete liberty for agitators against capitalism. In all societies there is a natural "defensive" reaction against hostile ideas, and there is no reason to suppose that socialist authorities will be more tolerant of dissent than are capitalist ones. Indeed, in the present stage of historical development it is doubtful that socialist governments in general can be expected to be as politically tolerant as capitalist ones, partly because many socialist economies are in the throes of forced growth, and partly because most socialist governments feel insecure in a world in which capitalist power is still dominant.

Whether socialism will continue to be less politically free than the most liberal capitalisms is a question about which little can be said at present. As we have seen, it is possible to guard against the company-town aspect of socialism by means of a guaranteed income. But that is not to say that even a wealthy and self-assured socialist society will *wish* to put political liberty, with all its risks, high on its agenda. In the final analysis, I suspect that the

---

[5] Cited in *The Business Establishment,* ed. Earl Cheit (New York: Wiley, 1964), p. 217, note 17.

degree of political liberty will vary from nation to nation under socialism, as it does under capitalism; and that the *economic* framework will have very little to do with the quality of political life in either system.

This complex relationship between economic structures and political liberty brings us deeper into the question of how "capitalism" as an ideal type differs from "socialism." Specifically it leads to the question of whether we can discover a basis for *social* difference between the two systems—differences in values or life styles that might find their origins in the economic systems characteristic of each.

At first glimpse, there seems no relationship whatsoever between the two. Indeed, if we were to compare "socialist" Yugoslavia with "capitalist" Italy we would probably find many *more* similarities of social tone, cultural life, and general atmosphere, than if we compared "socialist" Yugoslavia with "socialist" China. And in the same way, "capitalist" West Germany probably more closely resembles "socialist" East Germany in general life style than it does "capitalist" Australia. *National* differences in culture and tradition seem so overwhelmingly important that any common social traits traceable to capitalism or socialism recede far into the background, if indeed they are discoverable at all.*

This emphasis on national differences is, I believe, of the greatest importance, and we will return to it in full measure when we inquire further into the problems of American capitalism. Yet at this stage of our inquiry, while we are still seeking to divide all capitalisms from all socialisms, perhaps one distinctive element should be noted. It is the presence within all socialist countries of an ideal not to be found in any capitalist country. This is the ideal of Socialist Man—of man transformed from the competitive, acquisitive being that he is (and that he is *encouraged* to be) under all property-dominated, market-oriented systems, into the cooperative human being who finds fulfillment in unselfishness and who presumably can develop only in the benign environment of a propertyless, nonmarket social system.

It need hardly be said that this ideal of Socialist Man remains an unrealized goal in any socialist society, and may perhaps even be an unrealizable goal, comparable to the ideal of a truly religious community vainly pursued by centuries of Christianity. Yet, however distant, however vulgar-

---

* Merely as one indication of this diversity, let us look into the much discussed matter of suicide rates. Does "welfare capitalism" bring a high suicide rate, as President Eisenhower once suggested? The evidence does not show it. Suicides per 100,000 population are higher (18.5 per 100,000) in Sweden than in the U.S. (10.4 per 100,000), but they are higher here than in Norway (7.9) or the Netherlands (6.6 per 100,000). Denmark, on the other hand, has an even higher rate—20.3 per 100,000—but it suffered from this rate *before* it became a welfare state. See Alan Gruchy, *Comparative Economic Systems* (Boston: Houghton, 1966), p. 436.

ized in practice, however abused as a mere slogan for social manipulation, the conception of Socialist Man provides a spiritual basis for an ideology that is powerfully persuasive. Capitalist nations may be efficient, humane, democratic, permissive, creative, but they do not have a "vision" built on the elements of property ownership and the market—a vision comparable to that which is founded on the ideal of common ownership and sharing.

This absence of a capitalist ideal may strike some as a fact little to be regretted, in view of the human suffering that so many official ideals have brought in the past. But if we suspend our judgments and merely ask whether there is an ultimate difference between the worlds of socialist and capitalist values and goals, I think the answer must be yes, that socialism has a sense of high human mission—perhaps even redemption—that capitalism, even at its best, cannot quite match.

PROBLEMS AND SOLUTIONS

Our discussion suggests that the ideal types of "capitalism" and "socialism" *are* useful because they indicate different kinds of problems that the two systems tend to generate. But we have not yet inquired into an extremely important question that our findings pose. Granted that capitalism and socialism have common problems, *does this mean that they all find similar solutions to these problems?*

To ask the question is to answer it. Obviously, different capitalisms respond to their economic and social and political problems in very different ways, as do different socialisms. Take capitalism as an example. Two well-known Marxist critics of capitalism have written that genuine planning or resolute action to provide housing would be impossible in America because "such planning and such action . . . will never be undertaken by a government run by and for the rich, as every capitalist government is and must be."[6] They have obviously concentrated on the lack of an effective social sector in the U.S., and overlooked the planning and housing undertaken by Norway, Sweden, Denmark, New Zealand, Netherlands, and other governments presumably run by and for the rich, since they are certainly countries in which private ownership of the means of production prevails.

In the same way, because all capitalist systems do suffer from macro-instabilities, it does not follow that all therefore suffer from the same degree of unemployment. As we have previously seen, during the 1960s when unemployment here and in Canada reached levels over 5 percent, in West Germany unemployment never rose over 1 percent of the labor force, and in New Zealand it was considerably less than that.

This same variety of responses can be found in socialist economies. Oskar Lange's diagnosis of bureaucracy has proved all too true within all socialisms, but some have responded with a reliance on market socialism

---

[6] Paul Sweezy and Paul Baran, *Monopoly Capital* (New York: *Monthly Review Press,* 1966), p. 300.

(Yugoslavia or pre-invasion Czechoslovakia); others, in efforts to solve the problem with better computer-planning (U.S.S.R.); and still others, with a search for "moral incentives" (Cuba or China).

American Capitalism in Crisis

All this has an obvious relevance to the central issue with which we began this chapter. For we can see now that whereas many of the problems that beset America undoubtedly have their roots in our capitalist institutions, the fact that we have coped with them so inadequately is not a matter that can be blamed on capitalism as such.

Take, for example, the question of social neglect that is so dismaying an aspect of American life. If we compare the United States with, say, Norway in terms of various indicators of social well-being, there is no doubt that we show up poorly. Infant mortality in the United States is a full 50 percent higher than it is in Norway. Norway spends a higher proportion of its GNP on education than we do, even though Norway has a much smaller per capita GNP. Norway has more hospital beds per thousand population than we do. It allocates a larger proportion of its GNP to social security expenditures than does the United States. Its cities are essentially free of all slums. Although Norwegian citizens have a much lower GNP than American citizens, "poverty" as a relative condition—or poverty as a human condition of neglect by society—has been virtually eliminated there.

If we are willing to grant on the basis of these and other indicators that Norway has a record of social welfare superior to that of the United States, we would expect large differences in the economic structures of the two countries; for instance, in their income distributions. Yet, as Table 36-1 shows, there are not!

What the table shows is that the pre-tax distribution of income—that is the relative shares of rich and poor as determined by the market mecha-

---

TABLE 36 • 1

PRE-TAX INCOME DISTRIBUTION: UNITED STATES AND NORWAY

PERCENT OF INCOME GOING TO PERCENTILE GROUPS				
Lowest 20% of population	Second 20%	Third 20%	Fourth 20%	Top 20%
Norway (1950)	5.5	10.4	15.4	23.7	45.0
United States (1963)	5.1	12.1	17.6	23.6	41.6

Sources: Norway: Simon Kuznets, "Quantitative Aspects of the Economic Growth of Nations (VIII), Distribution of Income by Size," *Economic Development and Cultural Change* (January 1963). United States: U.S. Census Bureau, *Trends in the Income of Families and Persons in the U.S.: 1947 to 1964,* Technical Paper No. 17. Note that the years are not identical, but in view of the extreme slowness of movements in income distribution, this is not a serious consideration.

nism—is much the same in both nations. Indeed, in the United States the pre-tax share of the rich is *smaller* than it is in Norway, and the relative share of the second and third groups from the bottom (which includes the bulk of the working class) is *larger* than Norway.

But this surprising result would be totally altered if we now took into account the distribution of income *after* taxes and subsidies. In contrast to the generally nonprogressive structure of U.S. taxes, the Norwegian tax structure is one of the most progressive in the world and this progressive tax incidence is further emphasized by a system of subsidies to low income groups, which greatly lightens their net tax burden. The point, of course, is clear. It is that *the original capitalist dispositions of the marketplace do not leave an irretrievable mark on their societies, but can be radically modified by taxes and transfers.*[7]

CAPITALISM OR AMERICAN CAPITALISM

All this has a sobering, as well as an encouraging, implication. It is that much of what troubles America seems to be related to factors that, however much exacerbated by our economic system, cannot be uniquely attributed to capitalism as such. The low level of social services in America, the enormous role played by the military, the "rat-race" tempo of American life, the extent of our slums, the callous treatment of criminals, the obsession with "communism," and many other unlovely aspects of our social system are not predominant in many other capitalist systems.

The problem, in other words, resides more in those elements of our society that are *American* than in those that are capitalist. To put it differently, the significant question for us is to understand why capitalism here has not achieved the possibilities realized by capitalism elsewhere, rather than to compare the deficiencies of life in America with the presumed advantages that "socialism" might bring. For unless we understand and correct the failures of *American* capitalism, the likelihood is that a change of economic systems in this country would produce only an *American* socialism that would manifest many of the very failings of American capitalism.

Can we identify the elements in America that have brought about the failure of capitalism here to match the social achievements of similar systems abroad? Here we move from the reasonably firm grounds of empirical evidence to the quicksand regions of social conjecture. There are, perhaps, no "right" or "wrong" answers to this crucial question—only answers that are more or less useful in helping us think about an immensely complex and elusive problem. But with all the difficulties, let me try to suggest some possible explanations for the failures of our system.

[7] See Gruchy, *Comparative Economic Systems,* p. 338. See also his discussion of Swedish tax incidence, p. 402.

We might start by asking what is the most striking difference between the United States and the more socially responsive capitalisms we have referred to. One such difference that immediately suggests itself is sheer *size*. Is the greater social neglect of American capitalism simply the result of the scale of our continental country? Are we too big to create a genuine sense of community?

It is certainly plausible that a large country, with its variations in regions and interests, is less apt to feel a sense of shared responsibility than a small one. And yet at best, the explanation of size can be only a partial one. Canada, which is geographically larger than the United States, has a considerably more highly developed social welfare program and "point of view" than we do. Australia is another example of a large, regionally variegated nation with a high level of social services. Perhaps more to the point, our density of population (which is the way that "size" becomes translated into human experience) is 25 percent *greater* than Sweden and double that of New Zealand, so that our continental expanse does not physically separate man from man to a degree that might explain the lack of our "communal feelings."

A second hypothesis seems more convincing. It would explain the failures of American capitalism by the extreme diversity of our population— the many ethnic and cultural groups that have obstructed the formation of a socially-minded single community, comparable to the Danes or the Swedes.

Yet this hypothesis also loses much of its persuasiveness under scrutiny. Switzerland, for example, has three different language and nationality groups and yet maintains a very high level of communal concern. Canada, despite the political friction of its French- and English-speaking regions, has a well-developed social welfare system. Perhaps even more telling is a great deal of social neglect in certain areas of the United States where there *are* strong ethnic, regional, and racial bonds—the rich whites of Appalachia have paid little attention to the decline of their poor white kinsmen.

Yet, if our social heterogeneity does not provide a fully adequate reason for our inadequate social performance, it does point in one direction that sharply differentiates American capitalism from capitalism in other nations.* This is the fact that America is burdened with a *race problem* that is closely entwined with many areas of its laggard social performance.

There is no need at this point to rehearse the statistics of Negro poverty and neglect. Instead, it is necessary to link our deep-seated prejudice against the Negro with our national disregard of the (largely black) slums, our national neglect of the prisons (disproportionately filled with blacks), the

* With the exception of the Union of South Africa, which significantly also displays many of the same symptoms of social neglect that we do—and for the same reasons.

low level of welfare provision (roughly half of which goes to Negroes). To put it bluntly, one very likely reason for the continued failure of American society to clean up its ghettos, improve its prisons, and liberalize antipoverty programs is the unwillingness of many white Americans to allow their hard-earned dollars to be taxed and spent in ways that will tend to benefit black Americans more than white ones.

THE TRADITION OF DEMOCRATIC INDIVIDUALISM

The race issue, so central a part of our history, reaches deep into the core of American social neglect, but it does not account for every aspect of our problems. Racism does not explain our reluctance to deal generously with white poverty through higher Social Security levels, nor our militarism, nor our failure to cope effectively with the deterioration of the environment. To what special factors in American experience might we attribute these weaknesses of American capitalism?

The first answer I will suggest may be a surprising one. It is America's tradition of *democratic individualism*—a tradition born and nurtured on our frontiers, and perpetuated in the image of the town meeting as the ideal, democratic mode of government.

This is surely an odd suggestion, in that it is precisely this tradition that is one of the proudest claims of American society—indeed, the genuinely democratic quality of American life continues to impress visitors even from the most socially advanced European nations.

Yet, there is a price to be paid for this heritage. It is the lack of a tradition of strong central government and *noblesse oblige,* the duty of the benevolent ruler to provide for his less fortunate subjects. Both these traditions are woven into the cultural traditions of most European nations and have helped them create *welfare* capitalisms.

Alexis de Tocqueville, the great nineteenth-century French sociologist, wrote perceptively about the difference in traditions when he visited America in the 1830s:

Aristocracy [he wrote] links everybody, from peasant to king, in one long chain. Democracy breaks the chain and frees each link. As social equality spreads, there are more and more people who, though neither rich nor powerful enough to have much hold over others, have gained or kept enough wealth and enough understanding to look after their own needs. Such folk owe no man anything and hardly expect anything from anybody. They form the habit of thinking of themselves in isolation and imagining that their whole destiny is in their own hands. Thus, not only does democracy make men forget their ancestors, it also clouds their view of their descendants, and isolates them from their contemporaries. Each man is forever thrown back on himself alone, and there is a danger that he may be shut up in the solitude of his heart.[8]

---

[8] Alexis de Tocqueville, *Democracy in America* (New York: Harper, 1966), p. 478.

This is not to claim that European aristocracies were in fact more solicitous of their peoples in the nineteenth century than was democratic America. On the contrary, as the direction of immigration showed, quite the opposite was the case. Nonetheless, with eloquence and perception, Tocqueville points to a deep difference between democratically based and aristocratically based social systems. It is the presence, within the older governments of Europe, of a *legitimacy of authority* that, in the changed conditions of the twentieth century, made possible a much more vigorous and direct governmental attack on social problems than was possible in the American democratic-individualist environment.

But it is not only our tradition of small-scale local government that has handicapped us in dealing with large-scale, national problems. What Tocqueville alerts us to is an inhibition in the *feeling of social responsibility* of a democratic society, compared with one of more aristocratic lineage. This suggests that one of the reasons that Americans have not developed an effective attack on social problems is that there is no popular support for the idea that government should help the needy. The result has not only been an anaesthetizing of the American social conscience, but a paralysis of the mechanism by which that conscience might have been best expressed.*

LACK OF
A SOCIAL
DEMOCRATIC
HERITAGE

To this possibly heretical suggestion, let me now add a second, which applies to America at the other end of the socio-political scale. It is that American capitalism, unlike its European counterparts, never developed much of a tradition of *democratic socialism as a reformist force.*

Many observers have commented on the failure of the socialist ideal to implant itself in America, a failure due in part to our economic success and in part to our political (if not economic) stress on equality, at least for whites. "On reefs of roast beef and apple pie," as the economic historian Werner Sombart put it, "socialistic utopias of every sort [were] sent to their doom."[9]

It has been customary for Americans to congratulate themselves on the absence of a native socialist movement, for socialism has certainly brought sharp conflicts and severe social tensions within many nations. Yet, it has also brought an impetus for social change and a widened agenda for

---

* Sociologist Seymour Martin Lipset gives a telling illustration of the difference in national attitude between our highly individualist tradition and that of a more aristocratic society. Both the United States and Canada have created national folk-heros connected with the frontier that was so important for both societies. How suggestive that America should have chosen the free-wheeling cowboy and that Canada should have picked the scarlet-clad Canadian mounted police, representative of central authority and law and order! See Lipset, *The First New Nation* (New York: Basic Books, 1963), p. 251.

[9] Quoted in Daniel Bell, *Marxian Socialism in the United States* (Princeton, N.J.: Princeton University Press, 1967), p. 4.

discussion that has been missing from America. In Sweden, Norway, Denmark, England, Netherlands, New Zealand—in short, virtually everywhere that capitalism has achieved a high level of social welfare—the driving force for change has been a democratic socialist party, pushing against the limits of conservative capitalism. In America, with the important exception of the early New Deal, no such "socialistic" enlargement of the conception of what a society might achieve has ever significantly enlarged the conception of what "capitalism" meant. Hence measures such as the nationalization of industry where that might be useful, or the massive redistribution of income—both measures used by a number of capitalist nations—are avoided in America because they smack of "socialism."*

THE PROBLEM OF MILITARY POWER

There remains, however, one vast problem to which neither of the preceding suggestions directly applies. It is the question of the relationship of capitalism to the rise of an aggressive American military state.

Is militarism itself a specifically capitalist phenomenon? The evidence of history would hardly indicate as much. There have been pacific capitalisms (Sweden, Switzerland) and aggressive ones (prewar Germany, postwar United States); and the actions of the Soviet Union in its invasion of Hungary and Czechoslovakia or its border clashes with China are enough to indicate that capitalism has no monopoly on international violence.

Yet there is no doubt that in recent years American capitalism has become a military state that feels itself impelled to police the world. Since World War II, the United States has intervened in Lebanon, the Dominican Republic, Cuba, South Vietnam, Cambodia, and Laos; has clandestinely overthrown at least one government (Guatemala), and probably another (Iran); has actively supported repressive right-wing regimes in Greece and Brazil; has entered into a worldwide system of secret military arrangements even extending to the support of the government of Ethiopia; and (as we mentioned in Chapter 1) has "shown the flag" on a total of 50 occasions.

Whence derives this military commitment? The answer is not easy to give. In part it lay in a genuine fear of postwar Soviet intentions, hardly reassured by Russia's general truculence, by its walling-off East Berlin, and by its anticapitalist rhetoric. Yet, compared with the reaction of many European nations, the American response to these threats was exaggerated—indeed, so exaggerated that it undoubtedly helped to provoke the very Soviet (and later Chinese) belligerency by which Americans could then justify their uncompromising stand.

* The political scientist Robert A. Dahl has written that Americans are "half colorblind" when they think about such problems as how to control giant corporations. "An important reason," he writes, "is that our history has left us without a socialist tradition. . . . The consequence, I think, is a serious limit to our capacity for clearheaded consideration of how economic enterprises should be governed. Because we have no socialist tradition, our debates about economic institutions nearly always leave some major alternatives—chiefly 'socialist' alternatives—unexplored." (*After the Revolution?* New Haven: Yale University Press, 1970, p. 119).

The sources of this American response are many: clergymen who equated the rise of communism with the anti-Christ and who stirred the fears of fundamentalist religious groups; labor unions whose anticommunist feelings reached such irrational levels that longshoremen refused to unload Polish merchandise at the very time that Poland was trying to break *away* from the Soviet bloc; veterans organizations to whom patriotism meant an uncritical support of American "might"; Congressmen who subscribed to the belief that America must defend "freedom" everywhere, except perhaps for selected members of their own constituencies; military leaders who gradually enlarged the conception of American "defense" to the ability to wage two major wars and one minor war *simultaneously*; industrial circles for whom the arms economy provided a seemingly inexhaustible source of revenue; high government officials who saw America as the world's bulwark against "international communism," even after international communism had dissolved into mutually hostile nation-states; intellectuals and professors who applied the cool logic of "maximizing" national security but never questioned the premises on which security might be based.

In this multiplicity of causes, each of which has played its part in the American anticommunist stance, the role of "capitalism" is both central and elusive. Certainly capitalism all over the world has felt itself menaced by the rise of powerful socialist governments in Russia and China and the prospect of revolutionary socialism in the underdeveloped areas, much as the Catholic Church once felt menaced by the rise of Protestantism; or the British aristocracy, by the rise of democracy in France. Yet, as we know, Catholicism made its peace with Protestantism—differently, to be sure, in different countries—and the aristocracies made their peace with democracy—also differently in different countries. That private property and the market mechanism can also make a peace with public property and planning seems equally evident—but that, too, will take place differently in different countries.

In many capitalist nations that process of peacemaking seems now fairly far advanced. Various capitalist nations have long carried on trade freely with Russia, have begun to invest in communist nations, have recognized and traded with China, and while maintaining a healthy skepticism toward the national policies of these nations, have felt no need to mount an anticommunist crusade against them. Now, after the disastrous Indo-Chinese War that has been the price America has paid for its blind anticommunism, we shall have to see if here, too, we cannot find a pragmatic mode of coexistence, and become once again a citizen, and not the policeman, of the world.

If our discussion points to any conclusion, it is that we must seek to change many aspects of American capitalism in the direction that capitalism in other nations has indicated. This does not mean, of course, that America could or should set out to "copy" the achievements of other lands. Institutions, like good wines, do not always travel easily. We shall have to find our own ways of coping with the problems of health and the cities and national planning and the arts and pollution and education—ways that may take inspiration from foreign accomplishments, but that must in the end reflect our own ways of doing things.

Yet it may help if we have at least a general idea of what such a major effort would look like. There is such a "preview" in the proposed budget of government expenditure for the year 1976, drawn up by the National Urban Coalition. Envisaging a new program of National Health insurance, public service employment, family assistance for the poor, aid to students from preschool to college, grants for improving police departments, taxes to curb pollution, plus a wide range of other social services, the Coalition looks ahead to a total federal government expenditure in 1976 of $354 billion,[10] compared with $206 billion today.

Is such an enormous increase in expenditure imaginable in a capitalist society? Comparisons are helpful here. In 1967 the United States used 18.8 percent of its GNP for nonwar public purposes. The proposals above would raise the nonwar proportion of GNP used by government to only 20 percent, assuming that GNP will grow very rapidly (about 5 percent per year) under the many-sided stimulus of this new program.

But if GNP grew at only 3 percent, the "burden" of the proposed nonwar expenditures on GNP would be only 26 percent of GNP (and the addition of the defense portion would raise it to only 30 percent). In Table 36-2, compare the portion of GNP used by other nations for nonwar purposes only.

TABLE 36•2

NONWAR USES OF GNP, SELECTED NATIONS (1967)

Canada	26.7%	Italy	27.6%
France	31.6	Sweden	36.8
West Germany	30.9	United Kingdom	27.0

Source: *Counterbudget*, p. 313.

The problem, then, is not one of economics, but of politics, of will. The program will require increased tax revenues, and the Coalition proposals call for graduated increases in taxes on incomes over about $10,200, plus the closing of many tax loopholes. Thus a family earning $11,000 a year would pay about $100 more in taxes; one earning $20,000 would pay roughly $1,000 more; one earning $35,000 might pay as much as $2,500 more.[11]

---

[10] *Counterbudget*, p. 300. (The 1976 figure includes $94 billion of purchases of goods and services, $50 billion of which are allocated for military expenditure, and $260 billion of transfers to individuals and states and localities.)

[11] *Ibid.*, p. 10.

Will those influential Americans who constitute the 40 percent of all families above the $10,000 line assent to such an increase in their taxes to bring about a new America? Only time and effort will tell. Many Americans, particularly those who find themselves in the influential upper echelons in the nation, are not deeply disturbed by the problems of the remaining 60 percent, much less those of peoples many thousand miles away. Yet, others—including sizeable numbers who are aware of their good fortune—feel the urgency of the problems and the inadequacy of the American response. Indeed, if we judge by the past, the leadership for the reform of America's backwardness will come from those very groups who will have to make some sacrifice of their private income to achieve a greater public good.

THE MORAL CHALLENGE

Textbooks are not proper places for expression of political sentiment. They are not improper places, however, in which to give vent to moral sentiments, provided these are properly identified. Hence let me end our long discussion of the origins and character and problems and promise of our society by saying that I believe that American capitalism stands at the threshold of a crucial decade. For almost a generation our society has been identified in the eyes of much of the world as a nation that is rich but indifferent; peace-loving in rhetoric but aggressive in behavior; boastful of its economic strength, blind to the misuse of that strength. Now the years are at hand in which that image—and the realities that are uncomfortably close to the image—can be changed. We will continue to be a rich nation; we must cease to be in so many ways a poor one. We will continue to be a powerful nation; we must learn the limits of our power. We will continue to be an economic colossus, but our economic system must now become the undergirding for a good society.

In view of our heritage, our traditions, our deeply-rooted failings, this will not be an easy transformation for America to make. It may even prove to be an impossible one, although I strongly believe that this is not the case. But in any event, the all-important thing is to make the effort. The challenge is to change America today into a different and much better America tomorrow. In my view, this will be the most searching test of its character that American society has ever faced.